"Jesus charged us to preach the gospel to every cre[ature] evangelize with every ounce of strength and creativi[ty] what He is asking of us to see the nations discipled. This book is filled with wisdom from the Scriptures and from men and women who have been obedient in their generation, and looks at some of what God is saying and doing around the world in our day. May your faith be stirred and your wisdom increased as you consider what the Holy Spirit wants to say to you through these pages."

Loren Cunningham, *Founder, Youth With A Mission*

"These pages give new insight and motivation to the challenge of discipling the nations. It will give you a refreshing perspective on the totality of what God has called the church to be about. In a day when evangelized nations are collapsing from corruption, and people are crying out for authenticity everywhere, this book brings us back to the mission of God to 'bless the nations' and all that that involves."

Paul Eshleman, *Vice President, Campus Crusade for Christ; Director, Finishing the Task movement*

"This book will give you a new vision of what God's call to all means in the Great Commission. It is a delightful blending of the theological, practical, and spiritual challenges of making disciples of all believers, churches, and nations. I dare you to read it and not be changed in your thinking, your approach to ministry, and your efforts to impact the world."

Avery Willis, *Executive Director, International Orality Network*

"In *His Kingdom Come* YWAM has given the body of Christ an effective tool for fulfilling the mandate of Jesus to 'disciple all nations.' ... Through the inspired insights of servant leaders from the YWAM family around the world, [this book delivers] to *the body* what the Bible says, what history showcases, what ministry philosophy and strategy works best for transforming the nations in response to Jesus' prayer to the father: 'Your will be done on earth as it is in heaven.' Ever since founder Loren Cunningham envisioned the seven spheres of life that influence the values and beliefs of any nation thirty-three years ago, YWAM has been on the cutting edge of the formulation of a God-honoring approach for transformation for the nations."

Luis Bush, *International Facilitator, Transform World Connections*

"Youth With A Mission is one of the most phenomenal mission entities to emerge in recent decades. It defies definition as an organization, a strategy, and as a multinational movement impacting the world for Jesus Christ. This volume will reveal the vision, passion, and innovation that is enabling God to use YWAM to alleviate suffering, impact communities, and extend the kingdom of God all over the world. The reader will be impressed that the task of discipling the nations is not for an elite few who go as professional missionaries but is the responsibility of every church and every believer."

Jerry Rankin, *President, International Mission Board, SBC*

"The resources provided in *His Kingdom Come* are excellent—bar none. This will definitely be a resource that we will use extensively and one I wholeheartedly endorse."

Bob Roberts, *Pastor, NorthWood Church; author of* Transformation, Glocalization, *and* The Multiplying Church

"I have had the privilege of working with a number of YWAM leaders in the last several years and am very impressed with their love for the Lord and their wisdom in helping fulfill the Great Commission."

Steve Douglass, *President, Campus Crusade for Christ*

An INTEGRATED APPROACH *to*
DISCIPLING *the* NATIONS *and*
FULFILLING *the* GREAT COMMISION

EDITED *by* JIM STIER,
RICHLYN POOR, LISA ORVIS

HIS KINGDOM COME

yWAM
PUBLISHING
P.O. BOX 55787 SEATTLE, WA 98155

YWAM Publishing is the publishing ministry of Youth With A Mission. Youth With A Mission (YWAM) is an international missionary organization of Christians from many denominations dedicated to presenting Jesus Christ to this generation. To this end, YWAM has focused its efforts in three main areas: (1) training and equipping believers for their part in fulfilling the Great Commission (Matthew 28:19), (2) personal evangelism, and (3) mercy ministry (medical and relief work).

For a free catalog of books and materials, contact:

YWAM Publishing
P.O. Box 55787, Seattle, WA 98155
(425) 771-1153 or (800) 922-2143
www.ywampublishing.com

His Kingdom Come
Copyright © 2008 by YWAM Publishing

Published by YWAM Publishing
P.O. Box 55787, Seattle, WA 98155

14 13 12 11 10 09 08   10 9 8 7 6 5 4 3 2 1

ISBN-10: 1-57658-435-6; ISBN-13: 978-1-57658-435-4

Library of Congress Cataloging-in-Publication Data in progress.

The chapter "Fiji—A Dramatic Return to Life" by Loren Cunningham is adapted from Loren Cunningham, *The Book That Transforms Nations* (Seattle: YWAM Publishing, 2007), pp. 211–215. Used by permission.

Website addresses are offered as a recommended resource at the time of publication only. These websites are not intended to express the views of YWAM Publishing, and we cannot ensure the accuracy of the addresses for the life of the book.

Unless otherwise noted, Scripture quotations in this book are taken from the *Holy Bible, New International Version*®. NIV®. Copyright © 1973, 1978, 1984 by International Bible Society. Used by permission of Zondervan. All rights reserved.

Printed in the United States of America

Contents

Foreword 7

Preface 11

Contributors 13

Part 1: Introduction

Finding Your Place in the Great Commission 23
Jim Stier

Part 2: What the Bible Says

The Old Testament Template for Discipling Nations 31
Landa Cope

The New Testament Basis for the Discipling of Nations 47
David Joel Hamilton

Case Study: Second Thoughts on Galactic Domination 77
Don Grattus

Part 3: History of Discipling Nations

From Rome to Reformation 95
Todd M. Johnson

Calvin and Geneva 103
Thomas A. Bloomer

Revolutionaries and Anti-Revolutionaries 119
Jeff Fountain

Youth With A Mission and the Great Reversal 147
Debra Buenting

Case Study: Fiji—A Dramatic Return to Life 167
Loren Cunningham

Part 4: Philosophy of Ministry

The Church and the Kingdom   175
Dean Sherman

A Conversation on Calling   183
John T. Henry

Discipling the Nations—One Disciple at a Time   201
Danny Lehmann

Incarnational Evangelism   213
C. Lynn Green

Developmentoring   219
Kent Truewell

The Importance of People Movements in Discipling Nations   235
Steve Cochrane

From Vision to Reality   243
Howard V. Malmstadt

Case Study: Principles and Practices in Albania   257
Fraser Haug

Case Study: When Less Is More   275
Bráulia Ribeiro

Part 5: Strategy

Loving God and Your Neighbor   295
G. Stephen Goode

Healing the Wounds of the World   317
John Dawson

Family and Culture   325
Diane and Jeff Littleton

Transforming a Divorce Culture into a Marriage Culture   339
Larry Ballard

Bible and Government   353
Ana Roncal Villanueva

Discipling the Nations through the Sphere of Business   371
Susanna Shenk

Discipling the Nations through Journalism   387
    Alison K. Muesing

Media That Transforms Nations   399
    Calvin and Carol Conkey

Strategy Coordination   417
    Karine K

University Campus Ministries   427
    SungGun Hong

How Lovely   443
    Jose Joseph and Sarah Jose

Part 6: Conclusion

Reflections on the Kingdom   461
    Jim Stier

Appendix A: YWAM Statement of Faith   467
Appendix B: University of the Nations Founding Principles   469
Appendix C: The Lausanne Covenant, Section 5
    (Christian Social Responsibility)   471
Study and Discussion Questions   473

Foreword

We live in an extraordinary time. We've been given a new task for a new day, with new responsibilities that will require novel ways of doing things and extraordinary integration, working together as the global church.

Our history is important and must be remembered, but God is doing a new thing around the world and throughout the body of Christ. A large movement is coming. We can see a doubling of the church in a generation, a billion people added in the next fifteen to twenty years. Why do I say this? I am watching and listening to what the Spirit of God has been saying in these past few years.

In 2003 the founder of Campus Crusade for Christ, Bill Bright, was on his deathbed. He called together leaders from two hundred ministries and denominations and charged them to contend as one for the gospel. The goal became known as the Billion Soul Mandate. The means to implement it would be an international network of leaders, initially called the Global Pastors Network. Reaching this Spirit-inspired goal is only going to happen through a unified church. We must come together under his lordship. If we would see unparalleled levels of fruitfulness, we must be willing to live at unprecedented levels of unity. As we partner, we will actually accelerate finishing the Great Commission.

The Global Pastors Network became the Call2All, because we came to recognize that leaders in all spheres of life must come together to seek God for his strategies on how to influence and engage the world through their calling. According to Jesus, the responsibility to influence the nations is ours. When Jesus said, "You are the light of the world," he clearly expected us to shine for people to see! We don't ask them to come to us; we go to them, where they live, work, and play. We have to engage the public arena in government, education, media, the arts, entertainment, sports, science, and technology. We have to go public, to bring the gospel of truth where people can hear it.

God has used public proclamation of the gospel to shape society throughout history. In my lifetime I have watched public proclamation change people, families, cities, and even nations. When this public proclamation is accompanied by the demonstration of the Spirit's power, its effect is magnified. Successful evangelism depends on demonstrations of love. In the Youth With A Mission evangelistic campaigns, we noticed that many leaders in other religions ignored the physical felt needs of the people and demanded continual religious sacrifice. Our proclamation was accompanied by acts of mercy. Even civic leaders in closed, seemingly hostile nations opened their hearts to Christianity because of public examples of Christ's love.

We must commit to multifaceted, strategic evangelism in every nation, evangelism that includes everything from stadium events and television broadcasts to local church outreaches and individuals caring for their neighbors. We must commit to strategic nation discipling, asking God for insight, faith, and creativity as business-people, teachers, and artists to impact our nations, communities, and neighborhoods for the kingdom. We must commit to intense prayer and ongoing demonstrations of the love of God. Together we must move forward into all that God is saying he wants to do.

What will fuel this fire? The Moravian movement was birthed and sustained in prayer; for one hundred years there was ongoing prayer, fasting, and waiting on the Lord in one location. The birth of the modern Protestant missions movement resulted. Right now we have the equivalent of the Moravian prayer movement occurring, multiplied one thousand times over! Global prayer initiatives, national prayer movements, and whole ministries are dedicated to unceasing intercession. Local churches and individual believers stirred to new passion and expectancy in prayer abound. What do you suppose will happen because of these prayer meetings that are transpiring all over the earth? We will see pioneering, coordinated missions activity launched around the world. There will be an explosion into missions!

With prayer, faith, and unity increasing in the body of Christ, we can anticipate that things will begin to move rapidly. The fruit will fall off the tree suddenly and in great numbers. We must be ready. How will we disciple them all? We must grapple with issues like multiplication and how to mentor effectively and quickly. We must pray! Innovative models will come as we do so.

The word is coming in from all over the world: God is saying, "Here it is—go take this thing!" He will give us strategies to take hold of this season, but we must ask. We must ask daring new questions, listen for bold answers, and act with radical faith. We must commit to engage with what God has given us in the long term, and grow past a short-term mentality. We must plan with this great harvest in mind and look at what he says he *will* do, not just at what has happened in the past.

The Call2All is one mechanism to bring us all together. Look and pray for other inspired initiatives born from the same Spirit of bold faith, lavish unity, and fresh creativity. In this extraordinary season, what is he calling *you* to do with *your* gifts and talents in *your* nation and sphere of life?

If we reach out to the world the way the apostles did, we'll have the same results. Together, fervent prayer, public proclamation, and demonstration of truth and love really work—they change the world.

This book explores the mandate to reach out to the world as we look into his Word, the experiences of the church through the ages, and the events happening right here and now on earth. There is much to learn as we reflect on these pages and ask God to give us deeper and broader understanding of what is in his heart and mind for the nations. When we have a shared understanding and vocabulary to work from, we can move together into the new things he will reveal to us in these days.

MARK E. ANDERSON
President, Global Pastors Network
International Director, Call2All

Preface

This book is largely a discussion of what God has been doing in and saying to Youth With A Mission (YWAM) over the past thirty years regarding Christ's mandate to "make disciples of all nations" (Matt. 28:19). It originated with a desire to increase mutual understanding between workers in different streams of ministry, from frontier missions to discipling ministries. As the project unfolded, we realized that every believer, by understanding these ideas, could be more effective in discipling the nations, for we all are designed to resonate specially with our part or purpose in God's bigger plans. Our hope and goal is that through this book you would be challenged to do your part in God's kingdom, even as you understand and appreciate that your neighbors may be called to a different important focus. We have learned that in ministry and missions there isn't one answer, one way to respond, one strategy that "always works." Rather, our infinitely creative God has led YWAM in many ways, revealing different facets of his heart and mind as we have pursued him both individually and corporately. Other parts of Christ's body have yet further revelations, giftings, and callings. Our amazing Creator is weaving all this together to build a kingdom according to his good purposes.

While producing this book, we quickly realized that it would be impossible to cover adequately every possible topic in a discussion about the expansion of God's kingdom. Our topics cover some of our experience as a mission, and hopefully they will stimulate your imagination for further exploration in areas we didn't discuss. The topics of prayer, education, and science are obvious omissions. Prayer and intercession are vital to any undertaking. Education has long been recognized as a way to change peoples and nations, because youth absorb values and assumptions so readily. We must consider how to teach our children explicitly and implicitly. As for science, too often the church and scientists have been sold the lie that science and faith are at odds. How can that be if science is the study of God's general revelation to humankind? Increasingly, a secularized world looks to science to solve its problems. The technological imperative—if we can do it, we will do it regardless of the morality involved—is increasingly accepted as a basic truth. We desperately need Spirit-filled men and women gifted in science, who can humbly be salt and light through all the disciplines and endeavors of science. As you read, we encourage you to be aware of other omissions, such as the orality movement, which seeks to disciple nonliterate nations, or the megacities model for urban settings. Prayerfully ponder how God is calling you to contribute.

We want to thank all the authors for the labor that went into their chapters as they considered ideas, wrote, and rewrote. We want to say a special thanks to Barb Overgaard for her editorial assistance and insights with Alison Muesing's and Debra Buenting's chapters, and to Ed Sherman for helpfully reviewing the history section (Part 3). To Ryan Davis and others at YWAM Publishing, we extend heartfelt gratitude for unflagging encouragement and excellent contributions to the manuscript. Last, but not least, we thank all the family members, friends, and coworkers who listened, shouldered extra work, and persevered with us.

Contributors

Larry Ballard

Larry and his wife, Violet, joined YWAM in 1985. Since then, Larry has traveled to over forty nations, speaking at conferences, camps, and seminars. From 1994 to 1998 Larry was YWAM base director at Weyerhaeuser, Wisconsin. Now, Larry is the international director of family ministries for Youth With A Mission and the director of the University of the Nations Family Resource Centre.

Larry has been the Midwest regional director for Marriage Savers since October 2000 and the Wisconsin state chairman for Marriage Savers since 1997. He has been active in developing Community Marriage Policies (CMP) in five Wisconsin cities. The first CMP, established in Eau Claire in 1997, was signed by eighty-nine clergy from thirty-three different denominations and ministries. The Ballards reside in Eau Claire, Wisconsin.

Thomas A. Bloomer

Tom Bloomer studied archeology at the University of Illinois, and worked as a French translator, ladies' shoe salesman, and youth pastor before joining Youth With A Mission in 1972. In 1983 Tom and his wife, Cynthia, responded to a call from Loren Cunningham to help develop the University of the Nations (U of N). A master's degree in missiology from Wheaton and years of missions experience proved invaluable as Tom helped coordinate, refine, and improve the different courses developing through the U of N. Tom is now the international provost of U of N and has completed a PhD in theology of education at Trinity International University.

Teaching the Word is the primary thrust of Tom's ministry. The challenge before him is to discover what it means to love God not just with one's heart, soul, and strength but with one's mind as well. Tom's hobbies include aerobic history, extreme gardening, and prophetic composting.

Debra Buenting

Debra Buenting, BA, MA, PhD, joined Youth With A Mission in 1975 and soon became part of the audio and video ministry of Procla-Media Productions. She quickly saw the strategic potential of using mediated communication in missions. Eight years later, Debra returned to university to earn a BA in journalism and an MA in television and film. She also worked in the television field and business. In 1996 Debra returned to Procla-Media as a video writer, producer, and director.

Debra's focus is on the use of entertainment-education (strategically placed educational messages in entertaining media) to promote holistic development in places such as Eastern Europe and Africa. When studying for a doctorate in communication, she asked the key question, "What role can communication play in discipling nations?" Debra also teaches video production and visual communication at various University of the Nations campuses.

STEVE COCHRANE

Steve Cochrane has worked with YWAM in India for the past twenty-five years. He started YWAM's work in the nation and has also worked in church planting among Muslims in North India. Steve formerly served as the international director for frontier missions for YWAM. He also serves with his wife, Elizabeth, as the field director for South and Central Asia.

Steve resides in western India and has two daughters. He is presently working on his PhD by extension through the Oxford Center for Mission Studies.

CALVIN AND CAROL CONKEY

Calvin and Carol Conkey have been serving as full-time missionaries with Youth With A Mission since 1978. They each have a master's degree in international communication and are the founders and directors of Create International, a global ministry of YWAM with centers in Thailand, India, and Australia. They lived in Singapore for five years and now live and work in Perth, Western Australia, with the staff of Create International and YWAM Perth.

LANDA COPE

Landa Cope is the founding international dean of the College of Communication for YWAM's University of the Nations. She has a bachelor's degree in art and education and a master's degree in humanities and international studies. Joining YWAM in 1971, Landa has served in over 110 nations.

For eight years Landa developed communications and fundraising for Mercy Ships International. She then founded U of N's College of Communication. In 2005 Landa founded The Template Institute (TTI) to facilitate biblical thinking in the professions and public arenas. Living in Switzerland, she is executive director of TTI and director of the U of N Burtigny campus.

Landa Cope speaks around the world on discipling nations. She is the author of *Clearly Communicating Christ,* a book about Jesus-style communication, and *The Old Testament Template.*

LOREN CUNNINGHAM

Loren Cunningham is the founder of Youth With A Mission, an ever-expanding worldwide "family of ministries" which he and his wife, Darlene, began in 1960, and which has now served in every nation. He is also the president of YWAM's global University of the Nations, which has permanent training locations in more than 140 countries. In the line of duty over the last forty years, Loren has personally visited every nation on earth. He has spoken to millions and continues to speak in thirty to forty nations each year. He is also the author of five books: *Is That Really You God?* (translated into eighty-four languages), *Making*

Jesus Lord, Daring to Live on the Edge, Why Not Women?, and *The Book That Transforms Nations.*

JOHN DAWSON

A native of New Zealand, John Dawson has traveled and taught throughout the world for over thirty years. A well-loved leader in the international church, he gives oversight to diverse global ministries: Aglow International women's movement, March for Jesus International, and Youth With A Mission (as president). In 1990 John founded the International Reconciliation Coalition, a network of Christian leaders dedicated to healing wounds between people groups and elements of society. John hosted a two-hour television miniseries based on his book *Healing America's Wounds,* which has been broadcast in several nations. He regularly addresses stadium rallies and outdoor festivals, including gatherings of the Promise Keepers movement, in places as varied as Hong Kong, Natal, New South Wales, and Holland.

JEFF FOUNTAIN

Jeff Fountain has been director for YWAM Europe since 1990, when the political landscape radically changed with the collapse of Communism. Since then, he has been networking with leaders in the European body of Christ, promoting partnerships toward the re-evangelization of the "prodigal continent."

Originally from New Zealand, Jeff graduated with a history degree before working as a journalist and then a staff worker for a Christian university student movement. Jeff and his Dutch wife, Romkje, have three adult sons and live in Holland.

Since short memories breed short-sightedness, Jeff believes that knowledge of Europe's Christian heritage is key to gaining vision for the future. His book, *Living as People of Hope,* sketches past and future scenarios for Europe. He and Romkje lead heritage tours of people and places that shaped Europe's Christian past.

G. STEPHEN GOODE

Steve graduated from the University of Memphis in 1973 in radio, TV, and film. He and his wife, Marie, joined the YWAM School of Evangelism in Lausanne, Switzerland, in January 1974. For their Summer of Service, they assisted at the historic Lausanne Congress for World Evangelism sponsored by the Billy Graham Association. Then they went on staff at YWAM Lausanne.

In 1980, when Khmer refugees fled the Khmer Rouge genocide, flooding the Thai-Cambodian border, the Goodes moved to Thailand. For fifteen years, along with 700 YWAMers and 5,000 refugee staff, they served over one million refugees from Indochina.

Steve is vice president of YWAM Mercy Ministries International (MMI). MMI assists the needs of the absolute poor in relief, rehabilitation, and development, because loving God and loving your neighbor is foundational to the discipling of a nation.

DON GRATTUS

Don Grattus has lived and served in YWAM for most of his adult life. He dropped out of high school to join YWAM when he was seventeen. Since then he has staffed training schools, led a mobile evangelism and relief team in Central America, taken outreach teams into Cuba during the Pan American games, and helped pioneer a new work in a predominately Muslim, post-Soviet nation (called "Daristan" in this chapter). Don and his wife, Jo, live in Daristan with their four children.

C. LYNN GREEN

Lynn Green started the work of Youth With A Mission in England in 1971. He was director of YWAM in the United Kingdom until 1989, and continues as executive chairman.

Since 2004 Lynn has been YWAM's international chairman. In previous years he has been much involved in serving other movements and organizations. This has included chairing Challenge 2000 (the DAWN movement for England) and being a founder and director of March for Jesus. Lynn is also a trustee of CARE Trust. He has also directed the Reconciliation Walk, helping to defuse 900 years of bitterness between Muslims, Christians, and Jews.

DAVID HAMILTON

David Joel Hamilton, the son of United Methodist missionaries in South America, has served God for more than twnety-seven years in YWAM. He and his wife, Christine, pioneered the work of YWAM in Santiago, Chile, and the first School of Biblical Studies in Spanish in South America. He currently serves as the international associate provost of the University of the Nations, assistant to the president, as well as on the International Leadership Team of the U of N and the Global Leadership Team of YWAM. He is also currently director of training on the YWAM/U of N Kona campus. David and Christine have four children.

FRASER HAUG

Fraser and his wife, Puanana, have been in full-time international ministry since 1977, twenty-three of those years with Youth With A Mission. They have traveled to and ministered in over fifty nations.

The focus of their ministry is equipping national Christian leaders for the task of advancing the kingdom of God in all aspects of society and culture, primarily in the spheres of education, business, and church life. They have a special passion to serve poor and needy children in the developing world in practical ways.

Fraser was born in St. John's, Newfoundland in 1951. Since 1991, the Haugs have lived in Germany. During that time, they have focused much of their ministry in the Muslim and Arab world.

JOHN T. HENRY

John Henry is the international director of the University of the Nations Student Mobilization Centre. The Field Ministry Internship program, a principle program of the Centre, has mobilized university students from eight countries and over 100 universities to short-term mission projects in thirty nations. The Centre equips YWAM staff for student ministries through a twelve-week course, the School of University Ministries.

John and his wife, Mary, have two terrific boys, Justin and Nathan, and a beautiful little girl, Rebecca, whom they adopted in 1999 from China. John and Mary have served with YWAM for over twenty years. He is now completing a master's in global leadership at Fuller Seminary.

SUNGGUN HONG

SungGun Hong committed himself to the Lord as a teenager. Experiencing the power of the Holy Spirit in college motivated him to obey Jesus' Great Commission to disciple the nations. He presents Jesus to young people, inspiring them to also serve God.

SungGun Hong graduated from SeoGang University (BA) and Presbyterian Theological Seminary (MDiv). Joining YWAM full-time in 1978, he pioneered Campus Ministry in 1979. After serving as national director of YWAM Korea from 1986 to 2003, SungGun became the regional director of YWAM East Asia. He also leads the University of the Nations campus in Jeju, South Korea, where he lives with his wife, HyunJu, and their three children.

A well-known Bible teacher, SungGun has written four books: *Worship, Warfare and Intercession; Participants in Divine Nature; The Power of the Holy Spirit;* and *The Nation-Changer.*

Todd M. Johnson

Todd began his missions career in 1978 with YWAM. He worked all over the world doing relief work, evangelism, mobilizing college students across the US, and long-term church planting. He has spent years teaching, writing, and researching topics that include the biblical, historical, and present-day status of missions. For his PhD in international development from William Carey International University, Todd developed quantitative tools to analyze the past, present, and future of global Christianity.

In 2003 he launched the Center for the Study of Global Christianity at Gordon-Conwell Theological Seminary in Boston. In this role, he does research on the status of Christianity in every people, language, city, and country, and he monitors strategic plans for world evangelization.

Jose Joseph and Sara Jose

After training and performing for four years in India's Carnatic classical musical tradition, Jose Joseph joined YWAM. Jose copioneered the Indian School of Performing Arts (SOPA) and an Indian Arts With A Mission (AWAM). Jose's other dreams included the creation of an arts center with a professional-quality recording studio. The quality Christian music recorded there in India's diverse languages will help disciple the nation.

Sarah Jose is from the USA. Trained as an occupational therapist, Sarah married Jose in 2000 and found that arts-related ministry fits her more perfectly than she could have dreamed. Sarah is a painter and enjoys teaching art, worldview, and Bible classes.

Jose and Sarah have three boys—Bemin, Benjamin, and Isaiah.

Karine K

Born in Switzerland, Karine K gave her life to God at the age of sixteen and embarked on a journey of surprises, challenges, and miracles.

In her twenties, Karine and her husband, Joel, were dramatically called to an Asian country by visions that included fiery letters on a wall. They knew where but didn't know *how* they were to serve an unreached people group (UPG). Learning about strategy coordination in a YWAM School of Frontier Mission, they recognized the answer.

After training, Karine and Joel moved to their country to be strategy coordinators for a UPG, known as one of the toughest, most dangerous groups in the region. After twelve years, when indigenous people were catching the vision to spread the gospel in their own people group, they handed the strategy coordinator work to a local team.

Today, Joel and Karine serve strategy coordinators around the world, organize training, and promote strategy coordination.

DANNY LEHMANN

Danny Lehmann resides in Hawaii with his wife, Linda. They have two sons, Daniel and David, and are the proud grandparents of two grandsons.

While a surfer in California, Danny was confronted with the gospel of Jesus Christ on the beach and shortly thereafter was converted to Christ. After a few months of discipleship, he began to share his faith on the beaches and streets. In 1980 Danny joined Youth With A Mission. When not leading outreach teams to the South Pacific and Asia, Danny directs YWAM Honolulu and YWAM Hawaii. He also serves on YWAM's Global Leadership Team.

Danny has written three books on evangelism and many gospel tracts. He travels extensively, teaching on evangelism, the disciplined life, and missions.

DIANE AND JEFF LITTLETON

After completing a BS in sociology from the University of Wisconsin, Jeff Littleton went to Malaysia to teach English as a second language in 1968. Malaysia brought several life changes. Attending evangelistic meetings with his English students, Jeff himself entered a personal relationship with Jesus Christ after years of being a good churchman.

At the same time, Jeff realized—to his joy—that God was calling him to Asia. He loved Asian culture with its "rubber time" and indirect communication. But where would he find a wife with the same calling? A year later, in Malaysia, he met and married Diane, a Canadian serving as a missionary with OMF.

Since then, Jeff and Diane have been working with Asians. They have gained many insights into the challenges and opportunities of ministry in Asia and the Pacific. Their particular burden is for families.

HOWARD V. MALMSTADT

Howard Malmstadt distinguished himself as a world-renowned scientist, pioneering several areas of science and technology, including applied spectroscopy, automated chemical measurement systems, clinical methods, kinetic methods of analysis, and instrumentation for scientists. He was a teacher, mentor, author, and inventor. He wrote several textbooks used around the world, and more than sixty research students did their doctoral theses under his direction. In 1978, after this stellar career, he turned his energy to beginning the University of the Nations with YWAM founder Loren Cunningham. Howard spent the rest of his life laying out the foundational vision and principles that are so unique to the university, which now has over 400 campuses in 120 nations. He completed the chapter for this book just before going to be with the Lord in 2003.

ALISON K. MUESING

Alison Muesing pioneered and led the School of Journalism of University of the Nations in Washington, DC, and the School of Government & International Studies in Lausanne, Switzerland. She earned her master's degree in journalism from Northwestern University in 1983. She has taught seminars and courses in several nations on worldview and how to work with the media. Alison now works in Native American reconciliation ministry in the Southeast.

BRÁULIA RIBEIRO

Bráulia Ines Ribeiro has been working in the Amazon jungle for the past twenty-eight years. She has pioneered several YWAM bases in that region, during which process she and two other young people discovered a tiny, isolated tribe. Their efforts to bring these people the gospel has been key to new understanding of God's work in micronations. Bráulia and her husband Reinaldo later started YWAM Porto Velho, now a catalyst for many diverse mission initiatives all over the western Amazon basin. She is the author of *Radical Call* and writes for many Christian magazines. She was the president of YWAM Brazil from 2004 to 2007.

SUSANNA SHENK

Susanna Shenk, MBA, has a broad background as an international business consultant and CEO of two organizations. Her specialties are human resource development, organizational development, and forecasting. Susanna has designed tools for entrepreneurial testing, values transmission, marketing, and team building. She teaches internationally, and her work in establishing businesses with multicultural teams in cross-cultural settings is well known.

Susanna has pioneered diverse institutions ranging from a UN program for refugees to a rehabilitation program for former prisoners and drug addicts, from a successful gift-in-kind donor organization to the center promoting business as missions. Currently, she serves as a principal of a Great Commission business, and a co-developer of a business and organizational development program.

DEAN SHERMAN

Dean Sherman is the international dean of the College of Christian Ministries in the University of the Nations. He teaches internationally in the body of Christ to train pastors, church leaders, and missionaries. Since joining YWAM in 1967, Dean has led mission teams into most Asian and Pacific countries and helped pioneer YWAM in New Zealand, Australia, and New Guinea.

He has written two books: *Spiritual Warfare for Every Christian* and *Love, Sex, and Relationships.*

Dean is married to Michelle, an Australian. They make their home in Salem, Oregon, and have two married children, Cherie and Troy, and an undisclosed number of grandchildren.

JIM STIER

In 1975, during their first year of marriage, Jim and Pam Stier left their native USA and moved to Brazil. After enduring much hardship during their early pioneering efforts, Jim and Pam have seen the work in Brazil grow to 1,500 staff.

Brazilian YWAMers seem to thrive on the challenges of the "hard places" and serve on every continent. Some of the most impacting, innovative strategies in YWAM for discipling nations have come from Brazilians, focusing on such diverse areas as war refugees, tribal languages, malaria, and street children.

Jim has served as the international director of the frontier missions and executive chairman for YWAM. He is currently the director of the Americas field.

KENT TRUEWELL

Kent and Josephine Truewell have over twenty-five years of missionary experience in the USA, the Amazon region of Brazil, and Australia. The roots of Kent's ministry are in community development, from which he derives the word *developmentoring.*

Their family moved to Amazonas, Brazil, in November 1986 after training as cross-cultural missionaries through Youth With A Mission's frontier missions and community development programs. Together with their four children they worked in the Amazon region of Brazil until September 1998. For three of those years, the Truewells made their home aboard a 15-meter regional riverboat floating on the Purus River. Now based in Australia, their continuing missions work focuses on investing the experience they have gained into other missionaries.

Ana Roncal Villanueva

Originally from Peru, Ana Roncal Villanueva studied business administration. As an international banking officer, Ana wondered what her faith had to do with finance. Her questions led her to YWAM in 1987, where she served on three continents over a three-year period and experienced a total surprise concerning the meaning of "missions."

After returning to Peru and completing master's studies in political science, Ana founded and led the Association for Research, Spreading, and Application of Biblical Principles. This organization sponsors The Government Centre, an institution for research and teaching of biblical principles of government. Ana authored the book *Foundations of Government* in 2002. She describes her job as "an increasing passion."

A native of the Peruvian coast, Ana gets her best inspiration at the beach.

Part 1

Introduction

Finding Your Place in
the Great Commission

Jim Stier

Ephesians 2:10 confidently declares that all of us have a purpose in life: "For we are His workmanship, created in Christ Jesus for good works, which God prepared beforehand that we should walk in them" (NKJV). One of the most strongly felt needs of humans is for their lives to have meaning. God has designed us so that this meaning is found when we serve others in some way.

When Jesus taught the disciples to pray, his instruction included, "Your kingdom come. Your will be done on earth as it is in heaven" (Matt. 6:10 NKJV). This is not only our prayer; it is also the great work of the church and of every person who is part of the body of Christ. We're not only to bring salvation, but also the life of the kingdom of God to the earth. This was a consistent emphasis in Jesus' teaching, and I believe this is what he meant when he charged the disciples to "disciple the nations" in Matthew 28:18–20. This book is meant to help you find your place in fulfilling both that mandate and the very design God gave you.

As you will read, God is interested in all facets of human life. Involvement in your church as a dedicated layperson is certainly desirable, but God has more for you. Our authors assert that God wants us to be more than witnesses to his salvation. He wants us to be agents for the transformation of society, the general betterment of mankind in all honest and legitimate areas of human need and endeavor. Our work is much more than a way to get a paycheck; it is to be an act of worship to God and of service to mankind. Living this way will bring deep fulfillment to us as well.

This book was written by men and women who have served in Youth With A Mission, a nondenominational missions movement begun by Loren Cunningham in 1960. We've done ministry in every country of the world, and as of May 2007 we have a permanent presence in 170 nations.

In countless prayer meetings through the years, we've grappled with what it means to fulfill the Great Commission Jesus left us with in Mark 16 and Matthew 28. We have some understanding of preaching the gospel to every person, but what does it mean to disciple the nations? Most of us don't approach these questions as academics, but as practitioners of mercy and transformation. We're heavily involved in what we're writing about.

We offer our thoughts as those who have had to face hard realities in the trenches and wrestle with how to respond in a godly way. There is no final solution here, but there is a variety of responses from all over the world that have come out of the crucible of confronting human need.

In this book we have endeavored to lay foundations to understanding God's call to us as a church and as individual believers, including a look at both Old and New Testament teaching and examples, an overview of how the church has responded through the centuries, and thoughts on various strategic approaches to fulfilling God's call to disciple the nations. Some authors present inspiring examples, others strong values-based arguments in favor of working with him to answer our own prayers as he taught us to pray, "Your kingdom come. Your will be done on earth as it is in heaven" (Matt. 6:10).

In 1975 God spoke to Loren Cunningham, Bill Bright, and several other Christian leaders that there are seven spheres of life which influence the values and beliefs of any society: education, church, family, government, business and technology, the performing arts, and the media. These have since been slightly modified as: education; religion (church and mission); family; government; economy (including business, science, and technology); celebration (arts, entertainment, and sports); and public communication (media). I hope that the big picture revelation of God's love for the nations will inspire you and give you both encouragement and examples of ways you might contribute in the sphere of life to which God has called you.

Modern society is complex. In the midst of this complexity, God has promised that he has prepared good works for *you* (Eph. 2:10). You have a contribution to make. In this larger context of advancing God's kingdom on earth, what are the good works that he has prepared for you specifically? Uncertainty can keep us from stepping out and stepping up to the role of influence and service God has designed for us. We hope that this book will change that in your life.

Some have acted. Many of my friends and colleagues have given their lives to advancing his kingdom in obedience to his leading. Here are a few examples from the various spheres that might give you an inkling of the things that can be done. My hope is that these examples might make some links between this book and your life, sparking you to action.

I know a woman in Kathmandu who told me how the Lord asked her to take care of one sixteen-year-old ex-prostitute who was dying of AIDS. That led to further involvement, and soon she and her husband were taking care of nine of these girls, daily showing them the love of Christ. The government of Nepal began to seek them out to help find solutions to the tremendous social problem of child prostitution. This example includes influencing the spheres of health care and government.

I have friends who couldn't abide the lack of education for the children in Gabu, Guinea Bissau. They went there and started a grammar school based on biblical principles. Within a few years that school won an award as the best institution of childhood education in the country. In the process the Muslim parents of the students came to love and honor our Christian teachers. They even, with evident delight, call their own children "students of Jesus."

In the sphere of the church, I have a friend from India who converted out of a Hindu background. He was cruelly persecuted by his family and spent some years in exile from his homeland. Now he is back. The Lord has protected him and his family, and they are busy with the many churches that they and their workers have planted among his people group.

As an example of how to influence the sphere of the family, I know a girl from the Amazon region who was led by God to go to one of the most closed Muslim nations in Africa. Once there, she became the leader of prison reform for women convicts, most of whom had been jailed because of illegitimate pregnancies. A new prison was built, and programs were launched for the children who were in prison with their mothers.

My friend Lynn Green will tell this story in depth, but I want to mention the following example of the influence we can have in the sphere of business and technology. I know a man who was called by God to a certain nation, but he was denied a visa. However, he was able to get a visa and a job there as an engineer, and while serving, God led him to start a business. His business grew and became a place of Christian witness that contributed much to the nation. He went on to win a government award as the foreigner who most helped his adopted land during that year.

I have a colleague who loves the performing arts. He launched a ministry of dance, drama, and music that currently wins thousands to Christ every year. This is done primarily through live performances in schools and has now spread to four continents.

Media has a huge influence on our societies. I have a colleague and friend in Chile who was asked to be a guest on a radio program as a last-minute substitute because the original guest couldn't come. He did well and soon had his own program where he debated the leaders in Chilean society and government regarding the most pressing issues of their country. The radio program did so well that he was invited to do the same on television. One program focused on sex education in the schools, and my friend, a missionary and lawyer, was able to argue in the name of diversity that the Christian view of abstinence and purity needs to be taught as much as any other. He is influencing and teaching a whole nation.

It's true that those I cite above are almost all full-time missionaries. That is my context, after all, and those are the people that I tend to know. However, there are many who have no formal position in the church but involve themselves in advancing the kingdom of God. Here's one such story.

In the Brazilian city of Goiânia, six married couples became very disturbed by the problem of prostitution. It is widespread in their town and nation and often involves girls as young as twelve years old. These couples didn't just complain and celebrate their own superiority by criticizing the immorality though. They prayed about what to do and received what they believed was a strategy from God.

The couples arranged a nice weekend place in a rural setting and spent Saturday preparing. They cleaned, decorated, and prepared a feast. When the time came, the husbands went downtown to a house of prostitution in three teams of two. Each team prayerfully chose two girls and paid the fee, arranging to take them to another place as if to engage in prostitution with them. By all accounts, the trip back to the weekend place was quite confusing to the girls!

When they arrived, the wives came out and formally received the girls. The first thing these Christian wives did was to wash the feet of the prostitutes. By the time that was over, all of the girls were weeping. From there the couples took them to the table and served them a banquet. The prostitutes were so moved that they could barely eat. Finally they asked why these couples were doing such a thing, and that opened the door for the couples to talk about Jesus and his unconditional love.

At the time of this writing, all six of the girls have left their lives of prostitution, committed themselves to Jesus, and are being discipled by the wives who served them. Six prostitutes aren't a nation, but what if millions of Christians did similar things? What if we put our efforts into acts of extravagant love, the very law and nature of the kingdom? What if there were close to 100 percent involvement on the part of the billion or so Great Commission Christians around the world?

Not one of the people cited as an example in this chapter began as a celebrity or as a friend of those in high places of power. They all just got hold of a way to love others unconditionally in whatever sphere of life they were called to. We don't have to capture the reigns of the institutions of power in our societies in order to advance the kingdom of God. We just need to show the love that is the law of God's kingdom.

There are those who will be celebrities, those who will influence politicians and change governments for the better. There are those who will exercise vast influence through the arts. Some with great financing and organizational skills will launch megaprojects. Howard Malmstadt points out the need for this in his chapter. As you will see in the historical section of this book (Part 2), some Christians have brought change from positions of great power and influence. We fervently hope that many will read this book and be inspired to use their position and talent to serve the purposes of the kingdom.

Most of us, however, will have much humbler roles. This book gives the broad strokes. We encourage you to wrestle with the study questions in the back of the book in order to draw out of the text a personal answer for your own life.

Jesus began the Great Commission with "All authority in heaven and on earth has been given to me. Therefore go and make disciples of all nations" (Matt. 28:18–19). He passes on this authority to us. We have all we need to step out in faith and obedience and make a difference for God.

You are authorized by the King of heaven himself! Get involved. Find a group of friends to work with you. Have an adventure. Do warfare. Stir up some opposition. Win your victories. Be a part of something with cosmic implications. Love someone. Expand the kingdom.

Part 2

What the Bible Says

After undergoing personal travail over her perception of the small influence of believers on society, Landa Cope had some startling revelations from God about our problems and his solutions straight from the pages of Deuteronomy. Ponder carefully her insights into the breadth and depth of the counsel of God's Word. But be warned—her story might convince you to change your paradigms.

The Old Testament Template for Discipling Nations

Landa Cope

What's Gone Wrong?

I was channel surfing, mindlessly flipping through scores of TV programs to pass the time. I landed on a show where a British journalist was saying that Christians believe that many of their members being in a community will affect that community for good. The greater the Christian presence then, the greater the benefit to society at large. I agreed with the commentator. That is what we teach.

The journalist had proposed to select the most Christianized city (based on the largest percentage of believers actually attending church) and see how this influence worked out practically. Dallas, Texas, at that time had more people per capita in church on Sunday than any other community in the country. The journalist had therefore studied the social demographics of Dallas to see how this "Christian blessing" worked out practically in the community.

He presented various statistics and studies, including crime, safety on the streets, police enforcement, and the justice and penal system. We looked at health care: hospitals, emergency care, contagious diseases, infant mortality rate, and the distribution of caregivers. We reviewed education: equality of schools, safety, test scores, and graduation statistics. Jobs, housing, and general economics were evaluated. Were jobs available? Was housing available? Did potential income match available housing? We looked at homelessness and programs for those unable to care for themselves.

Each of these categories was evaluated using racial and economic factors. Was there equity regardless of color, creed, or income? And so on.

The program was perhaps an hour long and I watched it alone. I was devastated. No one would want to live in a city in that condition. The crime, the decrepit social systems, the disease, the economic discrepancies, and the racial injustice all disqualified this city from having an adequate quality of life. And this was the "most Christianized" city in America. I wanted to weep.

The program was not finished. The host now took this devastating picture of a broken community to the Christian leaders and asked for their observations. He chose leaders of stature and integrity. One by one, each pastor viewed the same facts about their city that I had just seen. With simplicity the narrator asked each minister, "As a Christian leader, what is your response to the condition of your city?" Without exception, in various ways, they all said the same thing: "This is not our concern . . . we are spiritual leaders."

The program finished, the room was silent, and my world began to crumble. I was shocked to silence—by the facts. I had no argument against the case that this journalist had built. As Christians we do say that our faith lived out will influence a society to good. We go beyond this. I have heard it said, and have taught, that it only takes 20 percent of a society believing anything to influence, even lead, the other 80 percent in a given direction. We teach that the gospel is good for a society, that its values will bless those beyond the members of faith! But the facts from nations with high percentages of professing Christians do not support this. We must look at the facts!

I was still grappling with questions: How could a community that is primarily Christian be in such abominable shape? How could the gospel result in such chaos? I began a four-month trip to Africa. I visited primarily Christianized nations—Togo, Ghana, Nigeria, Kenya, Uganda, and South Africa. My anguish increased. Mission statistics that I had quoted with joy burned in my mind. *Africa, 80 percent Christian south of the Sahara by the end of this century. Africa, the most evangelized continent in the world. Africa, the most churched continent by the end of this century.* Yet in each nation, the story was the same. Poverty, disease, violence, corruption, injustice, and chaos met me at every turn.

My heart was heavy as I traveled Africa, as I thought about my own nation. My prayer became, "Lord, what has gone wrong?" Nearly two thousand years of concentrated missions effort on this continent—how could it result in this? God spoke, simply and with a dawning revelation that would change my understanding of missions and my life calling, fundamentally and permanently. He said, "The devastation you see is the result of a gospel that limits itself to the preaching of salvation."

I was reeling over implications and questions. Why had I not been honest enough to see the discrepancy between my teaching and the visible results? If the gospel does influence all of society, how could America, possibly with more Christians per capita than any other time in its history, be slipping from biblical values in virtually every arena? Slipping into crime, immorality, poverty, corruption, justice, disease, drugs, homelessness, illiteracy, and more? How was it that I had never put all this together? Why had we not judged ourselves, and found ourselves wanting!

It had been clear to me for more than a year that as Christians we were missing a significant part of God's revelation. We were well on our way, in my generation, to reaching every creature with the salvation message, but what did it mean to disciple the nations? How could we regain the wisdom, knowledge, and influence to transform communities with the gospel as the church had done throughout history? What were the keys? I understood our gospel message was incomplete. But how would we restore the greater revelation?

In my search I had pursued men and women of God who seemed to see the same deficits in the impact of the church that I was seeing. One man who saw the need clearly was Tom Marshall. Pastoring a small church in New Zealand, this man of God had an enormous vision of the kingdom of God and the church's role in building its influence on earth. After he spoke at our university in Kona, I wept for hours with a broken heart over our diminished gospel message. As I wept, I prayed, "God, you must show us the road back. You must reveal again your great revelations of kingdom life beyond salvation." I was so constrained by the Holy Spirit it felt as if I was having a heart attack. "God, you must reveal yourself to me or I feel I will die of need."

Over the next few days I went to Pastor Marshall and asked the same questions I had asked others. The difference this time was that I was sure Tom Marshall would have the answer. "Tom how do we do it? How do we actually disciple the nations? How do we put feet to the vision?"

His answer was simple, short, and immediate. "I have no idea! God hasn't revealed that to me." That was all he said. To say that I was crestfallen is truly an understatement. The man I knew with the greatest vision in the area of my search had no answers for me. What hope was there?

I had come to Christianity reluctantly. As a college student I was a committed atheist and gave speeches on why not to believe the Bible. I longed for truth that could be lived on a practical basis, truth that could lead to justice and genuine love for others. I had never been a Christian for emotional or personal reasons. I am a follower of Christ because I believe the Bible is true and that whenever its teachings and principles are applied and measured, they will prove true. I was convinced, too, that based on God's character and nature, he is faithful and just, and that he would not command us to do something without telling us how to do it. If we ask him he will answer. My faith was on the line, and I believed that the God I knew was up to the challenge.

Cornfield Revelation

Within twelve months, I was traveling through the grain fields of the Great Plains of the US. I was on a seven-month trip visiting mission bases in America. Driving for a change, instead of flying, was a great relief for me, and it gave me wonderful time to process and pray. Before starting the journey I had asked the Lord to give me a plan for my time in the car. I had been reading through the Bible nearly every year and a half for over twenty years and had read most of the English versions at least once. During this drive I felt that God gave me a very specific goal of listening to the entire Bible from Genesis to Revelation during my trip. I will never forget the morning in the grain fields. I can still see the wheat and cornfields sliding by on both sides of the car mile after mile. The time of day, the angle of the light, the temperature, the clear blue skies are all as clear in my mind at this moment as they were the day God spoke. The penny dropped and everything in my life from that moment changed.

All of a sudden it was as though I were given ears to hear what I had read so many times in my life and never understood. Somewhere between Boise, Idaho, and Omaha, Nebraska, (which is about five days of corn and wheat,) I was driving along and all of a sudden I thought, *Whoa! Do you know what that chapter was about? It was about Law! Moses was teaching law. Moses was forming government.* A little farther through the corn I thought, *Whoa! Do you know what that chapter was about? It was about hygiene!* There was a passage on economics. Then one on family and health care. Now another on law, and on it went. The light flashed into my poor little brain. Revelation hit like a laser beam. Moses' job was to disciple a nation. His job was to teach people who had been slaves for more than three hundred years how to form and run their nation. Moses was to teach Israel God's principles of government, economics, the family, the priesthood, and every domain of human society. He had forty years in the wilderness to do it, and he had written it all down!

What had I been thinking when I had read the books of Moses for the first twenty or so times? I had been reading with "gospel of salvation" glasses! I had been taught to read the Scriptures looking for certain themes: salvation, sin, forgiveness, prayer, righteousness, and spiritual warfare. These great themes are there because they are major parts of the gospel message. I had been reading the books allegorically even though it is clear they are historical. They are records of events that took place in time and space. But with salvation glasses on, when I read of Israel in bondage to slavery, I saw a message on sin and life without Christ and salvation. When I read about the Jews in the wilderness, I learned about the "valley of decision" between the life of sin and God's great promise of salvation. When Israel entered the promised land . . . salvation! They were God's at last. They were saved! I preached these messages. The themes—these parallels of sin, decision, and salvation—are there. There is nothing wrong in teaching them. But they are not the primary message of the text. What was happening to Moses was real and not allegorical. He had a real population of Jews, in a real desert, with the real challenge of turning them into a prosperous nation. Moses was discipling a real nation in the truths that would make them great in every area of life. And God inspired him to write it all down—for you and me. I knew I would never be able to read the Bible in the same way again. My mind was turned upside down.

What a job Moses had! We think we have needy nations today! Look at what he had to deal with. We know that 600,000 able-bodied men left Egypt with Moses (Exod. 12:37–38). But what was the entire population? If we take the number of women and children for each man in Jacob's family of seventy (Gen. 46:26–27) when they entered Egypt, it is about 4.5 to 1. At that ratio the number of Israelites leaving Egypt would have been around 2,700,000 additional people. But remember the reason they were having problems with the pharaohs is because they were multiplying so rapidly they threatened the balance of population with the Egyptians (Exod. 1:6–7). Furthermore, Israel did not leave alone. The slaves that were not part of Israel left with them. They had alien members wandering with them from the very beginning of their wilderness history (Exod. 12). It is no exaggeration to say that Moses was leading some three and a half million people out of Egypt into the desert.

To give that number perspective, we need to realize that it is like the entire population of New Zealand. The largest refugee situation in modern history was that of the Afghans on the Pakistani border after the invasion by the former Soviet Union. They numbered in the area of two million. Yet, with all the resources of the United Nations, the Red Cross, and aid from developed countries combined, this refugee situation overwhelmed our modern agencies. The Jews had no outside help to come to their rescue. Moses' people were in far worse circumstances. The Afghan refugees had a country to go back to. They had homes and schools and businesses and institutions to return to. They had banks and roads and infrastructures to rebuild, even if the Soviet Union had demolished some of them. The Afghans were refugees. The Jews fleeing Egypt were people without a portfolio. They had no country. They had only a promise.

Imagine!

These are a people who have grown from a tribe of seventy people to more than three million in 430 years. They have been in exile this entire time. For the last three hundred years of their existence they have been slave labor under Egyptian pharaohs. They have just walked out of the nation of Egypt with what they are able to carry and what animals they own. Think about it:

- They are poor.
- They have no schools.
- They have no government.

- They have no economy.
- They have no land.
- They have no army.
- They have no industry.
- They have no religious system.
- They have a welfare mentality and no work ethic.
- They have been oppressed and victimized.
- They have a social system that is not developed.

They are, without a doubt, the most undeveloped large nation of people that has ever existed on the face of the earth. Compared to any nation I can think of today, Israel was in much worse shape. It is to these people that God says, "You are not a people, but I will make you a people" (Deut. 4:20; 14:2). He promises these people, in this condition, that they will become a great nation and other nations will admire their greatness and be blessed by them (Deut. 4:5–8). They have just left one of the great civilizations in human history, Egypt in its glory days under the pharaohs. The Jews are an impoverished mob in the middle of a wasteland. Yet, to them God says, "I am going to make you a great nation!" Can you imagine the unbelief, the bewilderment, even the cynicism they might have felt?

But, in just about three hundred years' time, God does it. He makes them one of the greatest—if not the greatest—nation on the face of the earth. They have such a notorious reputation within three centuries that the whole known world is talking about it. A queen from the Arabian peninsula hears of this great kingdom, and she decides to check it out firsthand. She travels north, passing the crossing north of the Red Sea leading to Egypt, the former "greatest nation." Her journey continues further north toward Canaan. Listen to her words:

> She said to the king, "The report I heard in my own country about your achievements and your wisdom is true. But I did not believe these things until I came and saw with my own eyes. Indeed not even half was told me; in wisdom and wealth you have far exceeded the report I heard." (1 Kings 10:6–7)

God had made a promise to build a great nation and he did it. He built a great nation in every category. They had just laws. They were economically prosperous. Their architecture and crafts were brilliant. They had superior education and wisdom. One of their kings, Solomon, was a great scientist. They were even admired by their former slave masters, the Egyptians. They were by no means a perfect kingdom. God never indicated he was promising that. But they were a great kingdom. This history of Israel is not written as an allegory from which we are to learn the benefits of salvation, although you could make that point from the text. This is history. It happened in time and space to real people, to a real nation. The point for us is that if God can do it once, he can do it again. There is hope in the Scriptures for every nation on earth, because if God could disciple Israel, he can disciple any country. God's truth can and does transform communities and can do it for any existing nation in any age, because not one community or nation in the world is worse off than the Israelites in the wilderness. But the question is, how?

The Old Testament Template

God has told us to reach every creature with the message of salvation, and he has taught us how to do that. He left us the model of Jesus and Paul and the New Testament church to guide us into the global vision of reaching every language, every tribe, and every people. But God has also told us to "disciple every nation." How do we do that? God, in his faithfulness, has not given us a mandate to disciple the nations and then left us ignorant as to how to accomplish it. He has left us a model in Israel and a teacher in Moses. Israel and its journey from slavery to greatness is the template of how to disciple a nation. The keys to the job are in the story and life of Moses, just as the keys to evangelism are in the story and lives of Jesus and Paul. We have an Old Testament template for how to disciple a nation!

A template—what is that? You use one in drafting. When you want to put shrubbery around a building for an architectural drawing, you don't draw all those little trees by hand, you have a landscaping template. It's an artist's "cheater." It allows you to draw the same bush a thousand times perfectly. The root word is temple. The temple is a template, or a model. It's something God uses to illustrate something. It's a small version of something greater. In the New Testament God says, "Here's how you reach every creature. Here's the message." In the Old Testament God says, "Here's how you disciple the nations, and here's how I did it with the most underdeveloped nation on the face of the earth." God wanted us to be encouraged so that by his grace and power we can do it. God is not silent on those things he's told us to do. In his justice he has left a witness for us that will guide us in the many decades it takes to disciple a nation.

I began to study Deuteronomy and the Old Testament from the perspective of what God taught about each area of influence in society. For example, what did the Word teach about government, economics, and so forth? I would start with the books of Moses because it was obviously his job to teach a nation these things. Then I would work my way through the rest of the Bible to see the whole counsel of God's Word on any given domain. I don't think I had been this excited about something since the invention of television.

I already had an idea of the domains I would try to study in Scripture, because our university had developed around the concept that certain "spheres of influence" disciple nations. The areas I chose were government, family and health care, economics, science and technology, arts and entertainment, communication, education, and, of course, the traditional work of the church. My thought as I began was that the very study itself would confirm whether these were primary categories in God's Word or not. I began to color my Bible by domain or sphere of influence, using eight colored pencils. As I studied, I began to realize, *My goodness, this chapter on government has basic principles in it. It's not that we are to transplant Israel's government on a nation, but we are to use the same principles and apply them today.*

Government

In my Bible Deuteronomy 1:9–18 is purple, for government. That is the domain this passage is talking about. It is all about government. I have underlined verses 13, 14, and 17, because in this passage you can see that Moses is pursuing some principles of government. He says, "Choose some wise, understanding and respected men from each of your tribes, and I will set them over you" (Deut. 1:13).

That means that it was representative. Every tribe was to have someone representing their tribe, and it was some sort of elective process. The tribe was able to choose for themselves whom they would send. In verse 14 Moses reminds the people, "You answered me, 'What you propose to do is good.'" If you translate that into modern political language, Moses had a consensus. You cannot govern a people who will not be governed. But there was consensus, representative consensus. Is this a democracy? No. There are many forms of government that include an elected representative and a consensus process. Whatever the form of government, these two elements must be present for it to be godly government.

In verses 16 and 17, Moses talks about the laws and the court system. He says:

> "And I charged your judges at that time: Hear the disputes between brothers and judge fairly, whether the case is between brother Israelites or between one of them and an alien. Do not show partiality in judging; hear both small and great alike.... Bring me any case too hard for you, and I will hear it."

What is Moses saying about law? He's saying that it is to be impartial and unprejudiced (because of race, color, or creed). It is to have a process of appeal. It is to be comprehensive. It is to deal with matters of justice, no matter how big or small. These are political principles we can preach and work for, because they are rooted in God's design for government.

Economics

If we move on to Deuteronomy 15:1–10 in my Bible, it is green—for money. As I started to go through Deuteronomy just for economics, it blew my mind! The principles here are so culturally unbiased. They are so basic to what will work and what will not work. They give such clarity as to where we, who are called Christian nations, have drifted from the ways of God. These principles give light and discernment to us. Although there are several verses, I have chosen to focus on verses 1, 4, 6, and 8.

In verse 1 it says, "At the end of every seven years you must cancel debts."

What does this mean? This means that there was not to be an economic system that put people into debt for unlimited periods of time. The loaner and the loanee were to think in terms of how this could be paid off before the seventh year. We won't go into detail, but there was also the fifty-year Jubilee. It was very important in God's economics that the people would not be burdened by debt indefinitely.

Verse 4 says, "However, there should be no poor among you, for in the land the Lord your God is giving you to possess as your inheritance, he will richly bless you, if only you fully obey the Lord your God."

The goal was that there would be no poor. Moses is not speaking to the government at this point. He is speaking to the nation of Israel at large. He is telling them as a nation, "Don't let there be any poor." It was to be a responsibility not of the government, but of society at large.

Verse 6 continues, "For the Lord your God will bless you as he has promised, and you will lend to many nations but will borrow from none. You will rule over many nations but none will rule over you."

This passage has so much to do with my own country. I mean, America is so far from Christian economics that it's unbelievable! The greatest problem is not the government. The greatest problem is that we will not live within our means. The Lord said to the nation of Israel, "You are not to be like that. You are to trust me to supply what you need from within your land. You may help other nations with generosity, because I am going to bless you so much you'll have abundance. But you are not to go begging to other nations. If you want more, you must come back to me. You must find a system within the land I have given you." And it was the working out not only of an economic blessing, but of a personal discipline.

Verse 8 says, "Rather be open-handed and freely lend him whatever he needs."

The Lord is not against lending. He even tells them when they can charge interest and when they can't. He wanted them to lend to the poor. He wanted them to lend to other nations, but to do it within constraints. And when they had lent to the poor, they were to lend what the poor could pay back within seven years or what they were willing to *give* them after the seven years.

Science, Technology, and Health Care

Chapter 23 is a fun chapter—one of my favorites. I have been meditating on this for the last six months. This is not one of those I call a "promise-box verse." This particular passage never makes it on Christian greeting cards. But I tell you, whenever I have gone to a place where they do not understand this principle, I have wished they had read Deuteronomy 23. In my early years in YWAM, I seemed to have had a special dispensation for these kinds of places.

Verses 12 through 14 tell us, "Designate a place outside the camp where you can go to relieve yourself. As part of your equipment have something to dig with, and when you relieve yourself, dig a hole and cover up your excrement." Now get this: "For the Lord your God moves about in your camp to protect you and to deliver your enemies to you."

This lends itself to visualization. Here's the Lord our God before Deuteronomy 23, tip-toeing around small mounds! Why is this here? Because God cares about these things. This is not outside the body of the laws. In fact, when you look at science and public health (which in my Bible is blue), you see whole passages that are simply about health and hygiene and how to be a clean community. Many times we read about being unclean and relate it to sin. The Jews needed cleansing in everything from "if you touch mildew" to "a priest who touches blood." Now, if you think about it, this is in the time of sacrificing! How often do you think a priest would touch blood? Every day, if he was working in the temple. When you take the sum total of all the things that are considered unclean, for which they must go outside the camp to wash, you go, "I get it! He means *unclean*, as in *dirty*, as in *take a bath—often!*" Our forefathers said, "Cleanliness is next to godliness," and we thought, *Sweet little old people. We know God is about much more important things.* No. They were saying, "Look! God is in our camp!"

Be clean. Your land is to be clean. Your cities are to be clean. Your bodies are to be clean. Before people knew the concept of germs, God was teaching them about germs. God could have said something far more mysterious. He could have said, "There are little things, not visible to the eye, growing on your skin. You don't see them, but when you breathe you take them into your body!" This would have been unbelievably mystical. So he gives them practical things. I think, if you were a doctor, you could probably extract from this list that these are all ways by which infection gets transmitted. We know this happens in refugee camps. The absence of soap and the contamination of water causes many to die. God is saying, "These things do not glorify me. I want to give you health. Obey these body laws, not because they have some mystical power, but because they follow the natural laws of the material world that I have made." He is simply causing Israel to be thousands of years ahead of every other nation on earth.

If you look at an overview of the book of Deuteronomy, you will get an idea of the emphasis on different domains. People in ministry don't need to worry; they still have about 46 percent of the book. But the second largest concentration of the book is on government and the military, and this is the first thing that is established. The religious context and the worship life come later. The Israelites have to have a government or they cannot be a people. Twenty-five percent of Deuteronomy is outlining governmental laws and the organization of a military defense. The arts have 6 percent. This is all primarily in one or two chapters. It's wonderful! I found the origin of opera. Moses wrote the first opera. It is the longest single song I can find at this point in time. He sings the entire history of Israel and says, "Learn this song." So, it was important to have the history of the people represented in more than just books and words. The arts are right there at the beginning of Moses' instructions.

About 6.5 percent of Deuteronomy is on the family; economics has 6 percent; 4 percent is on health and hygiene; education has 2.5 percent; 2.5 percent is on nature; and 1 percent is on communications. Or, if we consider the entire book to be relevant, communications becomes 100 percent!

Now these are not perfect numbers. But you'll know God inspired me when I tell you how I arrived at these figures. I counted all the lines in the book, because it was the only way I could get any accurate estimate. I took the number of lines on a given subject against the total number of lines in the book of Deuteronomy. If you know me, you will know that this was God! And so it gives us an overview. The body of laws is all of these things. It is not only the 46 percent of laws that applies to worship, the altar, the temple, and instructions in those areas. No, the body of law has to do with every domain.

A National Inventory

I discovered that chapter 28 gives us what I call a national inventory. It gives us a way of measuring how our nation is doing. It says if you are experiencing *these* things, you are being blessed. If you are experiencing *those* things, you are being cursed. When I drew out the different domains that are blessed when we are following God's laws, I realized that he talks about the whole of society. So he says, "You will be blessed in the city; you will be blessed in the country." When I hold American cities up to this, I know we are not being blessed. Our cities are a mess. He says, "You'll be blessed in the rural areas—the farming communities." He says, "Your children will be blessed." We are not blessed as children in America. Our farms are not blessed. The speed at which farms are going under is one of our national issues. He says, "Your economy will be blessed." He says, "Your going out and your coming in will be blessed." I call that obtaining a visa, and you can pretty well tell that some countries are not blessed in this area! For years it was nearly impossible for South Africans to get out to another country. But that's changed. Why? Because they have had a course-correction as a nation. God is beginning to bless them again. And their whole nation can see it. The world can see it, saying, "What's going on in South Africa? What's happening down there?" Deuteronomy in action.

God says, "Your military will be blessed." In Leviticus 26:8 we read of the blessed, "a hundred of you will chase ten thousand," and in Deuteronomy 28:25 we read of the cursed, "You will come at [your enemies] from one direction but flee from them in seven." In my country, that would describe the Vietnam War. We were not blessed—the largest military power in the world could not win the war.

God says that the weather will be blessed (bad news for California!). He says national debt will be blessed—by lack of it, that is. America is failing on this list. How is your nation doing? God basically says that if you obey this body of laws, your country will be blessed.

But in verses 15 and 20 of chapter 28, God says, "This is what your country will look like if I have cursed you." He says there will be "curses, confusion and rebuke in everything you put your hand to." Nothing will work. We can name countries like that, where nothing works. Haiti, for example, or Somalia, Rwanda, or Nigeria. And in only a short time, I believe, the United States. We are slipping quickly. He says, "There will be disease. Your weather will be cursed. Your military will be routed. You will have crime. Your families will fall apart." Does this sound familiar? Does this begin to describe some so-called Christian nations? Are these nations saying that they are the ones we need to model ourselves after because they are Christian nations? I think we have to look very carefully. Some aspects may be Christian, but where is the nation that can boast of these blessings without these curses? He says, "Your government will be cursed. You will have the reputation of being a cursed country. Your economy will be cursed." Basically, everything will be cursed.

You see, Christianity is not just revealed by the changes of hearts in men and women. Christianity is revealed through the corporate, through the people. It includes everything society needs. It is saying, "Here are laws you can plant your feet on. If you will build your nations on these principles, they will be strong." From Abraham on, God's plan was that every nation in the world would be taught these principles.

Lessons from Africa

I have a book which was given to me in Zimbabwe. It was written by George Kinoti, a professor of zoology at the University of Nairobi. It was amazing confirmation to me of what God has been saying, because this author has written my message, right down to the Scripture references and the points I was preaching in Africa. Let me share with you something Kinoti says:

Experts tell us that Christianity is growing faster in Africa than on any other continent. At the same time the people are rapidly becoming poorer, and the moral and social fabrics of society are disintegrating fast. Christianity is clearly not making a difference to the African nations. Thus, although a revival started in Rwanda sixty years ago, that country has known nothing but poverty and civil war since gaining independence in 1962. In the latest tribal violence between April and July of 1995, an estimated 500,000 to 1 million Rwandans were butchered and another three to four million were forced to flee to Zaire. Uganda, which soon became the heart of this revival, experienced about two decades of untold suffering. The Ugandan economy was shattered. Torture, murder, civil war and displacement of people reached unimaginable levels. And all the while Uganda had one of the strongest churches in Africa.[1]

We say, "Africa is 80 percent evangelized south of the Sahara." No, it isn't. Africa is 80 percent saved south of the Sahara. People have known a changed heart. There are hundreds of thousands of churches and evangelists. It is the most Christianized continent in the world, if you are looking at saved people. But does it fit any of the criteria for a blessed nation, as defined by God? The answer is no. In fact, thirty of the forty poorest countries of the world are in this region. God is wanting to teach us how to disciple nations. Africa is ready. You can say that in our normal sense of the word, they are evangelized. But now it is time to build the nations. God says the Africans need the holistic view of life; they need the Bible from Genesis to Revelation. And he says that it was not Africans who brought in this segregated view of life. The African view was, perhaps, more holistic prior to the arrival of missionaries.

Developing Community

We have some repentance to do before God is going to give authority. I want to look at a section in Numbers, the camp of Judah. This is an outline of what Moses describes as the community plan for the nation of Israel, as given in Numbers, chapters 2 and 3. Israel is divided into tribes. And so you have thirteen tribes. Then you have the tent of meeting in the middle. You have the Levites around the outside of the tent of meeting. This is a planned community. Why? Because planning how a community will live is important. It had emergency strategies for evacuation. You can imagine the chaos of 3.5 million people being frightened and taking off. No, they were instructed how to leave, tribe by tribe. There was a whole strategy for moving them as a nation. There was a defense strategy behind the way this was being laid out. And you see that the people being able to come together was a central issue to the community.

When you take this to the high-rise ghettos of the world, you can see that they are wrong. Not because of their size, but because they make no provision for people to be a community. And you see that the religious community is placed all the way around the people, circling the community meeting place. There was a worldview represented in their community development layout.

When you look at the Reformers' cities, like Lausanne, you see that they had a community development plan that was born out of the Word of God. On the highest hill was the cathedral. A little bit lower than that were the buildings of the government. And a little bit lower than that was the university. Then the city was built around those three elements of the society. They had done their homework. They knew what God was saying about discipling nations in his Word. They had extracted the principles from the nation of Israel that were needed for Europe at that point in time.

Disciple the Nations

When we study discipling nations as we have seen it demonstrated by the church in history, one is struck by a specific focus of the Reformers. Each of them discussed at least two things: they stressed a deep devotional life and a commitment to the Word of God. God wants us in his Word. We have to know first and foremost what the Word of God says about the discipling of the nations. He has left us a model. He has taught us how to extract the principles. They must be the principles we build on in every domain, because if we don't, we will disciple the nations in something other than eternal principles of truth. God has been faithful and just to you and me. He has left a record. He has said, "Here's how I did it. Now you apply these principles to the future generations." But we must be in his Word. We must be consumed with a love for God's Word. It must be like a mine for us, in which we will dig deeply to find the gold and the gems. May we make it a daily prayer, "God help me understand your Word and what you are saying about how to disciple the nations!"

God has given us a vision. He has given us a mandate to disciple the nations. He has given us a task for this generation. He has allowed us the privilege of being alive in a season when this is what the Holy Spirit wants to do around the world. We can build on no other foundation than the Word of God—the template that he has given us. We have no other message. This is what we are to disciple others with. It is unbelievably comprehensive. The principles are sure and sound, but he is not going to give them to light inquirers. He is going to require that we love him and acknowledge that this is his Word—that we obey him to meditate on it day and night. Then he will release to us the secrets of his universe. When we preach them they will be like a sharp sword bringing clear answers into darkness, setting captives free, giving sight to those who cannot see, and discipling nations into all of his blessings. When we are asked where we get this understanding, he will abide by no answer except from Jesus Christ, as we feed on his Word.

Will you do that? That is your responsibility. In order for that to happen, we have to be thankful that he's told us how to do it. And we have to be diligent, with the Holy Spirit's help, in studying and understanding what he reveals to us. Then he will open our minds and give us clarity. Then he will open our mouths and give us authority. We provide the faithfulness; he provides the revelation, because God is eager to disciple the nations of the world.

Notes

After writing this material for this book, Landa continued to expand on her understanding. More information can be found on her Old Testament Template Website: www.templateinstitute.com (accessed December 1, 2007).

1. George Kinobi, *Hope for Africa—and What the Christians Can Do* (Nairobi, Kenya: AISRED, 1994).

Just as Landa illuminated how God embedded principles for building godly nations in the Old Testament, David Hamilton leads us in an analysis of God's strategy for fulfilling the Great Commission mandate to disciple nations as it is revealed throughout the New Testament. David explores the breadth and depth of God's forever dream, and gives practical, inspirational insights into how we can play our part to see it realized.

The New Testament Basis for the Discipling of Nations

David Joel Hamilton

Growing up, I loved reading a good mystery. Whether it was reading about Sherlock Holmes or Hercules Poirot, the mark of a great mystery author is that the tale would grip my attention until the final page. I knew that as I read, the pages were littered with clues, which I avidly tried to detect and understand. But if a mystery was well written I wouldn't be able to figure out the ending until I got there. Once there, the clues scattered throughout the preceding pages seemed so obvious and so numerous I couldn't imagine how I'd missed them the first time through.

The first read of the mystery would produce a see-saw of conclusions. At one point I would be sure that the butler had committed the crime, but then a chapter or two later, I was certain that it was the cook. I'd have to keep reading, sifting through the details as they were revealed. When in the final chapter the crime was resolved, I often experienced two emotions, one immediately overrunning the other. First there was the sense of great surprise at the unexpected final twist of events that led to the discovery of the criminal. I'd think to myself, *How could I not have seen that coming?* Then I'd experience a sense of sheer satisfaction as the resolution became clear. I'd tell myself, *Of course, that's the way it was. It was so obvious. All the clues pointed in this direction.* And then I'd re-read the book. The clues which had previously been hidden seemed to jump off the page in light of the understanding gained from having read the final chapter.

So why not start by reading the final chapter? The idea crossed my mind more than once, but I resisted temptation. Why? Because the drama of discovery was ever so thrilling. Trying to solve the crime before the renowned detective was a challenge I wanted to undertake time and again. Besides, if the ending was known, the suspense along the way would be greatly diminished. The second reading allowed me the joy of savoring the mastery of the author who had so cleverly woven into the fabric of the tale all the clues needed for its resolution without prematurely giving away the finale.

God's Great Mystery

Similarly, for thousands of years—from God's first encounters with Abraham until Christ's death and resurrection—generations of God-seekers sought to understand the unfolding drama of God's redemptive actions in history. It developed like the best mystery, littered with clues obvious to the discerning reader who has read the "final chapter," but hidden to those who found themselves caught up in the story as it moved from generation to generation. Though God was clearly laying out his plan, even his archenemies did not rightly understand the clues which were given to reveal his purposes. Reflecting on this, Paul wrote, "None of the rulers of this age understood it, for if they had, they would not have crucified the Lord of glory" (1 Cor. 2:8). Satan and his henchmen misread the clues, they misunderstood God's design, and so the day they thought was their day of victory proved to be their downfall.

Jesus' advent is the culminating chapter of God's unfolding mystery. Paul speaks of the gospel as "the revelation of the mystery hidden for long ages past, but now revealed and made known" (Rom. 16:25). What was once mysterious is no longer a mystery. God has made known to us not only Christ's identity, but also the eternal purpose of his coming. "This mystery is that through the gospel the Gentiles are heirs together with Israel, members together of one body, and sharers together in the promise in Christ Jesus" (Eph. 3:6). *All* peoples, Jews *and* Gentiles reconciled, *all* ethnic groups redeemed, *all* nations transformed together by the work of Jesus—this is the mystery which was "made known" (Eph. 3:3). The objective of Paul's ministry was "to make plain to *everyone* the administration of this mystery, which for ages past was kept hidden in God, who created *all* things. His intent was that now, through the church, the manifold wisdom of God should be made known to the rulers and authorities in the heavenly realms, according to his eternal purpose which he accomplished in Christ Jesus our Lord" (Eph. 3:9–11).[1] So what is his eternal purpose?

The clues become evident after one reads the culminating chapters. After reading of Jesus' incarnation and earthly ministry, after reading of Jesus' death and resurrection, after reading Jesus' final words to his disciples before his ascension into heaven, all of Scripture becomes very clear. God has always had a redemptive purpose. The intent of his heart, that which has motivated all of his actions from before the beginning of time, has always been that he does not want "anyone to perish, but *everyone* to come to repentance" (2 Pet. 3:9). That is why Jesus Christ "was chosen before the creation of the world, but was revealed in these last times" (1 Pet. 1:20). God's eternal plan is no longer a mystery. God "wants *all* men to be saved and to come to a knowledge of the truth. For there is one God and one mediator between God and men, the man Christ Jesus, who gave himself as a ransom for *all* men—the testimony given in its proper time" (1 Tim. 2:4–6). This is God's forever dream.

Though clarified in the New Testament writings, God's forever dream is evident throughout the Scriptures. He tells the patriarch Abraham, "I will bless you ... so that you will be a blessing ... and in you *all* the families in the earth shall be blessed."[2] King David grasps God's dream when he writes, "*All* the ends of the earth shall remember and turn to the Lord; and *all* the families of the nations shall worship before Him."[3] The prophets Habakkuk and Isaiah envision the fulfillment of God's global dream, saying "the earth will be full of the knowledge of the Lord as the waters cover the sea."[4] Similarly, the apostle John sees around the throne of God "a great multitude ... from *every* nation, from *all* tribes and peoples and languages" (Rev. 7:9 NRSV). The pages of Scripture reveal a God who wants *every* individual, *every* family, *every* community, *every* town and village, *every* sphere of society, *every* people group and nation to experience the transforming redemption of the gospel.

Two Ways to "Go!"

This is most clearly seen in Jesus' final encounter with his disciples. His parting instructions to his followers, commonly referred to as the Great Commission,[5] clearly reveal God's forever dream. Let's consider the Great Commission passages as recorded in Matthew and Mark. They read as follows:

> "Go into all the world and preach the good news to all creation." (Mark 16:15)

> "Therefore go and make disciples of all nations, baptizing them in the name of the Father and of the Son and of the Holy Spirit, and teaching them to obey everything I have commanded you. And surely I am with you always, to the very end of the age." (Matt. 28:19–20)

As we look at these two passages, we note similarities and differences. Both contain the exhortation to go, but what follows from there illustrates the breadth of God's dream.

First, note the different verbs used in these two passages. Mark says "preach." Matthew uses "disciple." To preach or proclaim the gospel is an easily definable task. How long does it take to preach the gospel? The essence can be told in a few minutes or in a few hours or days. In contrast, to disciple is a verb that connotes a much longer process. To disciple means to shape, fashion, mold, teach, coach, model, instruct, train, mentor, educate, transform. How long does it take to disciple? To do it right requires years of intentional effort. While preaching has a defined beginning and end, teaching has an ongoing, progressive component. In discipleship, the mentor teaches "letter by letter, line by line, lesson by lesson" (Isa. 28:10 GNT). When is this process complete? Only when the disciple is fully "conformed to the likeness of" Jesus (Rom. 8:29). Until then disciples "are being transformed into his likeness with ever-increasing glory" (2 Cor. 3:18).

Second, note the different objects of the verb in each version of the Great Commission. In Mark the focus is on every single individual. *Every* person who is of sufficient age and reason to understand must have the opportunity to hear the gospel message. No one person is to be excluded. The scope is clear: it involves *every* creature, *all* individuals. Every. All.

But in Matthew the focus of the impact is not personal; it is corporate. The object of the verb is not every individual, but every nation. *Every* people, *all* ethnic groups must have the opportunity to experience the shaping, transforming, discipling impact of the gospel. No nation is to be excluded. The scope is clear: it involves *every* society, *all* peoples. Every. All.

Let's summarize what we've covered so far:

Mark 16	Go	Preach	Individuals
Matthew 28	Go	Teach	Nations

Can We Do It?

At this point we must ask a question of feasibility. Is the Great Commission doable? There are over 6.3 billion people on earth. Nearly one-third of them have never ever heard of Jesus. Does God really expect us to preach to every single one? Is it even possible? We must answer this question in the light of God's character. Would a just and loving God ask us to do something that is impossible to accomplish? Of course not! So, the fact that he has commanded us to preach the gospel to every human being clearly implies that this is a doable task.

If we can do it, then we must do it! Love for him who first loved us motivates us. For it is always the goal of the lover to make the dreams of their beloved one come true. This is why Paul writes, "I am compelled to preach" (1 Cor. 9:16) "for Christ's love compels us" (2 Cor. 5:14). Proclamation of the gospel is not to be seen as a laborious task to be fulfilled. It is a love gift offered back to God with gratitude for his undying love.

Clearly Jesus expected us to complete the Great Commission. This is evident in his prophetic words, "This gospel of the kingdom will be preached in the whole world as a testimony to all nations" (Matt. 24:14).

Mark 16 envisions a future in which every individual of sufficient age and reason to hear and understand the gospel will have had such an opportunity. This is like a snapshot of a digital camera. Only God will know when the last person on earth capable of hearing the gospel in some form has heard it. To this end we strive with a sense of great urgency, because the very nature of the command requires that it be fulfilled in the span of a single generation. We cannot preach to those who died before we were born, nor to those who will be born after we die.

Mark 16 will be fulfilled at some point in time. In terms of preaching the gospel to every individual, each generation is responsible for itself. If we don't do it in our generation, the next will have to pick up the task afresh. It's clear that this aspect of the Great Commission is a monogenerational task, which requires of us all the greatest zeal and commitment to see his dream become a reality. Jesus reflects this sense of urgency when he says, "As long as it is day, we must do the work of him who sent me. Night is coming, when no one can work" (John 9:4).

From Snapshot to Video

When we shift from Mark 16 to Matthew 28, we realize that this, too, must be a doable task, because the God who so commanded is just. Yet we realize Matthew 28 represents a different aspect of the fulfillment of God's forever dream. If Mark 16 is a snapshot of some future point in time, Matthew 28 is a rolling video. Mark 16 is a monogenerational task because it is focused on individuals who are "destined to die once, and after that to face judgment" (Heb. 9:27). On the other hand, Matthew 28 is a multigenerational task involving transforming a society, a task which transcends the life span of any one individual.

When we see God's dealings with the first nation he called to himself, we see that he employed a multigenerational strategy to transform the descendants of Abraham into the people of God. In each generation God revealed more and more of his ways. His goal was to see his kingdom principles implemented to bring transformation. His multigenerational strategy for the corporate expression of humanity is revealed in his name: "the God of Abraham, the God of Isaac and the God of Jacob. . . . This is my name forever, the name by which I am to be remembered from generation to generation."[6]

This corporate, multigenerational aspect of the Great Commission requires strategic, long-term planning and action. In terms of discipling nations, each generation is responsible not only for itself, but also for future generations. We must live not only for ourselves but also for our children and our children's children to the third and fourth generations. If we fail to do so, God's dream will go unfulfilled.

One of the saddest stories in the Old Testament is that of King Hezekiah of Judah. The end of his life is especially tragic, because for the most part, his reign was exemplary. It is said of him that he "trusted in the Lord, the God of Israel. There was no one like him among all the kings of Judah, either before him or after him" (2 Kings 18:5). After a lifetime of trusting God, experiencing his miraculous deliverance, and being a catalyst for spiritual revival among the people, Hezekiah could say to the Lord, "I have walked before you faithfully and with wholehearted devotion and have done what is good in your eyes" (2 Kings 20:3). Nevertheless, though he was pious, his unwise and short-sighted policies (2 Kings 20:12–18) sowed the seeds of the destruction of the nation in subsequent generations.

When Isaiah the prophet rebuked him and spoke of impending doom for his descendants, Hezekiah callously shrugged off the prophecy of judgment because "he thought, 'Will there not be peace and security in my lifetime?'" (2 Kings 20:19). Hezekiah's son Manasseh succeeded him and proceeded to become the worst of Judah's kings. He went so far as to offer several of his sons, Hezekiah's grandsons, in a fiery sacrifice to the pagan god Moloch.[7] This story is a sober reminder that we must not live for ourselves and our own times alone, but we must also give ourselves to create conditions which will further the well-being of subsequent generations.

Let us summarize what we have discovered about the Great Commission. Jesus' final words show us that he desires that every individual be redeemed and every society be transformed by the message of the gospel and the power of the Spirit. While the former requires urgent action to make sure the gospel is preached to all during our lifetime, the latter gives us reason to plan multigenerational strategies which will transform communities and peoples.

Mark 16	Go	Preach	Individuals	Monogenerational	Urgent
Matthew 28	Go	Teach	Nations	Multigenerational	Strategic

So we clearly see the individual and the corporate aspects of the Great Commission. God's concern for individuals and corporate expressions of humanity are present everywhere in the Hebrew Scriptures. Time and again, the prophets of old direct their words at times to individuals, at times to cities and nations. God's care for individuals like Abraham, David, the Shunammite, and Esther is clearly seen, as is his love for cities like Jerusalem and Nineveh, tribes like Benjamin and Judah, and nations like Israel and Egypt. Both the individual and the corporate are important to God.

This loving commitment to transform both individual human beings and their societies is exhibited throughout Jesus' life as well. The dual nature of the Great Commission is not a new concept expressed at the end of Jesus' earthly ministry; it is the passionate conclusion of a life lived caring for both individual and corporate expressions of humanity. Jesus ministered to numerous individuals. He also had a mission linked to a people. He thought strategically of nations. His mission was to touch not only individuals, but also a people with his grace. The people as a whole was important to him, as was every individual within the people.

Jesus took both seriously. In the gospels we are told of two instances in which Jesus wept: once upon learning of the death of his friend Lazarus (John 11:35) and once when he prophetically foresaw the destruction of Jerusalem (Luke 19:41). In both cases there was sorrow for the destruction that sin brings in a fallen world. Whereas he wept silently for Lazarus, he wept audibly over Jerusalem. In both, the anguish is deep and genuine. God passionately cares for lost persons and lost societies.

The Mystery Revealed

Reading Jesus' final words is like reading the last chapter of a mystery. This is the climactic point of revelation. This is when all the clues start falling into place. When we begin to understand God's unconditional love for individuals and nations, it gives us a framework to go back and reread the Scriptures, looking for clues which we might have overlooked at first. With each successive reading the picture becomes clearer, and we see that God has always intended that we cooperate with him in seeing individuals redeemed and nations discipled.

New sets of questions form as we go back to reread and rethink the Scriptures. Why the careful documentation of the catalogue of nations in Genesis 10 and elsewhere? Is this just due to a fascination with historical accuracy? Or do nations as nations hold a special place in God's heart? Why did God deal with the nation of Israel as he did? Was it only a pragmatic means for bringing the Messiah into the world, or were there other things he was attempting to teach us through his dealings with this particular nation?

If God were only concerned with spiritual salvation of the individual soul, why the many chapters of instruction in the Torah concerning every facet of both private and public life? God taught Moses' generation about:

- worship & economics
- personal hygiene & corporate ecology
- governmental leadership & judicial principles
- agriculture & nutrition
- family relationships & national celebrations
- education & caring for the needy
- land usage & military strategies
- music & clothing styles
- immigration laws & medical practices
- architectural guidelines & perfume fabrication
- communication principles & fiscal guidelines

Why would God go to all this effort to address diverse issues in the life of a nation if he were not interested in the nation per se? The more we read, the clearer it becomes that God's concern for nations permeates Scripture. The scope of his redemption, the holistic nature of his transformation, is much greater than what we have often considered.

For example, a closer look at God's first commandment to Adam and Eve, the progenitors of all nations, reveals a more global and more comprehensive mandate than what we usually consider. "God blessed them and said to them, 'Be fruitful and increase in number; fill the earth and subdue it. Rule over the fish of the sea and the birds of the air and over every living creature that moves on the ground'" (Gen. 1:28). God's mandate is global in nature and comprehensive in scope. We're to fill all the earth, and all areas of life are included within his holistic plan for his creation. There is no sacred-secular divide. We're to look to the horizons and see his kingdom displayed in every facet of the created order.

Similarly, God's first promise to Abraham, the progenitor of the chosen nation, expresses obvious care and concern for corporate expressions of humanity, from families to nations. "The Lord had said to Abram, 'Leave your country, your people and your father's household and go to the land I will show you. I will make you into a great nation and I will bless you; I will make your name great, and you will be a blessing. I will bless those who bless you, and whoever curses you I will curse; and all peoples on earth will be blessed through you'" (Gen. 12:1–3).

Jesus' Strategy Was Not Understood

This Old Testament framework of the kingdom of God sets the stage for Jesus' advent. It is not surprising that as he began his ministry, "Jesus went into Galilee, proclaiming the good news of God. 'The time has come,' he said. 'The kingdom of God is near. Repent and believe the good news!'" (Mark 1:14–15).

As Jesus began his ministry of personal redemption and corporate transformation, many did not understand what he was about. With the mystery metaphor in mind, this should not be overly surprising to us. They did not have the benefit of perspective that has been given to us, because we have the privilege of reading the final chapter. We are told in the gospels that the religious leaders did not understand him (Matt. 9:10–13; 15:12–14; John 3:10). Similarly, his parents did not understand him (Luke 2:50). Even John the Baptist did not understand him.[8] In fact, on many occasions, his own disciples did not understand him.[9] Time and again Jesus had to say things like:

- "Do you understand what I have done for you?" (John 13:12)
- "Don't you understand . . . ?" (Mark 4:13)
- "Don't you see . . . ?" (Matt. 15:17; Mark 7:18)
- "Do you still not understand?" (Matt. 16:9; Mark 8:21)
- "Do you still not see or understand?" (Mark 8:17)
- "You don't know what you are asking . . . " (Matt. 20:22)
- "Why is my language not clear to you?" (John 8:43)

Sadly, when it came to the most important subject of all, his upcoming death and resurrection, it was more of the same. "But they did not understand what he meant and were afraid to ask him about it."[10]

Because of their slowness to understand, Jesus had to pace his teaching. He shared with them only as far they were able to understand. "With many similar parables Jesus spoke the word to them, as much as they could understand" (Mark 4:33). When washing their feet during their last evening together, "Jesus replied, 'You do not realize now what I am doing, but later you will understand'" (John 13:7).

That final evening was filled with many expressions revealing his desire to share more with the disciples. He had not been able to fully pour out his heart to them. This was due not to his unwillingness to share but to their inability to understand. He longed to be able to go deeper in his communication with them.

- He told them, "All this I have spoken while still with you. But the Counselor, the Holy Spirit, whom the Father will send in my name, *will teach you all things* and will remind you of everything I have said to you" (John 14:25–26).

- He continued, "When the Counselor comes, whom I will send to you from the Father, the Spirit of truth who goes out from the Father, *he will testify about me*" (John 15:26).

- Then he made this very telling comment: "I have much more to say to you, more than you can now bear. But when he, the Spirit of truth, comes, *he will guide you into all truth.* He will not speak on his own; he will speak only what he hears, and he will tell you what is yet to come. He will bring glory to me by taking from what is mine and making it known to you. All that belongs to the Father is mine. That is why I said the Spirit will take from what is mine and make it known to you" (John 16:12–15).

Can you relive the drama of the moment? God had spent millennia preparing for the coming of the Messiah. Jesus had just spent three years pouring himself out to the disciples gathered in the upper room. It was his last moment with them, a final meal filled with intense love (John 13:1) and deep expressions of the heart. In a matter of hours he would be arrested and the final scenes of the divine drama of redemption would be played out. Now was the time to communicate the most important, the most climactic truths. It was a moment in which he would have carefully selected his final words to make sure that the disciples understood why he had come and what their mission would be now that he was departing from them. But what did he find himself forced to say? "I have much more to say to you, more than you can now bear" (John 16:12).

Can you feel his emotions, understand his dilemma? Having more to share, but not being able to, because they had not understood so much of what he had previously shared? What did he want to tell them? When would he be able to share those things with them that were weighing on his mind that evening? Though he had repeatedly told them that he would die and rise from the dead, they had no understanding of what was about to happen. If they couldn't understand what Jesus' role in God's redemptive plan was going to be, how could they possibly understand the role that he was preparing for them in seeing individuals redeemed and nations transformed?

It was one thing to think that God could use Jesus to do unheard-of miracles. It was something totally different to think that God intended to use them to do unheard-of miracles too. Even though that very evening he had told them, "I tell you the truth, anyone who has faith in me will do what I have been doing. He will do even greater things than these, because I am going to the Father" (John 14:12), they simply did not get it.

Before their minds would be open to understand the Great Commission mandate that Jesus would give them, they would have to see him as the risen Lord. First

Jesus would "wow" them with the reality of the resurrection. What he was going to ask them to do was so amazing, so out-of-the-box, so unbelievable, that the only way they could begin to believe his mandate was if first he did the most unimaginable thing possible—come back from the dead! Then and only then would they be in a condition to accept the mandate he would leave with them.

The Great Commission: Going in Depth

So, let us now look at the Matthew 28 passage in detail. First let us look at this crucial passage in the original language. In the following chart I've combined several tools to serve the non-Greek speaking reader. The first line in this interlinear text is the corresponding Strong's Concordance number identifying the original Greek word. The reader can use this number to look up Greek words in a variety of dictionaries and lexicons. The second line is the Greek text. The third line contains the grammatical codes which tell you what part of speech and what tense, voice, and mood each word is.[11] The fourth line in this expanded interlinear is the literal word-by-word English translation of the Greek original.

The Great Commission: Matthew 28:18b–20
Coded and Parsed Greek-English Interlinear Text[12]

1325	3427	3956	1849	1722	3772	2532	1909	3588	1093
ἐδόθη	μοι	πᾶσα	ἐξουσία	ἐν	οὐρανῷ	καὶ	ἐπὶ	[τῆς]	γῆς
VIAP-ZS	NPD-XS	A-NF-S	N-NF-S	PD	N-DM-S	CC	PG	DGFS	N-GF-S
Given	to me	all	authority	in	heaven	and	over	the	earth

	4198		3767	3100		3956	3588	1484	907
28:19	πορευθέντες		οὖν	μαθητεύσατε		πάντα	τὰ	ἔθνη	βαπτίζοντες
	VPAONM-P		CC	VMAA-Y-P		A-AN-P	DANP	N-AN-P	VPPANM-P
	going		therefore	disciple		all	the	nations	baptizing

846	1519	3588	3686	3588	3962	2532	3588	5207	2532	3588
αὐτοὺς	εἰς	τὸ	ὄνομα	τοῦ	πατρὸς	καὶ	τοῦ	υἱοῦ	καὶ	τοῦ
NPAMZP	PA	DANS	N-AN-S	DGMS	N-GM-S	CC	DGMS	N-GM-S	CC	DGNS
them	into	the	name	the	Father's	and	the	Son's	and	the

40	4151		1321	846	5083		3956	3745
ἁγίου	πνεύματος	28:20	διδάσκοντες	αὐτοὺς	τηρεῖν		πάντα	ὅσα
A-GN-S	N-GN-S		VPPANM-P	NPAMZP	VNPA		AP-AN-P	APPAN-P
Holy	Spirit's		teaching	them	to observe		all	how much

1781	5213	2532	2400	1473	3326	5216	1510	3956
ἐνετειλάμηγν	ὑμῖν	καὶ	ἰδοὺ	ἐγὼ	μεθ᾽	ὑμῶν	εἰμι	πάσας
VIAD-XS	NPD-P	CC	QS	NPN-XS	PG	NPG-P	VIPA-XS	A-AF-P
I commanded	you	and	behold	I	with	you	am	all

3588	2250	2193	3588	4930	3588	165
τὰς	ἡμέρας	ἔως	τῆς	συντελείας	τοῦ	αἰῶνος
DAFP	N-AF-P	PG	DGFS	N-GF-S	DGMS	N-GM-S
the	days	until	the	completion	of the	age

Second, let us look at this passage in outline form:

A. CONTEXT/PREMISE/FOUNDATION:

    18 Then Jesus came to them and said, "All authority in heaven and on earth has been given to me.

B. CONSEQUENCE:

    19a Therefore...

C. COMMANDMENT:

    19c ...disciple all the nations... (μαθητεύσατε πάντα τὰ ἔθνη)

        1. 19b ...go(ing) and...

        2. 19d ...baptizing them in the name of the Father and of the Son and of the Holy Spirit

        3. 20a and teaching them to obey everything I have commanded you.

D. COMMITMENT/PROMISE/FUTURE:

    20b And surely I am with you always, to the very end of the age."

The Context for Revelation

Now, let us go through this passage phrase by phrase. Let us begin with the immediate context. We read, "Then Jesus came to them and said, 'All authority in heaven and on earth has been given to me'" (Matt. 28:18). This passage begins with Jesus' initiative. Jesus, resurrected and reclothed in the full authority of his divine nature, comes to his disciples. It begins with a divine drawing-near; intimacy with the Resurrected One is the foundation of the Great Commission. What would follow was not their good proposal; it was his eternal purpose.

The resurrection reality of Jesus gives credibility to what will be shared. This was no mere preface to the final command; it was the absolute prerequisite. Only when face-to-face with the living Christ were they able to hear the next words, the culminating declaration of Jesus' earthly ministry, the most shocking and amazing of all the shocking and amazing things they had heard from him. These final words would embody the very core of his eternal plan. Undoubtedly, he carefully picked the moment and the company with whom to share his cherished dream. Every detail of his communication was carefully orchestrated so the disciples would catch the full import of what he had to share. Jesus had first to astound them with his resurrection in order to be able to share his heart's greatest dream. Otherwise they would have discarded it outright as a lunatic idea.

Jesus' opening statement is so uncharacteristic of the way he normally communicated. Throughout his earthly ministry, he regularly made statements that drew the attention away from himself and directed it to the Father or the Spirit, preferring them in honor over himself. During the final evening with his disciples, he said of the Spirit, "It is for your good that I am going away. Unless I go away, the Counselor will not come to you; but if I go, I will send him to you" (John 16:7). He deferred to and commended the Holy Spirit. In a similar way, when people would make a big to-do about the miracles he had done, he deflected attention to the Father with remarks like, "I love the Father and I do exactly what my Father has commanded me" (John 14:31). Rarely does he point to himself.

One of those rare times occurs prior to the Great Commission mandate when he is approached by the rich young ruler. Luke tells us, "A certain ruler asked him, 'Good teacher, what must I do to inherit eternal life?' 'Why do you call me good?' Jesus answered. 'No one is good—except God alone'" (Luke 18:18–19). Apparently, the young ruler addressed Jesus as he did out of cultural civility, without thinking through the full implications of what he said. Jesus would respond to the young man, but first he wanted him to wrestle with his identity. Jesus was not going to answer him as one more teacher amidst the smorgasbord of teachers of his day.

His question to the young man set up the beginning of a syllogism. A syllogism was a frequently used method of logic employed in the Mediterranean world of antiquity. It consists of two premises which then force a logical conclusion. If both premises are true, then the conclusion is inescapably true. The young man's greeting served as the first premise. He had declared that Jesus was good. Jesus then urges him to think implicationally and lays down the second premise: only God is good. It would have been obvious to the young man and to all the hearers present that the conclusion to these two premises was that Jesus is God! His answer to the question about eternal life must therefore be taken with due seriousness, for he spoke as the highest authority in the universe!

Similarly, when Jesus began the Great Commission mandate with the words "All authority in heaven and on earth has been given to me" (Matt. 28:18), it is to remind them of who he is in no uncertain terms. The One who was always pointing to the Father and promoting the Spirit said this to capture their undivided attention. He underlined his absolute authority as if to say, "Listen up. Take stock in who I am and what I have done. Take what I'm about to say to you very seriously. I am God!"

Because He Is Who He Is

Having set a context, Jesus establishes a consequence. Because he is who he is, he declares, "Therefore . . . " (Matt. 28:19). The Greek word translated "therefore" is οὖν (*oun*) (Strong's #3767). Jesus uses this word ninety-six times in the New Testament text. He uses it ninety-five times before his death; this is the only recorded cause-effect statement that he makes during these climactic forty days since Easter morning. What follows would be the paramount consequence of his resurrection and exaltation to the place of supreme power and authority in the universe. The scope and implications of the words to come were so overwhelming that the wonder of the resurrection (without which it would not be possible) would pale in comparison. The end (God's dream) would surpass the means (God's sacrifice).

When Jesus told the disciples that he would rise from the dead, they did not believe him. They discarded the concept outright, for how could such an impossible thing be done? Now they were confronted with the One who had accomplished the seemingly impossible and unimaginable. He had risen in authority and stood in power before them. Now he was talking to them about something even more inconceivable! If it were not for the fact that they were standing in his resurrected presence when he spoke to them of discipling nations, the thought would have been totally preposterous. But the powerful display of his resurrection gave him the means to finally share with them the desire that had been on his and the Father's heart since the beginning of time. Now he could tell them of his dream to see all of creation reshaped by the transforming revelation of the gospel. The disciples must have thought, *Resurrection? How can it be done? Incomprehensible! Impossible!* Most likely the call to disciple nations produced similar reactions: *How can it be done? Incomprehensible! Impossible!*

The concept he had introduced was so novel, so foreign to their way of thinking, that it required even a greater stretching of their heart and mind to believe this than it did to believe in the resurrection. Indeed, even as they had misunderstood Jesus' predictions about his death and resurrection, it would be decades before they would fully understand the mandate of the Great Commission.

Haven't Quite Got It!

Their lack of understanding of the nature and scope of the Great Commission is recorded in Acts 10. On this occasion Peter only reluctantly shares the gospel with Cornelius, a Gentile and a Roman centurion. Throughout the book of Acts, several Greek words are employed to communicate the idea of nation or people. The two main words are *laos,* which is used to refer to God's first people, the Jews, and *ethnos,* which is used to refer to all the peoples of the world, especially those who were not the chosen *laos,* that is, the Gentiles. When Jesus gave the Great Commission, he commanded his followers to disciple all the *ethnos.* However, for that first generation of Jewish believers, it was hard to embrace the cross-cultural aspect of his final mandate. From their vantage point God's redemptive work had always been experienced within the context of their own nation. The fact that he was calling them to go to all peoples was beyond their comprehension.

When Peter explains the Great Commission to Cornelius, he states, "[Jesus] commanded us to preach to the people and to testify that he is the one whom God appointed as judge of the living and the dead" (Acts 10:42). This sounds like a good summary of the Great Commission in English. However, the word translated "people" here is *laos,* not *ethnos.* Jesus had said the latter, but because of his cultural blinders, Peter had heard the former. In doing so he reduced God's dream to something much smaller than what God had intended it to be.

Before Peter went any further with his narrow, cultural reinterpretation of the Great Commission, God intervened. The Holy Spirit was poured out on these Gentile seekers, bypassing the normal cultural protocol of Jewish proselytism. Everyone was amazed by God's unexpected actions. Years of debate and persecution would be necessary before the cross-cultural dynamic of the Great Commission would be understood and embraced. More than three decades would go by before Paul would write, "This mystery is that through the gospel the Gentiles are heirs together with Israel, members together of one body, and sharers together in the promise in Christ Jesus" (Eph. 3:6).

What Are We to Do?

Now we are ready to look at the heart of the Great Commission. In Matthew 28:19–20 there are four key verbs, but in the Greek only one is a commandment, only one is in the imperative mood. The other three verbs are present participles, verbs that describe how the imperative is to be carried out. The commandment is: "disciple." The present participles are "going... baptizing... and teaching." Let's look at each of these four verbs in turn.

The Greek verb μαθητεύσατε (*matheteusate*), from the base form μαθητεύω (*matheteuo*) (Strong's #3100), is the sole imperative in this passage. It is best translated by the straightforward English word, "disciple" or "teach" as in the ISV, KJV, or Young's Literal Translation. To translate it as "make disciples" is unhelpful in English, because for most readers it confuses the corporate mandate with the act of personal discipleship. Thus, it incorrectly gives the impression that this is an activity that occurs *within* a nation, rather than one that occurs *to* a nation, a people, a corporate expression of humanity, an *ethnos.*

There are over nine hundred years of Greek literature from Homer, the first European author, to the New Testament. Despite all the extant Greek manuscripts, Jesus is the first person to ever connect the verb "to disciple" with the direct object "nations" in one sentence. When Jesus described God's dream, he introduced a totally new, radical, and revolutionary concept to human beings. Never before in recorded history had a teacher ever commanded his followers to make this task their intentional and deliberate aim. It had far-reaching implications that extended beyond what his disciples then—and now—could begin to comprehend.

The First "How To." How would the discipling of nations occur? Three verbs are used as adjectives to describe the means of discipling the nations. They lay out the "how to" of nation discipling.

First of all, it requires "going." Jesus' words require a global and mobile approach to life. As Loren Cunningham, the cofounder of Youth With A Mission, says, "*Go* means a change of location." Jesus understood that lack of mobility would hinder nation discipleship. If we do not go, if we reside comfortably within the paradigms of our own cultures, we are less likely to be change agents of culture. As people move beyond their comfort zones, whether they cross the street or cross the seas, that mobility opens them up to the work of the Spirit. Finding themselves in new and foreign experiences, followers of Jesus depend on him to be transformed so that they can in turn learn to be nation disciplers.

As we go to the nations of the world, there are two attitudes which must guide our strategy. To imitate Jesus, we must go incarnationally and we must go prophetically. Just as Jesus "became flesh and [dwelt] among us" (John 1:14), we must approach the people to whom we are called with incarnational love. There is no place for superiority or cultural imperialism. If we go like Jesus did, we strip ourselves of all that would hinder us from being servants who with grace and compassion identify ourselves with the people to whom we are called. Paul reflected this when he wrote, "Though I am free and belong to no man, I make myself a slave to everyone, to win as many as possible. To the Jews I became like a Jew, to win the Jews. To those under the law I became like one under the law (though I myself am not under the law), so as to win those under the law. To those not having the law I became like one not having the law (though I am not free from God's law but am under Christ's law), so as to win those not having the law. To the weak I became weak, to win the weak. I have become all things to all men so that by all possible means I might save some" (1 Cor. 9:19–22).

The next attitude needed for those going as nation disciplers is prophetic in nature. While we identify with cultures in love, we must hold up the standards of the kingdom of God, standards which will bring corrective transformation to every nation. Just as every individual reflects both the design of God and the destructive impact of sin, so also all nations, cultures, peoples, and societies bear both the mark of God and the mark of the fall. Those who go in response to the Great Commission must go like Jesus, "full of grace and truth" (John 1:14), exhibiting compassion while deliberately challenging the ungodly elements within fallen cultures. Jeremiah, the weeping prophet, is a great example of this principle. He never failed to speak "the truth in love" (Eph. 4:15), often anguishing over the corrective nature of the word he spoke, but never holding back for personal security or comfort. On the contrary, he states, "[God's] word is in my heart like a fire, a fire shut up in my bones" (Jer. 20:9), a fire that must have expression in bringing God's truth to bear on every aspect of society marred by the fall.

The Second "How To." The second "how to" in discipling nations is reflected in the verb "baptizing." It is difficult to envision how a nation can be baptized if we think of the sacrament of water baptism. You obviously cannot put all of Sweden in a baptismal font at one time! Water baptism is something that individual human beings undergo as a public expression of repentance and faith. So how do we understand Jesus' instructions when they apply to the corporate discipling of a whole nation?

It is helpful to consider all the times that Jesus employed the verb "to baptize" in the gospels. Jesus used the verb "to baptize" fifteen times. Nine times he used it to refer to suffering in general and his sacrificial death in particular.[13] Three times Jesus used it to refer to water baptism[14] and two times he used it to refer to Holy Spirit baptism.[15] That leaves us only this one occurrence in the Great Commission passage.

So how is it used in this passage? If it does indeed refer to water baptism, then it would seem to imply that the discipling of a nation begins with evangelism, resulting in conversions that lead to individual, yet public demonstrations of faith. This is one possibility.

The other possibility is that Jesus is simply using the word in its root sense: telling them to immerse the nations in the name—that is, in an understanding of the character and ways—of the triune God. This would mean that he has called us to flood the nations with the proclamation and demonstration of the gospel until all have come into transforming contact with the kingdom of God. This baptismal strategy could thus be seen to involve "saturation" evangelism or "immersion" education in the character and ways of God.

The Third "How To." This naturally leads to the third "how to" verb: "teaching them to obey everything I have commanded you." Permeating a culture with the teachings of the kingdom of God until the society's worldview is transformed by gospel principles is the essence of discipling a nation. To know God and to make him known is the foundation for transformation. Ideas do indeed have consequences. For this reason the revelation of who God is must produce a change in the beliefs, values, principles, and practices that reign in a nation and in every one of its corporate institutions. Every sphere of society must come to display the character and ways of God in its category of life. The spheres of society include:

1. Family (Clan/Tribe/People Group)
2. Church (Local church/Mission church)
3. Education (All levels, preschool through university)
4. Celebration (Arts/Entertainment/Sports)
5. Media (Electronic/Printed)
6. Economics (Business/Science and Technology/Research and Development/ Production/Sales/Service)
7. Government (Executive/Judicial/Legislative)

In Darrow Miller's book *Discipling Nations,* he describes the four "generations" needed in the process of transforming a society. In the first generation the key change agents are the thinkers (philosophers, theologians); in the second generation they are the balladeers (poets, playwrights, songwriters, musicians, actors, novelists, film-makers, singers, painters, sculptors); in the third they are the professionals (doctors, lawyers, engineers, professors, businessmen); and in the fourth the societal transformation impacts the broad masses of a people.[16]

Though ideas have consequences, ideas alone are not sufficient to see a whole society transformed. Societal transformation occurs when heart and mind, emotions and ideas, and values and concepts are embraced by a significant segment of the population of a nation. How do these transforming heart-and-mind elements get imparted in an integrated manner? Through the use of creative mass media and the arts to communicate the ideas of God. The arts allow truth to be spoken to the heart by touching the five senses and engaging the emotions. This allows for a holistic presentation of truth that engages the whole person in a transforming way.

It is particularly important to consider the first two of these generations as they set the framework for the multigenerational task of discipling nations. Clarifying worldview issues of the first generation is essential for change. Because our ideas do have consequences, it is crucial that we "be transformed by the renewing of [our] mind" (Rom. 12:2). Ideological change alone is not enough to produce a discipled nation. Propositional truth, though powerful, is not powerful enough to bring the needed transformation. It must be exhibited in story form. That is why Jesus had to come to earth and display God on the human stage. That is why today we need artists to express the biblical Christian world view in music, in film, through novels, in paintings, and on the stage. For when truth is experienced in a living story, it engages the senses, impacts the person, and reshapes the heart values of a people.

His Commitment Makes It Possible

With the core commandment of the Great Commission now expressed, Jesus concludes this epic moment with a declaration of his commitment to his followers. He says, "And surely I am with you always, to the very end of the age."

Thus, the Great Commission begins and ends with Jesus. He draws near to share his heart for the nations, and he promises to never withdraw his presence from his followers. His presence is the energizing means of accomplishing the task. He who commissioned us committed himself to us. Because he is Emmanuel, God with us, we can dare to dream of being coworkers with him to see the nations discipled. That is the only way in which this dream will become reality.

Let us summarize. We have discovered that redeeming individuals and discipling nations is at the heart of God's forever dream. It is part of the gospel mystery that has been revealed. Clues for this concept are threaded throughout the Scriptures but culminate in Jesus' post-resurrection Great Commission statements. The Great Commission has both individual and corporate elements, with monogenerational and multigenerational implications, requiring both urgent preaching and strategic teaching. The means by which we see nations discipled includes going, baptizing, and teaching. Though it presents a radical, revolutionary, almost impossible concept, it is doable because God is just in all his ways, and because in his loving commitment to us he promises to be Emmanuel as we commit ourselves to obey the call to the all. We must not stop until every individual, every family, every sphere of society, every community, and every people experience the kingdom of God, indeed, until the earth is "full of the knowledge of the Lord as the waters cover the sea" (Isa. 11:9; cf. Hab. 2:14).

So far, so good. But how do we implement this? Going, baptizing, and teaching are only the sketchiest of outlines. Didn't Jesus have more to say on the subject? Yes! Indeed he did! As we look to the Scriptures in light of the revealed mystery, things become clearer and clearer.

From Individuals to Nations: God's Strategy for Discipleship

As the body of Christ, we have a pretty good idea what it means to preach to individuals and even how to disciple and teach individuals, but how do we really go about discipling nations? How do we begin? There is such a big gap between "individuals" (*anthropos* in Greek) and "nations" (*ethnos* in Greek). Are there intermediate entities in the New Testament to help us bridge the transformation gap between *anthropos* and *ethnos*? Indeed there are. They help us break down the enormous task of discipling a nation into bite-size, achievable subtasks. There are corporate expressions of humanity that transcend the individual but that are not as big as a nation. The Bible speaks of transformation at these intermediate levels as strategic stepping-stones to seeing a whole society reformed and reshaped by the gospel. These intermediate entities are found in the concepts represented in the Greek words *oikos, koinonos,* and *polis,* as the chart illustrates:

Mark 16				Matthew 28
Anthropos	*Oikos*	*Koinonos*	*Polis*	*Ethnos*

Let's consider how these three words help us understand the process of discipling nations. Let's break down the biblical concept of peoplehood into manageable, doable, bite-size parts. The people of Jesus' day understood that the nation (*ethnos*) was broken down into the *polis*, which in turn was composed of *koinonos*, which had at its core the *oikos*, in which every individual (*anthropos*) had his or her place.

There were no nation-states in antiquity as we know them today. Our modern-day concept of the earth divided into 238 nations would have been foreign to the people of Jesus' day. One of today's nation-states may contain dozens of *ethnos*.

In antiquity, the identity of an *ethnos* was usually linked to a principal *polis*—a city like Babylon, Athens, or Rome. People identified themselves as belonging to a *polis*: e.g., Saul of Tarsus, Jesus of Nazareth. Even to this day we speak of a person's "citizenship," originally derived from the term "city." In fact, many English words are derived from the Greek word *polis*: "politicians" are the governors of a *polis*, "policemen" are the protectors of the *polis*, and a "policy" refers to the rules and regulations by which a *polis* guides itself.

So in order to disciple an *ethnos*, the *polis* would need to be transformed. The *polis* represents a strategic goal within Jesus' redemptive strategy for the discipling of nations. How do we see this evidenced in the gospels?

Transforming the *Polis*

The Great Commission was not an afterthought or a postscript tacked on hastily at the end of Jesus' earthly ministry. It was the compelling, guiding motivation of his life and ministry. From the very outset of his ministry, he was strategically thinking how to reach the "all." In the first chapter of Mark, we read of Jesus' initial ministry in Capernaum. Great things happened. The Word was preached, the sick were healed, the bound were freed, the sinners were forgiven. The town was in an uproar, and everyone wanted to be near Jesus. They crowded the house where he was staying. The disciples were thrilled—their rabbi was famous! No longer did they have to worry whether they could draw a crowd.

To their horror, they woke up early the next morning and they couldn't find Jesus. They desperately looked for him everywhere. This was a disaster! The crowds would soon be gathering, and without Jesus they would have nothing to give to the needy multitudes. Finally they found him on a lonely hill outside of town, spending time with his Father. They tried to hasten his return, but to their surprise "Jesus replied, 'Let us go somewhere else—to the nearby villages (*komopolis*)—so I can preach there also. That is why I have come.'"[17]

He had a plan! It did not involve staying in one place and building up a big, popular ministry, much to the disappointment of his disciples! He was called to the "all." And he knew that if he was going to impact the nation (*ethnos*), he'd have to reach every town and city (*polis*). He understood that in order to accomplish the larger task of reaching a whole people, he would have to break the job down into strategic, reachable subtasks. These "tasks within the task" are like Russian stacking dolls—the smaller components all fit into the larger.

This strategic, multitiered approach is reflected in Jesus' comments to the religious leaders of his day, "Every kingdom divided against itself will be ruined, and every city [*polis*] or household [*oikos*] divided against itself will not stand" (Matt. 12:25). In a similar way, Revelation 16:19 speaks of "the cities [*polis*] of the nations [*ethnos*]." For this reason "the Lord appointed seventy-two others and sent them two by two ahead of him to every town [*polis*] and place where he was about to go" (Luke 10:1). In the parable of the talents, Jesus tells us that those who are faithful in small matters are given responsibility to manage cities (Luke 19:16–19). Apparently, he wants his followers to lead out in areas of community development and urban transformation as part of his overall plan to redeem the nations.

A favorite Sunday school song is "This Little Light of Mine." It takes its inspiration from Jesus' words in the Sermon on the Mount, "let your light shine before men, that they may see your good deeds and praise your Father in heaven" (Matt. 5:16). But this exhortation to make sure that your personal life is a clear gospel witness follows an amazing comparison in the verses immediately preceding. Individually we are to be like lights on a stand, but corporately we are to be like a city on a hill. What a radical thought—he not only intends us to reach cities; he expects us to be one! We are to be the lit up *polis* of God standing in contrast to the dark cities of the world! Jesus said, "You are the light of the world. A city (*polis*) on a hill cannot be hidden" (Matt. 5:14). He expected our corporate life together as the body of Christ to be like that of a city lighting the way. We are to be an alternate society, a prophetic *polis,* modeling kingdom paradigms of transformation.

When my youngest son, Matthew, was three years old, we lived in Chile. One day I asked him a question that every father asks a son, "What do you want to be when you grow up?" He quickly answered, "I want to be a garbage collector." I was dismayed. I had hoped for him to say something like a doctor or a scientist or a football player, for these are roles more highly esteemed in our society. I was about to correct him, when I felt God correct me, "Don't reprove him, rather encourage him." Over the years I saw in Matthew a growing God-given desire to steward God's created order. His status-free, childlike answer in fact reflected God's initial command to Adam and Eve to steward and care for the earth.

Later, reflecting on Matthew's answer, I considered the political realities of the nation of Chile. Once a year all the mayors of the nation would gather in the capital to discuss policies and issues of mutual concern. I thought how very much I would love to be able to speak at one of those conventions. It would be a great platform to influence the whole of the nation. However, I realized that it would be very unlikely that I'd ever be asked to attend one of the mayoral gatherings with my credentials as a Christian missionary. If I could devise a new, better, cheaper, easier, more environmentally friendly way to solve the waste issues of the cities of Chile, perhaps I would be invited to attend and present my solutions. I could imagine myself talking to an influential mayor about this new waste removal solution and being asked by him, "Why have you dedicated your life to the development of this technology?" My answer would be, "Because my Father made this beautiful world and has asked us to help steward it."

I realized that if I were a garbage collector with a biblical Christian worldview and practice, my chances to influence the cities of Chile would be greatly enhanced. Upon realizing this, I repented of my dichotomized perspective of life and the status-driven aspirations I had for my children. If we are going to disciple nations, we must use every means possible to transform cities.

Breaking the Cities into Smaller Units: *Koinonos*

One of the global megatrends in recent generations has been the hastening pace of urbanization. Myriads of huge, world-class cities dwarf many nations and people groups. Cities like Tokyo, New York, Shanghai, Rio de Janeiro, Cairo, London, and Mumbai are many times larger than more than half of the 238 countries on earth! So the job still looks overly big, daunting, and formidable when we face the challenges of these immense metropolitan areas. So, how does the New Testament break down the challenges presented by the *polis?* A key lies in the Greek word usually translated as "fellowship." So let us now consider how the New Testament speaks of *koinonia* and its derivatives as part of Jesus' redemptive strategy.

What comes to mind when you think of the term *koinonia?* Today many Christian congregations have *koinonia* times in addition to their more formal church services. These *koinonia* gatherings in contemporary church life usually refer to a less formal meeting held in a home or in the fellowship hall of the church (as opposed to the sanctuary). When we think of *koinonia,* we tend to think of succulent potlucks and cozy sofas, of being able to hang out and chat with one another rather than have to sit in pews and observe someone else perform a religious ceremony.

This is not what came to the minds of believers when they heard the term *koinonia* in Jesus' day. This word referred to a voluntary association of human beings. A *koinonos* could be formed for political, educational, religious, athletic, or commercial reasons. It often consisted of a fiscal partnership, a for-profit society, a business corporation.

Plato, in his *Republic,* speaks of the *koinonos* as the foundational building block of society. "As a result of this, then, one man calling in another for one service and another for another, we, being in need of many things, gather many into one place of abode as "associates" (*koinonos* #2844) and helpers, and to this dwelling together we give the name city or state, do we not?"[18]

In fact, when Plato compares society to a body, he speaks of the *koinonia* as the basic parts of the body. "For example, if the finger of one of us is wounded, the entire *community* (*koinonos* #2842) of bodily connections stretching to the soul for 'integration' with the dominant part is made aware, and all of it feels the pain as a whole, though it is a part that suffers, and that is how we come to say that the man has a pain in his finger."[19] Notice how similar this language is to Paul's when he speaks of the followers of Jesus as the body of Christ: "The body is a unit, though it is made up of many parts; and though all its parts are many, they form one body. So it is with Christ. ... As it is, there are many parts, but one body.... If one part suffers, every part suffers with it; if one part is honored, every part rejoices with it" (1 Cor. 12:12, 20, 26).

Plato uses the term *koinonia* to describe "any *social institution* (*koinonia* #2842) whatsoever."[20] The voluntary nature of these partnerships is reflected in the related verb *koinoneo* as seen in this passage: "I highly approve of your purpose, and am ready *to lend a hand*" (*koinoneo* #2841).[21] He states that one can form these "dealings and *partnerships with* (*koinoneo* #2841) whom he will."[22] People linked together in a *koinonos* are called partners: "All people that are *partners* (*koinonos* #2844) in any action produce results that are fair and good whensoever they apply their minds to themselves and the action."[23]

The wide social diversity of these *koinonos* is pointed to by Plato. He speaks of when "the rulers and the ruled are brought together ... in some other *common undertaking* (*koinonia* #2842), either a religious festival, or a campaign, or as shipmates or fellow-soldiers."[24] As you read through Plato's writings, it becomes clear that within the thinking of the ancient Mediterranean world the *koinonos* had expression in every one of the seven spheres of society.

Plato, *Koinonia,* and the Spheres of Society

Family. With regard to the family, Plato writes, "Does not the starting-point of generation in all States lie in the union and *partnership* (*koinonia* #2842) of marriage?"[25] Indeed, the term *koinonia* is synonymous with marriage and the sexual union characteristic of marriage. He writes, "One certainly should not fail to observe that when male *unites* (*koinonia* #2842) with female for procreation the pleasure experienced is held to be due to nature."[26] He says that "girls over thirteen shall continue to take part [in sports] until *married* (*koinonia* #2842)."[27] Similarly, he speaks of "the *fellowship* (*koinonia* #2842) and intercourse of marriage."[28]

Religion. In the religious sphere, Plato also highlights the role of the *koinonos.* "In the case where the race is one, with the same language and laws, this unity makes for friendliness, since it *shares also in* (*koinonos* #2844) sacred rites and all matters of religion."[29] He writes of "all who *share* (*koinonia* #2842) in the worship of the tribal gods"[30] and of the "sacred *assemblies* (*koinoneo* #2841) of the Hellenes."[31] He says it is "most proper to sing hymns and praise to the gods, *coupled with* (*koinoneo* #2841) prayers."[32] The religious person is "a *partaker* (*koinonos* #2844) in [the god's] holy rites,"[33] and religion is described as "all sacrifices and ceremonies controlled by divination, namely, all means of *communion* (*koinonia* #2842) between gods and men."[34]

Education. *Koinonos* was also expressed in the sphere of education. Plato writes that the best friendship is the one resulting from "*association* (*koinonia* #2842) in liberal education."[35] In this regard he stated that "the female sex *must share with* (*koinoneo* #2841) the male, to the greatest extent possible, both in education and in all else."[36]

Celebration. The sphere of celebration includes the arts, entertainment, and sports. Plato makes frequent reference to *koinonos* as it relates to this sphere of society. He speaks of those "eager *to take a part in* (*koinoneo* #2841) that music which is noblest"[37] and of "the presence or *communion* (*koinonia* #2842) (call it which you please) of absolute beauty."[38] Similarly, he speaks of those "*taking part* (*koinonia* #2842) in ... sports."[39]

Media. Although there was no mass media in his day, Plato referred to the sphere of communication when speaking of *koinonos.* He writes of "that kind of oratory which *partakes of* (*koinoneo* #2841) the kingly art because it persuades men to justice and thereby helps to steer the ship of state."[40]

Economics. The sphere of economics is one in which the term *koinonos* is frequently used. Economic partnerships are one of the most common forms of *koinonos,* often described as the "business dealings *in any joint undertaking*" (*koinoneo* #2841).[41] In this light, Plato asks, "But again, within the city itself how will they share with one another the products of their labor? This was the very purpose of our *association* (*koinonia* #2842) and establishment of a state."[42] For this reason, Plato asserts: "It is necessary, in the next place, for the law-giver to keep a watch on the methods employed by the citizens in gaining and spending money, and to supervise the *associations* (*koinonia* #2842) they form with one another, and the dissolutions thereof, whether they be voluntary or under compulsion; he must observe the manner in which they conduct each of these mutual transactions, and note where justice obtains and where it is lacking."[43]

Government. In the sphere of government, Plato writes of "our *association* (*koinonia* #2842) in political affairs."[44] He writes of the man who "*has a share in* (*koinoneo* #2841) the chief offices of State"[45] and of those who "*have taken part in* (*koinoneo* #2841) elections to office in every department of State."[46] In the judicial area of government, he asserts that "all the citizens must *have a share* (*koinoneo* #2841); for the man who has no share in helping judge imagines that he has no part of lot in the State at all."[47] Regarding the executive branch of government, he describes kingship as "the art of caring for the whole human *community* (*koinonia* #2842) and ruling all mankind."[48]

Exploring Plato's use of the word *koinonia* gives the necessary background understanding to grasp the significance of the term to the New Testament readers.

Koinonia and the New Testament Church

We read this description of the early church: "They devoted themselves to the apostles' teaching and to the fellowship, to the breaking of bread and to prayer. Everyone was filled with awe, and many wonders and miraculous signs were done by the apostles. All the believers were together and had everything in common" (Acts 2:42–44).

At first this passage does not seem overly surprising to us, but when we understand all that which was implied in the Greek word *koinonia,* this image becomes shocking indeed. The early church devoted themselves to creating a *koinonia,* a voluntary association based on biblical teaching. The choice of this word clearly indicated to their contemporaries that they were intentionally establishing a corporate partnership with God and one another that would serve as the basic building block of an alternate, countercultural model society. This was a radical, perhaps even revolutionary term, going against the stream, challenging the status quo of the Greco-Roman world. This word did not indicate a passive retreat into comfortable evenings of food and fellowship with fellow believers, but a deliberate attempt to transform society by creating an alternate social model.

The new *koinonia* was not identified with the surrounding culture but challenged the surrounding culture prophetically. The new biblical Christian *koinonia* matched the old *koinonia* structures of the pagan world, offering distinctive alternatives to societal ills. Some of the distinguishing elements of a *koinonia* included a

- socialization process/education system (values, ethics, customs, belief systems),
- economic structure (greed vs. generosity; mammon vs. stewardship),
- leadership structure (domination vs. servanthood),
- conflict resolution structure (injustice vs. justice), and
- external relationships mechanism (coercion vs. conviction).

According to the *koinonia* model, we are to be distinct from but involved with and influencing the greater society around us. We disciple not through top-down, centralized control, grabbing the reigns of power. Rather, through serving we shape a nation as we become a minority significant in its influence to mold and reform the way a people educate their young, do business with one another, make decisions, solve problems, and relate to others.

Jesus compares this dynamic to leaven. "He told them still another parable: 'The kingdom of heaven is like yeast that a woman took and mixed into a large amount of flour until it worked all through the dough'" (Matt. 13:33). This image would have been shocking to Jesus' original Jewish audience, for within their culture leaven was often used as a symbol of all that was wrong with the world. When they celebrated the Passover, their feast of redemption, they would eat bread without leaven as part of their statement of commitment to God and his ways. Today many Christians think, "Don't get involved in politics. It's dirty." Or, "Stay away from Hollywood. It's corrupt." Or, "If you want to be holy, avoid business. It's full of darkness."

But you can't change darkness by standing at a distance and cursing it. The only way to transform the darkness is by turning on the light. For this reason God is asking us to get involved in *koinonia* structures that impact government, business, the media and the arts, education, and the home. It's time to be leaven and bring the influence of the kingdom of heaven into every sphere of society.

Bringing the Message Home: Transformation in the *Oikos*

We've gone from the *ethnos* to the *polis* to the *koinonos* on the way to the *anthropos*. But there is one more intermediate step on the way to seeing individuals redeemed and nations transformed. Let us consider the place of the *oikos* in Jesus' redemptive strategy for individuals and nations.

Oikos is the smallest, most foundational expression of corporate humanity. However, the New Testament concept of *oikos,* that is the "family" or the "household," is broader than the current idea of the nuclear family in the West. The *oikos* was a multigenerational expression of society which included not only those linked together by biology and marriage, but also those tied to the economic destiny of the household, including slaves and employees. Because business was a household industry in antiquity, the English word "economist" is derived from the Greek *oikonomos*—the manager or steward of the *oikos.*

Jesus cared not only for individuals, but also for members of their *oikos.* He healed Simon Peter's mother-in-law (Mark 1:30–31) and the slave of a centurion (Matt. 8:5–13). Jesus delivered the daughter of a Syrophoenician woman from demons (Mark 7:24–30) and commanded the man from the region of the Gerasenes whom he set free from demonic oppression, "Return home [*oikos*] and tell how much God has done for you" (Luke 8:39). From the dead he raised the son of a widow (Luke 7:11–15) and the daughter of a synagogue leader (Luke 8:49–56). He taught on marriage and parenthood (Matt. 15:1–9; 19:4–6; 21:28–32). The *oikos* was important to Jesus because he understood that transformation in the home leads to transformation in society.

This emphasis is evident throughout the New Testament. The angel of the Lord who appeared to Cornelius told him, "Send to Joppa for Simon who is called Peter. He will bring you a message through which you and all your household [*oikos*] will be saved" (Acts 11:13–14). Similarly, Paul and Silas tell the Philippian jailor, "Believe in the Lord Jesus, and you will be saved—you and your household [*oikos*]" (Acts 16:31). In this same city, Paul baptized Lydia and "the members of her household [*oikos*]" (Acts 16:15). Paul writes at length about the transforming impact of the gospel in household relationships (see Eph. 5:15–6:9).[49]

Think About These Things

God is seeking to bring redemption at every level of society. He not only wants to see individuals redeemed; he also wants to see nations transformed. In order to achieve this he targets the *oikos,* the *koinonos,* and the *polis* that comprise our societies. If this is his strategy, it must be ours as well.

The New Testament framework requires us to rethink how we understand the kingdom of God and approach the work of God. We need to be more intentionally integrative, more deliberately holistic, and more strategically relevant to all expressions of humanity around us.

Paul gives us great advice as we consider how to apply this new perspective. He writes, "Finally, brothers, whatever is true, whatever is noble, whatever is right, whatever is pure, whatever is lovely, whatever is admirable—if anything is excellent or praiseworthy—think about such things" (Phil. 4:8). He exhorts us to think. These eight adjectives become handles for creative biblical thinking when we line them up beside the five categories of *anthropos, oikos, koinonos, polis,* and *ethnos* as the following chart exhibits.

Discipling Nations Chart

Phil. 4:8	Anthropos	Oikos	Koinonos	Polis	Ethnos
True					
Noble					
Right					
Pure					
Lovely					
Admirable					
Excellent					
Praiseworthy					

Take this framework and think, reflect on, consider, and grapple with, "What does 'admirable' look like in an individual, a family, a *koinonos,* a city, a nation?" Do the same with each of the other words. Think hard and long. Wait before the Lord. Search the Scriptures. Discuss with others. Get specific. Break out of the box. Pray and reflect on the character of God. Think and rethink. Then, as you get the mind of the Lord, begin to act. Obey his call to the "all." Reach out to every sphere of society. Reach out to every nation. Reach out to every individual. Make a difference. Step out in faith. Transform your world with the redemptive love of God.

No Longer a Mystery

God's comprehensive plan for all peoples everywhere, for all areas of life is no longer a secret. Though we have much yet to discover about how to apply his ways into every arena and domain of life, the biblical story is clear. God's forever dream is linked to his undying love for individuals and nations and for every sphere of society. He does not want his redemption to have a partial, fragmented impact on this world. He wants to see every facet of life—both individual and corporate—transformed by the gospel message. So, let us make his dream our dream, his will our will, his goals our goals. Let us press on to know him and to make him known. Let us live to see individuals redeemed and nations transformed. Let us give God good cause to celebrate.

Notes

1. Emphasis added here and in Scripture references throughout this chapter.

2. Gen. 12:2–3 NRSV.

3. Ps. 22:27 NRSV.

4. Isa. 11:9; Hab. 2:14.

5. Matt. 28:18–20; Mark 16:15–18; Luke 24:46–49; John 20:21; Acts 1:8.

6. Exod. 3:15; cf. Exod. 3:6, 16; 4:5; Matt. 22:32; Mark 12:26; Luke 20:37; Acts 3:13; 7:32.

7. 2 Kings 21:6; 2 Chron. 33:6.

8. Matt. 11:2–3; Luke 7:20.

9. John 8:27; 10:6; 12:16; 13:28; 20:9.

10. Mark 9:32; cf. Luke 9:45; 18:34.

11. A–AF-P = adjective, accusative, feminine, plural; A–AN-P = adjective, accusative, neuter, plural; A–GN-S = adjective, genitive, neuter, singular; A–NF-S = adjective, genitive, feminine, singular; AP-AN-P = adjective, pronominal, accusative, neuter, plural; APPAN-P = adjective, pronominal, comparative, accusative, neuter, plural

CC = conjunction, coordinating

DAFP = definite article, accusative, feminine, plural; DANP = definite article, accusative, neuter, plural; DANS = definite article, accusative, neuter, singular; DGFS = definite article, genitive, feminine, singular; DGMS = definite article, genitive, masculine, singular; DGNS = definite article, genitive, neuter, singular

N-AF-P = noun, accusative, feminine, plural; N-AN-P = noun, accusative, neuter, plural; N-AN-S = noun, accusative, neuter, singular; N-DM-S = noun, dative, masculine, singular; N-GF-S = noun, genitive, feminine, singular; N-GM-S = noun, genitive, masculine, singular; N-GN-S = noun, genitive, neuter, singular; N-NF-S = noun, nominative, feminine, singular; NPAMZP = noun, pronoun, accusative, masculine, third person, plural; NPD–P = noun, pronoun, dative, plural; NPD-XS = noun, pronoun, dative, first person, singular; NPG–P = noun, pronoun, genitive, plural; NPN-XS = noun, pronoun, nominative, first person, singular.

PA = preposition, accusative; PD = preposition, dative; PG = preposition, genitive.

QS = particle, sentential.

VIAD–XS = verb, indicative, aorist, middle deponent, first person, singular; VIAP–ZS = verb, indicative, aorist, passive, third person, singular; VIPA–XS = verb, indicative, present, active, first person, singular; VMAA–YP = verb, imperative, aorist, active, second person, plural; VNPA = verb, infinitive, present, active; VPAONM-P = verb, participle, aorist, passive deponent, nominative, masculine, plural; VPPANM-P = verb, participle, present, active, nominative, masculine, plural.

12. Greek text taken from the *Nestle-Aland 26th Edition Greek New Testament* and the grammatical parsing code from the *Analytical Greek New Testament: Greek Text Analysis* and the *Greek N.T. for Windows with Grammatical Tags.*

13. Matt. 20:22a, 22b, 23a, 23b; Mark 10:38a, 38b, 39a, 39b; Luke 12:50.

14. Mark 16:16; Acts 1:5a; 11:16a.

15. Acts 1:5b; 11:16b.

16. Darrow L. Miller, *Discipling Nations: The Power of Truth to Transform Cultures* (Seattle: YWAM Publishing, 2000).

17. Mark 1:38; see also Luke 4:43

18. Plato, *Republic,* 369b-c.

19. Plato, *Republic,* 462c-d.

20. Plato, *Laws,* 639c.

21. Plato, *Laches,* 180a.

22. Plato, *Republic,* 362b.

23. Plato, *Laws,* 783e.

24. Plato, *Republic,* 556c.

25. Plato, *Laws,* 721a.

26. Plato, *Laws,* 636c.

27. Plato, *Laws,* 833d.

28. Plato, *Laws,* 771e.

29. Plato, *Laws,* 708c.

30. Plato, *Laws,* 729c.

31. Plato, *Laws,* 947a.

32. Plato, *Laws,* 801e.

33. Plato, *Letters,* 350b-c.

34. Plato, *Symposium,* 188b-c.

35. Plato, *Letters,* 334b.

36. Plato, *Laws,* 805d.

37. Plato, *Laws,* 667b.

38. Plato, *Phaedo,* 100c-d.

39. Plato, *Laws,* 834d; see also Plato, *Laws,* 950e.

40. Plato, *Statesman,* 303e-304a.

41. Plato, *Republic,* 343d.

42. Plato, *Republic,* 371b.

43. Plato, *Laws,* 632b.

44. Plato, *Letters,* 318d.

45. Plato, *Laws,* 856b.

46. Plato, *Laws,* 752b-c.

47. Plato, *Laws,* 768b.

48. Plato, *Sophist,* 276b-c.

49. See Loren Cunningham and David Hamilton, *Why Not Women?* (Seattle: YWAM Publishing, 2000).

Don Grattus shares lessons learned from experience in Muslim "Daristan." His honest assessment of theory and practice, and expectations and reality will be useful to anyone wanting to bring reform through the gospel to society.

Case Study: Second Thoughts on Galactic Domination

Don Grattus

I live in one of the most corrupt nations on earth. The international rankings change every year, but we are always near the top. Local cynics joke that we were actually rated number one this year, but we paid a bribe to be moved down the list. Unlike the joke, the situation is not funny.

Despite abundant mineral resources and universal literacy, the country, which I will call Daristan, is impoverished. A byzantine postcommunist legal system exists mainly to create a myriad of "gatekeepers" who must be bribed at every turn. Small children must bribe their teachers to receive grades. Young people pay bribes to enter the university and to receive their diplomas. Parents bribe draft officials to keep their children out of the army. Army officers sell equipment and food on the black market and extort money from parents begging the privilege of bringing food to their cold and hungry sons who are serving their country. Meanwhile, government officials build lavish homes on official salaries of two hundred dollars per month. Bribery and extortion are a way of life and few have any hope that it can change.

Many are willing to admit the root cause. "This is a Muslim country," they say resignedly. "Muslim countries are this way." Some of my friends have candidly told me that their country is incapable of freedom. "We need a strong leader. Democracy won't work here the way it does in the West." I once heard a government official use the word "Muslimness" as a euphemism for bribery. It has always seemed strange to me that so many can recognize the link between their beliefs and the dire condition of their society, and yet so rarely question the validity of those beliefs.

You may be surprised to learn that I am not pessimistic about the power of the gospel to change this nation. I continue to believe that the truth of God can radically transform a society on every level, and I believe that nations (both ethnic and political) are important to God. What has changed over the years is my perspective on the process by which this transformation will take place.

Does God Have Answers for the Problems of the Nations?

Arriving here in Daristan was the culmination of a long journey that began almost a decade earlier. My first experience in full-time missionary work was with Youth With A Mission (YWAM) in Central America during the violent political upheaval of the 1980s. During my three and a half years there, doing open-air evangelism through drama and music, distributing clothes to refugees, traveling in and out of guerilla-controlled territory, working with evangelicals and Catholics, I became increasingly troubled by a question that Christians seemed unable or unwilling to answer. People were asking, "What is God's (or the church's) answer to the problems in our nation?" Remember that these issues—violence, corruption, poverty, ignorance, disease—were not abstract or academic. In El Salvador, Guatemala, and Nicaragua, young people were taking up arms and staking their lives for or against one solution or another.

The church seemed to offer two alternatives. A portion of the predominant Catholic Church propagated liberation theology as God's answer. This seemed to me to be little more than "baptized Marxism," a thin veneer of Christian terminology and theological justification calculated to mobilize Christians to take up arms and put themselves at the disposal of Marxist-Leninist revolutionary movements led by militant atheists. I was in agreement with the most compelling aspect of this theology of liberation—the abundant scriptural evidence of God's special concern for the poor and downtrodden. The liberationist emphasis on *praxis* (works) over *doxis* (doctrine) also seemed valid to a point. My teammates and I were always looking for new ways to serve the poorest of the poor. For one six-month period we even lived in the homes of peasants on a coffee cooperative in El Salvador. But the fact that I was "for the poor" did not result in a conviction that violent class struggle resulting in state socialism was really in the interest of the poor or anybody else.

The other answer, or nonanswer, from the rapidly growing evangelical movement basically said that Christians need not (or should not) concern themselves with the structures of society, but should instead concentrate on the transformation of individual lives through salvation by faith. Some hoped that society would improve as more individuals were converted. Others felt things were bound to get worse no matter what we did, which was all the more reason to concentrate on eternity—getting as many people into heaven as quickly as possible. At its worst, this became a sort of "evacuation theology," a deliberate retreat from "the world" into a religious subculture. From this ghetto we might make occasional forays into enemy territory to rescue a few responsive individuals, who would in turn be extracted from "the world" and immersed in the subculture. There seemed no vision of victory and no effort to influence the corporate life of the nation. Even conversion itself was reduced to a mere cleaning out of the religious drawer in a person's life, with little emphasis on discipleship and ongoing spiritual growth. Any work, any effort that delayed us from getting as many saved as possible was suspect.

My search for answers, and the ability to articulate them, eventually took me out of Central America and into university, where I studied under the late Dr. Glenn Martin, a man who had given many years of thought and research to understanding how a Christian worldview expresses itself in all of life, particularly in the sphere of civil government. I came away feeling that I had begun to answer the question of how Christians should respond to the needs of society. I embraced a theology of engagement that rejected the dichotomy between "sacred" and "secular" and insisted that God is the rightful ruler over all of life, and that his truth should be applied in every facet of society. It was a theology of victory (not evacuation) which asserted that even a minority of truly biblical Christians can make a substantial difference in their society. Yet it was not utopian, because it acknowledged that perfection will never be achieved in this age and that each generation of Christians must renew its commitment to express biblical truth in their nation.

My wife and I assumed we would soon return to Latin American with our new daughter, Moriah, to begin to apply some of what I was learning. Instead, God began to stir our hearts in what seemed a completely different direction. With our reentry into YWAM in 1990, we were introduced in a deeper way into what was being called "frontier missions." Missions strategists had identified approximately 12,000 distinct ethnic and linguistic "people groups" which did not yet have a permanent Christian witness capable of evangelizing them. The vast majority of these groups were concentrated across a belt stretching from North Africa to East Asia. Missions mobilizers coined the term "10/40 Window" to describe this territory, where the vast majority of the least evangelized people lived and where only a fraction of the Christian mission force was working. A sanctified ambition began to rise up within my wife and me—we would be willing to give a significant portion of our lives to helping cross one of those 12,000 unreached people groups off the list.

As we continued to learn about frontier missions, we moved beyond this simplistic goal and began to form a more three-dimensional understanding of mission strategy through the excellent materials produced by the U.S. Center for World Mission, and others. Working together with a team of very sharp and motivated young leaders, we pioneered a YWAM ministry focused on equipping and launching teams into the unevangelized world. We strove to integrate the "missiology" we were learning with truths and principles that were part of our YWAM heritage and values. Intercessory prayer, spiritual warfare, hearing the voice of God in guidance, and the importance of multigifted, multinational "apostolic" teams were all important distinctives we sought to meld with the principles of strategic targeting and penetration church planting.

Most exciting for me, we tried to integrate all of this with "reform," the process by which the gospel transforms not only individual lives, but also whole societies and their corporate structures. This was heady stuff! We felt we were moving toward an integrated model—a "unified field theory" of mission! We even indulged in some testosterone-charged rhetoric about "total galactic domination." Of course, we had enough sense not to take ourselves completely seriously, but there was more than a pinch of triumphalism mixed up in it all.

Entering Daristan

My wife and I arrived in Daristan during the brief period of euphoria and optimism following the fall of Communism in Eastern Europe. The Communist leader had just been ousted in a coup, and a prodemocracy faction was put in control. We were the first Westerners most of our new friends had ever met. I saw immediately (which most of them did not) that democracy was not a panacea and that the situation would get much worse before it could begin to improve. Even so, I entered into the optimism in my own way. We had great hopes and "vision" for shaping the development of this newly independent nation. They were asking all the right questions and seemed open to new approaches. What was more amazing, we had access to young men and women who were obviously the leaders of tomorrow.

Since Daristan does not offer missionary visas, we had to find some other reason to be here. We soon learned that there was a strong demand for English-language learning and opened a course. As native speakers, this was something we could do reasonably well, and we have never had any problem filling our course, which has grown tenfold (in both size and quality) since those first classes over ten years ago.

As new team members began to join us, our course became a convenient way to bring staff into what was still a "restricted access nation." This was important to us because we believed in the value and power of team ministry. Although traditional missionaries have often worked as isolated individuals or couples, we were convinced of the wisdom of Paul's strategy of moving into an area with a multinational and multigifted apostolic team. This "missionary band" or "traveling church" can exercise the spiritual authority and the full complement of spiritual gifts that Christ gives to his body, even in areas where the local church does not yet exist. As YWAMers, this "community" is both who we are and what we do. So, before we even arrived, our strategy had included bringing many others into the country to work with us, and for this we needed visas.

Proverbs says, "A gift opens a way for the giver" (Prov. 18:16). Daristanis are wonderfully hospitable, but within their culture, a guest never comes empty-handed—he brings something, if only flowers or chocolate. Our English course is the gift we bring as guests in this land.

The course has proved to be more than a mere entry strategy for us. We see it as a valid form of community development. We might not have identified language instruction as the most pressing priority of this nation in crisis, but it is certainly a "felt need." On closer examination, it is not hard to understand why. With the fall of Communism, Russian is no longer the *lingua franca* for travel and interaction outside of this small nation. In this new era, some knowledge of English is essential for advancement in every field, whether business, education, medicine, or politics. Proficiency in English greatly increases one's chances of landing a paying job in the private sector. In a developing African nation we might dig wells; here we teach English.

The course has also put us in contact with English-speaking Daristanis with whom we can share our faith. (This has been especially strategic for short-term visitors, who do not speak the local language.) In the classroom we teach English and build trusting relationships. Outside the classroom we are free to discuss whatever we want, including what is most important to us—our faith.

Our Strategy

In the early days, our discussions would range from art to politics to religion to sex, back to spiritual matters and on to other issues. God was as interesting and relevant as anything else, and we rarely experienced that icy discomfort you feel in the West when the conversation turns to "religion." We saw some fruit—actual conversions— but they did not always "stick."

It was very stimulating to discuss politics, art, culture, and other issues with our Daristani friends (especially since we knew that many of them were, or would someday be, influential in their nation). But it was obvious that any solutions we could offer, or models we could point to, all relied upon a Christian foundation in the thought and practices of the nation. Republican government, democratic processes, the rule of law, civil freedoms, economic opportunity, and every other component of the ordered liberty which we cherish or take for granted in the West—all of these blessings sprang out of a certain soil and cannot simply be uprooted and transplanted just anywhere. Even the Daristanis themselves would say things like, "Our people aren't capable of living in a free society. Their psychology won't allow it." Or, "Corruption is a way of life. Our people are brought up on it. How can it ever change?"

They were right to be pessimistic—without widespread change in the hearts and minds of the people, structural change would be impossible. Even more important than the *breadth* of this change measured in numbers of converts would be the *depth* of the change. Many societal problems spring from deep in the psychology and culture of this ancient people—the roots go very deep.

The biblical word "repentance" is the Greek *metanoia*—literally, a "change of mind." This change of mind has little to do with mental assent. As Christ said, "Even the demons believe and tremble" (James 2:19). *Metanoia* begins with a realignment of the deepest motives of the heart—what Charles Finney called the "ultimate intention." It also includes a thorough uprooting and rethinking of those unquestioned ideas from which all our thinking and values flow, what Francis Schaeffer called "presuppositions." Only the presence of a transformed community, whose individuals have undergone this *metanoia,* makes structural change possible.

Someone said of the scholar and writer C. S. Lewis that he was "the most thoroughly converted man" they had ever met. His continuing influence both inside and outside the church is a testimony to the power of this principle. It is this "thorough conversion" we are after.

It soon became obvious to us that the first order of business was not "reform" but "church planting." William James said religion is what we do with our solitude. Religion may be private, but Christian faith certainly is not. The *corporate* expression of our faith and obedience together is essential. In fact, it is doubtful whether a "thorough conversion" is even possible in isolation. "As iron sharpens iron, so one man sharpens another" (Prov. 27:17). John says it is impossible to love God without loving a Christian brother (1 John 4:20). Jesus himself tells us to skip a "quiet-time" to repair a damaged relationship (Matt. 5:23–24). We are promised that when two or three gather in his name, he is there in some special way (Matt. 18:20). All of these passages and many more show that Christian faith is not a "me and God" proposition.

We chose as the pattern for the fellowships we wanted to establish what Dick Scoggins called "the virus model." A virus is about the most stripped down, basic life form. Some dispute whether it lives at all. What a virus does well is to multiply rapidly and mutate quickly. We did not want to plant one church or a group of churches, but a movement able to multiply across a nation and adapt quickly to different settings. We looked for the irreducible essentials of the New Testament church.

We have limited ourselves to a strategy and to methods that can be duplicated and reproduced by our disciples, with or without our help. For this reason we meet in homes. Any other venue would make these fellowships dependent on foreign subsidies for the foreseeable future and limit their growth and multiplication. These home fellowships are full-fledged "churches" in the New Testament sense of the word—communities of faith, following the commands of Christ. A typical gathering will include worship in song, much of the music written by Daristani believers. Those present are encouraged to speak out praises to God from their hearts. The high point of worship is when we "spread the Lord's tablecloth" (celebrate communion), which we do often. Someone will open a passage of Scripture, often a whole chapter, and lead the group to a deeper understanding and practical application in their lives, usually by asking questions. Everyone is encouraged to contribute to the discussion. The leader's function is primarily to bring the discussion back to the obvious meaning of the passage. Communion and the Word are usually led by different individuals, and if the group is more than a few months old, these will be nationals.

Community and Culture

The transformation of society is not merely the cumulative effect of isolated converts. Church planting is essential because a corporate expression of our faith is necessary to the transformation of what we call "culture"—that hard-to-define collection of habits, rituals, symbols, ideas, values, and preferences which, like language, binds a people together in an extended community.

Men and women are valuable because they are made in God's image. Culture is what people create together with that dimension of their beings which is made in the image of God. Culture is valuable because mankind is valuable. Although all cultures (like all men and women) are valuable to God, all cultures (like all men and women) are also fallen and need to be redeemed.

In Scripture, we read that the "glory" or treasures of the nations will be brought into the New Jerusalem (Rev. 21:24, 26). I believe that some of those treasures will be the magnificent music, poetry, and textiles of Daristan. The city of God will also incorporate many other wonderful customs, characteristics, and indefinable qualities that make up the unique cultural blend of this people.

Culture is a corporate phenomenon that can only be redeemed by a community of faith and obedience. For this reason, the unchanging truths of the gospel must be allowed to find an expression within the culture of every nation. Missiologists call this process "contextualization." Our goal and prayer has been that Daristanis would feel that they are "coming home" when they enter a fellowship we have planted. We know our efforts as foreigners to "contextualize" are clumsy, but even these inadequate gestures are significant.

Someone said that you can always tell if a church is culturally relevant by observing whether or not the missionary likes it. If he feels comfortable, it is almost certainly *not* contextualized. I remember the time one of our local disciples began to read out prayers in our home fellowship. We had been encouraging these new believers to speak out praises to God during worship and not just passively sing songs. One woman would wait till the appropriate moment and then pull out a notebook from which she would read out a prayer, sometimes almost a page long. I was concerned, and considered how I should approach her about this. Muslims tend to think of prayer as something done by rote, in a language they don't understand (unless they speak Arabic), with even the physical gestures prescribed for them. To my Western and Protestant eyes, she was obviously bound up in these religious forms.

I am glad I did not confront her about it. I waited and listened. Suddenly it dawned on me—she was reading poetry! These prayers were beautiful psalms she had composed during the week and was offering from her heart as a "sacrifice of praise." Nothing could be more biblical or more consistent with her culture. Daristan is a nation of poets. Nearly all of the many statues and monuments in the capital city commemorate not politicians, but writers and poets of their ancient and recent history. Poetry is a living art form, enjoyed by the masses, not just an academic elite. This woman was trying to bring this cultural treasure with her into the New Jerusalem. Thank God that I did not force her to discard it at the gate!

Transforming Society—Princes and People

But what about reform? What about applying Truth to every sphere of society? We have not given up on seeing this nation transformed. But my expectation of how the transformation will occur is now different than it once was.

I sometimes suspect that reports of our work here give the impression that we stride the corridors of power and engage in all manner of behind-the-scenes moving and shaking. It is true that our English course has put us in contact with many influential people in this society, not only political leaders, but also artists, journalists, and businessmen. These contacts and relationships sometimes develop into true friendships. They have also been valuable to our work in many ways. But I cannot say they have often resulted in a shaping influence on the structures of society.

I certainly understand the importance of friends in high places. Greg Livingstone, the founder of Frontiers, counsels missionaries working in Muslim nations to make a point of building friendships with people of influence. In many non-Western nations, which were not founded on the *lex rex* ("law is king") ideal, a friend in the right position can be the difference between an open front door and a kick out the back door. These relationships are an important way to build trust and protect the work from hostile attacks.

Here in Daristan, pressure on both foreign and local Christians waxes and wanes. A new wave of hostility usually begins in the newspapers, with a rash of articles denouncing Christian work in the country, complaining about conversions to Christianity, reheating some very stale lies, and calling on the government to take action against us. Whenever these articles begin to appear in official government newspapers, we know there is cause for concern. Pressure or persecution usually follows. On one occasion when the name of our organization appeared in a prominent article, many of our friends became concerned that the situation might be serious. About a week later, a friend of mine, who is an important journalist, stopped by to borrow a book. (I am afraid it was no more spiritual than Tom Clancy.) Before he left, he pulled me aside and said, "I was very upset when I saw the article about you. I want you to know it will not happen again. I talked to someone about it, and they told me, 'Mr. Grattus has nothing to fear. He has very important people, and the children of important people, studying at his center.'"

The stories of Joseph and Esther are biblical examples of how God works providentially in this way to guard or deliver his people, especially when they are aliens in an environment hostile to them and their message. But it does not necessarily result in a transformation of society on a structural level. God used Esther to preserve his people, but she does not seem to have shaped the governing structures in Babylon. Joseph, on the contrary, seems to have had a profound influence, but not necessarily in a good way. The narrative explicitly states that through Joseph's policy, all of Egypt became the property of Pharaoh. Joseph was certainly used by God to preserve the descendants of Abraham, and all of Egypt, from a severe famine. But the narrative does not tell us whether it was God's purpose to make the entire nation the property of one man. If it was his purpose, the result looks more like judgment than blessing.[1]

Over the years, we have learned not to "trust in princes" (Ps. 146:3). At times, friends in high places can present some disadvantages.

Sometime during our first year here, two members of the president's staff requested placement in our course, which was already full. We are habitually resistant to government officials asking favors, but because of the pressing need they had for English in their work, we made an exception for them. They turned out to be humble and idealistic men who had gained their posts on the merits of the courageous work they had done by running an illegal newspaper during the Communist period. We became friends, and talked about many things, including our faith and principles of civil government. It felt good to know that we had friends in high places. But we learned not to trust in princes. A *coup d'état* swept the president, and our friends, out of power. Suddenly our relationship with them became a liability rather than an asset.

At this point, our friendship actually grew much stronger through this opportunity to demonstrate that our affection and friendship had been sincere and unconditional. Over the course of the next year or two, we helped them in some simple but important ways, which resulted in both of them studying abroad. They both eventually found positions in important international organizations. Paradoxically, any shaping influence we have exerted through these two men is subsequent to their fall from power.

Even when friends in high places retain their positions of influence, the blessing is not unmixed. We met Yousif through his son, a student in our course. We helped his son improve his English when he was in a panic before a university exam. As a result, he felt in our debt and began bringing me a daily load of chocolate bars (which endeared him to my children). He further offered me the services of his father, who, we then learned, held a very high post in the government. We did not ask for favors, but a relationship did develop between Yousif's family and us.

Over a year later we asked Yousif to vouch for a new work we were starting in a rural area where officials, not accustomed to the presence of foreigners, were suspicious of our activities. Yousif opened some doors for us and we initiated a mercy-ministry project in an orphanage. We never learned what went wrong, but rumors began to spread, and the local officials became hostile. At this point we expected our influential friend to come to our aid. Instead, perhaps unsure what to believe, perhaps afraid of political problems for himself, he declined to vouch for us and asked us to withdraw the team. Ordinarily we might have been able to dig in our heels, face down the accusations, and weather the storm. But because we were associated with our prominent friend and did not want to be the cause of additional embarrassment or trouble for him, we were obligated to withdraw. We were not able to place a team there for another year. From this experience, we learned that the knife could cut in both directions. Or as a friend of mine says, "You gotta dance with who brung you."

When we finally established a team in that area, it was the direct result of sustained intercessory prayer. Our home-front team had worked tirelessly to establish a communications network linking our frontline work to intercessors in the West. As the team tried to return to the area, they again encountered opposition from the local authorities. Our home-front intercessors, having followed our progress and setbacks for nearly two years, responded with unusually energetic prayer and spiritual warfare. When the team reached an impasse, the team leader asked me to make a trip down to meet with the mayor. I was not optimistic, since he had met with me once before and had politely told me that our presence was not required in their region. The morning we left the capital, a local lawyer and friend handed us a newspaper containing a day-old presidential decree. It called on rural authorities not to impede the activities of foreign firms and organizations. The two departments that had opposed us were specifically mentioned. The content and timing was perfect, as if it the decree had been written for our benefit! When we arrived, the authorities were cordial and obliging. We thought of the scripture, "The king's heart is in the hand of the Lord; he directs it like a watercourse wherever he pleases" (Prov. 21:1).

We never know which of our actions is actually exerting an influence on the structures we seek to influence. I remember the day several years ago when two men walked into our office with a surprising proposal. They were academicians of the highest rank with impressive credentials from Moscow State University, the USSR's most prestigious school. One of them had stirred up some controversy with a series of newspaper articles decrying the state of higher education in Daristan and calling for the founding of a new Western-style university. The idea had gained the favor of the president, with the result that the government was ready to invest a large sum of money. The astounding thing was that these men wanted me to be a founding board member, and our English course to become the first year of study.

Today we might be able to flatter ourselves that it was the high quality of our course that had earned us this distinction. We have worked hard to make it one of the best in the country. But at that pioneering stage, we were just a handful of volunteers, learning as we went. As it turned out, our placement examination, not our course, had convinced them to invite us to be part of their important enterprise. When we give an entrance exam, we take pains to explain to each group that absolutely no talking or looking will be allowed and that at the first violation, the offender's test will be removed without warning or second chance. (When it comes to exams, Daristanis are shameless cheaters. Soviet Communists reinforced this characteristic because they viewed collaboration as a positive social trait. Evidently, not allowing others to look on and copy was considered dangerously individualistic.) On the occasion in question, several in the first group tested our resolve and reaped the consequences. One young woman actually stood in the hall crying as the next group came in, with the result that we did not have to pull another test for the rest of the day. One of the two visiting academicians had been tested that day. What he observed convinced him that only we would have the resolve to resist the ingrained habits of corruption in the Daristani educational system. When we subsequently met with the president's chief of staff, this educator again recounted his experience, which had obviously made a deep impression.

The story has a sad ending. Eventually the government money and the prospects of even greater profits drew in parties who finally excluded the idealistic academicians and convinced us that we should not be involved. After functioning a couple of years, the university closed down. The positive outcome for us, though, was that we learned that we never know which of our actions is going to influence our targeted structures.

We have also learned that we can never tell beforehand which of our friends and contacts will be strategic and influential in the future. Ali was a university student befriended by one of our young YWAMers. I remember clearly the first time he sat in my living room—an awkward kid from the village. He was a gentle soul but lacked social graces. In America we would have called him a "hick" or a "hillbilly." Later, he put his faith in Christ and was baptized. Another leader and I agreed that even though he was not particularly "strategic," the Lord could use him within his own circle of friends. Team members led him in Bible study and helped disciple him.

I was shocked when I learned that our young friend had landed an important staff position in the national government. I was even more surprised to learn the importance of his position and that he often accompanies delegations to important international conferences. The most exciting part is that he has actually been a witness in this position. He frequently prays for the specific needs of his high-ranking colleagues, and he has a standing pact with God that when the prayers are answered, he will speak to the individual and explain why. These high-ranking Muslim officials have asked him to pray for issues of national and historic significance. His busy schedule no longer permits the kind of intensive input we once gave him. Had I known the future, I would have poured into him everything I knew about how Christian pre-suppositions are expressed in the structures of civil government. Sometimes I wonder if I missed God. Other times I think it's for the best that we stuck to heart issues and left him to sort out how these principles should play out in his strategic responsibilities.

Transformation of a Nation Begins in the Heart of the Individual

So how can we reform the structures of society? The kingdom of God works from the inside out, not from the top down or from the outside in. This basic principle has almost endless social implications, touching every sphere of life. Virtually every other social program or revolutionary blueprint is designed to work the other way around—a perfected environment (economic, social, religious, physical) must result in a new man. Always the assumption is that we must transform mankind from the outside in.

For Karl Marx, the economic component was primary. Marxism literally promised that socialism would create a "new man." I remember a very sad article I read during a visit to Nicaragua during the Sandinista era. It appeared in the government paper *Barricada,* or "Barricade." In a tone of bewildered disappointment, the writer asked where to find the "new man" who should be emerging. On the contrary, he complained, people were getting worse—more selfish.

As Paul says in 1 Corinthians, the Christian social program is founded on the "foolishness of preaching." In other words, our revolution will be accomplished simply by talking to people about Jesus. This seems naive in the extreme to just about everyone else. Both liberation theology and its kinder, gentler predecessor, the social gospel, were fundamentally flawed. Not only were they "left wing," but they hoped to extend the kingdom of God through social action, to the extent that the biblical term "kingdom of God" is now discredited in some quarters. In the end, this kind of activity always becomes political. Anything else appears as "foolishness." Everyone wants their social action backed by the police powers of the state. There is always a temptation to reach for the "big guns"—sometimes literally. Even for evangelical Christians, the discussion of "dominion" and "discipling nations" is sometimes in danger of sinking to this level. But the kingdom of Christ will not work its transformation in this way.

The pessimism that doubts that Daristan can change is based on a pessimism that people can change. But we have seen radical changes in the lives of many Daristanis. One young man whom I helped lead to the Lord, is now completing his military service. Virtually no young person who has the financial means to avoid the "mandatory" draft actually goes into military service. The soldiers live in terrible conditions, and many return with chronic sicknesses from a combination of malnutrition, unheated and unclean living quarters, and inadequate medical care. My young brother is there because his conscience would no longer allow him to defer his enlistment through bribes and other means. During his military service, his refusal to collect bribes from those under him has brought him into conflict with his superiors who do not understand why he does not pass on a percentage to them. Even so, the integrity of his character is such that his superiors continue to give him significant responsibility over other troops. Those under his leadership have also recognized the difference. An officer even told him that soldiers were offering large bribes to be transferred into his platoon. An inner transformation resulting in a willingness to do right whatever the cost will transform a nation just as leaven permeates and transforms a lump of dough.

So, have I finally come full circle and returned to "evacuation theology"? Do we simply "get people saved" and let the world continue its inevitable spiral into corruption and judgment? Have we arrived back at a divided worldview that excludes Christians from penetrating every sphere of society? Absolutely not! The kingdom transformation must *begin* in the depths of the human heart, but *it must not stop there!*

Salvation involves a wholehearted submission of our lives to the transforming love, truth, and power of Christ. It is, as the poet T. S. Eliot said, "A condition of complete simplicity / (Costing not less than everything)."[2] A thorough conversion will touch everything we touch, and that means all of society. The worst expressions of "evacuation theology"—the secular-sacred split, the divided worldview, and the retreat from engagement with society outside the church—result as much from faulty evangelism as from a faulty social outlook. What evangelicals need is *not* a dose of the "social gospel" but a rediscovery of the lordship of Christ.

The gospel is "the gospel of the kingdom." Salvation is not merely a transaction with God in which we agree to go to heaven. If we simply encourage people to "accept

Jesus as Savior," we have truncated the gospel. It troubles me that Christian evangelists who would never gloss over Jesus' claim to be God will completely neglect to mention that he is "Lord"—the rightful and ultimate authority. You will search hard to find an evangelistic tract that even mentions repentance and lordship. Yet, the apostles and Christ himself emphasize his lordship far more often than his deity. In my experience, the Muslim who fully submits to *Isa Masih* (Jesus the Messiah) with only the vague understanding that he is "more than a prophet," will soon come into a full-blown understanding of Christ's deity—if he or she is truly submitted to follow him as Lord. On the other hand, we all know people who have slipped up a hand in an evangelistic meeting but never enjoy the blessings of God in their lives, nor bear any spiritual fruit, because they never truly submit their lives to him.

We must return to the great Reformed doctrine of the "sovereignty of God." The Reformers' conviction that no corner of the seen or unseen universe was out from under God's rightful authority empowered them to work tirelessly to understand every aspect of creation and extend Christ's dominion into every corner of human existence. They made some terrible mistakes along the way, but they also achieved amazing breakthroughs in science, civil government, and economics.[3]

When we invite people to come into the kingdom, they must understand that Christ is the King. He welcomes them as they are, but no corner of their lives will be exempt from his authority, truth, and transforming presence. The kingdom begins with a yielding of the heart, and moves out in ever-widening circles to transform not only moral conduct, but every relationship and sphere of involvement. Family, friendships, the workplace and economic activity, political associations, leisure activities, and aesthetic enjoyments all come under the dominion of Christ and his revealed truth. The reign of Christ *in* us results in the reign of Christ *through* us.

Christ prayed, "Your kingdom come, your will be done on earth as it is in heaven" (Matt. 6:10). An individual first gives up his rebellion against God's kingdom, and submits to Christ the King. Then, as each facet of the Christian's life comes under the reign of Christ, the kingdom of God begins to exert its influence through the obedient Christian. Not only do other lives come into submission to God through his or her witness, but in everything, the Christian strives to bring all things into conformity with the will of God. In this way the Spirit and Truth of God exert their leavening influence throughout every sphere of society. This influence may be expressed through Christlike courtesy at the checkout counter or courageous civil disobedience to social injustice or just by doing a good job.

I find that a clear presentation of the kingship of Christ does not drive away seekers, but attracts them. Why do we think we will gain anything by dimming the fierce beauty of the Lion of Judah or by diluting his rightful claims? Islam, whatever else it lacks, presents a unified worldview. It addresses all of life and not merely spiritual and religious issues. This unified worldview is much of its appeal, in both historically Islamic nations and Western nations where it is attracting converts. If we present a divided, stripped-down gospel, our message will be seen, or at least felt, to be inherently inferior to what they already have. What a tragedy! Islam does not even offer a relationship with God. Its top-down program for society results in bondage and tyranny, as Iranians and Afghanis have learned. Our message is not inferior unless we make it so.

In our context, baptism is the watershed issue. We do not even count converts until they have been baptized. Newcomers to our team are sometimes surprised at the emphasis we place on baptism. It is not that we endorse a doctrine of "baptismal regeneration." If practical considerations force us to delay baptism, we do not worry about it. But we have found over and over that if a new disciple is unwilling to be baptized, it is cause for serious concern. Spiritual progress will soon come to a halt, and often the individual will walk away from his or her faith. The issue is lordship. For Muslims, baptism is a big step and presents one of the first tests of the new believer's obedience to the commands of Christ. I have great respect for our Daristani brothers and sisters who take this step and live for their Lord courageously and without shame.

Still in Process

It has been over twelve years since my wife and I came to Daristan. I am not discouraged or pessimistic, though at the moment I am very tired. Our team and our work are better positioned than ever to deeply and widely influence this country. I truly believe that exciting times are ahead for us. But what we envisioned accomplishing will take longer than I expected.

Our work continues to diversify and to spread geographically into many regions of the country.

As I reread this chapter, I see how narrow my perspective is. Many others on our team could have spoken with more practical authority on many issues simply because they have had more hands-on experience in recent years. My Muslim-background Daristani coworkers could say much more about what does and does not need to be redeemed in Daristani culture. They are beginning to develop their own strategies for reaching their country and beyond. No doubt they will change the way we do things. But it is also exciting to see them getting excited about and passing on to their disciples some of the principles that have been important to us. Nothing is more gratifying than to hear one of our disciples expressing a confident hope that the good news is able to transform the whole man and all that he touches.

Notes

1. Is it reading too much into the text to connect this radical centralization of property and power in the god-king Pharaoh with the later enslavement of the Hebrews by one of his descendants who "knew not Joseph"?

2. T. S. Eliot, "Little Gidding," *The Complete Poems and Plays 1909–1950* (New York: Harcourt Brace & Company, 1967), 145.

3. I am, of course, aware that "the sovereignty of God" was and is also used to describe the Reformed belief that every detail of what occurs in the universe somehow expresses the will of God. Many great Christians of the past and present share this belief. I do not. On the contrary, I take at face value the many places in Scripture which imply or explicitly state that we live on a rebel planet in which God's will often is *not* done, hence Christ's prayer, "Thy Kingdom come, thy will be done, on earth as it is in heaven." In this view, God's sovereignty is dynamic, and not static or fixed.

Part 3

History of Discipling Nations

The call to disciple nations has within it the implication that we must be intentional both to disciple the nation we are in and to extend the discipleship to all nations. Todd explores the experiences of brothers and sisters who've gone before us as they grappled with the need for both breadth and depth in our response to God's purposes on earth. As with all history, we have as much to learn from their successes as from their failures.

From Rome to Reformation:
The Breadth and Depth of Christian Mission

Todd M. Johnson

From nascent Christian communities in the Roman Empire in the first century to the tumultuous seventeenth century in northern Europe, Christians have struggled with the inherent tension between offering the gospel beyond its current borders and the transformation of their own lives and the societies in which they lived. At the core of this struggle was the fundamental unity of the Christian religion: simultaneously planting communities in every people in the world *and* impacting the society Christians live in.

This struggle can be viewed from the context of Christian expansion into four major cultural basins over four 400-year periods in its first 1,600 years.[1] In each of these periods one sees a dynamic interaction between the extension of the faith by conversion of new peoples and the instruction and maturing process in those who had already become Christians. Andrew Walls utilizes a parallel motif—that of the indigenizing principle (emphasizing particulars of culture and group) and the pilgrim principle (emphasizing universal aspects of Christianity).[2] Thus Christians are to be completely at home in their culture (transforming it) and, at the same time, belonging to a global family of Christians (extending to every people). These two seemingly opposing streams of the *breadth* of mission (all peoples) and its *depth* (teaching all things) provide an apt backdrop for the story of global Christian expansion (Matt. 28:18–20).

Roman Era (0–AD 400)

Christians in and around Rome in the first century likely had little sense of how their faith might impact the Roman Empire. Not only were Christians viewed as "atheists" (for refusing to worship the pantheon of Roman gods) but, beginning with Nero in AD 70 and culminating under Diocletian by AD 300, were under increasingly intense and widespread persecution. Paradoxically, this period was one of significant geographic and cultural expansion of the Christian presence within the boundaries of the Roman Empire—Christian communities sprang up all around the Mediterranean Sea among dozens of peoples and languages. The breadth or expansion of the Christian community was largely due to four factors:

1. The Greek language was widely understood and used by early Christians as a lingua franca.
2. The Romans built thousands of miles of roads extending the trade routes the Christian faith would travel upon under Pax Romana.
3. Christians, following the example of the Apostle Paul, deliberately sought a home outside of the Jewish enclave.
4. Lay people participated in evangelism and church planting in huge numbers, particularly among the diasporic Jews and the God-fearing Gentiles.

Christians thus built upon the "mission" presence of the Jews, whose cultural and religious influence had already been felt around the Mediterranean for several hundred years.

Conversion was an often rapid and relatively simple affair. Theodoret, in witnessing the impact of Symeon's preaching on the pillar in the Syrian desert writes:

[Even the Bedouins] in many thousands, enslaved to the darkness of impiety, were enlightened by the station upon the pillar . . . They arrived in companies, 200 in one, 300 in another, occasionally a thousand. They renounced with shouts their traditional errors; they broke up their venerated idols in the presence of that great light; and they foreswore the ecstatic rites of Aphrodite, the demon whose service they had long accepted.[3]

These Bedouins came from at least 250 miles away. Their conversion was typical of so many others at the time. It entailed a change in allegiance from one spiritual power to another. What aspects of their previous culture and religion they retained, we do not know.[4] By the year 400, a majority of the empire's subjects were Christians.

Depth was dealt with in two major ways. First, Anthony's retirement to the desert of Egypt in the third century eventually gave rise to the monastic movement. The monastic communities (even most hermits lived close enough together to meet daily or weekly for worship) offered a structured daily discipleship plan, whereby any novice could grow in faith and maturity.

Second, the appearance of a young Christian with aspirations to rule Rome came just as the faith was gaining ascendancy in the Empire. Constantine, following a sense of call as well as the admonitions of his Christian mother, came to power in AD 312. Just a year later, with his coemperor at Milan, he signed into Roman law an edict ending imperial persecution. Constantine felt obligated to help widely flung Christian communities overcome stark cultural differences and engineered the first major council in Nicea in 325. This council and the many that followed offered a context for "depth" by clearly defining not only doctrine, but patterns of behavior.

In both these cases Christian discipleship was at the core. Two short generations later, Christianity was considered the state religion of the Roman Empire. This was not without a price. Winter writes:

> Thus, the political triumph of what eventually came to be known as Christianity was in fact a mixed blessing. The biblical faith could wear other than Jewish clothes; it was now dressed in Roman clothes; but if these new clothes were normative, it would not be expected to spread far beyond the political boundaries of the Roman Empire.[5]

Christians aligned themselves so closely with Roman political boundaries (e.g., doing evangelism only within Roman dioceses) that they failed to reach out beyond the Roman Empire.

Barbarian Era (400–800)

By AD 400, Christians were not only in the majority in the Roman Empire, but their leaders occupied the Lateran palace. Yet, only ten years later, after pressure from Huns moving into Europe, the first wave of Gothic barbarians under Alaric sacked Rome. This would have been a complete disaster for Christianity had not these northern peoples been long under the influence of Arius—a heretical Christian who believed that Jesus was not coeternal with God the Father. When these Arianized barbarians conquered, they did not wipe out the Christian leaders they discovered around the crumbling Roman Empire, because they recognized them as adherents of the same faith. This allowed the Roman pastors to disciple these believers away from the errors of Arius into an orthodox Christian faith. Thus, without deliberate attempts to evangelize by Roman Christians, the gospel made its way among new territories and peoples.

Broader expansion of Christianity was accomplished by two missionary groups, both far from the centers of Roman or Gothic Christianity. First, after the conversion of Ireland under Patrick, a surprisingly erudite missionary monastic movement under Celtic leadership arose. For several centuries after AD 500, Irish missionaries traveled throughout Europe, either planting churches where there were none or strengthening those that already existed. John T. McNeill concludes his masterful study of the Celtic Christian movement with these words: "Wherever they went, in their homelands or in far-off provinces of Europe, they planted active colonies of religion and culture, with lasting ameliorative effects that cannot be measured."[6] All of Europe benefited from Celtic mission well into the thirteenth century.

Second, Nestorius, a bishop in Constantinople, was accused of heresy (insisting that Jesus was two persons, human and divine, instead of a unified person) and banished to Egypt after the Council of Ephesus (AD 431). The Church of the East, a strong missionary movement based in Syria, aligned itself with Nestorius and sent its members as far as China by the seventh century. By AD 1000 the Church of the East was one of Christianity's most extensive branches, with over twelve million members in 250 dioceses all across Asia.

Depth in this period was achieved under the missionary movements above, both of which had strong monastic discipline, and with the introduction of the Rule of St. Benedict in AD 560. This balanced code of conduct was adopted by the majority of monastic houses. The Rule prescribed the reading of Psalm 67 every morning at daybreak. Thus the monks, while deepening their own spiritual existence, cried out first thing every day, "Let the peoples praise you; let all the peoples praise you" (Ps. 67:3). Monks often articulated the tie between the lofty goals of the Christian church and mundane daily life. Shenoute of Atripe, writing in the 420s, saw this immediate connection in the following passage:

> Try to attain to the full measure of this Name, and you will find it on your mouth and on the mouths of your children. When you make high festival and when you rejoice, cry Jesus. When anxious and in pain, cry Jesus. When little boys and girls are laughing, let them cry Jesus. And those who flee before barbarians, cry Jesus. And those who go down to the Nile, cry Jesus. And those who see wild beasts and sights of terror, cry Jesus. Those who are taken off to prison, cry Jesus. And those whose trial has been corrupted and who receive injustice, cry the Name of Jesus.[7]

These monastic movements (Celtic, Nestorian, Benedictine) provided a solid mooring for Christian mission and Christian discipleship in these early centuries of Christian development outside of the Roman world. They preserved learning, secular and spiritual, while promoting political and technological developments that deeply impacted their respective societies. Evangelical historian Mark Noll cites their contribution as "the most important—and in many ways the most beneficial—institutional event in the history of Christianity."[8]

Viking Era (800–1200)

By 800, a completely new experiment in Christian society was underway with the Frankish king, Charlemagne. In a period of renewal in politics, education, and theological reflection, with help from Celtic monks, Charlemagne essentially brought monastic structure and discipline to society as a whole—a clear example of depth in this era. This true "Carolingian renaissance" (renewal in northern European society) might have lasted longer had not unexpected external events intervened. The Scandinavian peoples to the north, virtually untouched by Christian contact or mission, suddenly and relentlessly burst on the scene—pillaging, raping, and destroying. One of the first places they landed was the missionary center Iona, where they promptly executed the sixty-eight monks living there. Their terrors indirectly led to a continent-wide monastic renewal based in Cluny.

More remarkable was the conversion of the Vikings themselves, effected mainly as the result of contact with Christian women they took as wives and monks they took as slaves. However, Viking wanderlust applied to a later and larger European mission resulted in a series of military crusades among the Muslims in western Asia. Not until the advent of the friars after 1200 were significant nonmilitary missions outside of Christendom initiated. Like the Barbarians in an earlier era, Vikings were not considered as part of the breadth of God's mission. Instead they invaded Christian lands and brought the gospel back to their homelands.

Mongols and Muslims Era (1200–1600)

The final four hundred years of this period set the stage for the largest single expansion of Christianity. The leadership of Francis, Dominic, and a reformed papacy gave the church in Europe its single greatest renewal. At about the same time, Genghis Khan and his successors had built up the largest empire the world had ever known. The Church of the East, an embattled minority among them, had nonetheless provided an essential leaven for Mongol affinity to the Christian message. Unfortunately, even with a royal Mongol invitation for Latin Christian mission (Kublai Khan and the Polos in 1266), there was minimal contact between these two great entities. The Black Death, and then the sword of Tamerlane, wiped out the Christian presence among Mongols and neighboring Muslims. The period ends with Europe rebuilding in the ashes and a promising reformation that would later plunge Europe into the so-called wars of religion.

In the sixteenth century, Roman Catholics launched the Society of Jesus and, in tandem with the Age of Discovery, sent missionaries to the Americas and Asia, once again extending the borders of the Christian message. Once again Christians in Europe struggled to balance the depth of Christian witness in their own society with the breadth of God's mission. The Catholic missionary orders (Franciscan, Dominican, and Jesuit) all contributed to renewal at home and mission abroad. But their work at home was continually compromised politically back in Europe (with greedy priests, cardinals, and occasionally popes). By the time Protestantism emerged, the Reformers had lost their understanding of God's breadth of mission, using almost all of their resources to transform Northern Europe.

Discipling Nations—a Process, Not a Plan

The extension of the Christian gospel can be comprehended in terms of geography and peoples. But how do we understand *discipling* these peoples from the standpoint of Christianity's first 1,600 years? We would not do well to look for some ideal pattern of social perfection to be used as a blueprint for all societies. Nor should we expect that clever plans or strategies can transform peoples. Instead we should first look at "the historic reality of Christianity as a living force," which has a transforming influence on both people and the societies in which they live.[9] Where there are Christians there is always the possibility of the transformation of society. However, transformation always begins as a spiritual process in the lives of believers, primarily in the context of Christian community. These spiritual achievements can result in society-wide cultural achievements, but there is always a significant time lag. One sees this clearly in the conversion of the Vikings. Whereas individual leaders converted and villages followed, only in succeeding generations were long-standing Viking patterns of behavior transformed. This was accomplished through a slow but steady movement of biblical literacy and spiritual renewal.

This time lag is also apparent in the earliest expansion of Christianity in Europe. Paul's earliest forays into Philippi involved nothing notable from the standpoint of contemporary culture. He was unpopular and only managed to convert a slave girl, a businesswoman, and a jailer. From these inauspicious beginnings, the church in Europe was born. It would be tempting to suggest that Paul's methods in response to a dream are incompatible with discipling the nations, but proper evaluation cannot be performed without the passage of a significant period of time. In retrospect, he was quite successful.

Christopher Dawson points out that "the great cultural changes and the historic revolutions that decide the fate of nations or the character of an age are the cumulative result of a number of spiritual decisions—the faith and insight, or the refusal and blindness, of individuals."[10] This leads us to believe that what decisions these are and who is making them is not always well known. The process of discipling the nations often involves unknown prayers and individuals who never make it into the pages of history books. Where there are Christians, there will be Christian community and Christian society. If their influence goes deep enough, there may even develop Christian civilization. But even then, the breadth emphasis of Christian mission would need to be at the forefront. An ideal Christian society is not one walled off culturally or socially from the rest of the world.

The geographic and cultural expansion of Christianity is in dynamic tension with the attempt to go deeper in the societies where Christians already exist. The Christian innovation most successful in navigating this tension was the monastic movement. Whether one examines the monks of the Egyptian desert, the Celtic *peregrini,* the later Benedictine and Augustinian monasteries, or the Franciscan and Dominican friars, one finds a deep commitment to both the spiritual life and the transformation of society. In all of these movements an equally profound commitment to missionary expansion and personal spirituality is apparent.

At another level it is important to realize that the transformation of society by Christians cannot be helped or hindered by human power or material catastrophe. This gives all Christians an equal chance of impacting the people that they live among—whether they be a persecuted minority or an overwhelming majority. A Christian president or a Christian king is no guarantee of a discipled nation. Some of the most effective Christian disciplers in its first sixteen hundred years were monks in the Egyptian desert, slaves in foreign lands, and captive Christian wives. The modern tendency has been to work for overarching reform on all fronts at once. Philosopher Michael Polanyi warned against the implications of this:

> To try to reform all the power structures at once would leave us with no power structure to use in our project. In any case, we will be able to see that absolute moral renewal could be attempted only by an absolute power and that a tyrannous force such as this must destroy the whole moral life of man, not renew it.[11]

Christians in the first sixteen hundred years were under a mandate to extend the gospel to new peoples and to see that these peoples were transformed by this same gospel. In both cases, there was no simple technique or method for achieving this. Christians have, on occasion, neglected their duty to carry the good news beyond its present borders. At other times they have not allowed it to transform either themselves or the societies in which they live. Their challenge is ours today—to do both and to do them well.

Bibliography

Bosch, David. *Transforming Mission: Paradigm Shifts in the Theology of Mission.* Maryknoll, N.Y.: Orbis, 1991.

Dawson, Christopher. *Religion and the Rise of Western Culture.* New York: Image, 1950.

Latourette, Kenneth Scott. *A History of Christianity.* New York: Harper and Row, 1950.

Notes

1. Ralph D. Winter, "The Kingdom Strikes Back: Ten Epochs of Redemptive History" in *Perspectives on the World Christian Movement,* ed. Ralph D. Winter and Steven C. Hawthorne (Pasadena, Calif.: William Carey Library, 1999).

2. Andrew Walls, *The Missionary Movement in Christian History: Studies in the Transmission of the Faith* (Maryknoll, N.Y.: Orbis, 1996).

3. Theodoret, *Religious History,* 26 quoted in *Christianizing the Roman Empire, AD 100–400,* Ramsey MacMullen (New Haven: Yale University Press, 1990).

4. MacMullen makes the point that we know little about what happened to these Bedouins after their conversion, but nonetheless they must be considered part of the remarkable early expansion of Christianity.

5. Winter, "The Empire Strikes Back," 202.

6. John T. McNeill, *The Celtic Churches: A History, AD 200–1200* (Chicago: University of Chicago, 1974), 224.

7. Shenoute, *Contra Origenistas,* 821, ed. Tito Orlandi (Rome: 1985), 62–3, quoted in Peter Brown, *Authority and the Sacred: Aspects of the Christianisation of the Roman World* (Cambridge, Mass.: Canto, 1995), 10.

8. Mark A. Noll, *Turning Points: Decisive Moments in the History of Christianity* (Grand Rapids: Baker, 1997), 84.

9. Christopher Dawson, *The Historic Reality of Christian Culture* (New York: Harper, 1960), 14.

10. Ibid., 18.

11. Michael Polanyi and Harry Prosch, *Meaning* (Chicago: University of Chicago, 1975), 213–214.

Tom takes us on a journey through the history of the city of Geneva as a model of what God can do when we work with God to disciple a nation. There are periods of great success to learn from and some important warnings to heed from the city's story, and from the ministry of its greatest discipler, John Calvin.

Calvin and Geneva:
Nation-Building Missions

Thomas A. Bloomer

Geneva, nestled at the foot of the Alps at the crossroads of several major traveling routes, has been a center of great influence, trading both goods and ideas throughout Europe. Today, this small city is actually the diplomatic capital of the world, as 70 percent of the work of the United Nations is done there, and powerful organizations such as the World Trade Organization have their headquarters there. Its story is a rich tapestry of all the elements of a blockbuster movie: violence, corruption, intrigue, and courage in the face of great risk and injustice. In Geneva we can learn important lessons on the process of discipling a nation, as well as vital warnings of what happens when the church fails in its mandate.

During the Middle Ages, Geneva was a wild town. The streets teemed with crowds, as people from the all over Europe passed through on their way to France, Italy, Germany, or Austria. With more inns per capita than any other city of its time, Geneva was full of partying traders, petty criminals, political refugees, spies, and sailors from Lake Geneva. Drunkenness was common, and the houses of prostitution did a good business. The city fairs were particularly famous; during those events the town was wide open and filled with people.

However, as the sixteenth century began, competition from France markedly reduced attendance at the fairs, and the walls of the city fell into disrepair. People were poor, families were falling apart, and the future looked grim. Geneva was called the smelliest city of Europe.

Much of the responsibility lay with the church. All over Europe people were turning away, disgusted by the corruption and hypocrisy. The church was literally selling salvation, as people had to pay large amounts of cash to be sure of escaping Hell. In Geneva, the priests were not only immoral themselves, but were also running houses of prostitution. *In losing its purity, the church lost its power, and so squandered its authority and its leadership.* The people actually ran the bishop of Geneva out of town in 1530, and most of the city's nobles left with him. The spiritual and moral vacuum soon had major political and economic consequences. Geneva was in crisis.

Europeans were grappling with life-and-death questions: "How can we live? Is there a better way to take care of our families? Run the economy? Take care of the poor? What about school for the children? How should we defend ourselves? What responsibility does each citizen have?" As in many countries of the world today, solutions were needed for government, the economy, defense, schools, family life, and morality. The people were asking and the church had no answers.

Stirrings of Reformation

As the church became increasingly corrupt and burdensome on people's lives, there were stirrings across Europe for a more biblical Christianity. The underlying beliefs of this Reformation movement were that the Bible must be the source of authority to shape every aspect of people's lives, and the foundation of truth for entire communities and nations. One vital step toward this goal was for the people to have the Word of God in their language and their homes. Sadly, but not surprisingly, resistance to this came from the church itself, which in turn incited the government to persecute these believers. Forced to flee their homes, they spread the movement around Europe as they relocated.

William Farel, the redheaded, hot-tempered French evangelist, came into the vacuum that was Geneva in 1531. His strategy was simple but very effective: go into a city, do some outrageous things, get everybody all stirred up, and then get run out of town. His overall goal: make sure that everyone was angry enough to be talking about this new religion of the Protestant Reformers.

Once, he stopped to go into a church service and got so upset about what the priest was preaching that he went up to the front, pushed the priest out of the pulpit, and began preaching himself. Another time he saw priests leading a procession with relics down by the side of the river, and he ran over and pushed both priests and relics into the water. He was literally run out of Geneva by the monks of the cathedral.

Farel always managed to get out just in time. A good sense of timing is crucial for that kind of ministry strategy!

After he was kicked out of Geneva, one of his coworkers, the Frenchman Froment, started a school to teach children to read by using the Bible. Many adults wanted to learn how to read as well, so they also came to his school. He got so excited one day in 1534 that he came to the market square and jumped up on one of the market tables and started preaching. Some of the authorities came to listen, and at one point he got carried away and cried out, "We must reform the church in order to reform the nation!" That offended the authorities so much they arrested him and then kicked him out of town.

Businessmen whose salvation was rooted in the Reformation had migrated to the city; they began small groups to meet for study and prayer. The simplicity and disciplined lifestyles of the Protestant reformers stood in stark contrast to the corruption of the church and nobility. City leadership fell to these new leaders; finally, on the 26th of August in 1535, the electors of the city of Geneva voted unanimously to become a Reformed Protestant city. They also agreed to the condition that they teach every child in the city to read. One implication of their decision was that the city came under the protection of the Lords of Bern, strong Protestants who continued to mentor the city leaders.

Once the decision was made, the Reformers proceeded to destroy all the stained glass windows and statues of the cathedral. They felt that the people had worshipped these images, and therefore they were considered idolatrous and needed to be destroyed.

However, in contrast to the Lutheran Reformers, they did not believe that all the citizens of a city should be considered Christians and served communion just because the electors had voted for the city to become Protestant. The French Reformers believed that every adult had to make a personal commitment to Christ to be saved. To ensure that every person had a chance to respond to Christ, there was a sustained, ongoing effort for many years to proclaim the gospel, even in the streets and marketplaces.

While the electors had been unanimous in their decision that Geneva become a Protestant city, intense debate went on among the population. It's hard to appreciate just how big a decision this was for the city. As Catholics, they were risking excommunication and eternal damnation if this new religion was leading them away from God and his truth.

When the Reformation was finally accepted, it was evident that a pastor-teacher was the crucial need for the city. Farel knew that he was an apostolic evangelist but not the builder who was so necessary for the reconstruction of the nation. When he heard that John Calvin was in town, Farel immediately went to visit him.

Commitment to a City

Calvin and Farel had both been students in the theological faculty of the University of Paris when the Reformation started to break out there. They had both been

Augustinian monks, and like many others who were reading the New Testament and deciding that the present church was not at all biblical in its practices, they had to flee France for their lives.

After Calvin left, he was shocked to learn that the authorities were proclaiming that the Protestants not only did not have the truth, they were just rebels against the church who had no coherent beliefs. Since no defense of the Protestant faith existed in writing in French Europe, this version of events was gaining acceptance. Calvin set out to clearly state what Protestants believed, and the result was the *Institutes of Religion*. He wrote it for the memory of his friends, as an apologetic in a time of intense conflict, and so that many others would turn to the Bible and to a living faith in Christ. To think of Calvin as an ivory-tower theologian is to seriously underestimate him.

In 1536, at age twenty-seven, Calvin was traveling through Geneva, and Farel found him in an inn down by the lake. Farel spoke to him about the situation in the city, and called Calvin to join him in rebuilding the nation. Calvin had weak health, and his only ambition at that time was to continue his studies. So he said to Farel, "No, I can't do that. I need rest and I need to study." Farel got very angry, pointed his long bony evangelist's finger at Calvin, and thundered, "May God curse you and your studies if you do not join me here in the work He has called you to!" This threatened curse made such an impression on Calvin that he remembered it until the end of his life. He consented to stay, and committed his life to the work of God in Geneva.

Calvin cannot be blamed for hesitating to accept Farel's challenge. Geneva was a very difficult place to minister for many reasons. The city government, influenced by the authorities from Bern who were of the German Reformation, believed that the church should be ruled by the government, including defining who was a member of the church and who could take communion. In contrast, the leaders of the French Reformation believed that there are different spheres within society, each with its own domain of decision making. They taught that the government held the right to provide for the people's defense and levy taxes for the common needs of society, and the church was subject to its authority only in clearly defined areas.

For twenty years after voting to become a Protestant city, the authorities wanted decision-making power over the church. Calvin had to argue with them for all those years in order to establish the principle that the church should run its own affairs. He also wanted to establish the principle that the church had a primary *teaching* role in society and was to hold individuals and institutions, including the government, accountable to biblical morality. Calvin wasn't always right in the way he saw things, but his noble attempt to rebuild the city on biblical foundations was history-making, and the first outside of Israel.

These differences between the two strains of Reformation theology quickly came into direct conflict. Two years after he came to the city, the Lutheran Reformation authorities requested that Calvin and Farel give communion to the entire population. As French Reformation theologians, they refused, reasoning that since some of the citizens were living in open sin, they were not about to give communion to people who didn't even pretend to be Christians. The authorities insisted that they serve communion to everyone on Easter Sunday in 1538.

Calvin went to preach in the cathedral that day, and Farel preached in the second parish of the city. They both taught on sin and judgment, and proceeded to publicly excommunicate the entire population of Geneva. Then they left town, knowing their ministry was over in the city. Farel went back home to Neuchâtel, and Calvin went to Strasbourg to continue his studies.

The authorities at first said, "Good riddance," but three years later, at a point of desperation, they came to visit Calvin and his new wife in Strasbourg. They explained to him that the city was threatened with invasion, which would mean a return to Catholicism, losing everything they had worked for. They knew that Calvin had stronger, clearer vision for rebuilding the city than the rest of the city leaders, and he alone had the personal influence to rally the people to fight and withstand an invasion. They asked him to return and help save the city.

Calvin knew that the cost would be great, but he agreed and went back to Geneva. Changing a nation requires a lifetime commitment, and he gave the rest of his life so that Geneva would be a city that was as biblically based as possible.

Geneva—Rebuilding a Nation

As the word went out that John Calvin had been named the head pastor of Geneva, Protestants all over Europe were electrified. He was well known because of the *Institutes,* and people knew that his ministry in Geneva could be a historic opportunity. In many countries the Protestants had been put to death or exiled and robbed of their lands and possessions. In others, such as England and some of the Swiss cantons, the Reformation seemed to be gaining a foothold. Geneva was unique, though, in that the deeply entrenched social order of church and nobility had been torn down, so in that vacuum there was a unique opportunity for the Reformers to rebuild a city on biblical foundations.

Geneva quickly became a city of refuge for the Protestants. Its streets were filled with Italians, Englishmen, and especially French. The population of the city, which was only five thousand before the Reformation, quickly doubled to ten thousand. They called it the "Protestant Rome," and "the city set on a hill." All the Protestants of Europe looked toward Geneva to see what would be built. This small city-state was the laboratory, the pilot project, for the vision of a nation built on biblical principles and living in peace, prosperity, and righteousness.

Even though the city was small, its influence spread far and wide. Two young men came to visit Geneva from Holland, were soundly converted, and went back to transmit this new message to William of Orange. Their visit is the reason that Holland became Protestant, as the king converted to the new faith.

Another example is found in Scotland. When Mary Queen of Scots began her persecutions, the number of Protestant refugees coming from Scotland increased dramatically. In 1556 the former prayer chapel of the bishop of Geneva was reconsecrated as the church for the English-speaking refugees. John Knox, who was also a refugee, was pastor of the congregation and preached in that church for three years. He studied what Calvin was doing in the city and took it back to Scotland; the influence of Geneva then went to Puritan England and from there to North America.

The strategy of the Reformers was based on three principles :

1. Preaching the gospel to individuals, so that people would be saved and start to be transformed, and the church would be restored to biblical purity;
2. Teaching the city, so that people would know how to live, the authorities would know how to govern, and all would know how to work in their different spheres; and
3. Accountability for individuals and the leadership in spheres of society, so that the teaching would not just be theoretical but applied in all areas of life.

The basis of rebuilding the nation was individual conversion so that the population would put its trust in God. The immediate second step was a systematic, daily, long-term strategy of teaching. The challenge was to build a nation on biblical principles, so Calvin and his team searched the scriptures and did their best to apply them to the crisis situations in the city. They taught in the churches, but they also pursued city leaders to bring biblical truths into society. Calvin had a legal background, so he approached the needs of the city as a lawyer, not just as a pastor. He had the gifts and training to see the issues holistically and understand the biblical principles needed to build society, such as defining the structure of the government and the role of the church. He taught across a wide range of issues. Examining several areas in some detail illustrates the depth and breadth of his thinking, and the impact his teaching had on the nation.

One example of applying the principles of the Word was when the Reformers called on all the populace to come and rebuild the broken-down city walls. Calvin told the citizens that while they must trust in God, they were also responsible to do everything they could to protect themselves. They could no longer hide behind a nobleman or the church to protect them; they needed to rebuild the walls, arm themselves, and resist the oppressors who were threatening to invade from outside. The pastors were there too, joining in the stone-by-stone reconstruction of the walls. Calvin taught them to be responsible and work hard to defend themselves, but he also insisted that only God could protect Geneva, and he exhorted the population to put their trust in the Lord for protection.

This teaching resonated well in the city. The people knew Switzerland had begun by citizens uniting and arming themselves against imperial armies. Calvin taught that this was profoundly biblical; in fact, until just recently, every Swiss male was required to serve in their citizen army and kept his automatic rifle and ammunition at home. While the Swiss maintain political neutrality in the conflicts between other nations, they have always been ready to defend themselves as a nation.

Another of Calvin's principal ministry concerns was the family. Many of the men of Geneva were irresponsible, prone to drunkeness, and dishonest. The disorder in their lives was one of the causes of the poverty and immorality of the city. So the Reformers began teaching the people about individual responsibility, which meant first of all caring for one's family. Each head of household must work hard, pay his bills, give his tithe, and save his money.

But this was not just a teaching about how to have prosperity. Calvin taught that your work was your worship. We tend to believe today that work is what you do until Sunday, when you go worship. But Calvin taught that every believer has a holy vocation, not just "full-time ministers." For example, if you are a shoemaker, that is your vocation. So you have to work as unto the Lord, since you are presenting that work to him as worship. Clearly, if your work is your worship, then it has to be done with the utmost integrity and excellence. In fact, a hundred years ago when Max Weber, the great German economist, was looking for the sources of the prosperity of the West, he pointed to Calvin's teaching in Geneva.

Another of the sources of Geneva's prosperity was Calvin's teaching concerning financial principles. Calvin told the bankers they couldn't charge high interest rates, as that was the sin of usury in the Bible. He fixed the interest rates at 4 percent so that the bankers could have a fair return on their money, but people could still afford to borrow and invest. The 4 percent interest rate lasted for four centuries in Switzerland, and this practice was one of the long-term sources of Switzerland's prosperity.

One of the most amazing things that happened in Geneva was in education. The citizens of Geneva had committed to educate their children as part of their decision to become a Protestant city. This commitment was the result of their theology that each person was created in the image of God and that each one could be in relationship with God directly and only needed to read the Bible to know how that was supposed to work. This was a real first in the history of the world—all children of a nation being taught to read, even the girls. Sadly, the people who train educators today have forgotten that literacy for all is a biblical idea.

Calvin also taught about caring for the poor. An organization was established which cared for newly arrived Protestant refugees, widows, and orphans. Anyone who *could* work *had* to work; the poor were considered accountable too (a principle forgotten in too many countries today). It is said that all Protestant charities have their source in Calvin's organizations in Geneva, since they were copied and adopted in all the Protestant countries.

In an attempt to bring accountability to deal with the crisis in the family, the Reformers established a kind of citizen's tribunal, organized by neighborhood. Any man who beat his wife, or any mother who neglected her children, would be brought before a jury of neighbors and called to account.

Today the excesses of these tribunals are better known than the good they did, and it is true that they provided an easy way for mean-spirited people to settle accounts with neighbors they disliked. But Geneva was in crisis, people did not know how to care for families or work or live morally. Invasion threatened, and Calvin knew that if the city was to survive, he had only a narrow window of opportunity to teach the populace to become a united, disciplined citizenry, able to care for and defend itself.

Accountability was woven into the government structures as well. The Reformers were convinced of the sinfulness of mankind, especially since they had had personal experience of the corrupting power of undifferentiated authority. In other words, the King of France, as an absolute monarch, could and did decide to put Protestants to death. They knew that any leader or structure that cannot be held accountable will slide inevitably into sin, so they built a separation of powers into the government, where power is divided among the executive, legislative, and judicial branches of the government. The judiciary is especially important and must be free and independent.

A further division of powers takes place between the national, or federal, government, and the cantons (or states) that make up the nation, and the towns, giving us a system of government called *federalism*. The Swiss system of federalism provided the model for the Americans who designed their government in the late eighteenth century, since they also mistrusted an all-powerful central government because of their experience with the King of England. Albert Gallatin, who actually wrote much of the American constitution while working for Thomas Jefferson, was born and educated in Geneva.

The church also had a defined role in the nation, teaching principles of justice and morality and calling the people and the government to account if the principles were violated. In later centuries the church backed away from this role, and the accountability vacuum that was left has been filled in most Western nations by the media.

Economists today know that any country that practices hard work, favors the family structure, has reasonable interest rates, and lives by systems of law and accountability will have prosperity. The economic level will start to rise within the first gen-eration, as was the case in sixteenth-century Geneva. Now institutions such as the International Monetary Fund and the World Bank teach these principles to the nations, but it was Calvin who first took these biblical teachings and applied them in an early modern context.

Revival to Reformation

What happened in sixteenth-century Geneva was really about teaching the nations how they should live, which is the difference between revival and reformation. In revival, lots of people get saved, new churches are started, and the Christians get com-mitted. But revival often stops there.

In reformation, the same first steps of conversions, church-planting, and com-mitment take place. But then someone realizes that people don't know how to live their lives by biblical truths, and they need to be taught. Then the reformers examine every part of the life of the nation, looking at it to see what could be a biblical alter-native to the cultural way of doing things.

John Calvin was not just a theologian. He studied and taught the Bible in order to rebuild the nation, so he was essentially an apostolic nation-builder. He forged a biblical worldview, not because he liked to discuss philosophical issues, but so that his adopted nation would survive. Calvin, like the apostle Paul, was essentially a mis-sionary. Missionaries who are interested in completely accomplishing the will of God will be committed not just to the saving of souls, crucial as that is as a first step, but to teaching the nation. People who are actually doing the work of God in the nations often write the best theology.

Calvin was a master communicator and effectively used the technology of the day. He preached weekly in the cathedral and also taught daily in the former chapel next to it. He taught about the biblical instructions for every area of life. All over Europe, people were grappling with the same questions being faced in Geneva, and were looking for ways to live out biblical truths. There was such Continent-wide inter-est in what Calvin taught that a scribe would sit in his class and take notes, afterward taking them directly to Calvin's printer. The notes would be typeset, printed, and on their way around Europe within the week. We can hardly publish this quickly today, even with computers and the Internet! Calvin and his team were completely com-mitted to teaching the nations.

The towns and villages round about were also asking Calvin and Farel to send pastors and teachers so they could start to live the Reformation. But there was nobody to send. Calvin's lieutenant, another Frenchman named Theodore de Beze (or "Beza" in some English histories), had started a training academy for pastors in Lausanne, but there was a split, and part of that academy was moved to Geneva in 1559. Calvin taught young ministers in training from an alcove in the chapel. The chapel, renamed "Calvin's Auditorium," remained the place of training for the future ministers of Geneva for two centuries. It was the birthplace of the University of Geneva.

When Calvin and the French apostolic team came to Geneva in the sixteenth century, a powerful teaching anointing was forged in the Spirit. But three generations after the death of the apostolic leadership, the Protestant church started to become more and more formalized, cold, and dead. Injustice was first tolerated, then institutionalized, as political power fell back into the hands of a few families. Education was available only for the children of the well-off, and the poor went hungry. Some of the same trends happened in the Protestant church that had happened in the Catholic Church centuries earlier: it lost its purity and power.

The Enlightenment: Reason Reigns Supreme

The Enlightenment, a new movement that is still affecting us today, began at that time as history repeated itself. Faced with the corruption of the church, people were again actively looking for a new way to live. When the church abdicated its role of teaching the nations, others picked up that mantle. The Enlightenment was brought on by a set of specific teachings, as a few men and women decided that the nations needed new teaching, a new light. The Enlightenment shaped the faith of the church for generations to come. Not only were the nations taught from Geneva, but the church in the nations was also taught from that city.

One of the principal fathers of the Enlightenment was the French philosopher Voltaire. He often came to Geneva, because his printer's workshop was located there. After he was exiled from Paris, he bought a chateau just outside of Geneva. During the years he lived there, his home was known as the intellectual capital of Europe.

Under his influence, the church accepted the teachings of the Enlightenment, which included that the supernatural did not exist, miracles don't happen, Jesus Christ was not really divine, and the Bible was not really inspired. Also, humans could and should discover truth without divine help, science was the new religion that would save humanity, and peace and prosperity depended on human efforts alone. God, then, was no longer really necessary, except as a distant, impersonal First Cause who got things going and then withdrew from the earth. The idea that the church should only worry about the souls of people instead of every aspect of their lives and society came from the influence of Enlightenment thought on the church.[1]

In Geneva, we see an important warning to heed: the church tries to speak to the culture, then in learning the language, accommodates the culture, then finally becomes captive to it. It is a lesson we must pay careful attention to today. In our efforts to be "seeker friendly," we must not lose our mandate to shape the culture instead of be shaped by it.

Romanticism: Experience Reigns Supreme

Reaction to the ordered, disciplined rationalism of the Enlightenment came quickly in the form of Romanticism, or elevating experience over reason as our ultimate definition of reality. In the second wave of French Protestant refugees, a clock maker named Rousseau arrived in Geneva and had a son named Jean-Jacques. This son reacted strongly against the church of his time and against any idea of law or sin.

It was no coincidence that Rousseau was born and lived the early part of his life one street away from what had been Calvin's house. He took up the mantle Calvin had created for teaching the nations. Rousseau is still one who teaches the teachers of the world. In practically any nation, including the Asian nations, you cannot become a school teacher unless you read what Rousseau said about teaching children.

The Romantic movement, fathered by Rousseau and others, still strongly influences the church today. The ideas that the church is there for my self-fulfillment, that my experience of God is the most fundamental reality in my life, and that whatever is spontaneous is more spiritual than what is planned, come straight from Rousseau's teaching. He also taught that we are not really sinners, but our problems come from our environment, specifically the structures and institutions of society. When we are surprised at sin among Christians, we demonstrate that we are more influenced by Rousseau than by Calvin.

Back to the Bible

This war of ideas in the eighteenth century highlights the fact that there are essentially two ways to think, whatever the worldview, world religion, or culture: rationalistic and romantic. Jesus warned against these two temptations, represented in the Pharisees and the Sadducees (see Mark 8 and Matthew 16). Sadly, these two views are still foundational to much of our Christian theology today, even though Jesus warned us about these faulty beliefs two thousand years ago.

The romantic temptation (of the Pharisees) is to believe that God's power is submitted to my desires for health, wealth, and prosperity. The rationalistic temptation (of the Sadducees) is to believe that God and his ways are subject to my reason. As the eighteenth century progressed, these two ways of thinking were taught through art, music, architecture, and philosophy. They were also concentrated and diffused through the university systems, and, consequently, powerfully discipled the nations and the church. Geneva was one of the high places for the transmission of these teachings to the nations.

In the theological corruption of the eighteenth century, a student could study in Calvin's academy to be a Protestant pastor for three years and never read the Bible (except when Hebrew was studied and a few Psalms would be assigned). For three years a student would study almost entirely Greek and Roman philosophy. The whole church was filled with the influence of rationalist, Enlightenment philosophy. In the early nineteenth century, a Bible was published in Geneva which, like the Jehovah's Witnesses' bible today, changed the references that said that Jesus Christ was the Son of God.

The changes in thinking were reflected in the architecture itself. Under the influence of Greek philosophy, in the late eighteenth century a neoclassical portico with Greek columns was added to the cathedral where Calvin had preached.

In 1815 a young Scotsman named Robert Haldane came to Geneva. After visiting for just a few days, he walked around the city with a theology student prior to departing. This young student was getting ready to become a Protestant pastor. As Haldane spent the day with him, he was appalled at the student's lack of knowledge of the Bible and his absence of relationship with God. So Haldane decided to stay, rented an apartment in the Old Town, and started holding Bible studies.

Haldane invited the theology students to come, and they were very interested because they had never been to a Bible study. He found out later that most of them had never even read the Epistle to the Romans! They started to get converted, and then some of their professors did as well. Revival started right in the city of Geneva. There were hundreds of people who were saved and then thousands more as revival went into the neighboring canton of Vaud.

Some of these new converts stayed in the Reformed Church and others started new churches. They are still called the Free Churches of Geneva. These churches had an incredible vision for missions. For example, they had a plan to reach every town, village, and farmhouse in France from Geneva. They would recruit farmers from the Jura Mountains who couldn't work in the winter, fill their backpacks with New Testaments, and send them door-to-door in France. They visited every house in France. They also sold a calendar that had agricultural advice and a Bible verse on it for every day. France in the nineteenth century knew the Bible better than France of the twentieth century because of the revival that started in Geneva and then went into France. Many of the missions to the French-speaking countries of Africa and the Pacific were begun out of Geneva.

One young man, Henri Dunant, from the principal church of the revival, seemed to be mostly interested in making money. He often organized investment schemes, going to North Africa to try to find mines that people could invest in. As he was coming back from one of these trips, he visited a field covered with wounded and dead soldiers from a battle that had just taken place between the French and Austrian armies. He was told that if anyone went out to try to help or even bury them, they would be shot at by the other side. He decided to do something about it, so he gave his testimony about that visit in the revival church.

He also published a pamphlet, *A Visit to Solferino*, which pricked the conscience of Europe. Henri and some of his friends founded an organization which later became the International Red Cross. A few years afterward they called the nations to Geneva, where the sixteen greatest powers at that time signed the treaty we know as the Geneva Convention.

This treaty is based on the biblical principles in the first part of the book of Amos, which show that God is very concerned with the just conduct of war and especially the righteous treatment of prisoners. The reason we are prosecuting war criminals from Serbia today is because the nations were taught from Geneva in this area. Sadly, this was the only area in which the Revival of Geneva produced teaching for the nations.

In terms of influence on Swiss laws, the Reformation has a bigger impact even today than the revival ever did, though the Reformation happened almost three centuries before the revival. In giving us the Great Commission, Jesus said there must be individual conversions (Mark 16:15) and this should lead to discipling the nations (Matt. 28:20), so revival alone accomplishes only half of the task he entrusted to us. Apostolic leadership must take the zeal of new converts and teach them the implications of their faith in every area of their personal lives and the spheres of society in which they serve.

Revivals happen regularly in the history of the church. True reformation is a costly and lengthy process, so perhaps this is why it is so rare. It may be that the enemy so feared another reformation in Geneva in the nineteenth century that he took very specific steps to bottle up the revival by bringing in the Enlightenment teachings. Under this influence, the revived church did not believe that it had much to say about government, poverty, or injustice. The church retreated, leaving a vacuum for the teaching of the nations.[2]

Adding to this, a new teaching in the church said that there was going to be a rapture any minute, so be sure you are ready and try to save all the souls you can. These are good teachings, but if studied exclusively they can lead to Christians not being concerned about the affairs of the nation. The believers of that day withdrew from the universities, from political life, and especially from the media. Years later they were amazed that all these places were filled with pagans.

Geneva continued to hold the mantle of anointing to teach the nations. Early in the twentieth century, a young revolutionary came to study in the city. He spent two years studying and writing in the University of Geneva library. Much of the organization and preparation for his revolution took place there. In the process, he picked up the mantle of the teaching of the nations.

His name was Vladimir Ilyich Lenin. Until 1989, 80 percent of the world's population was being taught by his ideas, known as the Marxist-Leninist system. It was not a very intelligent system and it didn't even work very well. But it was a unified, overall system and any country could adopt it. It told them what to do about their schools, economy, army, political system, about every area of life. Nations on every continent adopted this system because they didn't see any other comprehensive system as an attractive alternative.

Lessons in Reformation: Geneva's Legacy

In one generation during the sixteenth century Geneva was totally transformed. What can we learn from its story on the vital subject of nation discipling?

- The church responded to the moral and spiritual vacuum of the day with preaching the gospel to bring individual conversion over an entire generation. This was coupled with intentional teaching on how to live the Christian faith in every area of personal life and society.
- The church prayed and searched the Scriptures for biblical truths to shape every sphere of society, and was proactive in bringing this teaching and moral accountability to the leaders in every area. The church did not hide in its buildings but was a very robust presence throughout the city.
- The church leaders continued to seek God together with leaders from other nations on what God was doing around the world in this area of discipling every area of life in his ways.
- The church was deeply committed to the poor and needy, caring for immediate physical needs and training in skills to enable the poor to live godly, self-sufficient lives.

To reap all the benefit from a study of Geneva's story, we must also take an honest look at the mistakes that were made so we can work to avoid them in the future. One category of error had to do with crossing the biblical lines of authority, or domains. Every conflict in society can be traced back to the question of domains: who has the right to make the decisions in any given sphere. In Geneva, several examples illustrate this important principle:

- Neighborhood tribunals were intended to help disciple families, but instead, they demonstrated the negative effects of the church overstepping its bounds and exercising an inappropriate degree of authority in people's personal lives.
- One tribunal punished an individual who wouldn't convert, publicly disqualifying the person from a role of leadership in another sphere. These actions highlight two areas of error. The church is to be an influence for salvation, not

exert control over the personal right to choose. The church has a teaching role but is not to exercise direct control over the other spheres of society.

- There was a rigidity in applying scriptural principles, which led to legalism on external issues like dress or leisure time activities, for example.
- The church focused almost exclusively on the application of biblical truths to their city, demonstrating a poor understanding of missions, thus missing the opportunity to extend God's kingdom even further during their day.
- As the years went on after John Calvin had passed away, faith became overintellectualized.
- Although he preached about the priesthood of every believer and detested the Catholic practice of looking to a priest for salvation, Calvin still left too much authority in the person of the Protestant pastor. For centuries afterward, pastors were still seen as the ones who could have a ministry; it was not an avenue for every believer.

Today, the nations are looking for answers. Moreover, it is the commandment of Jesus Christ and the calling of the church to teach the nations. If we step back from it again, we will leave another vacuum.

Whenever the church leaves a vacuum, the enemy is very happy to fill it. He is probably working on another system for the nations even now. If it is like his other recent efforts, it will be a mixture of nationalism, racist scapegoating, economic hope, and fearmongering. But the next version might well include supernatural power, and it will be freed from the residual morality that existed in the twentieth century. It will not be nice.

Will the church be ready with an attractive, intelligent, biblical alternative for the way nations can live? The lessons of Geneva will help those who rise up to take on this challenge.

Bibliography

Bosch, David. *Transforming Mission: Paradigm Shifts in Theology of Mission*. Maryknoll, N.Y.: Orbis Books, 1991.

Danner, Daniel G. "Pilgrimage to Puritanism: History and Theology of the Marian Exiles at Geneva, 1555–1560." *Studies in Church History* 9 (1999).

Mangalwadi, Vishal and Ruth Mangalwadi. *The Legacy of William Carey: A Model for the Transformation of a Culture*. Wheaton, Ill.: Crossway, 1999.

McGrath, Alister. *A Life of John Calvin: A Study in the Shaping of Western Culture*. Oxford: Blackwell, 1990.

Monter, William E. *Calvin's Geneva*. Huntington, N.Y.: R. E. Krieger, 1975.

Prestwich, Menna, ed. *International Calvinism*. Oxford: Clarendon Press, 1985.

Notes

1. This emphasis on the power of the human mind is often called Rationalism, and gave birth to Modernity, the condition of the last two or three centuries. For an authoritative summary of how Modernity influenced the church and missions, see the chapter on the Enlightenment in David Bosch, *Transforming Mission: Paradigm Shifts in Theology of Mission*, (Maryknoll, N.Y.: Orbis Books, 1991).

2. See Vishal and Ruth Mangalwadi's book, *Carey, Christ and Cultural Transformation*, revised ed. (OM Publishing, 1977), for a fascinating study of the Reformation-oriented pioneer mission work of William Carey and the first wave of missionaries to India who were inspired by the teachings of the French Reformation out of Geneva. Mangalwadi contrasts this first wave of missions, which changed the history of India, with the more revival-oriented second wave, which in his opinion was not nearly as effective.

Men and women of God have wrestled through the ages with what it means to live lives of faith and obedience. Jeff Fountain introduces five men who made a huge difference not only in their own nations, but around the world and down through history by their courage and determination to see their nations transformed by kingdom principles. There is much to learn from their examples and insights.

Revolutionaries and Anti-Revolutionaries:
Discipling Nations in the Modern Era

Jeff Fountain

Grimy smoke signals heralded the irresistible march of the modern era across England's green and pleasant countryside in the eighteenth century. "Dark Satanic mills"—as William Blake branded them[1]—belched soot into the heavens as new industries muscled in on Britain's pastoral society. Social dislocation rippled through a nation in transition from the Age of Agriculture into the Industrial Era.

Since the Christianization of Europe in the early Middle Ages, cathedrals and parish churches had been the societal hubs around which life revolved. Church spires had been the central reference points in both town and city. The church calendar had governed the annual rhythm of community life.

Now the Industrial Revolution was changing all of that. "Life under the sacred canopy" in premodern times was giving way to "life in the iron cage" of the modern era.[2] New industrial machinery ruthlessly uprooted rural populations from their ancient patterns of life by luring them into urban ghettos. A new working class was emerging with little or no relationship to Christianity. Factory chimneys now blotted out spires.

Men, women, and children were fed to the coalmines and factories as fodder for the gods of progress and modernity. Efficiency and productivity were the new masters of the new age. The rigid routine of the work schedule now ruled the laborer's lifestyle. Workers' rights, safety standards, and healthcare were almost nonexistent. Life was cheap. Education was elitist.

At the same time, Enlightenment philosophy began to promise a better future through the application of reason, science, and rationality. Enlightenment thinkers were shifting the focus of life from heaven to earth; from God to nature; from revelation to reason; from the future to the present; and from the transcendent to the transient. Over the following centuries, the Enlightenment would give birth to a string of "-isms"—*rationalism, humanism, socialism, Marxism, fascism,* and *liberalism.* In this "bright promising future," faith and revelation would be confined to the private closet.

However, it was the dark side of this "better future" which seemed more obvious at the start of the Modern Era. Cartoons by the contemporary satirist, William Hogarth, graphically captured the abysmal social conditions of England at the start of the Industrial Revolution: overcrowded living conditions, poverty, drunkenness, disease, and death, in addition to the suffocating staleness and indifference of the church of the day.

Sometimes we may be tempted to dream of the "good old days" when everyone seemed to believe in God and went to church. But this is a romantic, misleading view of the past.

The only word revivalist John Wesley could find to describe the English society of this time was *godless.* From the royal palace to the worker's row house, life was lived without acknowledgement of God. The king and the prime minister both lived in open adultery. Deism, dominant in the churches, taught that the Creator was not interested in the daily human affairs. This, coupled with a fatalistic form of Calvinism, gave little initiative to disturb the established disorder of things.

As a believer, John Wesley could not and would not stand by and let his nation deteriorate spiritually, morally, and socially. The challenge Wesley and his followers faced to transform their society was in many ways far greater than today's challenges. Yet the Methodists believed God had raised them up to do nothing less than disciple their nation.

Wesley expressed the challenge this way: "to reform the nation, particularly the Church, and to spread scriptural holiness over the whole land."[3]

Wesley's outstanding life and ministry were driven by this passion. The resulting reform of individuals, families, churches, and communities profoundly influenced the development of the whole nation of Britain. Other nations, following Britain into the Industrial Revolution, adopted her solutions to the new problems of the modern age.

The "Methodist Revolution" lubricated the relatively smooth transition from an agrarian, traditional, and hierarchical society toward the industrial, liberal, and egalitarian modern age.[4] The Wesleyan teachings of free will and universal salvation—theological parallels to the revolutionary ideals of liberty and equality—were midwives at the birth of modern society.

In this chapter we will begin by taking a closer look at the life of John Wesley. We will then glimpse the lives of four other leaders from the Modern Era—William Carey, Hans Nielsen Hauge, Abraham Kuyper, and Frank Buchman—who, like Wesley, understood the Great Commission in terms of discipling whole nations. Carey's transforming role in India, Hauge's development of Norway, Kuyper's impact on Holland, and Buchman's unique role in the twentieth century are all examples for us to explore, reflect on, and glean from in our search to discover God's call to us in our day to disciple the nations.

These leaders grasped the length, the depth, and the breadth of the Great Commission. These three dimensions may be summarized as:

- the geographical dimension of going into *all the world,*
- the socioethnic dimension of reaching *all people groups,* and
- the life-sphere dimension of reconciling *all things under heaven and on earth* under Christ's lordship (Matt. 28:19–20; Col. 1:20).

John Wesley—England's Revolutionary

John Wesley (1703–1791) had a remarkable mother. Not only did Susannah Wesley give birth to seventeen children, she also held neighborhood Bible studies in her (presumably large) kitchen—attended at times by up to two hundred people, to the envy of the local curate!

Despite such a godly upbringing, however, when John and his brother Charles went up to Oxford to study for the Anglican ministry, they had not yet embraced the reformational doctrine of salvation by faith.

Nonetheless, they lacked nothing in religious zeal, and started a Bible club with fellow-student and future revivalist George Whitefield. Other students disparagingly called them "Bible moths," "enthusiasts," and other derogatory names. But the name that stuck was "Methodists," because of their emphasis on following a disciplined and methodical lifestyle, observing liturgy, and doing good works.

After John was ordained into the Anglican Church, he set off across the Atlantic to become a chaplain in the new American colony of Georgia, hoping to find "true religion among the natives."

But his sailing ship ran into a violent storm, and Wesley later described in his journal his fear that the ship would break up. In the midst of the storm, he thought he heard the strains of hymns. He stumbled across the heaving deck toward the singing and found himself entering the cabin of Moravian missionary families from Herrnhut in Germany, also headed for Georgia.

The scene he beheld, of men, women, and children serenely worshipping in the midst of the raging tempest, confident in their God, convinced the young English clergyman that they had something he lacked.

"Aren't you afraid we may be drowned?!" he exclaimed in agitation.

"Our times, brother," they calmly replied, "are in his hands!"

This encounter was to lead to what has been called one of the most significant conversions in history. In Georgia, Wesley met a leading Moravian, Augustus Spangenberg, who asked him if he had yet trusted Jesus as his personal savior. Wesley confessed in his journal that he had lied in his response. He realized that he did not have that sort of relationship with Jesus.

On his return to London after a somewhat failed chaplaincy, Wesley attended a Moravian Bible study in a house in Aldersgate Street. As Luther's preface to Romans was being read aloud, he experienced his "heart being strangely warmed." From that time on,[5] he wrote in his journal, he knew that Christ had indeed died for his sins, that Jesus was indeed his personal savior.

Anxious to learn more about Moravian spirituality, Wesley then traveled across the Channel to Germany to visit the Herrnhut community, which had experienced an outpouring of the Spirit in 1727, leading eventually to widespread missionary endeavors. He also wanted to observe firsthand the Pietist movement in Halle, stories of which his mother had read him as a boy. Early Pietism[6] had produced many faith-based social institutions such as soup kitchens, poor schools, libraries, and reading rooms for the underprivileged.

Wesley was back in London in time for the New Year's Eve prayer meeting on December 31, 1738, held in the Fetter Lane Society, attended also by George Whitefield and brother Charles. In the early hours of the new year, they, too, experienced an outpouring of the Spirit, a foretaste of the revival to come.

Outdoors

John, Charles, and George now began preaching the message of salvation by faith in pulpit after pulpit, scandalizing congregations who understood too well the implication that "churchianity" was not to be equated with biblical Christianity. Church door after church door slammed shut to these fanatical "Methodists."

Whitefield began to preach to miners near Bristol in the open air and invited John to come and help. John traveled to Bristol but confided in his journal that the prospect of preaching in the open air horrified him. He thought it almost a sin if someone should be converted outside of a church building. However, while speaking to a small society meeting on the topic of the Sermon on the Mount, he suddenly realized what he was preaching about—his Lord and Savior preaching to the masses, in the open air!

So the next day found John preaching to three thousand miners who had never before heard the gospel message and who now experienced the convicting work of the Holy Spirit in their lives.

John and George now had a problem. How would these men be discipled? Could they send them to the existing churches, temples of *Deism?* In the first place, working-class people would not be welcomed. Secondly, they would not be fed.

So Wesley and Whitefield set up small groups—called cells and bands—and societies to disciple the converts, following the example of the German Moravians and Pietists. These *koinonia*-based discipling structures added to the message of personal salvation and open air preaching to provide the basic elements of the revival to come.

Bristol thus witnessed the start of modern mass open-air evangelism. It also was the location of the first Methodist chapel. Wesley never intended that the thousands of chapels that followed become a new denomination.[7] Rather, he wanted a relevant "wineskin" with which to reach out to the unreached of British society.

Foundations were being laid for a movement that was to spread throughout the whole nation and beyond, and that would profoundly impact the previously unreached working classes. In London, Wesley leased an abandoned cannon factory, the Royal Foundry, as his headquarters and ministry center. In addition to a chapel holding fifteen hundred people and another hall for three hundred, Wesley established there a medical dispensary, a bookstore, a free school, and a shelter for widows. Up to sixty-six society meetings were held there weekly.

Wesley began to travel on horseback in a circuit from London to Bristol to Newcastle and back to London, preaching and discipling converts; organizing them into cells, bands, and societies; and opening Methodist chapels. Those with evangelistic gifts he trained and released into ministry without official ordination, sending them out at 5:00 AM into the "highways and byways" to preach to the crowds on their way to work.

Converts thus became preachers, pastors, and in effect "church planters" as they too began bands and societies and set up chapels across the country, following their energetic leader's example.

Becoming a familiar figure on horseback, Wesley traveled around the country, covering 250,000 miles in his lifetime and preaching 40,000 sermons to crowds sometimes of over 20,000 without the aid of a modern public address system. He raised up 10,000 society and band leaders, and by 1798, the Methodist movement was over 100,000 strong. Not without just cause has Wesley been called the Apostle of England.

Wholeness

The Methodist movement, with its strong emphasis on personal conversion and inner piety, awakened a national social conscience with the most far-reaching consequences. Wesley's message was not simply one of personal salvation. He had a deep sense of social compassion and concern. A 1744 sermon entitled "Scriptural Christianity" scandalized the fellows, scholars, and students of Oxford by exposing the sorry state of that university town's spirituality.

Wesley's biblical exegesis and preaching reflected his concern to see the lordship of Christ applied to every nook and cranny of society. He attacked slavery before William Wilberforce, the anti-slavery campaigner, was even born. He supported civil and religious liberty against growing radicalism. He warned the nation about economic practices exploiting the poor and the weak. The Foundry clinic was probably the first in London since the monasteries had been disestablished after the Reformation. He set up spinning and knitting shops for the poor. For over twenty-six years, he studied medicine and anatomy in his free time to help the sick who could not afford a doctor.

Wesley's concern was not simply to "save souls" and to lead people into holiness. His passion was for *wholeness*—physical, psychological, spiritual, and intellectual—and this shaped both the man and his movement.

Faith working through love was the key to Wesley's personal and social ethics.

Reforms

Wesley did not live to see the long-term results of the Evangelical Revival in which he and George Whitefield were the two key players. The Evangelical Revival and subsequent revivals in the nineteenth century led directly to the following major reforms and the development of institutions that are simply taken for granted in our Western society today.

1. The abolition of slavery. On both sides of the Atlantic, Christians influenced by the revivals led the fight against slavery. John Wesley wrote *Thoughts on Slavery* in 1774, a brave attack against an institution supported by the Establishment, including the state church. Three days before he died, Wesley wrote to the young Christian parliamentarian, William Wilberforce, urging him to persevere in his fight against slavery until that evil had been eradicated from England. Wilberforce's efforts led to the abolition of the British slave trade in 1807 and the release of all slaves in the Empire in 1833. Across the Atlantic, revivalists Charles Finney and Theodore Weld fought slavery a generation later when the American Civil War eventually led to the release of America's slaves.

2. The abolition of industrial slavery. Another English Christian politician, Lord Shaftesbury, fought for workers' rights in factories and mines, for the protection of women and children from exploitation, for safety regulations, and for the ten-hour working day. This workingman's hero is still honored in London City by a statue in Piccadilly Circus.

Former British prime minister David Lloyd George observed that for over a hundred years, the leadership of the trade union movement had been drawn primarily from the Methodist movement.

Samuel Plimsoll, a Christian entrepreneur, was troubled by the practice of callous shipping merchants who overloaded their vessels and made large insurance claims when their vessels sank at sea with the loss of all life onboard. He developed a symbol, called to this day the Plimsoll mark, to be painted amidships on the waterline of every ship registered with Lloyds Insurance to indicate the safe loading capacity. This simple innovation has saved countless thousands of lives through the years.

3. The emancipation of women. Recognizing Wesley's role in treating women as spiritual equals to men in the Methodist movement, socialist historians Sidney and Beatrice Webb acknowledged the Methodist founder to be the leading women's liberationist of the eighteenth century.

Wesley is considered the grandfather of the Salvation Army, founded by former Methodists William and Catherine Booth, who both championed women's ministries. "My best men are women," Booth often remarked.[8]

Other Christians at the forefront working for women's rights include Josephine Butler, Susan B. Anthony, and again Charles Finney, who was principal of Oberlin College, the first U.S. college to admit female students.

4. Education. Christianity has a long history in promoting education: from the monasteries and ministers, which gave birth to Europe's oldest universities; to reformers and educationalists like John Knox (sixteenth century Scotland) and "the father of modern education," Jan Amos Comenius (seventeenth century Moravia, England, and Holland); and eventually across into the New World where the American Ivy League colleges of Princeton, Harvard,[9] Yale, and Union were originally established by Christians for Bible-based education.

Following the Pietist example, Wesley set up a poor school in his foundry. But a major step toward the concept of free education for all came when Robert Raines, an eighteenth century evangelical, set up Sunday schools to give working children a chance to become educated and escape the prison of their menial jobs. A statue on London's Thames Embankment still pays tribute to his vision.

5. Orphanages, mental asylums, hospitals, and nursing and prison reform. Men and women touched by the revivals and motivated by the love of God saw needs in many areas of social care. These men included George Müller and Thomas Barnardo, who established orphanages for street urchins rejected by society; Lord Shaftesbury, who championed the Lunacy Act which transformed mental asylums from hellholes and places of entertainment for visitors into places where patients were treated with dignity and respect; and Florence Nightingale and Elizabeth Fry, whose names are associated with the development of the nursing profession and with prison reform.

J. Wesley Bready's oft-quoted assessment is that had it not been for the Wesleyan renewal, England may well have experienced a revolutionary bloodbath similar to what France endured in the late eighteenth century.[10]

Such transformation stemmed directly from understanding God's love and purposes for humankind. It went a long way toward fulfilling Wesley's vision "to reform the nation, particularly the Church, and to spread scriptural holiness over the whole land."

Over time, others set out to follow Wesley's example and spread scriptural holiness far beyond the shores of Wesley's England.

William Carey—A Renaissance Man in India

The Wesleyan Revival set the stage for the recovery of mission vision within the church. Baptist shoemaker William Carey (1761–1834) of Northampton, England, is often called the father of modern missions, although the Moravians and others were active in foreign missions long before Carey was born. Nevertheless, he is seen by many as the instrument through whom Protestant churches were awakened to the need and urgency of the missionary task.

"Sit down, young man!" Carey was told by a senior Baptist minister after suggesting that his fellow Baptists should consider taking concrete steps to reach out to the world's unreached. "When God pleases to convert the heathen, He will do it without consulting you or me."[11]

Carey did sit down—and started to write. What he penned became a sort of "Magna Carta of Modern Missions," called *An Inquiry into the Obligation of Christians to Use Means for the Conversion of the Heathen*.[12] It included a survey of the world's unreached populations and biblical arguments showing that the Great Commission was not only for the original disciples, as widely supposed in Carey's day, but was for every generation of disciples.

Carey was eager to practice what he preached. So after setting up the Baptist Missionary Society in 1792 (the year after Wesley died), he sailed out to India the following year with his family. Thus began a most remarkable mission career inspiring thousands from Europe and America to follow over the next decades.

Not only did Carey became the founder of the Protestant church in India, but together with his two colleagues, William Ward and Joshua Marshman—the so-called Serampore Trio—he completed six whole translations and twenty-four partial translations of the Bible into Indian languages like Sanskrit, as well as grammars, dictionaries, and translations of classical eastern books. That in itself was an amazing achievement! But that was not even half the story.

Carey's understanding of the Great Commission involved much more than translating the Bible, making converts, and planting churches. It involved the discipling of a nation, that is, teaching the people of a nation how to live under God's government. Like Wesley, his passion was *wholeness,* the lordship of Christ over every department of life and society.

Indian writer and social reformer Vishal Mangalwadi has chronicled the following achievements of Carey's life.[13] Carey, writes Mangalwadi, was the founder of the Agri-Horticultural Society in the 1820s, thirty years before the Royal Agricultural Society was established in England. He did a systematic survey of agriculture in India, wrote for agriculture reform in *Asiatic Researches,* and exposed the evils of the indigo cultivation system two generations before it collapsed. He did this because he was horrified to see 60 percent of India had been allowed to become an uncultivated jungle abandoned to wild beasts and serpents.

He was the first to write essays on forestry in India fifty years before the government made its first attempt toward forest conservation. Believing that God had made man responsible for the earth, he both practiced and vigorously advocated the cultivation of timber, advising on how to plant trees for environmental, agricultural, and commercial purposes.

He was the discoverer of *Carey herbacea* in the jungles of the Himalayan foothills, an Indian variety of eucalyptus now bearing his name.

He published the first books on science and natural history in India, because he believed creation pointed to the Creator: "All thy works shall praise Thee, O Lord" (Ps. 145:10 KJV). Nature was declared "good" by the Creator. It was not *maya* (illusion) to be shunned, as taught by Hinduism. Carey frequently lectured on science and tried to inject a basic scientific presupposition into the Indian mind that even lowly insects are not "souls in bondage" but creatures worthy of our attention.

He was the father of printing technology in India, building the nation's largest press. Most printers had to buy their fonts from his mission press at Serampore. In addition, Carey was the first to make indigenous paper for the publishing industry.

He also established the first newspaper ever printed in any Oriental language, because of his belief that "above all forms of truth and faith, Christianity seeks free discussion." His English-language journal, *Friend of India,* was the force that gave birth to the Social Reform movement in India in the first half of the nineteenth century.

He was the first man to translate and publish great Indian religious classics into English. He transformed Bengali—considered "fit only for demons and women"—

into the foremost literary language of India. He wrote gospel ballads in Bengali to bring the Hindu love of musical recitations to the service of his Lord. He also wrote the first Sanskrit dictionary for scholars.

He began dozens of schools for Indian children—girls and boys of all castes— and launched the first college in Asia at Serampore, near Calcutta. He wanted to develop the Indian mind and liberate it from the darkness of superstition.

He was a British cobbler who became a professor of Bengali, Sanskrit, and Marathi at the Fort William College in Calcutta where the civil servants were trained.

He introduced the study of astronomy into the subcontinent because he cared deeply about destructive cultural ramifications of astrology such as fatalism, superstitious fears, and the Indian inability to organize and manage time. He did not believe that the heavenly bodies were deities that governed our lives, but were created to be signs or markers, dividing space into north, south, east, and west, and time into days, months, seasons, and years. They made it possible for us to devise calendars, to study geography and history, to be free to rule instead of to be ruled by the stars.

He pioneered lending libraries in the subcontinent in order to empower the Indian people to embrace ideas that would generate freedom of mind. He wanted to encourage the creation of an indigenous literature in the vernacular. He believed Indians needed to receive knowledge and wisdom from around the world, to catch up with other cultures and make worldwide information available through lending libraries.

He was the first to introduce the steam engine to India and encouraged Indian blacksmiths to make indigenous copies of his engine.

He introduced the concept of a "savings bank" in India to fight the all-pervasive social evil of usury.

He was the first campaigner for a humane treatment of lepers. Such patients were often buried or burned alive because of the belief that a violent end purified the body and ensured the transmigration into a healthy new existence, while natural death by disease resulted in four successive births, and a fifth as a leper.

He was the first to stand against the oppression of women, reflected in the practices of polygamy, female infanticide, child-marriage, widow-burning (*suttee*), euthanasia, and forced female illiteracy, "religious sanctions" virtually synonymous with Hinduism in the eighteenth and nineteenth centuries. While the British rulers accepted these social evils as irreversible and an intrinsic part of India's religious mores, Carey researched and published, and raised up a generation of civil servants who changed the laws.

Carey was the father of the Indian Renaissance of the nineteenth and twentieth centuries, argues Mangalwadi. He challenged the grip of asceticism, untouchability, mysticism, the occult, superstition, idolatry, witchcraft, and oppressive beliefs and practices on the nation. His movement culminated in the birth of Indian national-ism and of India's subsequent independence. His "this-worldly spirituality" with a strong emphasis on justice and love for fellow men, next to love for God, marked the turning point of Indian culture from a downward trend to an upward swing.

He was an evangelist who used every available medium to illumine every dark facet of Indian life with the light of truth. He is the central character in the story of the modernization of India.

Yes, Carey—the visionary father of modern missions—had a vision that extended far beyond evangelism and church planting to embrace the discipling of whole nations.

Some guy, this Carey!

Hans Nielsen Hauge—Vagabond for God

When Carey was pioneering missions in India at the start of the nineteenth century, Norway was a poor colony of Denmark. Nine out of ten Norwegians were farmers, working small land allotments hardly capable of feeding their often large families. Bread sometimes had to be made from tree bark in times of famine. It was not uncom-mon to see people dead from starvation at the roadside.

No universities existed and the school system functioned poorly. Public meetings without governmental approval were forbidden. Passports were required to travel around in the country and were normally only given to merchants and official representatives.

Then in the first decades of the nineteenth century, a drastic change occurred. Norway entered into a period of major economic growth. A key figure in this trans-formation from national poverty to wealth was Hans Nielsen Hauge (1771–1824). What Wesley was for England in the eighteenth century, Hauge was for Norway in the nineteenth century.

1796–1804: First Years of Itinerancy

Born April 3, 1771, in Rolvsøy in southeast Norway, Hauge was an unschooled son of a poor farmer. As a young man of twenty-five years, he had a deep experience of spiritual renewal while plowing on his parents' farm in the spring. This personal vis-itation resulted in a radical change of heart and withdrawal into prayer. He felt a deep love for both God and neighbor, an intense desire to read the Scriptures and to bring the message of salvation to others. By that fall, Hauge started preaching at regular devotional meetings held in houses in the area, before traveling further afield.

Over the next eight years, the intrepid Hauge traveled all over Norway on foot preaching in homes, writing, and establishing businesses. He preached that the whole of life was to be lived for God. Christ's work consisted not only of saving people from the guilt of sin, but also from the power of sin. Transformation was possible. Jesus was Lord as well as Redeemer.

Hauge taught that Christians were called to praise God in their earthly occupations. He warned his listeners against escapism from the world as he traveled from meeting to meeting. One should neither idolize the world nor despise it, he explained. Jesus' instruction about letting one's good works be seen spoke of good works in society.

Although the popular conception of Pietism has often been associated with an emphasis on the spiritual life as opposed to the secular, Haugian spirituality was remarkably "secular," emphasizing Luther's vocational ethic, encouraging people to work diligently and for the improvement of society. Work, too, ought to be worship.

Prayer, fasting, and service may have been the call of the medieval monks, but now Haugian Pietism taught that saints were called to work in the world. Asceticism now involved one's stewardship of time and money in one's secular work.

Hauge, like Wesley, was not just interested in spiritual matters but showed a broad interest in practical affairs such as the standard of living, aspects of folklore, and how to improve industry. He taught himself the skills of cabinetmaking, carpentry, beekeeping, and blacksmithing.

Before long, the Haugian Awakening was underway as a national movement. With such teaching, Hauge quickly became a radical change agent, both in the church and in society. His arousal of lay people to fulfill their role in the life of the church triggered many renewals in local congregations. This awakening was to leave a lasting imprint on the basic structure of Norwegian church life for the next century and a half.

Although printing was relatively new to Norway and schooling was poor, Hauge was quick to see the potential of printing for spreading the gospel and teaching Christians. He learned the skills of printing and bookbinding and wrote extensively.

Hauge's books became very popular and stimulated literacy. Demand for his teaching grew so strong that by 1800 five printing presses in Copenhagen were engaged printing his books, one of them almost continuously for four months.

Within his first eight years of ministry, Hauge had become the biggest publisher in his time. Over 200,000 copies of his books were distributed up and down the country. Like Wesley's books in England, Hauge's writings provided his followers solid theological foundations. These included a hymnbook, a book of sermons, a prayer book, an explanation of the catechism, a periodical, and also the start of a Bible commentary. A remarkable result for a self-taught farmer's son!

Revolution was in the air across Europe as the nineteenth century began. The "people power" of the French Revolution had not gone unnoticed in Norway, where great tensions existed between rich and poor, the ruling class on the one hand and farmers and fishermen on the other hand. New political awareness was growing among the peasants.

Virtually all the farming communities of Norway became affected to some degree by the Haugian movement, while at the same time the upper class kept its distance. Peasants involved in the movement began to relate to other believers outside of their own village or valley for the first time in Norwegian history. Thus, Haugians began to rise above their parochial level of thinking to develop a national consciousness.

Transformed lives and behavior changed professional life. Farmers migrated to the towns to become craftsmen or start businesses, textile factories, printing houses, and paper mills.

The Haugians became a new elite among farmers, learning to read and write. They corresponded with fellow Haugians up and down Norway and so became better informed than their fellow farmers on all sorts of subjects. Overcoming the apathy of traditionalism, they, too, became innovative influences in both the religious and agricultural affairs of rural Norway. With a new sense of trust and brotherhood, some were prepared to pool their money and experiment with new cooperative businesses, such as a communally owned printing house in Copenhagen.

In 1801 Hauge became a certified tradesman in Bergen, which enabled him to combine both business and preaching as he traveled. In the companies he started, he gave work to the young, to unemployed men and women, and to handicapped people. He gave them a daily salary and was the first to develop a pension scheme for his employees. Hauge was the first Norwegian to champion the leveling of salary and income.

In yet another parallel with Wesley, Hauge recruited fellow preachers from mainly peasant and working-class backgrounds. Such recruits were in tune with ordinary people's concerns. Many had gifts in preaching and counseling. The release of this enormous latent reserve of human resources accelerated the spread of the Haugian awakening in a relatively short period. Traveling at quiet times of the year for the farm or shop, these preachers gathered people in homes for singing, reading from a collection of sermons, a short exhortation, and a closing prayer.

1804–1814: Imprisonment

Opposition, however, was mounting. Norway's class-structured society frowned on the threatening influence of this simple, unlearned farmer's son. A royal ordinance governing religious assemblies in Norway, called the Conventicle Act, prohibited traveling preachers. Lay people could only gather privately during the daytime in small numbers, in same-gender groupings, and no food could be served. Local ordained ministers had to be informed to monitor the teaching.

Hauge was detained ten times during these years of traveling and preaching, but no sooner was he released than he would resume preaching.

Unsettled by his growing national stature, officials began to fear his influence would eventually incite a spirit of insurrection and lead to a plot against the government. So on October 30, 1804, an edict was issued to arrest Hauge, and he was imprisoned in the capital, Christiania (Oslo).

He was charged with violation of the vagrancy law; of the business law (he had tried to establish an economic joint ownership enterprise with his followers, or the so-called "holy cash box"); and of the law governing the freedom of expression (he had made strong statements concerning clergy in his early writings). Hauge's publications were also confiscated throughout the country, a major setback for the whole movement.

After Hauge had served four and a half years of hard labor, the government temporarily released him to establish salt refineries along the southern and western coast. Apparently the authorities considered their prisoner the only entrepreneur in the land competent for this task. This bizarre development was caused by the British blockade during the Napoleonic war, preventing the import of salt, which was essential for preserving fish and agricultural products. The population relied on preserved food, and the economy depended on income from food exports.

When his case finally came up for review in December 1813, Hauge was sentenced to two years' imprisonment with hard labor in the Akershus fortress, for breaking the Conventicle Act and the law governing publications.

A year later, in December 1814, he was released on probation after being fined one thousand riksdaler, which friends helped pay off.

1814–1824: Resuming Spiritual Leadership of the Awakening

The decade during which Hauge had been imprisoned had brought significant changes in the mentality of the Norwegian people. The British blockade had caused physical starvation in many places, while spiritual hunger had also been awakened by economic hard times and the threat of war. Over the years, many state church ministers had become much more open to the work of Hauge and his followers.

Hauge himself was now too weak for any major traveling. Prison life had exposed him to several illnesses from which he suffered for the rest of his life. Yet through correspondence and meetings in his own home, he was able to resume a degree of leadership of the Haugian movement. He established a mill by the Aker River and began to engage in charity work.

Some years later, even the authorities acknowledged his good work and made him relief officer of his district. In January 1815 he married his first wife Andrea, who died after giving birth to a son. In 1817 he bought a large farm, Bredtvet, and married Ingeborg Marie Olsdatter, who gave birth to three children, all of whom died young.

Bredtvedt became a spiritual center for the movement over the final decade of Hauge's life. By now Hauge had become highly respected. Priests and theologians frequently visited his farm. Government officials reimbursed valuables confiscated when he was imprisoned in 1804. Despite his illnesses, he was able to write more than eleven publications during his last years.

Hans Nielsen Hauge died March 29, 1824, at the age of fifty-three.

An Enduring Legacy

Awareness of the significance of the Haugian legacy continues to grow in Norway. The bicentennial of his spiritual awakening in 1996 prompted fresh reflection on his key role in the building of the modern nation.[14]

Hauge is recognized as leading the first successful movement against the officials of the absolute monarchy in Norway.

He initiated societies and mission movements that continued to be active for more than 150 years, and whose members provided the core of the congregations in the Church of Norway.

Once more like Wesley, Hauge remained a lifelong member of the mainstream church, the Church of Norway. He encouraged his supporters to be loyal to—but not uncritical of—the church.

The Inner Mission Association, founded in 1868 as part of the Haugian legacy to be a renewal movement within the church, has had wide national influence through its many Bible colleges, folkehøgskoler (high schools), agricultural schools, and institutions training teachers for the Norwegian educational system.

Haugians and Moravians started Norway's first mission agency in Norway in 1842, the Norwegian Mission Society, a major factor in Norway becoming the top missionary-sending country per capita.

Haugians initiated many political and social tasks in the first half of the nineteenth century and continued to contribute substantial numbers of parliamentarians through the years.

If Wesley could be called the Apostle of England and Carey the father of modern missions, it is no exaggeration to acknowledge Hauge as a father of modern Norway.

Abraham Kuyper—Ten Heads and a Hundred Arms

Undoubtedly, one of the fathers of modern Holland is the remarkable figure of Abraham Kuyper (1837–1920)—journalist, theologian, educationalist, politician, and prime minister. His impact on the nation in the late nineteenth century and the opening decade of the twentieth century has left an indelible imprint on Dutch churches, schools, media, and politics a full century later.

What was the secret of this prolifically productive man, once described as having ten heads and a hundred arms?[15]

Kuyper, on the twenty-fifth anniversary of his editorship of *De Standaard* in 1897, said: "One desire has been the ruling passion of my life. One high motive has acted like a spur upon my mind and soul. It is this: That in spite of all worldly opposition, *God's holy ordinances shall be established again in the home, in the school and in the State* for the good of the people: to carve as it were into the conscience of the nation the ordinances of the Lord, to which Bible and Creation bear witness, until the nation again pays homage to God."

Kuyper was born into a Europe still transitioning from the rule of monarchies and aristocracies into the more democratic governments of newly emerging nations. The French Revolution in 1789 had triggered convulsions across Europe lasting a whole generation, overthrowing traditional élites ruling in territories overrun by the French armies. After Napoleon's defeat at Waterloo in 1815, there was widespread resistance to the restoration of the traditional rulers. The ideas of *liberty, equality, and fraternity* were spreading across Europe. Nationalism was on the rise. Belgium and Greece gained independence and nationhood in the 1830s, while three or four decades later, various principalities and kingdoms were unified to become the nations of Italy and Germany.

Modern Europe was taking shape. What forms of government would replace the ancien régimes that existed before the French Revolution, where power was shared by the church, the monarchy, and the nobility?

The twin processes of industrialization and urbanization were changing traditional European life forever. What forces would shape the future of Holland?

Two main secular options were to present themselves across Europe as the century unfolded. Liberal humanism would stress laissez-faire individualism. Socialistic Communism would declare the state to be savior.

Could there be a third option? This search for a biblical alternative—and its application to Dutch society—would become the driving passion of Kuyper's life.

Early Formation

Baby Kuyper was born in 1837, in Maassluis near Rotterdam, with a large head. His mother worried that he had a water head. The midwife, with remarkable foresight, assured her that all was well: that head was simply full of brains!

Following his childhood in Middelburg, the young Kuyper completed doctoral studies and a dissertation in theology at Leiden University under modernist[16] teachers.

After ordination into the Dutch Reformed Church, he was called to a country parish church in Beesd, outside of Utrecht.

He made a disturbing discovery as he went on his pastoral visits to the simple country folk of his parish: his learning did not impress them. They did not accept him as their spiritual leader. In their eyes, all he had to give was head knowledge of the "modern" sort.

It was a common laborer's daughter, Pietje Balthus, who "discipled" her own pastor. She helped him discover the heart of the gospel and introduced both him and his "worldly" wife, Johanna, to a personal relationship with God.

This life-changing encounter gave Kuyper a lifelong appreciation of the *Kleine Luyden,* the common people, who would later form the major part of his supporting constituency.

Reform

With his new personal faith, Kuyper began to study Calvin's teachings afresh, looking for a practical theology by which to approach the daily issues of life. He began to realize how much nonbiblical ideas influenced the thinking of church folk on life in general, including his own. The pervading influence of modernism—the assumptions of the Enlightenment and Rationalism—needed to be resisted in both the world and the church.

When as a thirty-year-old minister he moved to the Domkerk in Utrecht in 1867, Kuyper enjoined the battle for reform and to expose modernistic "lies in the church." There he made his debut into journalism as an associate editor, writing both religious and political columns for the weekly *De Heraut* (The Herald).

In 1870 he moved to Amsterdam, where he continued to agitate for reform in the church, and against the dangers of an aristocratic hierarchy on the one hand and modernism on the other. Within two years, he was appointed head editor of the daily newspaper *De Standaard,* of which *De Heraut* became the weekly supplement. By the end of the century, *De Standaard* was recognized as the most prestigious Dutch daily paper.[17] Kuyper was to remain chief editor of both journals for over forty years, in addition to all his other tasks!

In 1874 Kuyper was elected to parliament, but the following year poor health forced him to withdraw to Switzerland for a two-year sabbatical. In retrospect, this quiet period of retreat appears to have given him the opportunity to develop his theology of diversity. "Sphere sovereignty," as he called it, explained how Christ's lordship extended into the real world of politics, education, and society in general.

Domains

Calvin's teaching of God's sovereignty over all of life was the starting point of Kuyper's thinking on "sphere sovereignty." The church as an institution was not sovereign over other areas or "spheres" of life. She had not been given the mandate to "dominate" society, as was taught in the Christendom of the old traditional, hierarchical orders. Neither had the state been given the mandate to "dominate" society, as held by humanistic socialism. Nor surely were individuals free simply to do what was right in their own eyes, as in liberalism, without society suffering serious long-term consequences.

Kuyper saw five domains or spheres of government, each directly accountable to God and each relating to the other domains within God-given limits of authority.

The first was that of *self-government,* the accountability of the individual directly to God.

The second was *family government,* instituted by and also accountable to God. Parents were given primary responsibility for the upbringing and education of children.

Church government was the third sphere, relating to the management of church affairs, leadership structures, and church discipline. The church had not been appointed as mediator between God and individuals or God and families. When church leaders tried to play such a role, they stepped beyond their divine authority into tyranny.[18]

That was especially true concerning church-state relations. For the fourth sphere, that of *civil government,* involved the divine mandate of the state to bear the sword in order to limit the effect of man's fallenness. When the state meddled with church affairs, or vice versa, tyranny ensued.

Lastly, the domain of *societal government* or voluntary associations included clubs, businesses, societies, organizations—significant players in what is called the "social midfield," which flourishes in healthy democracies and is tightly controlled under totalitarian regimes.

The Long Haul

On his return to Holland, Kuyper had thus a framework to enjoin the battle simultaneously on multiple fronts: the media, politics, the school, the church, and the family.

He immediately resumed his work on the daily and weekly papers, using these channels to disciple his growing readership of *Kleine Luyden* in the application of Christian truth to social life.

Next, he proved his political acumen by reorganizing the Anti-Revolutionary Party (ARP). Guillaume Groen van Prinsterer, a Christian administrator in the cabinet of King William I, had started this party in the 1830s. Its name was drawn from the claim that every Christian should oppose the French Revolutionary ideas of exalting human reason as supreme authority.

Groen had envisioned a Christian education in which all subjects would be studied in the light of God's revelation, and all children taught to worship God with their minds. Kuyper now began building up a large lower-middle-class following, with a progressive social platform called *Ons Program,* based on conservative Christian doctrine.

True to Groen's vision, Kuyper rejoined the struggle for the rights for "free schools," i.e., the rights for parents to send their children to schools offering education based on the worldview of the parents' choice. "Special" education would thus be the norm, and government taxes would underwrite both schools with a secular curriculum and those teaching from a Christian perspective, *Scholen met den Bijbel.* This *schoolstrijd*—school battle—raged in the press and in parliament for several decades before being settled in favor of the ARP's platform. This unique concept of education, reflecting a plurality of worldviews rather than being a secular melting pot seeking the lowest common denominator, continues to shape Dutch education into the twenty-first century.[19]

In turn, the *schoolstrijd* became a catalyst for a process called "pillarization" (*verzuiling*) spreading to other social fields, producing newspapers, trade unions, political parties, broadcasting companies, and even goat-breeding clubs (!), reflecting a spectrum of worldviews.[20]

Elementary education was only part of Kuyper's vision for reform of education; higher education and science also needed to be reclaimed. As early as 1870, Kuyper had written of the need for free universities initiated by private parties.

A decade later, amidst much interest and support from the *Kleine Luyden,* Dr. Kuyper opened the Free University, *Vrije Universiteit* (VU), in Amsterdam. His opening speech, *Souvereiniteit in eigen kring,* was a public declaration of the concept of sphere sovereignty.

In addition to all his other roles, he was now the first rector of the Vrije Universiteit, which boasted a faculty of four other professors and a total student body of four! Kuyper had seen the need for such a far-reaching instrument for further transformation in church and society. Nine years earlier he had written in *De Heraut:* "We are working for the long haul. We aim not for the apparent triumph of the moment, but for the ultimate success of our cause. The question is not what influence we have now, but what power we will exercise in half a century; not how few we have now, but how many of the young generation will take a stand for our cause."[21]

With politics, journalism, and education now harnessed to his cause, Kuyper returned to the task of church reform, choosing Luther's four-hundredth anniversary in 1883 to launch a new phase of his many-sided "anti-revolutionary" campaign. He argued that to be true to Luther's Reformation, reformed churches should always be being reformed.

In addition to free schools and a free university, a drawn-out struggle called the *Doleantie* culminated in the founding of free churches in 1892. These Reformed Churches *(Gereformeerde Kerken)* were freed from what Kuyper saw as an overly aristocratic synodal hierarchy to become self-governing, confessional, presbyterian congregations.

Kuyper viewed the spread of such congregations throughout the nation as an essential base of operations for the light of the gospel to disperse in all directions, through all life-spheres, and for future generations. Soon after the founding of the *Gereformeerde Kerken,* Kuyper created the framework for both home and foreign missions for the newly freed churches.

Climax

Any one of these accomplishments would have been a significant life achievement, but for Kuyper, the climax of his lifework still lay ahead. In April 1894, he returned to Parliament after an absence of twenty years to began a seven-year period of political activity which amazed friend and foe alike. In addition to leading the Antirevolutionary Party, he was still editor of both the daily *De Standaard* and the weekly *De Heraut,* as well as teaching as a professor at the VU in two faculties, theology and Dutch literature.

In 1898 he made a long-promised trip to America where he received an honorary degree and delivered the now-famous Stone Lectures at Princeton University, outlining Calvinism as a comprehensive, integrated worldview.

After the elections of 1901, the queen asked Dr. Kuyper to form a cabinet and to become the prime minister. In his opening speech, the new premier declared his intention to continue to build the nation on the Christian principles of the national life.

In this role he was called upon to mediate a peace between the British and the Boers at war in South Africa.

Under Kuyper, many progressive social laws were introduced, creating rights for the poor, minorities, and workers. In the competition between capital and labor, liberalism and socialism, he defended the workers' rights to be organized.

Kuyper's coalition cabinet did not survive the 1905 elections, however. While he continued to be active in politics and journalism until the year of his death, 1920, his best years were clearly now past.

Although some of Kuyper's views, such as those of women and race, are now seen as politically incorrect, his achievements were remarkable. The man with "ten heads and a hundred arms" had lived an almost superhuman life, stepping into the breach to defend his nation against a godless modernism, and doing all in his power to reestablish a biblical heritage in his nation.

A century after his Stone Lectures, international scholars convened at Princeton to honor Kuyper's memory and assess his legacy, in itself a measure of the powerful influence exercised by this one man, not only in discipling his own nation of Holland, but also in providing an ongoing source of inspiration to students, scholars, and leaders worldwide. While on the one hand Kuyper was recalled as a child of his times, he was, on the other hand, clearly seen as a champion of minorities, a champion of the "little people," and a champion for God's rule over family, school, church, government, and media.

Frank Buchman—Global Revolutionary

If the names of Wesley, Carey, Hauge, and Kuyper are permanently linked to specific nations, the name Frank Buchman (1878–1961) has truly global associations. While Wesley's aim was to reform the nation, Buchman's passion was to remake the whole world.

"Three great tasks confront this generation," he wrote in his book, *Remaking the World*. "To keep the peace and make it permanent. To make the wealth and work of the world available to all and for the exploitation of none. And with peace and prosperity as our servants and not as our masters, to build a new world, create a new culture, and change the age of gold into the golden age."[22]

From German immigrant stock, Buchman was born in 1878 in Pennsylvania, into a Lutheran Reformed family. He graduated from a Lutheran seminary in 1902. His first job was as a social worker, and he opened a *hospiz* for the disadvantaged in Philadelphia in 1904. Within three years, however, he disagreed with board members and suffered exhaustion. The doctor advised a long holiday abroad.

Turning Point

Harboring bitterness in his heart toward the board members, Buchman left for England. There he attended a Keswick Convention and in a little stone-built chapel underwent a life-changing experience during a service led by Jessie Penn-Lewis.

"She pictured the dying Christ as I had never seen him before," he recalled later, "I saw the nails in his hands and I knew that I had wounded him. I thought of those six men back in Philadelphia who I felt had wronged me. I began to see myself as God saw me, which was a very different picture than the one I had of myself."[23]

He left the chapel set on asking the board members forgiveness for the way he had behaved. This experience became a turning point in Buchman's life. He had learned that a changed world begins with a changed heart.

Back in the States, he began work as YMCA secretary at Penn State University. There he began targeting influential figures on the campus, from the bootlegger to the president. His bold approach to these men, telling them of their need for a life change, led to dramatic conversions, with a corresponding impact on the whole campus. Over the next seven years, Buchman's targeting of key individuals yielded remarkable fruit.

The whole tone of the college changed, and campaigns following Buchman's methods began to be held on many other campuses where real awakenings occurred, including at Yale and Cornell.

In 1915 Buchman left Penn State for India to help set up an evangelistic campaign, and then went on to China to apply his methods of "sustained evangelism" using intensive work with individuals. His plan was to target key figures, the "leaders of China." The first fifteen included a general, an admiral, the minister of the interior, vice minister of justice, and the president of the Chinese assembly. Buchman and his colleagues aimed to reform a whole country! Their principle coworkers were to be not other missionaries, but influential Chinese. It was the first of his efforts to implement his conviction that *a country, no less than a person, could become God-directed.*

"Who can tell the power of a man won for Jesus Christ?" Buchman asked. The acting prime minister of China, Hsu Ch'ien, passionately believed that Christianity alone could bring the unification of the country and "national salvation." Buchman's emphasis on the importance of a close partnership with educated and sometimes high-ranking Chinese was also untypical of the missionary community. Most missionaries saw the Chinese as inferior and unable to carry on this work. Buchman's insistence on dealing with sin, plus his view of the Chinese as coworkers, led to tensions with the missionary community.

In 1918 Buchman met with Sun Yat-sen, the Chinese leader, and confronted him with having too many wives. Later Sun Yat-sen said, "Buchman is the only man who tells me the truth about myself."[24]

Consequences

Later that year, conflict with the missionary community came to a flash point at a summer conference at which Hsu Ch'ien also spoke about the need for Christians to be right with God in order to break the bondages of "despotism, militarism, autocracy, opium-smoking, liquor traffic, concubinage, foot-binding, and slavery."

When Buchman challenged the missionaries to deal with private sin and to get involved in personal work with individuals, they reacted to his perceived accusations of their spiritual bankruptcy. Buchman was eventually asked by mission leaders to leave China, and he returned to the States in 1919.

This premature departure from China may have had major consequences for the future of that nation. His influence on both Sun Yat-sen and Hsu Ch'ien was second to none. Sun Yat-sen had come to the place where he believed that Christianity was the only way China could be saved. Hsu Ch'ien wrote to Buchman back in the U.S. that "at present the missionaries are only preaching about the individual righteousness but nothing about society and nations as a whole. Why should people be only righteous individually but not in political affairs?"

Then, in 1923, an agent from Moscow called Michael Borodin arrived in Canton and, in due course, became advisor to both Sun Yat-sen and Hsu. Hsu felt that Borodin really appreciated his ability and idealism, whereas he got little cooperation from the formal Christians in his large schemes of applied Christianity. Borodin himself knew the New Testament well. On one occasion, speaking of revolution, he exclaimed, "That man Paul, there was a revolutionary!" He pounded his fist on the table sending teacups flying, and shouted, "Where do you find men like him today? Give me one example! No, you cannot!"

Borodin went on to influence a number of key Chinese leaders toward Communism, including Hsu Ch'ien, Sun Yat-sen, Chiang Kai-shek, Mao Tse-tung, and Chou En-lai. While some later broke with it, others went on to capture a whole nation with zealous idealism.

Little imagination is needed to realize that the history of China in the twentieth century could have been very different indeed!

Moral Re-Armament

Over the next three decades, Buchman continued to travel the world targeting rich and poor, high and low, powerful and marginalized with his personal approach. He challenged world leaders and chambermaids alike to commit themselves to the four absolutes of love, purity, selflessness, and honesty. So strong was his belief that changed individuals can change nations that he attempted to meet personally with Heinrich Himmler, commander of the Schutzstaffel (SS) in Nazi Germany, as the war clouds gathered in the late 1930s—in vain.

A global movement had begun to emerge, initially called the Oxford Movement, after the university where Buchman had enjoyed particular evangelistic successes. But with war looming, the movement adopted the new name of Moral Re-Armament (MRA). Buchman preached, "the God-controlled nation will add to her armament an army of life-changers, to her national defense the respect and gratitude of all her neighbors. Such a nation will demonstrate that spiritual power is the greatest force in the world."

Hope and Healing

One July day in 1946, Frank Buchman gazed out from high above Lake Geneva in Switzerland on the snow-dusted French Alps stretching before him along the blue lake waters toward Mont Blanc. Above him towered the turrets of the eight-storied Caux Palace, Switzerland's largest and most prestigious hotel when built in 1902. Surely this was one of the world's most breathtaking and inspiring vistas.

Yet what inspired the Lutheran evangelist most was a burning inner vision. He had no doubt what God's will was for a Europe emerging from the chaos, rubble, and suffering of World War II. For decades he had preached a message of submission to God's will for individuals and families, and also for kings, presidents, and nations. Now, after the turbulent years of global conflict, Buchman was leading MRA in the task of remaking the postwar world.

His vision of individuals and nations living in common obedience to God was becoming more of a concrete reality that day with the reopening of Caux Palace as a Center for the Reconciliation of the Nations.

Just weeks before, ninety-five Swiss Christian families had given sacrificially—family jewels, life insurance policies, holiday money, and even houses—to purchase the run-down asylum for war refugees. Renamed Mountain House, the palace was to become a refuge of hope, a place for healing the past and forging the future. Over the coming years, thousands upon thousands of politicians, educators, trade unionists, captains of industry, students, journalists, artists, businessmen, and religious leaders from across Europe and the world would come through its doors.

As Buchman entered the cavernous reception hall, he surveyed the colorful gathering where delegates from across Europe, some in national costume, mingled with flag-bearing youths, Swiss donor families, and volunteer workers.

Suddenly he asked out loud, "Where are the Germans?"

A stunned hush fell over the crowd.

"You will never rebuild Europe without the Germans!" he added, breaking the awkward silence.

Although a year had passed since hostilities had ceased, Buchman's question still shocked many of those present. But he knew if Germany were not embraced by Christian forgiveness and reconciliation, godless forces of anarchy or Communism would fill the postwar vacuum. For him, forgiveness and reconciliation were clearly part of God's will for Europe in 1946.

Transformation

"I hated Germany so much I wanted to see it erased from the map of Europe!" confessed Irène Laure, a member of the French Resistance at the next summer's conference. "But I have seen here that my hatred was wrong. I want to ask all the Germans present to forgive me."

Those Germans attending Caux that summer were among the first of over three thousand leading citizens given special permission by the Allied authorities to travel to Caux over the next four years to meet their opposite numbers from Europe and other continents. The message of forgiveness and reconciliation taught by Buchman and demonstrated by Irène Laure affected them deeply. They invited Madame Laure to address many of their Länder (state) parliaments.

The following year, 450 Germans visited Caux. Among them was Dr. Konrad Adenauer, the future German chancellor, who invited MRA teams to bring the message of forgiveness through traveling musical shows and arranged a series of official receptions for Buchman. In the heavy industry area of the Ruhr Valley, many Marxist trade union leaders were converted. The resulting moral transformation was seen as a significant factor in the recovery of postwar Germany.

Meanwhile, the French Prime Minister, Robert Schuman, had heard that remarkable changes of heart were taking place in industrial circles in the north, where tensions had led to talk of civil war. The changes were traced to Caux. So in 1948 Schuman arranged to meet the MRA leader.

Buchman's ensuing friendship with both Schuman and Adenauer fostered a change in attitude between the two leaders, from mutual suspicion to respectful confidence. This trust culminated in an event now celebrated annually throughout the European Union on May 9, known as Europe Day. For on that date in 1950, the French Government accepted a bold plan, proposed by Schuman and supported by Adenaeur, to integrate the coal and steel industries of France, Germany, and any other European country who wished to join. Since these industries would be the motor of any potential military machine, future war between the nations would be rendered permanently impossible.

This Schuman Plan gave birth to the European Coal and Steel Community, ECSC, the first major step toward the formation of the European Economic Community, which has grown to become today's European Union.

A few weeks later, Schuman decorated Buchman as a Chevalier of the Legion of Honour, in recognition of his role in helping "to create the climate in which the new relationship between France and Germany had been rendered possible."

Few Christians today seem aware of the climate of humility, forgiveness, and reconciliation that fostered the birth of the ECSC and thus the EU. Yet the Caux story demonstrates the role of a "faithful minority" in exercising a disproportionate influence on the course of history.

The story of Frank Buchman affirms that changed nations begin with changed hearts.

Robbed

Spanning the three centuries of the Modern Era, these stories of Buchman, Kuyper, Hauge, Carey, and Wesley remind us of our rich heritage of nation-changers.

Yet too often we have become creatures of short memories. And short memories result in shortsightedness. We have allowed ourselves to be robbed of this heritage and stripped of a confident expectation of God's future actions in our world. Deprived of the past and cheated of our future, we have often become orphans in history with little historical consciousness of the cloud of witnesses cheering us on for our leg of the race.

Without such perspectives, we are seriously tempted to shrink the gospel to simply its "salvation" component. Clutching our tickets to heaven as we sit in our comfortable church pews, we wait to be raptured out of this worldly mess. Mouthing the words of the Lord's Prayer, we mistakenly think we are praying for the Second Coming as we pray for God's kingdom to come.

Yet that is to miss the point, as Jesus explained in the next line. We are to pray for God's will to be done *on earth,* not in heaven. God's will, by definition, is for his will to be done *on our planet.* God's will is not, therefore, for things to get worse and worse, as many seem to believe.

Conscious of this surrounding cloud of witnesses, let us then resolve to join God's faithful minority and to obey Christ's commission to disciple nations—by going into *all the world,* reaching *all people groups,* and reconciling *all things* under heaven and on earth under his lordship.

Bibliography

For Wesley
Lean, Garth. *Strangely Warmed.* Wheaton, Ill.: Tyndale, 1964.
Semmel, Bernard. *The Methodist Revolution.* New York: Basic Books, 1973.
Snyder, Howard. *The Radical Wesley.* Downers Grove, Ill.: InterVarsity Press, 1980.
Wood, Arthur Skevington. *The Burning Heart.* Lexington, Ky.: Emeth, 2007.

For Carey
Culross, James. *William Carey.* Hodder & Stoughton, 1881.
Mangalwadi, Vishal and Ruth. *Carey, Christ and Cultural Transformation.* Carlisle, U.K.: OM Publishing, 1997.

For Hauge
Fjeldstad, Hilde. *Hans Nielsen Hauge.* Master's thesis, Free Lutheran School of Theology, Oslo (1986).
Magnus, Alv Johan. *Trailblazer with Gall.* Norway: Prokla Media, 1996.

For Kuyper
Kuyper, Abraham. *Lectures on Calvinism* (The Stone Lectures), The Kuyper Foundation (Somerset, England) www.kuyper.org (accessed December 9, 2007).
McGoldrick, James E. *God's Renaissance Man: The Life and Work of Abraham Kuyper.* Auburn, Maine: Evangelical Press, 2000.

For Buchman
Lean, Garth. *On the Tail of a Comet.* Colorado Springs: Helmers and Howard, 1988.
Mottu, Philippe. *The Story of Caux.* Grosvenor Books, 1970.

Notes

1. William Blake, "The New Jerusalem." Poem available at EServer, Iowa State University, poetry.eserver.org/new-jerusalem.html (accessed May 3, 2007).

2. Sociologist Peter Berger's phrases.

3. John Wesley, *Notes from Several Conversations between Mr. Wesley and Others, 1744–1789.* Quoted by Pan Methodist Cooperation and Union website, www.gccuic-umc.org/panmeth/commonheritage.htm (accessed May 3, 2007).

4. Bernard Semmel, *The Methodist Revolution* (London: Heinemann, 1974), 8.

5. May 24, 1738.

6. Early Pietism emphasized *wholeness* while a later Pietism earned a reputation for super-spirituality.

7. Wesley fought his whole life long to keep the Methodist movement within the Anglican Church. Only over his dead body did the movement became a separate denomination.

8. "Women on a Mission," *Central Connection* vol. 33, no. 9 (September 1, 2003) available at www.usc.salvationarmy.org under the "Central Connection" link (accessed May 3, 2007).

9. Comenius was invited to be the first principal of Harvard, a role he turned down in favor of pastoring his scattered Moravian flock and reorganizing education in England under Cromwell.

10. J. Wesley Bready, *England Before and After Wesley* (New York: Harper, 1938).

11. The Baptist Page: William Carey, www.siteone.com/religion/baptist/baptistpage/Portraits/carey.htm (accessed May 3, 2007).

12. William Carey, *An Enquiry into the Obligations of Christians to Use Means for the Conversion of the Heathen,* (London: Ann Ireland, 1792).

13. Information on Carey drawn from: Vishal and Ruth Mangalwadi, *Carey, Christ and Cultural Transformation* (Carlisle, Cumbria, England: OM Publishing, 1993).

14. See Alv Johan Magnus, *Veirydder med gnagsår: Hans Nielsen Hauge—og vekkelsen som forandret Norge (Trailblazer with Gall: Hans Nielsen Hauge and the Awakening That Changed Norway)* (Norway: Prokla-Media, 1996), and Hilde Fjeldstad, *Hans Nielsen Hauge,* an unpublished dissertation from which this chapter has drawn.

15. In 1897 a political opponent, Charles Boissevain, called him "een tegenstander, die tien hoofden en honderd armen bezit" (an adversary who has ten heads and a hundred arms).

16. Kuyper later described the creed of the Modernist as: "I, Modernist, believe in a God who is the Father of all men; and in Jesus, not the Christ but the rabbi of Nazareth. I believe in man who is good by nature and needs only to strive for perfection. I believe that sin is only relative, that forgiveness of sin is therefore simply a human invention. I believe a hope of the better life and salvation of all men, without a day of judgement." Quoted in Jon R. Kennedy, *The Reformation of Journalism* (Toronto: Wedge Publishing, 1973), 11.

17. Ibid., 1.

18. Advocates of sphere sovereignty defined 'tyranny' as exercising authority beyond one's divinely instituted limits.

19. The Dutch educational policy enabled YWAM to initiate Evangelische Basisscholen as a distinct educational stream in the 1980s, recognized by the highest court in the land, and which has since been expanded into high schools.

20. Pillarization (verzuiling) was the segmentation of Dutch society into social groups around worldviews or life philosophies. Pluriform Dutch society in most of the twentieth century was composed of different social pillars (zuilen) reflecting, for example, Catholic, Reformed, Socialist, Anthroposophical, Evangelical, and Liberal lifestyles and philosophies. The author's Dutch father-in-law was president of a Protestant goat breeders' club—which presumably bred Protestant goats!

21. "Abraham Kuyper," in *Christelijke Encyclopaedie,* 2nd ed., F. W. van Grosheide and G. P. van Itterzon, ed. (Kampen, Netherlands: Kok, 1956–61), 543, author's translation.

22. Frank N.D. Buchman, *Remaking the World: The Speeches of Frank N.D. Buchman* (London: Blandford Press, 1947).

23. The information and quotations throughout this section on Frank Buchman are drawn from a variety of sources. See the books listed in the resources section of this chapter.

24. Gabriel Marcel, ed., *Fresh Hope for the World: Moral Re-Armament in Action,* trans. Helen Hardinge (London: Longman, 1960), 159.

Two streams of ministry have developed within the body of Christ. One focuses on saving souls through evangelism, while the other works for social change. Through examining Youth With A Mission's (YWAM's) developing understanding of these streams, Debra Buenting articulates how God has been bringing greater understanding that both are vital responses to fulfilling the Great Commission.

Youth With A Mission
and the Great Reversal

Debra Buenting

I was in South Africa listening to a radio talk show just before a major election. One caller suggested that Christians should get involved in the political process to help bring about needed change in the country. What followed stunned me. The next caller articulated in no uncertain terms that the job of Christians is to convert souls! "Saving souls is our only purpose," he shouted, "and if we get involved in politics, we'll just save fewer souls!"

The worldviews expressed by these two callers epitomize a significant struggle in Christianity, one that has been especially heated during the past one hundred years. One view stresses the importance of bringing redemption to every aspect of life, while the other stresses saving souls as the only task to which the church is called. Though the personal salvation emphasis has been the bedrock of almost every mission society in recent times, some circles are rethinking how to *do* missions. Many are challenging the church to return to Christianity's more ancient roots, a holistic worldview which guided the ancients of the Old Testament and which was assumed by believers in the New Testament era.

In Jewish tradition there is a concept known as *shalom*. Though English has reduced shalom to simply mean "peace," the term holds a much broader meaning, described concisely by community organizer Dr. Robert Linthicum:

The Hebrew word "shalom" is much richer than its English equivalent. What particularly reveals its richness is the number of English words used in the English translations of the Hebrew Bible in order to translate the single Hebrew word, "shalom." It is alternatively translated as peace, prosperity, welfare, well being, wholeness, harmony. It is used to describe bodily health (Ps. 38:3), security and strength (Dan. 10:19; Judges 6:23), a long life ending in a natural death (Gen. 15:15), abundance (Lam. 3:17; Ps. 37:11; Zech. 8:12; Job 5:18–26), successful completion of an enterprise (Judges 18:5; 1 Sam. 1:17), and even victory in war (Judges 8:9).[1]

The Hebrew concept of salvation holds similar meanings, suggesting a more complete meaning than deliverance from hell. The Old Testament concept of salvation implies aid, victory, prosperity, health, help, and welfare. Similarly, the Greek words for salvation in the New Testament indicate healing, preservation, making whole, keeping safe, and restoration.[2,3]

In this chapter I will discuss how the Christian church has struggled with conflicting worldviews and how Youth With A Mission (YWAM) has shared the struggle. By looking at the historical roots of these opposing views and analyzing the rhetoric[4]—the use of language—concerning holistic ministry in YWAM through the years, I believe we can learn much related to Jesus' mandate to disciple nations.

Realizing that ideas have significant implication, I set out to study the key influences that have guided Youth With A Mission since its inception in 1960. I studied old brochures, books, and other writings, collected old television interviews, and talked with several long-time YWAM leaders to learn how the mission approached these theological and ministry issues. What I found was that the struggles that have taken place in YWAM are the same ones that have challenged the church at large.

By analyzing the rhetoric surrounding these issues, I believe people of faith can better understand the context in which we view ministry and how we might change to communicate a more complete gospel. This study is not exhaustive by any means, nor does it attempt to point out discrepancies between YWAM's rhetoric and its practice. As the old adage goes, those who cannot remember the past are condemned to repeat it.

The Roots of Dualism

The Christian church has a long history of involvement in all aspects of life including government, education, healthcare, the arts, and social action. Catholic monks carried their missionary message throughout Europe, encouraging converts to develop every aspect of their lives, from private devotion to academic scholarship.[5] Monasteries became centers of faith, learning, and technical progress. Pietists, Moravians,

Methodists, and Puritans fed and clothed the poor, established schools, and fought for social issues such as the rights of women and slaves. The Reformers, too, were concerned with foundational social issues. Author Ronald Sider describes the worldview of Luther and his colleague Karlstadt like this: "They were convinced that fundamental human rights of equality, freedom and brotherly love had their source in the Christian faith."[6]

However, these values have not been shared throughout church history. The predominant view since the time of Augustine (who lived from ad 354-430) has been one that elevated *spiritual* things above the rest of life. Before converting to Christianity, Augustine gave himself to worldly pleasures, idleness, and adolescent mischief which led to a lifelong obsession with things of the flesh revealed in his *Confessions*. He spent nine years following Manichaeism, an intellectual religion whose goal was to be set free from the "pollution of matter" or the physical world. Anything physical was seen as evil, so naturally sex and even marriage were condemned. It wasn't the pleasure of sex they disdained as much as "They regarded it as an evil in itself because the propagation of the human race meant the continual imprisonment of the light-substance in matter and a retarding of the blissful consummation of all things."[7] Manichaeism reinforced Augustine's struggles with guilt and "the things of the flesh"; he was tortured by the problem of original sin. Augustine eventually became disillusioned with Manichaeism and converted to Neoplatonism, a philosophy based on the ideas of Plato but which had evolved to include "religious ideals and mystic tendencies of Oriental thought."[8]

After becoming a Christian, Augustine continued to dwell on sin and promote a dualistic theology that divided life into the sacred (spiritual) and the secular (physical). He incorporated Manichaeist and Neoplatonic ideas into Christianity, and promoted the idea that Jesus' earthly purpose was to "release souls of light from the prison of their bodies."[9] An argument could be made that Augustine's influence on theology was due as much to the existence of his prolific writings as to his honest questions and brilliant ideas. However, no matter the reason, it is clear that Augustine brought into Christianity a dualistic philosophy, and the church has wrestled with the tension between the secular and the sacred ever since.

However, it was during a period between 1910 and 1930 that the most significant debate occurred, one that was to affect how Christian mission was carried out in the twentieth century. This period came to be called "The Great Reversal," a term coined by Timothy L. Smith[10] and explained in detail in a profound little book published in 1972 by David O. Moberg titled *The Great Reversal: Evangelism Versus Social Concern; Evangelical Perspective*. The Great Reversal refers to a theological shift that reduced a holistic concept of shalom to an overemphasis on the salvation of individual souls, thereby *reversing* centuries of Jewish and Christian history.

The Great Reversal

In the early twentieth century, several issues descended on the American church. Some Christians had begun questioning the reality of God and the authority of the Bible. At the same time, societies were faced with new problems that included a huge influx of immigrants, urbanization, and the industrial revolution. These issues brought great economic disparity and social ills to cities such as New York and Chicago. How to solve these problems became the focus of a fierce theological debate.

One side engaged in social reform, working to relieve crime, pollution, injustice, and cultural tensions. They fed the homeless, fought for workers' rights, championed minorities and women, and sought to change unjust structures that relegated people to chronic wretchedness. But their message was often void of the Christian themes of personal responsibility, repentance, and a relationship with God. Individual change, they thought, would result from corporate change. They called their work *restoring the kingdom of God.*

The other group took the modern (and Western) idea of individualism and applied it intensely to Christianity. They became preoccupied with saving souls, focusing on personal religious experience as the end-all of Christian work. These Christians began isolating themselves from almost any sense of social responsibility, choosing to involve themselves in creating and growing a church culture rather than working to bring redemption to society at large. They believed that if individuals would experience personal redemption, society as a whole would eventually change.

The extremism on both sides forced new language that carried great emotional baggage. Those who concerned themselves with personal evangelism became known as *evangelicals* and those who focused on issues such as apologetics and the inerrancy (exemption from error) of Scripture became known as *fundamentalists* (for defending what they called the fundamentals of Christianity). These "conservative" Christians belittled those who worked to solve social problems, viewing them as being driven by *works.* The evangelicals called them *social gospelers* and despised them for missing the true message of the Bible.

While evangelicals looked down on those who engaged in the *social gospel,* the more socially conscious "liberal" Christians began to despise fundamentalists for their narrow-mindedness and apathy. This Great Reversal had a profound effect on how Christians viewed themselves, as articulated by David O. Moberg:

Each group read different parts of the Bible; when it stumbled into the other's domain, it provided a different interpretative schema. The sharp polarization that developed during the conflict made it politically impossible to remain both an evangelical and a social gospeler, and emotional involvements prevented Christians from recognizing the fallacies of being impaled upon the horns of a false dilemma. Christians became either evangelistic or socially involved, not both.[11]

As Moberg then pointed out, "Many Protestants became identified with the prosperous, moved their residences and churches away from the inner city... and thus remained blind to many evils of their society."[12] These suburbanite fundamentalists would take their *gospel of salvation* to the ends of the earth, leaving, in a sense, the rest of their Bibles—which dealt with corporate and social concerns—at home. It was into this culture that Youth With A Mission was born in 1960.[13]

Birth of a Ministry

In an interview for a television special, "Birth of a Ministry," hosted by Graham Kerr (The Galloping Gourmet) and his wife, Treena, Youth With A Mission founder Loren Cunningham said, "We're a mission organization that is traditional in every sense."[14] Cunningham was attempting to paint Youth With A Mission—which he had started nineteen years earlier—as a credible Christian ministry. However, his mission was anything but traditional, as its very purpose was to construct a new model. YWAM recruited young people (most of whom had no formal university education) as well as non-Westerners, and formed a highly decentralized and innovative movement. YWAM would grow to become one of the largest Christian movements in the world, attracting many thousands of students and missionaries, both part-time and full-time, united by shared ethos and vision. The mission would emerge from and reflect the spiritual roots of the founder himself.

Loren Cunningham was the son of two Assemblies of God itinerant preachers. His mother had grown up on the road, living and traveling in a covered wagon and then a truck, crisscrossing the American south with her parents holding revivals and planting churches. His father had grown up in foster homes because Loren's granddad—widowed with five children—had answered the call to become a traveling preacher to save souls. He had turned down an opportunity to pursue an engineering degree in order to serve the Lord because it was considered a higher calling. Loren himself was only thirteen when he felt God calling him to, "Go ye into all the world, and preach the gospel to every creature" (Mark 16:15 KJV). This New Testament passage was to become the mantra of the mission he would found.

Wanting to channel the enthusiasm and uncomplicated faith of young people, Cunningham started Youth With A Mission in 1960 with the idea of mobilizing young people on short-term mission trips. Despite his ordination by the Assemblies of God, his untraditional ideas were met with considerable criticism as denominational leaders pointed out problems with his plan to send young, inexperienced youth from many denominations, overseas. Despite opposition, Cunningham recruited high school and college students to give up their weekends and summer holidays to go on evangelistic outreaches in the U.S. and Canada, the Caribbean, Latin America, and the South Pacific. These young "YWAMers," as they were called, would talk to people about God in their homes, on the street, and in special evangelistic meetings. In a 1969 book about YWAM, *Journey with the Followers,* the ministry was described as "an interdenominational movement of young people organized for the sole purpose of reaching this generation with the Gospel of Jesus Christ."[15,16]

However, despite a clear goal of *going* and *preaching,* the first YWAM outreach was actually more practical in nature. Cunningham recruited two twenty-one-year-olds to go to Liberia, in Africa, to help build a road through the jungle to a leper colony. The young men also transported U.S. government donations and shared their testimonies as they traveled with resident missionaries to neighboring villages.[17]

During an evangelistic outreach to The Bahamas in the summer of 1964, Hurricane Cleo killed over a hundred residents and left thousands of others homeless. Cunningham had a revelation, as described in his book, *Is That Really You God?*

> I realized that many of us were in danger of not stressing properly one major part of the Gospel message. Jesus told us there were two important things to do. One was to love God with all our hearts, souls, minds and strength—teaching people to *do*—that *is* evangelism. The other command was to love our neighbor as ourselves—to take care of people, as much as is in our power to do. These were the two sides of the same Gospel; loving God and loving neighbor. The two should be almost indistinguishable—so linked that it would be hard to tell them apart.[18]

During the 1960s YWAM's staff consisted of a few dozen volunteers who had raised their own financial support, a policy that is still practiced today. Real growth did not come until YWAM began its School of Evangelism in 1969. Cunningham's short-term, nonformal education model was innovative and served as an alternative to the years of formal schooling mandated by most missionary agencies. The first class included several key figures who would become the first generation of YWAM leaders.

The 1970s: A Decade of Discipling

The 1970s brought an emphasis on discipleship courses, short-term outreaches, and establishing operating locations all over the world.[19] Cunningham was gifted in recruiting young missionaries. The theme of "going" was emphasized in a message he preached entitled, "Go Means a Change of Location." "God says go," he would preach, "whether it's across the street or across the world." The theme continued in 1985 with the publication of *Go,* a coffee table–style book of photographs of YWAMers involved in ministry that coincided with the mission's twenty-fifth anniversary. It also contained basic information about the mission and listed operating locations. This was followed by the annual publication of the *Go Manual,* which continues to serve as an annual directory of international YWAM training and ministry opportunities. "Go Festival" recruiting events were held on several continents, and "Go Teams" served as YWAM's shortest mission outreaches.

A subtle shift occurred in the mid-1970s in the name of the entry-level training course required of all long-term staff. The School of Evangelism (SOE) was replaced by the Discipleship Training School (DTS). The new name accurately reflected the mission's training emphasis during that decade.

In 1978 YWAM started a nonformal university in Hawaii called Pacific and Asia Christian University (PACU), later renamed University of the Nations (U of N), which included nonformal training programs at YWAM centers around the world. The U of N was to be a missions-oriented university dedicated to fulfilling the Great Commission. The formation of colleges was to reflect a message Loren had developed in the mid-1970s. His *Seven Ways to Change a Nation* became *Seven Mind-Molders* and eventually *The Spheres of Influence.* The seven spheres were: church, family, media, government, education, business, and the arts.[20] Today, the corresponding U of N colleges are identified as: Christian Ministries, Counseling and Healthcare, Communication, Humanities and International Studies, Education, Science and Technology, and The Arts. Several U of N centers eventually started to serve the mission with additional resources, including Community Development, Environmental and Stewardship Resources, and Field Ministry Internships.[21]

Despite isolated opportunities to show Christian kindness and participate in small relief efforts, YWAM in the 1970s could not be accused of being overly holistic due to its emphasis on evangelism. However, visiting teachers from various denominations and ministries brought an increasing understanding to the mission of the nature and character of God as shown in the Bible as well as principles for theology and mission. Teachers such as Francis and Frankie Schaeffer dealt with the subject of dualism, challenging the mission to dispel the evangelical presuppositions of a secular-sacred dichotomy and to view ministry more holistically.

One YWAM ministry that did attempt to view life incarnationally (as the fleshly embodiment of God) was that of Dilaram Ministries. The group was composed of hippies, travelers, intellectuals, and religious seekers who had become Christians and who lived in community, extended hospitality to non-Christians, and befriended stranded travelers along the hippie trail from Europe to Afghanistan. Their motto was "People don't care how much you know until they know how much you care."

Incite was a magazine published by Dilaram in the mid-seventies which dealt with issues outside of evangelism per se. It tackled topics such as art, politics, and social concerns, which were nonmainstream ideas at the time. Though Dilaram often viewed itself and was itself viewed as somewhat fringe within the mission, it was in many ways where the majority of the mission would eventually go—toward a more holistic view of life and ministry.

During this time, Brazilian YWAMers started orphanages under the leadership of Jim Stier (who would later become YWAM's president and then CEO). "I can remember," Jim recalled, "not knowing if we ought to [start an orphanage] because I didn't know if YWAM did that sort of thing. The need was great though, and we went ahead."[22]

The 1980s: A Decade of Mercy Ministries and New Frontiers

In the 1980s, YWAM was a loosely organized yet vision-filled movement of mostly twenty- and thirty-somethings that had concentrated its efforts on evangelism and training. A high priority was placed on individual and team *guidance,* a belief in hearing God's voice through personal and corporate revelation. When news of the refugee crisis in Southeast Asia flooded the press in the late 1970s and early 1980s, YWAMers were moved with compassion.

John Dawson, a young leader who would eventually become YWAM's president, was overcome with emotion and wept over photographs of refugees in *Time* magazine. He began articulating a profound sense of shame over the inaction of the church and YWAM toward those suffering desperate physical and emotional pain.

Dawson's mother, Joy, a recognized teacher and prophetic voice in YWAM, developed a message entitled "The Christian's Responsibility to Help the Poor and Needy." Her remarks, based on biblical passages dealing with the poor, were based on verses in the book of Isaiah. These passages were to appear again and again in YWAM rhetoric throughout the 1980s:

> The Spirit of the Lord God is upon me; because the Lord hath anointed me to preach good tidings unto the meek; he hath sent me to bind up the brokenhearted, to proclaim liberty to the captives, and the opening of the prison to them that are bound; To proclaim the acceptable year of the Lord, and the day of vengeance of our God; to comfort all that mourn; To appoint unto them that mourn in Zion, to give unto them beauty for ashes, the oil of joy for mourning, the garment of praise for the spirit of heaviness; that they

might be called trees of righteousness, the planting of the Lord, that he
might be glorified (Isa. 61:1–3 KJV).

Cunningham said at the time that YWAM had been meeting human needs in
150 nations for more than nineteen years. "But," he said, "God is calling us to do it
in a new level because the need is greater, because of a new level of refugees ready to
receive the gospel of Jesus Christ throughout the world."[23] Certainly the publicity
surrounding the refugee crisis became a wake-up call to the ministry that, as a whole,
had previously suffered from little social consciousness. Despite short periods of fasting and prayer for the poor of India, it was the first time many YWAMers had seriously grappled with the issue of poverty and a Christian response.

YWAM Relief Services was born in 1979 and became a highly publicized ministry in the 1980s. Because guidance, obedience, sacrifice, and flexibility were values
already instilled in the mission, YWAM was able to quickly rally workers to staff
refugee camps along the Thai-Cambodian border. Doing new things in new ways
had been part of YWAM's history,[24] so learning to work with refugees was viewed as
a new and exciting challenge. YWAMers collaborated with the United Nations High
Commission for Refugees and various nongovernmental organizations (NGOs) to
distribute food and clothing, administer medical and dental services, provide primary education and vocational training, and offer banking and postal services in
refugee camps. YWAM also established Bible studies and churches, and offered counseling to victims of war and abuse.

Youth With A Mission had held a vision for a ship ministry for many years. It
failed in an attempt to purchase an initial vessel in 1973 but found another ship in
1978 and set out to raise funds and recruit an international crew. The vision was to
send various kinds of teams to the port cities of the world, bringing the good news of
Jesus Christ and obeying Jesus' mandate to "Go into all the world and preach the
good news to all creation" (Mark 16:15).

YWAMers all over the world prayed and sacrificed along with other Christians
to launch the ship ministry, though the vision lacked the impetus to actually begin.
However, when the refugee news hit and YWAM began to involve itself in Southeast
Asia, YWAM had the images and phrases it needed to communicate the heart of the
ship ministry. Photographs of wide-eyed refugee children, barbed-wired camps, and
feeding programs appeared in brochures promoting the ship. Plans to give medical
assistance and distribute food and construction materials were expressed in phrases
such as "Arms around the world," "Hearts and hands to help," and "Ship to serve the
nations." Financial resources were raised, a crew was assembled, and an old ship was
restored. After five years of hard work, the *Anastasis* finally sailed in 1982. She was to
be the first in a fleet of what came to be called Mercy Ships.[25]

While it was hard for evangelicals to criticize work amongst destitute refugees, the ship ministry struggled somewhat to justify itself. The eventual ministry focus was still vague in the early days, and there was enormous pressure to maintain YWAM's evangelical and Pentecostal roots, emphasizing individual salvation as the end-all goal. Was the ship ministry going to represent the dreaded liberal social gospel? Perhaps to dispel the notion, one brochure went so far as to call the *Anastasis* a "salvation ship."

Ship director Don Stephens encountered some opposition in the early years of the ship ministry as he spoke about the *Anastasis* in North American churches. One large congregation in particular "questioned whether giving blankets, clothing, and medicines for a hospital ship were Christian acts at all."[26]

Ship doctor Christine Aroney-Sine developed a message on the "Christian Responsibility to the Poor and Needy." She began, along with others, to form and articulate a theology of holistic ministry. "As I looked at the Bible," she taught, "I realized that it has little to say about the causes of poverty but much to say about [the church's] responsibility in alleviating it."[27] Evangelicals, who had stressed a salvation message for more than a generation, sometimes considered her theology shocking. Dr. Chris encountered opposition from within both YWAM and the church in general for her radical view that demonstrating the gospel by helping the poor was just as valuable as verbalization of the salvation message. Dr. Chris challenged the notion that acts of kindness were bait to attract the lost to Christianity, arguing that showing social concern is core to the gospel.

In a 1979 television interview, Loren Cunningham had said the *Anastasis* would serve in three ways: as a (1) salvation ship, (2) mercy ship, and (3) training ship.[28] Stephens, who had developed compassion for the needy from his mother, had coined the three-fold ministry of YWAM, that of evangelism, training, and mercy ministries, which Loren often quoted. Stephens was convinced that balancing these three was a key strategy for the ministry, quoting "a three-stranded cord is not easily broken" (Eccles. 4:12).

The three aspects of ministry were not always distinct or separable, though the ship's emphasis on medical missions was to become obvious. Stephens articulated the approach some years later in a television news interview:

> What we're trying to do on the ship is follow the pattern of the Lord Jesus in our ministry. He cared for the physical need and the spiritual need at the same time. Ninety-five percent of the hundred million blind people in the world could be given sight with a fifteen-minute cataract surgery. Can you imagine the opportunity to bring sight to the blind? We think the medical ministry is the quickest way to reach into people's hearts with the message of eternity.[29]

The language of *the two-handed gospel,* meeting *the physical and spiritual needs of mankind,*[30] continues to describe Mercy Ships' mandate. Stephens's goal is incarnational ministry: "We must live and model the life of Jesus equally as well as we articulate the words of Jesus."[31]

As the ship ministry grew and matured, so did YWAM Relief Services (later called YWAM Mercy Ministries). YWAMers worked in Southeast Asian refugee camps until they closed in 1995. While continuing work in that region, they also responded to crisis situations in other places including Ethiopia, Pakistan, Uzbekistan, Afghanistan, Iraq, and regions devastated by the 2004 tsunami.

Another compassion ministry called Mother's Choice was opened in Hong Kong to give unwed mothers (often ostracized by their families) a place to stay during their pregnancy. It quickly became a refuge for the mothers' babies as well as for children who had become wards of the state. A few years later, a similar ministry called Mother's Love was started in China. Throughout the world, *various acts of mercy* became aspects of both short-term and established YWAM ministries.[32]

During this time, several YWAMers were influenced by outsiders through books and seminars. Various Christian thinkers and authors expressed outrage over economic disparity between the *haves* and the *have-nots,* including Ronald Sider, author of *Evangelicals and Development: Toward a Theology of Social Change* and *Rich Christians in an Age of Hunger* as well as Tom Sine, author of *The Mustard Seed Conspiracy: You Can Make a Difference in Tomorrow's Troubled World.* Seen by some as theologically left of mainstream evangelical center, these authors helped balance YWAM's personal-salvation-oriented roots.

Until its twenty-fifth anniversary in 1985, "YWAM seemed to function more in an 'oral tradition' where decisions that affected the whole organization were made in joint strategy conferences and leadership councils."[33] "Since 1985 however, there have been increasing use of documentation and other methods of communication to facilitate corporate vision and values, international policies and regional distinctives."[34] YWAM leaders began publishing books that addressed various topics with which YWAM had experience.

Loren Cunningham's *Is That Really You God?* (1984) told the history of YWAM, highlighting Loren's personal experiences in founding and leading the ministry. *Nine Worlds to Win,* written in 1988 by YWAM Urban Ministries founder Floyd McClung and Pacific Islander Kalafi Moala, provided an overview of several values that had previously been communicated only through personally delivered teachings. It included chapters on several people groupings including Buddhists, Muslims, children, and urban dwellers. The 140-page book dedicated six pages to "The Poor and Needy."

However, perhaps the most innovative book was a holistic atlas that was the brainchild of University of the Nations advisory board member Frank Kaleb Jansen.

Copublished in 1989 by the U of N and Global Mapping International, *Target Earth* was a compilation of maps, statistics, and articles by YWAMers and various mission experts which promoted "the necessity of diversity in a holistic perspective on world mission." The foreword described the content as "both tragedy and accessible opportunity . . . undergirded and informed by vibrant hope." It was meant to serve as a strategic tool for Christians to implement change in various spheres through research and planning, prayer, encouragement, and action. On the back cover of *Target Earth* was an endorsement by Loren Cunningham that reflected a holistic mindset: "Creation is the basis for value and purpose because He made us in His image. That's why the Gospel affects every category of life. For this reason we must reach every person with the Gospel." This was consistent with Cunningham's *Spheres of Influence*, which he had preached for more than a decade.

Although YWAM had not released formal statements or papers, it had been a signatory to the 1974 *Lausanne Covenant*, which included a section on Christian Social Responsibility.[35] YWAM also affirmed the 1981 *Christian Magna Carta* and the 1988 *Manila Covenant*, the latter of which affirmed "the Lordship of Christ over every sphere of life" and expressed a commitment "to love people in both word and deed" and to "perform acts of mercy so that men and women will embrace the truth of the Gospel."[36]

The 1990s: More Integrated Thinking

By the 1990s, some of the more influential ministries in YWAM were Frontier Missions and Strategic Missions, which were at least partly influenced by the church-planting emphasis of the U.S. Center for World Mission and by pressure from more traditional mission agencies. YWAM's Frontier Missions described itself as "a movement within YWAM that focuses on church planting among the least evangelized peoples of the world."[37]

Because of the focus on church planting among unreached people groups, there had been some tension surrounding some Frontier Missions (FM) efforts that were not directly related to evangelism and personal discipleship. This struggle was further evidence of the Great Reversal's legacy in evangelical missions. However, at times YWAM Frontier Missions workers were convinced that meeting physical and other needs is a valuable component of demonstrating the gospel. As a former YWAMer involved in holistic work stated, "You can't try to do evangelism in India, for example, without being faced with overwhelming physical needs and the incredible sense that word without deed is not truly life giving."[38]

While YWAM Strategic Frontiers (SF) also planted churches, it differentiated itself from FM in two main ways: by (1) working closely with the Western church in forming strategic alliances with indigenous churches, and (2) empowering indigenous churches to transform all aspects of life. SF took its cue from the U.S. Center that planting churches is a key first step to societal transformation.

At the same time, YWAM Mercy Ministries (MMI) began to shift its focus from short-term relief to long-term development goals. In the 1990s, MMI staff began to grapple with strategic solutions to human poverty and to voice these concerns to the mission at large.

At a 1990 Mercy Ministries conference, a covenant was drafted and several key issues were discussed. They included integrating approaches to relief and development, trends for the 1990s, and focusing on unreached peoples.[39] MMI was starting to understand the rest of their "Go!" mandate, which appears more completely in the Matthew reference than in Mark's. "Therefore go and *make disciples* of *all nations,* baptizing them in the name of the Father and of the Son and of the Holy Spirit, and *teaching them to obey everything* I have commanded you" (Matt. 28:19–20, italics added). This is what David Moberg had described in his 1972 treatise on the Great Reversal:

> Too many Christians have failed to recognize the full import of the Great Commission of Jesus Christ. They emphasize the evangelistic and missionary commands of its first three instructions (to go, make disciples, and baptize them), but they totally overlook the fourth, "teaching them to observe all that I have commanded you" (Matt. 28:20). It is here that Christian social concern lies.[40]

YWAM's University of the Nations began to champion holistic ministry by inviting church leaders to address Christian holism, often referred to as "community development." In U of N courses and workshops, Darrow Miller of Food for the Hungry shared his perspectives on world hunger, explaining some of the less obvious reasons for poverty and proposing a biblical response. A disciple of the late theologian Francis Schaeffer, Miller sought to expose the fallacies of Christian dualism and challenged YWAMers to consider new ways of thinking about "discipling nations." YWAMers began to exchange their modernistic concept of individualized faith for a more communal and inclusive understanding of holistic salvation.

Miller was a key speaker at the U of N's 1997 international workshop in Korea, along with Indian philosopher and author Vishal Mangalwadi and Global Harvest Foundation's Bob Moffitt, both of whom also emphasized the broader understanding of the Great Commission. Moffitt said in an interview:

> Holistic ministry means ministering the fullness of God's intentions for all creation, not only for the brokenness of our souls, but to be His representatives

in the restoration of the social brokenness as well as the physical and spiritual brokenness.[41]

At the same event, YWAM Community Development Centre director Christine Colby also attempted to redefine community development:

Often when people define development, they think [of] physical [things]. They think of water systems, they think of latrines, they think of healthcare from the physical aspect. But if we look at it from a biblical perspective, we're looking at God's intentions for a people, and moving people toward God's intentions for their lives.[42]

Miller published a book in 1999 titled *Discipling Nations: The Power of Truth to Transform Cultures*. The book was endorsed by Loren Cunningham, who wrote, "Darrow Miller points the way to the frontiers of the twenty-first century for all who are committed to the Great Commission. *Discipling Nations* is a 'must' for mission leaders." The idea of discipling nations became a vital element of YWAM rhetoric in the late 1990s and into the new century.

Several YWAMers also began forming theologies of discipling nations and spread them through articles and teachings. Landa Cope's study, teaching series, and book on *The Old Testament Template: Relearning to Disciple Nations God's Way* underscored the need to understand and teach biblical principles for the domains outlined by Cunningham in the 1970s. Cope stressed the church's responsibility to implement and teach them at individual and corporate levels. Her website stated, "Our goal is to help bring vital, relevant, effective Christian thought and action back into the twenty-first century."[43]

In 1998 some of YWAM's Mercy Ministries, Frontier Missions, and Urban Ministries staff met to draft several documents that were subsequently ratified by YWAM's Global Leadership Team, and presented to the international staff. They included statements and recommendations concerning several issues including justice, gender, and life span. The collaboration on these documents was significant because it represented further steps toward a unified and coherent theology, worldview, and basis for mission.

At the time, MMI director Steve Goode expressed an effort by YWAM Mercy Ministries to articulate a cohesive message on social issues:

Issues that need to be looked at, for example, for women are poverty, education, widows, health, violence, armed conflict, economic empowerment; for children, for example, orphanages, education, poverty, infanticide and on and on. As we start to reach out to the poor and needy, the one billion that are living in absolute poverty, we're going to face these issues. So for us as a mission, we have to review how we're going to approach some of these areas.[44]

Mercy Ministries ratified a "Statement and Recommendations Concerning Issues of Justice" in 1998. The document drew attention to gender, race, economics, religious beliefs, social justice, health, education, and food and shelter. The paper affirmed principles and made recommendations for YWAM.[45]

The New Millennium

As YWAM entered the new millennium, a more holistic worldview began to exponentially permeate the rhetoric and ministry. The 2004 tsunami catapulted Mercy Ministries to yet another level as they sought to bring short-term relief and long-term development and recovery into predominantly Buddhist and Muslim regions. Long- and short-term teams worked in cleanup and rebuilding as well as counseling, providing kid-safe zones such as preschools and daycare centers, sponsoring community support programs, and aiding with livelihood restoration.[46] In other regions, they continue to "meet the felt needs of individuals and communities, children at risk, refugees and those living on the edge of survival in both crisis and long term development situations."[47]

The publication of this book, *His Kingdom Come*, was an effort to continue fueling a movement that understands and embraces Jesus' mandate to "go and disciple nations." It followed two significant YWAM events. The first was "Connexity," a conference on women's issues (not a women's conference) held in Malaysia in 2002. It focused on the unique needs of girls and women worldwide and how they are impacted by violence, armed conflict, economics, education, family, reproductive rights, and politics, as well as the special needs of the girl-child. A postmodern mix of dance, drama, visuals, and messages delivered from a diverse roster of speakers brought home the reality that girls and women are the poorest and most abused of humanity.

A year later, a University of the Nations workshop "Synergy 2003" in Singapore was focused completely on three topics: (1) children at risk, (2) the universal need for clean water, and (3) issues of justice. Both Connexity and Synergy were deliberate attempts by YWAM leaders to recognize global issues and to challenge YWAM ministries (no matter their emphasis) and University of the Nations courses (no matter what their title) to integrate holistic kingdom thinking into their core philosophy.

YWAM's staff magazine, *The International YWAMer*, published more than two dozen articles in recent years on the status of women, business and microenterprise, children, war, injustice, AIDS, and other challenges facing the world. These add to a steady stream of socially conscious rhetoric in YWAM, with statements such as: "We serve a God who suffers with those who suffer;"[48] "This is a hurting world,"[49] "Bringing help and hope to the downcast of our world;"[50] "To reach the poor with both medical and spiritual hope,"[51] and "Because we're a mission that's been called to impact the world, to share the Gospel with all peoples, we must address the issues that the world is hurting with."[52]

"Transforming Cultures through Kingdom Thinking" was the title of the YWAM North American Leaders Conference in 2001, with Darrow Miller as the sole speaker. Unlike colonial and paternalistic models of the past, the philosophy behind "kingdom thinking" is to *enable* people to "achieve all that God has for them." In other words, it is to help individuals and nations realize biblical transformation at every level. There is growing comfort with the phrase "the kingdom of God," one that evangelicals came to avoid because of ties to the social gospel during the Great Reversal.

Used increasingly in the mission, "kingdom of God" terminology describes a theology that seeks to transform nations using the entire Bible. YWAM International Chairman Jim Stier wrote in a 2001 article:

> We must preach both the gospel of salvation and the gospel of the Kingdom of God. [But] the Kingdom doesn't exist without personal salvation. To teach a type of personal salvation that doesn't produce integrity, compassion, and social involvement is to reduce the gospel to a mere ticket to heaven. . . . Many times you can only bring substantial and lasting help to individuals by changing the whole community or nation at the level of its collective conscience and values. . . . We need to show them the life of Christ in the way we love one another, the way we live, relate to one another, and do business. This will eventually effect society's institutions, laws, and attitude.[53]

Conclusion

In his landmark 1972 book, David Moberg stressed the importance of a holistic gospel. He wrote, "Evangelism and social concern are reciprocally linked in a number of ways. To see them as separate and antithetical is to be caught up in the false dichotomies that so often paralyze the Christian life and witness."[54]

It seems that despite the times in which he started Youth With A Mission, Cunningham understood this truth. Some believe he and his mission have played a significant role in bringing back a biblical balance, toward reversing the Great Reversal.

Others think the mission is in the initial stages of understanding the holistic nature of the gospel. The significance of this study is that it documents a process of maturing. YWAM, like the church at large, seems to be returning to a fuller understanding of the gospel, one that existed before the Great Reversal. Consequently, it is emerging as a mission better equipped to model Christ's example.

At the time of this publication, YWAM has more than 16,000 staff at some 1,100 operating locations in more than 170 countries.[55] The idea of discipling nations seems to be slowly moving from a wake-up call to bona fide holistic ministry in various parts of the world. Terms such as *business as mission* and *global response* are increasingly used as YWAMers talk about their ministry expressions. *Voice for the Voiceless* is a prayer initiative to draw attention to gender injustice.[56] YWAM is increasingly involved in HIV/AIDS, both raising awareness of the issue and working with orphans and others who have been affected. However, despite all these efforts in business, working for justice, and other compassion ministries, there is still much work to be done. The Great Reversal was a period of time where much of the church turned a blind eye to human need. Will YWAM help undo this trend, to reverse the Great Reversal?

It occurs to me as I complete this chapter, that Jesus' mandate at the end of his ministry, to "go and make disciples," only makes sense within the context of how he defined his own ministry. Note the passage from Luke 4 where Jesus explains his purpose:

> The Spirit of the Lord is on me, because he has anointed me to preach good news to the poor. He has sent me to proclaim freedom for the prisoners and recovery of sight for the blind, to release the oppressed, to proclaim the year of the Lord's favor.[57]

Curiously, Jesus' message here had seemingly little to do with what modern evangelicals identify as *spiritual* ministry. Rather, he showed concern for every aspect of humanity and proclaimed he would demonstrate as well as articulate a message of redemption to all the aspects of enslavement and dysfunction of earth.

Following Jesus' example, a handful of individuals throughout history considered it their Christian duty to build the kingdom of God on earth. Martin Luther fought vigorously for the education of poor children and for low-interest loans for workers. William Wilberforce dedicated his life to the abolition of the slave trade and the reformation of manners; he was a founding member of both the Church Missionary Society and the Society for the Prevention of Cruelty to Animals. William Carey was a missionary to India, translating the Bible into several languages and dialects. As a scholar and humanitarian, he also founded a university, an Agricultural and Horticultural Society, and a savings bank; published dictionaries and books on grammar and botany; and fought for the conservation of forests. Susan B. Anthony championed women's rights, and Martin Luther King Jr. led a nation to consider racial equality. These deeply committed people of faith led movements that brought redemption to millions.

Along with many Christians of the new millennium, the YWAM movement is realizing that it does not have to choose between the salvation of individuals and the redemption of society. Its workers are reconnecting with the reality that the kingdom of God is a central theme of the Bible that invites all people of faith to work toward shalom and help reverse the Great Reversal.

Notes

1. Dr. Robert Linthicum, personal communication, July 8, 2004. Dr. Linthicum is executive director of Partners in Urban Transformation—based in Los Angeles, California—and is the former director of the Office of Urban Advance for World Vision International. He is author of several books and the primary teacher of *Building A People of Power* video series (available from www.thinkagainresources.org).

2. *Biblesoft's New Exhaustive Strong's Numbers and Concordance with Expanded Greek-Hebrew Dictionary* (Biblesoft and International Bible Translators, Inc., 1994).

3. *The Online Bible Thayer's Greek Lexicon and Brown Driver & Briggs Hebrew Lexicon* (Ontario, Canada: Woodside Bible Fellowship, licensed from the Institute for Creation Research, 1993).

4. The term "rhetoric" is not a negative one, but simply a term that describes how language is used. This paper is a rhetorical analysis of the language used in YWAM concerning holistic ministry, revealing how YWAMers were both processing and articulating the struggle to understand ministry from a biblical perspective.

4. P. E. Pierson, "Missions and Community Development: A Historical Perspective," in E. J. Elliston, ed., *Christian Relief and Development: Developing Workers for Effective Ministry* (Dallas: Word, 1989), 7–22.

5. Ronald J. Sider, ed., *Evangelicals and Development: Toward a Theology of Social Change* (Philadelphia: Westminster Press, 1981).

6. The Catholic Encyclopedia, Volume 9, s.v. "Manichaeism," (by J. P. Arendzen), www.newadvent.org/cathen/09591a.htm (accessed November 3, 2001).

7. The Catholic Encyclopedia, Volume 10, s.v. "Neo-Platonism," (by W. Turner), www.newadvent.org/cathen/10742b.htm (accessed November 8, 2001)

8. www.faithnet.org.uk, "St. Augustine of Hippo," accessed October 10, 2001, from www.faithnet.freeserve.co.uk/augustine.htm, which was moved to www.faithnet.org.uk /Theology/augustine.htm (accessed April 16, 2007).

9. Timothy L. Smith was a pastor, historian, and prolific writer. His first book, published in 1957, was *Revivalism and Social Reform.* Many of his thought-provoking articles can be found on the Internet.

10. D. O. Moberg, *The Great Reversal: Evangelism Versus Social Concern: An Evangelical Perspective* (Philadelphia: Holmon, 1972), 34.

11. Ibid., 35.

12. There were some voices throughout the twentieth century who tried to steer the church back to a holistic perspective. One of the most notable was Carl F. Henry, who wrote extensively on moral arguments for evangelical and political activism. Much of his material is available online for further reading.

13. D. Hawkinson, producer, *Birth of A Ministry,* video, 1979.

14. N. Wilson and R. Wilson, *Journey with the Followers: A Story of Youth With A Mission* (Hong Kong: World Outreach Publishers, 1969), 2.

15. See recent YWAM Statement of Faith in Appendix A of this book.

16. Jennifer Esterly, "Dallas and Larry," in International YWAMer, February 2000, 4–6. Also available at: www.ywam.org/articles/article.asp?AID=71 (accessed April 16, 2007).

17. Loren Cunningham, *Is That Really You God?* (Grand Rapids: Chosen Books, 1984), 63.

18. By 1989, 366 operating locations had been established, 120 of which housed training programs, as cited in G. Dryden and A. Kim, *The Go Manual: Global Opportunities in Youth with A Mission* (Seattle: YWAM Publishing, 1999). YWAM boasted a worldwide staff of around 6,400. This number was to double in the next ten years.

19. The Mind Molders have recently been renamed respectively to: Church, Family, Media, Government, Education, Economics, and Celebration.

20. See Founding Principles of the University of the Nations in Appendix B of this book.

21. Jim Stier, personal communication, April 20, 2001.

22. Hawkinson, *Birth of a Ministry.*

23. Paul Martinson, "The Development of Leadership in Youth With A Mission: A Study in a Contemporary Mission's History, Leadership Development and Current Leadership Challenges," (Unpublished manuscript, 1996).

24. Mercy Ships remained a vital part of Youth With A Mission until it grew and eventually spun off as a separate ministry in 2003.

25. Don Stephens, personal communication, April 17, 2001.

26. Christine Sine, "Responsibility to the Poor and Needy" (unpublished message notes).

27. Hawkinson, *Birth of a Ministry.*

28. Debra Buenting, producer, "Mercy Ships," *Newsight,* CBN Cable, 1988.

29. P. Kirby, *Mercy Ships Is . . .* (Lindale, Tex.: Mercy Ships International, 1998).

30. Don Stephens, personal communication, April 17, 2001.

31. See article on Mother's Love in J. M. Lau, "To Save a Child," *Reader's Digest,* 909 (January 1998).

32. Martinson, "Development of Leadership," 19.

33. Ibid., 20.

34. See the social responsibility section of the Lausanne Covenant in Appendix C of this book.

35. The Manila Covenant 4. Available at www.ywam.org/contents/abo_doc_manila.htm (accessed April 16, 2007).

36. "What is Frontier Missions?" March 15, 2001, www.ywamfm.org/frontier.html (accessed July 8, 2004).

37. Jane Overstreet, personal communication, April 13, 2001.

38. Steve Goode, personal communication, April 27, 2001.

39. Moberg, *The Great Reversal,* 155.

40. Bob Moffit, video interview (Korea: Procla-Media Productions, 1997).

41. Christine Colby, video interview (Korea: Procla-Media Productions, 1997).

42. Landa Cope, *The Old Testament Template: Relearning to Disciple Nations God's Way,* video series, (Colorado Springs: Crown Ministries International, 1999).

43. Steve Goode, video interview (Fortaleza, Brazil: Procla-Media Production, 1998).

44. "Statement and Recommendation Concerning Issues of Justice" formed at the YWAM Mercy Ministries International Consultation in Jimtien, Thailand, April 1998.

45. Mercy Ministries International, "Tsunami Recovery Report—February 2006," www.ywam-mercy.org/slideshow/index.htm, www.ywam-mercy.org/tsunami_report.html (accessed April 14, 2007).

46. Mercy Ministries International, "About Us," www.ywam-mercy.org (accessed April 14, 2007).

47. B. Boorujy and J. Bull, *Faces of the Poor: YWAM Thailand,* video (Amsterdam: Procla-Media Productions, 1989).

48. *The YWAM Story,* video (Colorado Springs:Procla-Media Productions, 1994).

49. *Cargo: Compassion,* video (Lindale, Tex.: Mercy Ships Video Productions, 1996).

50. *Mercy Ships 20 Years and Counting: The History of Mercy Ships,* video (Lindale, Tex.: Mercy Ships Video Productions, 1997).

51. David Hamilton, video interview (Fortaleza, Brazil: Procla-Media Productions, 1997).

52. Jim Stier, "Disciple all Nations: God's Character Demands It," *The International YWAMer* (June 2001), www.ywam.org/articles/article.asp?AID=96 (accessed April 20, 2007).

53. Moberg, *The Great Reversal,* 152.

54. See complete list of YWAM statistics online at www.ywam.org/contents/sta_res _stats.htm.

55. See http://photogenx.net/index.htm for *30 Days of Prayer for the Voiceless* resources.

56. Luke 4:18–19 NIV. For a comprehensive explanation of this passage, listen to Dr. Gregory Boyd's sermon, "The Holistic Kingdom" from January 14, 2007, available as a podcast from iTunes or from www.whchurch.org/content/page_26.htm.

Throughout history God has been at work to bring transformation in individuals and nations. Our day is no exception. Recent events in the nation of Fiji are a stirring example of what can happen when a nation seeks God's face and looks to his Word for answers to all areas of life. In this encouraging example, we see that discipling the nations reaches beyond people, society, and culture to affect even the land.

Case Study:
Fiji—A Dramatic Return to Life

Loren Cunningham

Nations are grappling with matters of life and death on many fronts: racial tensions, environmental destruction, poverty, corruption, AIDS and other plagues, and the list goes on. They are looking for answers. If we as God's people have life-giving solutions, we can have a profound influence for the kingdom.

So where do we get answers for these difficult and complex issues? Discipling nations must be based on the truths of God's Word. He has given us counsel on how to live individually and corporately in all areas of life. However, when we come to his Word, it is not enough to scan its pages for solutions. We must go beyond that, inviting the Holy Spirit to give us revelation, to open our eyes to specific applications of his Word for our communities. When we do this, we will be surprised at how many issues God has addressed in his Word.

As we invite the Spirit to give us revelation, we *must* be ready to obey whatever he shows us to do. Then we will find the answers we need to see transformation. Sometimes the life brought by the Spirit and the Word can be quite literal and utterly amazing. In the case of Fijians seeking God's will, they saw transformation of individuals, their society, and even their land itself.

Fiji: A Dramatic Return to Life

In 2004 I had an unusual visit from three representatives of the nation of Fiji to our YWAM University of the Nations campus in Kona, Hawaii. The men were sent on an important errand by the government, the Great Council of Chiefs, and the pastors of Fiji.

We introduced our distinguished guests at a public gathering of eight hundred YWAM staff and students. The men wore Fijian *sulus*—tailored sarongs worn with Western-style shirts. With great dignity they sat cross-legged on the floor of our large pavilion and began to make solemn speeches in typical island fashion. First they honored me by presenting me with a whale's tooth. I learned later that they give out very few of these. Whales' teeth are passed from generation to generation in families of chiefs and royalty. To present a person with one is the highest honor Fijians can give. When they give you a whale's tooth, they are linking you to them and to their history in a deep bond of commitment.

As the men's speeches were translated from Fijian, we learned their purpose in coming. They were asking YWAM's help in fulfilling God's destiny for their nation. Would we come to Fiji and give them more teaching from the Word of God?

For the past few years, Fiji has seen the start of a national awakening. It all began after Fiji went through two violent coups in 2000. Although the authorities put down the rebellion and imprisoned the instigators, the leaders of Fiji felt their country had been diminished in the eyes of the world. Their economy was in trouble. Their youth were going astray. Their country was losing its direction in every category.

A Unique Foot-Washing Meeting

For those unfamiliar with this nation, Fiji is the number one communication, education, and commercial center of the South Pacific (Polynesia and Melanesia). Its population is just over half indigenous Fijian (mostly Christians) and nearly half Indo-Fijian (largely Hindus and Muslims), whose ancestors were brought to Fiji as laborers during the British colonial era.

In recent years, some Fijians began to resent the Indo-Fijians' financial and political successes. In an outbreak of violence in 2000, Fijians looted and burned Indian stores. Insurgents raped Indo-Fijian women and injured many. The violence left eight dead.[1]

During this terrible time for his country, the new prime minister, Laisenia Qarase, went to the pastors and godly leaders, asking them to end the quarreling between denominations. He felt that bitterness in the body of Christ had helped lead to the deep national divisions in the country. The spiritual leaders came together, asking one another's forgiveness for malice and slander.

Then Prime Minister Qarase asked the pastors to find out what God wanted the country to do. The church leaders began to fast and pray. The prime minister and the president joined them, also calling for the people of the nation to fast and pray.

After they restored political stability, Prime Minister Qarase organized a gathering in Albert Park in Suva, Fiji's capital. Virtually all the church leaders were there, as were the political leaders. They made formal apologies to the Indo-Fijian community and to the public. Then in a stunning act of public contrition, the prime minister got down on his knees before the opposition leader, Mahendra Chaudhry, a Hindu, and asked his forgiveness. Next, the prime minister reached for a basin and a towel and washed his political opponent's feet.[2]

Hundreds of Fijians followed their prime minister's example that day in Albert Park, going to one another, weeping and asking forgiveness.

Healing the Land

Repentance and restitution didn't stop after that day in Albert Park. Pastors continued to meet together, asking God how to bring healing to their land and how they should advise the government leaders.

As the pastors sought the Lord, they came up with a specific plan. This plan, now being implemented, includes a mobile team of pastors and lay volunteers called Healing the Land. This team is ready to go into any village whose chief invites them. There they fast and pray for a week on-site. Then they visit all the people, going from house to house. They hold Bible teaching every night. The schedule is structured and comprehensive, with teaching on basic subjects and opportunities for the people to respond in repentance and spiritual warfare.

Bill Efinger and a team from YWAM Kona recently went along with the Healing the Land team on one of their visits. They traveled to the village of Saunaka, population five hundred.

Repenting in the Hot Sun

Bill said, "Every night the entire village came out to hear the Bible teaching." After the team thoroughly laid out the conditions for repentance and reconciliation, they gave the people the chance to respond. The entire village made a covenant to serve the Lord Jesus Christ. Everyone. One hundred percent. On Saturday they gathered for a formal time of repentance and reconciliation. All day long they sat cross-legged on the ground in the hot sun. The heads of clans and subclans, their chief, and the people took turns publicly confessing their sins to the community.

"It was dignified, according to island protocol, but we could feel their passion," Bill said. "We were amazed as the interpreters kept us aware of what was being said. The Fijians were making themselves completely transparent, asking forgiveness." A widow confessed she had been living off of money that her late husband had stolen from the church over the years. The athletes of the village—the soccer team, the rugby players, and the volleyball team—got up in front of the community. All the lanky youths stood quietly with their heads bowed as their chosen spokesman asked forgiveness for their rebellion, drunkenness, and disobedience to parents.

George Otis Jr. tells in his documentary *Let the Sea Resound* of similar meetings going on in fourteen villages of Fiji.[3] In one village where their forefathers had killed and eaten a missionary in the nineteenth century, the Fijians were stricken with guilt. They paid for the airfare to fly the victim's descendants in from England so they could ask their forgiveness in person.

In other acts of repentance, marijuana growers uprooted and burned 13,864 plants in the highlands of Fiji, worth an estimated eleven million dollars. A leader in the reconciliation movement, Savenaca Nakauyaca, says, "They realized they were guilty of defiling the land and under God's curse, [so they] gave up drug farming and gave their hearts to God."[4]

Others have abandoned witchcraft rituals passed on from their forefathers. Bill Efinger told of watching the villagers of Saunaka burn all their idols and articles of witchcraft in a large field.

All of this process has been saturated with Bible teaching. The Healing the Land team holds intensive Bible studies in converted villages, showing them how to live their lives personally and as a group.

As the people have repented and started living rightly, God has brought literal life back to their land.

Healing the Environment

An incredible thing occurred in the seaside village of Rukua. The coral reef near this village had begun to die some years ago. Since their livelihood depended on the fish that fed off the coral reef, the villagers were becoming desperate. After they humbled themselves before God, their coral reef came back to life and the fish returned.[5] Think about that! It takes hundreds of years for a coral reef to grow. But God restored their coral reef literally overnight. Now the same thing has happened in another village, Nateleira.

In the village of Nuku, up in the interior of Naitasiri, the primary source of water had been polluted and acidic for more than forty years. Three days after the villagers' repentance, Nakauyaca says, "God healed the creek." It became clean and pure again.[6]

Fijians are telling similar stories all around the country. In some places, fish have returned to lifeless areas of the sea. In another place wild pigs were destroying the crops. They suddenly went away. As these stories have accumulated, chiefs and other leaders in the islands are inviting the Healing the Land team to their areas. In a number of places where they've ministered, the team has seen 100 percent of the people repent and declare their allegiance to Jesus Christ.

Rewriting the Scripts

The Word of God is not just affecting the interior, either. Vini Guanavinaka, a leader of YWAM's School of Biblical Counseling in Kona, says of her native Fiji, "There is an increased response to evangelism . . . and a new desire to integrate Christianity into everyday life." She said Indo-Fijians, mostly Hindus, are now coming to the Lord as well.

The number of believers has doubled. Revival is also bearing fruit on a personal level.[7]

In the business world, Fijian Kalara Vusoniwailala says, "In [the capital city of] Suva, almost every business has a Bible study going during the week. There is an awakening, and they want to understand the implications of their faith."[8]

Similarly, groups of professionals in the media meet regularly to delve into the Word, asking God how to conduct themselves in their industry. Vini tells of one prominent TV personality who rewrites the scripts to be sure the news presentation is fair.[9]

I don't think I've seen a more literal demonstration of 2 Chronicles 7:14 in my lifetime. We promised the Fijian delegates who came to seek our help to do everything in our power to help maximize what was going on. We will be giving more training in Fiji. Our goal is to help the people spread this transformation beyond their borders.

This kind of thing isn't just for Fiji. God promises every one of us, "If my people, who are called by my name, will humble themselves and pray and seek my face and turn from their wicked ways, then will I hear from heaven and will forgive their sin and will heal their land" (2 Chron. 7:14). I look forward to seeing what happens next. We'll see what God does in Fiji and in the nations where Fijians go as missionaries.

Notes

This chapter is adapted from chapter 30, "The Spirit and the Word," of Loren Cunningham's book *The Book That Transforms Nations: The Power of the Bible to Change Any County* (Seattle: YWAM Publishing, 2007). Used by permission.

1. "Mutinies of Fiji Coup of 2000," Wikipedia, http://en.wikipedia.org/wiki/2000 _Fijian_coup_d%27%C3%A9tat (accessed December 9, 2007).

2. Some may wonder why Qarase was asking forgiveness for something he didn't do personally—the coup and violent acts against Indo-Fijians. He was following a biblical pattern

demonstrated by Nehemiah (see Neh. 1:6–7) and Ezra (see Ezra 9:5–7). Even though you haven't personally done the sins committed by your nation or by your forefathers, you can ask God's forgiveness. This allows God to begin to heal your country.

3. *Let the Sea Resound,* DVD, directed by George Otis Jr. (Lynnwood, Wash.: The Sentinel Group, 2004).

4. George Otis Jr., "Pattern for Blessing," *Explorer Reports,* The Sentinel Group, http://sentinelgroup.org/explorer.asp.

5. *Let the Sea Resound.*

6. Otis Jr., "Pattern for Blessing."

7. Lisa Orvis, "Fiji," *Transformations* (October 2003): 8.

8. Orvis, "Fiji," 9.

9. Ibid.

Part 4

Philosophy of Ministry

What did Jesus envision when he prayed, "Thy will be done on earth as it is in heaven?" What role did he instruct and equip the church to take in response to his prayer? Dean Sherman brings clarity and insight to who we are as a church, and what it means to live in and usher in the kingdom of God.

The Church and the Kingdom

Dean Sherman

Huge amounts of dialog and controversy have swirled around the concepts of *church* and *kingdom* throughout history. These two words have come to mean many different things to societies and cultures. Yet it is what we understand about these two functions that determines how we are going to live and what we are going to do in obedience to Jesus' commands. This chapter probes our role in being the church and extending the kingdom.

What Is the Church?

The most basic biblical idea of *church* is the community of believers. The church includes everyone who has come to faith in Jesus Christ. Everyone who has passed from death unto life is a part of the church. Everyone who has accepted the benefits of the atonement of Jesus Christ by repentance and faith and thereby been forgiven, given eternal life, justified before God, regenerated, born of the Spirit, and saved, is a member of the church. All those in whom Jesus lives are the church. Therefore you are either in the world or in the church. According to Scripture, there is nothing beside or between.

Moreover, the church is always seen in the New Testament as something corporate: the body of Christ, the building of God, a holy nation, a people belonging to God. We are all baptized by one Spirit into one body (1 Cor. 12:13). We are built together to become a dwelling in which God lives by his Spirit (Eph. 2:22). So the same process that makes me individually a child of God, makes me also a member of the church. I become one with God and one with others in Christ by one act. There is understanding to be gained here for both individualistic and group cultures.

Through history, cultures have adapted the concept of *church,* and church now is viewed in several other ways. Some understand church as an authority vested in a hierarchical leadership, with the rest of us communing with "the church" for our life and direction. Others recognized the "priesthood of all believers," but have developed the idea of church to mean human institutions and corporate structures to assist with accountability for members and for society at large. We show practical commitment to the church entire by becoming a member of a particular corporate structure, "I belong to that church." We speak of church as a place to go, "I go to church"; or as a meeting of believers, "Church starts at eleven"; or as a building, "That's our church on the corner." This contemporary cultural terminology is here to stay. We must thus live with it, yet remain ever mindful of the scriptural meaning of church as the community of believers.

A Church or The Church?

To do the task of discipling nations, we need to be clear about how we use the word *church.* Sometimes we think of church as one of many spheres of influence in our society. Then it is the ecclesiastical structure, which may be placed alongside business, government, etc. That is accurate, and in that role we need to reach the lost and nurture the saved. The church has a job of self-propagation through evangelism and of building itself up in love through various ministries in the fellowship of body life (Eph. 4). Therefore, we have developed the idea of "church planting." Every place, people, and individual needs access to nurturing fellowships that can provide a vehicle of worship, care, growth, and sending. These groups could be called the congregating church.

Another way to look at church is as all believers, in all of life, functioning in all spheres. This is the view that we have let drop somewhat and have replaced by the Greek categories of secular and sacred. When Jesus said, "I will build my church," he wasn't just meaning the planting of groups to meet together on Sundays. When Paul wrote to "the church at Ephesus," he wasn't just instructing them on how to conduct their services. He was giving Holy Spirit directives to all believers who would ever read that letter about how they were to live and function in everything, on every day, and in every way.

If all who are alive in Jesus are "the church," then they are the church not only while they are congregating on Sunday. They are equally as much members of the body of Christ while at the job on Tuesday. Because all parts of a body have unique and important gifting, each of us, as parts of Christ's body, possesses gifts. These gifts are used during our congregating but are also used in marriage, for business, or as a diplomat for the nation. The gifts of Ephesians 4, for instance, are certainly needed to build up the body and to edify the saints. But they are also needed to equip the saints for works of service (v. 12). Are those works of service only intended to be applicable in the congregated "services," or are they given to serve the needs of humanity as a whole? Are the manifestations of the spirit mentioned in 1 Corinthians 12:8–10 only to function when believers gather, or should we start seeing supernatural knowledge used on the unconverted like the woman at the well (John 4) as Jesus did? Should we expect miracles at everyday events, such as the party in John 2 where Jesus met a practical and social need by turning water into wine?

As a specific example, let's examine the concept of Christian leaders. The congregating church has always had leaders anointed by God. We will, of course, continue to need leadership over and participation in the congregating function of the church. We will probably continue to call these leaders pastors, elders, deacons, etc., until Jesus comes. That's fine. Some are now again beginning to be acknowledged as apostles and prophets, primarily within the confines of the congregating function. Are we ready to also acknowledge an apostolic entrepreneur, a prophetic consultant, or a pastoral healthcare professional? In other words, did the Holy Spirit give the gift of leadership just for use within the body of Christ, or did he intend that these servant leaders use their gifts in and for all society? Again, I believe the answer is yes.

Does this mean then that every born-again person is functioning as church when they are in their places of career or employment? I don't think so. I think our body-gifting "kicks in" when we are being deliberate to build the kingdom of God. For example, an entrepreneur is functioning out of an apostolic gift; if that believer intentionally utilizes the gift to build the kingdom, then there is kingdom fruit. There has be to a sense of call from God and a intentional strategy to reach people and to meet the needs of society rather than just expanding the company to a foreign market or being a believer in the marketplace. This purposeful, anointed interface of a full-stature church-building kingdom in society is what we could call *discipling nations*. We all have irrevocable gifts and callings from God himself. We must encourage one another to seek God and his specific will for our lives. Perhaps this is even part of seeking first his kingdom as opposed to seeking first to feed and clothe ourselves (Matt. 6).

We easily accept that individual believers have specific gifts. Can we expand our concepts to see that not only individuals, but also various structures within the body are specifically gifted? For example, local churches are primarily gifted pastorally, missions agencies might be primarily gifted as apostolic or evangelistic, and training institutions or translators as obviously having a teaching anointing. If we continue to acknowledge only certain structures to be legitimately "church," it begs the question from 1 Corinthians 12: If the whole body were an eye, where would the hearing be? Or, if the hand is not the foot, is it any less a part of the body?

Are only a few gifts appropriate for using in these Christian structures? I think not! For too long we have allowed primarily only those who are theologically trained Bible teachers to be considered as having ministry gifts or to become missionaries. Even recently, when "lay" people have become increasingly involved, they find that the slots of expression are mostly evangelism, Bible teaching, and congregational oversight. Are we limiting our effort and effectiveness in changing society by not allowing the whole body and the full stature of Christ to be presented to the world? Have we cut our labor force by 90 percent by not encouraging all Christ's gifts to function in both the congregation and the whole of society? The day is upon us when leaders in missions could just as likely be an MBA as a seminary graduate. Could we not envision engineers as serving by helping, physicians by healing, and politicians by serving the common good? If followers of Christ are called to these or any other career, should they not be seeking God for vision and empowering to do their job well, for his glory?

Thy Kingdom Come

In Matthew 16:18–19 Jesus announced in simple form what he had come to earth to do. To paraphrase, he said, "I am actually here to build my church. The gates of hell will not be able to withstand it. To that church I will give keys to the kingdom of heaven." Notice, the church is not the whole of the kingdom, but it has the authority, the tools, to bring the kingdom. The basic foundation of every prayer, Jesus said, would be for the kingdom to come. What is the kingdom coming? It is his will being done on earth as it is being done in heaven.

Church does not exist just to have congregational meetings. Regarding the kingdom, church has been assigned the tasks of bringing the kingdom, praying the kingdom to come, preaching the gospel of the kingdom. Above, we discussed the need for church to intentionally influence society. This influence is part of working with Jesus to bring the kingdom. The word for church used in the Greek text of Scripture, *ecclesia,* was taken from Greek governmental meetings where the reason for gathering was to make decisions, not to be spectators.

We will not always have church meetings, but his kingdom is from everlasting to everlasting. "Of the increase of his government and peace there shall be no end . . . his kingdom [established and upheld] with justice and righteousness [will last] forever" (Isa. 9:7).

How do we build kingdom? Jesus said the kingdom is like yeast that is put into the dough. It disappears but soon has an amazing and obvious effect on the dough. He said the kingdom was like seed to be scattered. Initially, it also disappears, but the grains have life within that eventually manifests in vibrant, fruitful harvest. He said the field where we scatter is the world, not just the church. As we perform the work we are called to with love for God and man, seeking to honor him in all we do, we are acting like yeast. We may feel that our work is insignificant or dead, but God may use it as a seed that he will grow into a strong kingdom tree.

The kingdom, then, is an invisible set of principles, a way of thinking, a worldview with values by which to live. The kingdom comprises the principles of truth and the precepts of Scripture that, in the final analysis, are the only way things actually work. This is the wisdom of God spoken of in Proverbs, the salt that affects the taste and preserves, the light that automatically dispels darkness. It is living unselfishly, loving God with everything, and loving neighbor as self. The kingdom is whatever the King rules. When we understand and submit to his principles, we come in some measure under the reign of the King.

The kingdom cannot be contained in an earthly structure. The kingdom is controlled only by the King and is above all other structures. Even the human institutions that start well tend to disintegrate into arenas controlled by powerful people. Structures simply model, introduce and implement kingdom. Truth is God's truth. Truth is absolute and universal and cannot be owned by any earthly structure. "Jesus said, 'My kingdom is not of this world. If it were, my servants would fight'" (John 18:36). He surely got that right. Think of all the strife and even violent action that has been elicited by assuming the kingdom was earthly structure or dogma. Having a Holy Roman Empire or referring to a section of the map as Christendom only led to oppression, control, and lots of funerals. Having the church take over and have dominion over society has been tried. It failed. Scripture is clear on the aspect of the kingdom that includes world domination. That aspect only happens when the King returns to earth.

Even today, we must resist all subtle attempts to make the kingdom "our thing" through sectarian control or isolated withdrawal through special teachings or practices. The kingdom is bigger than our structure. It is to be scattered through the whole of society. That scattering allows truth to reign and makes Jesus Lord "over the whole earth" (Zech. 14:9). Wherever the principles of truth are enacted, the kingdom has come and the King is reigning to some degree.

The foundational principle of truth, of course, is to submit to the King by accepting his love and forgiveness through the Cross. That's why evangelism will always be the vital ingredient. Jesus told Nicodemus, "No one can see [enter into] the kingdom of God unless he is born again" (John 3:3). This is the unalterable link between church and kingdom, and why the two are often seen as the same. The church is to demonstrate and pray the kingdom in, but the way to fully join the kingdom is to become a part of the community of believers. So, the presentation of the kingdom should lead to the planting of the church, and the planting of the church should lead to further manifesting of the kingdom. Church is who we are, and kingdom is how we live. Church is the vehicle, and kingdom is the result.

Discipling a nation doesn't require that every citizen be a Christian. It means that a significant proportion of the society functions under the principles of truth, that the dominant mind-set in the various spheres of influence is biblical. Wherever government is working well, it is probably because the principles of the kingdom are being implemented. Wherever corruption is absent, kingdom is present. Wherever justice, serving, mercy, love, giving, and trust function, the kingdom is alive.

A grave problem, however, is that many Christians are not living by kingdom principles or seeking first the kingdom. The result is starvation, AIDS, fatalism, and corruption. Others, not yet saved, live to some degree under kingdom principles, so they find things going well for them despite their lostness. Our job is to rectify both of these paradoxes. We need to teach Christians how to live in the kingdom by applying their biblical truth to every area of life. We must develop kingdom principles in society as a way of attracting people to a personal relationship with the King. The principles themselves can, but should not, serve as a substitute for the King. Wisdom will be required.

Sometimes Jesus presented salvation first, and sometimes he demonstrated and presented the kingdom first. This was often highlighted by another important biblical aspect of the kingdom: the supernatural. Romans 14:17 says, "The kingdom of God is not a matter of eating and drinking (the natural), but of righteousness, peace and joy in the Holy Spirit (the supernatural)." Jesus said, "If I drive out demons by the spirit of God, then the kingdom of God has come" (Matt. 12:28). For the kingdom to come, there has to be a displacement of another who has dominion and control over much of society, both practically and philosophically (Col. 1:13; 1 John 5:19). Thus, supernatural intervention, not just good planning, is required. For this reason, Jesus said to wait in Jerusalem for power (Acts 1:4–8). That's why Paul said to the Corinthians, "My message and my preaching... were with a demonstration of the Spirit's power" (1 Cor. 2:4). As believers, we must overthrow in the spirit realm the one who holds the thinking, and therefore the practice, of millions of people in bondage. One of the reasons there is a strong church in places where society is still in chaos is that it takes time for new believers to bring their thinking and practice into line with biblical truth, and still more time for believers to influence those around them.

I regularly visit some friends in a limited-access nation. A few years ago they were led into an area without a church or Christians, an area where the government said they could not live unless they would do something to help the people and the economy. It was a place of great poverty, crime, and despair. God led them to start a factory, a business. They interviewed and hired the local village people to prepare the building that the government had given them after approving the business plan. These same people became the employees of the company. Through the factory interface and the just and righteous dealing by my friends, most of these village people became believers. Now, every day before work the workers have times of singing. There are classes for the employees on parenting, marriage, how to handle finances, how to live in harmony in the village, and how to serve others—all from the same book. The company has now expanded to include a training center to develop skills and has opened an orphanage. The workers consistently perform projects to serve the elderly and poor of the villages. The local economy has totally changed. The tone of the local society has changed. Everybody wants to know why these factory people are so happy, humble, and loving. The government is not suspicious but thrilled with what they see. The kingdom is coming, the church exists, but it perhaps would not be recognized by many of us who have a narrow view of how to fulfill the commission.

Let's expand our concept of church and the kingdom so that we understand church to function in the whole of society. Every believer must seek his irrevocable gifts and callings from the Lord, his or her unique contribution to answering our collective prayer for the kingdom to come. Let us be the church and live the kingdom for our King.

Where do you fit in discipling nations? God is calling you to do kingdom works that he has planned and prepared for you. The Creator of the universe desires you to work alongside him as he crafts his work on planet earth. John Henry shares about finding your place in fulfilling God's plans for your community and for the nations.

A Conversation on Calling

John T. Henry

K im sat at the edge of the bench holding his head in his hands. "What am I supposed to do now? My education has prepared me better than most to 'make a living.' But once I have that living, I haven't the faintest idea what to do with it."

This was not a time for a cliché response. Do you know someone like Kim? Do you know someone who has a gift to give to the world without realizing he can use it to be a message of hope for his generation? Kim knew Jesus' parting words to his disciples, "Go and make disciples of all nations" (Matt. 28:19), but he had not yet taken those words into his heart and soul. Do you ever wonder what you are called to do and to be—maybe a doctor, a businessperson, a political leader, or a scientist? Is it possible to serve God's purpose of bringing the good news to every person as a journalist? Can a professor participate in teaching all nations to obey everything Christ commands? Can an architect help build the kingdom of God? Could it be that Christians who run the race in one of these typically nonreligious courses of life are also participating in the Great Commission? Kim raised his head to look at me when I told him he could know his calling by beginning a journey with God.

Kim's story is like that of tens of thousands who have followed the world's prescription for success and found a sense of insufficiency at the end of their university experience. Like Kim, they wonder if their field of study, their career, is indeed their "calling." Too often, even Christian students are asking, "What contribution can I make to the kingdom of God through my life work?"

Calling is no trivial pursuit. When we do not know our calling, it is like being asleep behind the wheel at night on a lonely highway. To wake up we need to lift our head, open our eyes and ears, turn on our headlights, and pay attention to where we are going. We may not know where we are right away, but we can pay attention to the road signs and obey what we do know. Like reading road signs, we can stop, turn around if we are heading the wrong direction, and follow God's instructions to find out where we are and where we should be going. As God's light shines on the road in front of us, we can begin to learn why God placed us on this road, and we can fulfill our purpose. When enough people wake up and follow God's road map, their calling begins to influence every area of life.

Kim looked at me and asked, "So that's what it means to make disciples of all nations?"

"Yes, your calling is God's personal invitation to you to use the gifts and the talent he gave you to work on his agenda with eternal consequences."

Every Christian has three progressive callings:

1. *We are called to salvation.* Salvation is the call to reconciliation. First, we are called to be reconciled to God. Then we are called to be ambassadors of reconciliation (2 Cor. 5:18). Salvation is a call to know and love God in saving faith. It is a call to obedience to the Word of God generally, as well as those things that need immediate attention as we "walk worthy of our calling" (Eph. 4:1). The call to salvation goes out to all humankind, and some respond.

2. *We are called to discipleship.* Discipleship is the second call, extended to all who receive salvation. It is a call to be conformed to the likeness of Christ (Rom. 8:29). As the call to abide in Christ and to bear fruit (John 15), discipleship includes pruning. Discipleship is the call to offer one's body, gifts, talents, and abilities as a living sacrifice, and the call to be transformed by the renewing of our minds (Rom. 12:1–2). As disciples, we respond to immediate needs and learn through acts of service.

3. *We are called to a vocation.* Vocation is our unique call of purpose, the call to serve beyond our daily tasks. Vocation is more than discipleship. Vocation is deeper and wider than career. Vocation is our very personal response to the voice of God. Vocation is our lifework, our special gift of worship, which is the sum of all our gifts, talents, and abilities to serve God's purpose in our generation (1 Cor. 3:13–15; 2 Tim. 2:5; 4:8).

Calling begins as God rescues us out of abandonment and rejection into a new life of acceptance through adoption. As an international student we had met through our ministry, Kim knew that we had adopted our daughter Rebecca a few years earlier. Rebecca was less than a week old when she was found abandoned on the street in China. While visiting our summer interns at orphanages in China, my wife and I held abandoned babies and our hearts broke. We entered room after room of crying babies failing to thrive because no one could offer a loving touch. We adopted Rebecca when God opened our eyes and our hearts and called us to offer our family to one of those little abandoned girls in China. What Kim did not know about Rebecca is the often hidden, painful therapy required for adopted children. Because of rejection at the time of birth, children develop an attachment disorder, which requires long sessions of holding, struggle, tears, and prayers. When children are rejected, they resist affection because something in their brains did not develop during infancy. Therefore, they cannot accept the loving arms of their new family. Imagine God's heartbreak when so many people struggle in family relationships and fail to know and serve God's purpose. Responding to the call of adoption into God's family has tremendous influence.

Perhaps Christians today need to consider why their witness is not having more influence in many parts of the world. Kim had completed his degree at one of the finest universities in the world. His relationship with Christ was shaken and he was no longer sure what he believed. Ideas, whether they be true or false ideas, have consequences on society. False ideas have kept individuals and whole communities captive from knowing and experiencing God's purpose, and the liberty that comes from the truth. Truth is not merely an idea, but a Person. Jesus said, "I am . . . the truth" (John 14:6). Waking up to the idea of calling will transform us.

"As I learn God's truth," Kim spoke up, "and respond to his call, I can begin to influence the world around me with his truth." The call of God will lead us from our private world of devotion to the public world of influence as a witness of Christ's kingdom.

Kim opened his Bible with me as I asked him, "What have you added to your faith?" He was puzzled, but then we opened to the beginning of Peter's second letter where we found an outline of qualities to add to faith. Kim read the passage aloud:

> For this very reason, giving all diligence, add to your faith virtue,
> to virtue knowledge,
> to knowledge self-control,
> to self-control perseverance,
> to perseverance godliness,
> to godliness brotherly kindness,
> and to brother kindness love.
> For if these things are yours and abound, you will be neither barren nor unfruitful in the knowledge of our Lord Jesus Christ. (2 Pet. 1:5–8 NKJV)

Peter was an old apostle when he listed these character qualities to "add" to faith. He began this letter with an encouragement, "His divine power has given us everything we need for life and godliness through our knowledge of him who called us by his own glory and goodness" (2 Pet. 1:3). "Kim," I said, "because you know Jesus, you already have everything you need." He was unsatisfied. "It's true, Kim. Jesus told the crowd sitting on a Galilean hillside, 'You cannot add one hour to your life.' Without God's guidance, people attempt to "add" all kinds of things to their lives. They "add" hair color, clothing styles, education, cars, houses, jewelry, even a spouse and kids. Let's look again at the words 'giving all diligence.' Another version translates this as 'make every effort.' Could it be that our faith in Christ is only the beginning of a journey?"

Starting with Faith

Faith is the starting point. Jesus said, "Have faith in God" (Mark 11:22). He said, "I am the door," the way to enjoy friendship with God (John 10:7 KJV). Like Adam and Eve, we have two calls. First, they were called to serve in the garden with the instructions "to dress it and to keep it" (Gen. 2:15 KJV). Adam and Eve already enjoyed friendship with God. Then the two disobeyed God and sin entered the world, so God's second call became a cry seeking his lost friend, "Where are you?" (Gen. 3:9). Because Adam and Eve made a fatal choice in the garden, God's call to us is not for us to "tend to the garden." God's first call to all of us is to restore our relationship with him. Augustine, bishop of the early church in modern day Libya, put it this way, "Thou hast made us for Thyself, O Lord, and our hearts are restless until they find their rest in Thee."[1]

Kim shifted on the park bench uncomfortably as he looked down the path of the wooded park. We got up to walk. "So my calling is not just about what I do? It's about my personal relationship with God?"

"It's more," I said, "but without faith, any discussion of calling gravitates toward using our natural abilities for practical purposes. God wants you to know him, Kim. Hearing and obeying God's voice is part of a normal Christian life. Isaiah 43:1 says, 'I have summoned you by name. You are mine.'" Kim looked up as the wind blew through the trees. I could see he longed to hear God's voice, and I thought of Jesus' words, "The sheep listen to his voice. He calls his own sheep by name and leads them out" (John 10:3). "By faith," I added, "and through simple obedience to his voice, you will begin to cooperate with God's plan for your life."

The path through the woods led to an open field where clusters of people were enjoying the sun and playing catch on the green grass. "This walk through the woods," I explained to Kim, "out onto this field of people, is like our walk of faith. Our journey begins with a close encounter with God. Then he leads us out to serve his purpose by serving people." God calls us to know him first, and then he calls us to make use of our gifts, talents, and abilities serving others. This is what gives meaning to our lives. Kim would not find meaning in one of those self-help books. Not even a Christian book on spiritual gifts would answer his deeper questions. Studying spiritual gifts helps us know how God has designed us to serve him; however, all the recent attention on spiritual gifts seems to have overshadowed the more important questions: Why did God create me this way? What is his purpose for my life? Just like Kim, we must recognize the divine implication: the Gift Giver is the one who calls us.

"Kim, God gave you gifts for a purpose." Those gifts are like the one I gave my wife on a hot summer evening at the New Jersey shore, an engagement ring. She did not say, "Thanks for the gift." She said, "I will!" She immediately understood that I wanted to be her husband. The gift implied a call to be my wife. God's gifts are just like that. He invites us to know him and to be faithful to him. Kim and I reached the end of the field. He thanked me for spending the afternoon with him, and we agreed to meet again the following day.

Adding Virtue

A light rain was falling from the sky when I met Kim at the coffee shop. We sat by the window and picked up where we had left off. Kim asked, "What is virtue?"

"It is God's character of goodness," I answered. God is all-powerful and infinite, yet he invites us to know his character because he is also personal. God spoke and created the flowers, sunsets, waterfalls, and stars. He made all things beautiful. God's character is revealed in his words and acts, just as our character is revealed in our words and actions. It is not only the things you say and do, it is also the way you say and do those things that reveal your character.

Kim looked at me intently, after sipping from a large mug of his Guatemalan decaf, and asked, "What does that mean?" I told Kim about Annette, one of our medical ministry interns in Guatemala. During team introductions, Annette closed her fist and pounded her knee as she declared, "I am going to be a pediatrician!" Annette clutched onto her career goal with her obvious strong will. As I prayed for Annette that summer, I wondered if her passion was a reflection of God's calling. Would she open her fist and release her tight grip to trust God's goodness to lead her? Annette was using her fluent Spanish language and strong personality to take charge at the Guatemala City garbage dump clinic where our team and our staff nurse were serving. I received some complaints that Annette was "controlling." As I prayed for Annette, the words "She has a leadership gift" came to my mind. I met Annette to affirm her with those encouraging words. "But Annette," I urged, "God wants you to use your leadership gift his way. Jesus is a Servant-King and he wants you to find ways to encourage and release others in their ministry gifts." From that day on Annette served and encouraged her teammates to use their gifts and abilities. Like opening her fist, Annette began to trust God. She learned that her gift of leadership is a reflection of God's character.

Virtue is not something you can pretend to possess. It is a deep reflection of the character and goodness of God. We must first trust God to do a deep work in our lives, which is a complete surrender of self, before we truly reflect God's character. We must put off whatever may hinder us before we draw near to God.

Kim looked down at his feet, thinking. "What would keep me from getting closer to God?" he asked.

"Shoes," I said, half-teasing, then went on to tell of Moses.

When Moses encountered God, he was told to take off his shoes—a leather layer of protection around his feet. Could it be Moses also had a self-protective layer around his heart? Moses was a fugitive, living in fear of being found by the Egyptian king. He was trained to build cities, but rather than exercise his gifts and abilities, Moses tended his father-in-law's flocks. God called him to put aside his fears. God was about to speak from his heart and he wanted Moses to trust him.

Kim stared at the rain as it ran down like tears on the window of the coffee shop. "This encounter Moses had with God," I whispered, "must have been so intimate that it changed him forever." God shared Moses' longing to rescue the Israelites. God shared the pain in his heart for his people suffering in Egypt (Exod. 3:7). Moses met God and learned that he is good. When God called Moses, Moses was delivered from fear. Moses found his identity; he was the one who would deliverer the Israelites out of bondage. "Shoes," I said to Kim, "or any self-protection, may be preventing you from an encounter with God." The rain stopped and our coffee cups were empty. Standing by our cars in the parking lot, we prayed for a fresh encounter with God. Tears ran down Kim's face as he thanked God for being so good.

Adding Knowledge

Kim was beaming when we met after church services. "Something has changed in me. It is like the Holy Spirit has become my teacher." When we have a true encounter with God, we find out the meaning of the scripture that says, "You will be ever hearing, but never understanding" (Matt. 13:14).

"Kim," I explained, standing next to my car in the church parking lot, "we never really begin to learn until we are willing to learn from the greatest intellect in the universe. In Matthew 11:29 Jesus said, 'Take my yoke upon you and learn from me, for I am gentle and humble in heart, and you will find rest for your souls.' When we trust God, we begin to relax with him. Then he can teach us a new perspective of the world, a new worldview.

"God's calling is already at work in your life," I assured.

"My education filled me with so much cynicism and doubt," Kim responded with a big smile, "but now I trust God! He wants to be my teacher."

I pulled out my keys and grinned, "Think of it! He'll renovate your mind and show you how to make him smile." Kim's smiled contorted into a puzzled look. "What do you mean?"

I explained, "Do not conform any longer to the pattern of this world, but be transformed by the renewing of your mind. Then you will be able to test and approve what God's will is—his good, pleasing and perfect will" (Rom. 12:2).

"That's what I want," Kim shot out.

Learning about people and places, nations and nature, from the smallest particle to the farthest star, is an exciting discovery when you allow the Holy Spirit to be your teacher. Sadly, many very intelligent and highly educated people never place their trust in God and therefore never experience that joy. In fact, God declares, "I will destroy the wisdom of the wise; the intelligence of the intelligent I will frustrate" (1 Cor. 1:19). Scriptures often refer to the Jews and Greeks who opposed the truth, because they could not accept that the truth is both personal and knowable. However, Paul did not hesitate to tell anyone the truth of Jesus Christ. Paul even revealed some of his experience in the school of the Holy Spirit when he told his listeners how the things that make us different, whether generational or cultural, ethnic or economic, were designed by God for the purpose of calling us to himself:

> "From one man he made every nation of men, that they should inhabit the whole earth; and he determined the times set for them and the exact places where they should live. God did this so that men would seek him and perhaps reach out for him and find him, though he is not far from each one of us." (Acts 17:26–27)

"You are adding knowledge," I assured Kim. "As you respond to him, it is like taking a journey of learning with the Holy Spirit as your teacher."

To know our calling, we need to gain fresh revelation and understanding of the nature and character of God. "Jesus is a master teacher," I emphasized, "so you can expect him to teach you in surprising ways."

The disciples walked with Jesus, and he taught them through storytelling, through the text of the Scriptures, through the storms of life, through practical needs, through miracles, and by his example. We can learn through books, especially through biographies, but we must not limit our learning to the classroom or the library. God wants to show us his ways through the good times and the bad times of our life journey.

Kim looked straight at me, obviously hungry for more. "Knowledge was never supposed to be separated from relationship, especially relationship with God," I warned.

Those who do not accept the truth will wander in the social wilderness of fallen humanity, missing God's special purpose for them. Jesus told the people, "You are the light of the world" (Matt. 5:14). We are called to let that light, the reflection of our relationship with God, to shine out into the world. God teaches us so that we can be a light in public service, business, science, media, or the ministry.[2]

My wife, Mary, joined us at the car. "Would you join my family for lunch?" I offered to Kim. "Sure," he quickly agreed.

Adding Self-Control

Standing in our kitchen, Kim asked, "So when will I know what I am called to do?"

I opened the fridge. "Are you hungry?"

He looked at me as if I was ignoring him. "Uh, yes."

"He's given you the choice, Kim. It is your choice how many times a day you go to the refrigerator," I grinned, thinking of the next of Peter's litany of qualities, self-control. Self-control is a vital part of our journey because just knowing what we are called to do is not enough. We must learn how to choose what God calls us to do amid all the competing and distracting options.

"The degree of self-control you exercise in your private life will be the level of self-control you exercise in your public witness," I advised as I passed Kim a bowl of potato salad to place on the table.

We must pay close attention to Paul's words, "I beat my body and make it my slave so that after I have preached to others, I myself will not be disqualified for the prize" (1 Cor. 9:27). Self-control is developed as we appropriate God's grace to make quality choices, especially those choices to overcome personal temptations.

"Kim, too many Christian leaders have displayed their moral failure publicly because they failed to develop self-control in their private lives." No matter what I am called to do, self-control will keep me on the path toward God's plan for my life.

"Do you have a dream?" I asked Kim as I took a bite of a sandwich.

Some people have big dreams, like eliminating poverty, eradicating HIV/AIDS, reducing greenhouse gases, or influencing international politics. "No matter how big your circle of concern for the world, it's your circle of influence that matters." I pointed at the fridge again and smiled, "If you do not make the small decisions in your current sphere of influence, such as the thoughts you entertain, the words you speak, or even the simple task of balancing your checkbook, you will probably never make the harder choices to realize God's dream for your life."

Jesus said, "He who is faithful in a very little thing is faithful also in much" (Luke 16:10 NASB). Before the children of Israel could inherit the land God promised, they had to first gain the moral ground within their hearts and within their community.

It's the same for us—only after gaining a measure of victory as the people of God does he lead us into the public arena as his witnesses, to inherit his promises.

Four hundred years ago, a few courageous Christian Reformers changed history. They brought reforms to the Christian church, and they brought about a transformation in society. The Reformers' view of calling ran counter to the primary philosophy of the Middle Ages, when Christians were taught that priests, monks, and nuns were living the perfect life, while farmers, soldiers, and tradesmen lived a kind of secondary grade of piety.[3] This bizarre view of life and work excluded most Christians from any sense of divine calling and suggested that the hard work of a housewife or house builder was second rate. Even today, many Christians have the attitude that work is a demeaning activity.

I stood to clear the table, and Kim joined me with an armload of dishes. I stopped at the sink and said, "We are called to leave behind the world, so it no longer has power over us."

Jesus explained that what controls us should not be external, but internal. He said, "The kingdom of God is within you" (Luke 17:21). It is for freedom that Christ has set us free (Gal. 5:1). Therefore he does not call us to hide from the world, but he calls us to "go into all the world" (Mark 16:15). We are all called to be priests to the world, praying for and appealing to every person to receive the gospel of the kingdom.

Kim took a towel from the drawer and I handed him the first hand-washed dish. "Did you know Luther celebrated the religious value of housework?"

Luther writes, "It has no obvious appearance of holiness, yet these very household chores are more to be valued than all the works of monks and nuns."[4] This biblical perspective of work gives everyday worldly activity a religious significance. Thanks to Luther and Calvin, ordinary work has dignity and meaning.

Kim stared at the sign in our kitchen that says, "Services Held Here Three Times Daily." Then he mumbled, "I still do not know what I am supposed to be doing. I haven't gotten a single interview."

I knew how agonizing a job search could be. I sensed this was just the beginning. "Could it be you feel pressured to live up to expectations that God never intended?"

Calling is not about social or economic status. It is about trusting God and doing what pleases him. The biblical view of calling frees us to worship God through our life's work. God placed Adam and Eve in the garden "to work it and take care of it" (Gen. 2:15). Work is not something we do to keep up with the world's expectations. Neither is a career something we seek to make our lives meaningful. Work became harder when Adam and Eve made a fatal choice to disobey God; however, God did not remove the original dignity and meaning of work (Gen. 3:17–19).

I handed Kim a glass of iced tea, "Choosing a career is a heart-searching question." We settled on patio chairs as I challenged him with the words of Archbishop William

Temple. "If you choose a career on selfish grounds it is 'probably the greatest single sin any young person can commit, for it is the deliberate withdrawal from allegiance to God of the greatest part of time and strength.' [5] Seeking God, as you are, to know what he is calling you to do," I encouraged, "shows how much you value your relationship with God over what you do for a living. You are showing that he can trust you."

Self-control is also necessary as we engage the world around us. Self-control is like the sign that calls us to yield as we enter traffic. Before we engage the world as a witness for Christ, he calls for caution.

I prayed for Kim. Then he demonstrated even more how much the kingdom of God had taken control of his life. "Jesus, I just want to give you all my energy, my time, my talent, my abilities, and my relationships. I trust you to provide for me and I thank you that you gave me the desire to work for your purposes."

Adding self-control begins with personal choices. It leads us into a public witness, where we must learn to persevere.

Adding Perseverance

I hadn't seen Kim for a few weeks, so I called him hoping to meet again. "I didn't expect it to be like this," Kim said. I could hear in his voice that, whatever it was that discouraged him, he hadn't lost his resolve.

"How's the job search?"

He quickly replied, "Oh, I got a job. I knew it would be temporary, but I didn't know it would only last two weeks." Before I could ask, he revealed, "My boss is asking me to lie." Kim had taken a job as a salesperson at a local office supplies dealership. "I can't do that," he added, "So I've turned in my resignation."

Kim has pursued God's calling, adding qualities of faith, virtue, knowledge, and self-control, all of which began as a private response to God. However, in order for these qualities to continue to grow, he must engage the world. Self-control is necessary as he begins his public witness. Perseverance is the next quality necessary because engagement with the world will always involve a test. While imprisoned, Paul announced, "What has happened to me has really served to advance the gospel" (Phil. 1:12). As James writes, "Consider it pure joy, my brothers, whenever you face trials of many kinds, because you know that the testing of your faith develops perseverance" (James 1:2–3). As we follow God's calling into the public arena, we can be sure we will be tested.

God calls us to express the knowledge of him in every sphere of life, especially those places where his name, his character, and his ways are not yet known. As we emerge from a private into a public arena, we are tested. If our motives are selfish,

God will reveal that to us, too. Adding perseverance leads us to deeper commitment to God, a deeper faith, a deeper understanding of God's character, and a deeper surrender of control to the grace of God.

"Kim," I assured, "what you are experiencing is a normal testing phase of going deeper in the call of God. Of course, the test can be much more severe," I added, "but you must persevere through the tests if you are to fully know your calling."

Peter writes, "Dear friends, do not be surprised at the painful trial you are suffering, as though something strange were happening to you. But rejoice that you participate in the sufferings of Christ, so that you may be overjoyed when his glory is revealed" (1 Pet. 4:12). The test often comes as people oppose God's work through us. For example, Martin Luther was called to renounce his words of reform at the Diet of Worms. He stood firm, "Here I stand, I can do no other."

"Part of Jesus' ministry is to bring the fire of testing," I explained. John the Baptist proclaimed, "He will baptize you with the Holy Spirit and with fire . . . but he will burn up the chaff with unquenchable fire" (Luke 3:16–17).

"I don't understand," Kim questioned.

"The Holy Spirit empowers us to be a witness," I replied, "but not without the fire of testing." The phone was quiet. "That is how we are prepared to go to the hard places, whether it be to plant a church among unreached people or tell the truth as a journalist at the *New York Times*."

As the disciples prayed on the day of Pentecost, the Holy Spirit came with a "violent wind" and "tongues of fire" (Acts 2:2–3). Thus, the first Christians were empowered to go everywhere telling of the grace and power of God, and he continues to empower people to be a witness. The North American mission movement can be traced back to a few college students who persevered in prayer in a haystack when a thunderstorm whipped up on a sweltering August day in 1806.

"Imagine crowding into a haystack to pray with your four prayer partners over the crack of thunder." I described to Kim how Samuel Mills, a student at Williams College in Massachusetts, showed perseverance as he led his friends in prayer. "What would you do, Kim?" These students prayed for Asia. Then they shouted over the storm their prayer of commitment, "We can do this if we will!" It became known as the Haystack Prayer Meeting, and it marked the beginning of a great wave of missionaries streaming out of the United States. These few students became the answer to their own prayers and changed history.

"I don't know if I'll change history," Kim said, probably surprised that he said it out loud.

"Whether you are called to be a medical doctor or a missionary, a composer or a contractor, God will refine your work for his purposes."

Paul writes, "His work will be shown for what it is, because the Day will bring it to light. It will be revealed with fire, and the fire will test the quality of each man's work" (1 Cor. 3:13).

"You will change history," I encouraged him. "The question is whether your work will stand the test." Kim was being tested at his first job. He was learning he is no longer bound by the crisis of identity that haunts people with indecision.

Before hanging up the phone, Kim insisted, "I will not lie to keep my job. I know God has a better job for me."

Adding Godliness

By persevering we show that we have "set apart Christ as Lord" (1 Pet. 3:15), and by adding godliness we show that we live before an audience of One. Weeks passed, and Kim had demonstrated that he really did not care anymore what people thought about him being unemployed. As I prayed for Kim, however, I began to be concerned that he was missing something. I asked him to help me move some boxes of books. As we loaded the boxes into my truck, I asked what he thought about the words of Peter, "Be all the more eager to make your calling and election sure" (2 Pet. 1:10). He was quiet for a while. Then he set a box into the truck and said, "I think I understand calling, but I do not understand election."

"Election has been misunderstood for generations," I answered. "Too often people have mistakenly regarded themselves as God's special favorites. A wrong view of godliness has made them proud, arrogant, and even narcissistic. They have become too aloof to care about others." We put a few more boxes in the truck and stopped a moment. "To be godly is to settle the question of identity," I emphasized. "Godliness is knowing you are his chosen representative and there is no turning back." I set the last box in the truck and asked, "Can we meet again tomorrow?"

Adding Brotherly Kindness

Kim and I stepped out of the parking garage onto the downtown sidewalk. We paused, amazed at the number of people hurrying past the homeless person on the corner. The man was in tattered clothes, a hat, a scarf, and a grubby overcoat. "Sirs," the man asked us politely, "can you spare a dollar?"

I did not have cash on me, so I asked, "What can I do for you, sir?" Kim stood by quietly as I had a conversation with the man about his family and the job he lost. I invited him to join us in the café, but he refused. So we parted with smiles. "Hope to see you again soon."

Brotherly kindness seems so common, so ordinary. "After all these other qualities we've talked about, do you need a call from God to be kind?" Kim asked. We sat on wooden benches at a table in the back of the café and ordered lunch.

"I think the answer may be found when a teacher of the law came to test Jesus' knowledge," I replied. Jesus' reply to the teacher was simple, "'Love the Lord your God with all your heart and with all your soul and with all your strength and with all your mind'; and, 'Love your neighbor as yourself'" (Luke 10:27). Uncomfortable with the answer, the teacher of the law tried to justify himself. He suddenly feared his relationship with God was insufficient. To divert attention, the teacher followed up with a controversial question, "Who is my neighbor?"

"Did you know the Samaritans were hated by the Israelites?" I quizzed Kim. Everyone knows what it means to be a "Good Samaritan." Even so, we seem to miss the point of the story.

"Jesus seems to be pointing out that loving your neighbor is something everybody should do. It's nothing special," Kim observed.

"That's right!" I nearly shouted. "It does not require a special call." Showing God's kindness may be done by anyone, and often is done by those who are not even followers of Christ. Brotherly kindness is a common, ordinary act, which does not require any "special grace."

Brotherly kindness is a common grace, which is meant for the common good. Common grace is like the sun, which rises "on the evil and the good," and the rain, which falls "on the righteous and the unrighteous" (Matt. 5:45).

"Brotherly kindness is an act of common decency and caring for the needs of others," I said as Kim looked outside at the man on the corner.

"No matter who they are," he added. Our lunch order arrived at the table. We thanked God for the gift of our waitress and I plunged into my salad.

"The call to plant a garden is just as valid as is the call to plant a church," I sputtered as I chomped on a carrot. "Building a business is just as legitimate as baptizing a believer," I added. William Perkins wrote, "The true end of our lives is to do service to God in serving of man."[6] This does not replace the important work of church planting, evangelism, and the spiritual gifts and callings God has given to his people. However, coupled with the command to love God will all our heart, mind, soul, and strength, Jesus commands us to do the common, ordinary thing—to love our neighbor as ourselves. In this, Jesus encapsulates all the law saying, "There is no commandment greater" (Mark 12:31).

Jesus explains how the impact of brotherly kindness will eventually lead us to engage every arena of society. He said, "The kingdom of heaven is like yeast that a woman took and mixed into a large amount of flour until it worked all through the dough" (Matt. 13:33). We are all called to do the small acts of kindness. As we do, we become "the salt of the earth" (Matt. 5:13). Kim confided, "It is going to take some time to really do these things." We paid for our lunch and stepped out the door to find our homeless friend, Jim. Kim chatted with Jim this time.

Adding Love

I was away on a ministry trip when Kim received a call saying he was hired for a position with a telecommunications firm in Seattle. He left a message saying how much our conversations meant to him and that he really senses this job is part of God's leading for him right now. I did not have the opportunity to say goodbye, so I wrote a letter:

Dear Kim,

Congratulations! It has been so good to spend time with you, too, my friend. God has provided a job, but there is so much more he has for you. You are a quality guy. I know God is going to complete the work he began in you. I hope you will continue to "make every effort" to keep adding these qualities.

Press on to understand God's kind of love. Remember? Love is the last of Peter's list of qualities. Paul chose the Greek word *agape* to describe God's kind of self-sacrificing love.

We do not have many living examples of the meaning of love. Let me encourage you to read about Mother Teresa. Through her life, our generation has witnessed an unmistakable demonstration of God's love, the love that gives without thought of return. Mother Teresa's name has become synonymous with self-sacrificing concern for others. Mother Teresa lived beyond her vows. She sensed God's call to reach out to the poorest of the poor in India.

Mother Teresa loved people who were dying on the streets of Calcutta. "Mangy, covered in oozing abscesses, their festering wounds stinking and crawling with maggots, these people often had been thrown out of whatever hovel-like shelter they had known in the terminal stages of their illnesses by superstitious landlords or family members."[7] She said that those castoffs were Christ himself, but "in a most distressing disguise."[8] She cared for, cleaned, bandaged, and washed the bodies of these rejected people. Now, that is God's kind of love!

Where did Paul turn for his understanding of God's love? I think it was in his revelation of the cross of Christ. Paul writes, "What does 'he ascended' mean except that he also descended to the lower, earthly regions? He who descended is the very one who ascended higher than all the heavens" (Eph. 4:9–10).

Paul's letter to the believers at Philippi has two references to Christ's nature. Can you find them?

Each of you should look not only to your own interests, but also to the interests of others. Your attitude should be the same as that of Christ Jesus: Who, being in very nature God, did not consider equality with God something to be grasped, but made himself nothing, taking the very nature of a servant, being made in human likeness. And being found in appearance as a man, he humbled himself and became obedient to death—even death on a cross! Therefore God exalted him to the highest place and gave him the name that is above every name, that at the name of Jesus every knee should bow, in heaven and on earth and under the earth, and every tongue confess that Jesus Christ is Lord, to the glory of God the Father. (Phil 2:4–11)

Did you see them? The first is where it says he had God's *nature.* Jesus was secure in his relationship with the Father, so he did not try to prove it, even when he was tempted. Jesus told Philip, "Anyone who has seen me has seen the Father" (John 14:9). The second is where it says Jesus put on the *nature* of a servant. He humbled himself and became obedient. He showed us God's kind of love.

Kim, if Jesus had a need to prove his relationship with the Father, grasping for his identity as the Son, his sacrificial love would not have been completely unselfish. Then again, if Jesus had been content with his relationship with God, but refused to become obedient to become the perfect sacrifice, he would never have come to earth or gone to the cross. I think this is why Peter puts perseverance, godliness, and brotherly kindness, in that order, right before love. We need to go through the tests to settle the question of our identity as a child of God. Then, as his dearly loved children, we need to love our neighbor. We need to show how good God is with no expectation of reward. As we follow Peter's instructions to "make your calling and election sure," we will show the world the love of God.

I look forward to hearing from you again, Kim. I am praying for you.

Your friend,
John

Conclusion

God's call gives meaning to all of life. Around the world, young people listen to counsel to go to college so they can "get a good job." However, a good job is too often defined by its income or prestige. As a result, many young Christians yield to cultural norms and pressures. They enter the halls of higher education as the next logical step prescribed by a materialistic society. Many young people may thus be set up for frustration later in life. Many have already suspended their calling, and therefore a deeper friendship with God. God is calling everyone. Until we are prepared to face our unwillingness to respond to God's call, we will be frustrated in our work and incomplete in our relationship with God.

Peter instructs us to "be all the more eager" and to "make every effort" in pursuit of our calling (2 Pet. 1:5, 10). This pursuit must include a private devotion to God, with the qualities of faith, virtue, knowledge, and self-control as milestones on our journey. Giving instruction to the believers in Corinth, Paul writes, "Run in such a way as to get the prize" (1 Cor. 9:24). To get that prize, Paul continues, we must go "into strict training" (1 Cor. 9:25), because God's calling will lead us into the public arena of witness, with the qualities of self-control, perseverance, godliness, and brotherly kindness as milestones on our journey. The witness of those who know their calling has historically changed the social and political structures of their generation. This is why we must not be idle. We must pursue the call of God to the full measure of the outward expression of God's love, the most powerful gentle force in the world.

A surge of teaching and learning has followed every major revival. In their newfound faith, Christians have sought understanding of God's purposes for their lives and their communities. They became disciples of God's kingdom and diligently obeyed their calling in the midst of community. As they pursued God's calling, they established new institutions, hospitals, and schools that ultimately transformed whole communities. God intends that we love our neighbors, which declares God's goodness to the world. God also intends that we all participate, by all means, in the presentation of every nation before his throne.

Jesus said, "Go make disciples of all nations" (Matt. 28:19). For this to occur, leaders who know their calling are needed for every field of endeavor, every sphere of influence, and every nation on earth. Just as a mustard seed begins as a small potential, we can look into the Scriptures for special revelation of our call while looking at the needs of the world for general understanding of God's call. God's call may be to plant a church in a yet-unreached people group. However, for others, God's call may be to represent God's character and ways as a gardener or a financier, a carpenter or an engineer, an officer of the law or a politician.

God calls us first to restored relationship, to know him. Then he calls us to be his witnesses in the world. Following the call of God according to Peter's progressive qualities will eventually lead us to revelation of the love of God at the cross of Christ. The psalmist writes, "Be still, and know that I am God; I will be exalted among the nations" (Ps. 46:10). Calling is about intimacy with God, and it is about making his name known in all the earth.

Further References

Dawson, Joy. "Fire of God," U of N Workshop, Seoul, Korea, September 1997.

Kuyper, A. *Lectures on Calvinism* (The Stone Lectures) The Kuyper Foundation (Somerset, England), www.kuyper.org (accessed December 9, 2007).

O'Day, J. "Saving the University: Charles Malik" in *More Than Conquerors: Portraits of Believers from All Walks of Life*. Edited by John Woodbridge. Chicago: Moody, 1992.

Miller, Darrow. "Discipling Nations," North American Leadership Conference, Vancouver, BC, April 2001.

Schaeffer, F. A. *How Should We Then Live? The Rise and Decline of Western Thought and Culture*. Wheaton, Ill.: Crossway Books, 1983.

Weber, M. *The Protestant Ethic and the Spirit of Capitalism,* 1905 (first German publication). Los Angeles: Roxbury Publishing Co., 2002.

Notes

1. L. Cowan and O. Guinness, *Invitation to the Classics* (Grand Rapids: Baker Books, 1998), 83.

2. During the Reformation, Calvin taught about the sacred nature of work and the role of the church in discipling people to serve God in all spheres of society. See the chapter by Tom Bloomer for more detail.

3. Os Guinness, *The Call: Finding and Fulfilling the Central Purpose of Your Life* (Nashville: Word, 1998), 34.

4. A. McGrath, "Calvin and Calling," *First Things: The Journal of Religion, Culture, and Public Life* (June/July 1999), 31–35.

5. Guinness, *The Call,* 20.

6. P. A. Marshall, *A Kind of Life Imposed on Man: Vocation and Social Order from Tyndale to Locke.* (Toronto: University of Toronto Press, 1996), 41.

7. David Aikman, *Great Souls: Six Who Changed the Century* (Nashville: Word Publishing, 1998), 221.

8. Ibid., 101.

With clarity and passion, Danny Lehmann teaches the irreducible minimum of what it means to obey the Great Commission. You will love his two-edged, sharp-tipped sword of nation discipling. He explains why evangelism has primacy, though it doesn't always come first in sequence.

Discipling the Nations— One Disciple at a Time

Danny Lehmann

Awise man once said, "He who throws mud not only gets his hands dirty, but loses a 'lot of ground.'" Unfortunately, a lot of ground has been lost and much mud thrown back and forth between missions-minded Christians over the years. This conflict has been over the two main aspects of our missionary call. On the one hand there are those who see Jesus' last command as simple and straight-forward, "Go into all the world and preach the gospel" (Mark 16:15 NASB). With the gospel events,[1] gospel promises,[2] and gospel demands[3] defined clearly, what further evidence do we need? Let's roll. Preach it!

Then there are those who point to Jesus' command to "make disciples of all the nations" (Matt. 28:19 NASB) which suggests to some degree a more detailed process of teaching people(s) how to walk under the lordship of Christ. Those in this camp tend to see those in the first as being too heavenly minded to be any earthly good because they focus on the sweet by-and-by rather than the raw here and now. The evangelistic people counter with comparisons of time with eternity, and love to quote Jesus' question regarding the relative value of gaining the whole world while losing one's soul (Matt. 16:26). Thus, the debate goes on.

Babies and Bathwater

Charles Spurgeon, the great English preacher, was once likewise asked to reconcile the apparently contradictory teachings in the Bible regarding divine sovereignty and human responsibility. His response: "There is no need to reconcile friends." Evangelism and social action[4] are friends. We cannot take one singly without destroying them both. To use an American idiom, both sides need to be careful not to "throw out the baby with the bathwater."

Success in discipling the nations will require a "both/and" mentality rather than an "either/or" posture on these two issues. Both preaching the gospel and discipling the nations were commanded by Jesus and need to be obeyed. They have been intended by God to be partners working together rather than poles pulling apart. Two feet walking one step after another or two hands working together help to illustrate these dual ministries that have been described as "distinct, yet equal" partners.[5]

Amy Carmichael, the great missionary to India, was once chastised by some of her missionary leaders for spending too much time alleviating the temporal suffering of the girls she was working with at her orphanage in Dohnavur. In a kind but spicy letter back to her superiors she acknowledged the primacy of evangelism, but went on to make the pithy observation: "One cannot save and then pitchfork souls into heaven . . . souls are more or less fastened to bodies . . . and as you cannot get the souls out and deal with them separately, you have to take them both together."[6] William Booth, founder of the Salvation Army, once cautioned his soldiers not to preach to someone with a toothache. His reasoning was that their dental pain was so loud they wouldn't be able to hear the gospel. His remedy: fix the tooth—then get 'em saved![7]

Horses and Carts

Borrowing another expression from my culture, "Don't put the cart before the horse," I would like to suggest, however, that there is a "leading partner,"[8] an "equal among equals," a "horse that pulls the cart" when it comes to what we do when we go to the nations. When I say leading partner, I don't necessarily mean in sequence. In General Booth's "toothache" analogy, the social action came first and we also observe that Jesus' Good Samaritan didn't stuff tracts into the pockets of the Jericho-bound victim!

I do believe, however, that Jesus, the apostles, church history, and the Bible all point to the primacy of evangelism in the command to disciple the nations.[9] This can be demonstrated in three crucial areas and summed up in three words: history, theology, and eternity.

History

Someone has said that the one thing we learn from history is that we don't learn anything from history. Let's hope and pray that doesn't apply to us. There is too much at stake!

Catherine Booth, William's wife and Army cofounder, had a favorite reply when her contemporaries would try to draw her into controversy over their theology or practice: "My friends, all I know is—souls are dying, dying,"[10] she would exclaim with a passion for the perishing multitudes. The Salvation Army (who could never be criticized as being too heavenly minded) began as a model of evangelism and social action working together. General Booth told his officers, "Go for souls and go for the worst!"[11] The Booths and their followers also fed the hungry, clothed the naked, sheltered the homeless, and worked against corruption in government. William's landmark book, *In Darkest England and the Way Out,* outlined a plan to disciple the nation in dealing with its social problems. The Booths' driving passion, however, was the winning of the lost to Christ.

Throughout church history, the gospel-preaching, Bible-believing missionaries and church planters have been the most effective at initiating social and cultural change in the nations. Below is a random sampling:

Tertullian in the third century wrote, "Christians support and bury people... support boys and girls who are destitute of parents... old people, and those who have suffered ship wreck or are shut up in prison."[12]

In the Middle Ages, the monastic movements (the closest equivalent at the time to our modern-day missionary movements) of Benedictines, Celts, Nestorians, and later the Franciscans, Dominicans, and Jesuits promoted scholarly learning as well as agricultural advances. Well-known historian Thomas Cahill credits Irish monks with "saving civilization."[13]

John Wesley, the great British evangelist and church planter, is credited by many historians with saving England from a bloody revolution like the one endured by France just a few years before his time. He said, "Christianity is essentially a social religion. To turn it into a solitary religion is to destroy it."[14] A perusal of his sermons reveals his passion for the "national" issues of the day—wealth and poverty, war, education, medical ethics, sea piracy, free trade, slavery, and the liquor industry. He was also one of the greatest soul winners in history.

John Elliot, a missionary to the Algonquin Native Americans, not only preached the gospel with zeal and translated the Bible into their language but fought for justice and clemency for Indian prisoners, freedom for Indian slaves, and prevented Algonquins from being defrauded of their land. In addition he established schools for Indian children.

William Carey, the father of modern missions and a pioneer missionary to India, introduced the steam engine to India, taught the locals how to produce their own paper for publishing, built the largest printing press in the nation, and established the first savings bank. He preached against bribery and labored for the humane treatment of lepers. He lobbied to change the law concerning "suttee" or widow burning (no doubt many widows are grateful for that one), and taught economics, botany, agriculture, and mathematics. Further, he won souls, planted churches, and translated the Bible into several languages. Whew!

In the Sandwich Islands (Hawaii), New England missionaries followed Carey's lead and served the people's practical as well as spiritual needs. Medical work was done for people suffering from diseases brought in by Western whaling ships. Schools were established to provide educational opportunities for the Hawaiian people. The missionaries also translated the Bible and other books into the Hawaiian language.

Many of the outstanding universities in Asia, including Yonsei University and Ewha Women's University in Seoul, as well as a large percentage of the hospitals, orphanages, and hospices (like the Red Cross) were founded by evangelical missionaries.

Space here does not permit more examples. The historical record is clear. The people who have best discipled the nations were those who put the preaching of the gospel first. They labored to establish their converts as obedient disciples of Jesus and taught both the social and the individual demands of the gospel. The corporate transformation followed for two reasons. First, their lives radically changed by the power of God through the gospel. Secondly, they were properly taught that Jesus should be the Lord of every area of life.

Theology

Years ago one of my mentors, Michael Green, made a statement which has resonated within me as a life lesson: "Most evangelists are not very interested in theology and most theologians are not very involved in evangelism. I am committed to both."[15] With this in mind, a few crucial issues come up in our present discussion. What exactly did Jesus commission us to do? What did he mean when he told us to disciple the nations? What did his original hearers (the apostles) understand him to mean? What does the Bible in general have to teach us about the relationship between evangelism and discipling? We must allow our theology of discipling the nations to be shaped by the answers to these biblically based questions.

First, let's examine condensed versions of Jesus' all-important Great Commission, given to us five times on three separate occasions.

1. Matt. 28:18–20, The Inclusive Mandate: "disciple all nations"
2. Mark 16:15, The Exclusive Mandate: "preach the gospel to every person"
3. Luke 24:47, The Message Mandate: "repentance and forgiveness of sins should be preached to all nations"
4. John 20:21, The "Jesus Style" Mandate: "As the Father has sent me, so send I you"
5. Acts 1:8, The Geographical Mandate: "be witnesses . . . in Jerusalem, Judaea, Samaria, and the remotest parts of the earth"

Permit me the following paraphrase of the five texts: "Go in my name into every inhabitable place on earth and proclaim the good news of forgiveness and salvation to every person. Baptize those who repent and believe and disciple them by teaching them to obey all my commands." The above is the irreducible minimum that has to be done if we are to obey the Great Commission. Notice the preaching of the gospel is at the heart of all five passages.

Theological liberals have for years tried to excise repentance, conversion, baptism, and obedience to Jesus as Lord out of the Commission as they formed a theology of discipling the nations without these crucial elements. To apply Old Testament principles of justice, ethics, etc., while hurdling over the entire New Testament would have been ludicrous to the original apostles. To reconstruct a society on biblical principles without the cross of Christ at the center of those principles would have been the farthest thing from their minds. To do so would be to build a kingdom without the King. To return to our "cart and horse" analogy, this would not merely put the cart before the horse, but leave us with a cart and no horse!

Should we seek to improve the lot of people (Christian or non-Christian) and alleviate suffering whenever and wherever possible (as did the Good Samaritan)? *Yes.* Should we feed the poor, visit the prisoners, clothe the naked, heal the sick, and perform other expressions of the Father's heart? *Yes!* Should we, without partiality, love our neighbors as ourselves, be they individuals or nations? *Yes!* Should we be "salt" as well as "light" and bring godly influences even into the "secular" societies (nations) in which God has placed us? *Yes!* But biblical discipleship has to center around the Lordship of Jesus.

We've looked at the last thing he told us to do, now let's look at the first: "Jesus came into Galilee preaching the gospel of God and saying, 'The time is fulfilled and the kingdom of God is at hand; repent and believe in the gospel'" (Mark 1:14b–15 NASB). He also said the reason he came to the earth was to call sinners to repentance (Luke 5:32). Once, when a man was overly concerned about domestic duties, Jesus told him to "Let the dead bury their own dead, but you go and proclaim the kingdom of God" (Luke 9:60). When he sent his disciples out on a short-term mission, the first thing he told them to do was to preach the gospel (Matt. 10:7; Luke 9:2).

A short perusal of the book of Acts shows us what the original apostles understood Jesus to mean when he told them to disciple the nations. Their priority, especially when pioneering in a new location, was to preach the gospel and win people to Christ. Then they would build them up in that holiness without which no one will see the Lord (see Heb. 12:14). On the day of Pentecost when the respondents cried, "What shall we do?" Peter told them to repent and believe the gospel (Acts 2:37–38). This was how Peter applied his understanding and obedience to what Jesus had commanded just a few weeks before.

Shortly thereafter, Peter healed the lame man at the Beautiful Gate and straightaway told the people, "Repent . . . and be converted, that your sins may be blotted out" (Acts 3:19 KJV). Next was the Saduceean persecution in which Peter responded first with his preaching of Jesus as the only way of salvation (4:12) and then with boldness: "For we cannot but speak the things which we have seen and heard" (Acts 4:20 KJV). This was immediately after they were commanded "not to speak at all nor teach in the name of Jesus" (Acts 4:18 KJV). After they were threatened again, they prayed. What did they pray for? Boldness to speak the word (Acts 4:29).

After their backs were laid wide open with a whip, Peter and John were "rejoicing that they were counted worthy to suffer shame for his name" (Acts 5:41 KJV). And what did they do upon their release from the prison and its beatings? "Daily . . . they ceased not to teach and preach Jesus Christ" (Acts 5:42 KJV).

The sixth chapter of Acts gives us their first real social test between Hebrew and Hellenistic people groups in a matter related to unjust distribution of food. The apostles' response: preaching and prayer while they delegated the responsibilities for the food distribution to the seven Hellenistic leaders. We then observe the Acts spotlight shine on two of those leaders. Stephen was found preaching the gospel (Acts 6–7) and became the first martyr, while Philip became the first evangelist. He preached the gospel en masse in Samaria and individually to the Ethiopian eunuch. Meanwhile, the Hellenistic believers were scattered and preaching everywhere (Acts 8:4). In the next chapter we find the story of Saul's conversion. What was his response? "Straightway he preached Christ in the synagogues" (Acts 9:20 KJV).

For the sake of space, we will skip to Paul's ministry and give a short synopsis. The first thing he did when he landed in a new town was to proclaim Christ.[16] Even in Athens, when he saw the city "wholly given to idolatry," how did he respond? Did he try and change the customs and culture and work to reform the society? No, the text reads, "Paul was preaching the good news about Jesus and the resurrection" (Acts 17:18). What was the result? He was mocked and persecuted almost everywhere he went as he preached the gospel, healed the sick, cast out demons, gathered converts, and planted churches.

Let me take this opportunity to shoot straight. In the book of Acts, as today, the devil or his followers don't mind it when Christians love people, feed, clothe, or house them, or in general do something to improve the quality of their lives. Then, as now, when sinners are told they need to repent, when selfish people are told to deny themselves, and when the only Name that can save is boldly and exclusively proclaimed in a world of five major religions and hundreds of minor ones, it is then that Satan's wrath gets hot!

Is it any wonder why we shy away from evangelism, not only in the hard places, but any places? Who wants to get rejected or persecuted? Our flesh doesn't like the "offense" that the Cross brings (Gal. 5:11). We would rather win friends than take the risks required to win souls. We are thus tempted to transform social action activities—

good biblical *supplements* to preaching the gospel—into *substitutes* for preaching the gospel. Read any book on the history of great missions movements, and as one generation passes the torch to the next, observe how we sell our eternal gospel birthright for a mess of temporal pottage. But we must allow the message of the Bible to inform our theology, and in turn our theology must inform the way we see the gospel and what we value most. This brings us to the final and most crucial issue.

Eternity

In one scene of the blockbuster movie *Gladiator,*[17] the gladiator exclaims, "What we do in life will echo in eternity." This phrase, or at least something similar, should be at the forefront for every believer seeking to fulfill the Great Commission. Words and concepts like "endless time," "timeless eternity," and "everlasting life" seem to short-circuit our mental capacities as we try to comprehend them. Struggle as we may, we need to constantly keep in mind the apostle Paul's admonition to "fix our eyes not on what is seen, but on what is unseen. For what is seen is temporary, but what is unseen is eternal" (2 Cor. 4:18). He also encouraged the Colossians to "set your minds on things above, not on earthly things" (Col. 3:2) while James reminded us that our present life is "a mist that appears for a little while and then vanishes" (James 4:14). In light of the logical comparisons of time with eternity as well as the consequences of a hell to shun and a heaven to gain, an eternal perspective is absolutely crucial for those of us that are involved in missions. Even though it is impossible for our finite minds to comprehend eternity, with the eyes of faith we can apprehend it. I once saw a t-shirt that said, "It's not that life is so short, but that you're dead for so long!"

Early in the last century there was a debate in theological circles called the "Fundamentalist-Modernist" controversy. The Fundamentalists, on one extreme, had their eyes on heaven and had an attitude of "you shouldn't polish brass on a sinking ship" or "don't rearrange the deck chairs on the Titanic" and consequently failed to care about the here and now. On the other hand, the Modernists were those who blatantly dismissed the eternal issues of the gospel and got focused almost exclusively on social action. Again, we must emphasize it is the both/and rather than either/or and that there are eternal issues involved in gospel work. C. S. Lewis said, "Aim at heaven and you get earth thrown in. Aim at earth and you get neither"![18]

Scholars for years have debated the descriptions of heaven and hell given to us in the Bible. Is the New Jerusalem literally 1,400 miles cubed? Are the streets really made of pure gold? Are the pearly gates for real? If fire is a physical property, how can it burn souls, which by nature are spiritual? Are the descriptions of wailing and gnashing of teeth, everlasting destruction, and outer darkness literal? How can there be outer darkness and flames at the same time? Rather than debate these issues, I would just like to keep the truth of Scripture in our face as we seek to nurture a both/and mentality with regard to the temporal and eternal issues in missions. As we seek to disciple the nations in the here and now and bring the Lordship of Jesus Christ into every area of society, as well we should, we must keep the words of Jesus in the forefront of our minds. "For what profit is it to a man if he gains the whole world, and loses his own soul?" (Matt. 16:26 NKJV)

It is said that William Booth wished all his Salvation Army officers could hang over hell for twenty-four hours prior to their commissioning. He felt this would stir them to a deeper commitment to evangelism. Leonard Ravenhill[19] tells the story of Charlie Peace, a convicted criminal sentenced to die by hanging. On his death walk to the gallows, the prison chaplain glibly read him some Bible verses from a book called "The Consolations of Religion." Charlie was shocked that a minister who professed to believe in the Bible could so coldly and professionally read about hell without so much as a tear in his eye or a quiver in his voice. "How can he believe that there is an eternal fire that never consumes its victim and yet be so unmoved?" Charlie mused to himself.

Finally unable to hold his peace any longer, the convict snapped at the chaplain, "Sir, if I believed what you and the Church of God say you believe, even if England were covered with broken glass from coast to coast, I would walk over, if need be, on hands and knees and think it worthwhile living to save just one soul from an eternal hell like that." Charlie spent his last moments on earth with a passionless, unbelieving preacher and went on to his Christless eternity.

We may be tempted to think that such a focus on heaven and hell is some form of religious extremism, out of touch with reality and common sense. But how can we say we are eccentric and extreme in the light of the reality of eternal separation from God? The psalmist said, "Horror has taken hold upon me because of the wicked that forsake thy law. . . . Rivers of water run down mine eyes because they keep not thy law" (Ps. 119:53, 136 KJV). Jeremiah spoke of bitterly weeping over the pride of his people (Jer. 13:17). Certainly one of our main motivations for missions needs to be the fact that the world is going to hell, and Jesus Christ and his gospel are the only salvation for people assigned to such a fate. "Knowing therefore the terror of the Lord, we persuade men" (2 Cor. 5:11 KJV).

We must, like the prophets of the Old Testament and the apostles of the New, allow God to break our hearts with the very thing that breaks his heart: the eternal destruction of millions of people (and peoples) who, without believing the gospel of the kingdom of God, are headed for a Christless eternity.

In light of eternity, the value of a human soul, and the example and overwhelming testimony of the primacy of evangelism in the Bible and church history, let us resolve ourselves to a more aggressive posture toward both evangelism and disciple-making. As we go, however, let us not neglect to make a certain kind of disciple—one who would make new disciples—so that we multiply until "the earth shall be filled with the knowledge of the glory of the Lord, as the waters cover the sea" (Hab. 2:14 KJV). Let us also train them to be cross-carrying, obedient disciples who realize we preach the gospel of the kingdom and therefore should seek to permeate the world with kingdom influences much like salt and leaven in the dough (Matt. 5:13; 13:33).

Getting to the Point

Allow me the following illustration: the Bible tells us that God's word is like a "two-edged sword" (Eph. 6:17; Heb. 4:12). I like to picture the two edges as discipling (training) and mercy ministries, while the point of the sword is evangelism. All three move together at the same speed while the sword is thrusting forth into the nations. So the issue is not which comes first, but which is primary.

Surveys reveal that up to 95 percent of all Christians have never lead a soul to Christ while 86 percent of all those who become Christians were converted by personal evangelism through a friend, relative, or neighbor whom they encounter where they work, live, or play.[20] Most young missionary candidates will not be grooving with the movers and shakers of nations initially, if ever, so let's teach them first things first. They must learn to disciple the peoples of the world by discipling the people of the world—one at a time.

I'll close with a word picture that gives that average disciple some vision for discipling the nations one at a time. Two boys were walking on a beach where thousands of starfish had been deposited as the tide retreated. As far as the eye could see, starfish lay baking in the afternoon sun, teetering near death. One of the boys feverishly started throwing them back into the ocean as fast as he could, knowing he would save their lives in doing so. He was ridiculed by his friend for his seemingly futile effort: "Look at all those starfish. You're not making any difference!" At which time the rescuer held up another grateful starfish, looked his friend in the eye and confidently asserted as he chucked it into the sea, "I made a difference to that one!"

God's plan for "starfish" is that they would live in harmony in his glorious starfish kingdom where righteousness, peace, and joy (Rom. 14:17) abound in every area of society. There the starfish will have beaten their swords into plowshares, and every area of starfish society is under the lordship of Christ. First of all, however, let us get them where they belong—into the saving arms of Jesus. If you, my dear reader, are in any form of missionary training or leadership, I would challenge you to take your shoes off your beautiful feet (Isa. 52:7) and lead those under your charge to the beach. The starfish are waiting.

"Follow me, and I will make you fishers of men." (Matt. 4:19 NKJV)

Notes

1. The death and resurrection of Christ, 1 Cor. 15:1–4.

2. Forgiveness and eternal life, Acts 2:38; John 3:16.

3. Repentance and faith, Mark 1:14–15.

4. In this chapter "social action" will denote applying biblical teaching and values into every area of society: ministry to the poor, the family, education, government, business, media, the arts, etc.

5. "Although reconciliation with God is not reconciliation with man, nor is social action evangelism, nor is political liberation salvation, nevertheless, we affirm that evangelism and socio-political involvement are both part of our Christian duty" (Lausanne Covenant, Clause 5). The Lausanne Covenant is available on the Internet at www.lausanne.org/lausanne-1974 /lausanne-covenant.html (accessed January 9, 2006).

6. Quoted in Ruth Tucker, *From Jerusalem to Irian Jaya* (Grand Rapids: Zondervan, 1983), 241.

7. William Booth, "Famous Words," Salvation Army International Heritage Center, www1.salvationarmy.org/heritage.nsf/All?OpenView, under "People" tab, then under "William Booth – Famous Words" (accessed April 30, 2007).

8. See Samuel Moffett, "Evangelism: The Leading Partner," in *Perspectives on the World Christian Movement: A Reader,* ed. Ralph D. Winter and Steven C. Hawthorne (Pasadena, Calif.: William Carey Library Publishers, 1981), 729–731.

9. "In the church's mission of sacrificial service, evangelism is primary" (Lausanne Covenant, Clause 6).

"As we have seen it, (the church's mission of sacrificial service) includes both evangelistic and social action, so that normally the church will not have to choose between the two. But if a choice has to be made, then evangelism is primary." John Stott, *Lausanne Covenant: An Exposition and Commentary* (Minneapolis: Worldwide Publications, 1975), section 6.

10. Catherine Mumford Booth, *Papers on Aggressive Christianity* (London: Salvationist Publishing and Supplies, 1880), 177, Victorian Women Writer's Project: An Electronic Collection, www.indiana.edu/~letrs/vwwp/booth/aggchrst.html#Text, (accessed April 30, 2007).

11. William Booth, "Famous Words," Salvation Army International Heritage Center, www1.salvationarmy.org/heritage.nsf/All?OpenView, under "People" tab then under "William Booth – Famous Words" (accessed April 30, 2007).

12. Tertullian, "Chapter 39," *Apology,* Rev. S. Thelwall, trans., at New Advent, The Fathers of the Church, www.newadvent.org/fathers/0301.htm (accessed April 30, 2007).

13. Thomas Cahill, *How the Irish Saved Civilization* (New York: Anchor Books, 1996).

14. John Wesley, "Upon Our Lord's Sermon on the Mount, 4, Point I," Global Ministries: The United Methodist Church: The Sermons of John Wesley, http://new.gbgm-umc.org /umhistory/wesley/sermons/24 (accessed April 30, 2007).

15. Michael Green, *Evangelism in the Early Church* (Grand Rapids: Eerdmans, 1970), 7.

16. Acts 13:5, 7, 16–43; 14:1, 6–7, 25; 16:13–14; 17:2, 10, 17–18, 22; 18:5; 19:8.

17. *Gladiator,* directed by Ridley Scott (Red Wagon Entertainment and Scott Free Productions, 2000).

18. World of Quotes.com: Historic Quotes and Proverbs Archive, www.worldofquotes.com /topic/Earth/index.html (accessed April 30, 2007).

19. Leonard Ravenhill, Why Revival Tarries (Minneapolis: Bethany Fellowship, 1959).

20. D. James Kennedy, *Evangelism Explosion* (Chicago: Tyndale, 1993), 4.

Lynn discusses the importance of incarnational evangelism, or demonstrating the life and love of Jesus to a community. In this volatile period of history when religious tensions are running high, this is an essential strategy for fulfilling the Great Commission. Lynn explores what incarnational evangelism can look like in the sphere of business, a key sphere in both opening the door to the initial stages of evangelism and bringing discipleship, especially in areas of the world that are resistant to the gospel.

Incarnational Evangelism:
There Is No Law Against Love

C. Lynn Green

In an increasingly volatile religious atmosphere around the world, how can Christians interpret Jesus' last commandment? His final recorded words in the gospel of Matthew are: "Therefore go and make disciples of all nations, baptizing them in the name of the Father and of the Son and of the Holy Spirit, and teaching them to obey everything I have commanded you. And surely I am with you always, to the very end of the age" (Matt. 28:19–20).

To some, that particular aspect of Jesus' teaching doesn't seem as relevant as it once was. In fact, much of the world would see it as an inflammatory imperative. There was a time when Christian nations and peoples enthusiastically and without apology exported their faith and their cultures. It was a widely accepted idea that some faiths (especially Christianity) and the cultures they spawned were superior to others—that they possessed more truth and should therefore be gratefully embraced by less fortunate peoples and nations. And often, such was the case. Entire nations in Africa and some in Asia and the Pacific islands freely embraced the Christian faith as presented, usually by European and American missionaries.

In our day, entire tribes or communities still embrace the Christian message and become Christians, as Donald McGavran documents in his work on "people movements,"[1] but this is less common than it was one or two centuries ago. In spite of that, there is no denying that countless individuals and families convert to active

Christian faith from other religious backgrounds every year. But it is often against a backdrop of social and governmental censure against religious conversion of any kind.

Confrontational Proselytizing

This antagonism is often provoked by an approach to evangelism that might be described as "confrontational proselytizing." The early 1990s provided a prime example.

In the first few years after the collapse of Communist regimes in the USSR and Eastern Europe, Christian evangelists from Western nations poured into the social, religious, and political vacuum. One television news crew produced a damning documentary by recording, without a narrator's comments, the thinking and actions of one team of evangelists.

The mostly young evangelists displayed an embarrassing ignorance and assumed superiority over the Christian traditions of the peoples they were targeting, branding the Orthodox faith, whose Christian roots go back to the second or third century, as a satanic deception. Their approach was confrontational and offensive. When their street preaching was greeted with resistance, on occasion they condemned their audience as worthily destined for hell.

Even though those "evangelists" were not representative of the majority who went east at that time, the documentary served to reinforce a popular stereotype of evangelism. As a result of that kind of caricature, many people today have insufficient knowledge to be able to distinguish between appropriate evangelism and confrontational proselytizing. So it is understandable that evangelism is at the very least frowned upon and often legislated against in much of the world.

Incarnational Evangelism

Again we must ask the question, What do Christians do about the last words of Jesus? Interestingly, the world in which he uttered those words was also antagonistic to proselytizing. The Roman authorities promoted an official pantheon of gods, including Caesar, who claimed divinity for himself. When the religious leaders of the Jews demanded the death of Jesus, it was on these grounds—that Jesus' claims were in direct opposition to Caesar's declaration of divinity.

In spite of such a hostile environment, the Christian message spread at a rapid pace. When circumstances allowed, his followers proclaimed the message of salvation through the name of Jesus in places of worship and in the public square. Though only a few of their messages are preserved, it is worth noting that they aimed to connect with their audiences by respecting their cultural and historical milieux. In the

Acts of the Apostles, chapter two, Peter quotes Jewish prophecies when preaching in Jerusalem. But in Acts 17 when the apostle Paul is preaching to Greeks in Athens, he commends their religious zeal and quotes from their own poets. In both cases, the speaker presents a commendable willingness to understand and engage his audience.

When official policy changed and public preaching was not allowed, these disciples promoted their faith by actions more than words. This was entirely consistent with their Leader. He had described them as salt and light on the earth. He had told them to let their good deeds be seen by all men so they would glorify God (Matt. 5:13–16).

Later, when the apostles wrote letters to congregations of believers who were scattered around the Roman Empire, they urged submission to, and respect for, governmental authorities, but exhorted the followers of Jesus to demonstrate their faith by doing good to all (Rom. 13; 1 Pet. 2). The apostle Paul summarized his message when he reminded the Galatians, "But the fruit of the Spirit is love, joy, peace, patience, kindness, goodness, faithfulness, gentleness and self-control. Against such things there is no law" (Gal. 5: 22–23). They bore witness by the way they lived.

Theirs was not a mute faith though. The apostle Peter exhorted them to "always be prepared to give an answer to everyone who asks you to give the reason for the hope that you have. But do this with gentleness and respect" (1 Pet. 3:15). Their way of living demonstrated that something extraordinary had occurred within them. Then, when opportunity arose, they were ready with an explanation.

With this approach they were following the fundamental nature of their new-found faith. When God sought to reveal himself to humankind, he did not just send a book or letter, or even an inspired messenger. He chose incarnation. He became one of us. By that infinitely inspired method, he demonstrated his nature in a manner that words alone could never match.

Sadly, in much of the world today, the Christian faith appears to be so intermingled with Western culture that the two are indistinguishable. For Muslims in the Middle East, Hindus in India, and Buddhists in Thailand, Christianity is understood to be part and parcel of a culture of hedonism, consumerism, and scientific materialism. Films, television, music, fashion, and the Internet reinforce that message daily in all corners of the world. So it is no wonder that Christian missionary activity is often seen as a most unwelcome activity.

There has, therefore, never been a better time for Christians to rediscover the importance of incarnational evangelism. It is clearly not a new approach. Church history is full of believers serving others in ways that demonstrate the nature of Jesus Christ. Emperor Julian the Apostate is recorded as complaining, "How shall we stop them? Not only do they care for their own poor, but ours as well!" St. Francis of Assisi said to his followers, "Go about everywhere preaching Christ. Where necessary, use words." When plague struck North Africa in AD 251, Cyprian, Bishop of Carthage, exhorted his congregation to risk their lives by remaining in the city to care for the sick and dying while others were fleeing. He preached, "There is nothing remarkable in cherishing merely our own people with the due attentions of love ... one should love his enemies as well."[2] Pontius, Cyprian's biographer records, "Thus, good was done to all, not merely the household of faith."[3]

To some extent, Christians still continue in this rich vein of incarnational evangelism. Today, medical missions still thrive, especially among the poor, and missionaries have developed high-quality educational establishments in almost every nation. And who is not aware of the remarkable work of the late Mother Teresa and her Sisters of Mercy, just one of countless expressions of love and grace offered by Christians?

The world today presents Christians with more and wider opportunities than ever for incarnational evangelism lived out in every sphere of life. Where preaching evangelists are not welcome, honest businesspeople are. Where missionaries can't get visas, Christian sports stars, artists, or entertainers have a ready entrée.

Every sphere of society—government, the arts and entertainment, media, health care, education, family, church or religious organizations, and business—needs active Christians who will demonstrate, with God's grace, high standards in work practices and ethics. An examination of the influence of business on a nation can highlight principles of incarnational evangelism that can be applied to any sphere of society.

Love in Action: Opportunities through Business

For a number of reasons, business may well provide the most influential opportunities of all at this time. Every nation hopes that their economy will prosper as foreign and domestic businesses thrive, producing jobs and enhancing standards of living. As a result, even the most remote parts of the world are ready and willing to welcome new business ventures. On the other hand, too many communities and entire nations have been disappointed at the hands of businesses that proved to be exploitative. But when they find honest businesspeople whom they can trust, the red carpet is rolled out.

Good business offers a service that efforts in other social domains cannot match—an opportunity to work with dignity. For those who have not experienced unemployment, it's easy to underestimate how debilitating it is. We are created with a fundamental need to work in a productive manner and to thereby gain access to the basic needs to sustain life—food, shelter, and clothing.

When businesses that are governed by biblical principles (I will call them *transformational businesses*) begin to multiply in a community or nation, they have the potential to transform the lives of families, communities, and entire nations. When good business begins to provide income, that in turn can lead to improvements in health care, education, and, in fact, the entire standard of living.

Some development experts have begun to question whether or not material improvement is a worthy goal. There is no doubt that material wealth introduces different social dynamics and personal temptations that can damage the relational dimensions of society. But prosperity does not inevitably destroy moral foundations. While the debate about these issues is valuable, it should not obscure the simple questions: Would we want our children to be sick or well? Would we prefer a life expectancy of forty years or seventy-five years? Would we want to be hungry or satisfied? Would we prefer to drink clean water or dirty water? There is no question that economic development and the advantages it brings should be available to all.

Business also provides an ideal environment for incarnational evangelism. Unfortunately, business can have a reputation for being the domain of greedy, ruthless people who exploit others for the sake of ever-increasing profit. But those who are not motivated by greed and personal advancement will therefore stand out in welcome contrast.

Full-time Christian workers (an anachronistic and unhelpful term) often find it difficult to make and maintain comfortable relationships with people who have different beliefs. It is quite logical that most "normal people" find it hard to understand or relate to a church minister or youth worker or missionary. No such barriers exist between fellow employees or managers in the workplace.

This relational dynamic can provide solutions to another difficulty for the Christian faith. The checkered history of the missions efforts of the "Christian" Western nations has made missionaries suspect in many parts of the world. They are often assumed to be spies or other shady characters. Sometimes these suspicions are simply the result of their behavior which sometimes defies normal interpretation. When a foreigner who has no obvious job or source of income seems to spend his or her time trying to get to know local people and engage them in conversations, it is quite reasonable to suspect that they have a hidden agenda. Of course, normal employment or commercial activities prevent these doubts from arising.

These are just some of the advantages of transformational business. In light of these benefits and the dangerous rise in recent years of religious tensions, committed Christians should be seeking opportunities to demonstrate their faith in the world of commerce.

There Is No Law Against Love

Several years ago, I met a man who was deeply convinced that God wanted him to be a witness to the Christian message in a Middle Eastern country. He consulted with his wife, quit his engineering job, and entered Bible college. After graduation he tried to find a mission board who would sponsor him and his wife, without success. Finally, because he was so sure of the call of God on his life, he simply bought a one-way ticket and moved to the Middle East.

For months after his arrival, he tried to work out what a "missionary" should do, but nothing seemed to be very effective. He found it hard to get to know the locals and he had to keep going out of the country to renew his tourist visa. Eventually his meager funds began to run out, so he and his wife faced a difficult decision—should they return home or try to find a way to make a living there? As they grappled with the choices before them, a local businessman discovered that this foreigner had some engineering skills, so he asked him for help on a project.

Nearly four decades later, it is obvious that this first request for practical help turned out to be the beginnings of an engineering design company. In the decades that followed, those small beginnings developed into a firm with hundreds of employees, many of whom came to faith in Christ. Some local authorities and many religious figures were antagonistic to the idea of an outspoken Christian living and working among them. But their antagonism was tempered by the fact that this "failed missionary" was an honest, humble man who provided employment for hundreds of their citizens.

The host nation is still resistant to anyone wishing to enter its borders as a missionary. But this one faithful man-and-wife team have become honored citizens who have built a world-class transformational business which, in turn, has resulted in one of the largest churches in that nation.

There aren't many transformational businesses like this yet, although evidence suggests that the story will be repeated many times in the years to come. In recent years, more and more Christian businesspeople have developed a deep longing to use their skills more fully for God's purposes.

Surely we are seeing more than ever the fruitfulness of the body of Christ reaching out to communities through the many spheres of life where we live and work. As we build relationships and discharge responsibilities in our workplaces with excellence, integrity, humility, and love, we demonstrate the life of Christ in a compelling way. And against love, joy, peace, patience, gentleness . . . there is no law!

Notes

1. Donald McGavran, *The Bridges of God* (London: World Dominion Press, 1955).
2. Pontius, *The Life of Cyprian,* 9 (available online through www.ccel.org).
3. Ibid., 10.

Kent Truewell describes an integrated, purposeful approach to discipling nations one community at a time. His "Developmentoring" process incorporates elements from both community development and church planting. Developmentoring comes to life as Kent explains the process and shows how it worked among the River People of the Amazon.

Developmentoring

Kent Truewell

Developmentoring is the self-reproducing process of bringing the kingdom of God to a community. Developmentoring is a ministry framework that draws from the concepts of biblical development, community, sociology, and church planting. This paper provides an overview of this process with particular reference to how it has worked among the River People of the Brazilian Amazon.

In brief, the developmentoring process begins with prayerfully selecting a target community from among the cultural mosaic of humanity. The focus then shifts to development: improving the community's quality of life and moving the community toward God's intentions. The goal of this development is to genuinely benefit the target communities and effectively reflect and initiate God's truth into every realm of society. To this effect, community institutions are structured and strengthened with an emphasis on mentoring and leadership development. Next, the new leaders create, or are initiated into, a church-planting movement. As this movement gains momentum, the followers step out to disciple the entire people group by going, baptizing, and teaching a new target community. Thus, developmentoring renews itself and disciples the nation, community by community.

Discovering Humanity—The Cultural Mosaic

The developmentoring process must begin with prayerfully identifying the specific people group to target. Missions strategist Donald McGavran explains that until humanity is seen as a mosaic, it cannot be properly understood or effectively evangelized.[1] Like individual and distinct mosaic tiles, mankind must be conceptualized as small socio-ethnic groups. To refer to people groups solely as countries or metaphorically as the harvest field does not portray an accurate picture of humanity. The authors of the *World Christian Encyclopedia*[2] concede that dividing humanity into separate mosaic tile segments can be somewhat artificial. But at the same time, both they and their colossal collection of statistics and diagrams gathered in the encyclopedia affirm McGavran's conclusion that it "is essential in order to comprehend and enumerate this vast complexity and to properly appreciate its kaleidoscopic nature, also in order to focus ministry and develop mission strategies or tactics which are appropriate and effectual."[3]

Under the leadership of YWAM Amazon, my family went to work among the ethnic group known as the River People of the Purus basin in the Amazon jungle of Brazil. Geographically and politically they are rural Brazilians, but sociologically and culturally they clearly form a distinct subunit. Average Brazilians quickly identify the River People culture as distinct from their own, and frequently cite examples that differentiate themselves from River People. Of the forty million rural Brazilians, three million live in the Amazon region. Of these, the bona fide River People comprise only the one million rural people actually living on the banks of the Amazon River or its 200+ tributaries. During our years of living among them we observed that the River People lived much like the hunter-gatherer indigenous peoples. Further, they spoke their own sociolect—a distinct way of speaking among a particular social group. This sociolect contains numerous idiomatic expressions from their jungle lifestyle, combined with a type of "King James Portuguese" spoken at the time of their migrations into the region between 1888 and 1912. It has a special vocabulary and pronunciations that left even our Brazilian coworkers at a loss on some occasions. The multiple characteristics that unite the River People as one, conversely also separate them from mainstream Brazilian culture. The main shared traits are their common history, their shared sociolect and cultural influences, their vocational uniformity as subsistence farmers and fisherman, their geographic isolation, and their lack of political participation. Most importantly, they perceive themselves to be unique, and are proud of the fact that they, alone, are the River People.

Designing Development

After the selection of a target people group, the next task is designing development. But what is development? In rich nations, development in a community is normally equated with social work or initiatives in social welfare. In the poor areas of the world, development is traditionally defined as "improving the quality of life." These definitions are good, but they are limited as a development model for Christian missionaries. A biblical development model must be holistic, in no way limited by the Greek sacred-secular dichotomy common in Western minds and cultures, including the Western church. Christian missions and Christian community development can be, and should be, fully integrated into a unified expression. Christian development does not require a choice between preaching "the gospel of salvation," or "the social gospel." Jesus himself preached neither of these but only preached the gospel of the kingdom. "Jesus went throughout Galilee, teaching in their synagogues, preaching the good news of the kingdom, and healing every disease and sickness among the people" (Matt. 4:23. See also Matt. 9:35). The kingdom of God is "the divine rule in the lives of those who acknowledge Christ."[4] This is supported by Matthew 6:10, "your kingdom come, your will be done on earth as it is in heaven."

Matt. 24:14 says that "this gospel of the kingdom will be preached in the whole world as a testimony [witness] to all nations, and then the end will come." I feel this verse is less about the coming end and more about the gospel of the kingdom. The gospel of the kingdom is the development philosophy of missions, bringing the good news of the rule and reign of God into a community of people on earth, right here and now, through meeting their needs: intellectual, physical, spiritual, and social.

Addressing social challenges with the gospel of the kingdom is a very different reality to the preaching of a "social gospel" as originally articulated in *A Theology for the Social Gospel*.[5] A definition of Christian development work that summarizes the key concepts, stands firm on biblical truth, and is concise and useful in missions is "growth towards God's intentions."[6] We should remind ourselves that Jesus was raised in a small village of a poor nation. Yet, even in Nazareth two thousand years ago, a basic yet appropriate and sufficient development was provided for Jesus. Luke 2:52 says, "Jesus grew in wisdom and stature, and in favor with God and men." This verse provides a useful framework for biblical development, as it outlines God's intentions of growth for his own son. The involved and loving Father went so far as to fashion the worldview, culture, and institutions of an entire ethnicity, the people of Israel, just to ensure that his child benefited from this development.[7]

We should also remember that in spite of three marvelous years of ministry, the first 91 percent of the life of Jesus was basic development. That is, thirty years of slow, sociological, and unspectacular development. As far as God his Father was concerned, the 91 percent development was a precursor to the 9 percent of successful ministry. If it was obligatory rather than optional for God, shouldn't development remain an obligatory first component of any ministry?

Clearly, many avenues could be profitably followed in any society to facilitate "growth toward God's intentions." So the question becomes, how does the Christian missionary select the focus area(s) of development ministry? Among the River People, we determined that health care was the primary felt need of the people. We discovered this first and foremost through the incarnational ministry approach of "dwelling among them" (see John 1:14). Of course, this included diligently learning their language and culture. Additionally we engaged in observation and ethnographic study, community and health baseline surveys, as well as regular prayer for God's direction in regards to the development needs on which to focus.

Working in development via health care gave us legitimate roles and goals in their communities and granted us access into their lives in ways that we could not have easily achieved as "religious workers." In no way, however, was God left out of our work. Infant mortality was 25 percent in remote villages. While working in health care we would declare that it was *not* God's will or intention that so many children died. Through the development vehicle of health care we described and demonstrated a compassionate and loving Father who wanted the best for them and their children.

Benefiting Community

The book *Church Growth and Group Conversion* describes how the expansion of the gospel in India was halted by an invisible but very real social reality—the caste system.[8] The upper castes wanted nothing to do with a religion that forced them to mingle with those castes they considered to be inferior. This example clearly demonstrates that strategizing to reach a whole nation, or even an entire ethnic group, is usually too broad to be practical. Grandiose goals are indeed inspiring, but being overly generic, they prove to be impractical for designing ministry direction or concrete plans of action.

The most strategic focus for beginning any ministry is community. But what is community? Neither community, nor the biblical term *ta ethne,* which we translate into our word *nation,* refers to a mere aggregation of individuals. Sociologically speaking, the community, not the individual, is the essential unit of mankind that should be engaged through the missionary enterprise. Community is a microcosm of the larger *ethne.* Community provides a sense of individual identity within a group context. In simple social settings the community defines that identity. Community gives status, defines roles, and networks these roles into perpetual functions we call institutions.[9] Ethnicity is manifested at the community level through practical chores, daily social interaction, and the cultural expressions of the social group.

McGavran's general premise for his 1979 book *Ethnic Realities and the Church* is that the key for any mission enterprise is the social factor.[10] Understanding community and its basic sociology can make ethnicity and its local social realities one's partner, even one's greatest asset in ministry, rather than being one's greatest hurdle—or worse yet, one's greatest enemy. When assessing the degree of evangelization among the River People communities, I sought to learn about the amount and type of contact the communities already had with Christianity. I encouraged my friend and cultural informant to explain how they maintained order and structure in their lives. In doing so, he described how evangelical Protestant Christians made a *bagunça* in their communities. *Bagunça* is derived from the Portuguese verb meaning "to promote disorder and confusion." This was a strong indictment against the Protestant church workers who did not understand the River People communities and their social order and protocols. This lack of sensitivity was interpreted by the River People as a lack of respect and, in some cases, as outright dislike. Where the evangelicals were allowed to take root, they often brought such social disorder that previously harmonious communities became divided. Consequently, the River People communities sometimes drove visiting evangelicals out of their villages. This happened not because the River People hated Jesus Christ or the salvation message. It was because the methods of the evangelicals were inconsistent with the good news of the gospel. I learned through this insight that non-Christian communities do not want to trade their current social benefits on earth for some potential future spiritual benefits in heaven.

Much community disruption seemed to stem from the evangelical urgency of evangelizing individuals as opposed to the slower but historically more comprehensive approach of evangelizing the whole community. Generally speaking, in developed Western nations individual autonomy is a social reality. This means an individual can become a Christian in spite of community practice and tradition and even against family wishes. Individual autonomy, however, is not the cultural norm in the majority of nations and communities—yes, even in the twenty-first century! Communal and family authority remains the social context for most individuals in this world. The key for any mission enterprise is the social factor; evangelizing the community and family authorities is therefore the key to success.

Wooing individuals out from the authority of their family and bringing them under the authority of a mission or church organization is a recipe for spiritual and social disaster. If Christians are not contributing to the development and well-being of the community in other ways, then showing disrespect for family authority will be especially unwelcome. A pastor or missionary who evangelizes individuals usually gives status, defines roles, and quickly networks these individuals to carry out the functions of the church. But the defining and networking of roles in the community is normally assigned to the community leaders. Thus, in practice, the church creates a second community within the existing community and offends family and community authorities in the process. The local community is eventually divided when an ultimatum to choose allegiance is pressed by either the current community leadership or the new church leadership. As a result *bagunça* (disorder and confusion) is created in their communities.

Evangelizing individuals in this manner can therefore result in fractured relationships and communities and actually produce minimal long-term results for the church in family- and community-authority-based societies. Also, because imposing the mission or denominational culture often accompanies this approach, the second or "rebel" community (church) may only remotely reflect the culture of the larger ethnicity. This antagonizes not only the local community where the newly established church is located but antagonizes the larger ethnic expression as well, making further church planting in other communities even more difficult. In this scenario the Christian becomes a community destroyer rather than a community developer.

In our work we sought to evangelize the community as opposed to "snatching individuals from the fires of hell"—the usual justification for personal evangelism. After eighteen months of incarnational ministry and development work we still had no converts. At this time another church-planting initiative started in a large village six hours down river using the individual decision approach. After only four months a church building was built and the pastor had numerous converts. Within a year there was a seemingly vibrant church with twenty-five to thirty baptized believers. In the second year, significant community backlash came and many converts backslid. By the third year the membership seemed to level off at around twenty of the two hundred adults in the community. The nonlocal pastor then moved to the capital city while the church, then ten years old and without a pastor, remained at about 10 percent of the community.

On the other hand, in the twenty-fifth month of the developmentoring process, we saw a significant move to Christ. In the twenty-eighth month I baptized the community leader who in turn immediately baptized sixteen others. Within a year, seventy of the eighty members of the community were in the church, with thirty-one of the forty adults baptized—about 75 percent of the community. Ten years later this community was about 80 percent Christian, has the same original local pastor, and has started churches in neighboring villages. The community leader/pastor has baptized over 100 adults in the region and helps lead a network of churches totaling 400–500 in weekly attendance. All of these churches are under local community leadership and are viewed positively by community members and the River People subculture group at large.

Strengthening Institutions

Institutions are the infrastructure of all human communities. Because institutions vary greatly according to their purpose and cultural milieu, there are diverse institutions, including those dedicated to education, spiritual affairs, recreation, politics, etc. Institutions in urban and developed-world settings tend to express Western individualism and be subservient to distant state and/or national authorities. Communities in the developing world also organize and express themselves through institutions. Although far less subservient to distant authorities, and minuscule by comparison to the behemoth organizations of the developed urban world, they are institutions none the same. Because of this important aspect of human interaction and social organization, the developmentoring process logically transitions to the objective of strengthening institutions.

Institutions are "cultural procedures that have become formally organized and enforced by the groups serving the institutional function."[11] Individuals, even nuclear families, were never capable of meeting all their required and desired needs. Institutions therefore are required for families to meet their basic development needs. Although individual autonomy and distant political authority is characteristic of Western institutions, the process of families joining together under a common purpose is the heart of a community institution. Institutions are important to missionaries because any potential church will also be a community institution. By examining the process through which community institutions emerge, a sociocultural pattern for the emergence of a church becomes evident.

Community institutions emerge when community spirit, intertwined with a genuine felt need, initiates a process of community mobilization among representative families. Education is an example of this process. Parents are ultimately responsible for all of the development needs of their children, including education. Because individual nuclear families are generally incapable of meeting all their educational needs, the role of a teacher is created to educate the community children collectively. The authority of the teacher is a delegated authority from the parents, who set standards for the local institution for the benefit of themselves and their children. The institution (school) in turn holds members of the community accountable to the objectives given to it by the parents. This example, which indicates a social order in keeping with biblical principles, places the individual under community institutions, which in turn are under the authority of the family.

In addition to examining emerging institutions, the Christian development worker should scrutinize extant institutions and develop a response to the functions they provide the community. Upon arrival in non-Christian societies, Christian and secular development workers alike struggle with the pervasive sinfulness and lack of development. Many formally organized cultural procedures are sinful, don't work, or are even contrary to the desired progress! Too commonly the incoming inexperienced worker deems it easier to reject the existing system and start over.

Human communities are dynamic; therefore changing needs may render an institution redundant. Hence, some institutions do not appear to benefit anyone beyond those few in the institution itself. In this case, throwing out an institution may benefit a community. Often, however, compelling reasons constrain workers to retain community roles and work within existing institutions. Institutions and their procedures involve peoples' lives in a significant way. Though aware of institutional shortcomings, the missionary development worker should carefully count the cost of working to remove an institution. Community members should not be thrown out along with the problematic cultural system. An excellent illustration of this point comes from Bruce Olson's work among the Motilone tribe of Colombia. The tribal witch doctor concocted many strange and ineffectual jungle remedies in an attempt to cure a pink eye outbreak in the tribe.[12] Bruce Olson wisely did not provide the cure himself but offered his antibiotic anointment to the witch doctor. As a result the tribe was cured and the witch doctor's esteem was strengthened as a person and as health provider. Over time the witch doctor himself, and the precarious health institution he led, was transformed and redeemed!

Both the people that provide the service through the institution and the institution itself are key pieces of the community mosaic. Ideally, one should seek to redeem both the function and the person performing it.

The four components of Jesus' development listed in Luke 2:52 translate into four essential institutions needed in any community around the world. Wisdom represents the institution of education; stature, the institution of health; favor with God, the institution of religion; and favor with man, the institution of government. Without these four areas of basic development, a collection of families never will successfully create or maintain community. The Jewish community of Nazareth, even two thousand years ago, had these institutions functioning so that a sufficient development was provided for Jesus. Though not extravagant, it did the job well. The institutions enabled Jesus to grow toward God's intentions. All communities must have access to sufficient levels of development through local community institutions. It need not be comprehensive or costly, but the institutional role must function.

Our work among the River People endeavored to be instrumental in strengthening the institution of health. There were many erroneous ideas surrounding the origin of disease among the River People. Even more troubling, however, were the many outrageous, costly, and sometimes dangerous practices used for curing disease. In spite of the ill-founded science and practices of the River People's community institution of health, we called together all the local health workers and learned what we could from them. We learned much more than we had initially expected. Through our interactions, they also learned from us. We involved them in clinical visits and broadened every consultation from just the curative to an educational and even spiritual experience, where we taught and prayed for all patients. We used this relational, on-the-job training approach not only in health but also in the other three domains of Luke 2:52.

Mentoring Leaders

For institutions to function well they must have capable leaders. Therefore, an important component of strengthening institutions should be mentoring, or developing leaders. The relational, on-the-job leadership training described previously is the mentoring of leaders. Transforming change is not accomplished through just one great teaching or methodology. Mentoring is not a single event but a series of intentional actions to induce gradual changes leading toward an intended result. Jesus is the best example we have that outlines the process of mentoring and developing leaders. His ministry may be fruitfully examined for ideas on how to develop leaders.

The kingdom of God was unquestionably the ministry theme and message of Jesus. His public ministry constituted a brief 9 percent of his time on earth. Despite such a short time span, his ministry message and method were earth changing. What were they? "Repent" and "believe" comprise the two main elements of the kingdom message.[13] Significantly, the kingdom method that Jesus employed was developing leaders in the context of community. Jesus chose his leaders from among those he lived with every day. Like Jesus, they were minimally educated, blue-collar, western-Aramaic-speaking, Galilean men.[14] "Jesus challenged potential disciples with the words 'follow me,' he did not invite them to just link up with a certain system of thought or project, but to commit themselves to him as a person...into a life-transforming relationship."[15]

Jesus did not invite the disciples to join an organization; he called them into relationship. Relationship is the means through which people grow toward and into God's intentions. Others will not commit or entrust themselves to us if we do not first commit ourselves to them. Too often the tendency of the Christian worker is to commit in relationship only to community members after they are redeemed. This practice is not in keeping with the lifestyle of Jesus who befriended sinners.

In working with health care for the River People we practiced three key principles for mentoring leaders. The first key was teaching in and through relationship. Everyone who sought health care was treated and also trained to treat themselves and their family members. Thus, every consultation was a training session. Every consultation was also a personal, unrushed, and friendly visit. This built the relational base necessary for mentoring.

Modeling is a second key aspect of mentoring. For the institution of health, we sought to visibly model hygienic and healthy practices as a family. The parents in the community marveled at how our children, who lived and played with theirs, remained healthy while so many of their children repeatedly succumbed to sickness.

The third key principle of mentoring is appointing. Together with the community, we selected individuals to receive further training. Two people from each of seven different communities were appointed to be rural health agents-in-training. These fourteen, most with a second-grade education, had the following job description: (1) to learn and to do health care with our team, (2) to preach and teach health to others, (3) to cast out sickness through prayer, medicine, or both (Mark 3:13–15). This aspect of appointing created a formal commitment and a recognized role for the local person. It also highlights the importance of planned and intentional components of a mentoring program.

After almost three years, thirteen of the fourteen trainees successfully completed the rural health agents training and were formally commissioned to this task. They were not only mentored in health areas; they were mentored socially and spiritually as well. Almost half of the rural health agents became Christians in the training process. The impartation of values and beliefs easily occurred in a mentoring relationship. The newly Christian health agents easily embraced Christian mentoring, which "involves developing disciples through encouragement and sound instruction based on God's word (Titus 2:6, 15) and the formation of leaders (2 Tim. 2:2)."[16]

Even after three years our rural health agents did not appear fully prepared for the challenging job ahead. Amazingly enough, neither did the eleven apostles feel ready, even after three years with Jesus. The successful mentoring and leadership development method of Jesus was intense, but short. *Jesus modeled, trained, commissioned— then he left!* According to Jesus' methodology, the best leadership development is intensive mentoring followed by a quick, and total, release into leadership and responsibility. Our tendency is to demand perfection from others before trusting and releasing them into leadership.[17] Clearly, this is contrary to the approach Jesus used.

Whether it be for wisdom development or social development, health care or church planting, when you mentor people you call them into a transforming relationship. You expose them to your character, your integrity, your servant leadership, your compassion, your authority, your obedience, and even your righteous indignation. Of course, "Jesus Christ is the real and decisive agent in Christian mentoring. We cannot bring about change in our mentorees, yet we can influence them to be changed by Jesus Christ."[18]

Starting Movements

Too often mentoring in the vocational context focuses exclusively on doing—doing a job—while too often mentoring in the discipleship context focuses exclusively on being—being a good Christian. One key distinctive of the developmentoring process is to raise the eyes of the mentorees off themselves (a "being" focus) and off their immediate job (a "doing" focus), so they can set their gaze on the big picture of the overall system.

Developmentoring requires systems thinking. In the developmentoring process, leaders are mentored with the aim of starting movements. This requires taking into view the whole social system. The goal of the developmentoring process therefore is not just Christian health agents or Christian schoolteachers. The goal is changing the nation one community at a time.

Jesus did not just evangelize and mentor a few fishermen. From the beginning, Jesus set out to start a movement. In relationship, he mentored his disciples in the process of starting a movement. "Jesus prepared his closest followers thoroughly for future leadership responsibilities within the prospective movement."[19]

In Matthew 15:24 Jesus states, "I was sent only to the lost sheep of Israel." With the lost sheep of Israel as his target audience, it is noteworthy that Jesus developed his own leaders and movement among a distinct Jewish subculture—a sociopeople called the Galileans. These Galileans repeated the model of Jesus and started a movement among the larger Jewish ethnicity in the capital city. Successfully starting a culturally sensitive movement implies a social dynamic where a group enthusiastically adopts a new way of life, as if it were a natural expression of their ethnicity. Starting movements among a social group is essentially the same as the missions phenomenon of "people movements." "A people movement is a meaningful procedure or form of action by which communal people register symbolically their acceptance of cultural change."[20]

Donald McGavran describes people movements as "the supreme goal of a missionary effort."[21] People movements start most easily within a homogeneous group, such as the River People or northern Galilean fishermen, because identification and communication is so strong in a uniform community. People movements often start slowly through relationship building and practical work (development), but then grow quickly as spiritual manifestations of the kingdom of God begin to transpire among the people. When community members conclude that spiritual development, represented by the emerging institution called the church, benefits their community, they are more likely to experience a people movement. Expanding like the progression in Acts 1:8, this wildfire growth often spreads into culturally similar communities. Once started, people movements are relatively easily perpetuated. Because the movement fits the social structure of the people, the social structure reinforces the movement.

Discipling Nations

As a people movement gains momentum, new believers will naturally work toward an Acts 1:8 expansion of the kingdom. Following Jesus, they will do his works. Jesus started a movement that resulted in the Jerusalem church. This movement continued in Judea and Samaria, and in a generation spread throughout the Roman Empire. Although the local church is just one of the institutions of any community, the universal church, the collection of all believers committed to obeying Christ, is *the* vehicle for discipling the entire people group. With this thought in mind, the Great Commission command to make disciples can be restated as bringing the kingdom of God into ALL communities on earth. The Lord's Prayer can also be understood in this light: Our Father, who art in heaven, hallowed be thy name . . .

> God's kingdom come
> His will and intentions be done
> On earth—right here and right now—
> In every way
> As it is being perfectly done in heaven. (my paraphrase)

The mechanism for accomplishing this goal is the body of Christ. Christian workers should make the church the principle agent of development in a community. Some Christian workers suggest that development is a distraction to church planting, even contrary to discipling nations! This thinking, however, reflects pagan Greek dualism, where the physical is inherently bad while only the spiritual is good. Others argue that Jesus himself never did development work. To that I suggest rereading the gospels and counting all the times he assists somebody physically. In addition to this I would add that Jesus never engaged in what we often deem the most spiritual of all initiatives—church planting. That's right, Jesus never planted a church! Jesus' ministry met physical (healing) needs, wisdom (teaching) needs, and other areas of need that today we classify as development. The important consideration in all of this is to say that development work does not imply an unholy alliance or compromise with the world, nor does it necessitate a dilution of the gospel.

Discipling the nations as found in Matthew 28:19–20 is normally understood to involve making disciples by going, baptizing, and teaching. These are important activities to carry out for establishing a group of believers committed to obeying Christ. In light of the previous discussion about the kingdom of God and our examination of the developmentoring process, discipling a nation is clearly far more comprehensive than those three activities. It is the work of the church in every sphere of society; it is people growing toward God's intentions in every dimension of life.

> The Kingdom has to do with everything, every part of life, and every part of society. God is not just interested in redeeming our souls. He is interested in every aspect of our life. Everything comes under His lordship. We need to embrace the larger picture of God's call on the church, not just to preach the

gospel to every creature, which we must do, but [also] to make sure every creature has their inheritance through discipling their nation.[22]

Our health care and literacy work among the River People purposefully pointed to Christ and intentionally sought to start a movement. This eventuated in a locally led River People fellowship, which in turn led to a church planting movement among other River People communities. The developmentoring process combines the strength of "being-focused mentoring" (Christian character), with the action and productivity of "doing-focused mentoring" (vocational skills), all under the larger vision of starting a kingdom-transforming movement of change in the social system, in the people, in the nation.

Sustainability

Sustainability is a major concern among political and international development organizations. Essentially all development proposals drafted today build sustainability into the project design. Sustainability is a critical component in consideration of community intervention. It involves planning your exit before you even start. It entails working in a prescribed way now so that your work has the ability to continue in the future without you. Church planting and discipling the nations proposals should approach the discussion of sustainability very seriously. Scripture verbalizes this concern as "fruit that will last" (John 15:16).

Peter F. Drucker, in his book *The Effective Executive,* writes, "An organization that is not capable of perpetuating itself has failed. An organization, therefore, has to provide today the man who can run it tomorrow."[23] From this standpoint Jesus was a very effective executive. He strengthened institutions, mentored leaders, and started movements, so that the fruit (the church) could sprout, bloom, flourish, and multiply.

If a building, a person, or material goods are the sole fruits of the development work, keep in mind they will eventually wither, die, or become obsolete. However, *if a model of the process is instilled in the people, it may be perpetuated for generations to come.* Knowing the process of creating a product is actually more valuable than the product itself, because if the process is corrupted, forgotten, or unused, the product cannot be produced.

Developmentoring is a missions term created to describe the overall process of bringing the kingdom of God into a community and its larger ethnicity. Discipling all individuals in all communities in all nations is the desired final outcome. But often when we talk about discipling ALL the nations we do not develop mission strategies or tactics that are appropriate and effectual at the grassroots level of diverse human communities. The broad global discussion tends to focus on Christian leaders, organizational movements, and current staff but tends to forget about humanity, development, community, and institutions.

A danger common in discussing the discipling of nations is to refer only to the activity of discipling. Singular tasks or a collection of nonintegrated ministries fall short of achieving the desired final outcome. This narrow approach focuses on numerous varied activities without the context of the bigger picture. Developmentoring, in contrast, sequences key steps into an overall process for bringing the kingdom of God into a community while maintaining a wider view necessary for reaching the entire ethnicity.

As we have seen, developmentoring outlines a process of seven continuous stages: (1) discovering humanity (selecting the tile to serve), (2) designing development, (3) benefiting community, (4) strengthening institutions, (5) mentoring leaders, (6) starting movements, and (7) discipling nations.

One word of caution must be stated. With a developmentoring process it can be difficult to determine when success has been attained. Any overall process can be somewhat vague and invisible in comparison to tangible results like church buildings, agricultural yields, or other goals you achieve along the way. A common human tendency is to seek a finished product, a showpiece to exhibit. Often Christian workers also experience many external pressures from supporters and other constituents to produce quick, visible results. However, if the developmentoring process is instilled in those chosen and appointed to go and bear fruit (see John 15:16), and woven into the institutional fabric of their society, fruit will remain for generations to come.

Conclusion

Luke 2:52 is the foundation for developmentoring because it implies that our Father in heaven made certain that his Son's community in Galilee, and the larger ethnicity of Israel, benefited from sufficient development for Jesus to grow in wisdom, stature, and in favor with God and man. God did not stop short with insufficient and nonintegrated development for his Son. He wants nothing less for the billions of children on earth today.

All seven steps outlined in the developmentoring process are necessary for bringing the kingdom of God on earth right here and right now. Developmentoring's seven steps integrate the potential plethora of kingdom-related activities into a system for changing a community. Developmentoring is systems thinking, and systems thinking is developmental thinking. Such thinking is necessary to get the job of the kingdom done. A system integrates different processes into a workable whole. "This integrated way of viewing life is absolutely essential for a person to be a truly courageous leader, capable of transforming his/her world."[24]

The developmentoring process begins with discovering the ethnic tile of humanity to target for this project and then designing development based on the felt needs of that segment. Needs-based development benefits the target community while it strengthens local institutions by mentoring or leadership development. The larger aim of mentoring leaders is the social dynamic of a church planting movement. The church sprouting from that movement disciples the larger ethnicity by going, baptizing, and teaching in new target communities. The process is then reproducing itself. In short, developmentoring is the process by which the mandate to go and make disciples of all nations is fulfilled—one community at a time.

Notes

1. This is one of the predominant themes of McGavran's teaching that is more specifically highlighted in the two books *The Bridges of God* (UK: World DominionPress, 1955) and *Ethnic Realities and the Church* (Pasadena, Calif.: William Carey Library, 1979).

2. David Barrett, George Thomas Kurian, and Todd M. Johnson, *The World Christian Encyclopedia,* 2nd ed. (New York: Oxford University Press, 2001).

3. David B. Barrett and Todd M. Johnson, *World Christian Trends, AD 30--AD 2200: Interpreting the Annual Christian Megacensus* (Pasadena, Calif.: William Carey Library, 2001), 38.

4. John Stott, *New Issues Facing Christians Today,* 3rd ed. (London: Marshall Pickering, 1999), 9.

5. Walter Rauschenbusch, *Theology for the Social Gospel* (New York: Abingdon Press, 1917).

6. Bob Moffitt, "Moving Toward a Vision of the Kingdom of God," article in the Leadership Development Training Program I (Scottsdale, Ariz.: The Harvest Foundation, 1998), 241–245.

7. Landa Cope, *Discipling the Nations: The Old Testament Template* (Kailua Kona: University of the Nations, 1995).

8. J. Pickett, G. Singh, and D. McGavran, *Church Growth and Group Conversion* (Lucknow, India: Lucknow Publishing House, 1956).

9. Paul G. Hiebert, *Cultural Anthropology* (Grand Rapids: Baker Book House, 1976), 177–193.

10. McGavran, *Ethnic Realities and the Church.*

11. Hiebert, *Cultural Anthropology,* 189–193.

12. Bruce Olson, *Bruchko* (Altamonte Springs, Fla.: Creation House, 1973).

13. John Bright, *The Kingdom of God* (Nashville: Abingdon Press, 1953).

14. Gunter Krallmann, *Mentoring for Mission* (Hong Kong: Jensco Ltd., 1992), 43–49.

15. Ibid., 104.

16. John Mallison, *Mentoring to Develop Disciples and Leaders* (Adelaide, Australia: Open Book Publishers, 1998), 5.

17. Denny Gunderson, *The Leadership Paradox* (Seattle: YWAM Publishing, 1997), 135–136.

18. Mallison, *Mentoring to Develop Disciples and Leaders*, 39.

19. Krallman, *Mentoring for Mission*, 68.

20. Alan Tippett, *People Movements in Southern Polynesia* (Chicago: Moody Press, 1971), 219.

21. McGavran, *The Bridges of God*, 81.

22. Landa Cope, "Making Disciples of All Nations . . . What does that Really Mean?" *The Mandate* (July 1993): 6–9.

23. Peter F. Drucker, *The Effective Executive* (New York: Harper Collins, 1993), quoted in George Barna, *Leaders on Leadership* (Ventura, Calif.: Regal Books, 1997), 303.

24. James Halcomb, David Hamilton, and Howard Malmstadt, *Courageous Leaders: Transforming Their World* (Seattle: YWAM Publishing, 2001), 34.

From his many years of personal experience as a frontier missionary and a leader of hundreds of missionaries in South Asia, Steve takes us along for a more detailed look at a particular missions strategy for discipling nations: people movements. He also raises vital points of discussion around the importance of being engaged in both church planting and conversion as well as discipleship and being salt and light in a nation. There's no one sequence to disciple a nation, but it's a process that must be consciously pursued for all people groups.

The Importance of People Movements
in Discipling Nations

Steve Cochrane

As we consider the command of Jesus in Matt. 28:19, "go and make disciples of all nations," it is vitally important that we understand the place of people groups moving toward Christ. Throughout mission history one of the most common ways people have come to know Jesus is not one by one, but as a group or tribe together. Often this approach has been discounted in church and mission history with comments like "shallow growth" or "only motivated by socioeconomic reasons." While certainly true at times, it can be tempting to throw the baby out with the bathwater and miss an incredibly strategic and God-honoring way of the kingdom advancing.

When sufficient disciple-makers have been involved in these mass movements toward the gospel, the results have been very different than what the nay-sayers would want us to believe. Whole peoples and geographical areas have changed, with worldviews and behaviors impacted by the gospel. An important assumption in this whole topic must be that we always want to see an emphasis on discipling "nations" in spreading the gospel. This requires great cost and commitment, with people available for this task as well as for the initial church planting. In this chapter we will examine the importance of people-group movements by highlighting three movements: two in South Asia started in the late nineteenth century and one in the late twentieth century. We will also discuss how we can more effectively strategize with people-group thinking, bearing in mind the necessary connection to discipling nations.

People-Group Movements in South Asia

In India, mission historians estimate that up to 90 percent of today's Indian Christians can trace back to movements of their people group into Christianity. In 1955 Dr. Donald McGavran, a former missionary to India, published a significant book called *The Bridges of God*.[1] Dr. McGavran built on the work of another missionary, Watsom Pickett.[2] Both men stressed the positive results in India and South Asia of these movements, while not ignoring the negatives or dangers. Some of the greatest examples of these movements are in northeast India, with people groups like the Naga, Mizo, and Khasi. These historic movements primarily occurred between 1870 and 1940, but several are developing today among groups like the Banjara, Chamar, Koli, and Malto.

European Christianity can also look back in its history to many of its people coming to Christ together. We can see this especially with the Irish (and the overall Celtic movement of the fifth century onwards), the Germanic tribes, and Vikings (modern Swedes, Danes, Norwegians). Granting that a whole new dynamic of evangelization and discipling needs to happen among these people today, we can still see the tremendous power of these movements in their time.[3]

Let us look briefly at three examples of movements for Christ among groups in South Asia. None of these stories describes perfect success (is there ever?) and all three illustrate the need for continuing discipling of their "nations."

The first example, from the late nineteenth century, involves the Churhas in the region of modern-day Pakistan. The Churhas, a people group of low-caste Hindu origin, were agricultural workers and very oppressed. Starting with the conversion of one man who began to reach his relatives, a people movement began. After eighty years, virtually every Churha had become a Christian. While there were many exciting advances for the gospel among this group, many individuals also returned to Hindu groups. More workers were needed to help disciple the new believers and those who were seeking. Though insufficient outsiders responded, the Holy Spirit initiated strong prayer movements which helped to bring spiritual depth in the face of oppression and lack of discipleship. Missionaries and nationals, individuals and entire churches, gave themselves up to long periods of prayer, sometimes twelve hours at a time. They also fasted. Today, after several generations, we observe a need for renewal and for a missions challenge to the Churhas to encourage them to reach their surrounding society.

The second example comes from northeast India, where the Mizo people group saw tremendous mission advances in the early and middle years of the twentieth century. The Mizo, who primarily live in the Indian state of Mizoram, are a colorful, dynamic people. Some have said that there are more Mizo missionaries sent out per capita than from any other people group in the world. Today the Mizo are over 90 percent Christian, yet there is a deep need for discipling this new generation. Worldview and behavioral changes abound in the Mizo story as they responded to Christ and grew in him.[4]

Over the past twenty-five years in our ministry in India, we have had many Mizo Christians in our Discipleship Training Schools. Though they do have these powerful tribal memories of how God has worked in their midst, this generation often struggles with drugs, broken relationships, and a sense of rootlessness. We have seen these Mizos come to a much greater sense of their need for ongoing discipleship personally, as well as their people's need to walk closer to Christ.

Coming to more recent history, we have the story of the Banjara. A nomadic group found throughout central and southern India, the Banjara are experiencing an ongoing people movement that seems to be growing in power. In the past two years there have been large meetings of thousands of believers for encouragement and challenge, and several key Banjara tribal leaders have come to the Lord. It is crucial even now that committed disciple-makers be involved among the Banjaras.

These disciple-makers have an open door to come alongside even some of the Banjara tribal leaders mentioned above. One of the most exciting things about this movement is the number of village leaders who have responded to Christ. But ongoing discipleship is needed so this movement can grow in depth.

These movements and others (some of which have been arrested in the initial stage) show us that depth of commitment to Christ and Christlikeness in life are very possible, but ongoing discipling is vital. One mission researcher has said that based on studying many of these movements, an average time period of twenty-three years elapses from the entrance of the pioneer missionaries into the unreached group to the time when a self-sustaining, self-multiplying movement has began. To be more effective in discipling people groups, we must develop a specific strategy and way of thinking about people movements.

Defining People-Movement Thinking

People movements to Christ are not just social or economic transformations. They are caused by genuine stirrings of the Spirit of God. McGavran said that "Christward movements of peoples are the supreme goal of missionary effort."[5] There is a multi-individual decision involved, often led by the existing authority structures. As experienced by groups in the Pacific and elsewhere, there often is a "power encounter" between the gods of the people and the Lord God.

People-movement thinking means that the initial intent of the church planting effort is to see a whole people come to Christ, and then be discipled in every area of their personal and collective life. The discipleship process envisioned must include the emergence of new mission movements from the newly reached group to other unreached peoples. Strategies (discussed below) must be chosen and implemented to bring these goals to pass.

People-movement thinking and strategy will ensure that no people group is left untouched by the gospel. Rather than focusing on a few individuals, and perhaps missing their surrounding relatives, we enlarge our visual field to include the entire group. People-movement thinking is not a new concept in missions; however, in the early twentieth century, discussions centering on people movements became more frequent due to missionaries in India like Pickett and McGavran.

Some have used the term "mass movements," but this can falsely connote that these movements are a product either of mass hysteria or forced from the leaders above. A painful example (unfortunately one of many) comes to us during the Crusades of the eleventh and twelfth centuries, when Muslims and Jews, among others, were forced to convert or face death. As historian and missionary to the Pacific Alan Tippett said, "The term mass movement is a bad one. It envisages a fearful, hysterical crowd acting as an irrational mass."[6] Tippett and others have preferred the term "people movements" to describe people as a group making decisions for Christ. This movement is often led by the perceived leader, and then affirmed by the people themselves.

People movements have been misunderstood and even disregarded as a mission strategy today for various reasons. Some of these reasons include the thought that they are forced movements resulting in nominal belief. Another reason is that in these days of globalization, this approach can be mistakenly assumed to work only for remote or rural areas and peoples. Still a third objection, especially in the Indian context, can be that this approach is a misguided resorting to casteism. Outside of India, people-movement strategy can likewise be misconstrued as a wrong-headed attempt to keep people in their cultural and social boxes.

The first misunderstanding is that a people movement is forced upon a people and produces only nominal believers. Often this viewpoint derives from a lack of knowing how a group responds. The bias from highly individualistic, primarily Western societies makes it difficult for missionaries from these backgrounds to recognize and fully function within a context of group thinking.

Many of the unreached peoples in the world today still have strong group thinking. This can be seen in such matters as an emphasis on arranged marriage (rather than "love" marriages), seeing your group as more of a priority than your own individual needs, and a greater emphasis on honoring family and the corresponding shame when that family honor is violated. Granting that there can be a difficult "fine line" between a people being led into responding to Christ by their leaders or being forced, we must recognize that the former scenario does occur and is valid. Clearly, bribes or threats to convince new converts falls under the category of force. Again, even this potential pitfall illustrates the importance of teaching a good understanding of the Scriptures. Of course, the appropriate discipleship and teaching methods will vary with the group involved. For example, if the people group is illiterate, this teaching may take the form of "storying" the Bible.[7] There is no ironclad way to avoid nominal belief in *any* society (especially beyond the first generation), but a growing knowledge of the Word of God and Holy Spirit–inspired leadership will go a long way in preventing it.

The second objection to people movement thinking comes from those who interpret the trends of globalization and urbanization to mean that working to see people movements is no longer valid, except perhaps in rural or remote areas. But this denies the equally strong worldwide trend of peoples returning strongly to tribal roots. This move back toward tribal roots may even be a backlash against globalization. The world is not only becoming more "globalized" but also more "tribalized." On the one hand, the Internet and worldwide web links the world as never before into a "global village." On the other side, many Gujaratis in India are using Gujarati language on the Internet to communicate to the Gujarat diaspora worldwide. As the Internet embraces more languages, this is happening with increasing frequency.

The third strong objection to people movement thinking is the concern that praying and working toward people movements will only encourage tribalism, or casteism as observed in India. Casteism is an emphasis on the caste of the potential convert, or the caste of the whole people, to the exclusion of other groups. This mentality would keep the people locked into their caste instead of allowing them to embrace others and realize that in Christ there is no "Greek or Jew." This danger exists unless there is deliberate discipleship into an understanding of the whole body of Christ from the beginning of the new churches. If peoples' worldviews are to truly change, they must first be confronted by the living Christ.

This confrontation with the living Christ is where people movements and discipling nations (or peoples) interface. There must be a deliberate focus on the heart and Christward movement. Tribalism or casteism ultimately is a matter of the heart, and even in a globalized or urbanized person the best and the worst of their caste, tribal, or racial identities can live on unhindered. These identities may not be outwardly evident but reside nevertheless in the heart. The battle for change lies in the heart. Eating at a McDonald's in an urban setting with other tribes or castes does not guarantee that the person's heart has been transformed or that it will eventually change.

These are some of the primary objections that could be raised, and as more are shared they should not be disregarded. Rather, we must seek to provide solutions for each one with deliberate discipleship or from seeking a wider perspective. The debate will continue. As it is employed to bring godly change, it is valuable. Where it brings a halt to considering whole peoples at once, it is a hindrance. Regardless of the strategy we prefer, we need to initiate increasing work among the unreached to see Matthew 28:19–20 fulfilled.

Applying People-Movement Thinking: A Strategy

How can we apply people-movement thinking in a strategic way? As we have seen, people movements in history have led to significant movements toward Christ. When combined with intentional disciple making, people movements can result in multi-generational effects.

In recent years, a helpful emphasis developing in mission circles is to work toward seeing church planting movements among unreached peoples. In some ways this is not new, but as a concept and strategy it is gaining new momentum. A church planting movement can be defined as a "rapid and multiplicative increase of indigenous churches planting churches within a given people group or population segment."[8] This concept challenges us to see that as we work toward developing a movement of new churches among an unreached people group, we are cooperating with the Lord for the goal of people movements. The multiple indigenous local church movements growing worldwide are one of the most encouraging signs of the Lord's global work. Reports are coming in even from parts of the Muslim world like Indonesia, South and Central Asia, and West Africa.

One of the most difficult areas of planting church movements among unreached peoples concerns its interface with discipling efforts. As we consider the vast needs of the Muslim, Hindu, Buddhist, and tribal peoples, the question arises, Who goes in first—the church planter (recognizing that initially the church planter may need to be an outsider, even if from another people group nearby) or the teacher/discipler? In his book, *People Movements in Southern Polynesia,*[9] Alan Tippett speaks profoundly to this issue. He also discusses the nineteenth century's ongoing controversy between "civilizing" and "evangelizing." Civilizing was defined as bringing the fruits of Western civilization to unreached peoples, often under the guns of a colonial Western power. Evangelizing, much the same today, implied the verbal proclamation of the gospel.

The issue of who goes first brings up the complexity of priorities: Do we evangelize a people first, or lay the groundwork in a society of moral influence through the spheres hoping then for a positive atmosphere for the gospel? Or is it both? Does the choice depend upon the particular situation or is there always a preferred order? This is a much longer issue than this chapter can address, but it needs to be part of the vital ongoing discussions in every church and mission agency.

As we think of "civilizing" or "evangelizing," we realize that in the eighteenth and nineteenth centuries "civilizing" later became known as "colonizing." While the vast majority of missionaries that attempted to bring cultural change with the gospel did so from right motives, at times bringing the fruits of Western civilization also brought unwanted colonizing. As noted earlier, this became even more complex when foreign powers protected these same missionaries with their armies. We must be very careful today that "discipling the nations" does not mean imposing an external framework that is merely "colonizing" under another name. People movements or church planting movements arise from within, though in the early stages there will perhaps need to be cross-cultural witnesses. But, as we have already said, the discipleship process must continue all the way to cultural change and to new mission movements emerging to bless the nations.

John Williams, one of the key pioneer missionaries to the Pacific, was an important figure in the in the ongoing debate of the 1830s over evangelizing versus civilizing. Williams did believe in civilizing, positively defined as seeing a moral change in society, but negatively as the imposition of foreign cultural values which were not necessarily biblically based. But as Tippett says, "[Williams] was always conditioned by the practical requirements of the primary motive of church planting.[10] Some have called the need to disciple nations "applied Christianity" that should be an overflow of the indigenous churches' numerical and spiritual growth. Williams himself often had heated correspondence with his mission directors in London, emphasizing that the ongoing advance of the gospel must be always to the next village. He strongly believed that it was the responsibility of the new local believers to take the gospel to their neighbors and effect moral changes in their society. Involvement with the heart issues of the people and a concern for their discipleship and biblical worldview must be present right from the initial presentation of the gospel and discipleship.

There is room for cross-cultural influences (for example, Christian lawyers, medical workers, etc.) in the discipleship process of both individuals and the group, but we need to be clear strategically as to what their goal is and at what stage they are involved in the people movement. The goal must be to empower the local movement at every point, not to dominate or control it with outside influence or money. Cross-cultural influencers can be catalysts all along the discipleship process in a people-group movement.

Conclusion

People-movement thinking and strategy will ensure that no people is left untouched by the gospel. Not only will individuals be reached one by one but their networks of families and clans will be reached as well. A framework is provided to truly disciple each people while also encouraging them to constantly move beyond their own people to others in mission advance. Such apostolic church planting must go hand in hand with discipling and teaching ministries. One without the other is incomplete and will result in either shallow, inch-deep Christians or only influences of Christian values and worldview but no local Christians and churches. We must be clear and not confused in our approach and strategy. We must walk in a continuity of mission history while remaining open to innovative and creative breakthroughs.

In India today there is a continual need to disciple new generations of the church into people-group thinking. This discipleship must be sufficiently flexible to understand and adapt to the dynamics of urbanization and global influences on the emerging youth culture. India with its amazing diversity, perhaps more than any other nation, presents an opportunity for testing these innovative breakthroughs. As a leader in the twentieth century quoted in another context, "let a hundred flowers bloom."[11] Our challenge in missions today is to see a hundred movements bloom, indeed thousands of movements that will dynamically touch their own peoples and the ones around them.

Notes

Thanks to Omid Haqq, a South Asian researcher, unpublished article, 2000.

1. Donald McGavran, *The Bridges of God* (London: World Dominion Press, 1955).

2. J. Watsom Pickett, *Christian Mass Movements in India* (New York: Abingdon Press, 1933).

3. For further reading on this fascinating topic, see Thomas Cahill, *How the Irish Saved Civilization* (New York: Doubleday, 1995) and Richard Fletcher, *The Barbarian Conversion* (New York: Henry Holt & Co., 1997).

4. Personal communication from Mizo believers.

5. McGavran, *The Bridges of God*, 81.

6. Alan Tippet, *People Movements in Southern Polynesia* (Chicago: Moody Press 1971), 999.

7. For more information on this strategy, there are excellent resources at www.chronologicalbiblestorying.com.

8. David Garrison, *Church Planting Movements* (Richmond, Va.: International Mission Board, Southern Baptists, 1999), 8.

9. Alan Tippet, *People Movements in Southern Polynesia*.

10. Ibid., 26.

11. Chinese Communist Party slogan, 1956–57.

Earlier in this book, David Hamilton gave insight on God's strategy to disciple nations—one location, sphere, and level of society at a time. Howard now articulates valuable advice on how to actually put our vision into a plan that we can see come into reality. Howard describes the historical background and founding principles for the development of YWAM's University of the Nations as an example of a "megaproject" developed to disciple the nations.

From Vision to Reality:
Project Planning for Discipling Nations

Howard V. Malmstadt

Breathtaking Vision

On May 25, 1961, in the State of the Union address, President John F. Kennedy proposed an awesome challenge to the American people.[1] "I believe that this nation should commit itself to achieving the goal, before this decade is out, of landing a man on the moon and returning him safely to the earth." Wow! This statement set our imaginations soaring.

President Kennedy did not mince words as he described the cost and benefit of such an incredible undertaking: "No single space project in this period will be more impressive to mankind, or more important for the long-range exploration of space, and none will be so difficult or expensive to accomplish." He went on to outline the first incremental steps that would be taken toward reaching the goal by the end of the decade, less than nine years away from his proposal to Congress.

President Kennedy continued to put this vision before the American people. In 1962, in remarks at Rice University, he pointed out that the spaceship would need to carry "all the equipment needed for propulsion, guidance, control, communication, food, and survival on an untried mission, to an unknown celestial body, and then return to earth, reentering the atmosphere at speeds of over 25,000 miles per hour, causing heat about half that of the temperature of the sun—and do all this, and do it right, and do it first before the decade [of the '60s] is out ... we must be bold."

As a scientist, I recognized the immensity of this challenging project. My own research and development team at the University of Illinois, which included chemistry, electronics, and scientific instrumentation developments, made me aware of how bold the nation had to be to accept the challenge. I knew, too, that the president's statements were not the result of some weird dream. He had done his homework.

During the Second World War, I had served as a radar officer in the U.S. Navy, and after the war I remained in the Naval Research Reserve for the first part of the 1950s. This had given me an opportunity to learn about some of the amazing research already underway on space travel and preliminary ideas about flights to the moon and farther. All of the research and development (R&D) prior to 1961 had provided the initial information necessary to advise the president what might be accomplished under the best of conditions. The estimated billions of dollars, intense focus on the nation's research and development, and tens of thousands of skilled personnel who would accept the challenge were all part of the "homework" required for the president to make his gigantic proposal to Congress.

Many of us vividly remember the rest of the story. Hundreds of millions of people across planet Earth listened and watched in awe when on July 16, 1969, the Apollo 11 spacecraft with astronauts Neil Armstrong, Michael Collins, and Edwin "Buzz" Aldrin in the command module lifted off at the space center in Florida. After three days of travel through space, they began to orbit around the moon. The lunar module *Eagle* with astronauts Armstrong and Aldrin touched down on the moon's surface on July 20. As Armstrong emerged from *Eagle*, descended its ladder and stepped on the moon, he made his famous commemoration of the moment, "One small step for man, one giant leap for mankind."

The astronauts explored the moon's surface, deployed two experiments as part of the Scientific Experiment Package, and collected twenty-one kilograms of lunar rock samples for return to Earth. They then left the moon and guided the ascent stage of their module to a rendezvous with the orbiting lunar command module. They touched down safely on planet Earth on July 24, 1969. Kennedy's proposal for a super challenging space project had been completed within the nine year time frame— mission accomplished.

The Apollo project was extremely complicated, and certainly one of the most challenging attempted in all of the history of man. It required strong, bold leadership, brilliant planning, unity of thousands of personnel working in diverse fields, dynamic management, exhaustive research, and creative environments for the design and development of new systems and methods never before known in our world.

Great Commission Project

A more profound project was initiated millennia ago by the God of all creation. This world-transforming, life-changing project is described in the Old and New Testaments of the Bible. The important concepts and principles of the project were demonstrated by God's courageous Son, Jesus Christ, when he came to reside on earth for thirty-three years. Near the end of his appointed time on earth, Jesus told his disciples, "All authority in heaven and on earth has been given to me. Therefore go and make disciples of all nations, baptizing them in the name of the Father and of the Son and of the Holy Spirit and teaching them to obey everything I have commanded you. And surely I am with you always, to the very end of the age" (Matt. 28:18–20). These words of Jesus recorded in the Bible are referred to as "The Great Commission."

After receiving power from the Holy Spirit, Jesus' disciples were transformed and they proved very effective in discipling others. The body of Christ grew, missions flourished, and today over two billion people profess to be Christians. Unfortunately, recent reports indicate that most professing Christians have not been adequately discipled. There are pockets of dynamic disciples in many nations, but there is not one nation on earth today that could be called a truly discipled nation. A discipled nation would have Christians in every sphere of society who had been taught to obey every commandment that Jesus taught his original disciples, and they would be free and passionate to be teaching others in every realm of society.

Lessons to be Learned from Apollo

The Apollo megaproject required transformational leadership and creative planning and management so that personnel with a wide range of expertise could operate in unity as a huge team. Great Commission megaprojects have similar requirements. Since there are similar dynamics to aspects of these two megaprojects, it can be valuable for us to examine and adopt some of the effective methods that were used in the Apollo project.

The words used in planning projects often have different meanings. They are defined and presented here in the order of vision, overall objective (goal or target), allowable time from the start of project to reaching the goal, and preliminary information.

Vision

The word *vision* has multiple meanings; for projects, vision can be described as an inspired revelation of what is to be accomplished in the future.

For the Apollo project, the vision was an inspired belief by leaders of the U.S. space program and President Kennedy that the Apollo project was crucial for the welfare of the nation and the free world. It encompassed development of space leadership, awesome technical and facilities advancements, and the infrastructure for effectively operating in and exploring the universe far into the future.

For a Christian project, vision is inspired revelation of what God has communicated in one of his many ways, perhaps as supernatural revelation in a prayer meeting or a dream of what is to happen in the future. A Great Commission vision would relate to the words of Jesus and his commission to his disciples (Matt. 28:18–20): going, baptizing, and teaching the nations to obey everything he commanded them. Having vision that is truly from God, and not just our own good ideas, is the critical first step.

As vital as a compelling vision is, alone it is not enough to begin a project. It is important to note that a megavision into an undefined future is *not* a project, rather it is the catalyst which inspires specific projects.

Overall Objective (Goal or Target)

The overall objective is a project goal or target encompassing a portion of the vision. It is the goal that a leadership team believes it is called to accomplish within an allowable time frame, and describes the mission to be accomplished. The ongoing space vision, which is still very active today, has inspired many projects for ongoing and long-range exploration of outer space and the universe.

The overall objective of the Apollo 11 project was to capture the genuine interest of the public by the sensational accomplishment of landing astronauts on the moon and bringing them back safely to earth. In addition, the project would demonstrate the practical benefits of breakthroughs that would create new products and businesses to impact the economy. It would clear the way for future accomplishments in the ongoing vision of space exploration. The overall vision is space exploration, the objective in this case was the Apollo 11 project—the target or goal, the mission to be accomplished. It is impossible to reach a goal or hit a target that is not defined.

Perhaps many visions, hopes, and dreams for discipling nations are never implemented because they are never boiled down to the specific goal that God had planned for you and others who had the same vision. Is our Lord waiting for you and others to seek his plan for a specific nation-discipling goal on which you and your team can focus and which you can diligently move forward to reach?

Allowable Time

An overall objective or goal becomes a definable project when it is accompanied by a specific time frame stating the allowable time to reach the goal.

This concept of allowable time was illustrated by the Apollo 11 project. The target date was before the end of 1969, and it was reached triumphantly several months prior to that deadline. This required excellent project development leadership.

Preliminary Information

Following World War II there was considerable interest and activity in developed nations to gain more information about outer space and the universe. By 1957 the Soviet Union had a major lead in space travel, primarily because of their booster rockets for launching larger spacecraft. These rockets represented a military threat, so there was an urgency to develop a space project and to convince the U.S. government to approve the huge increases of funding needed for a rapid development in this area.

Between the Sputnik flight in 1957 and Kennedy's Apollo proposal to Congress in May 1961, the U.S. space leaders had gathered enough solid information about the possibility of landing a man on the moon and returning him safely before the end of the sixties. However, the nation had to be convinced that the effort would warrant the huge increase of resources to be made available immediately. Kennedy's brilliant decision to announce this goal was what Congress needed to move forward.

Clearly communicating the vision is vital to planning Great Commission projects as well. In the book *Courageous Leaders Transforming Their World*[2] which I coauthored with David Hamilton and Jim Halcomb, we discuss the importance of creating a written record of the vision, including Scriptures that came to mind during prayer and reflection, and subsequent confirmation from others for the person(s) with the original vision. This record will be a helpful reminder to pray for further revelation on details for the project goal when it's time to move into the detailed planning stage. The recorded preliminary information will also inspire others so they also can run with it (Hab. 2:2). The questions to answer are: What vision did God give you and what impact is this project to have? How did he give it to you? What confirmations have you had?

The leadership must all understand the vision and then together as a team confirm the goal or overall objective related to the vision that God is calling you to embrace. In this section we have introduced the first major step of project development. In the next section we will examine the essential leadership ingredients for reaching a discipling-a-nation project goal with a God-led plan following God's ways.

Leadership Skills Needed

If the Lord has confirmed your project overall objective, you have completed the transition from a God-inspired vision (doing the right thing) into the start of developing a God-led plan (doing things right). When you complete the plan you will be ready for the next big transition: from a God-led plan into God-motivated action (doing the right things right). It all seems so simple, but I've observed that for many of our leaders it is at these transitions from vision-to-plan-to-action that a project is often delayed or fails to proceed to a mission accomplished in ways pleasing to God.

In the late 1980s I launched yearly Project Development Leadership Seminars (three- to six-week intensive courses) and a twelve-week school, primarily for YWAM leaders and a few soon-to-be leaders or professional friends of YWAM. I designed it for leaders who wanted understanding of how to develop and oversee a major new project, and guidance on more effective planning methods. I noticed that men and women who had been very successful Christian leaders because they knew God's character and had committed to doing the right things seemed to shift into a different mode of thinking when they faced a huge project. They may have gotten the right vision from God, but then failed to seek him for the details on how to carry it out. It is vital to go back again and again to get the details and not presume to go on merely wisdom and experience.

Robert K. Greenleaf wrote and published an essay in 1970 called "The Servant Leader." He emphasized that "[servant leadership] begins with the natural feeling that one wants to serve, to serve first. Then conscious choice brings one to aspire to lead. The difference manifests itself in the care taken by the servant—first to make sure that other people's highest priority needs are being served. The best test is: Do those served grow as persons; do they, while being served, become healthier, wiser, freer, more autonomous, more likely themselves to become servants."

These concepts are profound. They are biblical, and they are essential if we are to be nation disciplers. Some of the major industries and institutions in the world have modified their operations to implement Greenleaf's recommendations. If they recognize the value of his words, how much more should we, as we follow the example of Jesus, the ultimate servant leader. He emptied himself of all divine power and privilege to be born as a baby, to be a member of a despised minority. He became flesh and dwelt among us, and shared his life with his disciples and lived in the same conditions with them. He demonstrated excellence as he healed the sick, fed the multitudes, and had compassion. He made the ultimate sacrifice of being executed on the cross so that we might be saved. Then he provided hope for the future with his resurrection. Indeed, he gave us the ultimate example of a servant leader, and he told us to follow his example.

There are many leadership principles that should be followed to remain on the right path for reaching the goal.[4] Leaders must adhere to God's ways from start to finish. Overlooking even one of God's principles can cause unexpected stumbling blocks and major delays in completing the project. God expects his leaders to be seeking his guidance throughout so that no principles are compromised. In the next section we will look at an example project from my own experience, observing how a megaproject can be used in discipling nations.

A Great Commission University

One megaproject that can move us powerfully toward discipling a nation is the university. Modern universities are major institutions. They encompass and impact essentially every area of society in their nation with a wide range of courses, seminars, research and development, publications, and community programs. They often interact with and influence government, industries, and other institutions. For better or worse, they are influencing and discipling their regions, nation, and sometimes their world. Each large university represents a dynamic development project usually consisting of multiple subprojects of the whole.

Many of today's well-known universities such as Oxford and Harvard started as Christian universities, but they long ago drifted away from their Christian heritage. This section presents the background of the early development years for what could be called a Great Commission university. YWAM's University of the Nations (U of N) believes it has a mandate to be a university that disciples nations, impacting every area of society with the good news and teaching the people to obey everything that Jesus taught his disciples.[5]

In what follows, some of the hopes and dreams for an ideal university are presented, followed by some of my own experiences in serving in a major American university for several decades prior to being called to help found the U of N. Those experiences provided a unique background as God was speaking to us about his vision and plan to develop a Great Commission university.

The Ideal Characteristics of a Great Commission University

When I was a professor at the University of Illinois I often asked my doctoral students at the end of their final oral exam, "What would be a truly *ideal* solution for your research project?" A few years ago at a scientific conference, several of these former students, now some twenty, thirty, and even forty years later reported that they are now close to the ideal answer to the question. They told me that the question about "the ideal" that I asked them to envision so many years ago had been a catalyst for them to seek for the *ideal*. Their comments encouraged me to reflect on the question, what are the characteristics that would make an ideal "Great Commission university"? Some of the characteristics I listed were:

1. All the people associated with the university, who truly are the university, would know God intimately, and their hearts would be on fire to make him known.

2. The people would be committed to and become engaged in the Great Commission given by Jesus in Matthew 28:18–20.
3. The campus community would express the love of Jesus in numerous tangible ways.
4. The people would work together in unity and would be a catalyst for unity in the body of Christ (John 17:20–23).
5. The people would be obedient to the Word of God.
6. The programs, courses, and activities would be inspired by the Holy Spirit and be designed to release God's gifts of creativity in students and staff, *and* the people groups they serve.

The list goes on and on. What would you add to the list?

Is it possible for YWAM's fledgling U of N to reach the ideal? Yes, I believe that it is, *if* we seek diligently to remain open to impartation from our Creator, his vision for each campus, his direction in planning the research and development projects and implementing the schools, programs, and outreaches worldwide.

I believe that our Lord is seeking for men and women to develop the U of N for his purposes and by his Word. He is seeking people who will seek him diligently in prayer and count the cost to be able to influence the future. Ever closer to him they will rejoice both when he confirms their thoughts and when he shows them a better way. These men and women will commit to programs and ministries only to the extent that all contribute to building a people—a people called and taught of God, a people of destiny, a people who will fully play their part in bringing a great multitude before his throne, a great multitude, which no one can count from every nation, tribe, people, and tongue, singing: "Salvation belongs to our God, who sits on the throne, and to the Lamb" (Rev. 7:9–10). We also see in Micah that the nations will come before him, and he will teach them (Mic. 4:2).

Until that day, he seeks for men and women to follow his plans, including his plans for developing campuses of the University of the Nations in all nations—branches connected to one perfect vine. Each campus must seek to embody his ways of teaching, of managing, of communicating, of living out his ways of working together in community. They are to be a people, young and old, committed and open to his commission and his empowerment to "therefore go and make disciples of all nations, baptizing them in the name of the Father and of the Son and of the Holy Spirit, and teaching them to obey everything I have commanded you" (Matt. 28:19–20).

What Makes Excellent Training?

Universities have a profound impact on their communities, nations, and even the world. Whether they are leading out with innovation and problem solving utilizing godly wisdom and values, or are motivated by worldly concerns, they have a role of great leadership. How can a Great Commission university intentionally exercise that leadership as an institution and through the individual contributions of its graduates? My own experiences in many university settings taught me much about effective training methods which are now incorporated into the U of N.

One experience during my years as a university student had a significant impact on my thinking about education. During the summer of 1938, between my junior and senior years, I took a six-week course, wherein only two of us were regular students. The others were trained professionals who were returning for an advanced short course. I found that the whole atmosphere was different. The participants were not worried about grades but were very anxious to learn something new. We enjoyed friendly relationships between the students while studying intently but in a relaxed atmosphere. They wanted to help each other and share their experiences and understanding of the course content. This course opened my eyes to the great importance of the learning environment.

The next discovery was in 1943, during my time of service in World War II. I was sent to MIT where I experienced a five-month module of intense classroom and practical laboratory work that shaped my understanding of what could be accomplished in a short time. The Navy had called on professors from MIT and many other universities to put together a program to train radar officers. The university contributed not only ideas, teaching materials, and personnel, but introduced an unorthodox and effective way of teaching. They used what I call a top-down approach. They gave an overview of radar and why it was so significant. They told us about the battles being fought and the way radar was influencing the results right at the moment they talked about it. They impressed on us that how well we listened could be a matter of life and death for many personnel. Giving that context and overview increased our attentiveness as we recognized the significance of our task.

At present we are in another very significant battle. It is a spiritual battle, and it is becoming more intense all the time. How well we listen and obey the Lord concerning education will be a matter of life and death for many. As with the military during wartime, a Great Commission university must be very deliberate in its commitment to maximize the effectiveness of its training.

While at MIT, I also noticed we were able to integrate and retain the information we were given far beyond a typical course. Perhaps some of the principles that were used by the MIT model would be good for us to consider.

One key was the very intense modular approach, where we studied one topic with great intensity for several months. These classroom sections included hands-on experience wherever possible, and they were followed immediately by a related field assignment.

Our schedule was often six days a week, day and night. We had four hours of lectures in the morning with only a five-minute break. In the afternoon we gained hands-on experience with the radar systems being used aboard ships and airplanes and on the ground. My field assignment was about eighteen months aboard destroyers in the Pacific. Skills learned in the classroom were immediately applied at sea. It was necessary to quickly learn new things not covered in classroom studies and adapt what had been learned to unusually difficult situations.

It was a demanding schedule, but it was a time of emergencies. In reality, we are also in a time of emergencies today. If young men and women were willing to train so intently for the cause of freedom and country, how much more can we call our Christian young people to a time of sacrificial, intense training for the goal of fulfilling the tasks God has given us in the Great Commission?

Another key lesson was learned by divine revelation in the midst of a fierce battle. I learned that God amazingly reaches out with grace, as he spoke audibly to me from Psalm 23. In a profound supernatural way he also pointed me to John 14:6, to the words of Jesus, "I am the way and the truth and the life. No one comes to the Father except through me." He gave me the gift of faith in the midst of battle in the Pacific Ocean, in his classroom. Imagine a university that provides an environment where in every course module and field assignment the Spirit of the living God can impart to us his wisdom, his faith, his words and directions.

Another benefit I experienced in graduate school was the wealth of resources and expertise that is available from many professional disciplines being in close proximity to one another. The overall environment stimulates creative thinking. A good university should provide exciting and stimulating environments that draw out the creative giftings of students and staff alike.

I then joined the staff at the University of Illinois in 1977, where I continued to learn about critical dynamics to maximize the university as a nation-discipling tool. Teaching was an important part, creating new courses to fill new needs. Research was equally important. Developing new courses and doing innovative research created many opportunities for me to consult with industries and government and take part on national and international committees. Widespread interaction with other institutions and government enable universities to influence, or disciple, communities and nations in major ways. I also discovered that working with research students every day gives the staff opportunities for one-on-one relationships with people from many nations. This one-on-one for ten to thirty minutes can often be more significant than several hours of lectures.

In general I found that the combination of teaching, research and development, and publishing articles allows university staff and students to influence policies, to show how to meet real and felt needs of people groups, and to take part in cutting-edge research and development that can impact the future.

In 1974 YWAM had a very important prayer meeting in Hilo, Hawaii, in which the Lord gave us a vision and prophecy that YWAM would develop educational resources that would impact every area of society, every age level, and every culture to serve in the discipling of nations. Because this is so "humanly impossible," I believe that God gave such a vision to YWAM. The Lord saw that YWAM had been faithful for many years to embrace vision that is "impossible," trusting that if they do the possible God will do the impossible.

The U of N has a responsibility to provide the environment and training to release the creativity of students. If we do so, they will help create the resources needed in the nations. We must stand up for truth and not withdraw, even when we encounter opposition as we step out on revelation for new materials and methods from the Spirit of God.

I believe that what has been happening at the U of N in the last twenty years is building a foundation that can provide nations with biblically based resources in areas related to each domain of society. Our colleges/faculties and centers, which relate to most areas of society, have been listening carefully to the Lord, and they are receiving revelation, insight, and understanding of what and how to communicate in the different cultures, nations, and age levels.

Ongoing Development of God's Great Commission University

The above brings us up to the birth of YWAM's university, beginning in late 1977 and continuing with planning meetings in 1978. The Lord provided revelation through staff and friends of YWAM in all areas. This was to be a university founded on the Word of the Lord; this was confirmed in dozens of different ways, from people in other YWAM ministries and leaders from outside of YWAM. We recognized that U of N was to be his university, a university of the Spirit, a discipler of nations. We quickly understood that regardless of how many of us would work in the university, how much background and experience all of us might have, even if we could pay salaries that would attract the world leaders including professors from Harvard, Oxford, and various other places, we couldn't put together the university the Lord wanted. We realized that this was not the strategy God had in mind to fulfill all he was showing us he wanted to do through the U of N. Rather, he wanted us to seek him, line by line, precept by precept, to gain understanding of what he wanted for the U of N.

This Great Commission is a life-and-death mandate impacting entire nations. Indeed, a Great Commission megaproject is to be our fitting response to the foremost, the greatest commandment: "'Love the Lord your God with all your heart and with all your soul and with all your mind and with all your strength.' The second is this: 'Love your neighbor as yourself.' There is no commandment greater than these" (Mark 12:30–31). He impressed upon us that if we somehow were to reach the goal of a nation-discipling megaproject, *but* the people do *not* have love, we have failed. Hearts and action can become focused on the project with little concern for the process or people. Like space travel, there is no room for a mistake if we are to disciple nations. We must resolve to "know and rely on the love God has for us" and to understand in greater depth that "God is love. Whoever lives in love lives in God, and God in him" (1 John 4:16) so that "being rooted and established in love, [we] may have power, together with all the saints, to grasp how wide and long and high and deep is the love of Christ, and to know this love that surpasses knowledge—that [we] may be filled to the measure of all the fullness of God" (Eph. 3:17–19). If we do, nations will be discipled.

To summarize, a few features of the U of N that were impressed on our hearts and minds in our early prayer meetings need to be kept at the forefront of our activities:

- The integration of evangelism and community reformation in our outreach operations.
- The development of biblically based educational resources which can be used worldwide at all levels. This major responsibility must not be neglected.
- Multigenerational relationships—genuine interaction between the generations. We don't want to isolate our students, teachers and administrators, staff, or their children. We want the U of N to operate in community as extended families.
- U of N is to operate worldwide in many cultures with unity in our relationships and diversity in our strategies. During the first years that we were praying for guidance about the university, the Lord continuously called us back to the "love passages" in the scriptures. We need those passages to be apparent in our daily lives.
- The dynamic of students and staff from many nations and cultures working together is to be maintained.
- We are to research, develop, test, and refine God-inspired prototypes that enable people worldwide to see living examples of discipling the nations.
- The University of the Nations is the Lord's university. We must continue to be alert to his voice and obey his directions. Every class, every hour, every moment should be open to teaching from the Holy Spirit.

I believe revelation will continue until he returns. The Lord is calling thousands upon thousands of people into the U of N. I trust that he will give understanding and insight on the roles he wants people to commit to in the University of the Nations, perhaps something way beyond their present calling. Maybe it will include revitalizing the dreams of the past which have been buried because of the apparent impossibilities. The U of N has been given an exciting opportunity to serve in the Great Commission. It is our mandate. Awesome! Let's stand firm, keep praying, and remember the Lord's promise in Matthew 28:20: "And surely I am with you always, to the very end of the age."

Mission Accomplished

Do you have a sense of satisfaction and joy when you complete a project, even daily tasks or small projects? Then imagine the overwhelming joy when you have been part of a team that completed a megaproject.

This chapter was started by reviewing some characteristics of the most awesome, exciting, expensive, and challenging megaproject ever developed by man. The mission of sending astronauts to the moon, then walking and collecting data on the moon, and returning safely to planet Earth was accomplished in July 1969, several months before the deadline set by the U.S. President in his May 1961 State of the Union address. Hundreds of millions of people across our world were amazed as they watched television or listened to the radio as the Apollo 11 project was reaching its goal. The mission had accomplished its objectives of generating public enthusiasm for manned space exploration, design and development of new materials with important new applications on earth, a dynamic space program, and infrastructure for continuing the ongoing vision for future space exploration of the universe—Mission Accomplished.

The exuberant joy of tens of thousands of those who worked on the project was televised worldwide.

Discipling-the-nations megaprojects can and should be even more exciting and certainly more rewarding than the Apollo 11 megaproject. Fulfilling the vision will undoubtedly require multiple discipling-nations megaprojects. Each project would lead toward a discipled nation where the people in every area of the nation's society had been taught what Jesus taught and commanded his disciples. Imagine the joy of our Creator and his children in accomplishing this God-sized, inspired project, a project that is humanly impossible but possible by collaborating with Jesus.

The integration of several Christian megaprojects could result in fulfilling the hopes, dreams, and vision for a truly discipled nation. The overall objective for each project and a plan for integrating all of the megaprojects would certainly require God's inspired plans, followed by God-motivated action and his involvement in the hearts and minds of the people called by him to be involved.

What type of new project would serve the catalytic role for a truly discipled-nation vision as the Apollo 11 project did for the space vision?

Ask and you will receive. The glory goes to him. Jesus said, "If you remain in me and my words remain in you, ask whatever you wish, and it will be given you. This is to my Father's glory, that you bear much fruit, showing yourselves to be my disciples" (John 15:7–8). Are we serious about working so as to see nations truly discipled? It will take people who are ready to commit their lives completely to him who was given all authority in heaven and on earth, and to ask him for a nation to help to lead toward being a truly discipled nation. Only when the project and the process have been done in God's ways and the commandments of Jesus have been followed can we say in truth "Mission Accomplished."

Notes

This chapter is published posthumously from material written by Dr. Howard Malmstadt for this publication. For more information on the life of Dr. Malmstadt, see John Feaver, *Into the Light: The Academic and Spiritual Legacy of Dr. Howard Malmstadt* (Seattle: YWAM Publishing, 2007).

1. John F. Kennedy, "Speech," May 25, 1961, Internet Archive: Presidential Recordings, www.archive.org/details/jfks19610525 (accessed April 30, 2007).

2. Jim Halcomb, David Hamilton, and Howard V. Malmstadt, *Courageous Leaders Transforming Their World* (Seattle: YWAM Publishing, 2000).

3. Larry C. Spears, ed., *Reflections on Leadership: How Robert K. Greenleaf's Theory of Servant-Leadership Influenced Today's Top Management Thinkers* (Hoboken, N.J.: John Wiley & Sons, 1995).

4. These are covered in depth in Halcomb, Hamilton, and Malmstadt, *Courageous Leaders.*

5. U of N. See Appendix B for the University of the Nations Founding Principles.

Fraser Haug was part of a team that served in Albania right after the Communists fell from power. The team's express intention was to "disciple a whole nation" through service and to develop an understanding of what discipling a nation looks like in reality. He shares some key principles as well as innovative methods and strategies that they field-tested in Albania.

Case Study: Principles and Practices in Albania

Fraser Haug

Introduction: Precursors to the Albania Project

I remember sitting around a table of YWAM leaders and business professionals. We were discussing the concept and implications of "discipling a whole nation"—particularly the business/economics sector of a nation. A YWAMer posed one of those simple yet profound questions: "What does a 'discipled' nation actually look like and how will we know when we have finished?" Almost simultaneously, major events were unfolding in Eastern Europe which would provide a practical theater for beginning to answer such an important question.

For years YWAM International, especially University of the Nations (U of N), had been wrestling with the idea of "discipling whole nations." We were (and still are) attempting to understand what it means to bring the gospel, the power of salvation, not only to every ethnic nation, but also to every arena of a geopolitical nation. We needed to garner yet more experience to test our interpretations and hypotheses. Then came the fall of the Berlin Wall.

The fall of the Wall in November of 1989 was not just an isolated political event in the history of Germany—it was a marker of profound ideological importance that reverberated around the world. The isolated Communist nation of Albania would also feel those effects. By late 1990 and early 1991, the Communist leaders of Albania saw the writing on the wall. With a little outside encouragement from the students at Tirana University, they initiated a remarkably smooth and (in light of the history and local conditions) bloodless transition toward a more democratic, free-market orientation.

By mid-1991, this ideological transition had progressed to the point where Christians were allowed to operate openly. Indeed, one of the significant events of that year was a large evangelistic campaign held in Tirana, the capital. At that meeting, government officials broached the subject of formal assistance from the international Christian community for the nation's transition. By this time, the actual needs in the country had become increasingly evident. Consequently, the invitations for assistance were for the fundamental rebuilding of all aspects of Albanian society, including their businesses and economic system, education, civil justice, and so forth. YWAM/U of N responded to these official invitations. Our response was twofold: First, we wanted to serve this nation as effectively as possible.[1] Second, we desired to develop practical models, if not prototypes, of what "discipling a whole nation" actually looked like in practice. Thus, the six-and-a-half-year "Albania Integrated Development Project," or A.I.D. Project,[2] began in November 1991, with our first exploratory trip to the nation.

Methodology of Presentation

Because the A.I.D. Project was not just an outreach project but also a test case for YWAM/U of N, we attempted to be deliberate about all we did: in the practices and strategies we employed, in understanding the principles behind those practices, and in regular, albeit cursory, analysis of the results.

This article is organized around three key "principle-practice sets." I will present a key principle, elucidate that principle briefly, identify and discuss any associated exceptions or caveats, describe the practice(s) employed, and, finally, close with a short analysis based on our Albanian experience.

Due to space constraints, I present only three key principle-practice sets that I believe to be strategic in promoting effective "discipling of nations." Many other principle-practice sets such as evangelism, or intercessory prayer and spiritual warfare could have been profitably included. However, these latter principles are commonly taught, understood, and practiced in YWAM, and therefore are not addressed here. Further "uncommon" principles could have been explained as well, but these three seemed among the most important. However, presenting the following three principle-practice sets as central to a theology and strategy of "discipling nations" in no way implies that these are the only critical principles and practices.

The material presented here is the most basic and summarized form of the broader content it represents. Indeed, the A.I.D. Project was for many of us on our team the culmination of many years of previous inquiry into the Scriptures, wisdom garnered from others, and insight into our own previous cumulative experiences. It is impossible therefore to convey the full riches behind the principle-practice sets presented here. Moreover, our work in Albania represents only one early foray into a field of ministry where there is still much to be discovered and learned. Readers would do well to continue seeking insights into this topic.

Principle-Practice Set #1: Comprehensively Advancing the Kingdom of God

The Principle

To "disciple a nation" means comprehensively advancing the kingdom of God in that nation. The kingdom of God is reconciliation to God, redemption from the destructive power of sin. The kingdom further includes the realization of his just and loving reign through his Word and his Spirit, in the hearts of individuals (evangelism and discipleship), in all of society and culture (sociocultural transformation), and, ultimately, in the natural order (environmental restoration).

Biblical Foundations and Explication

This first and foremost principle is tremendously pregnant with deeper and broader content. The New Testament forcefully presents us with the reality that "all things" belong to God by virtue of creation and should belong to his kingdom by virtue of his redemption through Christ. Colossians 1:20 declares that through Christ, God intends to reconcile to himself all things on earth. The things that need reconciling are those things lost in Eden through mankind's sin. In summary they form three complementary aspects of the kingdom: (1) man the individual, (2) human social relationships (i.e., society and culture), and (3) the natural order. When the Apostle Peter states in 2 Peter 1:3 that through Christ we have everything we need for "life and godliness," the original Greek word used for life is *zoe. Zoe* stands for every facet and aspect of life, from the basic physical necessities of organic (animal) life, all the way to eternal life.

In John 3:16, we are told that God so loved the entire *cosmos* (the original Greek word rendered "world") that he gave his only son. This Greek word *cosmos* stands for much more than just humanity or man the individual. Although the context of John 3:16 clearly centers on man and his needs, *cosmos* by definition includes the broader elements of sociocultural structures and the natural order.

The "kingdom of God" is the overarching theological, conceptual framework for all of our life on this planet, including missions.

Caveats

Although I have briefly stated the inherent breadth of God's kingdom and his kingdom intentions on earth, obviously a need for biblical balance exists in such sweeping assertions. Individuals, society and culture, and the natural order are to be redeemed from the power of sin. But the Scripture shows us there is no reconciliation or redemption for the devil and his minions.

Neither do I assert that the advancement of God's just and loving rule and reign on earth means a return to the innocence (sinless perfection) of Eden. I do, however, maintain that the church will be victorious in this age. We will see significant and dramatic redemption and reconciliation amongst the nations before the second return of Christ. Indeed, Matthew 24:14 tells us that the nonnegotiable condition of Christ's return is nothing less than a successful, victorious completion of the kingdom task.

Lastly, despite the biblical truth that the domain of the "gospel of the kingdom" is essentially threefold—man the individual, society and culture, and the natural order—we must still qualitatively distinguish the individual from societal institutions and structures of which he is a part. Educators, students, and administrators are created in the image of God. Based on their covenantal position with God through Christ, they will spend eternity either with him in heaven or separate from him in hell. The societal institutions of schools, classrooms, and ministries of education, on the other hand, do not die and go to heaven or hell. Moreover, though God will make a new heaven and a new earth, our responsibility to fulfill the stewardship mandate of Genesis 2 is not removed. Hence, we must maintain the highest priority on individual souls through evangelism and discipleship, while we seek to bring biblically based transformation to society and culture and the natural order.

The Practice

If the kingdom of God is to be a reality in all of life, then our planning should reflect that. In the A.I.D. Project, the basic "organizational" structure of our ministry reflected the significant sectors of Albanian society. After an initial period of orientation and learning we divided our ministry into twelve sectors or spheres: (1) Evangelism, Discipleship, and Church Development; (2) Family, Children, and Youth; (3) Education; (4) Business and Economics; (5) Public Administration and Leadership; (6) Law and Justice; (7) Communication and Media; (8) Agriculture; (9) Health and Dental Care; (10) Arts and Literature; (11) Community Welfare (Humanitarian Aid); and (12) Environmental Management.

This list was somewhat arbitrary. It reflected the realities and needs of Albania in the nineties. The point is that from the beginning we oriented our entire ministry into specific categories that reflected not only local need but also our understanding of the kingdom of God. Thus, we consciously planned, staffed, prayed, evangelized, budgeted resources, and so forth in terms of these ministry categories.

Evaluation and Critique

The conscious organization of our ministry in categories dictated by our understanding of the kingdom of God was an essential aspect of our ministry and success. One cannot bring biblically based transformation to society and culture by coincidence.

We thought it important to establish a sector for evangelism, discipleship, and church development. This reflected our conviction that biblically based transformation of society and culture can only be effected when the hearts of the individuals in those sectors are changed through conversion and the power of God.

In addition to our explicit plans for transformation in any given sector, we also planned consciously for evangelism in that sector. We discovered that being involved in concrete ways in people's daily lives, and in areas of acute concern for the nationals themselves, was an extremely effective means of evangelism (see Principle-Practice Set #3 for elaboration).

The sectoral approach revealed one unexpected weakness. We discovered a dramatic dearth of qualified Christian workers, particularly in the sectors associated with society, culture, and the natural environment. This hindered long-term effective ministry (producing fruit that remains). Our initial expectation was that we would be essentially "door openers" and "preparers of the way" for other professionally qualified Christians. We consistently established contacts and agreements with national leaders at the very highest levels of Albanian society. Unhappily, however, we were unable to fully follow up on many opportunities because skilled professional implementers with the requisite biblical understanding were lacking. This situation revealed an essential weakness in the body of Christ (also therefore reflected in YWAM and the U of N).

Historically, across almost the entire church, our theology of the kingdom has diminished to embrace primarily church and the Christian family along with a bit of Christian education and mercy ministries. Consequently, we have significantly lost the art and skill of "thinking" biblically in areas such as business, environmental management, the arts, et cetera. The constituency of YWAM also seems to mirror this bias. We have a relatively larger reservoir of educators and trained medical personnel. Consequently, professionally qualified workers joined our team, and those two areas were the most well-developed and successful. YWAM in Holland had also launched and supported a ministry called Agrinas which focused on biblically based agricultural development. The ministry in the agricultural sector was therefore quite effective, indeed exemplary.

In conclusion, a shortage of open doors for service in the societies of the world for Christians and missionaries is not the problem. The church has a profound shortage of professionals, prepared by education, experience, theology, worldview, and vision to enter those open doors of opportunity. Perhaps the primary recommendation from our experience would be for the body of Christ to train and equip more resource professionals for the relatively abundant open doors.

Principle-Practice Set #2: Strategic Modeling of the Kingdom

The Principle

The church is to be a "city of light set on a hill" (see Matt. 5:14). We are to preach the gospel of the kingdom to all nations as a testimony. We are to proclaim, to publish, to make manifest, to demonstrate, or to strategically model the kingdom of God.

Biblical Foundations and Explication

One assumption naturally emerging from a comprehensive view of redemption and the kingdom is that our job is bigger than it really is. The bottom line in all missionary endeavor is to present the gospel, not to take responsibility for its full acceptance. Our task is essentially communication, not complete implementation. What Jesus commanded us to do was to "preach" the gospel—that is, to "publish" it, or to make it effectively known so the world can see and the sinner can make an informed choice.

This is essentially the same method Jesus employed. He came to "incarnate" God the Father—to make him visible and known. He tangibly testified to the realities of the nature of God and his kingdom.

The word picture of a city of light on a hill (Matt. 5:14) is very instructive. Darkness is implied to be the prevailing condition, certainly on the periphery. But because darkness cannot overcome light, a huge or brilliant light is not required to present a contrast. In our context, we don't necessarily need to do something big, but our work must accurately and visibly represent the kingdom. Quality is more important than quantity. Hence, our strategy was simply to "preach" the gospel of the kingdom by establishing "cities of light." We chose to develop models of God's kingdom that clearly and accurately portrayed the substance and reality of the King and his kingdom.

This strategy has as a primary goal that each person of the targeted group have an opportunity to see, touch, feel, and experience the reality of the kingdom of God. Then they can make an informed choice for or against God and his kingdom. The kingdom task of Matthew 24:14 is finished not when we have "kingdomized" the last square meter on the planet, but simply when the last soul on the planet has had the opportunity to see the kingdom of God in action and in reality, and has had the opportunity to make an informed decision for or against it.

Caveats

This principle of "modeling" the kingdom must be held in complementary tension with the first principle presented, the comprehensive redemption and rule of the kingdom of God on earth as it is in heaven. When looking at the kingdom mandate from the perspective of communicating the gospel to lost souls through "modeling" the kingdom, we can indeed downsize and simplify the task. But the kingdom mandate is in no way a minimalist mandate. We should not settle for minimum candlepower in a world of darkness. Rather, we are to strive for maximization of kingdom redemption and rule on this planet.

Scripture, for example, uses the picture of the wilderness being radically transformed into a garden (Isa. 35:1–2, 6; 41:19; 43:19). It speaks of Christ returning for a victorious bride, without spot or wrinkle (Eph. 5:27). It declares the reconciliation of all things on earth (Col. 1:20; Heb. 1:13; Rev. 11:15). It points to the unconditional surrender of the enemy, not some sort of a standoff, or worse, the imminent rout of the forces of truth and light except for the last-minute intervention of Jesus rescuing us from the overpowering might of the devil (Eph. 1:20–22; Col. 1:13). Peter declares that we have been given all things for life and godliness (2 Pet. 1:3). None of these expressions can be construed as minimalist metaphor. In light of these scriptures, the biblical attitude must be one of pressing on to completion of the task and total victory over the power of sin in the lives of individuals, as well as in society, culture, and the natural order.

A caveat on "relevance" is also appropriate. To communicate the gospel of the kingdom effectively, relevance is an important consideration. We must communicate the kingdom such that it speaks to the issues, concerns, needs, and realities of the target group and their surrounding society, culture, and natural environment. We must scratch where they itch. However, relevance contains some built-in pitfalls. From a biblical perspective, one can be exceedingly relevant by standing in opposition to the status quo of a people or society. "A Christian must be a sign of contradiction in the world."[3] We are, indeed, to be relevant to real problems and issues. But biblical answers or alternatives are not necessarily found within a society's currently accepted norms or practices. The most effective kingdom model may present a stark contrast to the standard solutions and conventional wisdom proffered in that society. In other words, our task is to distinguish the holy from the profane. Initially, kingdom models that are "contradictory" to society's norms will almost certainly be viewed as irrelevant. Relevance therefore is a useful concept, but it is not a biblical absolute.

The Practice

This principle of building high-quality, visible models to communicate the substantive reality and truth of the kingdom and its King dramatically simplified our task. We applied it first to our selection of location for our work in Albania. In 1991 there were twenty-six regions or political subdivisions in the country. We determined that we would concentrate our efforts, that is, build "cities of light" or models of the kingdom, in only one of those twenty-six regions.

We consciously considered the alternative of staying in the capital because of its high degree of "visibility" (due to the centralized nature of the Albanian government structure, a holdover from the Communist system). Nevertheless, we chose to move away from the capital, primarily because the majority of the Albanians, approximately 90 percent, lived in the provinces. To be relevant to that rural majority, we selected one of the twenty-six regions that typified the realities of Albanian life and culture, the province of Pogradec.

The inherent "multiplication" factor was another reason we choose to set up our ministry in the provinces. Tirana, the capital city (and one of the twenty-six regions in itself) was qualitatively different to the other twenty-five regions. If we were successful in outer regions of Pogradec, we could relatively easily multiply those models into the other twenty-four regions. In other words, "multiplicability" is also one of the considerations in planning a model. If a model can be easily reproduced in similar contexts, its value is significantly increased. Moreover, a replicable model poses fewer barriers to initial entry since the model is already designed to suit the culture.

This "modeling" strategy was also employed within the respective twelve sectors. For example, in the education sector, our goal was simply to "model" the kingdom of God in various aspects of public education.[4] We selected representative or "model" schools in which to concentrate much of our educational ministry. In the region of Pogradec, there were over eighty schools. (By extrapolation, we estimated that there were approximately two thousand schools in Albania). We, however, chose only one preschool, one primary school, and one high school in which to focus our efforts at kingdom modeling. For example, we did physical renovation to display how an effective learning environment might appear. We established demonstration classrooms where Albanian teachers could observe class sessions based on a biblical philosophy of education. On the interpersonal side, we worked extensively with Albanian teachers to show them how to teach, plan, and resolve personal and professional conflicts in a team context.

Another critical component of the model school strategy was to secure not only government approval but also active cooperation. At the ministerial level in Tirana we formalized agreements which gave us official authorization. These agreements explicitly communicated that we were operating from a Christian value base, and that we were attempting to demonstrate something of the reality and nature of the kingdom of God as it would look in public Albanian education. A more implicit aspect of these formal agreements was that we were "competing" with other models, methods, or systems of education. Upon completion of our work, the Ministry of Education was invited to evaluate the quality of our version (the "kingdom" version) of public education against any other models or systems. We also encouraged them to then choose the best approach for the students, the parents, and the nation as a whole.[5]

Evaluation and Critique

The principle of strategically modeling the kingdom repeatedly proved an effective method in the six and a half years of our ministry in Albania. For example, despite working in only three schools, we had the cooperation and the eye of those who had the power to adopt biblical, kingdom standards across the entire nation.[6] An effective model works even if only three schools out of two thousand are involved. On one occasion, a newly appointed minister of education was so impressed by a brief presentation of our work that he wanted to make a TV documentary for the nation and to convince the other fifteen ministries of the Albanian government to adopt similar programs! Declining the minister's offer, we chose instead to work quietly behind the scenes.[7] But this incident demonstrated that an effective kingdom model doesn't need to be big. It needs to be relevant to the needs of the people and place, and to clearly communicate the substance and reality of the kingdom and its King.

Modeling should be employed frequently in our planning and implementation. A model, of course, is not in itself the gospel, but does reflect basic biblical values, strategies, and methods. Additionally, because available missionary resources are a perennial concern, it would behoove us to adopt strategies that would maximize our effectiveness in fulfilling the kingdom mandate while utilizing a minimum of resources. "Modeling" the kingdom is one of those strategies.

Certainly, inherent dangers or weaknesses affect any principle-practice. We can easily be tripped up in the "relevance" game discussed above. The danger of "overintellectualizing" this (or any) principal-practice set also exists. Selecting the most effective and strategic models may not necessarily be only the result of diligent data gathering and analysis. In fact, our choice of Pogradec, which later proved to be an effective and even wise selection, was largely predicated on a divine encounter with one man, the director of education for the Pogradec region. We had the principle firmly in grasp. That is, we knew we wanted to focus on building models in only one region. But we had few facts and figures in the classical sense. Nevertheless, through prayer and spiritual "watchfulness," we were sovereignly led to the right person(s) and place.

Demonstrating (preaching) the kingdom through "modeling" was an essential practice and contributed greatly to whatever success we garnered in Albania.

Principle-Practice Set #3: Sequences of the Kingdom

The Principle

The kingdom of God is anchored in the hearts of individuals and is mediated to the world through God's covenantal people, the church. This covenantal people are the means of evangelism and reaching the hearts of individuals. God's goodness concretely expressed in models of his kingdom by his people leads individuals to repentance.[8]

Biblical Foundations and Explication

One question frequently arising around this view of kingdom is in the form of the classical dilemma: Which comes first—the chicken or the egg, the church body or the kingdom? The kingdom is anchored in the heart of man. In terms of the flow of the redemptive power of his Spirit and the application of his Word into this world, God works through the heart of man. Men's hearts are the primary portal through which the kingdom of heaven enters this side of the cosmos. Yes, God is sovereign. He has intervened directly in human affairs, and he will continue to so. However, the body of Christ is crucial because it forms the community of individual "hearts" through which God normally works into the world.

Nevertheless, let us not confuse the primacy of the human heart and the church as "agent" of the kingdom with the sequence of development of the kingdom in any given locale. An enticing logic would say that the sequence of developing the kingdom must be, first, evangelism of individuals; second, discipleship with church planting and development; and third, when all that is finally in place, venturing outside the planted church into the spheres of societal transformation. While we always place man the individual as the highest priority because he alone is created in the image of God and he alone has the potential for intimate, eternal fellowship with God, to insist on the individual-to-church-to-society sequence of ministry and development of the kingdom is artificial.

In January of 1992, during the beginning phases of our work in Pogradec, it was estimated that in the entire region of approximately 75,000 there were only three believers, and no functioning churches of any kind. This seemed the norm for a nation that had so systematically eradicated any forms of "religion." It was true not only for the Christian church but also for Islam, the dominant religion for the 450 years prior to Communism.

Despite the complete absence of churches and a desperate need for planting local churches, we nevertheless felt that we were to focus first on the breadth of God's redemption and rule, which included all of society, culture, and the natural order. This was a decision of strategic sequence only, not one of inherent value or worth.

Our decision rested on two reasons. First, we are mandated to advance the kingdom on earth as it is in heaven. The kingdom, as I have explained briefly above, is God's redemption and rule in more than just individuals and the church. Therefore, to focus on the breadth components of God's kingdom was inherently biblical. Second, such a decision could be made only if we also held fast the complementary truth of the qualitative primacy of man the individual and the centrality of the church. Thus, we could sustain the broad, biblical perspective necessary for mutual inclusivity and long-term balance of all three complementary aspects of the kingdom.

So, there are (at least) two sequential paths or strategies leading to the fulfillment of the kingdom mandate. The first, and most frequently utilized, is to start with evangelism of individuals, then plant and develop the local church, and finally step into ministry to society, culture, and the natural order. A second option is to start with ministry in society and culture, and through those activities to evangelize individuals who can be gathered into a local church. The choice between these two options is based on the calling and giftings of the ministers and local variables of time, place, and people. The foci of individuals, church, society and culture, and the natural order are qualitatively different. Nevertheless, they are all aspects of the same kingdom order. They all connect and overlap with one another sooner or later. They are mutually inclusive and must all be operating to fulfill the whole of the kingdom mandate. This unity amongst the diversity of kingdom components is nonnegotiable. The sequence in which we approach the three components is flexible.

One of the main reasons we made the decision to focus first on ministry in society and culture, rather than on church planting, had to do with our understanding of the dynamic and power of Romans 2:4: "the goodness of God leads to repentance" (NKJV). When we first came to Albania in November of 1991, and for a number of years thereafter, the nation was a wasteland in almost every sense of the word. Very few of the normal aspects of life functioned, from food production and basic commerce to the political structures and systems. Even the natural beauty of the land had been decimated. Albanians were understandably focused on the very basic necessities of life: food to eat, wood to heat their homes and schools, and basic medical supplies. Our approach was to meet such needs while simultaneously building personal relationships and friendships as a basis for evangelism (and later discipleship and introduction into a local church). The promise of Romans 2:4 is that as people see the "goodness of God" (under which we could subsume models of the kingdom) they are attracted to the nature of God and the King of the kingdom. Their attraction eventually leads to "repentance," individual salvation, and entry into the kingdom. Simply put, as people see and experience the kingdom in terms of what is important and significant to them (food, shelter, education for their children, employment, civil justice, health care, etc.) they begin to concretely realize that God is concerned about their earthly condition and is not far off. Such demonstrations of the goodness of God through kingdom models are a powerful form of evangelism.

We experienced this dynamic in numerous contexts. Starting with societal realities and individual needs, we effectively entered people's lives, built friendships, and led many to Christ. Serving Jesus was a lifestyle rooted in the practical necessities of life. Our models stood in stark contrast to the Communist ideology and methodology. Under Communism, everyone was gathered into a room to hear one or two informed individuals communicate the tenets of the new faith. But that "faith" was never really connected to the needs and realities of the time, the place, and the people.

Caveats

Our tendency is to overlay our giftings and callings, hence our convictions, onto our theology about the best or only way to bring the kingdom. If I am called and gifted as a church planter, I will tend to elevate that aspect of the kingdom and see it as the most important element and the invariable beginning point. If I am an evangelist, I might do the same thing for my expertise. The reality is, there is no inherent biblical, universal absolute in determining the sequence! The ideal would be if the evangelist and church planter could work side by side with the "development" specialists, each recognizing the others' differing calls and priorities, while simultaneously holding on to the one overarching goal: the advancement of the kingdom of God on earth as it is in heaven.

The Practice

We formalized our process into a five-step sequence, a planning template. Planning began with the twelve sectors mentioned above. For each, we developed individual projects and programs which were collectively intended to fulfill the kingdom mandate. In the education sector, for example, twenty different projects of diverse magnitude and length might have run throughout any given year. Each project was planned and implemented using our five-step sequence:

1. Pilot Project: We performed an initial pilot project in partnership with local Albanians. Our goal was to concretely serve them at the point of their need. The pilot was designed to maximize the demonstration and communication of the substance and reality of God and his kingdom.

This first step enabled us to meet and work intimately with local nationals. We quickly "stepped into their world." Thus, we first established a basic platform of trust and then developed closer personal relationships and friendships with them. This led to the second step: friendship evangelism.

2. Friendship Evangelism: Albanians are oriented toward relationship and hospitality. After proving our commitment to them by serving at their point of need, we developed deeper personal relationships with relative ease. Within that framework of open friendship, our evangelism would be quite natural, often done around drinking coffee together, visiting their homes, and having a meal together.

In fact, this dynamic worked so well that after a while we noticed many people who had made a profession of faith had done it primarily to honor us as guests and friends! We trusted that God has his ways of pruning the church. From this stage, we needed then to move on to more intensive discipleship.

3. Discipleship: Discipleship is obviously of the highest importance. At this point our practice diverged into two distinct paths: partnership with church-planting entities and personal discipleship by our staff. Initially, we had settled on a "partnership" strategy to primarily accomplish "discipleship." On our very first visit in 1991, we had met a German missionary in Pogradec. His ministry priorities included a strong emphasis on church planting. We therefore agreed that he would plant and pastor a local church and that we would essentially focus on societal transformation. We planned to endeavor to channel all of the converts and inquirers from our work into his church. Later, when an American missionary planted another church, we also sought a similar relationship with that church.

In theory, we "delegated" discipleship to the church planters. In reality, however, our own staff ended up being intimately involved with much of the actual personal discipleship. This was a natural consequence of the depth of personal friendship and relationship which had been cultivated during the pilot projects and friendship evangelism (see Evaluation and Critique below).

4. Leadership Development: Basic Christian discipleship led to the fourth step of leadership development. For us, leadership development included two dimensions. The first dimension covered general leadership skills based on biblical principles. The second dimension comprised the specific leadership issues and skills necessary for Christians to move into leadership of the various sectors of society and culture. For example, we focused not only on prayer and Bible literacy but also on educational quality and learning theory, principles of ethics in business management, and project development methods in the government.

We mentored leaders through the ongoing projects and programs originated as pilot projects. Leadership development for Christian teachers, for example, took place in the various educational projects and programs that continued from year to year. Those projects and programs therefore had a twofold purpose: First, they allowed us to enter into the world of the Albanians, to establish trust and build relationship. Second, they were "real-world" discipleship and leadership development schools. Leadership development was critical because we had always intended to exit.

5. Exit: Not just redeemed individuals and planted churches, the kingdom of God is also the comprehensive redemption and rule of God in society, culture, and the natural order. In God's order, the nationals move into responsibility for the kingdom mandate in their own nations. We saw our role as "initiators" of the kingdom's growth process, not as the main resource to finish the task. Therefore, from the very beginning of our work, we always spoke about the "exit" point: that time when the nationals would be sufficiently prepared to take over the full breadth of the kingdom task, in all twelve sectors. Then we could leave.

For us, exit did not mean that the kingdom task was finished; exit indicated that our initial contribution was complete. We determined that our initial contribution for each individual sector was finished when there were adequate national leaders trained and equipped to continue the kingdom mandate without us. Therefore, exit clearly implied a turnover. Exit was the last step in our planning process, and the goal toward which we strove from day one.

Evaluation and Critique

This five-stage process was an effective way of making explicit—in the planning and implementation process—many of our foundational values and beliefs. However, from experience, there are two beneficial modifications that bear mentioning.

First, our scheme to transfer those who came to Christ under our ministry to another ministry did not work as well as we had hoped. This was apparently due, first and foremost, to the relational nature of the Albanian culture. Having come to Christ within the framework of friendship with us, many Albanians found it difficult to transfer their Christian "loyalties" to another group. Many simply never affiliated themselves with the church, but rather stayed with us in an informal way. Many factors in Albanian culture and recent history could explain this phenomenon. Having studied this further, I would venture to say that this is not a uniquely Albanian phenomenon. Rather, the issues of personal trust and relational bonding are a universal human dynamic. Within our team, we talked and prayed much about any corrective action that should have been taken. The primary alternative that we discussed was to simply start our own church. That church would have been a "cell-based" church, with the cells organized around the twelve sectors of society we had targeted. We never implemented this strategy for various reasons. We did actively seek to augment our staff with qualified church planters but were unable to find any who could come.

If someone with the requisite requirements had been available, and the conditions had been right, we probably would have added in this strategy at an opportune time.

Certainly, knowing what we know now, and finding ourselves in another situation similar to the Albania of 1991, we would probably start with a cell-church-planting strategy from day one. But we would also seek active partnerships with other local churches, because we found this strategy effective and fruitful. We gratefully recognize that the efficacy was due to the maturity and grace of the other Christian leaders in the regions. We also regretfully recognize that such a partnership is not always possible. Nevertheless, we would seek active partnerships, as much as possible, with other local Christian churches and action groups.

Second, based on over six years of experience, I would make a modification of our "theory": In each of the twelve sectors, it took much longer to work through our five stages than we first projected. Initially, we tentatively reckoned on a five-year span. Realizing midway through that this estimate was far too optimistic, we began talking about seven to ten years to exit point. If I were to start over again today, I would begin with at least a ten-year planning framework to realistically reach the exit point.

As previously mentioned, one of the main impediments to our progress was the shortage of trained and staged professionals in each of the twelve sectors. If there were a pool of such people out of which we could draw as needed, then a shorter time span could again be realistic. We had to develop the field work in Albania, and simultaneously find or develop the professional (and other) resources outside Albania. This significant complication beyond our original expectations affected the progress rate in Albania.

Final Conclusions and Recommendations

When the University of the Nations decided to respond to the newly opened doors in Albania in the summer of 1991, the idea was to develop a concrete prototype of discipling a nation. My wife, Puanana, and I had been actively engaged in such questions for many years prior, albeit on a smaller scale. Nevertheless, we entered Albania with our tool bag full of principles and practices garnered from years of previous ministry. In this paper I discussed three of those. After six and a half years of very rigorous "field testing," I am confident in saying, that with few exceptions, the A.I.D. Project "prototype" proved the validity and applicability of those principle-practice tools.

Our experiences, however, have also revealed some areas that require greater attention from the international body of Christ, including YWAM/U of N. First, we must put greater emphasis on the long-term nature of discipling nations. Second, we should deliberately build networks with skills and experience to disciple nations.

Third, we must continue to develop a theological understanding of discipling nations. I will elaborate on these three points.

Discipling nations is a long-term, resource-intensive proposition. It cannot be accomplished with a short-term mentality only. Short-term teams have an important and useful contribution to make, but only if there are long-term teams in place. We need to direct our efforts and resources to both sides of the equation. We must place teams on the field. At the same time, we must also establish the support foundations required for long-term success. Support would certainly include financial resources. But equally important are the resources of trained professionals (who have reinterpreted their discipline from a biblical perspective) and an active prayer support network. All are necessary to arrive successfully at the exit point when the nationals take over leadership with local resources.

Discipling nations, because of its inherent breadth and complexity, requires a conscious and diligent networking and partnering across the body of Christ. We desperately need one another's wisdom, experience, and spiritual gifts for such a task. Highly "decentralized" strategies have their place. Nevertheless, mechanisms to bring the various gifts, experience, wisdom, etc., together and to make them available where needed on the field are also required. This will require intensive teamwork, leadership teams, strategic planning, and cooperation at the center. Nothing else is sufficient to meet the challenges of the task.

The requisite theology of "discipling nations" is still quite obscure and misunderstood and, in some instances, contested by a *significant* majority of the church and the missionary community. Until we have more fully recaptured these theological foundations, we will need to invest proportionately larger amounts of time, prayer and other resources into educating and mobilizing Christian leaders and workers for the kingdom task. For now we are attempting to do a job with few of the theoretical and theological foundations and tools. We lack many of the technical or practical tools that depend on biblical clarity at the broader conceptual level, but happily, this situation appears to be changing. More and more Christian believers are addressing such issues. As this trend continues, as we continue to dialogue, pray, and work together, we can realistically hope to see whole nations discipled.

Acknowledgment

I wish to acknowledge the marvelous contribution of the other leaders and team members of the A.I.D. Project. They made it possible. They all played significant roles in not just an outreach, but in pioneering new methods and strategies for international missions work. Faleminderit shueme dhe gezuar!

Notes

1. As an organization, YWAM has historically had a very special relationship to Albania, provoked in part by the events of two of our workers in 1973 in Albania. This story is related in the book *Tomorrow You Die* by Reona Joly. Since then, thousands of YWAMers have prayed diligently for the opening of the country and the propagation of the gospel in what was a very closed nation.

2. This was the formal name we gave to this project. It is the name by which it is most widely recognized, particularly in Germany where most of the practical support came from.

3. Ascribed to Father Jerzy Popieluszko, a Polish priest martyred by the Communists.

4. During the entire duration of our project, private education was not permitted by law so we never had to choose between modeling in public and private systems.

5. We had much favor and support within the Ministry of Education during the six and a half years of the project. Ultimately, however, for a multitude of reasons beyond our control and often owing to the instability of the new republic, no explicit choice was ever made by the government to adopt or reject our model.

6. We later discovered that any educational standards or methods adopted by the Ministry of Education in Tirana would also very likely be adopted by the Albanian provisional government in Kosovo.

7. At the time this took place, there was a pronounced wave of money and influence from a number of Islamic nations. Their goal was clearly to reassert Muslim influence in this nation (which had been under Ottoman Turkish rule for 500 years). We felt, at that time, that we had the attention of the decision makers in the government and that was enough. To publicly portray our intentions and our relationship with the upper echelons of Albanian government would have exposed our strategies to those who would have vigorously opposed it. Hence, we made the choice to continue working behind the scenes.

8. Romans 2:4 (NKJV) states that "the goodness of God leads to repentance."

When Jesus charged us to disciple nations, the word he used was closer to the idea of "peoples" than to political borders. Some of the "nations" of the Amazon jungle have less than one hundred people, but they are worthy of our greatest efforts to bring them the gospel in a way that builds them as a people and does not tear down their unique identity. Bráulia draws us into the stories of three tiny nations hidden away in the Amazon. There is much to learn from these brothers and sisters and from those who have loved and served them, as they have wrestled together to see these nations discipled by the gospel.

Case Study: When Less Is More:
The Appropriate Role of Development

Bráulia Ribeiro

I was first attracted to the Brazilian song "In This Home"[1] by the rhythm. Once I digested and understood the words, I discovered that the song was as rich in wisdom as hours of missiology class. The words are:

In this home nobody wants your fine manners.
The days that we have food,
We eat it with our hands.
When the police, disease, distance,
Separate us from our brothers,
A heart could never contain such pain.
But we don't cry in vain.
But we don't cry in vain.

In this tribe nobody wants your catechism,
We may speak the same language,
But we don't understand your sermon.
We laugh aloud, we drink, we swear,
But we don't laugh in vain.
But we don't laugh in vain.

On this boat nobody wants your steering.
We know where we are headed,
But the wind is what guides us.
A life that drifts is our objective,
But we don't go in vain.
But we don't go in vain.

Why does this song move me so much? After all, it expresses a very non-Christian attitude. It seems to chase the missionaries away by insisting that they are not wanted in swearing, hungry, ill, disoriented Brazil.

Actually, I believe it is a cry for respect and dignity. It speaks for a people made in the image of God, people who want to be treated with respect by a gospel that should not strip them of their identity. Each verse declares: we have our own culture, and it must be valid too. We have our own way of eating, we have our own manners, and we suffer pains that you will never understand. Your conceptual message doesn't reach us, because it does not make sense in our world. Speaking the same language is not enough. We deserve respect. Your discipleship is not appreciated because we know where we are going in spite of the apparent drift of our boat. We do not live to make and strive for goals. Life, in and of itself, is our goal. The mystery of things is as important to us as the knowing.

The writer of the song, Arnaldo Antunes, confronts a deeper foundational thinking than I am able to explore in this short article. I have included his song to give us a glimpse into the heart of a non-Western person, to hear their longing for us to approach their world, bringing the good news to their culture with a teachable heart full of respect for who they already are.

It is important for us in cross-cultural missions to realize that walking with the Lord is not the same as performing brain surgery. We do not need to be exact or perfect. All we need is to be honest and humble. Mistakes are part of our humanity.

This chapter will examine three case studies of tribal microsocieties located in the Amazon basin of Brazil: the Sateré-Mawé, the Jarawara, and the Suruwahá. These tiny "nations" give us an up-close look at some of the issues we must be aware of as we engage with Jesus' mandate to disciple the nations. The Sateré case highlights community development issues, the Jarawara study gives us an insight into the role of education for discipling nations, and the Suruwahá example illustrates some of the dynamics we must consider to ensure the birth of a healthy, truly indigenous church.

Isolated from the majority of the Brazilian population, these three small tribes have kept their pre-Columbian lifestyle and worldviews for over 350 years while they have had contact with the outside world. Their languages and cultures are unique. Allowing these peoples to develop *apart* from our traditional discipleship efforts has given them room to find their own way, to incorporate into their culture the truths of who God is. My intention is to affirm the importance of proper contextualization of mission strategy, when "less means more" to the kingdom. Contextualizing and knowing when *not* to interfere is not merely an enhancement of mission strategy; it is the very backbone of love on which the gospel is incarnated.

Pre-Colombian vs. Modern Views of Economy: the Sateré-Mawé

The Sateré-Mawé do not make a good first impression.[2] Short and dark, they wear minimal, worn-out clothing, and have a sweet look that can be mistaken for the traditional servile humility of colonized peoples. A group of missionaries coming from southern Brazil or North America could easily think of the Sateré peoples' lives as miserable and needy. In our desire to serve these people in the name of our Lord, we might mistakenly determine that they need drastic intervention to improve the quality of their lives.

Despite 350 years of colonial pressure, the Sateré-Mawé people have preserved their ethnic identity, their social structure, and their love for and pride in who they are. They have chosen to absorb the technical skills needed to adjust to being surrounded by a technological society, and they have rejected those which they deemed would not make them a better people or give a better life to their children. They have not become alcoholic like many other tribes or servile beggars to the Brazilian government.

The Sateré-Mawé developed a unique way to cultivate the guaraná plant which is now known all over the world for its delicious flavor and many beneficial health properties. They developed a technique to transform the guaraná plant, originally a wild vine, into a small coffee-like bush that can be planted anywhere throughout the Amazonian basin. Processing the guaraná fruit takes several months; this process was also a Sateré-Mawé invention. Through a pre-Columbian tradition of guaraná commerce they interacted with neighboring people groups. Even Bolivian Indian groups, far from the Sateré native land, bought guaraná from them.

In order to accurately assess the condition of their lives and therefore determine appropriate goals and strategies for biblical development, a clear definition of poverty is essential to guide our task.

What is poverty? Under which criteria should a society be judged poor? Is there an absolute, universal standard that can be used to judge a people "poor," thus determining that we must "help them" to be in obedience to God? If we judge our own people and culture, the criteria for "poverty" are somewhat easier to define. Unless we are hardened of heart, we know very well what it is to be poor in our own social context. We know when our conscience hurts for a person we see on the streets or in a nearby neighborhood. In Deuteronomy 15:11 God teaches us not to harden our hearts and leave our poor neighbor empty-handed.[3]

However, when we talk about a people group of a different country or culture, everything changes. It becomes harder to differentiate poverty from a difference in lifestyle. First Timothy 6:8 says: "But if we have food and clothing, we will be content with that." The International Human Rights Declaration concurs, stating that every human being has the right to have food to eat and something to wear.[4] Is this a helpful working definition for us? We could define the poor as "those who are not able to decide about and supply their own basic needs."

The word "poor" in the New Testament is usually a translation of one of two different Greek words: *ptochos* and *penes*.[5] *Ptochos* means "one who is not capable of surviving by himself; beggar; one who depends on others . . . etc." *Penes* means "one who has to fight daily for survival," and it implies this person has sufficient, even if barely enough. Is *ptochos* the same as *penes*? No. The Bible clearly distinguishes between two types of poverty.

The word *ptochos* is used in almost all of the verses that mention the word "poor." According to Strong's concordance, the word *penes* is used only twice. In Luke 21:1–4, the *penes*-poor woman is shown giving to the temple. In 2 Corinthians 9, Paul quotes Psalm 112 as he gives a command to give to the *penes*-poor, but it is in the context of being generous and distributing resources to everyone, anybody. The command to give to the poor, in the sense of assistance, is always applied to the *ptochos,* the destitute, who, because of life's circumstances, has no means to support himself. This distinction needs to be made in our thinking about development, otherwise we might, in our efforts to help, really be transforming honorable daily-bread *penes*-poor people into helpless, dependent *ptochos*-beggars.

The Sateré in the village of Atuka were never *ptochos*-poor. They were not incapable of supplying their basic needs. Though they lived near the city of Maués, they did not depend a great deal on what the city could supply. Like all Sateré, they were proud of their "Sateré-ness," and carried on a unique and very Indian lifestyle despite the years of contact with a more powerful and more developed society.

One example of this has to do with their diet. The traditional Indian lifestyle does not require three meals a day. Instead, the people snack on a special type of mushrooms or on a handful of raw ants together with lots of guaraná drink. One main meal is prepared in the evenings, after the men return from the jungle or the river with the catch of the day. To our urban stomachs, it is quite difficult to adjust to such an exotic diet. Yet to the Sateré, this is the normal way to live. Their diet has kept them healthy and alert in the jungle for centuries. While many would find this diet repugnant and insufficient, it is not a sign of their poverty, but rather a choice they have made based on their culture and environment.

The pioneer work among the Sateré had been done by another YWAM team. Their main motivation had been to find godly analogies within the culture to lead the group to Jesus. After five years, there was a church with indigenous leadership, and a school running with indigenous teachers. The team decided that they had done their job. There were so many other Sateré villages that they felt the pressure to go to other places. In this very appropriate moment a second team came to give continuity to the work. They were motivated and well-trained in community development. Aware of their novice status in the Amazon, they started work carefully.

This team was trained to look for areas of need and design a project to improve the economic situation of Atuka village. They noted signs of acculturation such as "all wear clothes" or "some speak reasonable Portuguese" (the national language of Brazil). That is a common mistake outsiders make. The image of the stereotypical Indian, naked and free in the jungle, leads people to believe that tribes who wear clothing and know some Portuguese are "not Indian enough" or "have lost their culture." The development team misread these external signs to underestimate the value of the Sateré language and culture to that community.

Unfortunately, none of the team made the effort to speak the language or develop an in-depth understanding of the Sateré culture, including the intricate clan, kinship, and social structures. They came to the false conclusion that they were dealing with a community that would soon be totally integrated with the national society and therefore should be judged by the nation's standard of poverty in assessing whether they needed assistance. The Sateré were obviously a member of the *ptochos*-poor category by urban-Brazilian cultural standards.

The first YWAM missionaries had been intimately involved with the village for five years and had left when they determined that the people were able to keep growing in the faith without the direct help of a missionary group. Admittedly, the church was not very mature. Moreover, as an indigenous church, it had a different style of liturgy and different type of leadership than what the new missionaries had known. The new team had difficulty recognizing it as a real Christian movement. According to William Smalley, an experienced Bible translator, "Missionaries often do not like the indigenous church. Often a truly indigenous church is a source of embarrassment to the mission bodies in the area."[6] Smalley notes that missionaries require unusual insight and perception to recognize an indigenous Holy Spirit movement as coming from God.

In their misguided efforts to "help" the believers of Atuka, the missionaries of the second team began to control church life themselves, leading meetings, scheduling, and making the main decisions. The church leader, Cadete, was an old Sateré man from the clan that traditionally leads the village. One of the first decisions the team made was to remove him from his position in the church. Some of his attitudes did not seem "Christian" enough to the missionaries' cultural eyes. As time went by, it became obvious to Cadete that he could not continue to serve the village together with this new missionary team, and he stopped going to church. To the team, that was a clear sign that he had backslidden!

The development work focused on the perceived needs for a better daily diet and some kind of security for the future, since Atuka's proximity to town made it a difficult place to either fish or hunt anymore. However, the Sateré saw migration as the natural solution and began to migrate as they had in centuries past. The development team exhorted the villagers to stay, asserting that God would provide a way for them to survive in their present location. The government gave the village a one-time gift of rice and beans. This event was portrayed as evidence to the village that "God was in charge of the situation." Thus, the Sateré people who had been capable of supplying their own food by the daily work of their hands (*penes*), were now cast with the *ptochos*-poor, dependent on outside provision, supposedly from God.

Later the missionaries introduced a sewing cooperative with the intention of helping the Sateré to fight against a sense of inferiority and worthlessness. In reality, the Sateré had no sense of inferiority but rather a strong sense of pride and identity. The Sateré did not compare themselves with anyone, nor desire to have unnecessary things. This is what enabled them to stay strong and proud after so many years of colonial oppression. Ambition and consumerism are not common vices among Sateré people or even other tribes in general. This contentment with their simple lifestyle can be easily mistaken for weakness and a hindrance to the Indians' "progress."

In assessing the needs of those we long to serve, we must understand that values and priorities change from culture to culture. Western culture values *having;* possessing just enough for today is not sufficient. We need to have more than we can use to feel secure. However, as missionaries coming to "help" with development, we must ask God to help us assess our own values to determine whether they are reflections of our home culture or whether they are rooted in truly biblical values. Every culture has to develop its own expression of a biblical worldview, and we as missionaries must be very careful to allow this process to happen and not shape it by our own unconscious belief that our home culture is *the* best expression of biblical values and worldview.

The non-Christian development agency CTI implemented a guaraná cultivating and processing cooperative among the Sateré of another region. While implementing this project, they took great interest in the Sateré culture, social structure, and values. They studied for years, and then carefully introduced the project in a very cultural way that respected details of the economics and social values of the Sateré people. The Sateré perceived the project as their own, not as coming from outsiders.

The whole project was a textbook example of what has to be done to achieve a successful result on a development project. Nevertheless, contrary to the agency's original expectations, the project never became independent from outside funding.

The reason was understood and explained by the agency people themselves: "to radically increase the excess would only work if the Sateré stopped being Sateré."[7] The development agency staff understood that the Sateré were not interested in creating a profit. They worked in the guaraná production, but they also lived for the community by helping their friends and relatives to build huts or to clear the forest for planting manioc. They "wasted time" in the evenings and rainy mornings picking lice from their children's heads and doing little projects with their sons and daughters to prepare them for adult life. The guaraná production was always just enough to keep the project going and the community happy, but was not sufficient to become a profitable and productive enterprise.

The second YWAM missionary team worked hard to help the Atuka village, but building from their faulty understanding of the true condition of the people, they introduced economic and spiritual changes that actually ended up being destructive to the Sateré way of life.

The team introduced rice cultivation, when rice is not a common starch for the Amazonian peoples' diet. They introduced managing herds of cattle, when, according to the culture, whatever you raise you cannot eat (and milk is a very strange thing to drink). They "helped" a village leader get a bank loan, leaving this subsistence farmer tied up in debt with the bank. A few families "improved" their lifestyle, meaning they were able to buy more industrialized items from town. This is actually the beginning of a cycle that often leads these tribal families into a *ptochos*-poor lifestyle in a city somewhere.

In their effort to "help" what they saw as a floundering church, they installed a local non-Indian leader over the pastorate of the Sateré church. Other villagers that were not a part of the traditional lineage of leadership were discipled to be leaders in spiritual education and to provide counseling. That broke the Sateré's ancient leadership pattern, and after a couple of years the new leaders faced so much cultural resistance that there was no native leadership left. The newer Sateré pastor had to be replaced by an outsider whose leadership style did not work well for the Sateré.

Is this a picture of successful Christian development? Sadly, no. It is, instead, a picture of misguided efforts to change a lifestyle that was serving the needs of the people in their own unique expression of culture. As we can see, some of those well-meaning changes have actually destroyed aspects of the Sateré's uniqueness that the Sateré themselves would have to fight to restore. However, the project in Atuka was considered by some to be a model development project. The team left the leadership of the work in the hands of the community and moved out to supervise the project indirectly.

Years later on one sunny morning, the Sateré canoes were full, moving out slowly from Atuka. The paddles plunged into the water and rose up again, shining in the sunlight. As children played, confined in the tiny space of the canoe, mothers took time to craft one more necklace. As they paddled, fathers dreamed of their next hunting trip in a new place.

The final migration had to happen, as it had happened all over the Amazon region during years of Sateré pilgrimage. They left behind a worn piece of land, but also a lesson of persistence and love. In leaving our well-intentioned development program, the Sateré taught us about a people who know their own values and traditions and who want to keep themselves intact as evidence of the love for their Creator. For them, leaving the violated Atuka village was in itself an act of love for God. To leave behind Western patterns of economic development in order to regain a slow and family-oriented lifestyle is, in many cases, to be wise. The Sateré-Mawé have always been wise.

Are we prepared as Christians to love and respect people who have different cultures and values? We must sadly come to the conclusion that we are much less prepared than we think we are. There is a real tension between the benefits of moving toward development and retaining traditional lifestyles. We must ask ourselves how much of our efforts to help are actually interference, either from arrogance or from blindness to the real values of life. It is obvious that transforming daily-economy peoples into market-economy peoples has more to it than a better plate of food on their tables.

As much as I don't like the idea of an ethereal, abstract gospel that does not address all areas of life, the Sateré's experience is an example of the truth that the development principles we often package with the gospel have some serious drawbacks. I can only conclude that every tribe is a universe of its own and respecting their ways and learning from their traditions, even if they appear to be wrong according to our own view of life, is indispensable for good missionary practices.

So Man Is Not Just a *Tabula Rasa?* The Jarawara

The YWAMers trudged through a swamp for four to five hours. They had not realized it would be that far. First they had flown in a little airplane to Labrea, on the banks of the Purus River, a large tributary of the Amazon. Next, they had boarded a small boat to a Brazilian village five hours away, then crossed the swamp, and now, at last, were rewarded with their first sight of a Jarawara village. The name of the village was "White Water," a reference to the crystal-clear waters of a little stream that flowed nearby.

The team was composed of two women and one young man. The two women, Sandra and Beth, were both from the urban state of São Paulo and had joined YWAM not long before the journey to the Jarawara village. Beth had been a skilled teacher at a Bible college for many years when God called her to YWAM to work with tribes.

Sandra was a student at the college and a new Christian who had forsaken a past of left-wing causes passionately pursued. When Beth told Sandra about the situation of the Indians of the Amazon region and the opportunity to work with YWAM, Sandra felt like flying. Here was the great challenge, the cause she had been seeking. A year later they left the seminary to pursue working with tribes.

The young man, Afonso, was a Brazilian, also from São Paulo. The threesome formed a team without a lot of jungle expertise. Somehow they managed to arrive at the strange world of White Water. The Jarawara seemed very short to them, almost Pygmy-size. But once they became aware of the difficulties of life in the jungle and how the Jarawara had learned to cope with them, these urban YWAMers began to see the Jarawara as giants.

Months later an American named David joined the team; he and Afonso worked with various practical needs. Beth and Sandra knew that they had to lay good foundations for whatever God wanted to do with the Jarawara; they worked for five years preparing for a complete ethnoeducation project.

In White Water and the other Jarawara villages, all communication is in Jarawara. The only use for Portuguese is to trade with outsiders. However, merchants exploited them by making them pay repeatedly for the same merchandise. To counteract this, the entire tribe desired to learn to read and write in Portuguese and to study simple mathematics skills. However, Beth and Sandra understood that it was essential to maintain the mother tongue as the main language of the school if literacy was to become integral to tribal life. In fact, anthropologists had concluded that literacy could not succeed in becoming an integral part of a tribal community, but would always be relegated to a "foreign technique" used only in dealing with outsiders.[8] The Indians did not know the importance of this, but they agreed to start with Jarawara.

The village chiefs decided who would learn first. Four young men representing different families started receiving the literacy lessons whenever they could. The class schedule had to be flexible around hunting and fishing trips, rubber gathering, the annual event of clearing and burning of jungle for a new manioc harvest, and other important tribal events.

First the two missionaries worked hard to create an alphabet for the language; within a few months they had a functional version that would be perfected by the Indians themselves when they were able to write. Beth and Sandra worried that the people would need books to read to maintain motivation, so they started preparing little booklets about daily Jarawara life. After the men were able to write, they also used their students' own writing and drawings to make a few more books. The manuscripts were taken to town to be photocopied and bound so they could look like a proper book. They knew a great step was taken when they saw the first little booklets prepared by the Jarawara themselves.

Beth and Sandra returned to the tribe with the booklets, and told their pupils, "Now it's your turn to teach. Go and find someone of your kinship and teach him." The four young men were reluctant but accepted the task. Beth and Sandra had done their part of the job; it was essential for the success of the project that these first students now become the teachers of their own people. The period from the beginning of literacy through the preparation and production of reading material spanned the two years from 1989 to 1990.[9]

According to Beth and Sandra's previous training in the SIL program,[10] they had done more than well. The predominant missions' goal for literacy was that the "natives" would be able to read the Bible. But Beth and Sandra were hoping that education would include something more: survival for the Jarawara in the confrontation with the outside world.

Beth and Sandra next became involved in some other tasks including health care and informally reading Bible stories in Jarawara every night. They also started an intense time of spiritual warfare to show the Jarawara that they were not afraid of demons. But all the time they were observing to see whether anything would take root in the area of literacy.

One month went by, then two, then a whole year. To Beth and Sandra's frustration, nothing seemed to develop. The new "teachers" did not take any initiative to teach others. Beth and Sandra assumed the young men did not want to go to the trouble of becoming teachers themselves.

Moreover, the Jarawara women were completely out of the picture. Together with the four young men, Beth and Sandra tried to teach one Jarawara girl, but she showed no interest whatsoever in reading. The commercial interaction that motivated the men to read was not a part of the women's daily reality. Sadly, this is true even among tribes with successful educational programs.

Beth and Sandra, and YWAM throughout the Amazon, followed Don Richardson's[11] ground-breaking approach toward unreached people groups. Before his time, most missions believed that in order to "save" a tribe they had to begin evangelizing the children, because the adults were so wicked and corrupted by the tribal worldview that they were virtually impossible to save. His focus on reaching adults and redeeming the cultures through God's own self-revelation revolutionized the thinking of a whole generation of missionaries.

Another missionary author, Frank Laubach, had developed the second important principle Beth and Sandra followed.[12] Laubach began his work in the area of education in a Philippine tribe in the early 1900s. After years of frustration, God gave him a glimpse of his heart. He saw how much prejudice he carried and how that prejudice damaged his testimony. The Holy Spirit convicted him that he had to give honor and dignity to the people. A strategy to convey honor was to develop a literacy program that enabled the student to be a teacher as soon as he finished learning to read. "Each one teach one" became his motto.

Based on the inspiration of Richardson and Laubach and on their love for the Jarawara culture, Beth and Sandra decided never to teach children. The children would have to learn from their parents in order to maintain the Jarawara system of socialization and cultural values. The whole education program would instead target adults. That understanding later became a policy for the whole YWAM Amazonian tribal ministry.

Beth and Sandra had high expectations. They were expecting the revelation of God to come to the adults. More than that, they believed the Jarawara Indians would actually become good teachers and lead the education project that would eventually transform the tribe's slavery and marginality.

Despite their seemingly slow start, the Jarawara surged beyond the expectations of the missionaries, and the even lower predictions of anthropologists, to prove themselves capable of not only absorbing the new skills but also adapting them to their own communication needs. They made reading and writing useful in the context of their society, not just as a tool for relating to the outside dominant culture. Writing, not merely reading, is now a part of the daily life of 98 percent of the adult Jarawara. They were not dominated by the new technology as was predicted in most sociological books; instead, they were able to subjugate it to their own needs. They made it a real part of their culture, not just an adapted foreign skill.

The Word of God is now spread by letters. Personal testimonies of faith, prayers, and blessings all go back and forth between the villages. There are four villages besides White Water, with three to four hours' walking distance between them. The letters are the main means of communication between them, and very artistically folded and written in beautiful handwriting.

Formal schools are unnecessary among the Jarawara, at least in the area of literacy. The acquisition of writing is done in their normal social life while talking on top of the palafita huts, while cooking, while trying to read a letter sent by a relative living in another village. It is not the teacher who chases down the student, trying to hold his attention; it is the eager student who goes seeking for knowledge from his literate friend or relative. That is the ancient way of the Jarawara culture: "Whoever wants wisdom must seek it." Knowledge is granted to whoever takes the time and makes the effort to seek it out. This value explained the reluctance of the four young men to "go out and find someone to teach."

In their wildest dreams Beth and Sandra could not have conceived of such a perfect solution for the tribal need of learning to read and write in their own language. It took believing that the Jarawara would rise up in their own way, and having a patient heart to wait until their time came. The missionaries could have done it all.

In those years of waiting, they could have given literacy classes, keeping themselves busy and feeling very satisfied with their work. But by teaching the villagers themselves, they would have deprived the Jarawara of the opportunity to incorporate writing into their culture. Writing was not taught to them; to the Jarawara, it was reinvented by them.

Their story is a wonderful illustration of what happens when we as missionaries take the time to allow a people to find their own way forward.

What Makes a Church a Church? The Suruwahá

My father was a philosopher, and he taught me from an early age to ask hard questions. He frequently asked me: What is truth? Is it a concept? Is it a system of concepts? To find truth, how should we seek? With our minds? With our senses, or feelings? What kind of search will finally lead us to the true truth?

I became a Christian at the age of sixteen, but it took me several years to grasp the answer to these difficult questions. It is there in the Bible stated very clearly: there is only one Truth, and amazingly, this Truth is not a concept or a belief system but a person—the Jesus person. "I am . . . the Truth," he says (John 14:6). These seemingly abstract questions were foundational in developing a missions' mind-set that made room for God to meet little Amazonian tribes in his own unique way.

I had the privilege of getting to know the isolated Suruwahá tribe many years ago. When I first went there as a very young YWAMer, I was short on resources, training, and probably even on spirituality. Not many people from the outside world had been in contact with the Suruwahá before we arrived, and those encounters had resulted in a bloody, fearful reputation. Now, there were the three of us—myself and Thelma (both twenty-one years old at the time) and Eustaquio (a tall, slim black guy)—three naive YWAMers who believed God himself was leading them through the jungle to work with this "savage" people.

Contact was made, Eustaquio left Thelma and me there, and over many months we became accustomed to the ways of the people. We were sleeping inside the huge communal hut like everybody else, wearing the same clothes, or in this case, the same complete lack of clothes as everybody else, eating monkey whenever it was available, but eating nothing most of the time, crying when the people suffered, laughing with them—the whole incarnation bit. To me, that experience of almost five years (going in and out of the jungle) provoked a radical shift in my view of God, the church, and most of all missions.[13]

The gap between our two civilizations was huge! The differences were not merely in lifestyle, manners, clothing, or eating habits. Those were easy to spot and easy to overcome. What suffocated us was the overwhelming difference in thinking, feeling, understanding, seeing, and decoding the world itself. How could these wonderful people understand and embrace the gospel I knew? No bridge of communication between their world and mine seemed possible.

Of course, I had heard the story of Bruce Olson, the wonderful missionary hero who was faced with the same challenge in a similar context of jungle people.[14] Don Richardson's stories were also an inspiration.[15] But, in this situation, the missions strategy I knew was completely useless. I wish every missionary could have the same problem in interacting with a people group. This would probably prevent many common mistakes we make in world missions.

Thelma and I, and the other girls that followed, had no possible task to perform besides surviving. We had no way to preach, nothing to teach, no community development project to keep us busy, no worthwhile health care program, nothing. The only possible thing to do was to be present. It did not seem a lot to us at the time, but later we came to understand that our presence really made an impact, especially on the tribe's perception of the spiritual world. For many years no one would succeed in committing suicide (a common practice according to their worldview), while our team was in the village.

After two years, a Japanese-Brazilian man, Suzuki, joined the team "temporarily." Now, years later, he is so adapted to the Suruwahá culture that he is considered one of the native elders, even a member of the family. Suzuki married my best friend Marcia; the two of them, together with another two couples, have carried on the work with the Suruwahá for over twenty years.[16]

What door needed to be opened so they would know Jesus? Would it be the door of the mind, through which they would know intellectually that the powers of light were greater than the powers of Satan? Or would it be the door of signs and wonders, through which the Suruwahá would see a power encounter between Jesus and the devil and choose to join the winning team?

Working unexpectedly, Truth did reveal himself to the whole tribe and to the missionaries as well, much to our surprise. We often think of the missionary task as being a one-way street, where the missionaries are giving and the "pagans" are only receiving. The truth is that both sides receive and give a lot. I cannot imagine our understanding of who God is, or of what missions is about, without the wonderful revelations God gave us through the tribe. Jesus came to the village slowly, through several means.

One turning point was when an "Island Breeze" team visited. When the Suruwahá had first seen a picture of the Maori,[17] they automatically recognized them as being *inuwá*, capable of fighting and defeating the spirits of suicide that ruled over the tribe; so they were ready to welcome the team even for a short visit.

The few days were life changing for everyone. The Maori men danced their best death-defying dance, and shared the strength and beauty of God's redemption in their own culture with the Suruwahá. "All" the Island Breeze team did (as if it were insignificant!) was chant and dance and pray, and chant some more, and dance some more, and be Maori, strongly Maori, beautifully Maori, with all their masculinity, Indian-ness, molasses-colored skin, long hair, and beautiful full bottoms (to the Suruwahá, a very important feature).

It appeared to be a huge spiritual victory, but after the Maori left, things did not go smoothly. Suzuki and Marcia had to battle an immediate flu epidemic. Even worse, a chief, a good man important in maintaining the social-psychological balance of the tribe, committed suicide. Death, supposedly defeated, reared its horrible head again. Fear of chain-reaction suicide gripped everyone's heart. In the midst of a tremendous spiritual victory, their annihilation suddenly seemed closer than ever.

While pain and despair tried to drag more people to the grave, revelation came from heaven like rain. In this case, it came to the missionaries, especially to Marcia. This insight did not come as a result of in-depth research, but in prayer Marcia experienced a profound sense of what it is to be Suruwahá. She began praying in the Suruwahá language, and those prayers were so foreign that they barely made sense to her Brazilian mind. But, at last, their world began to make sense to her. She received a fresh image of God as he was to the Suruwahá, and the relevancy of this God-being to her was totally different than her Brazilian relationship with God. This new perspective brought understanding of all that God had been doing in the tribe.

Because of the relationship she could now have with the tribe, the Suruwahá began to tell Marcia their past experiences with the Jesus-person. Jesus reveals himself to the Suruwahá, at times as a physical person, as a tender, loving, tall Indian man. His body is painted red, a sign of power and dignity. They describe him as handsome.

Some people in the tribe see Jesus frequently. Some compose psalms to him; others receive powerful insight from him. Ainimaru, an old man who was bitten by a poisonous jararaca snake when he was young and had his leg chopped off, once taught Marcia about Jesus' different names. One of his names is *agijawadawa,* which means literally "He who takes care of me (in the sense of caring for a pet), releases me, then walks with me to freedom." Another name, *gia zubuni zamuna hawadawa,* means "He who transforms my heart into something Other."[18]

Another name is *hanadawa,* which means "He who calls out to me to assure me of his presence." Jesus once comforted a group of women who were alone one dark night. They had stayed behind while all the men went hunting. Staying in the communal hut surrounded by evil spirits was very scary. For many days the women resisted succumbing to fear, sensing the nearness of evil spirits. Then, one night they heard a sound coming to them through the jungle. The women somehow knew it was Jesus, calling so they could hear his voice and be comforted. They felt fear no more.

He once appeared to Axá, a witch doctor, who was on the path to committing suicide. Jesus said, "Don't kill yourself, Axá. Stay in this land. Be a good man to your

people." Since that day Axá has been a new man. One night, for the tribe's important time of meeting around the fire, Axá left the communal hut and strode deep into
the jungle. He previously had done this to receive evil spirits and then return their
message, in song, to the community. This night, after his first encounter with Jesus,
Suzuki and Marcia waited, wondering what would happen. Axá returned and sang
this song:

> Who left that cashew there,
> Lying in the middle of the trail?
> I want to know.
> It must be someone's heart.
> It is ripe. It is not green.
> It is ripe and sweet.
> How sweet is the ripe cashew!

Marcia and Suzuki were very disappointed. "What is this man doing? He is supposed to be a Christian! Why isn't he saying anything about Jesus, salvation, challenging the people's sinful life?"

What they did not understand at the time was that the cashew was a common
Suruwahá poetic figure for the heart, and the trail is the road to paradise. The green
cashew was a heart full of anger, unforgiveness, bitterness, disappointment, and
anguish that ended in suicide. What was obvious to the Suruwahá listeners was that
Jesus, walking along the path of life, could gather up bitter, acidic hearts and transform them into sweet fruit, worthy of paradise. Before there had been only death and
damnation; now there was hope.

Can we say there is a church among the Suruwahá now? If not, will there ever be
a church there that matches the expectations of our Western mind-set? The YWAM
couples have begun to translate the New Testament and have translated and recorded
a chronological account of the life of Jesus and Genesis. The recordings were played
to exhaustion and memorized by several of the Suruwahá. We hope they will be given
the New Testament in oral form. We think that this way it will belong to the
Suruwahá and will be incorporated into their oral tradition. Eventually the Suruwahá
will make the message of the Truth their own, so much so that Jesus will become an
authentic Amazonian.

Today we still see Jesus at work in the Suruwahá tribe. There are no formal meetings, but Jesus and his works are present in most of the conversations. The tribesman
remain self-sufficient and confident. We have seen him changing a foundational
belief for the tribe: defining who is a person and who is not. They used to practice

infanticide on babies who were born out of wedlock or with some kind of physical defect, but they are now striving to save the babies. Recently they were the protagonists in a fight against the government to be able to save a girl born with a physical defect. The Brazilian government was refusing to operate on the girl, saying that the surgery would create a change in their culture. One of the Suruwahá warriors pointed his finger in the attorney general's face and said: "I live in the jungle, I dress differently, speak differently, live differently than you, but I am not an animal." *Treat me with respect* was what he meant. His life is valuable, as much as anyone else. He is worth the blood of Jesus, and he knows that.

Is there a church among the Suruwahá tribe? I prefer not having an answer to this question. Wouldn't you?

Notes

1. "Nesta Casa" by Arnaldo Antunes. Translation into English by chapter author and Jodi Bunn.

2. This case study was coauthored with Márcia dos Santos Suzuki.

3. Deut. 15:11b says: "I command you to be openhanded towards your brothers and towards the poor and the needy in *your* land" (emphasis added).

4. International Human Rights Declaration can be found at www.un.org/Overview /rights.html

5. *Ptochos* is Strong's number 4434, *penes* is 3993 (and 3998 in the longer, related word used in Luke 21:2). Strong's Exhaustive Concordance of the Bible (Nashville: Abingdon Press, 1980).

6. William Smalley, *Readings on Missionary Anthropology* (Practical Anthropology, 1967) 147.

7. Sonia da Silva Lorenz, "*Sateré-Mawé, Os Filhos do Guaraná,*" (São Paulo: Editora Câmara Brasileira do Livro, 1992), 131. Translation into English by the chapter author.

8. Levi Strauss, the father of modern anthropology, said that the teaching of literacy has been an instrument of domination for governments around the world. Anthropologists have used the same line of thinking to criticize missionary work which prioritizes the teaching of literacy and the development of alphabets for tribes with oral tradition..

9. Lucilia Vogel from the WBT-SIL team also directly taught three young men in 1991. The alphabet was also approved by linguist Alan Vogel of SIL who later did an accurate phonological analysis of the language.

10. At that time YWAM was still in diapers in terms of cross-cultural training, so the first candidates to go to tribes were trained by the Summer Institute of Linguistics.

11. Don Richardson is the well-known author of *Peace Child, Lords of the Earth,* and *Eternity in Their Hearts.*

12. Frank C. Laubach, *Toward World Literacy* (Syracuse: Syracuse University Press, 1961).

13. You can read the whole story of the contact and our work with the Suruwahá tribe in *Radical Call,* my book to be published in English.

14. Bruce Olson, *Bruchko* (Lake Mary, Fla.: Charisma House, 1977).

15. Refer to note 11 above.

16. Moises and Lucilia Vianna, who have been enduring jungle life for the past seventeen years, with their three daughters, one of them an adopted Suruwahá girl, and Darci and Sandra who joined the team in 2000.

17. The Maori are the native people of New Zealand.

18. "Other" is the same word used for *holy,* so this also translates as "He who transforms my heart into something holy."

Part 5

Strategy

Jesus calls us both to preach and to live the gospel. Steve Goode explains the biblical foundations and historical significance of mercy ministry. His stories demonstrate love in action in an astounding variety of situations.

Loving God and Your Neighbor:
The Influence of Charity and Mercy Ministry upon Society

G. Stephen Goode

> *"The meaning of my life is the love of God. It is Christ in his distressing disguise whom I love and serve." —Mother Theresa*

> *The LORD ... remains faithful forever.*
> *He upholds the cause of the oppressed and*
> *gives food to the hungry.*
> *The LORD sets prisoners free,*
> *the LORD gives sight to the blind,*
> *the LORD lifts up those who are bowed down,*
> *the LORD loves the righteous.*
> *The LORD watches over the alien*
> *and sustains the fatherless and the widow.*
> *(Psalm 146:6–10)*

> *He has showed you, O man, what is good. And what does the LORD require of you?*
> *To act justly and to love mercy and to walk humbly with your God. (Micah 6:8)*

> *"You are the salt of the earth." (Matthew 5:13)*

> *"You are the light of the world." (Matthew 5:14)*

"Let your light shine before men, that they may see your good deeds and praise your Father in heaven." (Matthew 5:16)

"Whatever you did for one of the least of these brothers of mine, you did for me." (Matthew 25:40)

Ly Suan was abandoned by his mother at age six to live on the streets of Phnom Penh, Cambodia. To survive street life he joined a gang and became a pickpocket and a thief. He quickly learned that his life would be short unless he somehow got off the streets. One day, he met a Catholic priest who ran a home for street boys. The priest was initially wary of accepting Ly Suan into the home because he was a known a troublemaker. But after much pleading and many promises, Ly Suan was able to escape life on the streets. This was his first encounter with Christians. He liked studying, learned five languages easily, and used his hands cleverly. Ly Suan remembers one prayer from that time: "Lord, have mercy upon me and my poor family." God heard this prayer for Ly Suan's family and for thousands of other Khmer families.

This chapter describes how God hears and responds to the cries of a boy. Indeed, Ly Suan's story will be interwoven among the sections of this chapter as one example of God's redeeming love. YWAM has had a tripartite focus from its beginning in 1960—evangelism, training, and mercy ministry. Mercy ministries meet the practical felt needs of people, families, and communities, primarily through deeds. What does this have to do with discipling nations? When individuals, families, and churches love their neighbors, change occurs in society.

Several aspects of mercy ministry will be reviewed: its biblical foundation and history; how it shapes our view of the world; its influence upon society; and its role in extending the kingdom of God.

Our world is confronted today with two billion people living in or just above absolute poverty,[1] global health issues and disease, under- or unemployment, children at risk, family breakdown, war, terrorism, and crime. God is not silent. He hears and he weeps. He is moved. He acts, sometimes supernaturally, but mostly by using ordinary people. He sent Jesus as a compassionate, loving response. Today, Jesus' words to us ring loudly, "As the Father has sent me, I am sending you" (John 20:21)— to love individuals, families, and communities who have not heard. Jesus' commandments are to "Go into all the world and preach the Good News to everyone" (Mark 16:15 NLT) and "make disciples of all nations ... teaching them to obey all I have commanded you" (Matt. 28:19–20). His commands are summarized by the Great Commandment to love God and our neighbor (Matt. 22:37–40). How do we fulfill God's requirements for us today? How will this response to the Great Commandment affect nations? Let's explore some possibilities.

The Biblical Foundation of Mercy Ministry—Go and Do Likewise

Biblical examples of mercy ministries abound. Probably the best known is the story of the good Samaritan. An expert of the law questioned Jesus about eternal life. Jesus went to the heart of the issue through a story.

A Samaritan man, belonging to a people considered the sworn enemy of the Jews, came upon a man robbed and beaten. The Samaritan was moved with compassion and responded with help, in contrast to two religious Jews, who had previously walked past and done nothing. This Samaritan got involved in the emergency through medical care, transport, lodging, finances, and follow-up until the man was out of danger.

Jesus questioned the legal scholar, "'Which of these three do you think was a neighbor to the man who fell into the hands of robbers?' The expert in the law replied, 'The one who had mercy on him.' Jesus told him, 'Go and do likewise'" (Luke 10:36–37).

This parable raises a number of questions about our view of life and about the intersection of our faith and its practical outworking in our daily affairs. Mercy ministry is about the practical application of our faith upon people and society. Timothy J. Keller wrote:

> Obviously, there was no "ministry of mercy" per se before the fall of man since there was no human suffering or need. But it is clear that God's servants at that time were as concerned with the material-physical world as with the spiritual. After the Fall, the effects of sin immediately caused the fragmentation of man's relationships. Man becomes alienated from God. (Gen. 3:10). As a result his relationship with other human beings is shattered (vv. 12–13), and so is his relationship with nature itself (vv. 17–18). Now sickness, hunger, natural disaster, social injustice and death dominate. The first act of mercy ministry immediately follows the Fall: God clothed Adam and Eve with animal skins (Gen. 3:21). Man now needed protection from a hostile environment.[2]

Are we willing to go and do likewise? As we do, our societies will be affected like yeast or like salt and hopefully will be transformed.

The Historical Impact of Mercy Ministries on Society

Volumes have been written regarding the historical impact of mercy ministry. For example, in 1849, Mr. C. Schmidt, a professor of theology at Strasbourg, wrote about the early Christian impact on the Roman world in the first century. Christianity was at first small and totally surrounded by different religious beliefs and worldviews. "But though hidden and incomplete, this influence was also efficacious and unmistakable. At the time of all great changes in the history of the world, new ideas float in the atmosphere. One receives them without knowing how. They affect even those who resist them, until at last they leaven and transform the whole of society."[3] A new social principle had emerged—love.[4] The Roman Empire, indeed, the world, would never again be the same.

Martin Palmer's book *The Jesus Sutras*[5] documents the effect of the gospel of charity starting from the church in Antioch, or the so-called missionary church, as it moved along the silk route into Central Asia and eventually into the Taoist world of China. In AD 635 the Emperor of the Tang Dynasty opened the door for the church in almost every Chinese province, and perhaps every city, for two hundred years.

This practical love continued to make tangible influence upon society throughout the centuries. St. Francis of Assisi said in the eleventh century, "Preach the gospel and sometimes use words."[6] He was underlining the fact that meeting practical needs was at the heart of the gospel. The Franciscan ministry began with a call to those of financial means to voluntarily give up their wealth in service to the poor and to focus on serving the outcasts of their day—lepers.

An assessment of the past two hundred years of church history, revivals, and reformations also shows how deeply the gospel and the people of God, the church, have influenced civil society and its institutions. Charles Colson wrote, "At one point in the early nineteenth century in America, there were more than eleven hundred Christian societies working for social justice. Today, two of the world's largest private organizations caring for the hungry are Christian agencies: Catholic Relief Services and World Vision. And the Salvation Army alone does more for the homeless and destitute in most areas than all secular agencies combined."[7] Effects of these ministries include labor reform for children and adults, the abolition of slavery, and the emancipation of women.[8] Traditional cultures have also been transformed (e.g., the eradication of head-hunting Vanuatu.[9])

Nearly all mercy workers have been encouraged by the example of Mother Teresa and her order, the Missionaries of Charity. Their work has become synonymous with the word compassion. Over 4,000 Sisters are working in more than 126 countries. Their practical love and service has helped shape the world conscience about the poor and needy today.

Mother Teresa's acts of kindness and unconditional love took her before many government and world leaders. However, her goal was not to disciple and influence institutes and nations, but to love each poor person. She stated, "Ours is not a social work. We work twenty-four hours a day to express God's love. We evangelize by showing God's love. It is only through God's love that the poor can have their needs met."[10] At her funeral, kings, queens, and international leaders of nations laid flowers in tribute to what she had done for the poor. Her heart cry was, "We do it for Jesus."

Mercy Ministry in YWAM—Past, Present, and Future

The historical roots of mercy ministry in YWAM go back to the childhood of Loren Cunningham, founder of YWAM. He recounts hearing his father, T. C. Cunningham, share a story of a tan-skinned girl. She was a child, a Palestinian refugee, asking for alms, but T. C. saw her eyes begging for something far more than money. "She was reaching out for comfort, encouragement, for love, hope for the future. The Gospel. World Missions, Dad said, used to be a couple of words. But no more. From now on missions has a face. It is the face of a child."[11]

These words led some YWAM leaders from the early 1960s to the Caribbean, to Africa, and to Asia to serve lepers, the homeless, drug addicts, refugees, and others needing relief. Decades later, God continues to use the face of that refugee child, and those like her, to direct YWAM to the most needy and least reached.

Ly Suan continued

I met Ly Suan in 1990, years after he had left the streets. He worked with his wife and one daughter along the bank of the Mekong River in Stung Treng, Cambodia. Predominantly animist with Buddhist overtones, this remote, poverty-stricken area had limited electricity, no running water, and a 40 percent child mortality rate. We were assessing the local health needs. Ly Suan, proprietor of a bicycle repair cart, was repairing a tire.

As we conversed with Ly Suan, we were touched by his hospitality and graciousness. He invited us to his monsoon-flooded house. His family of five daughters and wife were very interested in the strangers' words. We heard more of Ly Suan's story over lunch. He told us about the only prayer he remembered. "God, have mercy upon me and my poor family." All of the sudden, I understood and with tears I responded. "Ly Suan, God is answering your prayer. You have been praying that prayer for years. God spoke to us in Thailand that we had work to do and people to serve here in Cambodia. Of all of the thousands of Khmer to meet, we met you." Our journeys had intersected. It was one of most memorable lunches that I have ever had.

I asked Ly Suan if he would like to read more about this God who hears the prayer of young boys. He said yes. We would bring him a Bible on our next trip. He asked us to meet him and his family at the river in the afternoon for a swim and to bathe. I had noticed that some of his daughters had skin infections so I took opportunity to see if these infections could be properly attended to with soap and water. In five days, these infections cleared up and a Khmer family and some foreigners had begun to bond in relationship.

God was answering the cry of a small Cambodian boy.

As William Booth said:

The exceeding bitter cry of the disinherited has become to be as familiar in our ears as the dull roar of the streets or as the moaning wind through the trees. It rises unceasing year in and year out, and we are too busy or too idle, too indifferent or too selfish to spare it a thought. Only now and then, on rare occasions, when some clear voice is heard giving more articulate utterance to the miseries of the miserable, do we pause from our daily duties and shudder for one brief moment at what life means to the poor.[12]

In contrast, Scripture often speaks about God hearing the cry of the child, the vulnerable, the afflicted, and the fatherless. His heart is moved with compassion. He acts, usually through his people. William Booth, the founder of the Salvation Army, was one such person. This compassionate man responded, particularly to the homeless. In the 1890s, he implemented a vision in England that changed the lives of three million homeless children and adults living in wretched conditions. Today the "Sallies," as they are affectionately called, impact the "down and out" in just about every major city in the world as they continue to implement Booth's bold strategy.

Booth's strategy had seven main points which can be summarized as: (1) Every project must modify the character and conduct of those served. (2) Circumstances need radical alteration when they are the source of wretched conditions. (3) Worthwhile remedies will be commensurate with the evil they propose to end. (4) Projects must be not only large enough, but also permanent. (5) The work must be immediately practical. (6) Indirect effects should not injure those being assisted. (7) Outreach to one segment of the community should not seriously interfere with the interests of another.[13]

We in YWAM also believe that we can and are to have a similar kind of impact upon today's families and children. It is slowly happening. Chan Kit Ying of Mother's Love, a sister organization that has operated in China since 1992, has literally touched the lives of tens of thousands of throw-away girl babies and handicapped children. Mother's Love has thus gained the respect of both the ordinary Chinese and the government.[14]

In 2004, YWAM Mercy Ministries were operating in more than 70 countries through 700+ projects. The problems tackled and the solutions implemented are diverse. Staff numbering approximately 7,000 were impacting more than two million people annually through projects such as caring for the homeless, abandoned, and children at risk; creating jobs; training people for vocational and microenterprise work; operating health care clinics; and educating in literacy. This is encouraging, yet the faces and cries of the vulnerable have increased.

With God's help, by 2020 and in partnership with the wider body of Christ, our goal in YWAM Mercy Ministries is to hear from God, respond with compassion, and impact one hundred million people annually. An audacious goal, you might say? Yes, and impossible without God and his people. Even if we fail, the attempt is worthy of all of our efforts. What will take place if we do not reach out to the poor? Is it not time? If not us, then who? What stands in our way? Do we need a change of heart or mind?

Mercy Ministry and Worldview

Our assumptions about the world and how it works form our worldview. Three foundational worldviews compete for our allegiance. Animism defines ultimate reality as spiritual, with the physical world being unimportant or just an illusion. Secularism defines ultimate reality as physical and assumes that the spiritual world is nonexistent or unimportant. Theism defines ultimate reality as personal, a deity who cares for and interacts with each of us. From one of these foundations we construct a worldview lens through which we "see" ourselves, our families, and our society. Our understanding (right or wrong) and our resulting choices flow from this worldview. A worldview sets direction and guides through life like a road map. It also shapes our identity in relationship to the world where we live.[15]

Steve Bradbury, the director of TEAR Australia, wrote of conversations he had with women in Cambodia, "'I must have been bad in a past life as this life is so awful.' This element of the Buddhist belief helps shape their understanding of what has happened to them. This is their lot in life. They have no understanding of human rights or justice and have no hope of a different future."[16] Similar comments can be heard in many countries.

Refugees, orphans, widows, prisoners, the sick, the poor, the lonely, the destitute, and the elderly often have several things in common. They are vulnerable, often afraid. They feel alone, unloved, and without value. They live without hope, are uncertain about today and even more so about tomorrow. Some have survived or continue in situations of terrible abuse, fear, or oppression. They may wonder, *Is this my karma? Am I cursed by the spirits? Is this God's will?*

We followers of Jesus have a message of good news to the poor. Transformation begins by the renewing of our minds, by changing our thinking. It is not enough just to put faith in Christ. We must seek to have his mind and his thoughts about our world. We must try to view the world through HIS eyes. Proverbs tell us, "As a man thinks in his heart, so is he" (Prov. 8:37 KJV). The poor have an even more desperate need to understand their history, their value, their self-worth and human dignity, and the true basis of their identity. When this occurs, the gospel really does become *good news.*

Vishal Mangalwadi of the MacLaurin Institute said, "Hunger is an obscenity and not what God intended. . . . We live in slums when He meant for us to live in a Garden."[17] This is not how God created the world. Poverty, like death, is an alien entity introduced to God's creation because of the Fall. Poverty has distorted how we view God, ourselves, and our world.

Ly Suan continued

Ly Suan was a responsible man and a good worker. His bicycle repair business expanded to a stall near the market to repair both bicycles and motorcycles. He also taught his daughters about the importance of work. Three of his daughters worked in "sales." Two were selling gasoline from glass Coca-Cola bottles and another was selling individual cigarettes.

When Ly Suan received his Bible, he read and started asking questions. During the Khmer Rouge times, he could have been killed for being able to read, owning a pair of glasses, or for asking a question. Within six months, Ly Suan decided that he and his house would serve the Lord. They were the first of eighteen believers who wanted to follow Jesus in that remote province. And thus began their worldview changes.

We influence one person at a time. Take Sopeah, an abandoned mother of four in Cambodia, as an example. Unemployed and desperate when she moved to Phnom Penh, Sopeah sold her daughter for US$150. As regret grew, she had a dream that God might help return her daughter. If so, perhaps he could also change her life. Later, she encountered workers with Hagar[18] who helped to redeem her daughter, gave them emergency assistance, and provided counsel and training at their shelter. She met the God of her dream. Now Sopeah is employed, her children attend school, and she is back with her husband. Times are still tough, but her changed thinking has brought hope.[19]

Transformation of individuals and communities is a process that requires a change of thinking, a new way of viewing our world. Restored relationship with God can provide that. God's heart is for all peoples, all cultures, and all languages to know him (Rev. 7:9).

Varied Strategies of Mercy Ministry

There are many examples in YWAM of service and impact upon the poor, too numerous and often too sensitive to even list here. In this section, a few expanded examples serve to demonstrate a variety of strategies that are employed in ministries of compassion.

Children at Risk

The homeless and destitute today include many children at risk. For these children, mercy ministry is indeed good news in the midst of much bad news. Abandoned children make up a growing number of "children at risk." Viva Network states that there are now more than 100 million children living on the street. YWAM in Contagem, Brazil, is a good example of the many YWAMers working with children at risk. They have schools and daycares, ministries to rescue kids from the streets and restore them to families, and a group home for children with AIDS. They train families and teens in God's principles to prevent further problems that come from drugs and extramarital sex.[20]

YWAM Uganda Reaches Out to Orphans

A special category of children at risk is the orphan. The church family has a significant role to play in educating, training, fostering, and adopting orphans. One of the huge challenges in orphan work today is AIDS. At the end of 2003, there were 143 million children orphaned by the death of one or both parents to AIDS in ninety-three countries.[21]

Africa has been particularly hard hit by AIDS. In Uganda alone, there are over two million AIDS orphans. YWAMers have responded by personally adopting hundreds of AIDS orphans into their homes and by establishing group homes for AIDS orphans. These ministries are a powerful witness of the love of God. YWAMers also meet regularly with government and church officials and other agencies to discuss what can be done to address this epidemic. YWAMers in Uganda have also been involved in developing a powerful tool called Living Positively with HIV, which will enhance the quality of life of those affected by or infected with HIV. The church is one of the largest institutions in Africa. Imagine the opportunity for impact in this huge HIV/AIDS crisis as the church serves infected individuals, prays, serves the orphans, and communicates the truth in love to help stem the spread of infection.

Refugee Ministry

Refugees require all kinds of compassionate ministry. Cambodians, affected by war since the early 1970s and crushed by the genocide of two to three million of their own people under the Khmer Rouge, are a case in point. Pol Pot, leader of the Khmer Rouge (KR), had a radical worldview. He wanted to create a modern Maoist society of one million peasants. For his vision to succeed, seven million people would have to die. He was well on his way to fulfilling this goal before the invasion by the Vietnamese in 1979. Within a year of taking power, the KR confiscated all property in the country and abolished money and all other major institutions.[22]

As Cambodian refugees trickled into Thailand and the atrocities became known, the international community responded. The refugee trickle swelled to a flood of over a million refugees. For years, half a million Cambodians lived in utter squalor in camps along the Thai-Cambodian border. Many said these camps were like paradise compared to what they had just left under the KR. All had the scars of losing someone. One refugee we befriended had seen the twelve other members of his family die from murder, starvation, or disease.

God spoke to YWAM to serve these Cambodian refugees and over 700 staff responded for more than fifteen years. Health services grew to include hospitals, clinics, and health care education. Preschools and vocational training in sewing, weaving, and traditional music were initiated. YWAMers provided emergency distribution, postal, and banking services, offered social services, and created jobs. Through these practical services, many Cambodians saw the gospel for the first time. And the refugees responded.

In Khao-I-Dang (KID) camp, two square miles in radius, there were 150,000 refugees. A mini revival occurred in the first few months and 30,000 Khmer became believers in Jesus. Many thousands were discipled into their new faith in Christ. Today, there are Khmer churches in Europe, North America, Australasia, and Cambodia because of what God did in the Thai refugee camps. Because of a past crisis, many tens of thousands are impacting their current locations. The Khmer church continues to be salt and light to Cambodia. Young believers in the early 1990s provided impetus to bring about change to the Cambodian constitution and laws in regards to the "freedom of religion" clause for the nation.

Kum Heng was nine years old when he and his mother made it to the Thai border. They were separated from two brothers and a sister, never to meet again. Arriving in KID when he was fourteen years old, he met a YWAMer from New Zealand. At age sixteen, Kum made a commitment to follow Christ. When he returned to Cambodia, he started work with YWAM's Hagar Project as a guard, then as a driver, and later as a program officer. In 2004, Kum was overseeing the building of 10,000 clean water filters in the province of Kompong Thom, a former center of Khmer Rouge activity. He had also started a cell group church of one hundred people.[23]

Crisis Intervention Can Influence a Nation

Probably no greater challenge exists than when a catastrophe strikes. An earthquake, cyclone, or hurricane shakes and rips homes and lives apart. Floods or mudslides wash away the security that seemed so stable just moments before. A drought may force millions to sell their meager possessions and to migrate in search of the basics of life. Civil war creates refugees who flee homes, families, and country with only what they can carry. People become internally displaced in their own land because of war, ethnic division, cultural genocide, or appetite for power.

During the midst of such crises, we can partner with churches, agencies, and governments to minister mercy. In crisis there is death, loss, pain, and separation. Unanswered questions, suffering, and injustices affect many. Both victims and decision makers are faced with many challenges. Opportunities abound for resilience, flexibility, courage, and hope. Surely believers can help in these times.

Don Stephens, founder and president of Mercy Ships, wrote how a crisis brought key players together to assist in the relief efforts after Hurricane Oscar.[24] While the flag ship, the *Anastasis,* was in New Zealand, news came that Hurricane Oscar had devastated Fiji and Tonga. Houses, schools, and churches were destroyed. Infrastructure was gone and the islanders were coming to grips with their losses. In New Zealand, the disaster galvanized a response from everyone, from ordinary people to national decision-makers. Churches, missions, civic clubs, and individuals pulled together to fill the hold of the *Anastasis* with relief materials ranging from lumber to fire engines. Diverse supplies were freely given and loaded gratis by the stevedores to help rebuild the devastated nations. Through many diverse people working together, one nation was able to touch other nations in need.

Hagar Project: Transformational Development in Cambodia

The Hagar Project was begun in 1993 by YWAMers Pierre and Simonetta Tami. Over the next decade Hagar impacted the lives of more than 100,000 women and children in war-torn and poverty-stricken Cambodia. Hagar is now an independent nongovernmental organization that serves those most at risk to trafficking. When Hagar began operations, the UN ranked Cambodia 147th out of 173 countries in human development. Now Hagar is being recognized internationally as an NGO that is making a difference in Cambodia.[25]

Hagar has become a model of transformation development through programs such as an emergency and development center, street-based screening and counseling services, foster homes, development villages, and creation of small businesses and new jobs. Development projects in four provinces include producing water filters, building schools, and providing emergency relief. Hagar works in partnership with churches, nongovernmental organizations, and government ministries.

The Queen of Cambodia opened their soya milk factory in December 2003. Hagar Soya employs formerly destitute women from the Hagar Shelter and young men who grew up in Hagar's foster care programs who have found jobs with the business. These transformed individuals have now touched royalty. This is not publicity; this is the gospel.[26]

Ly Suan continued

In northern Cambodia, God was speaking to Ly Suan. He queried us, "Do you think God might be saying that he wants me to help Khmer children, who like me, were abandoned or orphaned? Do you think that could be God?"

"It sounds like it might be God," we thought out loud. So Ly Suan and his family moved from Stung Treng to Phnom Penh to work with Hagar and start serving homeless mothers and children that were sold into prostitution.

At Hagar each woman and child is treated with love and dignity. Some were like Sopeah, mentioned earlier, who was reunited with her family. Others were like Sophal. She grew up in abusive foster care only to be abandoned at sixteen. She was gang raped, forcibly married, and eventually forced into prostitution. When she became too obviously pregnant to continue, she was turned out on the streets until she found shelter at Hagar. After giving birth, she learned she was HIV-positive. "Yet, Sophal commented, 'My life is not so bad, other girls are sold many more times than I have been.'"[27]

Sothy, abandoned by her husband, found a home at the Hagar shelter and learned to sew with Hagar Design to support herself and her toddler son. She began a new, independent life. Unfortunately, her health soon deteriorated and she learned that both she and her son were infected with HIV. Sothy died knowing that she had dignity, that she was loved, and that her son would be cared for by Hagar's Children's Rehabilitation Program.[28]

Leprosy Work in Chennai, India

YWAM workers in Chennai have a ministry among lepers, which includes small business ventures and compassionate outreach. In a touching example of this work, the team met sixty-six-year-old Ganesh, who had been suffering with leprosy and subsequent rejection since he was thirty-three. He and his wife, now also leprous, had been living on the streets, trying to please the gods so they could be healed, and watching his ulcers eventually remove his ability to walk. The team prayed for him, bathed his ulcers, and told him of Jesus' love. He joyfully received Jesus. On another visit, the team discovered that both leg ulcers had been completely healed, with the couple crediting the healing to Jesus.[29]

Microenterprise Development

In the last twenty-five years, Christians have been involved with the poor in a creative strategy of microenterprise development (MED)—loans to the poor for small businesses. These loans average less than US$100 but are enough for a family of six or seven to break out of poverty. The return rates have been high.[30] More than 80 percent of these loans go to poor women, which assures that the profits of these microenterprises go to families and communities. When a poor family's income rises, the increase usually goes toward better nutrition, clothing, housing, and education for children.

These loans also create an environment conducive to transformation. Presently an informal network of Christian microenterprise development organizations started by David Bussau includes more than 500 groups from fifty countries, including YWAM's work in ten countries. This network is annually impacting more than two million of the poor and their communities. These MED programs affirm human dignity and value as well as bring hope. They further empower the poor with a confidence that they can bring about change. This has great opportunity to significantly impact the two billion of the world's poorest.

Prison Work and Literacy

Jesus said that when we visit those in prison, we visit him. Philip Scott visited the local prison in the Cambodian northeastern regional capital of Stung Treng. He provided basic necessities for the prisoners, such as salt, eating utensils, and mosquito nets. He also taught basic Khmer literacy. Song, in prison for committing some petty crimes, was illiterate when he met Philip. They met regularly for nine months. Then Song was released and returned to his village ten hours away by boat on the Sekong River.

When he returned home his wife was so impressed that he could now read. He told her that he had learned how to read because of God. Song wanted to know more about this Jesus of whom he had heard and read. Later, when Philip visited this remote district, Song invited him to his house. When Philip arrived, he was surprised to see over thirty people interested in talking.

"So, tell us about your God," Song's wife asked. This is not a typical Khmer greeting and Philip inquired, "Why would you want to know about this God?" She said, "My husband went to jail in Stung Treng and he couldn't read and he returns here and he can now read. He says it is because of your God. We want to know about this God."

So Philip shared the gospel story. Now at least thirty serious inquirers in this village have started their journey in knowing God. Twenty-five of them were baptized, all because someone cared and took time to practically show God's love and mercy by meeting felt needs.

In fourteen years of service to the poor in remote Stung Treng Province, YWAM has worked with local, provincial, and national authorities. At one point the provincial government asked YWAM to provide some programs for the local youth in order to "give them a philosophy of life." YWAM assists with many programs in the province: HIV/AIDS education and prevention, English teaching, malaria prevention, mother and child health care, school health programs, emergency relief, community health training and development, and nonformal education. YWAM's health care programs have assisted in reducing infant mortality by the training hundreds of Khmer health care and development workers.

YWAM has planted seven churches. One area that the Khmer pastors have been "discipling" new believers in is the development of "smokeless" stoves that help reduce upper respiratory ailments. This is discipling the nation through mercy ministry.

Waste Management as Mercy Ministry

In Vietnam, one YWAM program is waste management. A solid waste management project is already affecting several hamlets with a resultant reduction of pollution and increase in health. A bio-gas project, affecting seven communes and district leaders, provides cooking fuel and removes pig waste in an environmentally sound way. Fewer trees are being cut for fuel. Women's work hours have been reduced by half because they no longer need to walk several kilometers for wood and because cooking is more time efficient. Hence, the women have more time for family. Other projects include clean water, sanitation, and education for school children.

Mother-Child Health Clinics

A YWAM sister organization in a poor region of a Central Asian country started a mother-child health (MCH) clinic. Prior to the opening of this clinic, local people had to walk several hours for medical assistance. Fifty percent of the children were dying before the age of five. Women had an average life expectancy of only forty years.

This MCH clinic had a life changing impact upon these women and children. The women received pre- and postnatal care, nutrition, vaccinations, hygiene and child spacing education, and outpatient consultations. This physical care opened spiritual doors; the women began asking questions about this God who would send Christian families from so far away to work with them. They asked for prayer. They started hearing about Jesus, many for the first time. The local population saw the gospel before they heard its message. The local mullah felt threatened and increasingly restricted the activities of these two families. In the end, the mullah put pressure upon the government to refuse the renewal of the visas for these families. Their departure was an indicator of their impact on the community.

Agricultural Programs

In the same Central Asian area, a related agricultural program had the same kind of impact on meeting basic human need. The agricultural team started asking questions of the local groups, helping local people to identify their needs and participate in solutions. Through teaching, coaching, and transferring skills, the agricultural team helped increase the income of the local population and developed relationships. Here, too, the local mullah began restricting the activities of these expatriates. The mullah began giving edicts, "You cannot pray before you work. You cannot pray over these seeds or over these fields . . . You cannot pray with these local farmers . . . You cannot!"

After ten years of service, the team was approached by the local mullah. He said, "We really like what you are doing. Your good deeds are very important and good for this community and district but we must ask you to leave." They asked, "Why are we being asked to leave? What have we done wrong?" The mullah said, "It is not that you are having an influence on this community but we are concerned that you are influencing our next generation in the ways of your God and they will follow you."[31] The mullah understood that their actions were the mustard seed of discipling a community or a nation.

Jesus Our Model—Our Ultimate Example

Jesus is our example, whether in showing acts of kindness, meeting felt needs, or discipling peoples and nations. He began and continued his ministry by meeting the needs of others. Whether at a wedding where the hosts had run out of wine or in a crowd of several thousand who had no food, Jesus met people's needs. He also helped to shape the spheres of influence in his day, such as the religious, political, and economic spheres. He left the task to his followers to complete by the help of the Holy Spirit.

Jesus called together a group of ordinary people to become his followers. He did not call the elite power brokers to be his disciples. His followers were common: fishermen, tax collectors, religious students, and activists. His message was simple, yet two-sided, like a coin. On one side the message was to love God, and on the other side the message was to love your neighbor. This was his single message that could not be disconnected without serious consequences. He began where people lived and met them where they had needs. It's a simple, yet profound, model:

1. He responded to needs.
2. He showed his disciples how to respond and they watched.
3. They responded and he supported.
4. He left and empowered them for the task.

In leadership terms, that is directing, coaching, supporting, and delegating. As C. Schmidt writes:

> We may be surprised that love is turned into a command, imposed with the authority of the law. How can this spiritual and spontaneous feeling be imposed, and why has Christ commanded it? The ancient order of things had a fundamental law, a principle that united its morality and institutions; the new order must also have its principles and law. It is not a law like that laid down by a State, but a condition that is to be freely fulfilled. It is a virtue of the soul, and in this view love becomes a duty for the Christian. We are only Christian while loving.[32]

The Future—What to Expect?

What will happen as we go and serve the absolutely poor? In many marginalized countries, Christianity is growing apace. However, such growth has not always been accompanied by the expression of integral kingdom values. As we focus upon this huge frontier, we must ask ourselves some questions:

- Have we accepted a model of poverty that is exclusively material and economic, rather than a model that includes the social, intellectual, and spiritual dimensions?
- What are the roles of Christian relief and development agencies in relation to the contemporary trends?
- How can churches and Christians become truly salt and light?
- How can churches become better educated in the issues that have contributed to the marginalization of communities?
- How can believers exercise advocacy on behalf of the marginalized?
- What are the global trends that will help our response?[33]

Ly Suan—a complete cycle

During the Pol Pot years, Ly Suan had to act like someone mute, crazy, or dumb in order to survive, even though he could speak five different languages. He worked in rice fields for sixteen to twenty hours a day. He did not know how he would survive but as he worked those fields, he remembered the prayer for God to have mercy on him and his family.

After surviving on the streets and then through the Pol Pot years, Ly Suan has worked with Hagar for more than ten years. His daughter, Chantou, heads up the handicapped unit of the rehabilitation program. Ly Suan is responsible for providing clean water to poor villages of the Kratie province and is a church leader. To an audience full of national government ministers and international dignitaries, he spoke at the ten-year Hagar anniversary celebrations about how his life had been changed.

God heard the cry of this boy to have mercy on his poor family. He spoke and sent others to demonstrate his love to them. Ly Suan and his family responded to the love of God. God spoke to them that they should love and serve those like themselves. Ly Suan led his family, in obedience, to serve others. A full circle.

When Is God at Work?

How do we know when God is at work through mercy ministries and that they are influencing people and the community? Vinay Samuel and Chris Sugden assert that seeing kingdom values replace other values in persons, movements, and structures is indicative of God at work. They give further indicators to help us recognize that God is at work:

- Where we see human dignity being affirmed and people discovering a sense of self-worth, self-acceptance, and a sense of having something to contribute to the world and to others, there God is at work.
- Where we see that people have the freedom to act according to their conscience without threat from others who control their actions and thus their attitudes, there God is at work.
- Where people are able to make their own contribution to the life of society, especially in participation in decisions that affect them in the family, in the community, in religious matters, and in political structures, there God is at work.
- Where people can live in hope, a sense that it is possible and worthwhile to plan for the future, where they can experience the respect of the community, and where there is sharing that enhances, not reduces, the humanity of the community, there God is at work.
- When people are committed to the struggle against evil and injustice, and where there is a sense of equity, there God is at work.
- Where women, the weak, and the handicapped find roles that give them dignity and equality, and where their needs get priority and power is shared to benefit all and dehumanize none, there God is at work.
- Where we find a sense of God's presence, a recognition of the power of evil without and within, and true humility about the limitations of our knowledge in the face of God's wisdom, there God is at work.

We should also look for God's work and influence as people make decisions, share information, help each other in emergencies, look for and work at jobs, attend social functions, direct the course of their families, help the under-privileged and marginalized, use resources, and worship. We should see the expression of God's work in social and family structures, in the political and government sphere, and in religious institutions. The temptation is to see God at work only in values, but he also works to transform structures to promote the values of the kingdom. While it is possible to be content with the expression of the values of the kingdom in the lives of individuals or small groups, if these values do not find structural expression they cannot bring lasting change.[34]

If we are to be obedient to Jesus' last commandment (Matt. 28:19–20) and his Great Commandment (Matt. 22:37–39, citing Deut. 6:5 and Lev. 19:18), we must go to the ends of the earth, to all peoples with that good news and teach all that he commanded. The full scope of human need[35] will challenge and facilitate the church in accomplishing this task. God is at work in the discipling of nations by mercy ministry. The Holy Spirit is changing people. Communities are being positively impacted. Systems and infrastructures are also being influenced for the common good. The poor are seeing the good news.

However, there are two billion that still cry out. Are we listening? What do we hear? God awaits our response.

Notes

1. The most commonly used definition of global poverty is the absolute poverty line set by the World Bank. Poverty is set at an income of $2 a day or less, and extreme poverty is set at $1 a day or less. From http://library.thinkquest.org/05aug/00282/over_whatis.htm (accessed April 11, 2007).

2. Timothy J. Keller, *Ministries of Mercy—The Call of the Jericho Road* (Grand Rapids: Zondervan, 1989), 40–41.

3. C. Schmidt, *The Social Results of Early Christianity*, trans. Mary Thorpe (London: Isbister Limited, 1853), 294.

4. Ibid. On pages 305–321 Schmidt discusses the Christian influence upon society in the first century as witnessed by nonbelievers. In summary, Christians submitted to human authority and laws; remained and worked in a society which despised them; appealed to emperors and government officials for principles of charity and equal administration of justice; condemned local barbaric acts of exposing children to death, prostitution, and slavery; voluntarily gave offerings for the poor, the sick, widows, orphans, and strangers;

responded to illness and disease with proper treatment of workers and slaves, particularly non-Christians; and elevated the role of women in society.

5. Martin Palmer, *The Jesus Sutras: Rediscovering the Lost Scrolls of Taoist Christianity* (New York: Ballatine Publishing Group, 2001), 51–52.

6. Attributed to St. Francis of Assisi. An Internet search via Google in July 2004 listed 212 websites that attribute this quote to St. Francis.

7. Charles Colson and Nancy Pearcey, *How Now Shall We Live?* (Wheaton, Ill.: Tyndale House Publishers, 1999), 137.

8. Winkie Pratney, *Fire on the Horizon: How the Revival Generation will Change the World* (Ventura, Calif.: Gospel Light Publications, 1999), 57–58.

9. Samuel Wilson, "Defining Development in Social Terms," in *Christian Relief and Development—Developing Workers for Effective Ministry,* ed. Edgar J. Elliston (Dallas: Word Publishing, 1989), 158.

10. Don Stephens, *Trial by Trial* (Eugene, Ore.: Harvest House, 1985), 192.

11. Loren Cunningham with Janice Rogers, *Is that Really You, God?* (Seattle: YWAM Publishing), 23–24.

12. General William Booth, *In Darkest England and The Way Out* (London: McCorquo-dale and Company, 1890), 15.

13. Ibid., 85–89.

14. David Aikman, *Jesus in Beijing—How Christianity is Transforming China and Changing the Global Balance of Power* (Washington, DC: Regnery Publishing, 2003), 282–283.

15. Darrow L. Miller with Stan Guthrie, *Discipling Nations: The Power of Truth to Transform Cultures,* 2nd ed. (Seattle: YWAM Publishing, 2001), 10. This book is an excellent starting place for helping one to better understand the world from a biblical perspective.

16. Steve Bradbury, "Where There is Hope," TEAR Australia *Target,* vol. 3 (2001).

17. *World View and Development,* YWAM Mercy Ministries International video produced by Debra Buenting (Colorado Springs, Colo.: Procla-Media,1999).

18. Hagar, a Christian NGO, serves abandoned women and children at risk to human trafficking in Cambodia. See www.hagarproject.org/ for more information.

19. *"Don't Be Afraid: Hagar's Promise to Cambodian Mothers,"* video by Hagar Cambodia, February 2004.

20. Isabelle Zwahlen. "Youth With a Mission Brazil," in *Mission as Transformation,* Vinay Samuel and Chris Sugden, eds. (Oxford: Regnum Books International, 1999), 416.

21. UNICEF, *Children on the Brink 2004: A Joint Report on Orphan Estimates and Program Strategies* (UNAIDS/UNICEF/USAID, July 2004), www.unicef.org/publications/files/cob_layout6–013.pdf (accessed April 12, 2007).

22. An excellent overview of Cambodian history in the Khmer Rouge era can be found in Elizabeth Becker, *"When the War Was Over—Cambodia and the Khmer Rouge Revolution"* (PublicAffairs, 1998).

23. Kum Heng, conversation with author, February 13, 2004.

24. Stephens, *Trial by Trial,* 142.

25. Victoria Silverman, "Hagar, an NGO, Helps Human Trafficking Victims in Cambodia," June 17, 2004. http://usinfo.state.gov/gi/Archive/2004/Jun/17–448703.html (accessed April 11, 2007).

26. Melanie Curless, Hagar Annual Report, 2003.

27. Steve Bradbury, "Development News and Insight," *Target* (TEAR Australia, 2001), Vol 1:9.

28. *Hagar Project Report, July–December 1999* (Youth With A Mission, Cambodia, 2000), 5.

29. Tim Svoboda, *YWAM Chennai Monthly Report,* October 2002.

30. Usually 97 percent return rates and above are considered acceptable in the MED sector.

31. Anonymous European missionary, conversation with author, May 2001.

32. Schmidt, *The Social Results,* 142.

33. Samuel and Sugden, *Mission as Transformation,* 393–394. A Christian Relief and Development conference in June 1996 reported the following global trends and consequences.

The global trends are:
- global integration of economy
- breakdown of political machinery
- emergence of global communication and information network
- growth in modern technological innovations and related knowledge
- increase in cases of AIDS, development of new clones of viruses, drug resistant bacteria and parasites
- environment degradation

The consequences of the above trends are:
- a widening gap between the rich and the poor
- movements of people for security and economic reasons
- diminishing sovereignty of the nation state
- marginalization of the nation state
- raised expectations which have no real hope of fulfillment
- major economic decisions which affect a majority of people are made by the emerging global economic community which not accountable to governments or the people
- increase in internal conflict and disintegration of communities and nations
- the high cost and unavailability of health care

34. Vinay Samuel and Chris Sugden, ed., *The Church in Response to Human Need,* (Grand Rapids: Eerdmans/Regnum, 1987), 193–194 as quoted in *Mission as Transformation,* 261–276.

35. The following list of basic human needs is adapted from Manfred Max-Neef, "Human-scale Economics: The Challenge Ahead," in *The Living Economy: A New Economics in the Making,* ed. Paul Ekins (London: Routlege and Kegan, 1986), 216–220.

1. Subsistence: food, water, income, infrastructure
2. Understanding: education and training, information, communication, conflict resolution
3. Protection: defense, prevention, cure, equity, and justice
4. Affection: sense of caring and being cared for, companionship, sense of unity with others

5. Identity: sense of belonging, feeling purpose in one's life, being of service
6. Participation: having a voice in one's own affairs, mutual support within a collective, contributing productively to family and community
7. Freedom: choice of values, speech, assembly, work, lifestyles, location
8. Creativity: release of one's social, economic, and spiritual potential
9. Leisure: social interaction, fun and laughter, sports, art

Broken relationships cripple us as individuals and as nations. Reconciling man to God and man to man is at the very heart of the gospel, the very purpose Jesus came to earth. Therefore, working to bring reconciliation to a nation's peoples is a key dimension of discipling a nation. John brings encouragement, instruction, and insightful examples on how we can wrap our hearts around the wounded nations we live in and minister to.

Healing the Wounds of the World

John Dawson

Paradigms That Shape Our Thinking

Today we live in a wounded world. Political ideologies and structures such as Communism have collapsed, and even the fanatical fervor of Islamic fundamentalism has been unable to bring Islamic regions and peoples together. Into this sociopolitical vacuum have rushed the much older claims of nationality, language, religious schism, and tribal identity. The old hatreds are back with a vengeance. Ancient fault lines that were briefly covered over are once again exposed.

Racial conflict in particular has had a dramatic impact on my own life. I am a white man. I have lived for the past twenty years in the African-American community in the United States. My neighborhood became famous worldwide as the place where officers of the Los Angeles police department were caught on video mercilessly beating a black man named Rodney King. Following their acquittal the city erupted. Fifty-nine people died in the rioting and more than 5,000 buildings were damaged or destroyed. Mr. King was later quoted in banner headlines around the world asking the desperate question, "Can't we all get along?" Mr. King's question hangs over us still. The answer, of course, is no.

Business as usual for the human heart is envy, fear, and contention. What an exciting time, then, to be a believer in Jesus and an intercessor involved in Christ's ministry of reconciliation! We have the answer! As 2 Corinthians 5:18 tells us, "All this is from God, who reconciled us to himself through Christ and gave us the ministry of reconciliation." It is as we are reconciled to God the Father that the "other-ness" of another gender, race, or culture becomes an attraction rather than a source of insecurity and division. This is why Jesus gives the ministry of reconciliation to the redeemed in Christ, the living church. Even the best efforts of humanistic peace-makers will disappoint. There is only one Prince of Peace.

Even now a wave of repentance is spreading through prayer movements around the world. Foundational sins that have hindered the progress of the gospel for cen-turies are being addressed through public confession and forgiveness. This season of particular grace for reconciliation began in the 1990s, starting with the issues that have wounded the New Zealand Maoris, Native Americans, and other indigenous peoples. I personally have witnessed stadiums filled with weeping Christians, where people flooded platforms to confess not only their personal sins but also the sins of their group against other groups.

In May 1995, for example, brokenness, repentance, and reconciliation swept the almost 4,000 evangelical leaders from 186 nations meeting in Seoul, South Korea. Leaders from Turkey and Armenia reconciled and embraced one another. Japanese leaders knelt and asked forgiveness from Southeast Asians. Such deep repentance, I'm convinced, not only demonstrates God's healing love but also robs Satan of ancient strongholds.

As the church of Jesus Christ, our goal, of course, has always been to see people reconciled to God through the gospel. The main hindrance to this end, however, has been us. The world has not been able to "see" Jesus because of the sectarian strife within the body of Christ.

For centuries, this spirit of religious controversy has made us part of the problem. But now I believe that we are finally becoming part of the answer. The growing wave of repentance over historic sins is leading believers of differing denominations, cul-tures, and movements to unprecedented affection and respect for one another. Jesus said that when this kind of unity occurred, the world would believe the Father sent him (see John 17:21). Ultimately, the world will "see" Jesus when a united church carries the ministry of reconciliation beyond its own walls.

The Wounds of the World

We know that two people can hurt each other through selfish and unjust behavior. It is also possible for a wound to be sustained by a nation or people within a nation. Animosity and bitterness can fester, unresolved for generations.

When we study human conflict, we see that Satan's method of getting one group to abuse another is rooted in the hardheaded collision of self-righteous people within each group. Take some truth, polarize the people with different sides of that truth, tempt them to unrighteous judgment, and then watch them wound one another with rejection, harsh words, injustice... and so it goes on.

At a Canadian conference in 1995, Christian delegates from over forty nations identified fourteen general categories of deep-rooted, systematic alienation between peoples and elements of a society.[1] These are fourteen areas in which reconciliation ministry must be applied:

1. Indigenous peoples to immigrant peoples (such as the Aboriginal peoples to European-Australians)
2. Residual antagonisms, when there is justice under the law but wounds continue (for example, between black and white Americans because of the legacy of slavery or the hearing and hearing-impaired because of a perception of society's continuing insensitivity)
3. People-group conflicts (such as the Kurds vs. the Turks or the Hutus vs. the Tutsis)
4. Nation-state rivalries (such as the border disputes between Pakistan and India)
5. Independence movements (for example, the Timorese resistance to Javanese Indonesians as a result of colonialism)
6. Civil wars (as in Bosnia)
7. Alienation between generations (such as a generation returned from war dealing with the countercultures of their teenage children)
8. Societal conflicts (for example, leftist vs. rightist ideologies on the environment or abortion)
9. Gender-based abuses (such as the forced prostitution of Korean, Chinese, and Philippine women by the Japanese military during the 1940s)
10. Industry, trade, and labor disputes (such as migrant farm workers vs. commercial agricultural enterprises)
11. Social-class divisions (such as those caused by the Indian caste system, socialist governing elites, land and business dynasties, or aristocratic cultures)
12. Interreligious conflicts (as between Christians and Jews)
13. Interdenominational conflicts (sectarian divisions)
14. Christianity to peoples (elements of Christian civilization have misrepresented God's character and put a stumbling block between those peoples and their Creator—an example is the impact of the conquistadors on Amerindian peoples)

How do we respond to such deep, gaping, sometimes ancient wounds? The simple answer lies in the humility of Jesus expressed through his body, the church.

A Model of Reconciliation

Although the Judeo-Christian ethos present in many national cultures gives us some basis for hope that reconciliation can occur through governmental or societal entities, I believe that reconciliation ministry is primarily the responsibility of the living church. There is, after all, no substitute for the atonement Jesus provided for sin.

During the great seasons of revival in the past, the church always placed a considerable emphasis on open acknowledgement of sin and called for changed attitudes and just actions. Likewise, today's Christians have the potential to demonstrate a model of reconciliation in today's troubled world.

What is that model? As Christians, we believe in confession, repentance, reconciliation, and restitution. In the context of healing the wounds of the world this means:

1. Confession: stating the truth and acknowledging the unjust or hurtful actions of myself or my people group toward other people or categories of people
2. Repentance: turning from unloving to loving actions
3. Reconciliation: expressing and receiving forgiveness and pursuing intimate fellowship with previous enemies
4. Restitution: attempting to restore that which has been damaged or destroyed and seeking justice wherever we have power to act or to influence those in authority to act

Sometimes we can begin this process by organizing events and ceremonies in which representatives of offending or offended cultures have an opportunity to express regret or extend forgiveness.

Of course, in initiating such acts we recognize that the issues involved are complex. Today's generation has inherited the task of both honoring righteous ancestors and seeking forgiveness for ancestral sins. Honesty dictates that we embrace both the guilt and the grandeur attached to our various identities.

It is also true that when we are redeemed we become part of the transcendent bride of Christ in which there is neither male nor female, Jew nor Greek (Gal. 3:28). While this might seem to dissolve our link to our national identities, the Bible teaches that as members of the body of Christ, we become even more responsible for dealing with the implications of our identity when new life is born in us.

Even though each person stands before God alone and is in no way guilty for the sins of their ancestors or any other group, God is looking for volunteers who will open themselves to experience godly sorrow and confess the sins of the land. Nehemiah did this on behalf of the nation of Israel, and his prayer released the power and favor of the Lord on that nation. This is where reconciliation begins.

God's Momentum

The reconciliation prayer movement seems to have found a God-breathed momentum far beyond human promotion. We are, I believe, in an unusual season of grace, a season of jubilee.

I work with the International Reconciliation Coalition (IRC) founded in 1990 as a fellowship of Christians attempting to deal with conflict in a Christian way. The IRC has grown rapidly into a worldwide network of like-minded but culturally diverse praying servants from all streams within God's church. There are intercessors, prophetic ministries, researchers, strategic planners, training ministries, and ambassadors of reconciliation who lead the way in public confession, repentance, and reconciliation at "solemn assemblies" and other special events.[2]

A reconciliation initiative is launched when people who trust each other form an alliance around a major reconciliation issue and determine to take action together. The IRC helps like-minded people find each other and learn from other reconcilers in the network.

As I write, there are dozens of ongoing initiatives and many more are gaining momentum. One of the most significant of the last decade was the Reconciliation Walk, coinciding with the 900th anniversary of the Crusades. European intercessors, along with others from all over the world, have walked the routes of the Crusades from west to east, carrying proclamations of repentance to Muslim and Jewish communities for the slaughter done in Christ's name.

The response has been encouraging. Identificational repentance is proving to be the key to opening doors that have been closed for centuries. I don't know why we waited 900 years to repent for the Crusades, but I'm glad breakthroughs among Islamic peoples are coming in our lifetime! Even in a post-9/11 world, the message of Jesus continues to find acceptance in surprising places.

In the United States, people are taking prayer journeys where Native Americans were oppressed or massacred. In addition, there are prayer journeys to the historical slave ports of West Africa where black and white Americans weep together, learn together, and find an intimacy that has eluded less radical believers.

Healing by the Power of the Cross

I have a Welsh friend named Rhiannon Lloyd who holds trauma recovery classes[3] for both Hutu and Tutsi survivors of the Rwandan genocide. If you were in her shoes, what would you say to these devastated people? Many have suffered rape or maiming or witnessed the murder of their family members *by those who were and are now again their neighbors, even part of the same church fellowship.*

This is what she does. In the shelter of a church house they meet for three days. Dr. Lloyd first persuades her grieving flock to write down on a piece of paper the worst experience that they had. When the awful facts have been confronted in this way, she has them come together in small groups to tell each other their stories. This is often the first trembling step toward trusting other people again.

Finally the terrible atrocities are listed on a large sheet of paper for all to see and the group is asked, "What does God feel about this?" She then draws a big, red cross through the list of hurts, symbolizing the cross of Christ.

"This is the only place we can bring our sorrows," she tells them. "This is one of the reasons Jesus came to earth, not only to take upon himself our sins, but also the sin of those who sinned against us. Stand and tell God of the pain in your heart," she tells them. "What you saw, what it did to you. If you're angry, tell him. If strong emotion comes, don't hold it back, because God will be weeping with you."

At first there is silence, but sobbing and wailing soon overcomes the cultural reserve of the Rwandans as people pour out their grief, anger, and hopelessness before the crucified Christ. A long time later, when quiet returns, they sing softly the old chorus, "What a friend we have in Jesus, all our sins and griefs to bear." Eventually Rhiannon brings in a big, rough, wooden cross and positions it on the floor with a pile of nails. One at a time, believers begin to slip forward and taking their tear-stained piece of paper with its record of horrors, they kneel and nail it to the cross of Jesus. All afternoon the hammer pounds, echoing the agony of Golgatha, a reminder of Jesus' complete identification with our sufferings.

On the third day an amazing thing happens. People begin to testify that in the midst of genocide, God was at work in the darkness. They talk of heroes, Christian reconcilers, who were the first to die. Anger at God begins to turn to empathy for God as believers contemplate his heartbreak over the way we humans treat one another.

With grief now resting lighter upon many, talk of forgiveness begins to emerge. Jesus is seen, not only as the innocent and suffering Lamb of God but also the resurrected and righteous Judge who will uncompromisingly administer justice. Even now his hand of vengeance is stretched out toward the wicked, the very persons haunting the memory of survivors.

"If they repent, is it all right with you if God forgives them?" Rhiannon asks. Each person contemplates this question. They weigh their testimonies of cleansing against their grief. Many finally conclude that if God forgave them, they must eventually forgive others. Truly this is "beauty for ashes," the promise of God (Isaiah 61:1–4).

Healing the Land

Finally Rhiannon tells them a personal story. "I come from a nation where two tribes have hurt each other," she says. "One day I was in a prayer meeting when an English Christian knelt at my feet. 'We have often made the Welsh our servants,' she said. 'Please forgive us.' And she proceeded to wash my feet. A deep healing took place in my heart that day because of the humility of one person who chose to identify with the sins of her people against my people."

Rhiannon's simple story contains a key. This is the key to the ancient gates that isolate peoples and elements of society from one another. She has given a wisdom gift to Hutu and Tutsi as they struggle to live together in the same land.

You see, Jesus didn't tell us to apply the cross to the other person, but to ourselves. This is what gives us power to be reconcilers. It is a mystery revealed in the cross of Christ. Each believer must take up the cross and apply it to his or her personal identity. Even now God is seeking for people like Rhiannon's humble English friend. He's looking for those who will express the humility of Christ and bring healing to the nations.

Rhiannon acts upon this truth. She does one more thing. As a white person surrounded by Africans, she takes a position of complete identification with Europeans. She cannot represent Europeans in any official way, let alone confess the sins of others, but she realizes that there are no "generic" Christians. We all come from somewhere and it is obvious to the Africans that she is from one of the European peoples that long held power in Africa.

Rhiannon knows that her very appearance reminds many Africans of rejection and unjust dominance. Instead of disclaiming all association with the colonial past by such statements as, "I'm not from Belgium," or "It was all in a past generation," or "My people have been oppressed too," she volunteers to stand in the gap as an intercessor. The Bible reveals that God is looking for such people. Not just people who will stand in the gap before him, but people who will repair the breeches in human relationships.

God does not put guilt on the intercessor. We are not individually guilty for what our group did or our parents did. However, he is waiting for the "royal priesthood," who are the redeemed in Christ, to openly confess the truth of a matter before him and before people, just as the ancient Hebrew priests once did over the sins of Israel. It is very difficult to forgive if you have never heard an open acknowledgement of the injustices that wounded you or your people. On the other hand, such grace for forgiveness is released when we are asked for forgiveness by those who identify themselves in some way with the identity of those who contributed to our suffering.

Reconciliation and Missions

I recently discovered the testimony of a missionary working in the Pacific in the 1830s. In his diary he describes early attempts to reach the warlike Maori tribes of New Zealand. To my amazement I found that these young followers of Jesus constantly risked their lives to avert intertribal conflict, often placing their bodies between war parties bent on *utu,* revenge killing. It was the ministry of reconciliation, more than anything else, which gave credibility to the gospel. Within a generation a large percentage of the indigenous population became believers.

What was effective then is even more important in today's missionary endeavors as we see from Rhiannon's powerful work bringing reconciliation after the horrific genocide in Rwanda. Conflict and unreconciled relationships within the national family is surely one of the most painful and paralyzing issues a nation can face. Discipling nations means bringing the truth of God's ways into all aspects of corporate life, so healing a nation's wounds is at the very core of the gospel message. If we will live out the mediating, reconciling life of Christ in a wounded, bitter world with no answers for its broken relationships, we will surely be the fragrance of Christ, bringing nations and individuals into reconciliation with both God and one another.

Suggested Resources

Dawson, John. *Healing America's Wounds.* Ventura, Calif.: Regal, 1994.

Notes

1. John Dawson, *What Christians Should Know About Reconciliation* (Ventura, Calif.: International Reconciliation Coalition, 2000), 29–32.

2. www.reconcile.org (accessed April 18, 2007).

3. Rhiannon Lloyd, *Healing the Wounds of Ethnic Conflict* (Le Rucher, Switzerland: Mercy Ministries International, 2001).

Family and Culture:
Keys to World Evangelism

Diane and Jeff Littleton

The Importance of Family

Family is recognized as one of the seven mind molders that shape society. As families go, so go our neighborhoods, our towns, our states, our countries, and our world.

We believe that God intends for families to be foundational to society. As the basic unit of society, family is culture's main unit for passing on important values for economic security, personal nurture, and support. The wholeness of a nation is contingent on the wholeness of its families because family teaches us patterns of expectation for how authority functions and how other institutions should be run.

One of our strongest felt needs is for family. From the beginning, the Bible tells us, "it is not good for the man to be alone" (Gen. 2:18). We all need to belong to a family and a community. The church is called "the family of God" (1 Pet. 4:17). "God sets the lonely in families" (Ps. 68:6). We are made for family. We cannot take the individual out of the family nor can we take the family out of the individual. Family gives us our identity (our surname), offers a place to belong, and provides the right situation for experiencing intimacy.

Ordained by God soon after Creation, family is the oldest human institution. Indeed, virtually all societies include a recognizable concept of family. Though the biblical definition of the nuclear family has been undermined these days, God's foundation for family is clear in Genesis 2:23–25 and Matthew 19:4–5. A biblical family is a man and woman with their natural or adopted children. Numerous verses could be cited to describe the role of parents in producing, nurturing, and training their children and the corresponding responsibilities of children to their parents.[1]

We began to understand the importance of family when we were helping to establish the University of the Nation's College of Counseling and Health Care (CCHC) before we began our work among families in Asia. When the University of the Nations was conceived, family was the mind molder assigned to CCHC. The roots of this emphasis on family go back to the pioneering health care work of Bruce and Barbara Thompson (the main developers of CCHC) during the 1970s in the primitive northern region of Ghana, West Africa. Primary health care and counseling to reduce the mortality rate among the extended tribal families in the region were important felt needs. Hearts were softened and ears opened because health care demonstrated genuine love and compassion while saving physical life. This became the most effective strategy for evangelism and church planting in that region.

Despite these beginnings, many years passed before we fully understood what a huge foundation stone family is for reaching the lost, particularly for being effective cross-culturally.

What does culture have to do with it? In Western culture we are egalitarians. We love our families but the individual is supreme. But for much of the world the family, or the group, is more important than the individual. To reach individuals effectively in these locations, our strategy must include the whole family. Some individuals, with great pain, may be able to separate from the group and come to faith in Christ. But for most group-culture people the thought of not being part of the group is utterly foreign. Their reasoning would say, "Surely if this is the truth, our family and elders would know it." To reach them we must reach their families.

As we reach families, blessing will extend to more than just the members of those families. Family is intended to be a light to a lost and fallen world. God told Abraham, "and all peoples on earth will be blessed through you" (Gen. 12:3b). God's purpose is always to bless us in order to make us a blessing to the world (not just to our own people). How careful we must be to make our families and the families to whom we go a part of God's great passion to reach a lost and dying world with his love.

We believe reaching and discipling families are major keys to world evangelism. By grappling with the family issues in a cross-culturally appropriate manner, we multiply our effectiveness many times over. In this chapter we want to share some cross-cultural keys that have enhanced our work.

Our Call to Cross-Cultural Work

Jeff Littleton first went to Malaysia in 1968 to teach English as a Second Language (ESL) in a mountain valley with a string of fenced-in "New Villages." The government had created these villages to house local farmers to prevent them from giving food to the Communists holed up in the jungle in the surrounding mountains. His ESL program was part of a church-planting outreach. Jeff taught everyone from kindergarten students to rice paddy farmers, from rubber tappers to high school students—anyone who was interested. Sharing a "duplex" two-room house on stilts just off the Village Green with a Malay family, Jeff ate all his meals in the food stalls in town and became immersed in the culture.

Diane went to Malaysia in 1969 with Overseas Missionary Fellowship. While studying Cantonese, she lived in a concrete row house in a small Malaysian town. We met and were married in Malaysia in 1971. Our call has been to cross-cultural mission work, with a particular burden for families.

Malaysian Cultural Expectations

We quickly discovered that Malaysian culture contained many opposites to our Western cultural expectations. To work most effectively among Malaysians, we had to learn to understand their basic assumptions about life. Five differences that particularly struck us were the group identity base, the obligation to family, the Confucian value system, the reality and significance of the spirit world, and "rubber" time.

Group-Identity Base

One of the most fascinating differences we observed was the importance of the group as opposed to the individual. Malaysians have a group-identity base. A thirty-five-year-old married son would come home to discuss a job change with his parents before proceeding with any change. The mind of the group was what counted, not the mind of the individual. How the job reflected on the group was far more important than how it suited the individual.

This affected more than jobs and careers. It affected the individual's choice of a marriage partner. The question was, "Would this marriage bring honor and prosperity to the group?" The personal happiness, fulfillment, or desires of the individual were eclipsed by the need for the match to be good for the group. Fulfilling desires was not expected. Serving the group was a duty.

Family Obligation

In addition to the group-identity base, Malaysians feel a strong obligation to their family. Not only did children consider their family's welfare and seek their blessing in employment opportunities and marriages but they cheerfully bore the financial support of their parents—sometimes giving their parents up to 95 percent of the paycheck.

Recently, when rereading the popular *Little House on the Prairie* book series about American life in the 1800s, Diane realized that America of one hundred years ago was largely a family-identity based culture. The individuals in the books made their choices in the light of the best for the family. Personal pleasure and satisfaction were secondary. How things have changed!

Confucian Values

Confucian philosophical values still rule a great deal of Asian thinking. Confucianism is a philosophical system developed by Confucius (551–479 BC) to confront the societal chaos of his time. He believed that right philosophy would bring order to society. Even Asian Christians may unwittingly adhere to Confucian values because they are part of their culture's world view.

Confucius thought that for society to function well certain relationships had to be given priority. In his view the father-son relationship took priority over the husband-wife relationship. Women were assigned to a role of servitude. We were amazed to see that the sons received honor and preferential treatment over their sisters, and even over their mothers.

Another Confucian value was the obligation to give honor to the elderly. The patriarch or matriarch ruled the entire family. In some cases, they even made choices about the lives of the grandchildren. When the patriarch or matriarch were benevolent, it was good. When they were not, it was not good. But either way this rule was accepted as right and normal.

The Reality and Significance of the Spirit World

The reality and importance of the spirit world were basic assumptions in daily Malaysian life. Certainly there was no widespread belief in demons in our American world prior to coming to Asia. Demons and the devil were cute characters that made Halloween spooky in a fun-loving way. There was nothing cute about the demonic spirit world of Malaysia. We came in touch with the absolute power of evil. We heard about material objects' levitation and people dying from a curse put upon them. We were immersed in a world where the spirits and their activity were all too real.

Spiritual significance was given to almost all the events of life. Obtaining the auspicious date for a wedding or any other important event was a high priority. Nothing happened by chance. There was always a good or evil spiritual cause. Understanding the spiritual cause was central to their concerns.

"Rubber" Time

Our rural Malaysian world was *event* oriented rather than *time* oriented. An event started when everyone got there and it finished when everybody left. Jeff loved this value. There was no rushing about. There was time "to be" as well as "to do." A high value was placed on relationships. In this context, who you knew was perhaps more important than who you were.

The Ancient Foundations of Asian Culture are Being Shaken

In the years since 1968, ancient Asian cultures have been shaken to their roots by the rise of worldly business culture and the accompanying materialism. Profit is the bottom line of worldly business culture. And surely profit (making money) is becoming more and more the governing force of Asia.

The inundation of the entertainment media has promoted the values of an individualistic culture. Personal fulfillment is becoming a new, important value. Marriages for "love" (actually it is lust—that which will meet my need to get) are desired. Marriages arranged for the status and enrichment of the family are diminishing.

Some children are neglecting their parents in their old age to the point where we are seeing a rising use of retirement homes for the elderly. For some of the young people the burden of the elderly distracts from the time needed to make money and to enjoy their pleasures and comforts as individuals. A new philosophy is arising—who needs the tiresome burden of aged parents!

The wholeness of a nation is contingent on the wholeness of its families. Not only in Asia, but all over the world families are feeling their foundations shaken. The divorce rate is on the rise globally. For example, in Korea the divorce rate is doubling every ten years. There is a desperate heart cry for something that will keep the family together. In most places, the source of that input is not nearly of so much consequence as whether that input works!

As Asians discover the emptiness of materialism and find insufficient power and answers in their ancient religions to grapple with this upheaval, they are left hungry for answers. People in transition are always more open to considering another perspective and Asia is definitely in transition. God's Word has the answer for the questions raised by all this social disruption. Asians are asking new questions about values and destiny. These queries open the door for the gospel to be shared. The Bible was written in an Eastern context and is very applicable sociologically as well as spiritually to the Asian heart cry.

As family obligation is shaken and tested under the new social pressures, in many cases it is found to be only dutiful obligation with very little heart commitment and care. Parents are left asking, "Must we lose our children?" Under pressure, family structures are sometimes found to be built on duty and fueled by guilt and intimidation. Control and manipulation can be strong forces. Some families are truly caring. But as obligation crumbles away, many are watching their family life erode before their eyes.

Many world evangelism strategies have historically begun with the "felt needs" of a people group and then moved to their "real needs," the needs of the spirit of a person. This certainly works in the area of community development or mercy ministries. And it will work as well if we care about the needs of families. Speaking to family issues is a major key to world evangelism because it meets the felt needs of people and opens the door for the gospel.

For example, a very real and also very felt need is the heartfelt struggle of some young families in dealing with elderly parents. The elderly parents use manipulation and control to deal with their children; they know no other behavior pattern. Something in adult children tells them that they should honor their parents, but they ask, does "honor" mean giving way to manipulation and control? Might God have something to say about the family crisis this causes?

What liberty and blessing can become theirs as they understand how God calls us to honor our parents, not out of mere obligation but with hearts that truly desire to show them love and honor. This love and honor is demonstrated by adult children being willing to listen to their parents, value their input, and care for their needs. But it is a healthy love that sets boundaries in family relationships. It does not allow the grandparent to overtake God-given responsibilities in the husband-wife and parent-child relationships.

The grace to love and honor in this way is only found in Jesus. Their conscience tells them they need to honor. Their experience knows that this is not possible without a power greater than their own selfish will. They know they need the salvation God offers to them individually and as a family to be what they should be to their parents while setting limits on their parents' dysfunctional patterns.

God has the answers to family needs, whatever they may be. However, our lack of cross-cultural understanding is often our major challenge in taking advantage of this enormous opportunity for sharing the gospel and communicating God's truth in a way that is culturally relevant.

Cross-Cultural Keys to Reaching Families

A few basic keys will help us leap over the hurdles of cross-cultural misunderstanding that we all face. The keys are simple things but they are not always so simple to apply. We need to understand both direct and indirect cultures. Turning our statements into questions will greatly help us to connect with others. We must learn to value listening, not just speaking. Understanding and valuing group-based-identity cultures is a major key. Appreciating that core values may differ in other cultures, we also must come to realize that the Western way may not always be the biblical Way. Lastly, we must recognize that group-identity-based cultures may struggle with a weakened conscience and address the issues involved in dealing with this. As you understand these keys, we hope you will be able to apply them and instruct others to "unlock" the hearts of people you seek to reach.

Direct and Indirect Cultures

We can leap over major hurdles in the communication areas of life if we understand that cultures fall into two basic groups: those that are direct communicators and those that are indirect communicators. Sarah Lanier's book *Foreign to Familiar* is an excellent guide to understanding our cultural differences in these areas. Basically, Western cultures are more direct, and Asian, Polynesian, African, and Latin cultures are more indirect. There are shades of direct or indirect in every culture. Direct cultures highly value time, especially other people's time; hence, people prefer to go straight to their point, asking a direct yes or no question with no concern that they will put the respondent in an awkward position. Respondents, in turn, may answer yes or no, politely voicing their own opinions, with no concern that the answer will be taken personally. Indirect cultures, however, value relationships over time, and extreme care is taken to avoid offense. Before getting to the main point of an exchange, people will take the time to be social and caring about the other's life. Every question must be asked in a way that the answer cannot be yes or no; otherwise the respondent will feel obligated to say yes (and potentially be unhappy about it). To say no could cause someone embarrassment, and the respondent would fear that the relationship could suffer. In indirect cultures, the process of learning what someone wants or likes can be time consuming, and it is often appropriate to use an intermediary so that the fear of shame for self or the other is decreased.

What happens when a missionary from a direct culture goes to an indirect Asian culture and shares about God's truth in a direct way? No matter how desperately needed the truth may be, nor how relevant it may be, it is not heard. To the indirect person our directness is heard as arrogance and pride. They may well take this pride as evidence that we have a gross lack of understanding of human life. So the reasonable assumption may follow that anyone so lacking in understanding about life can have nothing of relevance to share.

What is more, because we may be given the honor of being a teacher it would be impolite for the Asian to disagree with us. Therefore, rather than saying a direct "no"

to our teaching or request, they will say "yes" in a way that they hope we will understand to be "maybe" or "no." But for a Westerner's black and white worldview the
indirect answer may not be understood as "no."

Recently we were back in the USA doing some teaching on direct and indirect
cultures. Several times we were asked, "Why don't they just read the Bible and do
what it says?" Black and white Western minds do not understand that people may
need to hear a statement given several different ways.

People from indirect cultures may often need time to process a brand new truth.
Maybe it is not that the truth is as different as is the foreign presentation that allows
no time for process or repetition of information. We do not see the stark difference
between how we directly share truth and the indirect cultural norm that requires
some processing time to think through and apply such truths in the context of their
whole culture. In our direct culture stating the facts once or twice should take care of
the matter. In an indirect culture, truth must be considered in the context of their
whole culture.

Turn Statements into Questions

The question becomes, How do we overcome these cultural stumbling blocks so that
we can move from the felt need to the real needs? One simple answer will work wonders virtually every time: Turn every statement into a question. This is easy to say but
so difficult to do! We are so eager to tell all that we know.

If we really want to reach the hearts of those with whom we are sharing, the most
effective means is to ask their opinion. Asking questions shows our respect and con-
veys a humble heart that wants to learn. It destroys our "know it all" mentality and
opens others to hear what we might like to share. It helps to put our cultural pride on
the cross.

In turning statements into questions, our motivation is to put ourselves in a learning position. We want them to tell us, in their own words, the information we may
already know, or think we know. We want to understand their perspective and worldview. This gives them a sense of dignity. They feel respected by us if we really are being
respectful and not just using this as a technique.

We ask questions to gain understanding, not just to obtain information. We want
to understand their point of view and their world view. Asking questions in some
ways puts them in the place of instructing us and having an authority over us in bringing us into understanding of their worldview.

If we do not have the ability to ask the questions with patience and graciousness
then the whole process will break down. Asking questions puts us in the place of
being a learner and of wanting to be a servant to them. If there is any condescension
("I know better than you") in our attitude, it will immediately limit the interaction.

Telling people what they should do is a poor way to bring them to a place of being able to integrate any truth into their lives. A better way is to ask, "From your perspective how do you think this should be done?" and then share biblical principles that relate to their view. For example, a big area of interest and need is child discipline. We could make a statement of a fact such as, "This is the way to discipline your children . . ." The better way would be to ask the question, "How do you think children should be disciplined?" "Would you like to hear what the Bible shares as God's perspective on this matter?"

Value Listening

We must learn to truly value listening. Asking questions forces us to listen. Listening shows respect, gives dignity to the speaker, and increases understanding.

In asking questions the motive is to set up a reflective relationship. Therefore, it is wisdom to ponder what is said and to reflect back to the speaker what we heard her say. It is urgent not to run over an answer quickly to get on with what we have to say. When they have finished explaining, our response should be, "Am I hearing you correctly? Are you saying this . . . ?" In reflecting, we convey our desire to build understanding between the two of us. We want to understand them and we would like them to understand us.

A listening learner quenches the urge to finish the other's sentences. We should not rush to tell others what we think they are saying before they finish speaking. Often in indirect cultures the speaker will say things in a round-about way, so giving them plenty of time to express themselves is imperative.

Giving time for an answer is all the more important because attitudes are learned nonverbally. Consequently, they are often not consciously understood and are difficult to verbalize. It is hard for people in any culture to verbalize their values and beliefs. People tend to move along with the general flow, never really understanding what they unconsciously believe unless something causes them to think on these things.

When we ask enough questions, we begin to enable a person to verbalize the nonverbal values and belief systems of their culture. By verbalizing the nonverbal values and belief systems of their culture, they begin to understand what their culture thinks, feels, values, believes. As they deepen their understanding, they can see how it measures up to God's revelation and begin to affirm that which is good and whole, and look to change that which is not. Listening and asking questions is the key to understanding others and to helping them to understand themselves. As a bonus it may enable us to better understand ourselves.

More than once in our interaction with other cultures we have asked many questions and listened carefully to the answers, giving feedback as to what we thought we were hearing. We have then had people exclaim to us what a marvel it is that we understand them. One man asked, "How can you, a foreigner, understand my culture so well?" The truth is that we do not have large amounts of understanding but we know just enough to ask the right questions.

To save a family or disciple a nation we must have a heart attitude that *respects others enough to listen* to them until we gain understanding. As perception grows, we have the opportunity to discover, alongside those whom we would disciple, how God's truth applies in their family and culture and how it can save them corporately and as individuals.

Understand and Value Group-Identity-Based Cultures

Remember our discovery when we first moved to Malaysia that the family, rather than the individual, was the center of society? We can be much more effective in sharing cross-culturally if we realize that some cultures have a *group* (or *family*) *identity base* and others have an *individual identity base.*

Although Westerners are egalitarians, in the midst of Western individualism, especially among teenagers, we have the "peer-group culture" that esteems the values of peers above all else. So we do have this type of a "group" culture in the midst of our Western individualism. This should give us some small understanding of this difference. There is a real joy and security in knowing I am part of the group and knowing I have a place in the group.

Yes, God does meet us as individuals. Yes, our personal identity is important biblically. But we believe that biblically the family and group identity are also of great importance. Both are biblical. Both need to be understood and kept in balance. The church is called "the family of God" and is indeed a group.

Sometimes Westerners can feel that the family obligation of group cultures is an unbiblical encumbrance. Our Western opinion is that it infringes upon the individual's "rights." Rights are important to us in the West. Responsibility and relationship are of more consequence in other cultures. Is one more biblical than the other? Or do we need to understand *both* in bringing wholeness to families and indeed, in bringing the gospel to families?

Core Values Differ in Other Cultures

What happens when we do not understand that core cultural values may be different?

We have sometimes cringed when we have attended family seminars given by Westerners in Asia. The promised content has drawn a full house. Many of those attending are desperate, unbelieving parents who long for some straw of hope that they may regain their marriage or lost children. The Western speaker wrongly thinks that because of the evident desperate hunger of the crowd, if he just lists out the biblical principles, the truth will set them free.

He does not understand that in Confucian values, which often highly influence Asian Christians, the father-son relationship can far outweigh the husband-wife relationship. Personal friendship between a husband and wife can be minimal. Often it is a utilitarian relationship where she keeps the home, sometimes the money, and raises the children; he works and provides for the family. There is sexual intimacy but not personal intimacy. The man often finds his needs for relationships met by his friends or workmates and she finds hers with her children, siblings, and friends.

We have a close Asian friend. If we phone for him and he is out, we no longer ask his wife where he is. She does not know. He does not tell her. Day or night she has no idea where he is or when he will return home. And nobody but us thinks anything of it.

The Western speaker will tell this group of new Christian men how to love their wives. However, not having understood the low view of women and the low view of personal intimacy, the list is only followed legalistically. We remember one man who brought his wife flowers. We commented to her on what a romantic husband she had. We got the angry response, "A curse on his flowers. I want him to talk to me—not perform duties!"

If we are going to use the felt need for input on family life as a means of reaching group-culture people, then we need to start with an understanding of their values and beliefs. We must have an accurate understanding of the foundational biblical truths they already have, and which ones are needed. We should to be very careful when giving principles because they can so easily become a list of lifeless duties.

A family seminar allows the opportunity to discuss who God is. We can talk about his perfect Fatherhood and discuss his values and truths. We may talk about his Fatherly love that has made the provision for our sins and the sins of our children. An understanding of God's Fatherhood in the light of how fatherhood is viewed in the culture might be a good beginning point. From there we may go on to God's Fatherhood of women and children and his view of them.

These kinds of questions open rich opportunities to share scriptures on God as our Father and how he trains us as his children. We could look at the biblical obligations of being the child of our parents. We could discuss our "obligation" to God as our Father by Creation. This kind of discussion may lead to dialogue about relationships.

The area of self-control and anger can also provide excellent entrees to discussion. In Oriental culture self-control is highly valued. We have heard it said that to lose one's temper is worse than to commit adultery because losing your temper shows lack of self-control while adultery is a choice. Understanding this gives a wide-open door for sharing the gospel because the struggle with anger is a huge felt need, especially in family life all over Asia.

First, we desperately need to understand what people believe. What do they already have in their culture that is of God? What do they have that will not bring their family to God and his wholeness? We need to understand their values and heart attitudes. Then we can seek to enable them to understand these and compare them to God's values and desires for us.

The Western Way May Not Be the Biblical Way

When sharing in other cultures, we need to bear in mind that our Western way may not always be the biblical way. Ours may only be a shade of the biblical way. One Western woman, in trying to empathize with an Asian woman, began to ask her about how her husband met her emotional needs.

After some conversation the Asian lady spoke up and said, "You Western people put so much pressure on your marriages and husbands. I do not look for my husband to meet all my needs. I have my family. I have my friends. Most of what I need in relationships I get from them."

Personally we think that this woman had some understanding of biblical principles that could be helpful to those of us in the West. Perhaps sometimes Western people put too much pressure and expectation upon the marriage relationship.

Those from Group Culture Have a Weakened Conscience

A possible weakness of a group-identity-based culture is that the individual is asked to give up his conscience and let the conscience of the parent or group leaders become its replacement. The nonverbal message is, "You are too young, or too uneducated, or not of the right social status, or inferior to us older or more educated people in some way or form—so you cannot make your own decisions as well as we can make them for you. The group should choose for you." The giving over of the conscience is expected in many areas of life and can even extend into moral choices.

Sometimes the group (i.e., the family) is expected to make the choice of a person's mate. We are not altogether against "arranged marriages," but sometimes the suggested marriage is to an unbeliever or a person who is not suitable in some other way. In that case the person for whom the choice is being made needs the freedom to allow the burden of his conscience to be spoken out and honored.

Parents in some cultures give over their God-given responsibility for raising their children to the grandparents. Sometimes the eldest child may automatically be given to the grandparents to raise as their child. In other cultures the grandparents, rather than the parents, make the choice of values, discipline, and education. The parent's conscience in these matters is not considered.

An individual may even be asked to do acts that offend his conscience. How important it is for us, while affirming the importance of receiving the wise input of the family and the elders into their lives, to still call the individual to be responsible before God for his own moral choices. This takes the wisdom of God. God has promised that his word will divide between truth and error and bring liberty and wholeness where it is spoken out.

An understanding of these issues needs to be born in mind when appealing to the conscience of an individual. Great sympathy and wisdom is needed in helping them to divide between family/group loyalty and their individual opportunity to repent and know God. There is a need for individuals to realize that the group will not come to the liberty of the gospel until the individuals come first. God needs individuals to bring his love to the group through them as individuals. The cost may be very high for them—disowned by the family or maybe, in some cultures, killed for dishonoring the group.

Conclusion

The wholeness of the family is one of the strongest felt needs of all peoples. Biblical marriage and family principles are a shining beacon of hope in our confused and dark world. They give us a wide-open door for sharing the gospel and advancing the kingdom. Universally, apart from the power of Christ, we all soon discover that our human brokenness and sin keep us from all God has for us and our families. Perhaps our need for the cross of Christ is most vividly seen in our family relationships. These needs will lead us to him.

As we press on to understand how to effectively reach families, we will in the process begin to understand group cultures. This will give us a major key to cross-cultural evangelism. To make the gospel relevant in each culture we must care enough to understand its values and beliefs. We have the Bible, God's "manual" on marriage and family, and the power of the Cross to change individuals so they can follow it. By these means we can change nations.

The old chorus goes: "We will guard each man's dignity and crucify pride." The day in which God enables us to crucify our own cultural pride enough to give dignity to another man and the culture that has molded him is the day in which we can begin to win and disciple families and their nations for God. In that day, we will glory in how amazing God's family principles are and how sufficient his salvation, through the cross of Christ, is for families and their cultures to fulfill their God-given destinies.

Bibliography

Lanier, Sarah A. *Foreign to Familiar: A Guide to Understanding Hot- and Cold-Climate Cultures.* Hagerstown, Md.: McDougal Publishing, 2000.

Notes

1. A smattering of examples include Gen. 48:9; Deut. 4:9; 6:6, 7; 31:13; Josh. 8:35; 2 Chron. 20:13; Neh. 12:43; Ps. 127:3; Prov. 8:17, 32; 19:18; 22:15; 23:13; Isa. 8:18; Matt. 7:11; 21:15; Luke 2:42; 2 Cor. 12:14; Eph. 5:21—6:4; Col. 3:21; 1 Tim. 3:4, 12; Tit. 2:4.

Healthy families are critical to healthy societies. Larry Ballard works to save marriages and strengthen families as his contribution to discipling nations. In this chapter, he describes the issues our nations are grappling with as the commitment to family is deteriorating around the world. His overview of the multifaceted efforts around the world gives principles and insights which can spur our thinking about transformation in many spheres of life.

Transforming a Divorce Culture into a Marriage Culture

Larry Ballard

Family plays a key role in defining a culture, and marriage is the relationship central to strong, healthy families. Why are families so key to the overall health of society? Families are the socializing agents in a culture; for most children, the family is where they learn language, discover their identity, develop relationship skills, and form their values. It is the place where they develop their view of the world and their understanding of what is acceptable in the culture. They, in turn, live out those values and beliefs as they mature into decision-makers in their communities and parents of the next generation.

By targeting families and strengthening marriages, we can effectively transform civilizations. Healthy families lead to healthy churches, communities, and cultures. Conversely, when families are torn apart and marriages break up, social institutions within culture are weakened. Families, in the words of James Sheridan, chief district judge of Adrian, Michigan, are "small civilizations" and "the death of a family is the death of a small civilization."[1] It is also true that family is the one "cultural molder" that affects everyone, no matter what level of involvement one may have in the spheres of society: science and business, media, celebration and the arts, politics, education, health care, or the church. Everyone has a family, and everyone is affected by his or her family.

Sadly, over the past forty years, America has shifted from a "marriage culture" to a "divorce culture." Until recently, this shift has been largely ignored by the public. In the words of George Gallop Jr., "If a disease were to afflict the majority of a populace, spreading pain and dysfunction throughout all age groups, we would be frantically searching for reasons and solutions. Yet this particular scourge has become so endemic that it is virtually ignored. The scourge is divorce, an oddly neglected topic in a nation that has the worst record of broken marriages in the entire world. Divorce is the root problem in our country and is the cause of any number of other social ills."[2]

America is in the midst of a marriage movement that is turning the tide of this devastating problem. Clergy across the nation are joining together to implement programs that are decreasing divorce rates and increasing marriage rates in their communities. Federal, state, and local governments are committing resources to promote healthy families and strengthen marriages. Educators, policy makers, community leaders, clergy, human service providers, and counselors are in the midst of rethinking their approaches to this critical issue.

The Divorce Culture: What Is It?

The divorce culture has developed social institutions, public policies, and lifestyle choices in the general population that weaken and devalue the marriage covenant. Couples are encouraged to remedy their marital pains and conflicts by quickly dissolving their marital bonds instead of seeking to overcome difficulties. Divorce culture, at its root, is the shift from the virtue of remaining committed during difficult times to a refusal to tolerate discomfort and pain.

Obviously, no one should be encouraged to remain in an abusive and life-threatening relationship. However, in a divorce culture the threshold for terminating a relationship is so low that the majority of marriages break up over solvable issues and not over issues such as serious abuse, persistent infidelity, and chemical addictions. The laws and the judicial system actually favor the termination of relationships and tip the scales in the direction of divorce; in America we have "no-fault," unilateral, divorce laws. If one of the marital partners concludes there are "irreconcilable differences" in the marriage, the courts will almost always grant a divorce, even if the other partner believes the marriage can be repaired and wants to continue working on the relationship.

In divorce cultures, increasing numbers of people (young and old) opt out of life-long marital unions and instead choose live-in relationships that require less commitment. Engaged couples in increasing numbers sign prenuptial agreements and keep separate bank accounts so they can easily get out of the marriage if things break down. Cultural icons and popular role models drift in and out of matrimony as often as "regular" people change cars. All such actions and attitudes lead to a weakening and devaluing of the marital union in the society.

How Divorce Affects Society

Between 1960 and 1981 the United States of America went from a pro-marriage culture to a divorce culture:

- Divorces skyrocketed from just under 400,000 annually to over 1,200,000 annually according to the National Center for Health Statistics.
- By 2001, over 19 million currently divorced people were living in the United States.[3]
- Between 1960 and 2000 the number of cohabiting couples soared from under 500,000 to over 5.5 million.[4]
- Meanwhile, out-of-wedlock births climbed sixfold.[5]

These high rates of marital breakup are having disastrous consequences upon the affected children and American society:

- Children from a divorced home are 12.4 times more likely to be incarcerated than those from intact homes.[6]
- Children born out of wedlock are twenty-two times more at risk of being incarcerated.[7]
- A child living with a single biological mother is fourteen times more likely to suffer serious physical abuse than a child living with two parents.[8]
- A child is twenty times more apt to be abused by cohabiting parents and thirty-three times more likely to be abused if the mother is cohabiting with a man who is not the biological father.[9]
- High school dropout rates for children in single parent homes are double those of children raised in two-parent families.[10]

Judith Wallerstein, a world authority on the effects of divorce on children, conducted a twenty-five-year comparison study of 131 children of divorce. She reports that "it's in adulthood that children of divorce suffer the most. The impact of divorce hits them most cruelly as they go in search of love, sexual intimacy, and commitment."[11] Through the documented life experiences of these children, she illustrates how they struggle with fear that they will suffer the same fate as their parents.

Lacking an internal template of what a healthy relationship looks like, they are often left to invent their own models of intimacy in a culture that offers few guidelines. "Only 7 of the original 131 children in her study experienced stable second marriages in which they had good relationships with a stepparent or stepsiblings on both sides of the divorced family. Two-thirds of the children grew up in families where they experienced multiple divorces and remarriages of one or both of their parents."[12]

America's judicial system and human service departments are being overwhelmed by the results of family breakdown. In many social agencies, close to three-quarters of the children in treatment are from divorced families. The economic cost of broken homes is staggering. Millions of taxpayers' dollars are being spent dealing with the consequences of broken homes.

"Divorce is not a religious issue; it is a community issue," according to Judge Sheridan. "Who pays the taxes for the results of these broken marriages? Atheists, Catholics, Protestants, and agnostics. The color of money is green, not religious. Probably half of the criminal caseload comes out of broken families somehow or another, or badly dysfunctional families."[13]

Transformation: One Marriage at a Time

The dramatic story of Dan and Paige Wiersgalla illustrates some of the challenges and elements for restoration which must be addressed if we're to see change on an individual and corporate level.

Little did my wife and I realize that the couple sitting in our living room on February 7, 1999, was less than thirty-six hours away from the end of their ten-year marriage. The papers had been signed, the divorce had been granted, and all that stood between them and the end of their marriage was the 120-day required waiting period. Paige and the four children were already living in Texas and she returned to Eau Claire, Wisconsin, just to sign the final papers.

Dan's most recent adulterous episode had been the final blow for Paige and she was unable to forgive him for yet another betrayal. They had enjoyed several good years together, but things had deteriorated during the previous two years. Dan's job had taken him out of town and the ensuing temptations eventually took their toll. Before long, he found himself involved sexually with other women.

When Dan's conscience could no longer bear the guilt, he confessed to Paige what she already feared. They tried to salvage their relationship, but the depth of pain and anger was more than Paige could bear, and the decision to divorce was made. It was the only way out . . . or so it seemed.

In desperation, Dan reached out to the faith that had once been a vital part of his life. He found himself in a Wednesday evening church sobbing uncontrollably, asking God to save his marriage. The next day he called us, pleading for help. Paige reluctantly agreed to that initial session, primarily because she thought it might look good in court, not because she was motivated to save the marriage. They actually arrived in separate cars, sat on opposite ends of our living room and "were like two enemies in the same room."[14]

From that initial session, however, Paige noticed that Dan seemed to be undergoing a profound and genuine change in attitude. By the second session she sensed God prompting her not to give up on the marriage. Paige began asking God what he wanted her to do. She heard the Lord encouraging her to trust him and to let him do the impossible. His presence in her life became so real that she decided not to sign the final divorce papers, but rather to agree to a thirty-day extension.

With lots of perseverance, painful choices, support from others, and a rich measure of God's grace, those thirty days have turned into more than eight years. It hasn't been easy since agreeing to reconcile. However, today they both enthusiastically testify to being happy, inwardly peaceful, and closer to one another than ever before.

Their children suffered tremendously during this painful process. However, the relief and joy in hearing that their parents were staying together quickly began to heal the wounds inflicted on their tender hearts. Paige is quick to acknowledge that she hasn't forgotten Dan's betrayal, but the power of God's forgiveness has enabled her to forgive him completely. Today Dan and Paige are reaching out to help other couples who are struggling with the very things that once threatened to tear their marriage apart.

There are many "success stories" like Dan and Paige's. Retrouvaille, a popular weekend retreat for couples in crises, reports that four out of five couples that complete their program end up staying together. This movement originated in Canada and grew out of the well-known Marriage Encounter movement. Over 60,000 couples have attended Retrouvaille weekends. Many of these couples were on the brink of divorce or were already separated from one another. Their encouraging results confirm that even the most broken marriage has the potential to be saved with proper help.[15]

Reconciling God's Way,[16] a program developed in 1990 by Joe and Michelle Williams of Modesto California, has seen over half of the 700–800 couples attending their program reconcile with each other. A significant number of couples had already separated. Joe and Michelle had each gone through the pain and heartbreak of three divorces before becoming Christians. They once even separated from each other after they came to Christ. God has healed them to such a degree that they now give hope to others in crisis. Their personal pain has been transformed into an effective ministry to couples in crisis.

Transformation: Multifaceted, Multigenerational Strategies Needed

Seeing individual lives and marriages changed is possible, but it takes time. Transforming a divorce culture to a marriage culture takes place even more slowly and must include a comprehensive plan to involve all sectors of society. Faith-based organizations, local churches, community organizations, social service departments, policy makers, public officials, educators, and the media must all partner together. Nothing short of a full-scale commitment from each of these sectors will achieve the desired results.

One example of the body of Christ responding to this issue is a national marriage-saving initiative birthed in 1986. Ninety-five pastors, priests, and a rabbi in Modesto, California, signed the nation's first Community Marriage Policy (CMP). These clergy took this historic step at the encouragement of Mike McManus, a syndicated columnist and former *TIME* magazine correspondent. Later, in 1996, Mike and Harriet McManus cofounded Marriage Savers, Inc., to help other communities implement the strategies first embraced by the faith community in Modesto.

The spiritual leaders agreed to require a four-month premarital preparation process before they would marry anyone. They also required couples to take a premarital inventory and then receive a minimum of two feedback counseling sessions prior to the wedding. Older mentor couples were enlisted to come alongside younger couples and assist them in their premarital journey. Couples were also encouraged to attend an Engaged Encounter seminar to enhance their communication skills.

Since the signing of that first CMP, there have been some startling changes in the community:

- Modesto's divorce rate has dropped 52.6 percent. In the three years prior to the signing of the marriage policy, Stanislaus County (where Modesto is located) averaged 6.68 divorces per 1,000 population. In the year 2000 the rate was 3.16 per 1,000 population.
- The marriage rate in Stanislaus County also rose 12 percent during a time period when the marriage rate in the United States dropped 18 percent.[17]
- Between 1991 and 1997, the high school drop out rate in Modesto declined 20 percent.[18]
- The teen pregnancy rate dropped 30 percent, as compared to a 15 percent decrease in the general population of the United States.[19]

CMP have been adopted in other communities with positive results as well. More research is needed to determine if these trends are related to the CMP, but initial studies suggest they may be. Researchers Stan Weed and Paul Birch compared the divorce rate five years before and up to seven years after adoption of a Community Marriage Policy in 122 counties throughout the United States. For comparison purposes, they also looked at divorce rates in demographically similar counties without a Community Marriage Policy.[20] Their study found that counties with a Community

Marriage Policy averaged a 17.5 percent decrease in divorce as compared to an 8.1 percent decrease non-CMP counties. This decline holds even when accounting for such factors as poverty rates, cohabitation rates, and whether the county is urban or rural.[21]

"We've looked at this data 100 different ways and the bottom line for us is a Community Marriage Policy signing, and all other activities associated with it, brings the divorce rate down and creates a stronger culture for marriage."[22]

Another powerful example of a comprehensive plan is the marriage initiative in Grand Rapids, Michigan. In 1996 the Greater Grand Rapids Marriage Policy was put in place when clergy and civic leaders, under the leadership of Kentwood Mayor Bill Hardiman, made a public commitment to promote marriage and stable families in their community. Four task forces were formed under a fifty-member steering committee to determine ways that different sectors of the community could help reach the goal of a 25 percent reduction in divorces and a 25 percent reduction in the number of children raised by one parent.

- A judicial/legal task force encouraged judges to require premarital counseling for any couples seeking a civil ceremony of marriage. This task force also encouraged lawyers to suggest counseling for couples initiating divorce proceedings.
- A clergy task force adopted a strategy similar to CMP, and worked to strengthen the scope of premarital counseling and workshops for engaged couples. Local churches have been encouraged to offer enrichment seminars and other programs to strengthen existing marriages. Seminars for couples in crisis and programs for separated couples were also promoted by the clergy in the community.
- A health/mental health task force sought to develop programs to strengthen marriages, as well as to lobby insurance companies to make premarital counseling a covered benefit.
- Business task force members worked on studies to show businesses the positive impact of successful marriages on companies. They also looked into business practices that would encourage more successful marriages amongst employees.

Since 1996, YWAM Family Ministries and Marriage Savers have collaborated in numerous American communities to organize coalitions of clergy and civic leaders for the purpose of strengthening marriages and lowering divorce rates. At least three communities have achieved a 50 percent drop in their divorce rates. However, most gains, though substantial, have been more modest. Even with 219 communities embracing this initiative, we are still a long way from seeing a 50 percent drop nationwide. These initiatives require intensive time investment from a few committed people and a rich measure of the grace of God. Developing a broad-based community coalition requires patience, perseverance, and good communication skills. Community leaders usually agree about the importance of marriage and family, but there is vast range of opinion on what steps should be implemented to create and maintain healthy families.

A Marriage Movement Is Born

Thankfully, these wonderful examples of change in communities are not isolated events. The divorce culture that dominates American society is beginning to be transformed by a growing and influential marriage movement in the United States. Another marriage initiative, First Things First,[23] is taking place in Chattanooga, Tennessee. This nationally recognized program received a large federal grant to help them promote healthy families. First Things First has successfully organized a multifaceted, multisectored coalition of over one hundred agencies and organizations in the community. Their shared goals are to reduce divorce, to reduce out-of-wedlock pregnancies, and to increase the involvement of fathers in the lives of their children.

Some American states have proposed comprehensive plans to address the devastating social and economic impact of broken marriages on the lives of its citizens. In 1999, then-Governor Keating of Oklahoma launched the Oklahoma Marriage Initiative with the stated goal of reducing the divorce rate in his state 30 percent by the year 2010. Oklahoma at one time had the second highest divorce rate of any state in the nation. Keating's broad-based innovative plan is seeking to effect society for the public good by working through faith-based initiatives, public-sector programs, educational thrusts, and media campaigns.

Bringing transformation involves education as well; we must target young people before they announce their engagements and start planning their weddings. For example, several years ago, the state of Florida implemented a program requiring high school seniors to complete a marriage preparation and relationship skills course as a prerequisite to obtaining a high school diploma.

A handful of states have focused on premarital counseling and "covenant marriage" legislation. Louisiana, Florida, and Arkansas are seeking change through the sphere of government; their elected representatives have enacted legislation giving couples the option of entering into a "covenant marriage." Couples choosing this type of marriage waive their rights to a no-fault divorce and commit themselves to counseling prior to the granting of any future divorce. Minnesota and Florida offer incentives for engaged couples by reducing their marriage license fees if they complete premarital counseling programs.

Some states even require premarital education before a wedding license will be issued. Judge Sheridan successfully convinced those who perform civil wedding ceremonies in Lenawee County, Michigan, to require couples to participate in premarital training and counseling before conducting the wedding. Thus, Lenawee County became the first county in the United States where couples could not obtain a wedding license without first going through some form of premarital education.

These are encouraging stories on a local community level, but we must also engage this issue on a national level to increase the speed of transformation. A culture-changing coalition of policy makers, government officials, researchers, family life educators, mental health professionals, clergy, and mentor couples have come together with the goal of strengthening and preserving marriage. The movement's most identifiable national expression is the Washington, D.C., Coalition for Marriage, Family and Couple Education (CMFCE).

"The CMFCE serves as an information exchange to help couples locate marriage and relationship courses; to help professionals, clergy and lay educators locate training programs and materials; to connect those with an interest in continuing development of the field; to build community partnerships and support legislation and research; to promote the effectiveness of the courses and increase their availability in the community."[24]

Understanding Truth Will Support a Marriage Culture

There is no way to estimate the number of couples who pull back from the brink of divorce. But recent research shows that couples who do stick it out through difficult times are often rewarded with a far better relationship than they could ever imagine. The story of Dan and Paige Wiersgalla is only one illustration of how a couple can go from the brink of divorce to a satisfying and fulfilling marriage. Linda Waite, a professor of sociology at the University of Chicago, surveyed 3,500 couples whose marriages were in trouble and came up with these results: "Three-fifths of those who said their marriage was unhappy in the late '80s and who stayed married, rated this same marriage as either 'very happy' or 'quite happy' when reinterviewed in the early 1990s. The worst marriages showed the most dramatic improvement: 77 percent of married people who rated their marriage as very unhappy (a '1' on a scale of 1 to 7) in the late eighties said that the same marriage was either quite happy '6' or very happy '7' five years later."[25]

These statistics don't prove that couples who divorce could have developed a better marriage by staying together. But they do confirm that bad times in marriage are not as permanent as is sometimes assumed. Many couples in trouble say the marriage is going downhill and don't stick around until it rebounds. Instead, they invoke the no-fault divorce laws available in all fifty states. No-fault divorce laws, around since 1969, were intended to help couples avoid permanent unhappiness, but they did not take into account the fact that the majority of marriages in trouble can actually be turned around with the proper input and support. Ultimately, no-fault divorce laws touched off a national divorce epidemic that would leave women and children in poverty, kids emotionally devastated, and the institution of marriage crippled.

Policy makers, lawyers, and the judicial system embraced the myth that divorce was the best way to extract couples from a painful destructive relationship. However, several recent studies reveal a different picture. Less than a third of divorces result from marriages where abuse, neglect, or highly volatile fighting are the norm. Instead, over 60 percent of marriages break apart because of increasing loneliness, boredom, or small, unvoiced resentments.[26] Marriage experts say most of these symptoms can be repaired and marriages restored, but couples often lose hope before getting the right kind of help.

What Does This Mean for the Nations?

YWAM Family Ministry workers on six continents are offering marriage and parenting seminars regularly. Family and marriage issues are universal felt needs that transcend cultural and personal diversity. Everywhere, people are concerned about their families. The specific areas of concern may be dissimilar in different societies, but the burden for family life is universal. People care about their children, their marriages, and the breakdown of family life taking place around them.

Why should a predominately American initiative be of interest to the rest of the world and how does this relate to the Lord's mandate to "make disciples of all nations" (Matt. 28:19)? First, although America leads the world in divorce rates, it is not unique as a divorce culture. The rest of the world, unfortunately, is moving in the same direction. Korea, for example, now suffers a 42 percent divorce rate even though divorce was almost unknown there a few years ago.[27]

Second, the body of Christ can adopt the two-fold strategy of establishing Community Marriage Policies and training of mentor couples, which are transferable to most cultures. As clergy work together to strengthen marriages, they demonstrate the heart of Jesus' prayer in John 17:21 "that all of them may be one."

Mentoring, another word for discipling, is central to our Lord's call to effect change among the nations. What better way to impact a nation than to send out mentor couples, two by two, similar to what Jesus did with the disciples in Luke 10:1? We can imagine nothing more effective than a seasoned, committed, godly husband-and-wife team mentoring young men and women in relationship skills and the ways of the Lord. Older couples can help younger couples create models of marital life that demonstrate the "great mystery" of "Christ and the church" that Paul mentions in Ephesians

5:32. Training these couples to love the Lord with all their heart and to love one another as themselves is at the heart of transforming cultures and discipling nations.

YWAM has also helped promote this marriage-saving vision in a limited number of countries outside the USA. We conducted a Marriage Savers training session for over 1,500 pastors, Christian leaders, and mentor couples in Seoul, South Korea, in January 2001 in partnership with Sarang Church and the Family Ministry Institute of Korea. Reports and interviews from this seminar were widely distributed among Korean pastors around the world.

Marriage Savers training seminars and informational workshops have been conducted across Europe and North America as well. Students that attend YWAM Family Ministry Schools around the world are exposed to the basic concepts and are trained in the resources used to mentor couples. Those students are going back to their countries and are beginning to impact their culture with these tools. Our involvement is still in the embryonic stage, but we anticipate further growth in this ministry. Working with community-based coalitions of clergy and civic leaders is one practical way for YWAMers to disciple nations and influence societies.

YWAM's Family Ministry network is currently working in over thirty nations of the world promoting strong marriages and healthy families. More than one thousand families participated in family camp programs throughout Western, Eastern, and Central Europe in the summer of 2006. Participants were challenged to live out the kingdom of God in their families and marriages and to reach out to the nations as a family. These families are the hope for change in their own and other nations.

Through these dedicated workers around the world, marriages and families are being transformed in such diverse places as Mongolia, Rwanda, Kyrgyzstan, France, and Argentina. In Minsk, Belarus, two of our workers addressed the issues of healthy families, marriages, and parenting in a seminar for sixty-eight psychologists and social workers. The interest among people was so high that these YWAMers were interviewed on national TV and were able to speak to the entire nation about marriage and family issues.

Hope for the Future

Cultures are being transformed as marriages and families are changed. Divorce cultures can be transformed into societies that honor the marriage covenant. As a result, social institutions are being changed. Nations currently moving toward a divorce culture can be turned around. There is hope for individual families and there is hope for the societal institutions that are built on the foundation of healthy families. This hope, of course, is found in the redeeming power of God's love and the transforming grace of Jesus Christ.

Since, in Judge Sheridan's words, families are "small civilizations" and "the death of a family is the death of a small civilization," it is our hope and belief that the "rebirth of families" will lead to the "rebirth of small civilizations." These "small civilizations" have the capacity to transform the larger civilizations of the world and to extend God's kingdom into the uttermost parts of the world.

Notes

1. Chief Justice James Sheridan, conversation with author.

2. George Gallop Jr. quoted in Michael McManus, *A Manual To Create A Marriage Savers Congregation* (Potomac, Md.: Marriage Savers, 2003), 1.

3. National Center for Health Statistics, www.cdc.gov/nchs/ (accessed February 2004).

4. "America's Families and Living Arrangements, 2000," United States Census Bureau, www.census.gov/prod/2001pubs/p20–537.pdf (accessed February 2004).

5. Ibid.

6. Patrick F. Fagan and Robert Rector, "The Effects of Divorce on America," The Heritage Foundation *Backgrounder* no. 1373 (June 5, 2000): 5.

7. Ibid.

8. Robert Whelan, *Broken Homes and Battered Children* (Family Education Trust, 1994), quoted in Fagan and Rector, "The Effects of Divorce on America," 5.

9. Ibid.

10. Sara McLanahan and Gary Sandefur, *Growing Up With Single Parents: What Hurts, What Helps* (Cambridge, Mass.: Harvard University Press, 1994).

11. Judith S. Wallerstein, Julia M. Lewis, and Sandra Blakeslee, *The Unexpected Legacy of Divorce, A 25 Year Landmark Study* (New York: Hyperion, 2000), 299.

12. Ibid, 29.

13. Sheridan, conversation with author.

14. Barbara Souters, "Hanging Together," *World* 16, no. 5 (February 10, 2001): 29–30.

15. For more information about Retrouvaille, go to www.retrouvaille.org.

16. International Center For Reconciling God's Way, www.reconcilinggodsway.com.

17. Michael J. McManus, "Why Is It in Government's Interest to Save Marriages?" Public Hearing on Marriage Sponsored by The New York Family Policy Council, January 14, 2002.

18. Ibid.

19. Ibid.

20. Brooke Adams, "Could 'Marriage Policy' Cut Utah's Divorce Rate?" *The Salt Lake Tribune* (January 11, 2003).

21. Ibid.

22. Ibid.

23. First Things First, 701 Cherokee Blvd., Suite 230, Chattanooga, TN, 37405, or www.firstthings.org.

24. "Smart Marriages, Happy Families," brochure, The Seventh Annual Conference of the Coalition for Marriage, Family and Couples Education, Reno/Lake Tahoe, June 26–29, 2003.

25. Linda J. Waite and Maggie Gallagher, *The Case for Marriage: Why Married People Are Happier, Healthier, and Better Off Financially* (New York: Doubleday, 2000), 148.

26. Paul Amato and Alan Booth, *A Generation at Risk* (Harvard University Press, 1997).

27. Dr. Dong Sup Chung, lecture, Marriage Savers conference at Sarang Presbyterian Church, Seoul, South Korea, Jan. 16, 2001. Note: Divorce rates are generally calculated by comparing the number of new divorces to the number of new marriages in a given time period.

God, who created us, best knows how we would best govern ourselves. So what does the Bible teach about government? Ana takes us on a journey to examine God's purposes for government, the values and principles which shape the way a government operates, and how we as believers are to relate to it. Government touches every sphere of life, so understanding God's perspective gives us new insight on how to pray and what to work toward as we interact with the authority structures of our nations.

Bible and Government

Ana Roncal Villanueva

Throughout the history of Christianity, Jesus' mandate of Matthew 28, "therefore go and make disciples," has remained the source of inspiration for thousands who engage in missions worldwide. However, his mandate to "disciple the nations" is not just a matter of mobilization. If our expectations of change are to see whole nations prosper in all spheres of life, we must consider the second part of the mandate: "teaching them to obey everything I have commanded you" (Matt. 28:20). The devastating struggles of today's world in international politics and economic justice constitute a call to review the principles of government given in the Bible. These principles provide the keys to moving nations toward enjoying the peace and prosperity of biblical Christianity.

In today's wide spectrum of political alternatives, democracy is shown as the one rendering the best results, and it is presented as a universally valid system. However, many troubled nations discover that what has worked in other places fails for them[1] or is extremely hard to achieve. Our intention here is to discover a biblical alternative, a foundation from which those societies can achieve stability and grow without crippling dependency on others. With all of today's sophisticated global politics and international finances, the Bible is still the source of ideas that uphold individual freedom and development, the source of wisdom that has proven to bring blessings to individuals and nations alike.

Ideologies and descriptions of the term *ideology* abound.[2] They are formulated from different perspectives about the nature of man, where life originates, and whether it has a purpose or not. The ideology that underlies this discussion is based on the Bible as the Truth revealed by God to man in order to understand all issues pertaining to life, civil government included. Our perspective then is *theistic*;[3] this implies that these principles are universally valid in all times and places, for they emanate from the Creator of everything (Col. 1:15–20). Let us then look at the development of the underlying values and principles of the biblical frame of government through God's dealings with Israel in the Old Testament, and then how Jesus and the early church embraced that in the New Testament. We can then obtain a comprehensive biblical view of government and what that might mean to bring blessing to the nations in applying its principles today.

The Old Testament: The Purpose of Civil Government

Where do we start to understand the origins and purpose of civil government? Let us consider briefly the earliest records of man's history according to the Bible. Following this we will explore biblical principles and values in the account of Israel's becoming a nation in the book of Exodus.

According to the account of Creation in Genesis, in the beginning government was no issue for humankind. Being in close relation to God, Adam and Eve had a command to subdue the earth and rule over everything given to them so that they could be "fruitful" in all aspects of life (Gen. 1:28). Human dominion, however, was to take place within a certain frame of instructions given in order to protect them from a harmful choice (Gen. 2:15–17).

At this point, government had no connotation of men ruling over other men. Freedom and order in a way we cannot fathom today were the conditions of the world God had created for mankind's delight and development. But man's original sin broke the basic order of relationship between himself and God and the way creation should be governed (Gen. 1:28–30). What we see after Genesis 3 are the progressive consequences of sin.

As the face of God vanishes from man's conscience, he loses the ability to rule himself and rule over creation. Following Adam and Eve's original sin, Cain kills Abel. To stop men from self-extermination, God puts a mark on Cain so that anyone could know there would be a harsh punishment for taking his life. In this way, the first measure of civil protection was given on earth in order to protect man from his own fallenness (Gen. 4:15).

In Genesis chapters three to eleven, we see the intended order for relationships between individuals, marriage, family, and the local and international community deteriorate rapidly as the progression of sin affects dominion and authority in every level of society. Government was established by God to protect life according to his principles, but it can easily become corrupted by humanistic *politics,* or the striving for power in a society. This definition is commonly used in the discipline of political science at secular universities; in that environment there is no explicit goal to find solutions for societies, just to understand the strife for power among different groups. Nations founded upon a humanistic perspective view politics—as Cain, Lamech, and Nimrod did in these early chapters—as the means for power to achieve personal or group interests, not as a source of God's authority on earth to protect societies from the fallen nature of man. We must pray and work to restore biblical foundations to the nations.

The Biblical Principles of Government

God's instructions to Israel in the earliest days of their becoming a nation give much insight into the foundations of biblical practices for governing a nation.

> And God spoke all these words: "I am the LORD your God, who brought you out of Egypt, out of the land of slavery." (Exod. 20:1–2)

With those words God gave the whole of Israel a covenant law they would have to observe. At the time of Israel's birth as a nation, authority and tyranny were almost synonymous, as seen in the empires of Egypt, Assyria, and others. Into this context God brings in a completely new foundation for government. He gives Israel a set of laws that are for the protection and blessing of all, and even the leadership of the nation is bound to obey them. The biblical principles of government are shown in Israel's story in almost sequential form.

1. The beginning of the ideology: a Person. God addresses Israel in the wilderness very soon after their dramatic release from slavery in Egypt and says, "I am the LORD your God." God begins not with the law but with his self-introduction, and this draws the people's attention toward himself as Creator of life, to a relationship rather than a list of laws to follow. Because of who he is, *he* stands as the best source of ideas to govern a nation, defining the ideology of absolutes that will make any nation successful.

The next phrase, "who brought you out of Egypt, out of the land of slavery," complements God's self-introduction. God wants to lead them into a new stage, but Israel does not have to make a blind leap of faith or risk the unknown. They have a record of what God has already done for them, which shows that following God benefits the whole of the people.

A great difference between Judeo-Christian faith and other religions lies precisely here: Christianity is not a faith only for eternity, but for here and now. God is present as *immanent,*[4] active in history with wisdom and truth for all aspects of life, even on a national level. In the Old Testament we see God is involved not just in Israel's history but in the history of all nations. The prophet Isaiah mentions, in a passage that deals with difficult international affairs for Israel, the wonderful presence of Emmanuel in the midst of men and their worries (Isa. 7:14). As no other god, he has never left humankind alone, but keeps showing his power to bless nations as they embrace his principles.

God's intention for the proper role of authority shows in the Old Testament, both through modeling the proper use of authority as he is Lord over Israel and in the statutes he gives them to live by. Authority is to be exercised on behalf of the people for protection, guidance, and deliverance. The New Testament, through the life of Jesus and the teachings he leaves his people to follow, also demonstrates that the purpose of authority is for the ultimate good of those governed. In contrast to God's model, genuine commitment to the people's welfare is greatly missed by political parties, politicians, and world economic organizations today.[5] Governments easily sink into corruption as they serve the interests of favored groups which in turn provide the government officials with special benefits.

2. Education. Exodus narrates an event that would be challenging for any society at any point in history. A people who had known slavery for 400 years was now invited to function as a free nation. In Exodus 18:5–27, before Moses begins to lead the nation, his father-in-law, Jethro, gives him some crucial counsel, the most important of which is:

> Teach them the decrees and laws,
> and show them the way to live,
> and the duties they are to perform. (Exod. 18:20)

The first "measure" taken as Israel started a free life in the wilderness was that of instructing the whole of the people. When God gave Israel a law he did not call a few elders who later could dominate the rest. He summoned up the whole of Israel for all to hear, learn, and be empowered to live free and productive lives according to that law (Exod. 20:1–17).

Jethro's instructions also provide a complete perspective of what education is all about. The content of education is first to address all aspects of life, and then the practical aspects of conduct and their duties as members of their society. It is important to notice that the people would be instructed both about their "rights" and their obligations, a perspective of mutual responsibility which is missing in the human rights rhetoric today. This event takes place before any other, in order that every individual may take responsibility and exercise self-government, so that the need for a coercive government would be minimal and Israel would be a governable society.

Besides the charge to instruct all the people, God establishes a method of education by which all were to be instructed. Israel was an oral, illiterate society at that time, as many needy nations are in our day. The extensive use of electronic communications has also created an oral culture in the midst of literate nations today, so it is worth time and effort to review the characteristics of God's way of communicating and teaching a whole nation.

As God did through Moses,[6] parents are to repeat the stories and instructions as they live out the values before their children in all instances of family life (Deut. 11:19–21). This will establish a cultural heritage of values and knowledge leading to godly living pertaining to every aspect of life, which ensures generational blessings. They, in turn, may delegate a portion of their children's education to individuals and a system outside their home, but these values must be consistently passed on in every venue in order to maintain a strong consensus of values throughout society.

3. Self-government. An uneducated people ignorant of a moral law will conform to a society where lawlessness reigns. This is the condition of nations where education of the majority has been neglected due to a discriminatory view of society by those in power. The resulting discontent carries those nations to conditions where the law has no effect at all. The people, abandoned and turned into masses with no dignity, resent their authorities and laws which do not bring any satisfaction to them. The situation is the seedbed for general corruption, internal conflict, vindicating ideologies, and terrorism.

The biblical concept of "civil government" starts with the individual, empowered by his obedience to the moral law of God as expressed in civilized behavior; this system of law requires that authorities uphold it. The idea given in Exodus 18 is that the need for force to ensure that citizens obey the nation's law decreases as more individuals exercise self-government.

When campaigning for elections in troubled nations, candidates deal with issues like internal security, terrorism, or sexual abuse with promises of increasing the numbers of internal police, or of applying the death penalty to rapists and terrorists the same. As much as this may seem to meet the felt needs of the nation at the time, they are ignoring the basic problems at the basis of society, which are to be dealt with by the principles of education and inculcated values we have mentioned before.

4. National identity. Modern social sciences recognize the need for a society to build on two foundations in order that their civil institutions, the state, and the social order may be stable and effective.[7] A society must be able to count not only on individuals with a strong sense of identity and personal values, but also on the fact that those individuals are united by a collective conscience.

Any attempt to find consensus about the source and nature of human rights will face difficulties in the world today. There is diversity of opinions about the status of women, ethnic and social groups, foreigners, and segments of society. The reality is that international organizations which promote human rights actually see these rights hindered by the nonbiblical aspects of culture and religion in every society. Nations are confronted with the need to discover and build their societies on common principles and values, valid for all societies. By providing absolutes originating in the person of God, biblical Christianity constitutes a sure source for individual and collective identity. As more individuals find identity in Christ through evangelism, this identity becomes a collective, mutual conscience of a people who consider themselves equal, with the same rights.

In nations where discrimination has been the cause of a fragmented national identity, there is a need for national reconciliation. This is a biblical concept[8] that places Christians in a key role to achieve national unity. This may require actions ranging from symbolic public acts of repentance and forgiveness to government plans to make restitution and restore legal and economic justice to those sectors of society which suffered historic discrimination.

5. *Authority.* One of the greatest errors of interpreting biblical history in many authoritarian cultures concerns Moses as a leadership figure. He is exhibited as a model of absolute authority, a *caudillo,*[9] the hero who leads a group to victory by his unique leadership gift. In this model, it is taught that the people of Israel had to completely submit to Moses; therefore the church and society must completely submit to a dominant individual in authority as well. This faulty perspective condones a "theocracy" which quickly becomes an authoritarian style of government exercised by one "anointed" person, "used by God" to dominate people. Because of this theology, the church has been plagued with authoritarianism, alliances with political authorities, and abuses of all kinds in the name of religion.

This interpretation misses the fact that Moses was strongly discouraged from standing alone as an authority in the beginning of Israel's civil life as a nation. He led as part of a core team of three, in consultation with a group of seventy, with authority delegated to thousands who administered justice at a local, regional, and national level. The true model God gave Israel was the law given to the whole of the people, regardless of age, sex, and condition, so that the authority of the law might rest in all and everyone, not just in one man or even a group of them. This is what constitutes a real theocracy, the real kingdom of God: God reigning over every individual's conscience and behavior so that his government is manifest through every individual's actions in society. Likewise, the *elected* authorities should defend, by *delegation,* the authority and sovereignty of every individual over his own life, and therefore of all the people.

The pagan scheme of authority, by which sections of the population are deprived of their God-given authority by imposition or by a mentality of dependence or fear, is as ancient as the history of man separated from God. When deeply rooted in the history and culture of a nation, the authoritarian mentality will be the main hindrance to all attempts to turn a nation toward freedom and responsibility.

6. Consensus or "social contract." Adding to the principle of collective identity, most philosophers and sociologists since Jean Jacques Rousseau in the eighteenth century have argued that a society requires a set of rules by which they can govern themselves. These rules embraced by at least a majority must be considered and compiled by the authorities so that they constitute the legal framework sustaining a society in all its spheres.

Rousseau is widely known as the first who formulated the concept of a "social contract." But when societies attempt to implement such a contract without a foundation of biblical truth, they face a problem. If that contract originates in human will, who decides what are the best norms for all? This is a huge hindrance in society, for what seems right to some is seen from a different standpoint by others. That is the case with the status of foreigners, the death penalty, abortion, nuclear development, and other issues in both internal and external affairs.

However, about three thousand years before Rousseau, a social contract or covenant which could overcome that hindrance was made in the nation of Israel. The fact that its stipulations come from a supreme source, and that they are based on each person's identity in God, made it agreeable to all.[10] As explained below, the tenth commandment points to the transforming work of Jesus Christ in the inner man, which makes it possible to achieve the abolishing of differences and discrimination, not by external regulations, but from the heart of every individual (Eph. 2:14–22). The need for consensus upon which to build the social contract necessary to function as a society points again to the need for evangelism and education instead of imposition of rule by a civil government.

Authorities, as well as the people, must take into account that any government effort to achieve consensus will succeed only in the measure a society knows the source of reconciliation and understands the nature of true integration in Christ. Otherwise it will be a powerless effort consisting of a few material restitutions, which will not make a long-range impact in the individuals' consciences and therefore, will not achieve permanent unity.

7. Property. Throughout history we see a common element in many societies: poverty of the majority goes along with ownership by a minority. No wonder property is an issue of first importance in the law God gave to his people.

God has given man stewardship over his possessions. A primary "property" is his own conscience, by which he enjoys freedom of thought and opinion. Material property is protected as well, when the Decalogue (the Ten Commandments) states "you shall not steal ... you shall not covet" (Exod. 20:15, 17). It is also clear in the Scriptures that the whole of the land is God's, allotted to each family. The laws to preserve the property in the hands of the original owners, and those to avoid unlimited indebtedness made sure Israel would be a nation of *owners,* who could create wealth derived from their own possessions.[11]

We see a process by which Israel undergoes an amazing transformation from a group of slaves into a society of entrepreneurs. The idea has been "rediscovered" by contemporary economists, and considered a real revolution bringing hope to poor nations of the world.

Values from the Decalogue

Next to God's self-introduction, affirming himself as the source of life and truth from which any society must start, we find a list of commandments. These commandments affirm *values* of human life, authority, family, and property as aspects of life that must be respected and protected by all. Although other nations had similar codes, the law of Israel affirmed the greatest good and protection for the rights of every man, without discrimination of sex, age, social condition, or ethnic origin, something unthinkable at that time. This code would defend and champion absolute values, which in turn would ensure a just and stable order for society.

First Commandment: true morals. "You shall have no other gods before me." In Exodus 20:3 God requires Israel to follow him alone. God required them to build their lives and their nation on the foundation of his truth, not a mixture of many ideas and values derived from the cultures around them. The truth that man has been created by God and in God's own image ensures dignity and value for every member of society. It is the foundation for all moral concepts upon which formal law and social norms must rest.

Second Commandment: foundation of absolutes. In Exodus 20:4 God adds "you shall not make for yourself any idol." Representing God by any created thing is qualified as sin with very bad consequences, and Paul explains why in the book of Romans:

> [They] exchanged the glory of the immortal God for images made to look like mortal man and birds and animals and reptiles. Therefore God gave them over in the sinful desires of their hearts. . . . They have become filled with every kind of wickedness, evil, greed and depravity. (Rom. 1:23–24, 29)

God forbids Israel to create a different god, a process which he knew would lead to their building on a different source of values for individuals and societies. His intention was to protect them from the consequences described in Romans 1 when man worships idols of his own creation. Humanistic relativism, where each one determines what is true and valuable and the means to achieve it, leads to worshipping the gods of power, reputation, and material prosperity. The outcome of a society where money and power are supreme values is easy to foresee: a small, privileged elite with tremendous economic and social gaps between the rich and the poor, leading to conflicts as the powerless rebel.

Commandments 3–9: building on absolutes. Any society needs to build on true principles and values upon which all its members can agree. Who God is, and what he has said is valuable, are the absolutes upon which we must build all aspects of life. The first two commandments, which establish God as the sovereign, uncreated Ruler of the Universe and man being made in his image, impart value and dignity to every human life. From this foundation, eight other commandments follow. Together, these Ten Commandments point to universal values a society must uphold to empower individuals and protect them from exploitation:

	Content	*Value*
Third Commandment	Misuse of the name of God	God's image/Integrity of faith
Fourth Commandment	Observance of rest	Communion with God/ Quality of life
Fifth Commandment	Honoring parents	Family/authority figures
Sixth Commandment	Against murder	Individual life
Seventh Commandment	Against adultery	Marriage
Eight Commandment	Against stealing	Private property
Ninth Commandment	Against false testimony	Reputation/integrity

Tenth Commandment: cornerstone of civil government. Obviously, good laws are no guarantee of effective government. Almost all nations have laws defining behaviors that must be followed in society. The elections of many countries are based on promises of reform in specific areas of corruption. So why is there corruption in nations with many good laws, and why do promised reforms prove ineffective? In Exodus 20:17 we have the key: God gives Israel a law that not only defined behavior but spoke to the heart attitude behind it.

This brings the idea of law into another realm. "Thou shall not covet" requires obedience to the law from the heart, not only good external behavior. If we are honest enough to acknowledge the constant fight with personal sin, we must conclude that perfect obedience to the law cannot be humanly fulfilled. In that way, the law points to the need for man's redemption. God is instructing a nation to be governable, but is also pointing to the fact that the fallen human race cannot guarantee its governability.

Reconstructing a model of principles in an attempt to gain the benefits of stability and prosperity will not be enough for a nation or an individual to build on. While living apart from God, man can only be influenced from outside of himself through the promise of benefit and the threat of punishment, requiring more and more external controls to ensure conformity to society's laws. Christ at work within the human heart enables people to follow the law from the heart. No system of government can replace that moral foundation which Christianity provides. This links the Old and New Testaments and provides a perspective of biblical government: God's model is made possible only to the degree that societies experience Jesus' redemption.

The Biblical Way of Government: A System Shaped by the Right Ideas

As biblical principles and values are embraced by a society, they will be reproduced in the way it organizes its institutions in order to satisfy the needs of a people which knows its rights and duties. A people who has embraced biblical values will ensure certain basic elements are included in their framework of government: constitutionality, representation, separation of powers, decentralization, justice, and national defense.

Constitutionality—Fixed law

It is common for nations suffering constant political turmoil to continually change their basic constitution. Laws are issued to accommodate the interests of the government in power at the moment. The idea of a basic, fixed constitution originates when Moses presents the people a law in the form of a covenant with God. Throughout Israel's history, the law given by God remained as the first and ultimate norm, and all authorities were supposed to know and respect it. The importance of respecting that fixed law is mentioned around forty times in the Old Testament, including here:

> Hear now, O Israel, the decrees and laws I am about to teach you. Follow them so that you may live and may go in and take possession of the land that the Lord, the God of your fathers, is giving you. Do not add to what I command you and do not subtract from it, but keep the commands of the Lord your God that I give you. (Deut. 4:1–2)

Juridical stability, a set of laws that will not be changed easily by different governments, is necessary not only for the order of society but to guarantee the best atmosphere for business and investment in a nation. Investors will not risk their money nor their properties in a country where laws change with the governments.

Representation

Today's democracy is based on the people electing authorities to represent them in the decision-making process. The biblical model of government is one of close representation. To achieve this does not seem easy in view of the increase of population, but the biblical model shows two key elements: popular elections and local authority.

Popular elections. The Greeks were not the first to promote this means of selecting leadership. The true history of free popular elections began around the year 1500 BC with Jethro's advice to Moses. Jethro's counsel was to "select capable men from all the people—men who fear God, trustworthy men who hate dishonest gain—and appoint them as officials over thousands, hundreds, fifties and tens" (Exod. 18:21). However, in Deuteronomy Moses recounts following a different means of selecting leaders: "Choose some wise, understanding and respected men from each one of your tribes, and I will set them over you" (Deut. 1:13). He understood that the people needed to select their own leaders, those they knew and trusted to oversee justice dispensed throughout the nation. A group of recently freed slaves had free elections as the first act of its political life. Nobody—not even Moses, educated according to the best standards of the time in Egypt—dared to suggest that it was too soon to vote.

Local authorities. The same passage on elections shows the people voted in every tribe and the authorities were elected in proportion to numbers of population. The "representation" purported by democracy is usually pure metaphor as voters and those they are voting for rarely meet or have any degree of relationship. In contrast, the representation in the Old Testament model was real, as leaders were chosen from the people they were to lead, which ensured the people would have authorities who understood and identified with their issues. Although in principle that's what our democracy is like, and it used to be more locally representative, nations now have such large populations that this principle is not as closely adhered to as it should be to make an effective representative government.

Separation of powers

It is commonly accepted that the separation of powers, a basic condition in any modern state today, is a French contribution to politics. Although Montesquieu mentioned it in 1748 in his work "The Spirit of the Laws,"[12] such separation was present in the model of government for Israel about 3,300 years prior to his writings. The different functions of government were clearly defined in the Hebrew mentality. In Isaiah 33:22 we read:

> For the LORD is our judge,
>   the LORD is our lawgiver,
>   the LORD is our King;
>   it is he who will save us.

As we read the Old Testament history, we find judges who legislated and applied the law. Moses was accompanied by a group of seventy elders who represented the tribes[13] and by other leaders in areas of administration and in the army.[14] He was instructed by Jethro not to remain alone as authority over the people.

Even as God gave instructions for a representative form of government, he laid out the boundaries for a monarchy in anticipation that the people might ask for this form of government at some point in their future. The king's power was to be limited by a superior fixed law and his functions as ruler were limited (Deut. 17:14–20). However, as Israel abandoned God's law, distortion of the social and economic structures of the nation are recorded in the judgments of the prophets and the succinct accounts in the books of Kings and Chronicles (see, for example, 1 Kings 21).

Decentralization

Underdeveloped nations commonly have centralized administrative schemes. Most of their institutions of government are situated in the capital city, which contributes to the underdevelopment in other geographical areas of the country. With time, not only government institutions, but the best schools and universities, the businesses, and the best of the arts and entertainment will be also centered in one or a few main cities. The centralization of institutions favors the centralization of power which leads to corruption and indifference toward the needs of the people.

Jethro's counsel in Exodus 18 ensured people would have accessible authorities to attend their needs. We see the outworking of this principle in Deuteronomy where Moses states that in every trial "all the elders of the town nearest the body" (Deut. 21:6) should officiate as judges. That means that authorities were found in every city of Israel. In the beginning of Israel's history there was nothing like an imperial palace, typical of pagan empires. The judge Deborah administered justice under a palm tree (Judges 4:5).

Justice—Primary role of the State

Another foundational principle we can draw from Exodus is that the priority for government institutions was to preserve justice. Today underdeveloped nations have copied the structure of developed nations, assigning the state many different roles—aid to the needy, health, education—and commonly, the judicial system is deficient and fails to provide justice. In Israel, the state's main function was that of preserving the order of society so that the population could have peace and stability in all other spheres. The concept of justice was extremely important in the Hebrew mentality and recognized as basic for the welfare of the nation.[15] A complete judicial system with two key elements, due trials, and laws of restitution, was installed for all to have access to justice (Deut. 19:1–21).

National Defense vs. Internal Security

In the Bible, an army is a need of first order to serve the people by defending them from foreign attack (Num. 1:3; 10:9). The army wasn't permanent but was called upon in times of danger; therefore, taxation was not needed. Today we find very different ideas about the military:

- A support for a dictator to stay in power in a subjected nation
- A force to face increasing internal corruption
- A permanent force ready to invade nations for economic objectives
- A bulwark to install a system of government in an alien nation

None of these purposes correspond to the biblical model. Israel did not have internal police forces to keep order or exercise internal domination. The moral problems and corruption of some nations are the reason why there is a perceived need for increasing numbers of national police, while their foreign defense is extremely weak.

Conclusion: An Open System of Government

The biblical principles of government do not promote a rigid system but allow a diversity of systems—constitutional monarchy, presidential, parliamentary—which do not endanger freedoms. The various instruments of government champion participation and the responsibility of the citizens, while the state simply preserves the legal framework that sustains society. They are means for the power of the people to be expressed in authorities and institutions so that these both can achieve the goals of the whole of society for the benefit of all.

The New Testament: Believers and Civil Government

So how did Jesus and the apostles view civil government? God gave clear principles and a model in the Old Testament as Israel began its existence; as a sovereign people they had their own laws and systems. During the time of the New Testament, the Jews were a conquered people, so Jesus' and the apostles' teaching focuses primarily on how to respond to unjust government.

Jesus: Addressing political issues

Jesus' final words to his disciples were to "make disciples of all nations . . . teaching them to obey everything I have commanded you" (Matt. 28:19–20). In order to clarify an important aspect of that mandate, we will consider another passage where Jesus speaks:

I tell you the truth, until heaven and earth disappear, not the smallest letter, not the least stroke of a pen, will by any means disappear from the Law until everything is accomplished. (Matt. 5:18)

Here is the measure of greatness: obedience and the teaching of certain commandments. And if Jesus said "not the smallest letter," what was then implied? During his years of earthly ministry, Jesus preached repentance, drove out demons, and healed many. He also instructed his disciples on issues such as the separation of the spheres of government and church (Matt. 22:15–22), the divine nature of government institutions (Matt. 17:24–27), helping the needy (Matt. 25:42–46), and the right perspective on economic issues (Matt. 6:25–34). He did it holding the Law and the Prophets as his authoritative source.

As Jesus gives us the task of teaching the nations, we may ask for the content of such teaching. We can immediately connect that mandate to what he taught about the Law of the Old Testament, for that would be the standard of greatness in the kingdom of heaven, according to his teaching.

The nature of that discipleship becomes clear observing a few instances in the New Testament. The first one is recorded in the Gospel of John. The Roman governor Pilate, in a desperate attempt to set him free, inquires of Jesus: "Do you refuse to speak to me? . . . Don't you realize I have power either to free you or to crucify you?" Jesus answered: "You would have no power over me if it were not given to you from above. Therefore the one who handed me over to you is guilty of a greater sin" (John 19:10–11).

Jesus addresses an important issue of government all societies must face. The power of authorities comes from God, and despite the potential evil that could come from it, government is an institution to be respected. He will not break that order, for "in Him all things hold together" (Col. 1:17).

The Apostles

The same understanding causes the apostle Paul to write an exhortation in his epistle to the Romans: "Everyone must submit himself to the governing authorities, for there is no authority except that which God has established" (Rom. 13:1).

Paul affirms the authority of government, even distorted as it was by the corruption[16] of Roman and Jewish authorities. Today, as it was then, many sectors of the church disregard aspects of civil government out of disgust for the perversion of true justice. Paul and Jesus both restore the concept of civil government as an institution created by God for the benefit of men, to be exercised by the principles shown in the Old Testament.

In the same way, Peter addresses believers dispersed throughout the Roman world who were facing persecution. By noting the topics he touches on, we can "read" the effect the political and social forces were having on the believers of that time. In his first letter, Peter addresses three common situations, beginning each exhortation with the term "submit." The first exhortation reads:

> Submit yourselves for the Lord's sake to every authority instituted among men: whether to the king, as the supreme authority, or to governors, who are sent by him to punish those who do wrong and to commend those who do right. For it is God's will that by doing good you should silence the ignorant talk of foolish men. Live as free men, but do not use your freedom as a cover-up for evil; live as servants of God. Show proper respect to everyone: Love the brotherhood of believers, fear God, honor the King. (1 Pet. 2:13–17)

The second exhortation addresses behavior in the realm of labor relationships (slaves and masters in 1 Pet. 2:18–25), and the third exhortation deals with keeping the right order in marriage (1 Pet. 3:1–7). Secular history asserts that the early Christians hid from Roman society, but Peter's instructions call believers to active engagement with their society. They were not to hide from the "evil" pagan world and remain indifferent to government issues. Peter makes a strong point of supporting the civil order for the benefit of the whole of society.

"What do you think Simon?" asked Jesus, as Peter returned from a disturbing encounter with the tax collectors where they had raised the question, "Doesn't your teacher pay the temple tax?" (Matt. 17:24–25). Only shortly before, Peter had had an amazing revelation about Jesus' identity (Matt. 16:15–17), and coming to grips with the obligation of paying taxes would surely be difficult for him. We could well imagine the disciples expected the Lord would manifest his authority in power and for their benefit in the midst of the pagan, Roman rule which dominated their world. Jesus didn't resist the authority of the government but rather encouraged Peter to comply with the requirement even though it came from an unjust, ungodly government.

Jesus demonstrated an appropriate response to government as an institution through his submission to unjust treatment. Paul exhorted believers to respect authorities. Peter instructed the believers to be an influence on the civil order in the midst of a pagan world. In doing that, they were affirming a model given hundreds of years before, when a needy, dispossessed nation was given principles and structures for a new kind of government.[17] Integrating the Old and New Testaments, the key to follow the "model" would come not by the law but by the unexpected, unfathomable way of Jesus Christ.

Conclusion: What We Need

… and through him to reconcile to himself *all things*, whether on earth or in heaven, making peace by the blood of his cross. (Col. 1:20 RSV)

A few decades later, we glimpse the radical change Peter has experienced from his confusion over Jesus paying the temple tax. He writes, "For it is God's will that by doing good you should silence the ignorant talk of foolish men" (1 Pet. 2:15). We don't know how many times during those years Peter remembered his Master's words, his voice, his attitude . . . and his cross. We know it all led to a change, the one needed for a Simon to become a Peter, and for a Saul to become a Paul. The thirst for vindication, personal, and national ambitions for power that had marked Peter's life earlier (Acts 1:6) are far behind. What resounds in Peter's words is a dream of a different kind, one that can transform the world when Jesus' disciples understand the purpose and the means to do so. That is the change we need to reflect Jesus' dream to see the nations transformed as we teach them like Peter did.

> Love the brotherhood of believers,
> fear God,
> honor the King.

Should any of his disciples do less than that today?

Notes

1. Hernando de Soto, *The Mystery of Capital: Why Capitalism Triumphs in the West and Fails Everywhere Else* (New York: Basic Books, 2000) and *The Other Path: The Economic Answer to Terrorism,* reprint edition (New York: Perseus Books Group, 2002). In *The Other Path* De Soto exposes the failure of governments to establish an adequate legal system that works for all sectors of the population, and in *The Mystery of Capitalism* he looks at the failure of the capitalist system in most poor nations.

2. Francois Chatelet, "Concept of Ideology" *Visión de Ciencias Sociales* (Lima, Perú: 1978), 82.

3. For a comprehensive understanding of ideology and worldview see Darrow L. Miller *Discipling Nations: The Power of Truth to Transform Cultures* (Seattle: YWAM Publishing, 2000).

4. Ibid.

5. See Joseph Stiglitz, *El Malestar de la Globalización* (*Globalization and Its Discontents*) (Madrid: Santillana Ediciones, 2002).

6. The whole of the Pentateuch from Exodus 18 on shows an oral repetition method to instruct Israel.

7. Hernando de Soto, *The Mystery of Capital.*

8. See Isa. 2:1–5; Mic. 4:1–3; 2 Cor. 5:11–21; Eph. 2:11–22.

9. "Caudillo" is a typical term used to denote a leader who, by his special and unique gifts, can lead a group or a nation with an almost-Messiahlike quality. The political history of Latin

American nations is full of this kind of leader, mostly men in the military who fought against the Spanish dominance.

10. Deut. 4:1; 8:1; 11:8–9; 26:18–19; 28:1–14.

11. Lev. 25:8–18; Deut. 15:1–10.

12. Charles-Louis de Secondat, Baron de Montesquieu, *The Spirit of the Laws,* http://etext.virginia.edu/toc/moderng/public/MonLaws.html.

13. See Exod. 3:16, 18; 4:29; 18:12, 24:1, 9.

14. See Exod. 18:21; Num. 1; Deut. 1:13.

15. Isa. 1:21; Jer. 7:5–7; Dan. 9:7–14; Amos 5:7; Hab. 1:4.

16. For examples of corruption, see Luke 19:2; 23:5, 11; John 19:13–16; Matt. 9:11; 18:17.

17. Landa Cope, *Old Testament Template: Rediscovering God's Principles for Discipling Nations* (Burtigny, Switzerland: Template Institute, 1999). Also see www.templateinstitute.com.

We each have a vital role to play in seeing both facets of the Great Commission fulfilled. Susanna takes us on an in-depth look at how one sphere of society can disciple a nation. She identifies principles and characteristics of both individuals and ministries that are successful in discipling their communities through the sphere of business. Her examples give clear instruction and encouragement that we can have a profound influence on nations as we follow God's ways.

Discipling Nations through the Sphere of Business

Susanna Shenk

The age of communication is upon us. Technology has advanced so swiftly that it is now possible to correspond in most languages through the computer and the Internet. Communication is instant to almost any place on the globe. The Internet is a tool as revolutionary as the printing press, which enabled the Reformation. With this phenomenal rate of change and such rapid communication, the completion of the Great Commission becomes possible within this generation.

A tremendous opportunity exists in the new millennium for increased wholeness in Christian missions and a great mobilization of Christian workers into a worldwide harvest. Not only do most people work in some form of business, but with the onset of globalization, business is becoming the transcendent global culture, making it an open door to all parts of the world. Best practices and standards for business are becoming universal. Business is the common denominator today among people of almost every culture, language, and geography. Business is a new world language that provides an opportunity for the gospel of the kingdom to influence every creature and nation.

This new global business culture has great potential for either good or ill. Will it be used to dominate, exploit, and demean or to bring justice, dignity, and freedom from oppression? The answer will depend to a great degree on how radically and creatively businesspeople will follow Christ into the marketplaces of the world. Jesus said, "Go." It is up to us as his ambassadors to extend the victory of the Cross, a victory based on serving, into every people and sphere. We are to pervade business with God's ways and the display of his nature and character.

The command of Christ to "seek first his kingdom" (Matt. 6:33) applies as much to the Christian businessperson as to a full-time minister or missionary. Business is a key to unlock nations for the kingdom of God. Around the globe, nations that have closed the door to traditional missionaries are lining up to attract professionals who can advance their economies. Building opportunities for missions through business is a strategic, indeed critical, means of creating with God toward fulfilling the Great Commission of Christ to "disciple all nations."

In some areas considered closed to the gospel, traditional forms of evangelism simply will not work. Missions in the form of business may be the only practical way to develop contact with the local population. Peter Tsukahira, author of *My Father's Business,* states, "Practically, it is only those who have already been called by God to business who will be able to fully take advantage of these opportunities. It is an important priority in God's kingdom to identify and mobilize such persons for the worldwide harvest in our day."[1]

Great Commission Businesspeople

People who are called to disciple nations through the tool of business are called "Great Commission businesspeople." They plant "Great Commission businesses" as a strategy for discipling people groups. Increasing numbers of individuals identify themselves in this way. This section introduces a few of them to illustrate some diverse strategies that God may inspire.

One modern example of a Great Commission businessperson is Ken in Israel. Ken, accompanied by his wife, Margie, and their children, was first a tentmaker in Israel through an assignment as a Motorola engineer. After returning to the U.S. to complete Bible school and seminary, Ken and Margie desired to return to Israel. Because conventional doors to missionaries were closed, Ken and Margie started a business. They decided to locate the business in an area that had only a handful of believers.

The business was begun with three goals: to bless the nation of Israel, to provide employment for believing nationals, and to provide an incarnational Christian witness. They started small, with Ken baking antennas in Margie's oven. Early on, Ken began to mentor a young Messianic believer named Daniel. Daniel became the general manager of the company. As the business grew, the congregation that developed alongside the company also grew. After years of struggle and persecution for both the congregation and the business, the company won the prestigious Kaplan Prize, awarded by the Israeli government to the business judged to have contributed the most to the nation. The congregation had grown—it is now a fellowship of over 400 believers—and Daniel left the company to become the full-time pastor.

Other businesses were launched out of that company, all formed with Great Commission goals. Recently, the company planted and established a branch of the business among an unreached people group in a closed Asian nation. The congregation in Israel sent out missionaries to be involved in operating the business and in church planting.

Through planting a business, Ken and Margie succeeded at what many missionaries have failed to do after thirty years of service. They enabled the planting of a thriving congregation of believing nationals. They also provided a service that so blessed the nation that the nation publicly recognized the contribution, thus opening up many other doors of opportunity. They multiplied themselves through many other believers, even into Asia.

Harold is another type of Great Commission businessperson. As a businessman in Florida, he received a vision from God as he was praying one day. In the vision he saw fix-tuned radios—radios preset to the gospel stations for their region of the world—being used to propagate the gospel in unreached nations. In a distant land, moving in obedience to a similar vision, Ken had already been working on a fix-tuned radio design. The two met and they formed a corporation called Galcom to handle the production and distribution of the radio. Ken started a new branch of the business in Israel, hiring Russian immigrants, a large number of whom were believers.

After production, many of the radios were tuned to "Voice of Hope," a gospel station. They were distributed throughout the Middle East. Sometime later, in Beirut, Lebanon, when a ministry advertised a phone number in the newspaper for people who wanted a Bible, there were so many calls and requests for Bibles that another organization had to be started to handle the demand. When the people calling were asked why they wanted a Bible, they replied that they had been listening to "Voice of Hope" on their radios. Today, sixteen years later, Galcom is a household name among many mission organizations who have helped distribute 420,000 solar fix-tuned radios in 116 countries. By giving the gift that they had in obedience to God, these businesspeople are reaping a greater harvest than they could have through conventional missionary strategies. George Otis, founder of Kingsworld Ministries, says, "I consider the achievement of Galcom's founders to greatly exceed the spiritual harvesting of my own work."

Today, a new product called MegaVoice is being produced by Ken and Margie. This is a "talking Bible." Statistics say that over half the world's population is illiterate. It takes years to develop a written language or teach people to read and write.

MegaVoice is a hand-held digital audio player able to store speech. The size of a credit card, less than one inch thick and weighing in at only 114 grams (4 ounces), it is rugged and water resistant. It is self-powered, solar rechargeable (powered by the sun), and is therefore not dependent on batteries or an external power source. There are no moving parts to wear out and the user cannot erase the message. The gospel message, the New Testament, or even the whole Bible can be stored on the microchip and when played, the message comes over clearly, in the listener's own language.[2] Now the time it takes to get the Bible into the hands of people who cannot read or write is reduced by a fraction. Because these people have given their gifts through business and the production of technology, the Bible will reach millions who have never heard.

Another Great Commission businessperson is Seng of Singapore. Seng was a CEO of a multinational firm in Singapore for years prior to becoming a believer. After his wife and daughters prayed him into the kingdom, Seng wanted to somehow be involved in missions. When he spoke with the church's missions department, he was told that he could lead a Bible study. He knew that was not his gift. Seng approached a missionary named Bill and told him that he would like to start a business for missions. God had prepared Bill by telling him that he was going to give Bill a business. Seng and Bill formed a company with multiple business ventures that not only provide employment and a professional environment but also support and train Christians who are involved in missions through the businesses. The various businesses of the company send out new business ventures and businesspeople into restricted access areas.

The first business venture they launched specialized in creating franchises. The franchise business placed personnel in several nations, including two in the Middle East. They also acquired a human resources company that identified expertise and qualified persons to work in Singapore and surrounding nations. People came from India, Pakistan, and the Philippines. When Seng and Bill acquired the human resources business and began to bring in people from other nations, they recognized an opportunity for making disciples. They purchased a large apartment complex to house the employees and others. Missionaries trained for these people groups were placed as managers in the apartment complex. Two churches, including a Filipino church, were given space in the buildings to meet for worship. In the first three months of operation, there were ten new disciples, some from Muslim nations. Many more followed. The company has "outreach" and business in a number of 10/40 Window[3] nations, and many lives are being impacted.

Tom and Char were working for YWAM first in Germany and later in Hong Kong. When they began to look closely at sending people into closed Asian nations, they realized the need to create a business platform so they could legitimately place people in long-term assignments. They formed a business that placed many long-term workers on the field and created both a financial covering and self-supporting basis for their ministry.

Dwight is both a missionary and a businessman. An evangelist at heart, he has had a call to China and the 10/40 Window since he was eleven years old. Dwight learned the Chinese language by playing professional basketball for the nation of Taiwan. After completing an MBA and a degree in international law, Dwight went as a tentmaker to China in the role of manager for a large multinational corporation. While there, Dwight led many people to the Lord and participated in planting an international church in Beijing. After a number of years, Dwight returned to the United States to start a Great Commission company. His goals for the company were to enable Christian professionals to do strategic and significant Great Commission work; to reach unreached peoples; to reproduce other Great Commission companies in creative-access[4] nations; and to find a mutually agreed-upon rate of return for investors.

Dwight has helped form twelve businesses in China with hundreds of employees, and his company has trained and placed more than thirty foreign persons in long-term business planting assignments. In addition, similar businesses have been planted in other restricted-access,[5] 10/40 Window locations.

Dwight finds opportunities to share his faith regularly as he runs his business. He shares his faith as he talks about why it is important to have honest and ethical standards and best practices in a business. He shares his faith as he explains to the customer why he is in China and the heart he has for the people. He shares his faith in everyday encounters with the people with whom he works. Dwight reports that new believers do not come mainly from among his neighbors but rather from customers, suppliers, and employees.

Ken and Margie, Harold, Seng, Bill, Tom and Char, and Dwight are just a few of the many examples of the pioneers who are serving God around the world as missionaries through business. These businesspeople have a passion to pursue the call of God, to fulfill the Great Commission and display the kingdom in the realm of business by utilizing all their business skills and resources. Galen Burkholder, international director of Global Disciples states, "The call of God is to fully invest everything we are, everything we do, and everything we have"[6] in seeking first the kingdom of God.

Characteristics of Great Commission Businesspeople

Great Commission businesspeople, knowing they are called to disciple nations through business, have certain characteristics that distinguish them from business-people who merely wear a Christian "hat" or label. This section describes many of those traits.

Called

The first characteristic shared by Great Commission businesspeople is a sense of call-ing. To understand that business is a calling of God, a person first realizes that all of life is to be dedicated to God. God has gifted for and spoken regarding all domains of life. He expects discipleship in and through each field. The invitation to follow Christ takes a definite form of calling.

> In Jesus Christ every believer—lay and clergy alike—has a kingdom vocation that should be reflected in every dimension of his or her existence—as it was in the lives of the first disciples. Every Christian has a ministry and a calling. ... We are called by God to share in His life and His kingdom. Each one of us is called to a special place in the kingdom ... For each one of us there is only one thing necessary: to fulfill our own destiny, according to God's will, to be what God wants us to be.[7]

Many are called to reflect the image of God in and through the realm of business. The Great Commission businessperson senses a call to be involved in the creation of wealth, in providing for needs, and in discipling others through the sphere of business.

Intentional

Great Commission businesspeople can also be identified by intentionality. Inten-tionality is the active shaping of one's life around a defined purpose. This virtue causes businesspeople to be motivated by eternal values. They have decided to follow the call of God and to obey the commands of Jesus. They have placed their vocation as a businessperson under the lordship of Christ and submitted wholeheartedly to his standards and requirements.

Although they may be excited and passionate about their business vision, they are aware that the call of Christ is first of all to take up the cross of Jesus. They know that to obey God will mean going against the grain of the world. Obedience could require making choices for the overall good of their Great Commission goals even if it causes the business not to be as profitable. These decisions could cause their professional reputations to be sacrificed, their motivations to be misunderstood, and their liveli-hoods to be put at risk or even lost.

A traditional missionary is expected to suffer and go through hard times. The Great Commission businessperson is not exempt from trials. The only way into the kingdom is by way of the Cross. The principles of life in this kingdom are encapsulated in the words, "unless a kernel of wheat falls to the ground and dies, it remains only a single seed" (John 12:24) and, "they did not love their lives so much as to shrink from death" (Rev. 12:11).

Faith-Filled and Persevering

Great Commission businesspeople must have faith that God has called them and that he is faithful. The Great Commission businesspeople described above also faced death of a vision, suffering, and loss. Each person was tested to the point of giving up and facing complete failure. Each person found that if there was major sin in any key player of the business, God caused the business to fail until there was repentance or discipline. They also found that failure could come from the normal reasons for which businesses fail, such as an inadequate market, delivery or supply problems, or problems with their products. The primary characteristic which distinguishes those who continued on to be successful is simply faith with perseverance. Determination is unrelenting thinking and follow-through. As Hebrews 10:35–36 says, "So do not throw away your confidence; it will be richly rewarded. You need to persevere so that when you have done the will of God, you will receive what he has promised."

Biblically Based and Holy Spirit Empowered

Great Commission businesspeople and businesses must operate by the rules of God's kingdom. Fortunately, the principles governing truly successful business have been set out by God. To operate in obedience to Jesus, the Great Commission businessperson must also be constantly listening and receiving specific instruction from the Master. The Bible does not give a blueprint for the myriad complex tasks and decisions that make up the corporate world. The Great Commission businessperson must steep himself in the Word of God so that the principles of God become part of his life. He or she must walk in the power and guidance of the Holy Spirit to accomplish the appointed task. Moreover, he or she must garner wisdom and counsel from others with similar callings. In today's world, the need for the wisdom of the Word of God is perhaps greater than at any other time.

Prepared

A Great Commission businessperson responds to the call of God by preparation. Just as opera singers, pianists, or scientists must practice and study so that they can be successful in their chosen professions, one who plans to be of service through business must gain experience and expertise. In entrepreneurship and in all types of business, success comes when preparation and opportunity meet. The Bible tells us to be ready in season and out of season (2 Tim. 4:2). "Do you see a man skilled in his work? He will serve before kings; he will not serve before obscure men" (Prov. 22: 29).

Marked by the Fruit of the Spirit

Ultimately, what distinguishes one who merely wears the title of Christian businessperson from one who is genuinely a Great Commission businessperson? The Bible has instructed us how to discern. We are to judge by the fruit in a person's life and work. Personal characteristics of an individual are the fruits of the Spirit as listed in Galatians 5:22–23: "But the fruit of the Spirit is love, joy, peace, patience, kindness, goodness, faithfulness, gentleness and self-control." We are to prefer others in love and not be governed by selfish ambition, which is so contrary to and destructive to the purposes of God's kingdom.[8] Utilizing these guidelines, we can observe when the fruits of the Spirit are displayed and discern when we, or others, are not operating in the power of the Holy Spirit.

Perhaps the key scripture, however, for the biblical entrepreneur is Isaiah 61:1–2. Christ quoted this passage when he first announced his purposes: "The Spirit of the Sovereign Lord is on me, because the Lord has anointed me to preach good news to the poor. He has sent me to bind up the brokenhearted, to proclaim freedom for the captives and release from darkness for the prisoners, to proclaim the year of the Lord's favor."

We are to bring good news to the poor. Part of the good news to the poor is that God has provided for them by giving them a way to create wealth. He has sent us to bring healing for those without hope and to give freedom to those oppressed by slavery or the imprisonment of their abilities. We are to proclaim Jubilee by providing new beginnings and the means for freedom from financial and economic bondage to those who work.

The Great Commission businessperson bears the fruit of the Spirit and ultimately multiplies both himself and the blessings of God into the lives of others.

Characteristics of Great Commission Businesses

Business is an association of people who are working together for common purposes for both their company and their community. Each person's work is naturally interrelated and dependent upon the work of others. A Great Commission business exhibits fruits that influence the community.

Michael Novak says, "Business people are constantly on all sides involved in building community. In their own firms, they must build a community of work. For practical operations the firm depends on the larger community of suppliers and customers, bankers and government officials, transport systems and the rule of law. The modern business system expresses the interdependence of the whole human race."[9]

Therefore a business must be judged as to whether it makes products and bears fruit that are beneficial to mankind.

A single manufacturing business planted in a nation will, on average, cause at least eight other businesses to spring up. This is only one way a company affects the community and builds community around itself. A kingdom business that is immersed in the values of the kingdom can multiply itself in a society indefinitely through the creation of new enterprise, wealth, and righteous practice.

There are fruits in a community that is blessed by kingdom business. These fruits are a validation of the incarnational witness of the business. A true Great Commission business will display the kingdom of God through a variety of characteristics. The business and its messages are good news to the needy. It brings hope and healing. The dignity of work is reaffirmed and established. A sense of freedom and ownership, rather than slavery, exists. The business makes the people glad and creates praise for the production they see taking place.

Isaiah 61:3–6 says,

They will be called oaks of righteousness, a planting of the LORD for the display of his splendor. They will rebuild the ancient ruins and restore the places long devastated. They will renew the ruined cities that have been devastated for generations. Aliens will shepherd your flocks; foreigners will work your fields and vineyards . . . you will be named ministers of our God. You will feed on the wealth of nations, and in their riches you will boast.

A business—working, creating, producing, and multiplying wealth—causes transformation to take place in the community. What was previously dead takes on life. The poor become rich, the weak become strong, cities are rebuilt, houses and dwellings spring up, children are enabled, and the next generation is strengthened.

As businesses grow they become oaks of righteousness, demonstrations of integrity and strength. They display God's splendor. In some situations the community begins to rebuild the ancient ruins and the places long devastated. The community will very likely become increasingly cross-cultural; "foreigners" will gather to them and will find employment in the community. As products are exported and traded with other nations, the wealth of the nations will be brought to the community. It will become rich, and righteousness and praise will spring up.

Isaiah 58:11 says, "You will be like a well-watered garden, like a spring whose waters never fail." In a kingdom or Great Commission business it is difficult to tell where the business ends and the community begins. The business becomes a part of the community and the people it employs, the customers it serves, and the suppliers from whom it buys. In this way it reflects and models the way the kingdom grows.

The story of the business in Israel illustrates this principle of fruit that affects the community. Ken and Margie's company has become linked to business all over the globe. At least seven businesses have been started that are directly linked to the original business, and others have benefited indirectly. Hundreds of Russian immigrants to Israel have been employed, enabling them to flourish in their new land at a time when employment was very hard to find. A Messianic school was started for the children of believers in the company and the congregation.

The ripple effect from Ken and Margie's obedience is hard to measure and will go on for generations. The congregation that has been planted will endure. Many have been discipled in God's ways and have themselves led others into the kingdom. Both the community and the nation have become more prosperous and the wealth will continue to be reinvested in the next generations. The kingdom of God will multiply by means of the witness of those in the factory established among the lost in China, or through the ministry of the fix-tuned radio, or through the countless people who hear the good news from MegaVoice. The effect of their faith will be impossible for us to measure.

Business and the Great Commission

> Then Jesus came to them and said, "All authority in heaven and on earth has been given to me. Therefore go and make disciples of all nations, baptizing them in the name of the Father and of the Son and of the Holy Spirit, and teaching them to obey everything I have commanded you. And surely I am with you always, to the very end of the age." (Matt. 28:18–20)

Clearly, Jesus' Great Commission applies to every believer. In this final section, we will dissect the passage to examine how it may be specifically applied to businesspeople and their businesses.

"All Authority in Heaven and Earth"

"All authority in heaven and on earth has been given to me." This means that Jesus is in authority over business, trade, nations, governments, and people. He did not say "except in business." As God is the creator of all things and Jesus has been given all authority, then a Christian must not be dualistic in thinking about the domain of business, relegating it to the unspiritual or secular. For the Christian businessperson there can be no separation between sacred and secular because all God's earthly creation has been pronounced "good." Since Jesus' life, death, and resurrection it is all under his dominion. The same principles of life in God must be applied whether one is operating in the sphere of business, the family, or the church.

Jesus gained his authority by the manner in which he lived. His resurrection from the dead was evidence that death could not keep him as it had no hold upon him. Mammon and death only have power over mankind through the sinful choices we make. Based upon the authority of Christ gained through his life, death, and resurrection, we are called as businesspeople to live as Jesus lived, in business and every sphere of life. As we do so, we will extend the influence and power of the kingdom of God into the realm of business.

"Therefore, Go"

Based on his authority, Jesus said, "Therefore, go ... " Often in missions teaching a great deal of emphasis is put on the word *go*. The translation of the word means, "As you go," or "as you journey"—do this.

Mark 16:15 gives the church the mandate of world evangelization: "Go into all the world and preach the good news to all creation." We are commanded to take the gospel (good news) of the kingdom to every person from every tribe, tongue, and nation. This command applies to every believer regardless of age or occupation.

Kenneth Smith has said, "Taking the gospel into the marketplaces and classrooms of the unreached world is not only the main, and some cases the only, strategy to grant us access, but also more importantly takes the gospel of the religious affairs of men into the arena of relationships, and real life. Here is where the gospel needs to be lived, heard, and seen. Here is where it will make its greatest impact. Indeed actions born in faith will speak louder than words."[10]

Abraham is a biblical model of an entrepreneur who was called by God to leave his family "business" and go out in faith to a foreign land. Hebrews 11:9 says, "By faith he made his home in the promised land like a stranger in a foreign country." Abraham established his livelihood and did business in this new country. Genesis 14 and 21 record negotiations and contracts Abraham made with the Canaanites and Abimilech over land and water rights. The price for the land, the contract made in front of witnesses, and the awarding of the deed is recorded. Abraham, a man of faith, God's friend, and the first "missionary" of God's redemptive plan, was referred to as a prince because he was "very wealthy in livestock and in silver and gold" (Gen. 13:2). The first missionary was a businessman!

Abraham was recorded as faithful to God because he continued to trust in God as the source of all provision, even to the extent of being willing to risk losing it all by following the call of God.

"Make Disciples of All Nations"

Whereas the Great Commission passage in Mark 16 instructs us to "preach the good news to all creation," the corresponding passage in Matthew 28 tells us to "make disciples of all nations." Discipling the nations involves bringing the presence of the kingdom into every sphere of life and society. When the Soviet Union opened up, the evangelists went in and thousands were converted. Unfortunately, the area of business was not discipled by followers of Christ, but by organized crime. With Communism as the old way and organized crime as the new way, financial and societal havoc ensued.

"Make disciples of all nations" is a command; it cannot be ignored. We must disciple nations in the arena of business as well as all the other spheres of society. While the criminalized societies of Eastern Europe and Russia remain and human beings cry out for discipleship in the very ethics that the Bible teaches, we have the duty to disciple them. When the peoples of the African nations suffer under unjust economic systems and lack of enterprise while deserving the same rights of the family of God that the Western nations share, we cannot ignore our responsibilities to "our own flesh and blood."

What about societies that already operate by several kingdom principles? They often have wealth produced, community created, and a basic morality accepted. If their discipling stops there, doing business only in that society will focus business on wealth accumulation rather than wealth creation. This moves the society toward greed and other related sin. God's economic principles are similar to the principles of water flow. If the water accumulates without an outlet, it begins to stagnate and produce death rather than life.

Making disciples is the process of transforming beliefs, values, and ultimately, behavior. Discipling a nation is a process that generally occurs over several generations and through all domains of life and society. Making disciples in the area of business means bringing the power of God incarnate through our lives and examples to transform the business culture's values and mores, and to establish the multiplication of disciples. The wealth and relative prosperity that Western nations enjoy comes from previous generations and foundations built on biblical principles woven into the fabric of the society. (This is not to say that *all* the practices have been ethical or righteous!)

The majority of the poorest nations of the world, which can be found in the area known as the 10/40 Window, are those where the gospel has penetrated the least and which have had the least exposure to righteous biblical models of trade, commerce, government, and judicial systems. While providing income for missionaries and local believers, a "planted" kingdom business demonstrates commitment and concern for the local people in a fashion more visible and more easily understood than sermons. The adage is true: people don't care how much you know until they know how much you care. Business empowers people while reinforcing dignity, bringing hope, and providing the means to create a better future.

The message of salvation is just the doorway into the life of the kingdom. If we preach the gospel of salvation and not the whole gospel of the kingdom, it is like telling a couple that the goal of marriage is to have a wedding ceremony, but neglecting to mention that lifetime of joy together which comes after.[11] Calling someone to be a Christian businessperson without recognizing that Jesus desires to transform not just their name, not just their business, but also their entire identify and life practices, is parallel to adopting a child and then leaving him in a foster home. Let's help people move from the doorway of salvation into the kingdom proper.

"Baptize" and the New Kingdom Identity

Jesus went on to command that his workers would be "baptizing them [new disciples] in the name of the Father and of the Son and of the Holy Spirit." Baptism symbolizes cutting all ties with old allegiances and coming under a new authority, becoming part of a different kingdom that operates by a different set of rules.

Applied to the businessperson, baptism signifies the cleansing away of the old identity and worldly system of doing business. The Christian is a new breed of businessperson whose ultimate allegiance is not to state, culture, or business. These are false deities or idols, and ultimate allegiance to them is not compatible with following Jesus. As Jesus said, "You cannot serve both God and Money" (Luke 16:13). No longer "business as usual" or walking in the old ways, rebirth requires a totally new beginning with Christ as head. In Colossians, Paul says, "See to it that no one takes you captive through hollow and deceptive philosophy, which depends on human tradition and the basic principles of this world rather than on Christ . . . you have been given fullness in Christ, who is the head over every power and authority . . . having been buried with him in baptism and raised with him through your faith in the power of God, who raised him from the dead" (Col. 2:8, 10, 12).

"Teaching" the Ways of God in Business

"Teaching them to obey everything I have commanded you." Implicit in the command to teach all that has been commanded us is that we first must learn and become disciples ourselves in the ways of God in business and economics. Jesus spoke about economics and stewardship of resources, including finances, more than any other subject except the kingdom of God. Therefore, the business enterprise becomes an ideal learning environment for teaching principles that Jesus taught.

Teaching takes many forms. Instruction involves modeling, coaching, mentoring, lecturing, illustrating, and giving others experience. A leader or manager in business teaches the stewardship of resources, ethical practices, teamwork, and many examples of best business practices based on God's Word.

Jesus lived and modeled the kingdom of God by including all types of people who followed him, people of different gender, social status, and race. He allowed freedom of expression. All these actions ran contrary to the society of the day. The value of people goes beyond economic worth or skill sets. This principle can be expressed in business through the respectful treatment of employees.

All that Jesus said and did in his ministry was focused on the training of his disciples. "In the business world a company may have beautiful office buildings, powerful factories, and a smoothly operating financial system, but if these functions do not result in production, the company will soon have to shut its doors. The business of the kingdom is the production of discipled lives."[12] If a business owner or manager does not do a good job of multiplying the ethos and practice of the business to the employees and coworkers, the business will not succeed in multiplying its product. The kingdom businessperson must therefore make it his or her priority to multiply kingdom values and practices into employees.

The business environment is an all-day, almost-every-day opportunity for teaching and transmitting values to other individuals. A business is also an ideal learning environment because there are high moral requirements which depend on the employees having certain standards of moral and righteous behavior as part of their value system. Judicial law has banned a significant range of immoral business behaviors because international business is a highly regulated field. High moral standards are often a competitive advantage. Far from being an impediment to success in business, moral conduct is in the long run more likely to result in success than is immoral behavior. Business is dependent on building habits of righteousness. The lack of business success in Eastern Europe and the former Soviet Union has been credited to the unethical foundations of their society. The business world at large recognizes that judicial law and ethics need to pervade a society before new business can succeed in any measurable capacity.[13]

Teaching employees and others how to succeed in business therefore demands that we teach them moral and ethical behavior. As they try to apply the standards of behavior to their practice, we can introduce them to our handbook for best business practice, the Bible. And as they struggle to practice, we must introduce them to the power of the Holy Spirit who enables us as Jesus promised at the end of his command to go and disciple the nations: "And surely I am with you always, to the very end of the age."

What a tremendously exciting time to be alive. These are days of great upheaval and shaking. Uncertainty and fear increase as international events unfold. The events of September 11, 2001, have taught us that the whole world's perspective can change in an instant. The world economy has proven to be a risky and uncertain venture even for the best of businesses. Yet for believers these are days of great opportunity. In the midst of all of the shaking, those who are built on the solid rock of the will of God will stand firm, and their lights will shine more brightly in the darkness.

As believers in Jesus, we know that he has not changed. He still commands us to disciple, teach, and baptize as we journey. He has promised that he is always with us. His Word is still constant; his faithfulness continues. Surely he is with us.

Conclusion: Let Us Do Business in the Nations

Many studies of successful businesspeople have shown that they have two traits in common: risk taking and perseverance. Jesus asks these two qualities of us as his followers. As the writer of Hebrews says, "So do not throw away your confidence; it will be richly rewarded. You need to persevere so that when you have done the will of God you will receive what he has promised" (Heb. 10:35–36).

When we truly fulfill the command of Jesus to disciple all nations we will see the transforming power of God in society at all levels. We will grow in our understanding of what it means to live and function in the kingdom of God. The power of the gospel will radically change both our own lives and the communities in which we serve. What God has in mind for us as we take the risks of faith, invest in the kingdom, and persevere in service, is far beyond what our imaginations can conceive.

As the Word of God says, "No eye has seen, no ear has heard, no mind has conceived what God has prepared for those who love him" (1 Cor. 2:9). GO therefore![14]

Notes

1. Peter Tsukahira, *My Father's Business—Guidelines for Ministry in the Marketplace,* 2nd edition (Haifa, Israel: Carmel Communications, 2007).

2. www.megavoice.com.

3. The 10/40 Window has been identified by missiologists as being that part of the world between the tenth and fortieth degrees latitude north and stretching from West Africa to the Pacific. In this "window" are located 85 percent of the poorest nations of the world.

4. "Creative access" is a term referring to nations where traditional missionary activity is forbidden. Creative strategies are then employed to continue to spread the gospel while minimizing hostile attention from authorities.

5. "Restricted access" refers to a similar situation, with the emphasis on the degree of care which must be exercised when seeking to extend the gospel.

6. Galen Burkholder, "Editorial," *Global Disciples Newsletter,* vol. 2, no. 1 (1999).

7. Tom Sine, *The Mustard Seed Conspiracy* (Waco: Word, 1981), 137.

8. Phil. 2:3; James 2:1–9.

9. Michael Novak, *Business as a Calling* (New York: The Free Press, 1996), 8.

10. Kenneth Smith, editorial in *International Journal of Frontier Missions,* vol. 15 (1998): 1.

11. Loren Cunningham, "The Great Commission," address to the University of the Nations (1999).

12. Chris Sugden, *Fair Trade as Christian Missions* (Cambridge: Grove Books Limited, 1999), 9.

13. Novak, *Business as a Calling,* 8.

14. For more information on biblical approaches to business as mission, I suggest the following resources:

Evangelical Commerce Institute: www.ec-i.org

YWAM Business As Mission: www.businessasmission.com

Centre for Entrepreneurship and Economic Development:
www.CEED-UofN.org or CEEDcentre@cs.com

Scruples: www.scruples.org/bizetmiz

Marketplace Leaders: www.MarketplaceLeaders.org

When you hear the word media, what's the first thing that comes to your mind? Make a note of that and see if it changes after you read this chapter. You may be surprised at the roots of American journalism or at the breadth that Christian magazines and newspapers used to cover. Alison Muesing encourages us to pray for and build bridges of friendship with journalists. If you ever need to work with the news media to publicize or report on an event, you'll find encouragement and numerous helpful tips in this chapter.

Discipling the Nations
through Journalism

Alison K. Muesing

U of N Students Influence the Media

Several years ago University of the Nations Chancellor David Boyd boarded an airplane and while walking to his seat, tripped over a piece of luggage in the aisle. Looking up to apologize, he was surprised to see the bag belonged to Ted Koppel, host of the popular ABC News public affairs show *Nightline*. After introducing himself, David and Ted talked briefly about a mutual friend, Enock Freire from Brazil. Enock had interned with *Nightline* after completing his U of N journalism school in Washington, D.C.

Not long after this Enock was contacted by a Los Angeles producer who needed help in Beijing, China, with a documentary focusing on Western holidays such as Easter, Thanksgiving, and Christmas. Soon Enock was on a plane headed for Beijing and living in a dorm with Chinese university students while working on the documentary. Following production, Enock was surprised at how much of the Christian message was left intact. He was told that the documentary was to be required viewing for all middle-school teachers in China.

Only the Lord could have arranged the circumstances and opened the doors which eventually paved the way for teachers of the largest nation on earth to be presented with the message of Christ through their own TV documentary, produced by Chinese for Chinese . . . with the help of a Brazilian student.

Another U of N journalism student from Canada, Judy Wark, landed a job as assistant editor for *The Australian Printer,* a Sydney magazine targeting the printing industry. She suggested to her editor that the magazine needed an article on printing Bibles in China since a segment of its audience was Chinese printers. Making no promises, the editor encouraged Judy to write it. Her work became a featured article containing a quote from the president of a cultural organization in the former Soviet Union who stated that anyone who considers himself educated must have first read the Bible. Only God knows how many people picked up a Bible for the first time because of Judy's article.

Nabine Poadi, as a boy growing up in Togo, West Africa, often listened to the radio and dreamed of being on the radio himself one day. Following his schooling he joined YWAM and pursued a journalism degree with University of the Nations.

Nabine's memories of listening to Voice of America by shortwave radio while in Togo prompted him to apply for a journalism internship with VOA in Washington, D.C. He was accepted and soon found favor with his supervisors because of his integrity and character. His supervisor told him, "We don't normally allow interns to do this, but we want to give you a special opportunity to do interviews on the air." Soon Nabine was doing live interviews on the phone with politicians and educators in French-speaking West Africa.

After his U of N graduation Nabine started working for a radio station in France. He was then invited by VOA to share his childhood memories of Christmas and the significance of the holiday for him during one of their broadcasts. What an awesome opportunity to share the message of Christ by radio with millions in many nations.

These stories of U of N students sowing seeds through the news media present one strategy in discipling the nations—the profession of journalism. As Darrow Miller states in his book *Discipling Nations: The Power of Truth to Transform Cultures,* "Every area of human life is to be under Christ's lordship, and every aspect of culture is to be redeemed for God's glory, the advancement of His kingdom, and the development of nations."[1]

Truth and Objectivity

In the arena of the news media, the primary value is truth. The journalist bears the responsibility to report truth as closely as he or she can grasp it. But in our post-modern age, belief in objective unchanging truth is eroding. We are told that we can no longer "discover" absolute truth because it doesn't exist and instead need to "create" our own truths for ourselves. Though young journalists often enter the profession as idealists in search of truth, they often succumb to the syncretism of truth and error.

In addressing graduating seniors at Duke University several years ago, Ted Koppel said of the television business he represents, "In the place of truth, we have discovered facts. For moral absolutes, we have substituted moral ambiguity. We now communicate with everyone and say absolutely nothing. We have reconstructed the Tower of Babel, and it is a television antenna: a thousand voices producing a daily parody of democracy, in which everyone's opinion is afforded equal weight, regardless of substance or merit. Indeed, it can even be argued that opinions of real weight tend to sink with barely a trace in television's ocean of banalities. Our society finds truth too strong a medicine to digest undiluted."[2]

Only God is completely objective because only he can see the whole picture. In contrast, every human being is finite and subjective. If a journalist views the world through the lens of "God doesn't exist," everything will be perceived from that presupposition. It's as if he is wearing sunglasses that distort reality and affect his reporting of the world around him.

Our foundational assumptions about life, society, and nature form our worldview—in effect, the designer sunglasses through which we view people and events around us. A person's worldview determines how he or she lives and works. For the journalist, worldview affects what is perceived to be true or false. The journalist's worldview influences his choice of events and issues to cover, sources to interview, quotes to use, and placement of stories in the newspaper or TV news program. Conversely, worldview also influences the choice of what *not* to cover, which sources *not* to interview, and which quotes *not* to use. Often these choices are deliberate. Sometimes they are just the outcome of unconsciously living out one's worldview.

Dean Merrill, in his book *Sinners in the Hands of an Angry Church,* says, "There is much evil in the modern news media to avoid. But there is also some good. Every column, every interview, every sound bite must be tested to see if it enlightens, benefits, and educates, or if it demeans, distorts, and darkens. The media, after all, are merely the voices of human beings in a fallen society."[3] Merrill has captured the essence of God's intentions for the media in his tests for good reporting.

Jesus said, "I am the way and the truth and the life" (John 14:6). Of the Holy Spirit he said, "But when he, the Spirit of truth, comes, he will guide you into all truth" (John 16:13). It is the Christian journalist who can be most objective if he knows the One who is the Truth and is asking the Holy Spirit to guide him into all truth.

But if a journalist doesn't believe in Jesus or acknowledge the Spirit of God, he has missed the greatest Truth of the ages and has built his life on a faulty foundation. Yet this same journalist is expected to report the truth, even when blinded by deception. In effect, unrealistic expectations are placed on the journalist—knowing that the journalist doesn't believe in the Truth, yet criticizing him for missing the truth in many news stories.

Media Bashing

In general, Christians hold a deep-seated mistrust and negative attitude toward the media. In fact, media bashing has almost become a competitive sport among Christians. You've heard the complaints: "Their coverage is so slanted," "Why don't they cover the good news for a change?" "Their reporting is so anti-Christian." Perhaps you've voiced similar statements.

If you're wondering how you really feel about the media, take this simple test: When you hear the word *media,* what's the first thing that comes to your mind? Your answer (and emotional response) will reveal a great deal.

Several years ago I asked that question of a group of YWAM leaders from several nations. They responded with the following list of adjectives: humanistic, biased, negative, selective, powerful, influential, educational, perverted, manipulative, value-molding, immoral, sensational, divisive, and untrustworthy. They commented further: "They've always been a threat," "I run in the other direction because I'm not comfortable with them," "I'd communicate better if I wasn't fearful of them," and "I didn't know I had such a hatred of the media."

Yet Christians' perception of journalists was not always negative. In fact, at one time, Christians were the prominent reporters, editors, and publishers in America. What in the world happened? For the answer we need to flash back 300 years.

Christian Foundations of American Journalism

The year was 1690. The city was Boston, Massachusetts. A printer named Benjamin Harris had emigrated from England and published the first American newspaper, *Publick Occurrences.* On the front page he boldly outlined his objectives for his newspaper: (1) that memorable occurrences of Divine Providence may not be neglected or forgotten, (2) that people everywhere may better understand the circumstances of public affairs, and (3) that the newspaper might help to cure the spirit of lying.[4]

Publick Occurrences reported how the Christian Indians had declared a day of Thanksgiving to thank God for the bountiful corn harvest that season. Those objectives and such articles were the historic Christian foundations of American journalism. Today American journalism influences every nation on earth, for better or worse. Wouldn't it be encouraging to return to our roots and influence journalism in that direction?

When this first American newspaper was published in 1690, the United States did not yet exist. Almost a century would pass before the Declaration of Independence would be written and the new nation birthed in 1776. Despite the influence of Deism and rationalism in the early American republic, the Christian worldview remained dominant in the news media of the young country. Christians were at the forefront of journalism as editors, reporters, and publishers of major newspapers.

In 1830 the *Christian Advocate* of New York claimed the largest circulation of a weekly newspaper in the United States. In just one city, New York, there were 52 Christian newspapers and magazines.[5] These Christian newspapers covered all the news, not just church news and Christian events. This stemmed from the belief that all of life is under the sovereignty of God. "Christian newspapers through the mid-nineteenth century attempted to provide a Biblical worldview on all aspects of life."[6]

The New York Times, founded in 1851 by a Presbyterian, Henry Raymond, exposed political corruption in the city as well as abortion practices in a news story headlined "The Evil of the Age."[7] The journalist reported the horrific details of a young woman who died during an abortion. University of Texas journalism professor and author Marvin Olasky says, "Many early Christian journalists showed an awareness of how the Bible uses bad news to show us the wages of sin and to prepare us for understanding the necessity of the Good News. The journalists knew that general statements about man's corruption were far less gripping than coverage with specific detail of the results of sin and misery."[8]

Despite its Christian roots, journalism strayed far from its biblical base. A major reason was a change of thinking among Christians that led them to conclude that it was unspiritual to be a reporter or newspaper editor. Thus, the Christian "movers and shakers" in journalism defaulted on their positions as editors and publishers of major newspapers and retreated to the church.[9]

No longer did they sense a call from God to be journalists and began to leave the newsroom en masse. Their worldview had changed, and as a result, their godly influence in a strategic profession diminished radically. While non-Christians were advancing in journalism (as well as every other arena of society), Christians were retreating, evacuating their positions of influence. We are living today with the consequences of these worldview changes 150 years ago.

This departure of Christians from society is known as the great "cultural reversal," a paradigm shift that led Christians to withdraw from the world and retreat into "spiritual enclaves." Today, we desperately need another paradigm shift that will spur Christians to once again occupy the spheres of influence until Jesus returns. Change must come first in the hearts and minds of Christians, then there will be changes in the culture.

Our responsibility as Christians is not only to share the gospel so that souls might be saved but also to live out God's kingdom principles in every sphere of life, including the influential domains of society—the family, church, education, business, government, the arts, and the media. Chuck Colson writes, "We need prayer, Bible study, worship, fellowship, and witnessing. But if we focus exclusively on these disciplines—

and if in the process we ignore our responsibility to redeem the surrounding culture—our Christianity will remain privatized and marginalized."[10] As we influence the surrounding society toward kingdom principles, we will be fulfilling the words of Jesus in the Lord's Prayer: "Your kingdom come, your will be done on earth as it is in heaven" (Matt. 6:10).

Colson continues, "Turning our backs on the culture is a betrayal of our biblical mandate and our own heritage because it denies God's sovereignty over all of life. Nothing could be deadlier for the church—or more ill-timed. To abandon the battlefield now is to desert the cause just when we are seeing the first signs that historic Christianity may be on the verge of a great breakthrough. The process of secularization begun in the Enlightenment is grinding to a halt, and many people believe that the new millennium will mark 'the desecularization of world history.'"[11]

Dutch Christian Penetrates Spheres of Society

When Christian influence in society was waning in the late nineteenth century in the United States, the same was also occurring in Europe. Abraham Kuyper of the Netherlands chose to swim against the dominant European intellectual currents of rationalism and romanticism. After receiving theological training, he served several years as a pastor.

Then, while many Christians were leaving the newsrooms to become pastors, Kuyper did just the opposite. He left the pastorate to become editor of two newspapers: *The Standard,* the official paper of the Anti-Revolutionary political party, and *The Herald,* a Christian weekly newspaper. It was a daring step. Perhaps the church of his day criticized him for "leaving the ministry" when he left the pastorate to work as a journalist, but through these newspapers Kuyper reintroduced biblical principles to Dutch society.

Kuyper's influence was later felt in other arenas of society—higher education and government. In 1880 he founded the Free University of Amsterdam, using the Bible as the basis for every area of learning. Later, he was elected a member of the lower house of the Dutch Parliament. Soon after delivering his famous Stone Lectures at Princeton Theological Seminary, he became prime minister of the Netherlands.

By Kuyper's seventieth birthday celebration in 1907, he was recognized as having had an important influence in the Dutch state, society, press, education, and even the sciences.[12] What a tremendous legacy he left! He certainly would have given a hearty "amen" to these words of Chuck Colson nearly a century later: "The only task of the church, many fundamentalists and evangelicals have believed, is to save as many lost souls as possible from a world literally going to hell. But this implicit denial of a

Christian worldview is unbiblical and is the reason we have lost so much of our influence in the world."[13]

In 1925 the widely publicized Scopes "monkey trials" occurred in Dayton, Tennessee. At stake was the teaching of creation versus evolution in the public schools. Because of a lack of viable Christian reporting at this strategic trial, evolution was given an esteemed position in the press across the United States while creationists were debunked as unintelligent. On July 22 *The Atlanta Constitution* editorialized about the trial coverage's potential effect: "The world has been broadcast with the seeds of doubt and skepticism, and only the future can tell what the harvest will be."[14]

Today the results are clear. Several generations in many nations have been discipled in evolutionary theory. The rapid spread of evolution was the direct consequence of Christians withdrawing from the news media 75 years earlier. Ideas do have consequences!

Stop Cursing the Darkness, Begin Lighting Candles

Christians might feel they have the right to criticize the media. But though their complaints are often valid, isn't the present situation the result of Christians defaulting on their role as "salt and light" in the newsroom? An admonition worth heeding is: "Stop cursing the darkness, begin lighting candles." Instead of contributing to the problem by complaining, how about becoming part of the solution? Here are several things that every Christian can do:

1. Guard your tongue against speaking negatively about journalists.
2. Pray for the salvation of journalists and that their eyes will be opened to the truth about God and the world around them.
3. Adopt a journalist or two. Pray for them and send a letter or email commending them when their coverage is fair and accurate.
4. Build bridges of friendship with journalists and help tear down the dividing walls that separate Christians and the media. Be kind and compassionate when you come in contact with them.
5. Encourage Christians who sense a call to the media to get training and become a journalist. Or become a journalist yourself!

Suppose Jesus walked into the CNN newsroom. Would he harshly criticize journalists as "blind scribes" or would he show compassion for "lost sheep" who haven't yet met the One who is the Truth? Jesus was consistently harsher with the religious leaders of his day than with blatant sinners. The leaders were poised to hurl stones at the woman caught in adultery until Jesus intervened and said, "If any one of you is without sin, let him be the first to throw a stone at her" (John 8:7). Christians, too, are quick to condemn the journalist who distorts the truth. Yet Jesus might challenge us, "Cast the first stone if you've never lied."

One young woman who chose to build bridges was Judith Cespedes, a U of N journalism student from Peru who interned with CNN's Washington bureau. Because of her willingness to serve by doing whatever task was required, she stood out among the other CNN interns who felt it was beneath them to make coffee or photocopies for the employees. Her intern coordinator took notice and offered her a special opportunity to train as a production assistant. During training, Judith's supervisor was perplexed and asked her, "Why is it that you don't yell back at the boss like all the other employees and interns?" Judith thought a moment and then said, "Because I try to respond in the opposite attitude."

She was applying a teaching by YWAM founder Loren Cunningham on ministering in the opposite spirit. She merely removed the "Christian-ese" to make it more understandable to her supervisor. Judith was later offered opportunities to work with several CNN shows. The Lord had honored her servant's heart and response in the opposite spirit—simple yet powerful lessons she had learned during her YWAM Discipleship Training School (DTS) training. As journalists sense a change in the attitudes of Christians from antagonism to respect, many will undoubtedly begin to see the love of Jesus through his followers, perhaps for the first time.

Washington for Jesus

Although becoming a journalist is an excellent way to serve as "salt and light" in the media, most Christians will not follow this path. How then, in addition to praying, can one be a godly influence? One way is through contact with the media when promoting church-related or Christian events. We had such an opportunity when developing a media strategy for Washington for Jesus 1988.

Pastor John Gimenez of Virginia Beach had sensed the Lord's leading to call Christians of many denominations from all fifty states to the Washington Mall on April 29, 1988, to fast and pray for America. It was the same vision he had had for a similar gathering eight years earlier when hundreds of thousands gathered on the Mall. Prior to the 1988 event, organizers asked Landa Cope, director of YWAM Washington, D.C., if she would coordinate the strategy for the mainstream non-Christian media. She agreed. Then she asked me, a YWAM Washington, D.C., staff member with a background in journalism, to pray about handling the daily details of contact with the media.

I struggled with the decision because of the potential ramifications of inaccurate media coverage of the event. Driving through the countryside of northern Virginia,

I prayed for direction. My thoughts flashed forward to April 30, the day after the event. I imagined people reading the morning newspaper. Would Washington for Jesus even be covered in the paper? I presumed it would be because most editors would consider the event newsworthy, if only because of the projected attendance of hundreds of thousands of Christians.

But the next question was more difficult to answer. *How* would it be covered? Would the reporter write that the gathering not far from the Capitol Building had a political agenda? Or that Christians were complaining about congressional decisions? I knew this was not the objective. Yet if the media were not clearly informed about the purpose of the event, then it was possible that this day of prayer and fasting might be portrayed as political. To further complicate matters, two prominent televangelists had just been exposed in the national media for unethical financial practices and immoral behavior. I pictured the media gloating, "Now what do you have to say, church!"

I gulped, thinking of the responsibility. Clearly, the job had to be done. Though I didn't relish the thought of doing it, I sensed the Lord calling me to rise to the challenge. From that day through the event, we cried out, "Lord, we've never done this before. We don't know what to do. Please help!" God was faithful to lead us every step of the way.

Our first task was a meeting with those who could provide wise counsel in developing the media strategy. Landa and I met with *TIME* magazine correspondent Dr. David Aikman and Regent University journalism professor Dr. Cliff Kelly. Because the organizers' purpose for Washington for Jesus (WFJ) was to repent, pray, and fast for the nation, David suggested writing the news releases from a humble position, stating that we as Christians had failed.

We hammered out the initial news release which read, "This second Washington for Jesus event will focus on acknowledgment of failure as individuals and as the church to provide adequate concern for the social, economic, and spiritual problems which face the nation and the world, and to join in prayer for positive solutions." I imagined this statement would disarm journalists who would certainly agree that the church had failed. Perhaps some editors would even place the release in their "futures file" until the end of April.

The news releases were sent to 250 media personnel, then follow-up calls were made to assignment editors, bureau chiefs, and station managers to ask if they had any questions. Almost without exception they were very cordial, expressing their gratitude for the information. Only a few said they weren't interested in covering the event.

As the big day approached, we prepared a press kit which included news releases focusing on the various angles of Washington for Jesus (the main event, youth rally, the week of prayer on the Mall, and international delegations coming for the event).

We included a schedule of events, list of speakers and musicians, and an aerial photograph of WFJ 1980 showing hundreds of thousands of people gathered on the Mall. Even if all the words didn't convince assignment editors, surely they would send reporters just by observing the size of the event from the photo taken eight years earlier.

A press conference was held at the National Press Club the day before the gathering, and three press conferences were held during the event on the Mall in a tent set up for the media. Inside the tent was a registration table, chairs for press conferences, telephones for radio correspondents, a TV monitor with a live feed from the stage and, of course, a long table filled with homemade goodies, sodas, coffee, and tea. We had learned in advance to keep the media well-fed and watered!

Not only did the tent provide shelter from the chilly rain but it also provided a "home base" where journalists could attend press conferences, do interviews, and phone in radio stories. The thirty media-tent workers (YWAMers and local Christians) were briefed in advance with the following instructions on how to work with the journalists:

- Serve the media by providing them with the information they need to accurately cover the event. Don't try to control or manipulate them to get positive coverage. Direct them to the right source for the information and leave the results with the Lord.
- Communicate clearly without using "Christian-ese," terms that they may not understand.
- Protect journalists from "hostile" Christians who are antagonistic toward the media.
- Treat our media guests in the tent with professionalism and warmth. Treat them as you would guests in your own home.

The tent workers followed these guidelines and at the end of the day, several journalists stopped to thank us and comment that they really felt served in the tent. That was our goal and it was worth all the hard work!

So how did the media cover the event? A New York–based press clipping bureau had been hired to identify WFJ stories printed in newspapers across the nation. They sent us more than 500 newspaper articles from most states. In addition, local Washington TV stations, national radio networks, and TV networks (NBC, ABC, CBS, and CNN) all covered the event. The news stories were overwhelmingly positive, fair, and accurate. A Christian correspondent for Newhouse News Service, Roy Beck, said he was quite skeptical of coverage the event would receive, but after it was over, was pleasantly surprised by the positive tone.

In almost every one of the hundreds of contacts with the mainstream media, both by telephone and in person, reporters and editors were genuinely appreciative for the information provided. Only in a few cases were they defensive or antagonistic. The major lesson we learned is that media do an excellent job of covering Christian events with fairness and accuracy when we (1) serve them instead of looking for what we can get from them, (2) treat them with respect as Jesus would, and (3) work within their system (realistically consider if the event is newsworthy for the general public, submit well-written news releases, and respect their deadlines).

Just prior to WFJ, a French journalist for the Paris newspaper *Le Monde Diplomatique* traveled to Washington to do an interview with me about the upcoming event. She had spent the previous week in Louisiana investigating a scandal surrounding a televangelist and was quite skeptical about anything the American church might have to say. At the beginning of the interview, she was quite antagonistic toward American Christians.

I shared that many Christians' expectations of this spiritual leader were shattered, but the need was to focus on God, not man. Then I added that we've all sinned and now Christians are gathering in Washington to ask for God's forgiveness and help. This woman visibly softened as we talked and then she confided, "I've seen a difference in America morally since the last time I visited." She added, "With all the abuses, it looks like it may be time for prayer!"

WFJ National Chairman John Gimenez said that during the first WFJ in 1980 he felt like he was in the lion's den fighting with the media. But eight years later he felt a real breakthrough in relating with the media to the extent that he even joked with them!

As we refuse to become defensive with the media, steps can be taken toward renewed trust, understanding, and communication between Christians and the media. Christians must take seriously the ministry of reconciliation entrusted to them, taking the initiative to build bridges with journalists.

Conclusion

Discipling nations in the area of the news media must incorporate a two-pronged approach—reaching individual journalists with the gospel of Jesus Christ as well as restoring the biblical value of truth-telling to this influential sphere.

First, to reach journalists with the gospel, we must see them as lost sheep, people for whom Christ died. In effect, they are an unreached people group, not bound together by geographic boundaries or ethnic backgrounds but by vocation. Yet the need is the same—Jesus Christ. This people group, representing many nations, has largely been ignored by Christian missionaries.

The same strategies used to reach other people groups—prayer and reaching out in love with the gospel—are also effective among journalists. Unlike in past generations, Christians must now do pre-evangelistic work by building bridges and tearing down walls of division before sharing the gospel.

Second, to restore truth to the media, more Christians must take the initiative to cross over into their world. The U of N students from Brazil, Canada, Togo, and Peru mentioned earlier provide excellent examples of this. They have responded to the call to disciple nations by influencing the world of media, fulfilling their God-ordained assignment to "salt" this sphere with truth and the love of Christ.

For those who will not become journalists, it may be necessary to work with the media to promote truth when covering church or Christian events. Christians must combine respect and compassion for journalists, praying for them and building bridges of friendship, trust, and understanding.

The challenge is great. The laborers are few. Yet is anything too hard for the Lord? The questions the Lord presented to Isaiah still demand a response from us today: "Whom shall I send? And who will go for us?" (Isa. 6:8).

How will you respond? "No, Lord, not me. Not to the media!" or "Here am I, Lord, send me!"

Notes

1. Darrow L. Miller, *Discipling Nations: The Power of Truth to Transform Cultures* (Seattle: YWAM Publishing, 1998), 35.

2. "Nightline Host Ted Koppel Challenges Students at Duke," *The Forerunner,* July 1987.

3. Dean Merrill, *Sinners in the Hands of an Angry Church: Finding a Better Way to Influence Our Culture* (Grand Rapids: Zondervan, 1997), 134.

4. *Publick Occurrences: Both Forreign and Domestick* (Boston, Sept. 25, 1690), 1.

5. Marvin Olasky, *Prodigal Press: The Anti-Christian Bias of the American News Media* (Westchester, Ill.: Crossway Books, 1988), 17–18.

6. Ibid., 19.

7. "The Evil of the Age," *The New York Times,* August 23, 1871, quoted in Olasky, *Prodigal Press,* 20.

8. Olasky, *Prodigal Press,* 19.

9. Ibid., 25.

10. Charles Colson, *How Now Shall We Live?* (Wheaton: Tyndale House, 1999), x.

11. Ibid.

12. "Abraham Kuyper: Lectures on Calvinism," The Kuyper Foundation (Somerset, England) website: www.kuyper.org (accessed March 10, 2007).

13. Colson, *How Now Shall We Live?,* 296.

14. *The Atlanta Constitution,* July 22, 1925, quoted in Olasky, *Prodigal Press,* 208.

For wherever you work and whoever you're called to reach, Calvin and Carol Conkey give insightful advice for crafting effective communication tools and strategies. They also discuss the very practical questions of selecting the medium that will be most effective for the message and the audience. Their stories from years of field experience bring the principles to life. They further give a quick overview of current and upcoming communication technologies.

Media That Transforms Nations

Calvin and Carol Conkey

Media—It's Everywhere!

Small roadside fires lit our way as we walked dusty, cobblestone lanes in the foothills of India's Himalayas late one cold winter night. We passed villagers squatting around steamy pots of rice and lentils, women selling meals to local passersby, and others warming their hands near the open flames while discussing the days' events. Flashing lights in the distance caught our eye, so we followed the path past several yaks tied to a post. Entering a dingy room, we saw an unlikely sight: several Tibetan youth crowded over video arcade games. The next shop held floor-to-ceiling videos, including *Back to the Future 2*, which at that time had not yet been released to theaters in America! Media had captured the attention of these remote, unreached people.

Crafting the Message

Since we started the media ministry Create International in 1989, the many documented accounts we've received have convinced us of the essential role of media in discipling the nations. From the interest stirred by new technologies like iPods to the heart response to a message communicated through traditional art forms, the Spirit-led use of media to impact individuals and nations is an enormous factor in our effectiveness to fulfill Jesus' mandate to disciple the nations. The acid test of effective media is not how nice it looks nor how many compliments are given; the proof is in seeing souls enter the kingdom of God and communities transformed.

Below we will look at four defining aspects of our ministry: our goal, vision, strategy, and process. First, however, and throughout this chapter, we will explore how media and technology have been used and are still being used in discipling remote and unreached people around the world.

Discipling the Nations: The Komering of Indonesia

Not long ago, a short-term ministry team nervously stepped into the small home of a Muslim family in the highly restricted area of South Sumatra, Indonesia. The two team members sat on the only stools available as the others gathered around on the dirt floor. Through an interpreter they explained that they had come to show a new video in the Komering language. The family smiled approval and removed a lace cloth to reveal a large television set! As the visitors silently prayed that their video would be a powerful testimony, the family's excitement grew with the anticipation of seeing a video in their own language for the first time.

The father watched skeptically as the culturally adapted video of the "Prodigal Son" began, but he kept inching closer to the screen as the story unfolded. As the truths of Christ's sacrifice and the great love of God were explained in their own heart-language, everyone in the room watched intently. At the end of the showing, the father's nose was nearly touching the screen as he exclaimed excitedly, "This is the very first movie I have ever seen in my own language, and I like it very much. Everything in it is true. It is very good!"

In response to the family's open hearts, the team provided follow-up through long-term missionaries, and as a result, home fellowships were formed to study the life of Jesus. There is now an indigenous Komering church in Sumatra—the least evangelized island in the world.

The Goal: Communication to All Peoples

When we think of utilizing new technologies for furthering the kingdom of God in all the nations, it is vital to present the message in a way that is both understandable and relevant to the culture of the people.

Consider the implications: four billion people—about two-thirds of the world's population—are oral learners. Orality refers to the ways people think, learn, remember, and communicate because of their reliance on orally expressed stories, narratives, songs, and proverbs. They do not convey or receive information through written means such as books or tracts, or any form of communication that utilizes linear thinking. Included in this group are those who may read a written language, but it is not the way they prefer to interact with the world—and the Word of God. Surprisingly, the latter group includes millions of young men and women, a generation called "postmodernists" who live in "literate societies" but prefer nonliterate means of communication such as television and the Internet. With today's technology, many nonliterate peoples are moving directly into visual and oral means of learning and communication without ever learning to read and write their own heart language.

If these oral learners are truly to "hear" the gospel of Christ (understand, internalize, and recall the message), it must come to them through proverbs or carefully constructed stories compatible with their cultural thinking and presentation style.

We must contextualize our message to the worldview of those we seek to reach. Jesus modeled how to impart truth in culturally relevant ways; we can learn from him how to discover, interpret, and employ redemptive analogies (the witness which he has left for himself).[1] This ability was also displayed in an Athenian cultural context by one of the New Testament's most effective cross-cultural missionaries, the apostle Paul: "Now what you worship as something unknown I am going to proclaim to you" (Acts 17:23).

Discipling the Nations: East Java, Indonesia

A tiny Indonesian village house soon filled with cigarette smoke from the men who had gathered to play a part in our drama. Only recently had their language been put in written form. One of the actors could not read at all, and others were struggling to make sense of the translated lines. In the middle of casting, a distinguished-looking Islamic leader entered the room. Our hearts raced as he scolded us, "You can't do this drama here!" We innocently inquired, "Why not?" He scoffingly replied, "These are a bunch of uneducated fools. You will never be able to do any sort of worthwhile drama with them." He then stormed out of the room. Sighing with relief, we remembered God's Word: "But God chose the foolish things of the world to shame the wise" (1 Cor. 1:27).

During the filming, the Muslim participants would stop and pray or go off to the local mosque whenever they heard their call to prayer. Our Create crew decided to use this time in like manner. The actors would watch us, sometimes mock us, but we knew the truths of the script and Scriptures they were dramatizing were affecting them. We fervently interceded that they would become followers of *Isa al Masih*—Jesus the anointed Savior.

A few months after our return to Australia, a missionary to that people group came to report to us, "Your evangelistic film is working me out of a job!" He went on to explain that after our departure, the whole cast of seven became believers through further discipleship with our Indonesian cultural advisor! They formed home groups and had already distributed a hundred copies of the evangelistic video to their friends and family. Many workers have reported that this dramatic film is very relevant to the culture and has gained wide acceptance among this large unreached people group of East Java. Because this film is produced in the local language, it is now on the top of the charts in the area video rentals and sales.

The Vision

Stories like these point to the fruitfulness of developing contextualized media tools for unreached peoples. The vision for nation discipling is to see men and women reconciled to God, released into their gifting and finding their place in fulfilling the Great Commission. They will do so as they are free to worship and work through their cultural expressions, in order to impact their people group to see transformation in every sphere of their shared life.

"As we pursue the task of world evangelization, we must identify the major priorities that will be integral to ensuring that all the peoples of the world will have the opportunity to hear the gospel, in their 'heart' language, near where they live, with access to a healthy, indigenous church to help them grow in faith."[2]

The Strategy

How do we get there? There are keys to discovering the most strategic way to bring heart understanding and transformation to a people group. We must understand the needs, the most effective media to use, and the cultural context for the message in order to create a strategy, message, and tool that are unique for each people.

In our dramatic film stories, we show people coming to crisis through a real, current issue in their culture, and then being exposed to Christ as the answer. They may meet a believer, have a dream, or find Scriptures that speak to their problem. There's often an invitation given within the context of the story, actually showing the main character coming to Christ, then sharing his or her new faith with family and friends, and entering into fellowship. This is a key to the evangelism, because community-oriented cultures shy away from individual conversion, which can mean complete isolation. Seeing families open to the gospel and to believers from their own culture in contextualized fellowship is very reassuring and gives them the courage to step out, regardless of the response of those immediately around them.

The stories continue, showing the outworking of the character's new faith to address the crisis, and then being an influence on those around them. In this way we're able to sow the seed that personal transformation should lead to social transformation

(Matt. 28:19–20). Until the church exists in a people group, kingdom transformation of the spheres of that society cannot occur.

Discipling the Nations: Banjara People of India

Filming in the Banjara village in central India gave us the opportunity to become living witnesses for Jesus. Our team was often asked to pray for people in their homes. Only a few families in this village were Christian, so it was not uncommon to be praying beneath photos or shrines of Hindu gods. As Hindus/animists, the Banjara look to the supernatural to demonstrate the reality of one's faith in God. Less than 1 percent of over 20 million Banjara were believers.

Our team scripted and produced a film that spoke into a critical issue for the Banjara: community conflict. Many lives were lost from the cycle of retribution and vengeance the Banjara were caught up in. Our film, entitled *Transformation*, did just that in the Banjara community. As the only film in the Banjara language, they were immediately drawn in as they saw their culture and language honored. National leaders have reported that this film is an historic event in effective outreach to the Banjara people and that tens of thousands of Banjara have given their lives to the Lord. We're seeing transformation take hold as well: drunken men have turned from alcohol and are rebuilding their lives and families; home fellowships have started. National workers are requesting more copies, projectors, and greater distribution throughout India to further spread the gospel among the nomadic Banjara.

Discipling the Nations: The Turks of Turkey

A critical stage in the process for an individual or a people group is moving from salvation to growing as a Christian. As we wrestled with the needs of new believers, God led us to use the same principles we had in creating evangelistic films to develop a DVD depicting a Turkish home-fellowship in a Turkish home, with believers dressed in local clothing and speaking Turkish.

After creating the DVD highlighting the home-fellowship group, we were filming an evangelistic drama for the Turks, and we noticed several of the actors excitedly reading a major Turkish magazine. To our surprise, we saw shots of our home-fellowship film as illustrations for one of the feature articles in this nationwide magazine. The actors translated the articles for us; it was describing the recent home-church movement in Turkey in a positive manner! We were a little nervous that this massive publicity might deter the Turkish believers' participation in this present film. Instead, one of them declared, "It is positive; the media is doing the job for us!" Because our film was very Turkish and adapted to the culture, the local media and Muslim leaders were open to receiving the presentation into their society.

The Process

In creating any new communication piece, the process begins with an invitation from field workers and nationals to insure that the media tools will be used and a distribution plan for ongoing usage exists. Much time is spent prayerfully hearing God's direction and advice for what media tools to develop as well as the overall message to reach the intended people group.

Creating communication pieces is a partnership between the Holy Spirit and us. As we do the research, we are continually in prayer asking the Lord to give us revelation about the people and the keys to reaching them. We find he says to us: "Come join me in what I'm already doing among this people." We need to do our best to be skilled workman to know how best to communicate to a people. And when we pray, God will highlight what's key for that time for that group from the research we've done.

It's important to do extensive research before all projects. There is usually at least three months of research and gaining knowledge from field missionaries about effective communication, i.e., what has worked, what hasn't, how the people communicate and share knowledge with each other, what their felt needs are, what hinders them from being a follower of Christ, and so on.

Every script is tailor made for the specific audience. In the scripting process, our team addresses community issues such as revenge killings, unforgiveness, superstition, ancestor worship, and stealing. The salvation message is interwoven with a drama of conflict and resolution. Local cultural advisors are key to the film's authenticity. We look for a local person, preferably but not necessarily a believer, who is not highly Westernized and has a great love for the culture. If we're able to find more than one, we look for a range of ages, from both sexes, and from various walks of life to get the widest perspective possible.

Key tasks to identify the message:

- Gather information from libraries, the Internet, people profiles, and outreach experiences.
- Look for reccurring themes and patterns.
- Study cultural stories, sayings, legends, and life stories.
- Analyze the social needs and problems among the people (felt needs or longings).
- Look for redemptive ideas, gospel bridges or themes, morals.

- Discover what the people strive for in life—what do they want to be or accomplish?
- Build on biblical truth, biblical values, and biblical themes found in the culture.

Key questions to identify the method/media:

- What is everyday life like for this people group? Occupations, living conditions, educational levels, literacy, and use of technology?
- What are some of their unique and cherished art forms?
- What kind of media is most popular? What do they use to communicate with each other?
- How do the people celebrate ritual events, especially religious ones?

Then:

- Begin to create a believable story and test its validity with cultural advisors.
- Identify the key people of influence in the culture and portray them as the role models for communicating the gospel.

During production, we regularly ask for input from our cultural advisors to determine the best usage of symbols and other cultural preferences, appropriate gestures and body language, realistic costuming, props, settings, and appropriate emotional expression. After editing the presentation, we field test it for linguistic and cultural accuracy. Once the presentation is being used on the field, we stay in touch with those who are using it to evaluate our effectiveness. Did the audience understand the message of the film? How did they respond? How can other media help their growth in coming to faith in Christ and being discipled in God's ways?

Selecting the Media

After selecting a message, the next step is to select the media which will have the greatest impact. Options range from the "wow" of new technology to the comfort and authority of familiar art forms. It's also vital to seek God for how to effectively put together different media for different parts of the process, from salvation to discipleship to community transformation.

We must package the good news in a way that our target people group can unwrap in order to hear with understanding and pass on with accuracy. Until we learn to share information as local people do, we will have little impact on their community.

Let's look at a few media forms as tools of communication which are effective for reaching oral peoples, including this current generation.

Film

Films are a powerful medium that attracts a wide audience of viewers. Watching a film is a community activity; therefore it is an effective means for a group of people to be exposed to the same message at the same time. It's a powerful way to get the message across because everyone loves dramatic stories. Jesus knew this, and that's one reason he spoke in parables.

"Dollar for dollar more people come to the Lord through films than any other way. It's inexpensive if it's done right."[3] One example of an effective use of film is the "Jesus Film." Campus Crusade for Christ reports that the film has been translated into 950 "heart languages" of the unreached peoples with estimates of 6.1 billion "exposures" and over 200 million conversions.[4] Many agencies and churches have partnered together to distribute millions of their films in video compact disc (VCD) and DVD formats worldwide.

Radio

Shortwave radio has been used widely to propagate the gospel all over the world for many years. There's been a tremendous response to broadcasts, and many people who would otherwise not have access to the Word of God have received it in their own language through this technology. However, fewer and fewer commonly used radios are being manufactured with the ability to receive the shortwave frequencies, shrinking the audience of major radio ministries each year. Most of these ministries are shifting their focus to more attractive communication technologies like the Internet, where podcasting is rapidly becoming the new tool of choice. Streaming audio and video is becoming commonplace, while those who can afford to are moving to high-quality satellite radio broadcast.

Internet

The continuing growth of the Internet is phenomenal. In many countries, Internet usage is doubling every one hundred days![5] Internet usage is increasing in several Middle Eastern countries by more than 200 percent each year.[6] Most students worldwide have free access to the Internet; among graduates and young professionals, Internet access in many countries may be as high as 90 percent. Even in impoverished countries, citizens have access through their schools, government offices, and businesses. Internet cafes are popping up all over the unevangelized world and are particularly popular in poorer countries where "pay-for-use" phone shops are very common. This is strategically significant information for those wanting to influence the new generation of unreached peoples. The challenge to the church is to use the Internet for evangelism! "The Internet is the first medium that allows anyone with reasonably inexpensive equipment to publish to a wide audience. It is the first medium that distributes information globally at almost no cost."[7]

Mobile phones

The "high-touch, high-tech" nature of mobile phones has sparked a revolution in communications in developing nations around the world. Many so-called high-touch cultures that are highly relational are attracted to technologies that will improve their feeling of connectedness. Turn off these people's electricity for a day or so and there is little complaint, but take away their mobile phones for five minutes and you'll have a riot on your hands! With the advent of high-speed-Internet-capable mobile phones, much of the two-thirds world will bypass the need for computers to access the Internet's vast resources.

Microchip Players

Solar powered microchip players provide audio Bible stories with no need for electricity, and are only the size of a credit card. Christian organizations are using these audio players to bring God's message of hope and love to nonreading people all over the world. For evangelism to pastoral training, the solid-state MegaVoice audio players can be programmed in any language.[8]

Wireless Technology

Wireless technology is another development that is rapidly revolutionizing the way we access the Internet. There are now a plethora of technologies such as Bluetooth and Wi-Fi which connect computers with mobile phones, PDAs (personal digital assistants), printers, digital cameras, refrigerators, and every other type of electrical appliance. This has been called the beginning of the second wireless revolution.

Satellite Linkage

The use of satellite in the propagation of the gospel goes far beyond just TV to include radio, cellular communications systems, the Internet, and more. We can be in touch with people thousands of miles away in an instant. Even in some of the least developed nations satellite dishes are surprisingly prevalent.

Communication technology is reshaping the world around us. Previously, to communicate with tens of thousands or even millions of people in their own language, one needed to use very expensive, high-tech electronic media. Now, with the ability to capture the message using new digital technology combined with careful cultural research, reaching the masses cheaply and effectively is possible!

Cultural Arts

Serious consideration must be given to the nontechnical media already available in the audience's culture. The Christian message conveyed through a familiar indigenous expression is far more likely to be embraced by the audience than the same message introduced through a strange or foreign medium. New Christians who have received the message through a familiar medium can quickly pass the message on to others, without needing to spend time learning a foreign medium. Traditional cultural forms such as music, art, storytelling, and dance can be redirected to reveal one's true relationship with God and to communicate his message of love and salvation.

Discipling the Nations: Tibetan Buddhists

Tibetans, for example, portray their Buddhist teachings in a circular type of artwork called a *thangka* painting. A missionary working among the Tibetans in Nepal gave the Gospel of Luke to a professional thangka painter, and asked him to paint what he read. What he painted was truly amazing! In the typical circular format, this thangka depicts the life of Christ with meticulous clarity, showing the birth, miracles, teachings, last supper, death on the cross, burial, resurrection, and ascension. The artist clearly presented how Jesus broke through the futility of the "Karma chain" by his resurrection.

We used this local medium in one of our evangelistic films created to reach Tibetan Buddhists. After viewing it, Tibetans say things like: "Jesus can really liberate me?" "There are other Tibetans that believe in Jesus?" "How can I become a believer in this Jesus?"[9] To add to the excitement, the painter of the thangka became a Christian and is walking with the Lord today.[10]

The Tibetan case study illustrates an important principle: to be effective communicators, we must not only translate what we want to say into the appropriate language, but also communicate our message using the appropriate cultural symbols so that our audience is able to readily understand.

Contextual media is also the best form to insure continued use by the audience. We learned this during a project in West Sumatra, where our team was filming a dramatic rendition of the "Prodigal Son" parable.

Discipling the Nations: Minang, West Sumatra

One of our actors was Muslim, and by the end of the filming he gave his life to the Lord. Part of what impressed him was that our team cared enough to make a film adapted to his Minang culture. When this actor, a prominent singer and entertainer in the Minang culture, proudly showed us some of his music cassettes, we challenged him to produce and sing music for his culture that would glorify the Lord. For the next few years, we prayed for him and challenged any team going to Sumatra to visit him and encourage him in producing music that would help bring people to the Lord.

Two years later, a team from Singapore was visiting that same area in Sumatra and heard of a local dance and music performance. They all attended and were overjoyed to hear the gospel woven into the presentation in a way that was nonoffensive to the majority Muslim audience, and was very professionally done. After the show they talked with the manager of this dance troupe and found out he was the former actor from our film! He shared that our team had challenged him and showed him how to use the arts to present the gospel. He continues to rise to the challenge, winning people to Jesus using Minang cultural art forms.

We are continually discovering ways in which we can best use the indigenous arts of a culture to convey the gospel message—but so much more could be done in this area. Christian workers around the world should be paying special attention to how this can be encouraged and promoted in their work, especially among unreached peoples.

What an Integrated Media Plan Could Look Like

Since no single medium can do the whole job effectively, focus-groups and other research methods should be employed to establish which media work best for each stage of the discipling process. It would be worthwhile to survey both nonbelievers and new believers with the following questions:

- Which media attracted you to know about Jesus?
- Which medium was most effective in communicating the gospel message to you?
- Which media helped you grow in your faith?

Missions' current need is not for a new, one-time approach, but for a coordinated process that combines various media forms over a period of time.[11] The combined use of multimedia elements, e.g., music and visuals, increases the emotive and persuasive appeal of the presentation. It's also key to remember that media alone is not enough; "media combined with human interaction is one of the most effective means of communication."[12] A follow-up with group discussion also increases retention and allows for clarification of the message.

Media can optimize every level of church growth and discipling nations. For instance:

- Radio spots and flyer distribution could spark community interest in attending a movie or short video showing.
- At the movie showing, tracts or audio cassettes could be distributed. Having a printed tract or audio tool in hand for people can help bring the message home to them as individuals, giving them something to take home and reflect on privately.
- The distributed literature or verbal request could extend an invitation to a home Bible study. Christians in the Bible study could then develop relationships that lead to a conversion of the attendee.
- After conversion, a workbook and video for new Christians could be used to enhance the Bible study during the week; radio and TV programs could help the new believer grow in faith.
- A multimedia kit (cassette, VCD, workbook, and correspondence) could be given to the new leaders providing discipleship in some aspect of biblical education, or in place of a kit perhaps an Internet Bible training course including streaming video of lecturers and graphic illustrations of the lessons could be made available.
- A short film might be helpful to depict a home group studying the Bible. A group of believers might find it helpful also to have a workbook for their times of Bible study so each can prepare beforehand and record personal thoughts and prayers.
- A new church could learn evangelism and cross-cultural ministry through video profiles and prayer booklets as they go out to minister to another unreached people group.

The 6,500 distinct unreached people groups of the world[13] reflect the incredible complexity, diversity, and greatness of our God. One media form, or one message, will not reach them all. Several mission organizations get some help with the necessary research and planning of the effective use of media through media strategists. These strategists can help missionaries consider how to use media effectively in six different tactical areas: evangelism, conversion, discipleship, leadership training, church planting, and initiating church-planting movements.

From Evangelism to Church Planting: Discipling New Believers

Discipleship tools are being created to help new believers in a particular people group understand how they can start contextual home fellowships that are both faithful to

Scripture and relevant to their culture. The response to these videos has been dramatic. The local actors, themselves believers from a Muslim background, told us that these films would also be very effective for evangelism. This is confirmed by testimony after testimony of people who have given their lives to the Lord after viewing these presentations. In South Sumatra, a new believer was viewing the contextual worship video with his wife who was not yet a believer. After the presentation, his wife exclaimed, "If that is what you have been talking about, then yes, I am interested. I could worship Jesus like that!" One of the participants in the film, an actual church-planting leader in the community, showed the Indonesian contextual gathering film to the Islamic evangelistic association in his area. After viewing the film, one of the Muslim leaders said, "I believe in Isa al Masih [Jesus the anointed Savior]. How can I become a believer and be baptized?"

One of the greatest hindrances for Muslims to come to Christ is their preconceived idea about the nature and practice of Christians. If they can see that there are followers of Jesus who look like and worship like they do, they see how they too could be a part of this new family—a family who love and follow the teachings of Jesus (*Isa* in Arabic) and who also remain "fully submitted to God" (which is the call of all Muslims). God knew that this type of presentation was just what many Muslims were waiting to see and hear. Contextual worship videos are available for Indonesians, Algerians, Kurds, Turks, Urdus, Hindis, and Thai peoples.

Discipling the Nations: Urdu Speakers of India

"Yes, we're using the same Create International teaching VCD on contextual worship. We used to plant just one fellowship every week. But now, every day we go to a different house and tell them to invite their friends and family to come in, and we're starting a new *jamat* (contextual house church) every day in our area." This exciting report was told to us while on a recent trip to India.

National church-planting leaders have seen a tremendous breakthrough among the Urdu-speaking Muslims of India. Reports indicate they have recently baptized 750 new believers and around 7,000 are waiting to receive baptism. They have started 180 *jamats* in one area and 120 in another area, which already had 2,000 baptized believers.[14] It was incredible to hear of real breakthrough among the peoples of Northern India.

God is actively working in each people group and invites our participation with him. He is revealing himself through dreams and visions, miraculous healings, and other manifestations of the Spirit's power. As workers we also need to be involved in bold and abundant proclamation of the Word, demonstrations of love, humble service, transformed lives, and relationship. It is these realities that bring many people to Christ—and we rejoice in the fruit that we are seeing. Greater contextualization of the gospel message will lead to lasting fruit as the community embraces the message within their cultural context.

Putting It All Together

At this point in history, while we carefully select the most effective technologies for each context, there is an even larger movement toward integrating the technologies themselves. The convergence of television, satellite, mobile telecommunications, and the Internet will spark a revolution in how we see and interact with our world. It will literally launch the world into an unprecedented free-flow of information that will dwarf the effect experienced by the invention of the printing press!

Almost overnight, the simplest evangelistic websites will have an international television ministry. Those who have a presence on the Internet now, will be first in line to reap the rewards. All of this has brought the Internet closer than ever before to over a billion people. As Christians we stand at a very important point in human history and the evangelization of the world. We must be prepared to take advantage of this exciting new innovation.

Discipling the Nations: Hindus of India

India. In a land of one billion, mostly without Christ, the gospel's progress needs to be accelerated—instead of hindered. The family and social community of the 700 million Hindus of this nation will provide a natural relationship for worship and church gathering. Working in partnership with several mission agencies, Create International has produced a culturally adapted evangelistic film in the Hindi language, as well as a follow-up discipleship film that demonstrates how to start contextual home fellowships. Along with these two media tools we have also created a Hindu evangelistic website which contains additional contextual evangelistic and discipleship materials.

These three communication technology tools are woven together as a holistic transformational media package. When the evangelistic film is viewed, it gives links to the discipleship materials that include the contextual home-fellowship training video and the website, which is in Hindi and English. When the website is accessed, both of the video tools are available for viewing as streaming media, as well as downloadable for duplication and distribution.

Because of the popularity and low cost of VCD technology in India, thousands of copies of these two films have been distributed all over the country. In addition, millions of households are able to view it, as several Christian TV ministries are showing the film. These ministries are doing follow-up response with their viewers and referring them to the website and other discipleship materials available in their heart languages. Field missionaries and national workers report that Hindu people are contacting them for more information after viewing the film or website.

Call to Action

Passion and determination are two keys to being an effective communicator: passion for the Lord and his heart to reach all peoples, and determination to keep pressing on despite obstacles. We must never give up until all have heard! When the goal is clear, the creativity, energy, and resourcefulness are released to get the job done effectively. As communicators of the good news, we must constantly be seeking to utilize all forms of technology to ensure wider and more efficient communication of our message worldwide. Communicators must work hard to choose the appropriate media to communicate a contextualized message for salvation, discipleship, and community transformation.

All the passion and determination in the world still falls short unless our ministries are anointed, and only humility will generate the blessing of God. He wants our involvement, using all of our gifts, by all possible means, to bring all the nations the greatest story ever told. Let's take full advantage of the multiplicity of media forms, ask God for new insight and creativity, and together with him create new communication tools that will bring the message of salvation and transformation to the unreached.

God has millions of new ways to reach the peoples of this earth, and he will give them to us if we seek him earnestly. The apostle Paul's words ring true for us today: "so that *by all possible means* I might save some" (1 Cor. 9:22).

Have we exhausted all possible means? In discipling all nations, and finishing the task of world evangelization, we must follow the admonitions of the apostle Paul, "It has always been my ambition to preach the gospel where Christ was not known, so that I would not be building on someone else's foundation. Rather, as it is written: 'Those who were not told about him will see, and those who have not heard will understand'" (Rom. 15:20–21). Paul's ambition and devotion to God's call to extend the kingdom of God ignited a passion in him that could not be quenched, a passion that drove him to the frontiers.

Following his example, let's take the gospel to *all* peoples, discipling *all* nations.

For more information and resources see www.createinternational.com and www.indigitech.net.

Bibliography

Barrett, David. *Our Globe and How to Reach It*. Birmingham, Ala.: New Hope, 1990.

Engel, James. *How Can I Get Them to Listen?* Grand Rapids: Zondervan, 1977.

Hesselgrave, David. *Communicating Christ Cross-Culturally*. Grand Rapids: Zondervan, 1978.

Hiebert, Paul. *Anthropological Insights for Missionaries*. Grand Rapids: Baker Book House, 1985.

———. *Cultural Anthropology*. Grand Rapids: Baker Book House, 1976.

Klem, Herbert. *Oral Communication of Scripture*. Pasadena, Calif.: William Carey Library, 1982.

McLuhan, Marshall. *Understanding Media: The Extensions of Man*. New York: McGraw-Hill, 1966.

Nicholls, Kathleen. *Asian Arts and Christian Hope*. New Delhi: Select Books, 1983.

Nida, Eugene. *Customs and Culture*. New York: Harper and Row, 1954. (Reprinted Pasadena, Calif.: William Carey Library, 1975.)

———. *Message and Mission: The Communication of the Christian Faith*. New York: Harper and Brothers, 1960.

Richardson, Don. *Eternity in Their Hearts*. Ventura, Calif.: Regal Books, 1984.

Roper, Don. *"What is Group Media?"* WACC Journal. London: World Association of Christian Communication, 1983.

Shaw, Daniel. *Transculturation*. Pasadena, Calif.: William Carey Library, 1988.

Smith-Morris, Miles, ed. *The Economist Book of Vital World Statistics*. New York: Economist Books, 1990.

Soggard, Viggo. *Applying Christian Communication*. Ann Arbor, Mich.: University Microfilms, 1986.

———. *Media in Church and Mission*. Pasadena, Calif.: William Carey Library, 1993.

Tsering, Marku. *Sharing Christ in the Tibetan Buddhist World*. Upper Darby, Penn.: Tibet Press, 1988.

Notes

1. See Don Richardson's *Eternity in Their Hearts* for wonderful stories of discovering the truths already in the culture which point to God and his ways.

2. From "A Northstar for Evangelization Strategy" by Paul Eshleman, chairman, Strategy Working Group, Lausanne Committee for World Evangelization, 2007 report.

3. Mark Snowden, IMB Media strategist, media conference, 2000.

4. "About Us," *The Jesus Film Project,* A Ministry of Campus Crusade for Christ, International, www.jesusfilm.org/aboutus/index.html (accessed April 2007).

5. Tony Whittaker, *Bulletin of Web Evangelism,* Web-Evangelism Guide, SOON Ministries, http://guide.gospelcom.net/resources/bulletin.php (accessed 2000).

6. www.internetworldstats.com (accessed April 2007).

7. Whittaker, *Bulletin of Web Evangelism* (accessed 2000).

8. www.megavoice.com.

9. Tibetan worker's personal communication, letter in 1992.

10. Report from field missionaries in Tibet, 2000.

11. Viggo Sogaard, *Everything You Need to Know for a Cassette Ministry* (Minneapolis: Bethany House, 1975), 34.

12. Don Roper, "What Is Group Media?" *World Association for Christian Communications Journal* (1983).

13. www.joshuaproject.net.

14. Report from Paul Eshleman, strategy leader for Finishing the Task, quoted in *Update,* 2007, an e-mail communication of Create International. For other reports and streaming evangelistic videos in a variety of languages and cultural settings, see www.createinternational.com.

Strategy coordination is a relatively new and fruitful phenomenon. Strategy coordinators help the body of Christ to work together more effectively to start church-planting movements and serve and bless nations. By telling the story of Anna, an imaginary strategy coordinator, Karine K explains the roles and functions of this diverse position.

Strategy Coordination:
Opening a Door to the Unreached

Karine K

Amazing News about Unreached People Groups

Let your imagination go wild as you read the following news items—amazing statistics from the mission fields:

- In an unreached people group (UPG)[1] of Southeast Asia, in just four years the number of believers soared from 85 to 55,000—in over 550 new churches.
- In one Central Asian UPG, over 15,000 baptisms were performed in one year.
- In a South Asian UPG, 300,000 new believers and 4,000 new churches were established in less than a decade.
- In an African UPG, 600 home churches were started in two and a half years.
- Elsewhere in Asia, 100 churches were planted in four years among a certain UPG.
- In South Asia, 90,000 converts were recorded within eight years.
- In China, a UPG was reached with the gospel. The result was thousands of converts, hundreds of new churches, and members of this UPG carrying the gospel to other groups.
- In South America, thirty churches were planted in a UPG during a three-year period.

Are you excited about these statistics? Do you wonder if they are true, or just the fruit of my imagination? Praise God, they are true! These events have been and are still happening today! You may wonder how this is possible and who participated in making this happen. In each of those events a Strategy Coordinator played an important role in what took place. To learn more, read on.

"What is a Strategy Coordinator?" you may ask. Good question. Basically a strategy coordinator (SC), sometimes called a strategic coordinator, is a believer who humbly seeks to develop and implement a comprehensive, multifaceted strategy in order to see multiple church-planting movements[2] (CPMs) initiated and nurtured in an entire unreached people group, city, or segment of a population. The SC job description can be incredibly broad and varied.

Initially, the future SC is just an ordinary man or woman who has become so passionate for the unreached that he or she wants to see church-planting movements happen among them. To make this task more manageable, our future SC will prayerfully choose to serve a particular unreached people group, a city, or even a 4K zone.[3] To provide the big picture, let me create a case study. Let us follow Anna as she undertakes the ministry of an SC.[4]

Anna the Strategy Coordinator

Through Anna's story, from her preparation to the growth and multiplication of her ministry, we will see the role and functions of an SC.

Anna's Preparation

Anna's heart has been touched by God and is beating with his for the unreached. She has learned about the work of strategy coordinators and definitely desires to become one. Anna has chosen the Milian people group in Asia as her target group. She has heard that a small church-planting team from her organization is working among them and needs help. She contacts the people who will train her, and they recommend that she go on an information-gathering trip before coming to training.

Following their advice, Anna takes an information-gathering trip to the region where the Milian live. She also discovers plenty of interesting data through the Internet. Among many other bits of information, she learns that the Milian are a proud people group of about two million. They are Buddhists, and apparently have only ten Christians among them. There is no indigenous church as yet; the few actual believers have joined other ethnic churches.

Next Anna goes for one month of training where she learns how to become a fully functional SC. The SC curriculum is wide ranging. Students learn about methods for reaching the lost, ways to disciple new believers, and skills for humbly partnering with various types of organizations.

During her training, Anna learns that she will always need to have the end goal in mind and that her end goal is to see a church-planting movement happen among the Milian.

She is encouraged to start by asking herself the question, "What will it take to reach this people group with the gospel?" instead of "What will I do to reach this people group?" The difference between the two questions is very important. The second question implies that Anna is alone and will do something on her own. But the first question deliberately looks at the overall "big picture" situation and implies that the strategy coordinator will not be working alone.

Indeed, Anna is not going to be working alone. Firstly, God is in the situation, he is at work, and he has plans for the future. Secondly, there is the body of Christ. If Anna just went to the field ignoring the rest of Christ's body, she would start a compartmentalized ministry; maybe she would try to plant a church with the team from her own organization. However, as an SC, she will first assess what is already happening among the Milian, and she will ask God how she can participate in that. One of the preeminent words in strategy coordination is *partnership*. The SC cannot just promote her own ministry. Her ministry extends far beyond her personal church or organization and seeks the unity of the body of Christ.

While in training, Anna does more research on the Milian people and on groups who are working to reach them. She confirms that her own organization has a church-planting team working among the Milian. This team is formed of people from the same country as the Milian, but they are not Milian; they come from other people groups. Apparently, they have had little result so far in seeing Milian come to Christ. She also discovers that in another area, a different team is translating the Bible into the Milian language. After a period of many difficulties, the team experienced the death of their main translator. Their translation is progressing very slowly. About this same time, in Australia, a church hears about the Milian and decides to adopt them. Not knowing how to get started, the church contacts their local adoption program office. Because Anna has also just contacted them, the adoption program office helps link Anna with this church body.

During her training, Anna starts writing a master plan. The master plan is like a road map that will help her go the right direction and not be sidetracked by less effective activities. In her master plan, she states her goals and gives target dates for each of them. She also states her end vision: to see a church-planting movement happen among the Milian people. Everything she does in her SC work must contribute to helping make this CPM happen. She will have to constantly reevaluate what she is doing to ensure she is on track.

What types of activities might sidetrack Anna from her main goal? If a local church wants to adopt the Milian, it would be great if they asked Anna to advise and help them. However, if they start asking Anna to do all kinds of other things like preaching on Sundays or teaching the new believers' class, she needs to recognize that these activities are not very effective in starting a CPM among the Milian and graciously decline. Enabling a church to adopt the Milian effectively is a key activity for her; becoming a teacher in this church would be a sidetrack. Or, as a second example, suppose that a community development project organized by XYZ organization plans to reach out to the Milian. As Anna facilitates XYZ, she realizes that a different people group is the one actually being served. She should bring this to the attention of XYZ and try to convince them to return to their original target. If they want to stick with the new people group, then Anna should bless them and not spend too much time on their project because it is no longer helping to create a CPM among the Milian.

Getting Started

After having written her master plan, Anna works at implementing it. She chooses to live among the Milian.[5] She starts learning the language and the culture to make sure she is as efficient as possible.

Intercessory Prayer

Following her master plan, she prays for the Milian and asks others to pray. She enlists intercessors and makes sure the Milian are a prayer and intercessory target. Anna knows that prayer and intercession are the key to seeing the Milian reached for Christ. No activities among the Milian should be started without them. Spiritual warfare is also a must. The territory has belonged to Satan for years, so she knows she can't expect him to leave unless prayer, intercession, and spiritual warfare are strong. The Lord himself has asked his disciples to pray for the Master to send out more laborers in Matthew 9:38, "Ask the Lord of the harvest, therefore, to send out workers into his harvest field."

Networking and Working Together

Anna continues by contacting the church-planting team on site[6] and introduces herself to them. She listens to what they are doing and how they are doing it. She prays with them, and she tells them that she is here to serve them.

While talking to the team, Anna discovers that they have had four people come to Christ recently, but the team is struggling to disciple them. She takes the liberty to offer some advice and asks the team if she may demonstrate something she learned in her SC training: how to conduct a home church that will lead the new believers to become true disciples and to share the gospel with others. Although the team leader is a bit reluctant at first because he sees Anna as an intruder, Anna's gentleness and humility wins his heart. She has the team members pretend they are new converts;

then Anna models to them how they could effectively conduct home church meetings. At the end of her stay with them, the team leader is very enthusiastic and says he will try her method. The other team members are willing to give it a try too.

Anna is about to leave when one of the team member tells her that one of the new converts has in his heart to help translate the Bible into his language. Anna's heart jumps as she remembers the Bible translation team that has just lost their main translator. She asks the team leader if she can connect this Bible translation team with this new believer. The team leader happily agrees. Anna promises to visit again and tells the team not to hesitate to contact her if they need anything.

Next, Anna visits the Bible translation team. They are quite discouraged because of their many setbacks. One member is on the verge of quitting. Anna listens to their stories and struggles. When she tells them about the church-planting team and their potential translator, the translation team is very encouraged by her news. Anna prays with them. By the time she leaves, the team member who wanted to quit is reconsidering his position and seeking God for courage to stay. Anna also encourages them to link with the church-planting team. She suggests that they even try to see each other occasionally to pray together. She assures them that she is here if they need her.

Anna also sends an e-mail to the Australian church who has adopted the Milian. In their reply, they are very excited to hear about her SC ministry and are wondering how they can help. One of their ideas is to send a street-evangelism team. Anna grimaces when she reads that. Street evangelism is definitely *not* an option among the Milian, unless the church's team wants to end up in jail. However, she also knows that she cannot stop them if they just want to come and do it. She can only explain the situation to them and hope they will understand. In her next e-mail, she gently clarifies why it is not advisable to do street evangelism. She recommends a few other options instead. Among the options are intercession and prayer drives, and putting together a medical team. Anna also spends time in prayer for this church.

The pastor answers that he understands perfectly and is glad to have her advice. It just happens that they have one medical doctor and two nurses. Could they put together a medical team and come? Anna promises to research how to organize this. She contacts the department of health of the Milian region and is told that they would be very eager to receive such a medical team. They would even provide a guide. Anna becomes the bridge between the medical team and the health department until the medical team arrives on the field together with an intercession team.

Before coming, these two teams received a brief training from Anna regarding the Milian culture and the goals of their trip. Now they swing into action. The intercession team travels ahead of the medical team praying and preparing the ground, while the medical team goes around with their official guide. This guide makes them a bit nervous because they do not feel they can share freely. However, he proves to be a very nice man. He slowly realizes that the team members are Christian and soon starts to ask questions about their faith. At the end of their stay, the team has taken care of numerous sicknesses for people of all ages. Most of all, they have shown the love and kindness of Christ in a practical way. The guide has heard the gospel and is identified as a possible man of peace by the medical team. Anna had asked them to look for this kind of person according to Luke 10:5–6, "When you enter a house, first say, 'Peace to this house.' If a man of peace is there, your peace will rest on him; if not, it will return to you." The gospel had not been preached openly to all the sick and their families. However, when some families asked the team why they had come, it provided an opportunity for sharing.

As soon as the team leaves, Anna passes on the names of the guide and the villages that were visited and touched to the church-planting team. After waiting for some time, the church-planting team contacts the guide. He proves to be a true man of peace. He soon gives his life to Christ after some contact with one team member. Soon his immediate family follows. The team member starts to disciple them according to the method Anna had previously shared. The guide and his family immediately start sharing the gospel with friends and family.

This is when the head of their region becomes angry. He tells the guide to stop talking about Jesus or be denounced to the police. Some other people in the area are angry too. One night they surround the guide's house and scream threats. They say that they will kill him if he doesn't stop sharing the gospel. The frightened family starts praying. Suddenly, everything becomes silent again; no one is seen outside anymore. The next day, the guide meets one of the assailants, who asks, "Who were these men dressed in white around your house yesterday?" The guide replies that he doesn't know who they were. After these events, he quickly contacts the church planter who explains to him that these men were probably angels. What an encouragement to everyone involved!

Wise Reporting

From that story, Anna writes a quarterly newsletter about what is happening among the Milian. The letter is sent to her supporters and to the Australian church that has adopted the Milian. The church distributes the letter among the church members. Since names and places have been changed, there is no security concern.

Growth and Cooperation

The pastor of this church has been talking with another pastor. The second pastor has become very interested in their involvement among the Milian and decides to persuade his church to adopt the Milian, too. This second church wants to send a missionary directly to the field. They have an agriculturist in their midst who is ready to go. Anna connects this agriculturist with the church-planting team. Networking with the believing guide, the team eventually connects the agriculturalist to an interested village headman. The headman makes an official invitation and helps with the necessary papers so that the agriculturist and his family can live in his village.

Progress and Setbacks

Meanwhile, the church-planting team is doing well with two of their four new believers. They have taught them, and these two disciples have started to share the gospel with the people around them. The humility that they have shown in their families by apologizing for past wrong attitudes has really affected one family; some who aren't yet believers have even apologized to others. Forgiveness is beginning to be more common in their small community. Anna remembers from her SC training that biblical values and attitudes will affect a UPG as a true understanding of the gospel spreads.

The third convert has joined the Bible translation team to help as a translator. He is being discipled by that team as they work together.

The fourth new believer, however, created some problems after he came in contact with a pastor jealous of the work among the Milian. This pastor told the Milian convert that the church-planting team is using him to make money. This lie created a difficult situation. The church-planting team tried talking to the pastor, but to no avail. He could not accept that "intruders" were sharing the gospel with the Milian, although he himself, from another people group, has never done it before. The church-planting team calls Anna to ask for prayer and support. She relays the information to the two churches who have adopted the Milian. Everyone prays. It is decided to bless this pastor, forgive him, and continue the Milian ministry.

Further Growth

The church-planting team has contacts with a non-Milian church inside the Milian area. The Lord has touched the heart of this local church, and they want to be part of sharing the gospel with the Milian. The church has a few members who already have befriended Milians; some of them are very interested in the gospel. In one case, the pastor was invited to visit the wife of a Milian witch doctor. She was very sick and her husband, the witch doctor, had not been able to help her. She wanted the pastor to pray for her. When the pastor prayed, the woman was healed. The witch doctor admitted that the power of Jesus exceeded his own. This encounter opened the door for the whole family, including even a member of the extended family, to become saved and be discipled. They shared the gospel further among the Milian. One home church was planted and then another.

Anna is still busy visiting the CP team and helping them to organize discipleship and training for the new converts, whose numbers are increasing rapidly. House church numbers are also on the rise as recent converts themselves plant churches and start to lead them.

Radio and Movies

In the same time frame, following her master plan, Anna contacts a radio broadcasting organization to encourage them to start an evangelistic radio broadcast. Almost every Milian has a radio. Further, because there are no broadcasts in their language, a Milian language radio program could be quite effective once the word had spread about the program. Convincing the radio broadcast company is not easy, but Anna succeeds by working from the top leaders on down. One of the Milian converts is eager to become the announcer for the broadcast, and another convert offers to help. The frequency of the broadcast is publicized on free calendars, small cards, and pens. When listeners have questions, they write to an address given on the program. Their names are then passed along to the leader of the closest home church.

One of the adoptive churches has heard about an organization that creates promotional movies *and* contextual movies for the unreached. This church is very enthusiastic about funding a Milian project. They ask Anna if she could help locate the right Milian actors for the movie and organize the shootings. Anna finds a man who wants to help organize the project on site. Actors are signed on and soon the filming starts. Some problems arise during the shooting, but through prayer and humility everything is settled. The contextualized movie is used as an evangelism tool among the Milian. The promotional movie is for a very different audience. It is used in the Christian world to encourage people to pray for and adopt the Milian people.

For the Milian, radios and movies are appropriate ways to facilitate a CPM. Another SC, working with a different UPG, might select a different way to help reach his UPG. Or, another adoptive church might set up an Internet site in the language of a different UPG. The SC encourages his partners to select appropriate tactics.

Multiplication and Unity

Anna's SC work continues, keeping the focus on seeing a church-planting movement happen among the Milian. Portions of the Gospel of Mark are translated and distributed, touching the hearts of many. After three years, 200 people have become believers and many new churches have been planted. A church-planting movement is beginning! New believers are taking ownership of evangelizing their own people. A local SC has also been identified and formed. He specializes in SC work on site, concentrating on church-planting coordination. Outsiders continue to be involved but are careful not to create dependency or push their own way. A partnership has been formed to foster the unity of the body of Christ among the Milian.

Opening Doors for the Unreached

In this simple story, we can see that Anna joins with what God is already doing and is planning to do among the Milian. She also partners with the whole body of Christ.

Some people have been there before and have seen little fruit, some have prepared the ground for years in prayer for the Milian, and some are willing to go. As an SC, Anna has the privilege of helping bring everything and everyone together to facilitate a church-planting movement. She is very aware of what Paul says in 1 Corinthians 3:6, "I planted the seed, Apollos watered it, but God made it grow."

Strategy coordination is a wonderful and fascinating work, a ministry which makes the difference for the unreached. May the Lord bless you abundantly as you seek his will for your life.[7]

Notes

1. Throughout this chapter I will refer to unreached people groups, usually by the acronym UPG. A people group is a social grouping sharing a common language and sense of ethnic identity. An unreached people group is one who has yet to be presented with the gospel.

2. A church-planting movement is a Holy Spirit–controlled process characterized by rapid, multiple reproduction of indigenous churches among a specific people group. In a CPM, virtually every individual within that people group has an opportunity to hear and respond to the good news of Christ.

3. 4K is a global framework created by Youth With A Mission to give us a new way to see the people of the world and to respond to their needs. For more information, see www.ywam4k.org.

4. Anna's story is inspired by true facts put together to illustrate the SC ministry. However, these events did not necessarily happen in the same people group and to the same SC. For security reasons, names, places, and details have been changed.

5. Although some SCs choose to live outside their UPGs, many SCs choose to live inside.

6. When SCs actually introduce themselves to teams on the field can vary widely. Sometimes, teams even recruit one of their members to become an SC. Other SCs may meet teams during their pre- or post-training visit to the region.

7. Did the story of Anna touch you? Does your heart vibrate to be a part of such a work? Are you an ordinary person who seeks to do an extraordinary work for God? Then consider becoming an SC for an unreached people group. You will never regret your involvement. You will get a wonderful reward here on earth when you see people come to Christ. Your heavenly reward will be even better when, according to Revelation 7:9, you will see "a great multitude that no one could count, from every nation, tribe, people and language, standing before the throne and in front of the Lamb." Among that crowd you will recognize thousands of members from the people group you served on earth as an SC.

If you or someone you know desires to work among an unreached people group, or as a member of a church-planting team you would like to see someone become an SC, or you are a leader who would like to raise up SCs and see them trained, please contact us by e-mail at scserviceteam@bluewin.ch.

The Korean Campus Ministry program has been highly successful in Korea and several other countries. SungGun Hong describes what they do, why they do it, and how they expect this ministry to affect Korea and other nations. University student movements have historically been tied to frontier missions movements. Note the well-planned approach and the areas the Koreans have chosen to emphasize.

University Campus Ministries

SungGun Hong

Universities are filled with young people open to change and challenge. Often, campuses are a microcosm of culture, ethnicity, and nationality. Today's diverse students will become tomorrow's leaders in every sphere of influence and in every nation. Hence, ministry to university students is a key component to discipling nations.

The first section of this chapter describes the model of Campus Ministry Korea (CMK). The Korean model has been successfully multiplied to several nations. A second section elucidates goals, strategies, and reasons for campus ministry.

The YWAM Campus Ministry Model in Korea

Overview and History

University classes begin at 9:00 AM, but by 8:20 many students are gathering in pairs to share insights from their morning meditations. Then they pray for each other and intercede for their campus. This scene repeats itself on many campuses as students meet in dining halls, outside classrooms, or on lawns.

Weekly these young people host a two-hour evening meeting open to all interested comers. The students intercede, welcome newcomers, pray for one another, and enjoy fellowship. After a brief message given to the assembly by a YWAM staff member, everyone studies the Bible in smaller groups. On Friday evenings, the students actively involved with campus ministry meet from 6:30 to 9:00 PM for more intensive teaching, worship, prayer, and fellowship. These energetic students further participate in various outreach activities on their campuses.

This is a brief sketch of the activities of campus ministry as developed by YWAM Korea. How did this ministry begin?

In September 1979 YWAM Korea decided to start YWAM's first campus ministry from the Seoul base. I was assigned to give leadership to the program. A camp meeting of seventy students in February 1980 marked the beginning of this ministry. Now held each July, this missions camp has experienced steady growth in participation. In 2000, approximately 2,800 students gathered at the camp. Twelve bases had campus ministry to a total of two hundred campuses. Approximately 1,200–1,400 students were attending the Friday-night meeting regularly—just in Seoul! One hundred fifty full-time campus ministry staff and many volunteers were actively engaged in this work.

Main Activities of Campus Ministry

To achieve the goal of discipling nations, Campus Ministry Korea has developed eleven specific activities and emphases that go beyond the few already described. Activities include elements to train the students in godliness, to involve them in worship and intercession, and to prepare them for spiritual warfare. We desire nothing less than fully discipled Christians who will impact their society and their world for the kingdom of God.

1. Campus activities. Five key activities occur regularly on each campus. The most basic event, requiring the minimum commitment of the students, is the weekly meeting on campus for worship and hearing God's Word. All who attend are considered members of the campus ministry. Many students will stay for the second key activity, an intercession gathering to pray for their campus, for Korea, and for the world. Weekly training meetings of two to five students for Bible study and fellowship provide the third opportunity. These groups progress through two specially developed training books: *Seven Steps* and *Six Foundations.* The daily QT meeting is the fourth key activity. Gathering before classes, students share about their morning meditations and pray together. This meeting helps train them to develop a habit of starting each day in God's Word. Fifthly, as regularly as scheduling permits, students organize activities to evangelize their campus.

2. Leader training. Leader training is a critical area of activity for CMK because student leaders are the ones who run the show at each campus after the initial pioneering efforts of YWAM CMK staff members. Of course, CMK staff gladly assist in the work and provide training, but the majority of the responsibility should rest with the student leaders. A student becomes a leader after going through leader training.

Campus leaders meet on Mondays to learn biblical principles of leadership. They also discuss how to manage their groups and influence their campuses, and they spend time praying for God's will to be done. Every student leader participates in a leadership training camp during winter and summer breaks. A time of restoration and renewal in each leader's life, the camp also provides a venue for intense strategy discussions with CMK staff.

3. Friday-night joint campus meeting. Fridays evenings, students actively involved on different campuses gather at the local YWAM base. They pray for Korea and their campuses, have a time of corporate worship, listen to the Word of God, and cultivate a kingdom vision.

4. Missions conference. The annual missions conference is held on the first week of July. All the staff and students involved with campus ministry throughout Korea are invited to assemble in one location. Because students only stay at the university for four years, approximately 50 percent of the attendees are newcomers each year. Equipping participants with a missions-oriented mind-set and giving them opportunity to commit themselves to God are the two chief goals of the conference. We make the most of the time with a full schedule. Before breakfast, from 6:00 to 7:30 AM, we meet for worship, preaching, and meditation. After breakfast, we gather from 9:00 to noon for more worship, lecture, and prayer. Between 2:00 and 3:30 PM, we offer tracks on diverse subjects (often geared to the mind molders or different mission frontiers), campus meetings, or small group meetings. The day ends with a 7:00 to 10:00 PM assembly for more worship, preaching, and prayer.

Every time the conference is held, great blessings flow because God loves the young people of this generation so much.

5. Minischool of evangelism. We run a two-session minischool of evangelism. The spring session primarily targets freshmen or new believers. Teaching topics include God's calling in each person's life and how to live as a disciple of Jesus on campus. The fall session focuses on renewing the participants. Subjects include worship, intercession, spiritual warfare, listening to the voice of God, godly life, inner healing, and so forth.

6. Outreach. Every campus develops its own campus outreach program. Furthermore, each campus group goes on outreach for one to four weeks over their summer or winter break. About two thousand students annually participate in outreach with CMK. Campus teams have visited almost every area and city of Korea, as well as more than eighty other countries (mostly in the 10/40 Window). These short-term mission trips are a good opportunity for the students to develop a vision for world missions.

7. University Discipleship Training School. University Discipleship Training School (UDTS) is designed for university students. It lasts for eight months, and the students go through the process of becoming disciples of Jesus both in the classroom and on an outreach. In UDTS, students do not have to leave their university studies to be trained in discipleship. By taking advantage of the winter vacation (December to February) and summer vacation (end of June to August), they can have twelve weeks of lecture and eight weeks of outreach. The outreach weeks consist of two weeks of campus outreach and six weeks on a foreign mission field. In January 1984 the first UDTS was held. By 2000, there had been fifty-six UDTSs with a total of 2,100 graduates.

The UDTS is open to anyone involved with the campus ministry. This school is recognized as a first course for those who want to become a disciple of Jesus, especially for those who want to become missionaries. A registered course of University of the Nations, the UDTS has topics based on the curriculum of YWAM International. Lessons include subjects such as relationship with God, relationship with others, relationship with self, and relationship with the world.

8. Multiplying campuses within our nation. Campus ministry in Korea has grown rapidly during the last twenty years. It began with a few campuses in Seoul, but now every university and college in Seoul is involved. Bases in Pusan, Kwangju, Junju, Mokpo, Taejun, Chunchon, Taegu, Chonan, Chongju, Suwon, and Jeju have all developed campus activities. Our goal is to continue pioneering campuses until CMK serves the students in every Korean university and college.

9. Frontier missions and Target 2020. Campus ministry does not merely produces well-discipled Christians; it also can be a tool to achieve the vision in the book of Revelation, where multitudes from every nation, tribe, people, and tongue sing praises to God. In the 1990s YWAM Korea began to pioneer campus ministry outside of Korea. By 2004 campus ministry had multiplied to six other countries: Thailand, India, China, Japan, Mongolia, and Kenya. In each country campus ministry comes under the authority of the local YWAM leadership, not under that of YWAM Korea.

Until 2020 CMK will participate in the project Target 2020, YWAM Korea's comprehensive frontier mission strategy. Because of CMK's expertise in discipling nations through university ministry, our 2020 target is to pursue evangelism and mission activities in universities of the 10/40 Window, especially in unreached nations. This will involve pioneering new locations and multiplying the universities reached within those new regions. CMK will continue to send workers and will help provide strategy for each location. Based on taking initiative on mission frontiers, our Target 2020 project is an important strategy in achieving the Great Commission. We hope this ministry will multiply into and within many nations.

10. Alliance Movement. Another important emphasis of CMK is the Alliance Movement, a program of YWAM Korea. Alliances with local churches and other missions are a high priority. The students involved with campus ministry are highly encouraged to be active members of their own local churches. When a person accepts the gospel, we introduce him or her to a local church. To support church participation and to leave students free for their church meetings, we have no official meetings on Sundays. Even the annual missions conference runs Monday through Saturday so the students will not miss time in their home churches.

As part of the Alliance Movement, we also encourage and facilitate interaction with other Christian groups on campus or in the region. When the new school term begins, many campus Christian groups benefit from corporate activities. For example, Christians from various groups have a combined opening worship service. They also participate throughout the year in a mutual March for Jesus, joint seminars, and shared concerts. These united activities can be important factors in campus evangelization.

11. Vision groups. For devoted Christians who want to share the gospel in the 10/40 Window, we instituted weekly "vision groups." Ideally, these groups enable students to follow through on their desire to serve the Lord in missions. Each vision group focuses on one country, and students choose a group according to their vision. The members pray for that country and study about God's heart for the nations. They also go on an outreach to the vision location so they can have first-hand experience of the people, their culture, and their needs. In 2003 there were vision groups for South Africa, Taiwan, the Democratic Republic of Congo, North Korea, Europe, Egypt (Middle East), India, Indonesia, the Philippines, Japan, South America, Central Asia, China, Kenya, Turkey, Thailand, and North America. There was even a group for those who did not yet have a specific vision!

Vision groups are one step in the process of becoming missionaries. From freshman to those who are definitely preparing to go as missionaries, various people join the groups. Membership is not limited to people in YWAM, but open to graduates and experts in various areas. We want to set up a structure that can mobilize the manpower of students and graduates alike.

The Influence of Campus Ministry in Korea

Campus ministry has influenced YWAM, the local Korean church, the families of student members, campuses, and Korean society as a whole. We are encouraged to see such widespread results coming from this ministry.

CMK has greatly influenced YWAM Korea and provided many resources for the work. Over thirty Discipleship Training Schools (DTSs) run annually in Korea. Numerous applicants are graduates previously involved with campus ministry. Many of these have continued on to become full-time YWAM staff. Among the twenty-two National Leadership Team members in 2003, fifteen members were trained in campus ministry. Several former campus ministry students are included among the missionaries sent from Korea. Clearly, ministry on the campuses is producing efficient leaders and many committed, obedient workers.

CMK has helped to build up the local churches by discipling students. During their university years, most active members of campus ministry are also involved members of local churches. They bear much fruit in their ministry. When they graduate, their Christian life continues to edify the local church. They can become pillars of their local churches, because they are well-discipled Christians.

The students of campus ministry have been positive influences in their families. Many Korean families suffer from hatred, fear, bitterness, and unbelief. Youth discipled in campus ministry bring love, forgiveness, trust, an attitude of thanksgiving, and other godly virtues back to their homes. Many non-Christian families have become Christian through the influence and example of their family member who started following Jesus at the university.

Members of CMK also work toward creating a holy and godly atmosphere on campus. Our universities usually have a secular humanist framework that naturally worships worldly values like knowledge and fame. Hedonistic pleasures are often sought as thrilling and fulfilling. Through the intercession and witness of committed believers, the universities are being influenced to become places of light.

Further, the influence of CMK members extends beyond YWAM, their families, their campuses, and their local churches. When these discipled students graduate, they become the salt and light of the society in their specific areas of calling. Some work as doctors or nurses, others as teachers, professors, diplomats, lawyers, reporters, pastors, or missionaries. Having a biblical worldview, they labor to extend God's kingdom in their life's vocation. CMK graduates influence not only Korea, but also the nations.

How to Have an Effective Campus Ministry

From our experience, Campus Ministry Korea has learned that an effective ministry to students requires clear and appropriate goals. We have honed our goals to three essentials: evangelizing our campus, preparing students to be change agents in society, and evangelizing the world. To attain these goals, several strategic elements have proven to be of great benefit. These will be explained in "Effective Strategy for Campus Ministry" below.

The Goals of Campus Ministry

The first and most obvious goal of campus ministry is campus evangelization. In CMK, campus evangelization is not defined as causing every student to confess Jesus as his or her Lord and Savior. Rather, it means giving each student at least one opportunity to hear the gospel on a personal level. Further, influencing the campus toward godly values and lifestyles is considered a part of campus evangelization. We want to influence all students toward a Christian worldview.

Our numerical target is to have at least 25 percent of the student body confess Jesus as their Lord. We further seek that 25 percent of the Christians attend the meetings regularly, live out the life of a disciple, and be devoted to world missions.

From our experience on Korean campuses, approximately 3 percent of the students are extremely ungodly. They are absorbed in communism, socialism, humanism, or atheism. They use violent demonstration to achieve their goals. Another 20–22 percent of the students are their followers. We have also observed that around 3 percent of the students are devout Christians. They meditate on the Word of God and pray for their campus daily. They share the gospel with other students. While Christians often compose around 25 percent of the whole student body, only the devout 3 percent become involved in active evangelism. Roughly 50 percent of the students stay neutral or undecided. It is the 3 percent at either extreme that decides the atmosphere of the campus. The godly Christian group can take initiative to lead the campus toward holiness and biblical values. When we change a culture of alcohol, smoking, drugs, sexual immorality, violence, lies, cheating, and unfaithfulness into a godly culture, we can call it campus evangelism.

The second goal of campus ministry is preparing students to be societal change agents. We are not only concerned with the spiritual life of the students or with their campus. We also focus on preparing the students to lead their lives according to biblical principles before and after they graduate. Then they can be change agents in society. It is strategic to disciple university students. They are potential leaders in every field of endeavor. Moreover, in a multiethnic country, the leaders of several ethnicities may study together on one campus. Often, the best students from countries closed to the gospel come to universities where we are free to do campus ministry. So campus ministry aims not only at sharing the gospel with the students but also at discipling them, and, through them, ultimately discipling their ethnic groups and nations (Matt. 28:19). Further, campus ministry deliberately seeks to teach the students to influence each area of society (politics, economy, education, arts, religion, science and technology, family) through their majors. We teach them the Bible so that they can understand the kingdom of God, Christian worldview, and God's principles and character. Basic understanding of these areas can be translated into any sphere of society.

The third goal of CMK is world evangelization. This may be practically achieved in two ways. First, university revivals are a powerful impetus to world mission. Campus revivals have historically led to dramatic steps forward in world missions. Usually, 90 percent of campus ministry students take a traditional job and influence society after graduation. The other 10 percent devote themselves to cross-cultural missions. Second, universities are mini mission fields on our doorstep because the best and brightest of many nations, tribes, and tongues come to university at a key time in their lives, when they are seeking truth and open to new ideas. Universities are at the heart of the people. I believe the university is the most strategic and influential field in evangelizing unreached peoples. Even if they do not become Christians at this time, many of these diverse students go on to become influential leaders who can welcome or reject kingdom influences in their spheres of influence. Their university experiences can make them more open or closed to Christian influences in the future.

Effective Strategy for Campus Ministry

We need effective strategies to fulfill these goals. I would like to suggest eleven elements of strategy that lead to an effective campus ministry.

1. Keep prayer as a priority. We should pray whenever we meet. Prayer should be our top priority, even higher than fellowship. We should pray for revival and awakening in campus. We should pray that the Holy Spirit will shed the light of Christ to unbelievers so they will understand that life without Jesus is vain and that the pleasure they are seeking is not the true answer. We should pray for the students and their families. We should pray for the nation, and each area within it. We should pray for missionaries and the mission fields.

I was influenced by the prayer life of Dawson Trotman, who founded The Navigators. He and his friends went to a small cave at 5:00 AM every day. He hung a small map of the U.S. and prayed. God showed him that he would raise young people from all fifty states. Trotman prayed that he would be able to train those young people and send them to all nations. Since God gave him this specific vision, he prayed mentioning each state.

At some point, before he even had enough workers to start The Navigators, he became free from the burden of this particular prayer. Finally sure that God had answered his prayer, he began to thank God. He then hung a world map and began to pray. Later on, when he checked the list of workers of The Navigators, he realized that they were literally from all fifty states! His type and attitude of prayer is what we need.

2. Exalt the Lord with praise and worship. We should seriously, joyously, and enthusiastically praise Jesus, the Lamb. Many ministries in the campus have a short time of praise, because they are intellectually oriented. But we need to exalt Jesus Christ by our praise. When we praise him, we can draw near to God and Jesus Christ, and we can know God better.

3. Study the Word of God. We should study the Bible. Each meeting should focus on the study of God's Word. This is not a time merely to discuss the latest ideas and philosophies. Our Bible study should include an emphasis on application, on each of us trying to live out the Word of God in our individual and community lives.

4. Disciple students. We should focus on deliberately training disciples. Campus ministry should challenge the students to take the Bible as the plumb line in each area of their lives. It is easy to develop a selfish and egotistical attitude during the campus years. So, we should help the students to learn the life of community.

5. Emphasize the local church. Campus ministry should emphasize the importance of local churches. Campus Christian groups are usually more dynamic and active than local churches. Understanding campus culture better, campus groups can adapt rapidly to a quickly changing youth culture. Young people may thus consider the local church to be inferior. Yet, after graduation, the students must center their life of faith around their local church. Hence, we seek to connect students with local churches.

6. Empower student leadership. Campus ministry should be led by the students themselves, not by the YWAM staff. CMK staff do their best to empower and encourage the students to take initiative. When staff members take too much initiative on campus, students can become passive, and their spiritual growth may even be stunted. Leading stretches students to be proactive and to grow in their faith.

7. Aim to produce world changers. Campus ministry should produce future leaders who will influence society in a godly ways. God shows us an example in King David: "He chose David his servant and took him from the sheep pens; from tending the sheep he brought him to be the shepherd of his people Jacob, of Israel his inheritance. And David shepherded them with integrity of heart; with skillful hands he led them" (Ps. 78:70–72).

When God prepared David to become the king of Israel, he provided two things: one was the integrity of his heart, the other was the skillfulness of his hands. The former is formed by discipleship training, the latter is specific knowledge or skills acquired through study or experience to influence society in that area. Campus ministry provides the discipleship and also stimulates acquisition and use of university learning for godly reasons.

8. Focus on freshmen. We attract students as soon as possible by focusing on the freshmen. Students stay in college for only four years, and each year they gradually change. Before college they are very open-minded about the gospel and willing to commit their lives to Jesus. But each year their heart is hardened by 25 percent. So, as time goes by, it becomes difficult to lead them into commitment to the Lord. Thus, we should try to reach them while they are still freshmen. If they are already believers, we should encourage them to join Christian groups without delay.

9. Challenge them from the start. Someone once asked me, "What is the difference between YWAM and other student missions?" I answered, "In general other missions focus on converting the students through summer camp. But our aim is to challenge them to serve the Lord throughout their lives." So, in our camp, we pray for the baptism of the Holy Spirit and the power of the Holy Spirit. We guide members to devote themselves to campus evangelization and, ultimately, to world missions.

10. Emphasize the power of the Cross and the power of the Holy Spirit. Evangelization of campuses and spiritual growth are possible only through the power of the Cross and the Holy Spirit. A systematic Bible-study program or strategy will not be enough. Our zeal is not enough. A multitude of activities is not enough. These things can be useful, even necessary, but the foundation of campus ministry should be the power of the Cross and the power of the Holy Spirit. The power of the Cross brings people together. The power of the Cross changes human beings. The power of the Cross changes the world.

"When I am lifted up . . . I will draw everyone to myself." (John 12:32 NLT)

"But you will receive power when the Holy Spirit comes on you; and you will be my witnesses." (Acts 1:8)

"'Not by might nor by power, but by my Spirit,' says the Lord Almighty." (Zech. 4:6)

There is always the danger of getting involved with too many activities and human effort, of ignoring the power of the Cross and the power of the Holy Spirit. We should always put the power of the Cross and the power of the Holy Spirit first.

11. Maintain outreach as an integral part of the ministry. Outreach is an essential part of a vital ministry. We have all experienced how outreach helps us to practice what we have learned, to change our selfishness into selfless service, and to become world Christians with a burden for the nations.

Campus Revivals and World Missions

Campus ministry is a strategic part of world missions. Campus revivals have historically led to dramatic steps forward in world missions and the accomplishment of the Great Commission. God has always used committed young Christians to evangelize the whole world in fulfillment of his promise from Psalm 110:3: "Your people will volunteer freely in the day of Your power; In holy array, from the womb of the dawn, Your youth are to You as the dew" (NASB). To complete world mission, God sends revival to campuses, calls his people, trains them, and works with them.

In the fourteenth century, John Wycliffe and his friends at Oxford University began a ministry that eventually influenced the reformation movement in England.

Then, the true age of *world* missions began in the eighteenth century. Campus ministry provided a driving force for each of three missionary thrusts: coastal missions, inland missions, and missions to unreached peoples.

William Carey, also called the father of modern missions, started the coastal mission period (1792–1910). This movement sent missionaries to the easily accessible coastal regions of unreached areas. Several campus ministries influenced the beginning of this coastal movement. Count Zinzendorf started one movement as a student at Halle University in Germany. Later, with the Moravians, he began the first organized Protestant missions work. The Wesley brothers and George Whitefield led the Holy Club prayer meetings at Oxford University. Their influence reached America, and Jonathan Edwards started the Great Awakening movement from Princeton University. The resulting student movements, like the Haystack prayer meeting led by Samuel J. Mills Jr. and his friends in William State University and the Society of Brethren movement, played an important role in maintaining the momentum of the coastal mission period by generating prayer, missionaries, and funding.

Spearheaded by Hudson Taylor, the inland mission period (1865–1930) focused further inland to less accessible areas. Cambridge University in England was the center of the student movement in this period. The famous Cambridge Seven, which included C. T. Studd, were active in promoting missions throughout England. In the United States, D. L. Moody initiated a college-student volunteer movement at Mt. Hermon camp in 1866. John Mott of Cornell University and other student leaders officially started the Student Volunteer Movement (SVM) in 1888. Their motto was "The evangelization of the world in this generation." The SVM saw 100,000 students commit themselves for missions and 20,000 students actually go to mission fields. Mission activities in Africa and Asia, including Korea, were the direct outcome of this movement. The other 80,000 original volunteers stayed in the home country, worked to change their society, and helped the missionaries by their prayer and material support.

These student movements in the U.K. and U.S. provided manpower, prayer power, and material support for mission activities in unreached areas. They also served as a call to the local churches to wake up and get involved in world missions.

Cameron Townsend and Donald McGavran initiated a third focus on missions among the unreached people groups (from 1934 to the present). This is the movement to reach ethnic groups that still have no indigenous church. Many college students in North America have devoted themselves to missions to unreached people groups.

From these brief examples, we can clearly see that campus ministry is connected with missions movements.

Today, we are called to finish the Great Commission of Jesus: "Then Jesus came to them and said, 'All authority in heaven and on earth has been given to me. Therefore go and make disciples of all nations, baptizing them in the name of the Father and of the Son and of the Holy Spirit, and teaching them to obey everything I have commanded you. And surely I am with you always, to the very end of the age'" (Matt. 28:18–20). There is no better source for carrying out Jesus' commandment than Christian college students. To disciple nations means to renew every area of society according biblical principles. Discipling the nations involves fundamental changes in every area of society, bringing them into alignment with the principles of the Bible. When students graduate from college, they work in all these areas. If we can equip them adequately, we can disciple the nations.

Why Do We Need Campus Ministry?

I believe it is important to pursue ministry on university and college campuses for five primary reasons. I have already alluded to them, but in this section I will briefly summarize and explain the reasons.

First, we believe God's promises in the Bible to raise up youth. Remember Psalm 110:3 in the previous section? When God raises an army, he uses mostly youth to fulfill his will. As we have seen, most world mission leaders have come from campus ministry. We have to mobilize and challenge college students to be involved in world missions. What a privilege to work alongside God to fulfill his promises.

Second, we need to carry out his commandments, specifically the Great Commission. God has called us to influence each and every area of society in a biblical way. College students can be efficient agents to carry out his plan because they are skilled and knowledgeable in their fields. We need to help them pursue their calling into all the domains of society and to build God's kingdom wherever they go.

Third, God has historically sent revival among students to raise up his workers. As already described, mission movements may arise from student revivals. Since the eighteenth century, many college students have committed themselves to world missions. We must pray for revival and for God to thrust his laborers out into the field. In campus ministry, our challenge is to cooperate with God in raising up and sending out laborers.

Fourth, university campuses provide highly accessible locations full of potential new believers. A campus is a fixed location. A person ministering to students can visit the same people repeatedly over their four years of education. Monday through Friday, we can train them intensively. In addition, we can equip and send them for outreach during summer and winter vacations. Moreover, students may come from diverse tribes, tongues, and nations. In campus work, we have the privilege of serving them.

Fifth, we can meet future YWAM leaders and workers at the university. Many current leaders of YWAM Korea were trained in campus ministry. Likewise, today's campus ministry may produce future YWAM leaders. Of course, many people

without a college education become YWAM leaders too. But too often we have neglected the role of campuses in producing leaders for YWAM, other Christian organizations, and society as a whole. We need to pioneer campus ministry.

Characteristics of College Students

Understanding the characteristics of college students will facilitate our understanding of campus ministry. The unique needs and desires of this group help focus our
message and methods to high efficacy. We do not change the gospel; but even the
apostle Paul was all things to all men that he might win some (1 Cor. 9:22).

College students like to have vision. Indeed, they need to have vision. Without
it, their lives do not have a sufficient energy source. They need vision to know the
meaning of their lives, to select goals, and to have direction.

> Where there is no vision, the people are unrestrained, But happy is he who
> keeps the law. (Prov. 29:18 NASB)

> And it shall come to pass in the last days, saith God, I will pour out of my
> Spirit upon all flesh: and your sons and your daughters shall prophesy, and
> your young men shall see visions, and your old men shall dream dreams.
> (Acts 2:17 KJV)

Youth can assess visions. They search for one that is valuable enough to require
a lifetime commitment. Then they willingly commit themselves to see its fulfillment.
We can offer them a vision worthy of their whole lives, one from the Creator of the
universe:

> After these things I looked, and behold, a great multitude which no one
> could count, from every nation and all tribes and peoples and tongues,
> standing before the throne and before the Lamb, clothed in white robes,
> and palm branches were in their hands; and they cry out with a loud voice,
> saying, "Salvation to our God who sits on the throne, and to the Lamb."
> (Rev. 7:9–10 NASB)

If any location or philosophy provides a better vision than that, I will move there
today!

Second, college students will respond to Jesus the King like warriors.

> I write unto you, fathers...I write unto you, young men, because ye have
> overcome the wicked one. I write unto you, little children...fathers...

young men, because ye are strong, and the word of God abideth in you, and ye have overcome the wicked one. (1 John 2:13–14 KJV)

Students have the traits of mighty warriors. They can do the most difficult jobs. They are looking for the great commander who will lead them to do mighty works. When they hear from us how wonderful Jesus is, they willingly devote themselves to him.

Third, students love adventure. They want to face challenges that will demand their energy and creativity. The bigger the challenge, the more it excites them. Global missions, unreached peoples of the 10/40 Window, strongholds with giants like the sons of Anak are challenges that require people like Caleb with the spirit of a faith-filled pioneer. College students like to see themselves as Calebs. They crave the adventure of meeting these challenges.

Fourth, students seek truth. We should introduce Jesus Christ, who is the Truth (John 14:6). He has the answers for all problems. We can find true joy and satisfaction in him. His truth sets us free. When we help youth to know Jesus, they can always go to him for the truth they need.

Fifth, today's students have a global mind-set. We should teach them about God's plan for the entire world. They can understand it better than anybody else. They need to recognize that God gave a name to each people. They are excited to reach the different cultures, languages, and peoples. In Psalm 2:8 God said, "Ask of Me, and I will surely give the nations as Your inheritance, And the very ends of the earth as Your possession" (NASB). In Genesis 12:3 he promised, "And in you all the families of the earth will be blessed" (NASB). In Matthew 28:19 he commanded us to make disciples of the nations. College students are ready to face God's challenges for the entire earth. Let's make sure they comprehend the scope of God's desires for the nations.

Sixth, youth are unwitting enemy targets. The enemy is trying to attract youth into his camp so he can destroy them. The enemy tries to confuse them with evil distractions and sophisticated but worthless ideas. Drugs, alcohol, extramarital sex, wrong values, wrong worldviews, and deceitful philosophies are the tools Satan is using to capture them. But we must lead them into light so that they may live as messengers of light and ambassadors for Jesus.

Seventh, they are searching for their identity. The world cannot give them proper identity. The world incorrectly bases our identity on education, social position, possessions, and background; so youth may be confused and go astray. In contrast, the Bible gives us a clear and compelling identity. In the Bible our identity is based on our position as beloved children of God. We are created in the image of God. This is a unique, precious thought.

Eighth, students instinctively search for active examples rather than verbose teachers. True teachers, who are an example before trying to teach, engender their respect. They respond better to servant leadership than to authoritarian dictators; they prefer a brother or friend to a distant instructor.

Ninth, university students desire revolution. They yearn to attempt something new, to create something fresh and unique. Youth thrive on the excitement of pioneering novel methods. They prefer innovative worship. The dynamic and informal worship of YWAM often suits students well. Jesus, never changing but always doing a new thing, can best satisfy their cravings to transform themselves and their world.

Four Important Messages for Students

I believe that the Holy Spirit has given me the four following messages to share with students.

1. They need a revelation of holiness. Students often do not know how to control the energy within them. So, they may abuse their own bodies. Their hearts are too often filled with destruction, confusion, and emptiness. To have a revelation of holiness, we should seek God's face earnestly. Whenever I have preached the message of holiness in the student camp meetings, I have seen the Holy Spirit work among those assembled. He has always revealed holiness to their hearts, healed them, set them free, and purified them. We should teach them the power of the blood of Jesus, so that they may keep themselves clean and lead holy lives.

2. They need to know their true identity. This world gives deceitful standards of identity. They cannot satisfy, because they are false. God wants students to know that they are precious because he created them in his image, and that they are so valuable to him that he sent his Son, Jesus Christ, to die for them. They need to know that they are worthy of being loved. Then they can enjoy true satisfaction. Evolutionary theory brings confusion to our identity. Only when we realize that God created us according to his sovereign plan can we have freedom. Our Creator is good, he never makes mistake, and he is righteous.

3. They want to know their mission. They are in search of something worth dying for. When they realize their mission is to bring good to the country, people, and the whole world, they will be passionate about it. When they recognize that God had a good plan for them even before they were born, their eyes are opened. We need to help them to commit their lives to the calling of God for them. When people comprehend that they have a purpose from the Creator, they come alive.

4. They need to be taught about the power of the Holy Spirit to accomplish God's mission. We need to teach them about the personhood and work of the Holy Spirit and about receiving his power—the baptism of the Holy Spirit, gifts and fruits, and callings and ministries. In camp meetings I do not aim at students' conversion, but at leading them into victorious life through the power of the Holy Spirit. We need to teach them to rely on his power rather than their own. We must teach them how to hear his leading in their lives.

Prospects for the Future

Campus ministry is an important segment of YWAM Korea. We commit this ministry to the hands of God with intercession. When I first began this work, I prayed earnestly and called out the name of each campus. I prayed that God would allow us to share the gospel on them, and that he would raise up young people for himself on each campus. Our ministry began with just one campus, but by 2004 there were 144 campuses where the YWAM group was recognized by the university and over 100 campuses where pioneering work was in process. More than 5,000 students were being trained and equipped to work for the kingdom of God. Because God has promised the land and the offspring to Abraham, we should pray for campuses and committed Christians.

I expect three things will happen through campus ministry. First, campuses and nations will be changed. College students are the most important element in that. They will become nation changers. Second, we will have increased ministry personnel and resources for all kinds of Christian ministries. Third, campus ministry will become an important ministry of YWAM International. God has raised up several important ministries within YWAM. He raised up U of N for training. Mercy Ministries, Frontier Missions, and King's Kids are also important. Now it's time for campus ministry, as a transnational ministry, to influence other bases and ministries.

We should train students through university campus ministry to accomplish world missions. God will surely listen to our prayers and will send revival in campuses, societies, and nations. Devoted disciples will arise through campus ministry.

Jose Joseph and Sarah Jose explain how dance and music are the way to an Indian's heart of hearts. A performing arts team, even a Christian one, is welcome where a more traditional "ministry team" might not be welcome. Redeeming and working through traditional art forms, they disciple young believers and seek to reach their nation.

How Lovely:
Performing Arts in India

Jose Joseph and Sarah Jose

*How lovely on the mountains
are the feet of him who brings good news.
Isaiah 52:7 NASB*

Picture This

Imagine the scene in a typical Indian city: masses of people—old and young, rich and poor, light and dark; a palette of colors—vivid, pale, bright, somber; a medley of odors—fragrant spices, pungent animals, diesel fumes; often a cacophony of languages; dust, potholes, vehicles on the sidewalks and pedestrians on the road. It is easy to draw a crowd in the busy streets because of the sheer quantity of people. But attracting an audience is especially easy when music is playing and costumed dancers begin to appear. Curiosity causes clerks, owners, street vendors, shoppers, children, and a myriad of others to temporarily stop their tasks because something more important is happening. Entertainment!

The dust swirls around the bare feet of the dancers as they rhythmically stamp with the energetic beat of the music. The jangling of bangles, perfectly accompanying the beat of the tabla, immediately follows each lively stamp. The vibrant colors of the traditional costumes bring the movements of the dance, the strains of the music, and the energy of the moment all together into a rainbow of sensations.

The lyrics of the song speak of a Love that puzzles the crowd. They do not recognize this love that cares for others more than for itself. An unfamiliar yearning for something or Someone they do not know rises up in them. It is strange sensation.

The crowd watches eagerly. They get lost in the rhythmical motion of the dancers' limbs. In their own bodies, they feel the music surging. Excitement flows through their veins. They love this. The dance finishes and some of the dancers are speaking. Curiosity keeps the audience listening. Although they are attentive, inside they are hoping for another dance.

The break from their mundane and burdensome life comes to an end. Reluctantly, they head back to "normal life." But something inside them is different. A small fire of hope has been kindled. The next day many come again to the same street corner, with their friends in tow, because the dance team had announced that they would return.

Breaking Down the Picture

Many elements of this active picture may not seem obvious at first. Why is this dance team performing in the streets of India? Who are they? How is this picture meaningful in a Christian context? Let's examine the elements of this image to understand why such entertainment is an extremely valuable tool for discipleship in an Indian environment.

First, the art form being presented to the crowd is one of the forms of Indian classical dance. These dances are primarily used by high-caste Hindus to worship their gods in temples. Classical dancers are generally trained from childhood. When one wants to learn this dance form, she or he must approach the potential dance "master" and lay offerings at his or her feet. It is a very serious endeavor to submit oneself to a dance master. The master will curse a pupil who is deemed insufficiently or improperly respectful. Once cursed by a dance master, one is expected never to achieve success in this area. Very rarely does someone take up classical dance as an adult. People are shocked to learn that our team learned these dances in three short months.

Second, the artists themselves are a mixture of skin tones and facial features. They came from all over India to Pune, India, to study in a YWAM School Of Performing Arts (SOPA). Many are from the northeastern states of India, commonly referred to as the Northeast. These states are largely Christian because of people-group movements of the late nineteenth century. Because of their relatively new Christian heritage, the serious complications in the 1950s when India gained independence from Britain, and their closer affinity to other peoples of Southeast Asia, the peoples of the Northeast have long desired independence from India. Many don't want to even call themselves "Indian." Several churches in the Northeast wouldn't allow SOPA teams to perform South Indian dances inside the church because of the strong anti-India sentiments. For our Northeastern students to learn a South Indian classical dance and then to perform alongside South Indian brothers and sisters in front of their own people is an act of humility and cultural reconciliation deeper than many other superficial acts.

India is a land of many cultures. Running a school in India, even when the students are all Indian citizens, is a major cross-cultural experience. Students come to the SOPA from all parts of India and from extremely different life situations—financially, socially, and religiously. It is beautiful to see our pupils coming together to work, learn, sing, act, sweat, and dance as a team. When we take this newly established unity on outreach, it makes a major statement to the audiences. Even so, Northeastern students and staff think twice before going on stage with these dances in front of their own people. Gulping down feelings of humiliation, they step on stage and dance, knowing that Jesus has called them to the kind of lifestyle that has no racial or cultural boundaries.

Third, let's examine the audience. This particular scene actually happened on the streets of a town in Nagaland, a state in the Northeast. The "on the street" factor made this performance available to all—the rich, the poor, the disabled, and the homeless. Throughout India, people are irresistibly drawn to music and dance. They come out of curiosity and as they watch intently, their hearts open and become more vulnerable than if they had entered a church or hall to hear a message about Christianity. Art speaks directly to the Indian heart and rouses emotions of which the audience was previously unaware. We are opening our nation up to hear the truth by communicating in a language they understand and in a style they enjoy and can appreciate. We are contextualizing the gospel.

One of the most exciting elements of a SOPA performance is that many of the onlookers are from lower castes who are not even allowed to view this beautiful act of worship in a temple, let alone participate in it. By performing for them in the street, we are giving them back their culture in a redeemed form. For those who live on the streets, we are bringing it into their very home. We are showing them that *their* cultural expressions of worship are beautiful and valid and that they can be used to worship the One God who cares for the weak, the lowly, and the poor of the earth.

Dancing in the streets is such a rich act. It could be classified as evangelism, spiritual warfare, acts of reconciliation, or intercession. The Hindus would use these specific types of dance primarily for worship, and worship can also be one of the highest purposes we have for performing this art. Classical Indian dance takes tremendous skill and is beautiful. It is a "glory" of the Indian people. In fact, it is not only this form of dance but also all of the different Indian dances, music, and even fine art forms that can be used as worship to the Most High God.

Is God jealous for the worship of the Indian people? Yes. Should these beautiful art forms be used for his glory? Yes!

> I did not see a temple in the city, because the Lord God Almighty and the Lamb are its temple. The city does not need the sun or the moon to shine on it, for the glory of God gives it light, and the Lamb is its lamp. The nations will walk by its light, and the kings of the earth will bring their splendor into it. On no day will its gates ever be shut, for there will be no night there. The glory and honor of the nations will be brought into it. (Rev. 21:22–26)

Since Indians currently represent about a quarter of the earth's population, it stands to reason that they will be well represented in heaven. All the people groups of India will be represented in heaven and will be worshiping God by bringing their glory and splendor to his throne. What a glorious day that will be!

By redeeming this art form, we bring a bit of heaven here to earth and right into the lap of the Indian people.

Is It Necessary to Use the Arts to Reach the Indian World?

The disciple Thomas originally brought the gospel message to India. Yes, "doubting" Thomas. Not only did he come to India, but Thomas traveled all the way to the southern tip and established a number of churches who now call themselves the *Marthoma* church. (Be encouraged that even a doubter can become an ambassador for Christ in the far corners of the world!)

Despite having a Christian presence for almost 2,000 years, India still lists fewer than 3 percent of its population as Christians. Yet, churches and mission boards often consider India a "reached" country. True, many churches are in each of the main cities, and charity work abounds. But 3 percent seems terribly low. Maybe it is easier to consider India reached than to face its huge challenges. Name any social, political, religious, or economic problem and India has it. Our challenges include language differences, poverty, leprosy, AIDS, homeless families, illiteracy, tribal warfare, caste discrimination, drugs, alcohol, wife abuse, and orphans.

Despite the long-term Christian presence in India, the structure of Indian society has remained virtually untouched. Why? *Because we have failed to access the roots of the Indian heart.* Indian cultural art forms comprise a big part of the root. These cultural expressions form the basis of who we are and how we live and think. The Indian mind-set and traditions are ancient.

Transformation in the hearts of Indians and in the mind-sets of missionaries is required. In the past, missionaries have preached the gospel, told people that what they are doing is wrong, and replaced their cultural traditions with what is "right."

This has been the correct thing to do in some cases—for example, in outlawing the practice of a widow throwing herself on her husband's funeral pyre. Too often, however, instead of having their culture transformed by the gospel, different peoples in India have had their culture ripped away from them.

"What is culture without art?" Culture has been defined as "all learned behavior," a broad definition covering anything from food, dress, marriage customs, and child-rearing to how one behaves in a traffic jam! Can one adequately describe the culture of any people without mentioning art forms? Religious dances, arts, and craftsmanship of various cultures are always highlighted in National Geographic documentaries. Art forms are one of the main ways people express their identity and set themselves apart from other people. Observing cultural celebrations is an excellent way to observe what defines the people. By helping people understand their particular identity, art's important role affects all the other learned behavior. Art helps lift people above the pain and trials of life to meditate on what is beautiful. Further, art communicates to people about the meaning of life as they understand it from their traditions.

Why is this important? Jesus loves people from all cultures. And Jesus loves the cultures—he created them. Jesus loves each individual, and we believe he wants to speak to them through their own art forms. The Jesus revealed through these art forms will be their very own Jesus—a Jesus who makes sense to them, a Jesus who originally gave them life, then gave them their culture, the One who redeems them and teaches them to redeem their cultures. Then these specific cultural art forms can be offered as a form of worship to him, the Author of all, as the people give back to him the beauty of their culture.

Going Deeper

> [Jesus] got into one of the boats, the one belonging to Simon, and asked him to put out a little from the shore. Then he sat down and taught the people from the boat.
>
> When he had finished speaking, he said to Simon, "Put out into the deep water, and let down the nets for a catch."
>
> Simon answered, "Master, we've worked hard all night and haven't caught anything. But because you say so, I will let down the nets."
>
> When they had done so, they caught such a large number of fish that their nets began to break. (Luke 5:3–6)

Simon (Peter) and his partners had worked hard all night before this incident. Maybe that night had felt as long as ten nights due to the discouraging results of their labor. In a similar way, church growth in India has been discouraging. For a long two thousand years many people have worked hard and glorified God with their service. But for the most part, the nets are still empty.

But then Jesus asked Simon to do something unexpected. Simon wasn't too excited about the task, but Jesus' authority called for obedience. As always with our Lord, obedience was rewarded. Simon immediately reaped the fruit of obeying Jesus. A striking aspect of this passage is the unexpectedness of what Jesus asked Simon to do. Normally deep fishing is done at night, but here was Jesus, in full daylight, asking Simon to fish in the deep. What thoughts flew in and out of Simon's head before he took the step of obedience? "Who does this guy think he is? Amateur fishermen—think they know it all!" What Simon didn't know was that this was the beginning of an exciting relationship with Jesus, a relationship that would demand of him many more unexpected things.

God has spoken to our ministry through this passage. We believe he is asking us to do some "unexpected things." We are called to go deep into the culture of India and find the keys to reaching these people. We are not claiming to have found *the* key, but part of the key. Believing that the Indian people will respond to the gospel message, we are using their heart language—the art forms which have always been a vital part of their life.

Using the arts of India to reach the Indian people is more controversial than using arts forms in the Western world. Most classical Western art forms were originally inspired by Christianity, and therefore their use in Christian practices is rarely questioned. Not so in India. India is enormously rich with varied traditions and cultural expressions. A Christian tourist seeking to purchase a religiously "neutral" Indian artifacts or artwork will soon discover to his dismay that most art forms are dedicated to the gods of Hinduism or other religions. Gods or goddesses in strange, and often sensual poses, are a dominant theme in sculptures and paintings. As for performing arts, all forms of classical dance are performed in worship of gods. Each time these pieces of fine art are created and the dances performed, the participant grows closer to and becomes more dedicated to the god. It is a legitimate religious experience because of the power of Satan to deceive minds and hearts.

The traditional missions approach has been to eradicate these art and worship forms, considered evil because they glorify false gods. Many new Indian Christians do find it necessary to break from their art forms for a time because they have such negative connotations. But many other Indians categorically reject the gospel message because Christianity, as the "religion of the West," has often forced them to abandon their cultural traditions.

How do we go deeper and use these arts to reach the people of India? What is this unexpected thing that God has called us to do? *We simply change the object of worship from the gods of India to the true God.* This means learning these art forms well, understanding the meaning of each gesture, movement, and sound. The old message of the dance or song is replaced with an appropriate message of God's character and plan. When people hear the sounds of the tabla or mrudangam playing familiar rhythms or see the classical dances they have grown to love, they are interested and feel comfortable coming forward.

India—A Land Locked Up

It is hard to get in and out of India. A foreigner coming to India for the sake of the gospel may find the experience very challenging. The distance from many lands makes it an expensive journey. Expatriates coming for the long-term face difficulties in obtaining and maintaining visas. The extreme conditions can be daunting—the heat (or the cold in some places), the dust, the pollution, the mosquitoes, the language barriers, and of course, the sicknesses that seem to jump on any unsuspecting foreign stomach. Then, any person who has a heart for the poor and needy finds himself feeling guilty for struggling when there are so many who obviously have it so much worse.

For Indian citizens, the opposite story prevails. It is hard for us to leave India. Visas are often denied to Indians. Raising the finances to travel internationally is an extremely daunting task for the average Indian YWAMer.

But the most daunting way that India is "locked up" is not these climatic, geographic, or other physical aspects. It is the fact that the people's hearts are closed. How to reach them? The barriers often seem insurmountable, especially for a foreign team coming on a short-term basis.

There are two primary "Indian experiences." Gandhi once explained that to see the "real" India, you need to go to the villages. In the village experience, the people's hearts are locked up due to the lack of education and the generations of idol worship. People stubbornly want to stick to their own ways. However, India is also in the midst of drastic change. A whole new urban life is available for Indians complete with middle-class housing, car ownership, college educations, and so on. These dissimilar lifestyles make India even more of a challenge to reach. Different spiritual strategies are needed for each area.

In the city, where our AWAM (Arts With A Mission) ministry is located, people's hearts are not locked up in the same way as in the village. They tend to be well-educated and aren't interested in worshiping in the family's traditional way. The materialistic spirit, which has taken the hearts of many in the Western world, is entangling the hearts of India's city dwellers.

Hollywood has had a huge impact on Indian society. Attending a movie in an Indian city is a strange event. One feels as if they have stepped out of India for a short time when they enter the plush theater. The way people (young and older) dress is startling. Who are these people? They look Indian, but their clothes and mannerisms and expressions of speech (mostly copied from the actors and actresses) betray the influence of the Western motion picture industry. The most distressing aspect of this influence by Hollywood movies is how readily Indians are throwing away their traditions and morals. The movies show and glorify immoral values of illegitimate sex. The youth of India are embracing this lie. Not that Indians were pure and untainted before these movies came, but they are highly influenced by the free sex and "anything goes" attitude of movie stars.

India's own center for producing movies, Bollywood, is located in Mumbai. Bollywood is also responsible for this great shift in behavior and dress invading Indian cities. Indian-made movies increasingly resemble Western movies in both subject matter and the depiction of violence and immorality. Indian actors and actresses proclaim publicly that the single life is better and marriage just doesn't work any more.

India is rapidly changing. The Western and Indian media are largely responsible. Certainly, many more complicated, sociological factors are also involved but they are beyond the scope of this chapter. Hollywood and Bollywood have, to some extent, "unlocked" urban India. People want to change to become more modern and open-minded.

Is this "unlocking" of India by the media a positive thing in the context of our mission? In some ways, the answer is yes, and in many ways, no. *Confusion* is the current state of people's hearts. This unlocking has come very quickly and is desperately lacking in positive role models to demonstrate how to become "modern" while retaining moral standards. Many people have outwardly jumped on the bandwagon, but generations of traditions do not die so easily. Self-confessed secular agnostics may pray and give sacrifices to Hindu deities when their lives are stressed. Their outward appearances and even their words may not line up with what is truly going on in their hearts.

Inwardly, the people are still Indian. Indians love being Indian. Many of them, even though they may be dressing and even acting in the Western fashion, never want to leave the country. When the inward state of being and believing doesn't match the outward state of behaving, a great void arises and, as we have said, *a state of confusion ensues.* Our job as workers in India is to bring good from this confusion by speaking Truth into the hearts of the people. Christians in India need to consider these factors: the influence of media, the changing state of India, the isolation of the people in the villages, the confusion in the cities. Then we need to consider our God, who is so *big,* who is the God of creation and of creativity. Can't we, as his creatures, find creative ways to influence people positively using the same media as the enemy is using to influence the people in such a negative way?

SOPA/AWAM—Discipling India through the Arts

Discipling nations. How do we do it? How do we know we have done it effectively? A big part of initial discipleship is to get the message out. Then comes the task of getting the message to stick—for people to continue to believe it and apply it to all parts of their lives. How many of us have been encouraged in our faith through music and other art forms that stimulate us to think beyond the daily grind? On the other hand, how many of us have been negatively "discipled" by art forms of which we shouldn't have partaken? The arts communicate, teach, and disciple people largely without their awareness of what is happening. That is why it is so effective and that is why AWAM came about.

The ministry of Arts With A Mission came about in an interesting way (as do most YWAM works!). It is no surprise that our God would bring a man deep from the heart of South India's jungle and a woman from mountainous northeastern India to meet at a School of Evangelism and Pioneering (SOEP). While strategizing, Jose Joseph and Rosie Sorhie realized that, despite their extremely different upbringings, they both understood the need to utilize the arts of India to reach the Indian people with the gospel.

The SOEP leaders, Mike and Lora, encouraged these two in their vision and directed them toward the School of Performing Arts (SOPA) in Tyler, Texas. Miraculously, provision came in and they went. After participating in the SOPA as students, and staffing it for a year, Jose and Rosie were ready to bring the SOPA to India. They felt the call, were prepared and willing, and God did the rest.

As of 2006, the Indian SOPA had run successfully for seven years. Outreaches have been sent to north, south, and central India. Each outreach realized similar results: when the team went in the name of being artists, doors flew open left and right. They were invited to schools, colleges, and churches and given more contacts than they could effectively develop. They have taken their message of the freedom that Jesus brings into places other teams had not been able to penetrate.

Each year, about one-third of the SOPA students desire to return as staff. Although they initially give a two-year commitment, many of them decide to work long-term with the department, now called Arts With A Mission. This high growth rate can be attributed to the fact that Indians are so attracted to the arts and are so artistic. It is in their blood! Young adults are excited and amazed to find out that they can use their talents to serve God. Through AWAM, they learn that they can participate wholeheartedly, using their gifts to bless God and the people of India.

As the ministry and number of staff have grown, the department has expanded to include separate ministries; each is specialized in specific art forms to reach various target groups, such as the youth of India. As an example, for many years members of AWAM had been interested in starting a performing dance team with a higher skill level than is possible in the SOPA. After years of planning and doing tasks which weren't especially their "first love," the performing team was established. The team consists of five members who have a heart for dance and for the confused urban youth. By performing at conferences and for youth groups, churches, and schools, they have been able to educate people about the use of arts as a valid form of worship.

AWAM Strategies

Arts With A Mission uses music, dance, and other art forms as strategies to reach the people of India and fight against spiritual oppression.

Music

Because of its powerful effect and Indians' deep love for *their* music, music is one of our primary strategies for reaching and discipling people. Christian youth of the West, especially America, grow up able to listen to Christian lyrics in whichever music style they prefer—from R & B to hard rock. Contemporary Christian Music (CCM) has a large presence. Christian artists produce such high quality music that even non-Christians are often attracted to it.

The situation, however, is different in India and many other countries. Those same CCM CDs are available for sale and distribution in these countries, but the language is foreign. Wouldn't it be exciting to see high-quality Christian music for the youth of India in the Hindi language—music that the kids can dance to and even be confident to share with their friends? For the older generation, there could be music in their own language and favorite classical style—Hindustani or Carnatic. Let's not let the "devil get all the good music"!

In 2000 our team produced one CD in Malayalam, a language of South India. Conveniently, Malayalam speakers live all over India (in fact, all over the world), so this album has been appropriate for use in more places than just South India. However, producing just one album leaves us far from satisfied. We are currently working on building a music-recording studio, which will be available to Indian Christian artists at a very reasonable cost. So many talented Christian musicians in India "have the stuff" and are ready to record, but alas, have no money! We believe that building this recording studio will be instrumental in releasing hundreds of worship albums in the many different languages of India.

An AWAM team traveling by train in Bihar gives a great example of how influential and attractive music is here. Lawless Bihar state is notoriously called "the graveyard of missionaries." To pass the hours away, one member got out his guitar and started singing English songs. A crowd began to gather and then started asking for

Hindi songs. Another member told the crowd that they only had "Christi bhajans" (Christian worship songs in traditional style) as a disclaimer, but the crowd insisted that he sing. So he did! Now, traditional bhajan songs are sung in a call and response format. So Jose would sing, "Yeshu naam pyra naam," (Jesus name is Love) and the crowd would respond by singing back those same words. This continued for hours until the team was too tired to sing. Guaranteed, those lovely Indians in the train had some good songs stuck in their head on returning to their home. *Imagine,* if upon leaving the train, the AWAM staff all had those same songs on CDs to hand out to their new friends.

Imagine other musical possibilities . . . a team of musicians works alongside a church-planting team to study the targeted people's music. Then the music team can involve local musicians and record a worship album just for that people group in their language and style!

Imagine quality songs written and produced at such a high standard that they can be played on the radio and music videos can be made to accompany them. These songs can address topics like prostitution, justice, corruption, and even traffic! Let's use catchy music to teach India that there is a better way of doing things.

Dance

The strategies of music and dance go hand in hand. If there is music in India, dance naturally follows. Indians love dance. We could highlight this and put it in bold print, and still be understating the Indian love for dance. A quick look through the sixty or seventy TV stations available on Indian cable TV reveals about half showing some type of dance. Almost every movie coming out of Bollywood includes dancing. To be an Indian film star, one *must* know how to dance.

A church-planting team relayed that after showing the "Jesus" film to an Indian audience, the people said it was nice, except that there were no dance scenes! Contextualizing the gospel message for an Indian audience may require some sort of dance form. Now isn't that thinking out of the box!

An Indian film director explained that Indians insist on dance scenes in a good movie because they provide a happy escape from reality. Theatergoers hope to forget their pain and sorrow for a few hours. They don't want to watch a movie that only deals with the harsh realities of life. This shows us that people are looking for a "way out." The Hindu religion says that all hardship is to be accepted as karma or fate. Even if people say they believe that, the reality of it is that they still want to escape their pain—even if just for a short time.

Watching a dance scene in a movie (or a dance performed by a SOPA team on the street) lowers the guard of the audience. This is familiar territory, so they don't need to be on the defensive. Dance creates the prime opportunity for us to communicate to them the Way to be saved from their pain and burdens. These dances may only provide a temporary escape, but through them we can communicate a permanent salvation.

A popular praise song says, "Open up the doors and let the music play."[1] The reality in India is the opposite: "Let the music play and then the doors will open up!" This is exactly what our SOPA teams have found on outreach. They enter as "artists from the School of Performing Arts in Pune" and people are so excited to see them perform. A typical response is, "Oh, you are a dancer. I need to take you to meet my dance teacher!" Or, "Let me introduce you to the school principle so that you can perform in his school." So many doors, which were locked to other Christian teams, have flung open for ours. This is not a way of bragging but just to share with you a "secret" we found—people are very open to the gospel message when it comes in a different form. We are speaking their "heart language." On one outreach the team was in a hill station known for its high-quality international schools. The team got an opportunity to perform in the one considered the best international school in India, the very school where many Hindu (and radically anti-Christian) leaders send their children.

In urban settings, youth love to see hip-hop style dances. Christian youth find it very releasing and exciting to learn that dance isn't intrinsically bad as many of the traditional churches in India assume. These youth watch our performances and then want to learn how to dance. Discipleship through dance—another good, out-of-the-box idea!

Recently one of our staff was asked to teach dance each morning at a local Catholic school. Using all Christian songs, he taught the Christian, Muslim, and Hindu children some hip-hop dances. The music and this young man's influence on the children caused a stir. The children were impacted by the lyrics of the songs and began asking their teachers to pray with them. In a school performance for all the parents, the name of Jesus was glorified and the children danced in his name.

In villages and with more traditional crowds, people are delighted to see classical dance forms. If they are not Christian, they are usually very interested in why Christians are performing their dances. To say the least, a dance performance in a village causes a stir and creates great interest.

Art as Spiritual Warfare

Any serious intercessor or Christian in touch with spiritual warfare tactics senses the oppression in India. In the postmodern West, idolatry is covert—primarily abstract things like individualism and materialism pull people into idolatrous lifestyles. But in India, temples full of idols are up front, visible everywhere on the street corners, in every village, along back roads, as though one has stepped back in time to the day when the nations worshipped Baal and golden calves. Evidently, these idols and even the cows that roam the streets are valued more than human life. Children are left on train tracks to die, while in parts of India, a person could be put in prison for life if they even accidentally kill a cow. It is impossible to ignore the need for spiritual warfare in India. Ignorance could be deadly. By dancing in the streets and performing in prisons, hospitals, and other places where a Christian message is not normally allowed, we go into the "front lines" of spiritual warfare.

In North India the Buddhist influence hovers over the mountains like a dense fog. Buddhist monks are constantly humming out their worship and allegiance to Buddha. By doing so, they are locking in his influence over the land. However, in the opposite manner, we can unlock it through Christian praise and worship. Creating worship music in the same musical style and in the specific language of the people is especially effective for the simple reason that the people are attracted to it and can understand it. One friend of our ministry imagines all the negative Buddhist and Hindu sound waves being countered by the positive sound waves of the true worship of Jesus Christ. The very image spurs us on to want to create more and more beautiful praise music to invade the territory of the enemy.

Music and dance are currently the primary strategies for our work in India. However, the possibilities are endless. Some people groups of India have their own specific art form, such as puppet making, by which they relay their traditional folk stories to the coming generations. Why not relay the gospel message through the medium of puppets? On a larger scale, what about making very Indian movies with Christian themes of love and forgiveness? Could we make a Christian movie with dance scenes instead of always having just a crucifixion scene to mark it as Christian? What about painting and sculpting? How can we use these fine arts among an Indian audience? There are so many children in India—how about more art programs for children teaching them to respect their traditional art forms and use them to worship the true God? Using the arts with disabled and hurting people of India is a terrific and relatively unexplored idea. Art coupled with Christian counseling has tremendous power to bring restoration and healing to people who are emotionally or physically damaged. Isn't it our God who brings beauty from ashes? The possibilities are numerous, for our God is large!

Challenges Faced by Our Performing Arts Team

"Who are we?"
"Where are we going?"
"Are we being effective?"
"This is a hard journey. Is it really worthwhile?"

Questions haunt every person working for God. Our time on earth is short. We desperately want to make the best of it. Even those with traditionally recognizable missionary tasks such as planting churches, translating the Bible, or caring for widows and orphans must face these questions. The constant needs of the world around us require us to make sure we are doing something worthwhile. But when a person is in a nontraditional and less accepted role as a missionary, the questions seem to multiply:

"What are we doing, just dancing in the streets?
"Is that making a difference?"
"What will people think?"
"What will I tell my family?"

Our staff in Arts With A Mission faces these and many other questions. They can't escape from the truth that God has put something different inside them. If they aren't using these talents God has given, they can't find satisfaction. But others, and even we ourselves, often challenge our identity as "real missionaries." Many people, including fellow YWAMers, churches at home, and families, don't fully understand what we are doing and why it is so important. Because of this, the potential impact of our team is often minimized. But we take heart in knowing that Jesus was ridiculed and misunderstood by the leaders of his day. Many biblical characters were given unexpected tasks that put them on the receiving end of ridicule.

Our ministry is in the spotlight. If a simple mistake in a dance is made, it is obvious to many. If a person has a character issue, it is evident to all. Anybody serving in the public eye has experienced this. They are held to higher standards of purity and holiness. Those in front need to carefully examine themselves regularly, but they shouldn't shy away from the job because of fear of making a mistake. Satan's best tactics include encouraging artists to be overly proud and thus ineffective or to become overly "humble" and fearful to perform at all. The world is in desperate need of people who can live godly lives and be examples. This is not a job for the faint-hearted.

Many artists are guilty of stifling the artistic urge inside of them in the name of doing something more "worthwhile." Daydreaming about teaching the Bible or feeding the hungry may seem much more holy, but the fact is that may non-Christians have followed their dreams of making it in the art world and have had a tremendously large impact. Why can't Christians have the same kind of impact in the art world in a way that glorifies God? Artists, you are warriors for the Most High God! It is time for you to take your place in God's army and fight the spiritual battles that are already raging. Maybe some of you feel like the joy of creating and doing artwork was stolen from you. Maybe trauma in your life robbed you of that glory. It is time to get it back. Ask friends to pray with you about using your artistic talents for the Lord.

Our individual staff members have their own identity issues to deal with, but as a department we also have had many challenges defining who we are and then defending that. We are a pioneer ministry. We have all kinds of dreams and visions of new ways to reach India. But since the concept of discipling India through the arts is relatively new, it can be difficult to communicate its importance or worth.

Nonartists often view art or artists as an afterthought, a sort of a tool used to accomplish the mundane—only necessary to make a poster, write a little article, or draw a bulletin cover. The giftedness of the artist and the power of art can be overlooked quite easily. Art does not have to be the primary method of evangelism or discipleship, but some form of creative arts could enhance the vision and scope of many ministries in many countries. India is not the only country that can benefit from skilled artists using the glory God has put inside them.

Conclusion

Art is an extremely powerful communicator. It communicates the philosophy and root beliefs of people. As Christians who serve the Creator God who made humans and gave them minds to think and bodies to use, isn't it time we communicated our powerful message?

More and more, art is being used globally as a powerful medium. This is exciting but has been a long time in coming. It has been even slower in India, a country with two thousand years of Christian history. Let's make up for lost time and use the arts to communicate the gospel to this very needy nation of India and to the nations of the world.

Notes

1. Martin Smith, "Did You Feel the Mountains Tremble?" © 1995, Curious? Music UK.

─────────────── *Part 6* ───────────────

Conclusion

Reflections on the Kingdom

Jim Stier

D o Christians have a role to play in the institutions of society? Are our values
and beliefs relevant to nonreligious questions, or are we to restrict ourselves
to matters of the soul? These are ancient questions that are being renewed
and are now surfacing as a major concern in the body of Christ worldwide.

There are also more modern versions of these ancient questions. Will we lose
the focus on the spiritual if we involve ourselves too much with the systems of this
world? Aren't those systems so polluted that the Bible presents them as irredeemable?
Are we wasting our time in trying to improve the world? Wouldn't it be preferable
just to get as many people as possible out of the world and into our churches and let
the world proceed to its inevitable judgment? Aren't utopian visions dangerous, often
resulting in great cruelty as the vision takes precedence over the sanctity of individual lives?

These questions arise out of the central concern of understanding what the kingdom of God is and how the gospel of the kingdom is to affect the world. Many
churches and denominations have held different and even contradictory views of
Christian missions. Yet God is speaking to many throughout the body of Christ
about holistic ministry and the impact that the gospel of the kingdom should have
on the nations of the world. Many are discussing and acting upon the sorts of insights
and points of view that are presented in this book. Through a discussion of history,

Scripture, and the experiences of different streams of ministry, the chapters of this book have uncovered many aspects of the kingdom of God and the role we are to play in fulfilling the Great Commission. It is our hope that you come away from this discussion seriously considering how the kingdom advances and what God expects from us as Christians.

What Does God Expect from Us?

To answer the question, what does God expects from us? we must understand both his character and his kingdom and, in turn, how these should affect our view of our lives and work.

First, we are taught everywhere in Scripture to participate wholeheartedly and vigorously in bringing about the will of God on earth. The Bible doesn't encourage us to passively wait for the right things to happen or for Jesus to return. We are to get involved as fully participating partners with God.

Second, the God of the Bible is interested in everyone and in everything that affects people. God nowhere indicates that he sees the world in terms of a dichotomy between the spiritual and the secular. Scripture is clear in telling us repeatedly that God wants impartial justice, efficient hygiene, quality education, good business practices, good government, responsible care for the planet, and so on. As we bring his truth and presence into everything we do for individuals and communities, we are doing his work.

Third, when you think about serving God, the question isn't whether or not you are involved in specifically religious activity, but whether or not you are living the values of the kingdom of God in loving service, whatever your sphere of action. God's entire character is love, and our work is an expression of worship to God. The kingdom advances not just by our witnessing about Jesus but by the very way we do our work and live our lives.

Lastly, the Bible shows that God cares for us not only on a personal level but also on a corporate level. God deals with individuals and also with tribes, social groupings, and nations. If we are sincere about his will being done, we can't help but be concerned with the improvement of whole societies. Individual salvation is of great importance, but that is only a part of God's will. We are instructed to pray and work for all of his will for all of humanity.

These are values we believe express the very character of God. They are discussed and demonstrated throughout his Word and characterize his involvement in our human story.

How Does the Kingdom Advance?

In regard to the question of how the kingdom of God advances, we have discussed some of the "how" of responding to God's very clear command to actively disciple the nations. As you reflect on this process, carefully consider how you can be involved.

We must begin, first of all, by teaching the people to do all that Jesus commanded. Being born again by the Spirit of God is indispensable. The truly transformed individual and the corporate expression of a group of individuals will act like salt, finally permeating and giving flavor even to that which isn't itself salt. The salt (converted and transformed individuals with new values) has to be there for the flavor (an entire society or nation) to be changed.

Secondly, from the very beginning these individuals should be taught to apply their new spiritual insights and values in their everyday lives so that changes in their families, their businesses, and their spheres of influence will begin to happen immediately. As the number of deeply transformed individuals grows, God's values become more and more widespread in the nation/people. Those who are serving God with a whole heart bring the values and the truths of God's ways to media and communications, law and government, education, family, commerce, entertainment, and the church. The number of Christians continues to grow, and at the same time there is a growing unease throughout society with the old ways of doing things. Corruption and injustice become more and more unacceptable. The public mentality begins to change as the kingdom spreads like leaven.

Finally, we must be clear on what role the church as an institution has in this process of discipling the nations. The church as an institution is not to take over the institutions of power in order to become the ruling class. The church should be, among other things, a prophetic and loving voice of conscience and wisdom for all of the processes of a society. It must be clear that it doesn't stand to profit from direct involvement in the spheres when it is speaking into them; otherwise conflicts of interest, whether real or imagined, will weaken the church's authority. When the church has overstepped its role, violated the spheres, and attempted to bring change through coercion, society has been oppressed and the kingdom has lost ground.

However, while the institution of the church does a disservice to the cause of Christ if it tries to govern over other spheres of influence, the individuals that are sent from that institution into society will be integral parts of other spheres. As followers of Christ they will influence all spheres, not with a spirit of dominance, but through loving service. These are the ways of God.

If we try to force a "final solution" upon society, we run the risk of taking the institutions of power and using them in an evil way to persecute those who oppose us. History abounds with such stories. We must disciple nations with the spirit and methods of Jesus. He could have crushed all opposition, but he died instead. In doing so he established an unbreakable moral authority and opened the way for us, for the entire world, to have peace with God. Although no one could see it yet, his kingdom won.

When we turn away from the methods of our Lord and resort to force, duplicity, violence, or manipulation, the kingdom of God is already dead in us, and we have lost the battle. We must continue to serve by the Spirit, in truth, with unrelenting love.

His Kingdom Come

We face an almost infinitely complex task that is hard to define. It can be difficult to get our minds around even small parts of it. Yet we must not allow our vague ideas to inspire fatalistic noninvolvement. We must instead pay close attention to God's instructions for our actions at this present time.

However far we progress or fail to progress in changing nations, the church itself needs the constant struggle of trying. It is out of a life of struggle that we fervently call out for the grace of God to empower us. When we seek him with all of our heart, wisdom and holiness grow. As our values are challenged and our principles fail in the midst of conflict with other religions, ideologies, spiritual entities, and political and financial interests, we are constantly stimulated to examine, fortify, redefine, and develop our understanding of our work in God's kingdom. Our dependence on our living God grows as we recognize that we cannot do without such dependence.

What greater challenge exists than that of Isaiah 61:1–3, to bind up the brokenhearted, to proclaim freedom for the captives and release from darkness for the prisoners, to fight for beauty in place of ashes, the oil of gladness instead of mourning, and a garment of praise instead of a spirit of despair? And yet Christ came and fulfilled this very Scripture (Luke 4:21). To fully understand our role in God's kingdom, we must look to him who accomplished the impossible.

When Jesus called out to God on the cross, the bystanders thought that he was appealing to Elijah. Most scoffed, but one man had more faith than all the rest. He ran and got a sponge with a soporific in it and gave it to Jesus, waiting to see if Elijah would come. No sooner had he taken these steps of faith than Jesus died. He must have been overwhelmed with disappointment and felt himself a fool, looking at the circumstances. In reality, however, at the moment that Jesus expired, a decisive victory over sin and death was won.

Are we, like the bystander who had faith, willing to be scoffed at for our hope?

God doesn't teach us to wait for heaven, where we will finally see his will done. He inspires us to pray and act for his will to be done on earth right now. We are to go in the authority of Jesus and disciple all nations, teaching them to apply his teachings in their lives and in their societies.

The gospel of the kingdom is entirely relevant and extraordinarily powerful. God promises us in Isaiah 9:7 that the kingdom's advance is inevitable: "Of the increase of his government and peace there will be no end. He will reign on David's throne and over his kingdom, establishing and upholding it with justice and righteousness from that time on and forever. The zeal of the Lord Almighty will accomplish this."

God's zeal will accomplish this! He is committed. He is all-powerful. He is our hope and our motivation to do as much as we can.

Matthew 6:10 is to be both our prayer and our purpose: "Your kingdom come, your will be done on earth as it is in heaven."

Appendix A

YWAM Statement of Faith

Youth With A Mission (YWAM) is an international movement of Christians from many denominations dedicated to presenting Jesus personally to this generation, to mobilizing as many as possible to help in this task, and to the training and equipping of believers for their part in fulfilling the Great Commission. As citizens of God's kingdom, we are called to love, worship, and obey our Lord, to love and serve His Body, the Church, and to present the whole gospel for the whole person throughout the whole world.

We of Youth With A Mission believe that the Bible is God's inspired and authoritative word, revealing that Jesus Christ is God's son; that people are created in God's image; that He created us to have eternal life through Jesus Christ; that although all people have sinned and come short of God's glory, God has made salvation possible through the death on the cross and resurrection of Jesus Christ; that repentance, faith, love, and obedience are fitting responses to God's initiative of grace toward us; that God desires all people to be saved and to come to the knowledge of the truth; and that the Holy Spirit's power is demonstrated in and through us for the accomplishment of Christ's last commandment, " . . . Go ye into all the world and preach the gospel to every creature" (Mark 16:15).

Appendix B

University of the Nations
Founding Principles

Founded upon biblical principles, the University of the Nations (U of N) fulfills its commitment to Christ's Great Commission by equipping men and women spiritually, culturally, intellectually, and professionally, and inspiring them to use their God-given abilities to communicate and demonstrate the Good News in all nations.

The University of the Nations sees the world as its classroom. It is committed to developing Christian men and women who are called to reach those who do not know Christ. Special attention is given to nations, cities, and people groups without the Gospel. Evangelism and concern for the poor are presented as ways of life.

The university seeks to broaden the scope of evangelism by equipping students to serve worldwide in various domains of life. Opportunities are provided for students to grow and learn in their area of calling in order to serve effectively in the profession or vocation to which they are called. Believing that the command of Jesus to be salt and light in the world means Christian service and witness in all walks of life, the University of the Nations endeavors to equip students to take the Gospel to their profession by learning to think biblically, discern spiritually, and act humbly.

The University of the Nations' approach to education is based on 2 Peter 1:5–8, which stresses balanced development in every area of life: in faith, virtue (character), knowledge, self-control, perseverance, godliness, brotherly kindness, and love. By God's grace and surrounded by the love of Christ, students increase in their faith and worship of God. They are fortified with knowledge, turned toward wisdom, and inspired to be obedient to God's calling on their lives.

While the University of the Nations is committed to educational excellence in every aspect, its aims are achieved through knowing and loving God and seeking His revelation and guidance. Intercession, worship, and praise are integrated into every course. The living out of God's ways are to be apparent in student and staff relationships: in forgiveness, openness, repentance, honoring the gifts and abilities of each person, unity, teamwork, hospitality, servant leadership, and loving one another as commanded by Jesus.

Every course in every college/faculty of the U of N is a multiplier for missions, serving to increase the training locations, workers, and resources available for the mission fields. International in scope, each course is to provide cross-cultural training as it relates to the course's specific educational content. Courses are designed to be applicable in real-life situations. Each area of study includes field assignments and cross-cultural experiences for every student.

Appendix C

The Lausanne Covenant, Section 5 (Christian Social Responsibility)

We affirm that God is both the Creator and the Judge of all men. We therefore should share his concern for justice and reconciliation throughout human society and for the liberation of men and women from every kind of oppression. Because men and women are made in the image of God, every person, regardless of race, religion, colour, culture, class, sex or age, has an intrinsic dignity because of which he or she should be respected and served, not exploited. Here too we express penitence both for our neglect and for having sometimes regarded evangelism and social concern as mutually exclusive. Although reconciliation with other people is not reconciliation with God, nor is social action evangelism, nor is political liberation salvation, nevertheless we affirm that evangelism and socio-political involvement are both part of our Christian duty. For both are necessary expressions of our doctrines of God and man, our love for our neighbour and our obedience to Jesus Christ. The message of salvation implies also a message of judgment upon every form of alienation, oppression and discrimination, and we should not be afraid to denounce evil and injustice wherever they exist. When people receive Christ they are born again into his kingdom and must seek not only to exhibit but also to spread its righteousness in the midst of an unrighteous world. The salvation we claim should be transforming us in the totality of our personal and social responsibilities. Faith without works is dead. (Acts 17:26,31; Gen. 18:25; Isa. 1:17; Psa. 45:7; Gen. 1:26,27; Jas. 3:9; Lev. 19:18; Luke 6:27,35; Jas. 2:14–26; Joh. 3:3,5; Matt. 5:20; 6:33; II Cor. 3:18; Jas. 2:20)

Study and Discussion Questions

Part 2: What the Bible Says

"The Old Testament Template for Discipling Nations" by Landa Cope

1. Landa talks about the "gospel of the kingdom." What is included in this concept besides personal salvation?

2. What do you think of the response of the pastors when interviewed about Dallas's social problems and the church? What response would you have given? Has reading this chapter changed what you might have said?

3. Everyone needs to participate on some level in discipling the nation to which he or she is called. What is God asking you to do in your target community? If you aren't yet sure, begin asking for his leading, and praying for the needs in your community. What would God's hopes and intentions for your community look like?

4. How does Landa's chapter bring new insight into God's dealings with nations in the Old Testament?

"The New Testament Basis for the Discipling of Nations" by David Hamilton

1. Explain the "Two Ways to Go" shown in Mark 16:15 and Matthew 28:19–20.

2. Define the various levels of society: anthropos, oikos, koinonos, polis, and ethnos. Give an example of how you are related to each one. How could these different levels of society help us break down the task of discipling a nation into bite-size, achievable subtasks?

3. Describe the seven spheres of society. Which ones do you interact with the most? Which ones have been more a part of your life in the past, or will be more of your life in the future?

4. Using David's Disciple the Nations Chart (copied below) as a framework, ponder and grapple with "What does *true* look like in an individual, a family, a

koinonos, a city, a nation?" Your process may include prayerfully waiting before the Lord, searching the Scriptures, discussing with others, reflecting on God's character, considering and reconsidering, etc. You are encouraged to be specific and break out of the box.

Phil. 4:8	Anthropos	Oikos	Koinonos	Polis	Ethnos
True					
Noble					
Right					
Pure					
Lovely					
Admirable					
Excellent					
Praiseworthy					

5. How can you begin to implement some of the insights the Lord gave you in the process of filling in the chart in question number 4? What levels and spheres of society can your obedience transform with the redemptive love of God?

"Second Thoughts on Galactic Domination" by Don Grattus

1. Briefly describe liberation theology, evacuation theology, and a theology of engagement.

2. Why did his team consider church planting to be essential? Explain why you agree or disagree with their approach(es).

3. Cultural treasures, like poetry, will be offered to the King of kings. What treasure does your culture bring? If you have worked in others, what are some of the treasures they will offer to the King?

4. Don Grattus discovered that you never know who or what will be strategic in the future. How can you live your life faithfully each day?

5. What principles or ideas for discipling nations stood out to you from reading this chapter? Is there a practical way you need to apply any of them?

Part 3: History of Discipling Nations

"From Rome to Reformation" by Todd M. Johnson

1. What is one lesson that we can learn from each of the four historical periods Todd discusses? What principles did they learn? What did they do well to expand the gospel and to disciple the believers in each era?

2. The breadth and depth of our call to disciple nations must be embraced by every believer, regardless of the particular ministry God has given us to do. Are you functioning primarily in the breadth or the depth of God's call at this time? What are some practical ways you can embrace the dimension you are not as directly involved with right now?

3. Todd points out that the great transformations we can see throughout history were effected by men and women whose names we will never know as they labored in prayer and faithfully served their communities without stature or position (think of the captive wives and enslaved monks!). What role has God given you in discipling the nation you are called to?

"Calvin and Geneva" by Thomas A. Bloomer

1. What's the difference between revival and reformation? Can one happen without the other? Why or why not?

2. Tom states that the strategy of the Reformers was based on three principles. How could you incorporate those principles into your strategy to influence your nation or community? How would your community change if those three principles were implemented?

3. Calvin and the Reformers saw the role of the church as teaching the different spheres of society. What spheres of society did Calvin and the Reformers address in Geneva (i.e., family, business/banking)? What nation-building concepts did they teach to each sphere? What areas of society would God want to address in your community or nation?

"Revolutionaries and Anti-Revolutionaries" by Jeff Fountain

1. God has repeatedly raised up people of faith and insight to disciple nations. What character qualities do you see these five men having in common? How did those qualities contribute to their efforts and impact the discipling of nations?

2. What understanding did each contribute to the question of what it means to disciple nations? Which of the principles or strategies they operated from might be effective to bring transformation in your area of ministry? What might God be asking you to do to implement them?

3. How does Kuyper's understanding of domains help us in our efforts to disciple nations?

4. In targeting influential individuals, Buchman had a slightly different approach to discipling nations. How do you see that working together with the strategies employed by the other reformers? What key individuals could you begin to pray for in your nation or sphere?

"YWAM and the Great Reversal" by Debra Buenting

1. Describe the Old Testament concept of *shalom* and the New Testament revelation of salvation.

2. What did you initially understand to be the gospel? Was it focused on a personal decision to follow Christ or did it include more of a holistic approach? What is your current understanding? Did you recognize any of your personal journey of understanding in this chapter?

3. Where you live and work, are there issues you feel called to address? Remember it doesn't matter whether these have traditionally been called religious or nonreligious issues; we are committed to seeing every area of life under the lordship of Christ.

4. The type of ministry about which we are passionate tends to reflect our personal calling. To what ministry have you felt drawn? What steps are you taking, or do you need to take, so that your activities will demonstrate God's commitment to the whole person and community?

"Fiji—A Dramatic Return to Life" by Loren Cunningham

1. What events and actions were significant in bringing such sweeping change to Fiji? What can you do to help bring a similar movement toward God and his purposes in your nation or community?

2. As individuals grow toward God's intentions for them, their lives change in every area. As Fiji is growing toward God's intentions for them as a nation, what changes in aspects of their corporate life can we observe from this case study? What

other indicators could show that a society is becoming more discipled? (Make sure you can give biblical, not just cultural, reasons for your answers.)

3. The stories of miraculous restoration of Fiji's environment demonstrate God's holistic concern for individuals, nations, and creation. What examples do you find in Scripture of God's concern for the environment, and the effects of humanity's obedience or disobedience upon the environment? In light of the stories from Fiji and your discoveries in Scripture, what might our responsibilities be in regards to the environment?

Part 4: Philosophy of Ministry

"The Church and the Kingdom" by Dean Sherman

1. How would you have described the church prior to reading this chapter? How would you describe it now?

2. How would you define the kingdom of God? What are some ways we as believers are to bring the kingdom of God "on earth as it is in heaven?"

3. Describe ways you have seen people operate in their giftings outside of a church function. How do you see this in your own life?

"A Conversation on Calling" by John T. Henry

1. What are the three types of calling? Explain how "being called" relates to discipling nations.

2. Describe your understanding of God's calling in your life. Have you sought God for guidance on your vocation? If not, is it too late?

3. The qualities listed in 2 Peter 1:5–8 are a framework for growing in our calling, in our response to The Caller, and in our fruitfulness. Which of these qualities spoke the most deeply to you? What is God calling you to do in response?

4. How does God use you in your vocation? How might he be asking you to step out in faith to increase your kingdom impact?

5. Think back to David Hamilton's revelation that even a garbage man could speak for the kingdom of God under the right circumstances. In other words, any career we are called to is holy to the Lord when we walk in obedience. Prayerfully ask the Lord to reveal to you areas where you wrongly exalt or debase certain callings.

"Discipling the Nations—One Disciple at a Time" by Danny Lehmann

1. Summarize what Danny Lehmann means about the primacy of evangelism.

2. Danny described evangelism, discipling, and mercy ministry as the tip and edges of a two-edged sword. How would you explain the role of each to a friend who

was a new believer? Don't forget to expand the picture to include the discipling of nations and the kingdom of God.

3. Where has God primarily gifted and placed you: evangelism, discipling, or mercy ministry? What do you do now or what could you start doing to incorporate and make room for the other areas? Who could you ask to work with you to bring more wholeness to your work?

4. Do a personal assessment with God about your evangelism and how it may need to change.

"Incarnational Evangelism" by C. Lynn Green

1. Define incarnational evangelism as Lynn uses this term. Describe a time when have you seen this practiced, either by yourself or others.

2. How is incarnational evangelism an inherent part of fulfilling the Great Commission?

3. Discuss three principles from Lynn's discussion on the sphere of business which you found particularly insightful or encouraging. How can you apply those to the sphere that you are called to?

"Developmentoring" by Kent Truewell

1. Summarize the developmentoring process in your own words.

2. Kent wrote, "However, if a model of the process is instilled in the people, it may be perpetuated for generations to come." Reflect back on and describe an example where you have seen this occur. Ask God if there is an area where you need to be instilling a model in others.

3. Kent's steps can be utilized to reach any community. How can you begin to engage with your community in this process? Mentally envision and describe how your process might appear. First, prayerfully select the "tile" or group of humanity you feel called to impact. Second, design your development, or select your focus area. (Keeping Luke 2:52 in mind may help.) Third, how will your service benefit the community, respecting community roles and institutions as possible, without creating a *bagunça?* Fourth, what is/are the institution(s) you will strengthen? Fifth, how will you mentor leaders? Sixth, what movement will you deliberately be seeking to create? Seventh, how will this movement travel into and disciple a larger region than your community?

"The Importance of People Movements in Discipling Nations" by Steve Cochrane

1. "People movements" has been a mission strategy applied to ethnic groups with a strong value on community and community-based decision making. Are there

elements of group thinking and decision making along other lines of identity, such as profession (dentists or professional athletes), hobby (motorcycle gangs or surfers) or generation (teenagers)? How can we utilize the insights gained from the people movements strategy in reaching peoples in a nontribal setting?

2. What safeguards do we need to keep in mind to avoid the hazards Steve identified in his discussion of historical missions efforts? How can those be of help to you in your ministry efforts today?

3. Steve discusses the role of evangelism and church planting along with the value of discipleship and being salt and light to set a moral foundation for influencing a nation. All these elements come into play in the process of preaching the gospel to every individual and discipling every nation. What aspect of fulfilling the Great Commission do you see as your calling and ministry? How can you be more intentional to engage with those involved in other aspects of this process to maximize the impact of each effort?

"From Vision to Reality" by Howard V. Malmstadt

1. Describe a megaproject. What are the steps to design a megaproject and bring it to completion?

2. What portion of fulfilling the Great Commission has God put on your heart? What would God's ideal look like in that category of life at the level of society you are envisioning? (Consider using the chart David Hamilton created [copied above in the chapter 3 study questions] if you haven't already done that.)

3. We must intentionally seek God often for specific plans on how to proceed in fulfilling the aspect of the Great Commission he has entrusted to us. Spend some time now asking him for his wisdom and plans about the what, how, where, and when of your part in discipling nations.

4. Howard believed the U of N has a key role in discipling nations. What principles can you draw from its development? How can you implement those principles in what God has called you to?

5. Reflect on a time where you undertook a large project and were unable to complete it as you had envisioned. With what you understand now, what could you have done differently to keep the project on track?

"Principles and Practices in Albania" by Fraser Haug

1. Why do you think that Fraser Haug's team found a lack of qualified environmental specialists, but plenty of doctors and teachers for their work?

2. In your current location and roles, how can you become a more effective and strategic model of the kingdom of God?

3. What skill sets would you like to develop to be a more effective nation discipler?

4. Do you agree that the kingdom can be advanced in different sequences? Where do you tend to fit in a sequence?

5. Have you reinterpreted your discipline according to biblical principles? Better yet, are you always in the process of doing so? What things have you learned that may go contrary to what you were initially taught?

"When Less Is More" by Bráulia Ribeiro

1. In the case of the Jarawara, Beth and Sandra's patience to wait for their first language students to teach others to read and write paid rich dividends, as the tribe made literacy their own. How could you apply this example to your own discipleship efforts?

2. The question of "more is less" as a guideline for when and how to "help" has implications beyond the Sateré and the Amazon jungles. What application can you see in your own field of ministry?

3. A key issue for the Suruwahá tribe was the need to recognize a church that looked very different than the cultural expectations of the missionaries. How is this issue reflected in the various "cultures" you work with, e.g., youth culture, ethnic groups, or even denominations?

4. From each of the tribes discussed, name one mistake which endangered the tribe's ability to develop a biblical worldview and preserve their cultural identity. What can we learn from those mistakes? How can what you have learned be applied to your own situation?

5. Name one strategy used by the missionaries in each of the three tribes that allowed the tribe to develop a culturally unique expression of biblical Christianity.

Part 5: Strategy

"Loving God and Your Neighbor" by C. Stephen Goode

1. Summarize the Salvation Army strategy for making a difference. Could any of these principles be fruitfully applied to your work? Can you think of other principles that might make you a more effective nation changer?

2. Is mercy ministry a valid way to preach the gospel and/or to disciple nations? Defend your answer.

3. Should all Christians be involved in some form of mercy ministry? Discuss why or why not.

4. Do the needs of the world create a moral obligation on us to be involved in some form of mercy ministry? What sort of moral obligation does the condition of your community create for you?

5. Vishal Mangalwadi says that we influence one person at a time with a change of heart. Explain why you agree or disagree.

6. As you read, were you challenged to do anything new or different? If so, prayerfully write down the first step in how you feel led to change.

"Healing the Wounds of the World" by John Dawson

1. What is the role of forgiveness and reconciliation in discipling a nation? Compare insights and stories Jeff Fountain (chapter 7) shares about Frank Buchman with John's comments in this chapter.

2. From the list of issues and the stories John tells, what wounds and issues of conflict do you think exist within your nation at this time? What has been done to reconcile issues of injustice from the past?

3. How can you begin to pray for your nation to be discipled in this area? What is one practical step you could take to live out a ministry of reconciliation in your community?

"Family and Culture" by Diane and Jeff Littleton

1. Did you grow up in an individualistic culture or a group-oriented culture?

2. How would you summarize the importance of family to an individual? To a nation? How can you use this understanding to multiply the effectiveness of your ministry?

3. Since families prepare children for future social interaction, how do you think other social institutions in society might be affected if parents use manipulation and control to achieve their desires?

4. Diane and Jeff encourage us to come humbly to other cultures, to crucify our cultural pride, and give dignity to the other person and his culture. Jim Stier and Lynn Green both promote going to others with a great deal of love. Think of an example where you have seen people minister in pride and one where you have seen them minister in humility and love. Without naming names, tell what lessons can be garnered from these examples.

5. Compare some of the Littletons' suggestions for coming in a humble, cross-culturally sensitive way to the way Jesus interacted with people.

"Transforming a Divorce Culture into a Marriage Culture" by Larry Ballard

1. How is a family a small civilization? What did you learn in your family that you brought into other institutions with you? What are today's families unconsciously teaching their children? From your understanding of this chapter, describe the relationship between the health of families and the health of society. How do you see that reflected in the nation you are called to impact?

2. Why are so many agencies willing to work together to solve the problem of divorces for minor reasons?

3. Can you think of other issues where believers might need to facilitate so many institutions working together to solve common problems?

4. In the case of the Greater Grand Rapids Marriage Policy, there were many task forces with different focus areas. Choose a problem and outline how different task forces could work together by focusing on various sectors of society.

5. Larry describes many initiatives that seem to be bringing dramatic change through strengthening marriage and family. What elements do these initiatives have in common? How could some of these elements be incorporated into your prayer and strategy for your community?

"Bible and Government" by Ana Roncal Villanueva

1. What is the purpose of civil government?

2. Ana gives seven biblical principles of government. Briefly define each.

3. Summarize the values that come from the Ten Commandments (the Decalogue). Which ones are strong in your society? Which ones are weak or missing?

4. What does the New Testament add to our understanding of government and our interaction with government?

"Discipling Nations through the Sphere of Business" by Susanna Shenk

1. Describe how you have seen business being used by God for discipling the nations. What principles did the business follow? What effect did the business have in the community?

2. We are all called to a role in seeing the Great Commission fulfilled. How can you develop the characteristics Susanna highlights for Great Commission businesspeople (called, intentional, faith-filled and persevering, biblically based and Holy Spirit empowered, prepared, marked by the fruit of the Spirit)? How would you live them out in your area of calling?

3. If you are called to be a Great Commission businessperson, how could others affirm and encourage you? If you are not called in this area, how could you affirm and encourage those members of the body who are?

"Discipling the Nations through Journalism" by Alison K. Muesing

1. Before reading this chapter, what words and emotions came to your mind when you thought of "media"?

2. How did journalism interns highlighted in this article influence nations by their positions and work?

3. Does that idea of adopting a journalist appeal to you? If not, from what other profession would you choose to adopt?

4. Describe what you think God's intentions would be for news media. How would you recognize articles and broadcasts that fit within his intentions?

5. Christian newspapers originally covered a variety of domestic and international affairs. If you were to publish a magazine or newspaper, what topics would you address if you wanted to be a part of discipling your nation?

"Media That Transforms Nations" by Calvin and Carol Conkey

1. Create International works hard to contextualize the transforming message of the gospel. Describe the elements you saw that made their contextualization effective. What is one adjustment you can make to contextualize your or your church's message to a different segment of your society or to a different generation? How could their insights on orality help in this process?

2. The Conkeys give principles and stories to stir our thinking on choosing the most effective medium for our message. They also point out that different media can be most effective for different points in the process from evangelism to discipleship to community transformation. What considerations could shape your decisions as you seek to be effective reaching those God has called you to?

3. The Conkeys address the various aspects of the discipleship process, from evangelism to salvation to personal and community transformation. Couple this with the levels of society David Hamilton explored, and Steve Cochrane's encouragement to address entire communities with the gospel; there are many implications in how we utilize these principles, examples, and information. What are some areas God is speaking to you about that will bring adjustment to your ministry strategies?

"Strategy Coordinators" by Karine K

1. Describe the job of a strategy coordinator. What practices, principles, and personal qualities struck you as important for being effective at this calling?

2. In John 17:23 Jesus prayed, "May they be brought to complete unity to let the world know that you sent me and have loved them even as you have loved me." How do strategy coordinators become part of the answer to that prayer? Jesus' final command in Matthew 28:19 was to go and make disciples of all nations. How do strategy coordinators help to fulfill that command?

3. What principles or ideas from this chapter could you apply right now to the community where you live?

"University Campus Ministries" by SungGun Hong

1. Under the heading "Effective Strategy for Campus Ministry," SungGun Hong gives eleven proven strategies or tactics to make campus ministry effective. Look them over carefully. Could you benefit by adding any of those to what you do? Would you add any other elements to his list?

2. The Korean strategy is quite deliberately geared to forming well-discipled students who will serve the Lord in church and society, both in Korea and abroad. How could you have a more deliberate approach to discipling nations and raising up missionaries for unreached peoples?

3. If you were to start a vision group to be composed of people with a calling similar to yours, what would that group be? Who would attend? What difference would this make for the members of the group and people outside the group?

"How Lovely" by Joseph Jose and Sarah Joseph

1. Jose and Sarah make their case for how important performing arts are to reaching the Indian heart. Explain why you do or do not think this is a key to reaching all societies.

2. What other keys have you seen in Indian or other cultures? How could one or more of these be deliberately used for discipling that nation(s)?

3. Are you an artist who needed to read this message? What are you encouraged to do about what you have read? Are you a leader with frustrated artists on your team? Has this chapter expanded your vision for helping them grow their wings? How? If you are neither an artist nor a leader, how has this chapter affected your thinking?

4. Jose and Sarah comment that pioneers often feel they are out on a limb. How could this encourage you the next time you feel called to a step of faith? When was the last time that God called you out on a limb?

For bulk orders of *His Kingdom Come*
call YWAM Publishing at
1-800-922-2143.